A CITY CALLED

HEAVEN

MUSIC IN AMERICAN LIFE

A list of books in the series
appears at the end of this book.

A CITY CALLED

HEAVEN

CHICAGO AND THE BIRTH OF

GOSPEL
MUSIC

ROBERT M. MAROVICH

University of Illinois Press
Urbana, Chicago, and Springfield

Publication of this book was supported by the AMS 75 PAYS
Endowment of the American Musicological Society, funded
in part by the National Endowment for the Humanities and
the Andrew W. Mellon Foundation.

© 2015 by Robert M. Marovich

Manufactured in the United States of America

1 2 3 4 5 C P 5 4 3 2 1

∞ This book is printed on acid-free paper.

Library of Congress Control Number: 2015931904
ISBN 978-0-252-03910-2 (hardcover)
ISBN 978-0-252-08069-2 (paperback)
ISBN 978-0-252-09708-9 (e-book)

CONTENTS

ACKNOWLEDGMENTS

I am indebted to all the following who in one way or another made this book possible. Everyone I interviewed for this book (listed in the bibliography), I am forever grateful to you.

Blanch Adams
Libra Nicole Boyd
Ronald and Ramona Branch
Ambassador Carol Moseley Braun
Mark Burford
Rev. Walter Butts
Bil Carpenter
Ken Ciocco
Charles Clency
Aaron Cohen
Dennis Cole, Yvonne Wesley-Seabrooks, and the Chicago
    Area Gospel Announcers Guild
Robert Darden
L. Stanley Davis
Cies de Tieje
Ronnie Favors
Ken Flaherty Jr.
Suzanne Flambeau
David Frost
Gregory Gay
John Glassburner and the Mighty Gospel Friends
Cleave Graham
Ronald Greer
Danielle Gunn and the staff of WLUW 88.7 FM Chicago
Irma Gwynn

Linwood Heath
Patricia James-Holloway
Bishop Otto Houston III
Rob Hudson, Carnegie Hall Archives
David Jones
Rev. Dr. Stanley Keeble
Marilyn Moats Kennedy
Robert Laughton
Eric LeBlanc
Pastor Lamont Lenox
Annette "Queenie" Lenox
Christopher "Kip" Lornell
Pastor and Mrs. Mack C. Mason
Horace Maxile
Willie J. McPhatter
Joseph Middleton
Reginald Miles
Rev. Stefanie Minatee
Mildred L. Mondane
Cherli Montgomery
Opal Nations
Deborah Pollard
Lorenza Brown Porter
Robert Pruter
Robert Sacré
Glen Smith
Nancy Stachnik
Steve Strauss
Arthur Sutton
Dolores "Honey" Sykes
Robert Termorshuizen
Shirley Wahls
Marie Wakefield
Sharon Roberts Walker
Romance Watson
Marcel West

Rev. Dr. Issac Whittmon

Rev. Joseph Williams

Veronica Williams

Michael Wojcik

Kenneth Woods Jr.

Bobby Wooten

Alan Young

The staff of the Chicago Historical Society Archives

The staff of the Vivian G. Harsh Collection, Chicago Public Library

The staff of the Harold Washington Library—City of Chicago

Brenda Nelson-Strauss, Portia Maultsby, and the African American Archives of Music and Culture at Indiana University

The staff of the Center for Black Music Research, especially Janet Harper and Laurie Lee Moses

The staff of the Hogan Jazz Archives, Tulane University, especially Lynn Abbott

The staff of the Smithsonian Institute of American History Archives

The staff of Fisk University Library Special Collections, especially Aisha Johnson

My very special thanks to

The AMS 75 PAYS Endowment of the American Musicological Society.

Gospel historian and author Anthony Heilbut, whose *The Gospel Sound* is still considered the premiere history of gospel music, more than four decades after its initial publication. His comments, edits, and suggestions not only saved me from myself on more than one occasion, but his expert commentary—much of it gleaned firsthand from the gospel singers themselves—has also added a great deal of depth and color to the story.

Gospel historian L. Stanley Davis for his thorough review of the manuscript and many essential comments and additions.

Ronald Weber, Barbara Allen, Lynwood Montell, and Donald Critchlow at the University of Notre Dame, for kindling within me a passion for scholarship.

Laurie Matheson, editor in chief at the University of Illinois Press, for championing this book from the start. She patiently and good naturedly answered my endless questions, calmed my misgivings, and skillfully steered the project in the right direction.

Carol Terry, my copy editor, deserves to be draped in James Brown's cape for her hard work, patience, and counsel.

Carol Hobbs, whose assistance in transcribing nearly half of my tape-recorded interviews, was a gift from heaven; and to Robert Darden for recommending her.

Barbara Wojhoski, for her marvelous final editing work.

Attorney Harold Berg and accountant Lynn Rubin.

John Bealle, for his indexing genius.

My parents, Robert Sr. and Diane Marovich, who taught me to read, encouraged me to write (even when the outcome was illegible), and fostered my love of music and recorded sound.

My late wife, Patricia Andrews Marovich (1960–2000), who kindled the gospel music spark within me and was a more effective drum major for justice than I could ever hope to be; and my new wife, Laurel Delaney Marovich, without whose entrepreneurial spirit, encouragement, and dinner-table consultations this book would never have come to pass. I owe you dozens of day trips to Lake Geneva.

Finally, to the angels who assisted me along the way but have gone on from earthly labor to heavenly reward:

DeLois Barrett Campbell

Irma Gwynn

Geraldine Gay Hambric

"Father" Charles G. Hayes

Margaret Aikens Jenkins

Rev. Cleve Minter

Rev. Dr. Wealthy L. Mobley Sr.

Myrna Ordower

Nash Shaffer

Eugene Smith

Charles Walker

Robert Wooten Sr.

I regret they did not have a chance to see their story in print. If there is a library in heaven, and I hope there is, I pray they are pleased with the results.

To the Chicago gospel community: this is your story.

Introduction

Chicago is the capital of gospel and always will be. This is where
the great talents come to learn, this is where the great singers live.

Albertina Walker, *Chicago Tribune*, May 27, 1990

Friday, January 6, 2006, was a typical winter day in Chicago.

The temperature hovered around freezing as the sun shone through patches
of clouds. People returned from the holidays to the bustle of their workweek
routines, while big retail stores licked their wounds over disappointing holiday sales. Senator Barack Obama was about to finish his freshman year in
Congress. Nothing was unusual about the day until around 3:00 p.m., when
Pilgrim Baptist Church suddenly and rapidly became an inferno.

The blaze evaded all attempts by approximately 180 Chicago firefighters
to quench it. Decades-old stained-glass windows exploded onto Thirty-Third
Street and Indiana Avenue. A stone wall collapsed. The roof crashed to the
ground, hurling a wave of thick, hot air through the side streets. Rising twenty
to thirty feet, the flames were so intense that passengers in airplanes descending
into Chicago's O'Hare and Midway Airports could see them. As acrid smoke
wafted from the embers, what remained of Pilgrim were charred sections of
exterior walls and the first level of its stone facade. The conflagration had erased
115 years of architectural and historical significance in two hours.

Often referred to as the birthplace of gospel music, even though the title
belongs to Ebenezer Baptist Church two miles south, Pilgrim Baptist Church in
the city's Bronzeville community nevertheless served as a touch point for gospel's acknowledged father, mother, king, and queen. Pilgrim had hired Thomas
Andrew Dorsey, the father of gospel music and one of gospel's most prolific
songwriters, to organize its gospel chorus. Dorsey served the church's music
department for the next fifty-plus years. The National Convention of Gospel
Choirs and Choruses, the first organization to develop and propagate the new
sacred music, held its first gathering at Pilgrim. Sallie Martin, the mother of

gospel music, was an early member of the Pilgrim gospel chorus. At Pilgrim, James Cleveland, the king of gospel, sang as a boy soprano, so small he stood atop a box to be seen by the congregation. Mahalia Jackson, queen of gospel, opened a beauty salon up the street and often sang at Pilgrim-sponsored gospel musicals. When Dorsey's first wife and day-old child died—inspiring him to write "Take My Hand, Precious Lord," one of the most beloved gospel songs of all time—the funeral was held at Pilgrim.

The building was in the final stages of a major renovation at the time of the fire, but by the evening of January 6, all that was left of the structure were walls that resembled giant tombstones surrounding an empty gravel space that had once housed one of the South Side's most beautiful sanctuaries. What would the Pilgrim congregation do without its worship home? What happened to Dorsey's archives of music and papers—were they destroyed by the blaze? Rev. Hycel C. Taylor, Pilgrim's pastor at the time, had recently gathered college students from neighboring Illinois Institute of Technology to catalog and box the church's collection of Dorsey sheet music. Taylor rued that the boxes were likely stored in the church at the time of the blaze. They were not seen again.

Nevertheless, the destruction of Pilgrim Baptist Church was a sobering reminder of the vulnerability of history, of the urgency to chronicle the recollections of those who were the architects of the gospel sound before they, like Pilgrim, returned to dust.

What Is Gospel Music?

Gospel music was an artistic response to the Great Migration, one of the most significant cultural episodes in twentieth-century American history. Thousands upon thousands of southern African Americans who migrated to Chicago in the early and middle part of the twentieth century confronted economic, social, and cultural challenges that were bewildering, daunting, and disempowering. The prejudice migrants withstood was in many ways just as insidious as the discrimination they experienced down South. Gospel songs, and the gospel music community, provided the catharsis and affirmation they needed to feel less like strangers in a strange land. Borrowing from the lyrics of Rev. W. Herbert Brewster's "How I Got Over," gospel music enabled migrants to literally "shout troubles over." Wrote Horace Clarence Boyer, "It was . . . not unusual to witness a singer *singing* through her problems."[1] Gospel music was, in many respects, the only freedom migrants found. It offered them freedom from the daily indignities of being a black southern migrant in an unforgiving urban North, and freedom for a better condition spiritually, emotionally, socially, and—for some—financially.[2] The tight-knit gospel music community that coalesced in Chicago starting in the 1930s and 1940s established its own foundation by reclaiming the cultural identity and association they had formed and fostered in the South.

But bettering one's condition did not mean clinging single-mindedly to the past. It also meant embracing the new, urban, cosmopolitan society. The duality of the migrant experience—to cling to one's southern roots while striving to be part of the cosmopolitan northern urban black culture—was never as evident as when gospel singers and musicians swung hymns and spirituals to the steady rolling beat of urban jazz or the Hammond B3 organ. In other words, the gospel community was southern by roots, northern by circumstance, and cosmopolitan by choice.

In academic terms, gospel music refers to both a performance aesthetic and a type of sacred song composition. As a performance aesthetic, gospel music is the product of West African rhythmic, emotive, and improvisational antecedents; the uncomplicated lyrics and melodies of spirituals and revival and camp-meeting songs; and Baptist lining hymns. It also incorporates the urbanity of music genres such as jazz, swing, and blues in its use of blue notes, flatted thirds, and lyrics culled from the vernacular of everyday life.[3] It is a musical elision of the past and the present used to articulate messages of hope, encouragement, praise, and worship—a cathartic experience for the singer/musician as well as the listener.

Gospel music's progenitors, however, described the new music more simply and poignantly. Sallie Martin wrote that gospel songs "are the result of sleepless nights and care-worn days."[4] Kenneth Morris described gospel as evangelical songs that carried "soul and heart messages" about "everyday experiences."[5] Mahalia Jackson explained that "blues are the songs of despair. Gospel songs are the songs of hope."[6] Thomas A. Dorsey simply referred to gospel as "the good news."

While gospel as a composition style traces its roots back to the nineteenth century, Methodist minister Charles Albert Tindley is considered the African American hymnist who launched the twentieth-century gospel music movement. His earliest songs, written in 1901, forsook lofty lyrics for the language of the common person. They included "What Are They Doing in Heaven" and "I'll Overcome Someday"—upon which the civil rights anthem "We Shall Overcome" is based. His songs were included in the National Baptist Convention's *Gospel Pearls* songbook, first published in 1921. From Tindley on, gospel songs have articulated a straightforward message by borrowing the rhythm and phrasing of the folk preacher, phraseology from church vernacular, mother wit passed from generation to generation, and the expressions of the poor and working-class African American migrant.

Both Tindley and Lucie E. Campbell-Williams are considered the "Progenitors of the Gospel Song." A schoolteacher from Memphis, Campbell wrote enduring songs such as "Something within Me," which gospel historian L. Stanley

Davis calls a "National Anthem" in black churches. As a leader in the National Baptist Convention, Campbell was a significant force behind the 1921 publication of *Gospel Pearls*, the first African American songbook to use the word "gospel" in the title. Songs by Campbell were included in *Gospel Pearls*.

It is instructive to define gospel music also by the sociopolitical role it played in the African American community. Sociologist Robert Lee Sutherland noted in 1930 that "religion, as found in Negro churches in Chicago, provides salvation for the individual . . . giving him higher goals to work for . . . or by attacking his problems directly in an effort to make his life here and now more endurable and satisfying."[7] He added that, for the poor African American, if "insults, orders and scrub brushes remind him of his place" during the week, on Sunday the black church leader could mount "the rostrum in his store front church to become the spokesman of God."[8] Indeed, churches provided black Chicagoans leadership opportunities within their congregations, on usher boards and in athletics, women's and men's groups, the senior choir, and eventually gospel choruses and music departments that included gospel singers and musicians. Migrants with little or no voice in their employment, housing, education, and social status could achieve rank as respected gospel singers, choristers, directors, songwriters, musicians, and eventually owners of sheet music and record companies.

At its roots, gospel music was a populist activity. The first gospel choruses organized by Thomas A. Dorsey and Theodore R. Frye were social organizations that not only welcomed everyone, especially the transplanted southerner, to participate but also were managed by migrants. By establishing leadership offices such as president, secretary, and treasurer, gospel choruses adopted the formal structure employed by other church associations. Most importantly, gospel choruses and gospel singing were expressions that belonged to the people, a democratic means to elevate the lowliest worker during the week to star status on Sunday morning when he or she put on a long robe, marched down the aisle with the gospel chorus, stood proudly behind the pastor, and sang the glory down. The least talented singers and musicians in the smallest storefront church could get a hand clap and an amen for their attempt.

Within a decade after Dorsey and Frye's first gospel chorus, gospel music became a commodity created, presented, and sold by blacks with minimal reliance (at least initially) on white commercial interests. For example, Sallie Martin and Kenneth Morris's Martin and Morris Music Studio gave unknown but talented writers the chance to have their song-poems set to a melody and included in a song folio that would offer both song and songwriter national exposure.

After the Second World War, gospel music ascended to a new level of commercial appeal. Historian Jerma Jackson observes that the intersection of gospel and commerce transformed the gospel community of amateurs into professionals who grasped for the brass ring to further their artistic accomplishment. In many cases, their visibility came at the cost of diminished control over their music and the trajectory of their career. And while gospel afforded some practitioners a measure of financial gain, others, including many talented and respected singers and musicians, struggled under the crushing weight of economic poverty. The most poignant gospel songs and performances often arose from their personal struggles.

Music that survives the test of time is not a means to its own end. It is an expression of the human spirit at a specific period in time, but it also transcends time. It expresses with simplicity the universal emotions of joy and thanksgiving, sorrow and hope, hurt and aspiration, desperation and rebirth. If early gospel songs were resplendent with personal pleas for assistance and mercy, the 1960s witnessed gospel singers joining popular and folk artists in raising their voices against personal and universal wrongdoing. Artists such as Mahalia Jackson rolled up their sleeves and participated actively in the civil rights movement at the local and national level.

The songs, performance styles, and arrangements produced by men and women in Chicago's African American churches, high school auditoriums, and community centers forever altered the sound of popular music. Today, any singer in any genre who bursts forth with a mouthful of melismatic runs, trills, blue notes, and bent notes owes a debt of gratitude to the pioneers of Chicago gospel music.

Implicit in *A City Called Heaven* are five main arguments:

First, gospel music became a way for African American migrants to express personal frustration with the class-preoccupied status quo and establish their place and status within the city's church and social communities, even if it meant starting new churches. But gospel music was not simply meant to transplant the soul-stirring church music enjoyed back home. The gospel performance aesthetic, and even how the music was transmitted, expressed individual aspirations to be part of the cosmopolitan landscape. Like the postwar blues scene, gospel music combined the emotion of southern religious worship with the exciting, swinging rhythms of the city, thus enabling migrants to retain their traditions while establishing their place within modern urban society.

Second, gospel music as developed in Chicago transcended denominational boundaries. By singing wherever and whenever they were welcome, gospel singers and musicians moved seamlessly from Baptist to Pentecostal to Holiness to Spiritual to nondenominational churches, picking up songs and techniques along the way. Besides live performances, which have always been the bedrock of gospel music, the communication of the music in sheet music form and on recordings, radio, and television assisted greatly in its ecumenical sweep. These means of expanding a church's ministry beyond its four walls also broke through racial and cultural boundaries. In so doing, gospel influenced musicians of all walks of life as it made its way across the country and ultimately around the world.

The ecumenism of gospel suggests, and rightly so, that many church denominations brought their styles to bear on the development of gospel. While Baptist, Holiness, and the Church of God in Christ were early adopters of the new music, one cannot omit the contributions of musicians, singers, and pastors from the Churches of the Living God, Spiritual churches, Apostolic churches, community churches, and nondenominational churches.

Third, the gospel music industry grew out of the necessity for entrepreneurship among African American migrants. Since few job opportunities were available for the city's growing black population, the alternative was to find one's own way. In *Selling the Race*, social and cultural historian Adam Green posits that blues, rhythm and blues, and gospel artists in Chicago used their music to speak to the collective consciousness of African Americans while providing a model of entrepreneurship and mobility on their own terms.[9] Singers as well as musicians, songwriters, publishers, record company owners, distributors, record store proprietors, radio broadcasters, television hosts, and even pastors could craft their own Promised Land through the medium of gospel music. While most did not achieve significant financial success, some did, notably Mahalia Jackson, Sallie Martin, Roberta Martin, and Rev. Clarence Cobbs. Still, Green's premise that the vernacular (e.g., gospel music) "tied communal culture to commercial interest" underlies the Chicago gospel story and, in many ways, forever changed the genre's landscape.[10]

Fourth, like most styles of music, gospel music was periodically altered by the young. The first half century of Chicago gospel produced two generations of practitioners, each carrying the ball further down the field. But if the body of gospel changed, its soul did not. Gospel music was, and continues to be, a worship expression that reflects the socioeconomic circumstance of the times and uses the music of the times to articulate it. The revolution Dorsey started by swinging the sacred is not unlike today's gospel artists adding the rhythmic thump of R&B. Kirk Franklin's "Stomp" is distant kin to the sanctified beat of the Pentecostal Church. The street-corner evangelism of Sister Rosetta Tharpe—her inventive guitar licks and sassy, staccato lyricism—can be found in the street talk of today's Christian rap and hip-hop artists. As early as 1949, Morris recognized that gospel music should meet the "requirements and demands of the modern Christian," and that the music of the church should "keep step with modern progress, culture, and the times."[11]

And finally, six historic tipping points helped establish what is known today as gospel music. All of them occurred in Chicago:

1. Arizona Dranes's 1926 recording of "My Soul Is a Witness for My Lord," the first known commercial recording to combine several performance techniques attributable to the gospel sound.

2. The formation of the first modern gospel chorus at Ebenezer Baptist Church by Thomas A. Dorsey and Theodore R. Frye in December 1931.

3. The establishment of the Roberta Martin Singers, which gave gospel its signature ensemble sound.

4. The debut of the First Church of Deliverance radio broadcast in 1935, which spread gospel music across several states and across cultural and denominational lines.

5. The founding of the largest African American–owned gospel music publishing enterprise, Martin and Morris Music Studio, in 1939.

6. The 1947 release of Mahalia Jackson's best-selling record "Move On Up a Little Higher," which stimulated the gospel music recording boom.

A City Called Heaven is by no means an exhaustively detailed study of gospel in Chicago. Its intent is to chronicle the development of Chicago gospel music during its first five decades, from pioneers such as Thomas Dorsey and Sallie Martin to the start of the contemporary gospel era of the 1970s, when the focus shifted from Chicago to California. The book also paves the way for a thorough treatment of the city's gospel community since the 1970s, a story that in some ways compares to what the pioneers experienced, and in other ways is completely different but nevertheless is richly deserving of its own volume. I hope that this work stimulates a renaissance of scholarship on Chicago gospel music. There is so much more to be learned, so many more stories to be uncovered. Meanwhile, the reader will gain a greater understanding of, and appreciation for, a fascinating time in American history, and a people who moved physically to better their condition, only to discover that betterment rested within themselves, and in their songs, services, musicals, and believing community.

Finally, *A City Called Heaven* seeks to settle the long-standing argument about which city can properly claim the title "Birthplace of Gospel Music." I argue that the birthplace is Chicago, but there was no instantaneous musical fission, no big bang that brought gospel into being. Rather, gospel was a steady, incremental work in progress from the 1920s onward, starting with the Pentecostal and Holiness churches and spreading into mainline Protestant churches during the 1930s.

Because this story is essentially about the quest for freedom, let us begin our narrative with that universal symbol of freedom: the train.

PART ONE

Roots

CHAPTER 1

Got On My Traveling Shoes
Black Sacred Music and the Great Migration

> Rise, shine, and give God the glory, glory;
> Rise, shine, and give God the glory, glory;
> Rise, shine, and give God the glory in the Year of Jubilee.
>
> **"Do You Think I'll Make a Soldier," Wiseman Sextet version**

The Gospel Train Is Comin'

The Illinois Central passenger train screeched to a stop at the Twelfth Street depot on Chicago's South Side, its smokestack coughing up frothy puffs of soot as if the fatigue of traveling 1,126 railroad miles north from New Orleans had caused it combustible indigestion.[1] From among the train's human cargo, black men, women, and children trudged slowly through the passenger car doors and made their first footfalls on the platform.

The Promised Land.

Once inside the Illinois Central station's bustling lobby, the new arrivals searched the sea of faces, looking for family members, friends, and neighbors who had already settled in Chicago and promised to meet them when their train arrived. Those who had nobody waiting for them could hail a porter or redcap and seek explicit directions to their final destination

For the majority of arrivals, that destination was Bronzeville—the "city within a city," the Black Metropolis—the primary residential and commercial district for Chicago's black population during the nineteenth and early twentieth centuries.[2] In those days, Bronzeville was an eight-and-one-half-square-mile community concentrated between Roosevelt Road (1200 South) as the northernmost border, Cottage Grove as the easternmost border, Wentworth Avenue as the western boundary, and a southern border that shifted over time, from Thirty-First to Thirty-Fifth, then to Forty-Seventh and eventually Sixty-Third Street.

Many of the earliest southern migrants got their first eyeful of Bronzeville from the streetcar as they traveled the few miles south on State Street from the IC Station at Twelfth Street into the heart of The Stroll, Bronzeville's main entertainment district during the 1920s and 1930s. The area along State Street between Thirty-First and Thirty-Fifth Streets was packed with entertainments of every kind, a Chicago equivalent of Beale Street in Memphis or Rampart Street in New Orleans. Patrons of the Grand Theater enjoyed generous helpings of classic blues from Gertrude "Ma" Rainey, who made her entrance onto the stage by bursting forth from a giant papier-mâché Victrola. On the same block as the Grand were the Lincoln Theater and the Vendome Theater, where Louis Armstrong and Carroll Dickerson's Orchestra got patrons dancing after the motion-picture show. For fourteen-year-old Wealthy L. Mobley, who migrated with his family from Minter City, Mississippi, on Christmas Day 1935, the sight of Chicago was "awesome!" He explained, "Well, you know, coming out of the country, the only light we saw was the lighting up of a lightning bug!"[3]

Squeezed between the come-hither facades of dazzling theaters, cafés, and restaurants were furniture stores, funeral parlors, beauty shops, and sparse, somber storefront churches. As if to underscore the difference between them and their gaudier neighbors, these churches were minimally furnished with wooden folding chairs facing the pulpit in meticulously arranged rows, reverently awaiting the next service. On Sunday mornings and evenings, the rhythmic singing and shouting coming from Pentecostal and Holiness churches along State Street were so exuberant that one might suspect the buildings' proximity to the clubs had infected their congregations with the jazz bug.

Passersby were as much an expression of the area's contrasts as the buildings. Walking along State Street were men in sharp suits, women in smart dresses, factory workers in overalls covered in grease and dirt, and slaughterhouse employees splattered with animal blood. On one corner might be a battered man in an even more battered fedora, a cigarette dangling from his mouth while he played bottleneck country blues on guitar. On the other corner might be a sturdy, serious woman dressed in a long, dark dress, somber hat, and black Oxford shoes. Like the bottleneck guitarist, she sang with passion, but whereas his repertory was blues, hers was the gospel hymn and evangelistic song. He sang about hurt, she about salvation, but both strummed the same chords, sang with the same raw and genuine feeling, and hoped for a few coins in their cup or tambourine by day's end.

Chicago did not look or feel like the Promised Land as proffered by the *Chicago Defender*, the largest weekly newspaper by and about African Americans. The streets were not paved with gold, and some were not even paved. Still, Chicago did not have lynch mobs, sharecropping, or "Colored Only" signs. You could ride the streetcar and not have to move when a white person sat down next to you.

Starting around 1916, but given an official start date by the *Defender* of May 15, 1917, the Great Northern Drive, or the Great Migration, sent wave upon wave of black men, women, and children crashing upon Chicago's shores.[4] Between 1910 and 1920, the Great Migration swelled Chicago's black population from 44,103 to 109,458, placing the city fourth among all U.S. cities in total black population by 1920.[5] Of blacks living in Chicago in 1920, more than 80 percent—some 91,000—had been born outside Illinois, with the largest percentages arriving from Kentucky, Alabama, Arkansas, Tennessee, Louisiana, Georgia, and Mississippi. Most came from Alabama and Mississippi.

The Great Migration was called an exodus for good reason. Entire families evacuated plantations, small towns, and rural villages, but mostly left the cities of post-Reconstruction Alabama, Louisiana, Mississippi, Arkansas, Georgia, Tennessee, and Kentucky. In 1918, an adult could purchase a one-way ticket on the Illinois Central from New Orleans to Chicago for $22.52; by 1927, the one-way fare rose to $37.76. Individuals unable to afford the fare from savings sold property and personal goods or sought financial assistance from family or friends already established in Chicago. Especially enterprising individuals organized family, friends, and neighbors into "emigrant clubs" that enabled them to negotiate group discount fares with the train companies. When police began patrolling southern train stations to prevent the black labor force from leaving, ticketholders hid behind trees and brush north of the station. As the train lumbered past, the entire area seemed to spring to life, like jubilee: black men, women, and children, bags in hand, darted from behind cover and ran toward the train doors.

Regardless of the way migrants traveled, Chicago was the destination of choice, particularly for those from Atlanta, Birmingham, Mobile, New Orleans, and Memphis. Myriad reasons were given for leaving the South, but they could all be summarized as "to better my condition." That is what Chicago promised, what the *Defender* screamed from its front pages and editorials, what Pullman porters spoke about, and what relatives, friends, and neighbors—the pioneers who traveled to Chicago to test the waters—described in postcards, telephone calls, and during occasional visits back home.[6] Some things told about Chicago were not true, but as one newcomer noted, "So much of it true, don't mind the other."[7]

The Promised Land?

Substandard housing was one of the migrant's first disillusionments in the Promised Land. Blacks who moved to Chicago prior to the Great Migration found living accommodations without much difficulty, even though the city's restrictive housing covenants kept them within the confines of Bronzeville's narrow rectangular border. But by 1920, when more than one hundred thousand African Americans had settled in the city, Bronzeville was packed to bursting. When demand for flats outweighed supply, landlords subdivided already subdivided housing stock, creating the kitchenette—a cramped, dingy, and unsafe efficiency unit.

Employment was another disappointment. Many men toiled under the same backbreaking work in the northern steel mills and slaughterhouses as they had endured in the South. Migrants had also not escaped domestic servitude by coming north. The work available to them included jobs as janitors and wait staff, and maids and laundresses for women. When funds were available, women entered beauty schools, trained to become teachers, or studied nursing at Bronzeville's all-black Provident Hospital or the city's Contagious Hospital. Jobs in Chicago paid better than those in the South, but with higher wages came long, arduous hours of manual labor.

Resistance to new migrants sometimes escalated to violence. The Race Riot of 1919, during which 38 persons were killed and 537 injured, proved that race relations in Chicago were on shaky ground.[8] Further, between July 1, 1917, and March 1, 1921, 58 black-inhabited buildings in Chicago were bombed.[9] In 1925, a Baptist church on Michigan Avenue was bombed so repeatedly that the congregation took out insurance against bombing.[10] One Congregational church on South Michigan Avenue received national attention for placing a bulletin board in front that stated "A White Congregation Worships Here."[11]

If unemployment, substandard housing, and hostility weren't bad enough, the new migrants faced prejudice and discrimination from within the black community as well. Some "Old Settlers," members of the black middle-class establishment who were born or settled in Chicago prior to the Great Migration, believed the migrants' country behavior compromised any real or perceived racial harmony that existed in the city. One Old Settler commented, "There was no discrimination in Chicago during my early childhood days, but as the Negroes began coming to Chicago in numbers it seems they brought discrimination with them."[12] Others criticized the uncouth manners of some newcomers. One unattributed article in the *Defender* declared, "When in Chicago, for goodness sake, do as Chicagoans do!" The writer admonished black workers for "riding busses and trains in their overalls and dirty clothes used at work" and advised them to wash before coming home and leave dirty clothes at the workplace.[13]

The intraracial friction boiled down to class differences. Old Settlers did not work in factories—they were never afforded the opportunity. They developed stable incomes as postal employees, Pullman porters, housekeepers for wealthy white families, and doormen. In keeping with their urban middle-class standing, they cultivated a sense of refinement and respectability. They belonged to social clubs, were active politically, and fostered an appreciation for classical music. They favored highbrow performances of the all-black Apollo Chorus, Umbrian Glee Club, William E. Myricks's Federal Glee Club, and the women's Laredef Glee Club (Federal spelled backward), and Professor J. Wesley Jones's Metropolitan Prize-Winning and Radio Choir. They were embarrassed by southern migrants' folk mannerisms. Since restrictive covenants forced Old Settlers and new arrivals to live side by side, every wave of migrants found the middle class fleeing further south within the city's black belt boundary. They clustered in communities around Forty-Seventh Street, then around Sixty-Third Street.[14] As the black population continued to swell, Old Settlers moved southwest into the Englewood neighborhood. The more affluent made their homes in Morgan Park. It was not long before the migrant population was so pervasive that the Old Settlers could not go anywhere without finding new settlers living on the same block or in the same building.

It might seem that the one institution to which the new settlers could turn for solace was the church, but class differences were just as pronounced in the religious community as elsewhere. The worship style of the established Protestant churches in the urban north was dramatically different from what migrants practiced down South. The Great Migration and the resulting clash between the Old Settlers and the newcomers ultimately changed the religious order as profoundly as it did the social order, raising questions about what it meant to be black, religious, urban, and modern in the twentieth century.[15]

"How Shall We Sing the Lord's Song in a Strange Land?"

Communal worship, with its emotional music, preaching, rhythm, singing, and dancing, originated in West African sacred and secular traditions. Black gospel music in particular retained African-derived aesthetic markers, including falsetto, religious dancing or shouting, improvisation, repetition, hand clapping and foot patting, dynamic rhythms, communal participation, antiphonal response (call-and-response), and oral transmission of the music.[16] West Africans recognized spirit possession, a hallmark of the sanctified church, as the supreme religious experience. They regarded music and dance as both religious *and* secular, central to daily life and participatory.

Further, the folk preacher is a descendant of West African tribal leaders, serving as a spiritual leader and spokesperson and carrying musical elements into ritual. Jon Michael Spencer has observed that the "African rhythms of black preaching" gave the traditional black sermon its "melodiousness" as well as its "momentum and its momentousness."[17] It is also easy to hear the folk preacher's melodiousness, momentum, and momentousness in the delivery of a gospel song sung by a soloist or lead singer.

The black church evolved from the combination of "habits of belief" carried by Africans to the New World and "religion they were taught here."[18] "Brush arbor" or "brush harbor" meetings, named for the slaves' practice of gathering to worship under cover of brush or bushes to escape the notice of plantation owners, combined several African indigenous practices, including antiphonal, or call-and-response, singing and exhortations, impassioned oratory, and extroverted body movement. White Methodist missionaries taught psalms and hymns to slaves as they traveled the South and Southeast during the eighteenth and nineteenth centuries in search of converts.[19] The conversion process or "seekin' the Lord," a rite of passage similar to African initiation rites, encouraged slaves to make public testimonies or confessions of faith.[20] As slaves Africanized Christianity, they brought biblical themes of escape and deliverance into their own repertory of slave songs and spirituals. They were especially attracted to the mournful long-meter, or "lining out," psalms and hymns, in which a church leader recited or "called" a stanza of a psalm or song and led the congregation in a sung response. This practice, developed in mid-seventeenth-century white New England congregations in the absence of hymnbooks or instruments, was introduced to slave communities around 1750 by Samuel Davies, a New Light preacher. "Doc Watts" hymns—in essence, any long-meter hymn written by Isaac Watts and other hymnists—can still be heard "raised" or "lifted" by a deacon for congregational participation prior to a worship service in black Baptist churches.[21]

The songs and oratory of fundamentalist preachers and evangelists who pitched revival tents in rural areas and cities in nineteenth-century America also appealed to the black community. The use of vernacular language, emotional persuasion, and impassioned preaching echoed the slaves' brush arbor and plantation mission meetings and pray's house experiences.[22] The sprightly camp meeting spirituals and revival songs were crafted, like the long-meter hymns, so that attendees could learn them easily and quickly.

To facilitate congregational singing, gospel hymns and camp-meeting songs sometimes incorporated a portfolio of movable couplets and single lines that floated from song to song. For example, the opening verse of "Amazing Grace" was so well known by Christians that song leaders could incorporate it into any gospel hymn or set it to any melody with complete confidence that the congregation could join in.

Gospel Hymns and Sacred Songs, published by white evangelists Ira D. Sankey and Philip P. Bliss in 1875, was the first book to use the phrase "gospel hymns" in association with religious songs. Their *Gospel Hymns No. 2* followed a year later. Both hymnals attempted to capture the spirit and ardor of antebellum camp meetings, the Protestant City-Revival Movement of the 1850s, and the Sunday school songs that accompanied the revivalism.[23] More often than not, they seemed more solemn than celebratory. Nevertheless, they were far more popular among free blacks at the time than the spirituals, which served as embarrassing reminders of servitude's indignity.[24] More than a dozen of the hymnbook's songs, including "Pass Me Not," "I Need Thee Every Hour," "Come Ye Disconsolate," "The Solid Rock," and "Jesus Keep Me Near the Cross," remain popular hymns in the African American church.[25] Walter Pitts noted that worshippers often referred to these songs as "Sankeys."[26]

Independent black churches in southern states were established after the abolition of slavery. Individuals affiliated with one of several Protestant denominations, such as African Methodist Episcopal (AME), Baptist, Methodist Episcopal (ME), Colored (Christian) Methodist Episcopal (CME), and AME Zion. Regardless of denomination, the African American church was more than a house of worship. It was the most important black-centric institution— "the only institution," according to historian Carter Godwin Woodson, "that the race controls."[27] The church was a house of worship, a community center, youth center, senior center, social service center, news and information bureau, arbiter, mediator, and entertainment venue. Generations were born, baptized, married, and buried in the same church. According to Leroi Jones, "The Negro church, as it was begun, was the only place where the Negro could release emotions that slavery would naturally tend to curtail. The Negro went to church, literally, to be free, and to prepare himself for his freedom in the Promised Land."[28] Church congregations were communities within communities, sufficiently intimate that members knew one another by name and family genealogy. Membership was an important measure of status, and volunteer positions held within the church conferred additional standing.

The African American Church in the Urban North

While African American Protestant churches in northern urban centers served a similar role to their southern counterparts as community, social, and entertainment centers, migrants discovered that the African American church in the urban North had by and large distanced itself from the southern worship experience. The northern worship style tended to reflect the refined tastes of its upwardly mobile middle-class membership. Some educated black preachers winced at the "spontaneous improvisation and antiphonal chaos" of congregational singing.[29] AME bishop Daniel Alexander Payne and others sought to tamp down exuberant expression during services and replace the practice of lining out with "well trained church choirs" and classical musical instruments.

Just as the spirituals were shunned by former slaves, educated preachers considered antebellum worship practices involving excessive body movement and vociferous exclamation to be voodoo, superstition, or, at the very least, not in accord with racial uplift.[30]

Interestingly, Elizabeth Kilham, a white teacher of freed blacks, predicted as early as 1870 that the traditional worship practices and hymns were in danger of disappearing: "The distinctive features of negro hymnology are gradually disappearing. . . . The cause for this lies in the education of the younger people. . . . Already they have learned to ridicule the extravagant preaching, the meaningless hymns, and the noisy singing of the elders. . . . In the cities, the young people have, in many cases, taken the matter into their own hands, formed choirs, adopted the hymns and tunes in use in the white churches."[31]

Gradually more northern AME, Baptist, and other mainstream African American Christian denominations came under the influence of university-educated pastors and ministers who delivered learned homilies and integrated classically trained choirs into the worship service and musicals. Still, as blacks assumed full control of their churches, some pastors were amenable to congregants expressing "spontaneous religious emotions through active participation in worship."[32] Sutherland notes that among Chicago's black church congregations in the late 1920s, "a large share of the members recognize[d] that they [were] in a changed environment and that their rural religious practices [were] out of accord with the generally accepted standards," but that "occasional demonstrations occurred at Olivet, Metropolitan, Berean, Greater Bethesda, and others," though "usually of a mild degree."[33] On the other hand, Rev. Elijah J. Fisher, pastor of Olivet Baptist Church around 1915, said he believed "in enthusiastic religion but did not countenance a church in demoniac pandemonium."[34]

Sociologist Vattel Elbert Daniel categorized black churches in Chicago according to worship style: liturgical (e.g., Roman Catholic and Lutheran, in which the pastor or priest followed "liturgical ceremonial"), deliberative (e.g., Baptist, AME, CME, and ME, which preferred "sermon-centered services"), semi-demonstrative (e.g., Baptist, AME, CME, and Community, which "indulge in demonstrative assent"), and ecstatic cults (e.g., Church of God in Christ, Spiritual, and Church of the Living God).[35] Liturgical and deliberative churches preferred refined singing and worship practices, while semi-demonstrative churches did not mind a shout or two. Ecstatic cults encouraged demonstrative worship and singing. Daniel felt that of the four categories, semi-demonstrative churches were most closely related to the traditional (southern) African American church.

To black progressives, indigenous religious practices were more than embarrassing reminders of slavery times. They reinforced the very racial stereotypes that leaders such as W. E. B. Du Bois fought to eradicate.[36] Echoing the stern pronouncements of influential religious leaders such as Bishop Payne, who instructed his congregants to "sit down and sing in a rational manner," W. A. Blackwell of Walters AME in Chicago argued that "singing, shouting and talking" were the "most useless ways of proving Christianity."[37] Bertha Curry, a member of Chicago's Pilgrim Baptist Church, recalled that shortly after Rev. Junius Caesar Austin Sr. arrived from Pennsylvania to assume the pastorate, he declared, "We are intelligent folks here and we don't do a lot of hollering and so forth and carrying on."[38] Such a pronouncement did not preclude Austin or his contemporaries from interjecting a measure of emotion into their sermonic presentations, but in general public expressions of emotional worship during the formal service were discouraged as unbefitting behavior for people who wanted to be citizens of a modern urban community.

The Old Landmarks of Chicago

Refined worship was the norm in 1920s Chicago, and as the decade progressed, six deliberative Protestant churches organized by African Americans held the majority of the community's religious power. The first, and oldest, was Quinn Chapel AME. Founded in 1847, Quinn moved from its original location at Lake and Canal Streets to its present site at 2401 South Wabash in 1891. Metropolitan Community Church was established in 1920 by disenfranchised Bethel AME leader Rev. W. D. Cook. Organized in 1850, Olivet Baptist Church was considered "the largest single Protestant church in the world" by 1928 with 9,763 members. Its pastor, Rev. Lacey Kirk Williams, was a significant political force within the National Baptist Convention. Organized as prayer bands out of Olivet, Pilgrim Baptist Church and Ebenezer Baptist Church boasted the second and third largest congregations among African American churches in Chicago with 7,500 and 6,000 members respectively. Bethel AME, founded in 1862, was tied for third with 6,000 members.

Regardless of the facility, a church's reputation, its political might, the size and sophistication of its membership, and its financial sustainability depended on the pastor's scholarly homiletics and rhetorical skills, as well as on the prestige of the music department and the quality of its monthly musicals. The competition was fierce in a city brimming with educated, trained musicians, many of whom were associated with the National Association of Negro Musicians, founded in Chicago in 1919 and headquartered on the South Side. Pastors competed with one another to hire the finest conservatory-trained music directors to teach their senior choir oratorios and anthems. For example, spirituals preservationist Edward Boatner was director of music at Olivet during the 1920s and early 1930s. James A. Mundy, whose contributions to Chicago's music scene went back to 1912, held music directorships at Olivet, Pilgrim, Bethel AME, and Quinn Chapel.[39] Mable Sanford Lewis, who opened her own music conservatory in the 1930s, was the organist for Ebenezer Baptist Church. Voice instructor Omega Jane King, who, like Lewis, founded her own music school in the 1930s, was in charge of the Greater Bethesda Baptist Church senior choir.

The musical numbers these professionally trained music leaders programmed were culled from the western European–influenced classical repertory, including pieces written by black classical composers such as Samuel Coleridge-Taylor and concert spirituals arranged by John Work II and Harry T. Burleigh. Churches sponsored monthly musicals to spotlight the accomplishments of Bronzeville's classical elite. The community's preoccupation with classical music training and performance was prompted by not only middle-class upward mobility but also the expectation that the world would at last recognize that blacks could write, perform, and appreciate classical music.

Of the scores of religious music artisans who held positions of power in Chicago churches prior to the advent of gospel music, none was as well regarded as J. Wesley Jones. His "Prize-Winning and Radio Choir" from Metropolitan Community Church represented the apex of middle-class classical artistry in Chicago's black community. Their repertory, comportment, and prestige embodied the spirit of racial uplift as well as the economic and social aspirations of middle-class black Chicago. The ensemble was one of the first black choirs to record, to be heard on radio, to perform before a mixed audience, and to win a major choral competition. They performed arranged spirituals and well-known choral literature by western European and African American composers. Bach's "Sleepers Wake," Handel's "Shout the Glad Tidings," Christensen's "Beautiful Savior," Johnson's "Oh Southland," were some of the staples of the choir's monthly programs.[40]

Rev. Esther Greer offered a glimpse into the celebrity status of Jones and his choir: "Every fourth Sunday, if you didn't get to Metropolitan by five—and of course the musicale didn't start until 7:30—wear some comfortable shoes because you were going to stand up. . . . We used to try to keep the doors closed until six, but it was always so many people on Grand Boulevard [now Dr. Martin Luther King Drive] at that particular time that the police department demanded that the doors be opened."[41]

"The Songs Was Proud-Like"

In 1920s Chicago, the congregational singing that was popular in southern churches "had been all but obliterated" and relegated to prayer services prior to the main service.[42] Instead, the focus of the main service was the senior choir's singing and the minister's intellectual oratory. Thus, it was the highly formal, cultured singing by groups such as Jones's Metropolitan Prize-Winning and Radio Choir and other anthem-raising senior choirs that greeted migrants attending Sunday-morning services at deliberative Protestant churches on the South and West Sides in the 1920s.

Some migrants appreciated and admired the professional and semiprofessional senior choirs. Like their Old Settler brethren, they enjoyed Bronzeville's fashionable Sunday musicals, respecting Jones and Mundy as much as they did other black men and women considered "race leaders." Thomas A. Dorsey eagerly shook hands with Jones after attending one of the choir's performances.[43] These performances were the preferred form of entertainment for any of the saved and upwardly mobile who could not fathom spending time at the Grand or the Vendome, although to be sure, there were those who danced at the Plantation Café on Saturday night before taking in the uplifting sounds of the Metropolitan Choir on Sunday afternoon. Further, the rise in membership of the six major Old Landmarks during the Great Migration makes it safe to assume that not all their congregants were Old Settlers. The Sunday services of Chicago's deliberative Protestant churches, in fact, were packed to overflowing. Mary Fluornoy told interviewers that at Olivet, "We couldn't get in. We'd have to stand up. I don't care how early we'd go, you couldn't get in."[44] Mobley concurred. "Ebenezer, Pilgrim, all those big churches, if you didn't get in there at 10:30 [for the 11:00 a.m. service], you didn't get a seat."[45]

Although some demonstrative expression was allowed at the Old Landmarks, newly arrived migrants were nevertheless perplexed by the formal services that had more in common with their white counterparts than with churches in the rural South. For example, congregants were not encouraged to sing; that was the senior choir's responsibility. Rural southern blacks had been reared on what Woodson called "manifestations of the spirit."[46] They were accustomed to, and preferred, intimate, communal worship services that encouraged congregational singing and prayer. The church was the center of their community, and they were active participants. Conversely, Chicago's progressive and culturally refined Protestant churches were large and impersonal. One Louisianan who attended Pilgrim Baptist Church found it to be disconcertingly quiet. "Nobody said anything aloud but there were whispers all over the place."[47] The migrants felt that the deliberative churches and the "trills and flowery airs" of their senior choirs were haughty, and that their members were as interested in showing off their Sunday finery as in worshipping.[48] A woman who joined Olivet complained that she "couldn't understand the pastor and the words he used." She rued: "I couldn't sing their way. The songs was proud-like."[49] "Brother Brown," interviewed for the landmark study *Black Metropolis*, noted: "I haven't enjoyed a good service since I left the Southland. The meetings down home were soul-stirring."[50]

Although Paul Laurence Dunbar's "The Ol' Tunes" was not written about migrants worshipping in the Old Landmarks of Bronzeville, it nevertheless captured their sentiments:

You kin talk about yer anthems

An' yer arias an' sich,

An' yer modern choir-singin'

That you think so awful rich;

But you orter heerd us youngsters

In the times now far away,

A-singin' o' the ol' tunes

In the ol'-fashioned way.[51]

"Islands of Southern Culture"

Not finding a comfortable home in the Old Landmarks, migrants created their own "islands of southern culture," establishing churches that welcomed newcomers and encouraged congregational participation.[52] Southern migrants seeking a ritual that gave them the feeling of being back home was not unlike the experience of European immigrants who adjusted to urban life in Chicago by remaking their neighborhoods into microcosms of familiar culture.

Some migrants even went so far as to petition their home preachers to migrate and transplant their former community church in Chicago. For example, Christ Temple Mission in Chicago was reconstituted from members of the Christ Temple Church in Jackson, Mississippi.[53] The First Baptist Church of Hattiesburg, Mississippi, was re-created in a Chicago storefront, after its migrant members finally persuaded the pastor to move north and resume his duties as their spiritual leader.[54] These are literal examples of Sutherland's comment: "When the Negro migrated North his church came with him."[55]

Others departed from the big, impersonal churches of the denomination into which they were born to organize small, informal worship communities called prayer groups or "prayer bands."[56] This was not a new concept. Deliberative churches such as Pilgrim and Ebenezer started as prayer bands of disaffected Olivet members who met initially in South Side living rooms. While disagreements about church policies prompted the organization of the Pilgrim and Ebenezer prayer bands, the substance of the worship experience itself was often the factor leading migrant prayer bands to form. Some prayer bands received a tongue-lashing from bourgeois, middle-class individuals. As early as September 1921, the *Defender* chided that the exuberant sound of prayer bands in residential areas was inappropriate: "These religious enthusiasts do not seem to realize that residential neighborhoods are liable to have people living there who do not share with them in their demonstrative manifestations of religious devotion. Loud and noisy declamations and moans and groans from sisters and brothers until a late hour in the night are not only annoying but an unmistakable nuisance."[57]

Most of the islands of southern culture, whether Baptist, Methodist, or another denomination, were housed in cultural halfway houses—rented, bare-bones storefronts located along busy avenues on Chicago's South Side.[58] Storefront churches appeared on State Street as early as 1904.[59] By the late 1920s, storefront churches (113) outnumbered traditional churches (91), and by the late 1930s, Chicago had 266 storefront churches.[60] Like their larger counterparts, storefront churches understood that inspiring music, effective preaching, and a variety of social services built church membership among newcomers and disaffected Old Settlers alike. More members meant more tithe revenue, which in turn meant burning the mortgage or building a bigger temple, developing larger programs, and securing greater political clout for the minister in a community where the most revered pastors moved comfortably in the company of Bronzeville's power brokers and entrepreneurial kingpins. The difference was one of membership and methodology. Whereas the Old Landmarks catered to a middle-class membership, the storefronts were what Milton Sernett has called "religious outposts of southern culture," a "southernization" of African American religion in the urban north.[61] Their migrant clientele reveled in the familiar services. Also, by providing a participatory outlet for youth, the churches kept them from falling prey to The Stroll's enticements.

Storefront churches provided new settlers with opportunities for recognition and status that the larger, more established churches could not. Said one migrant: "There is not as much friendship [in the larger churches] as in one of these store-fronts. In a big church the preacher don't know you unless you make big donations or you are an officer of some kind. With my church, it is different. We are more like churches in the South—everybody is recognized."[62] Leadership spots in smaller churches were also more plentiful for newcomers. One pastor said: "In a little church there is something for everybody to do. Every man in the church, as well as every woman, can have an office."[63] "When you've been mistreated all the week," said civil rights attorney Benjamin L. Hooks, "called 'boy,' given inadequate wages, Sunday morning was the only time you were a man."[64]

The worship music of the storefront church—spirit-inspired in the case of the Pentecostal and Holiness churches and hymn-based in deliberative Protestant denominations—articulated the process of migrant adaptation to the urban environment. It would be a huge assumption, however, to suggest that all Chicago storefront churches allowed for spontaneous expression and sang in a fiery manner. Not all storefront churches were sanctified, nor did all churches rock to the sound of sanctified singing and preaching. Deliberative denominations found early refuge in rented storefronts as well. Sernett writes, "Many [storefront churches] housed congregations with memberships made up of migrants with Baptist or Methodist predilections who were seeking to create a cultural oasis in their environment."[65] Sutherland notes, "More Baptist congregations worship in store and house front churches than any other denomination."[66] Mobley recalled, "The first church that I joined when I came [to Chicago in 1935] was called Pleasant Green [Baptist Church]. That was a storefront church down there on the 2900 block of Cottage Grove. [We sang] the hymns and spiritual songs." Although gospel was gaining ground by 1935, Mobley remembered the Pleasant Green congregation staying faithful stylistically to Baptist hymnody, including songs such as "Jesus Keep Me Near the Cross" and "Blessed Assurance." "None of the boom-de-boom-de-boom," Mobley said. "No, we didn't have none of that."[67]

On the other hand, the congregational singing of the sanctified church incorporated the structured informality of the black rural communal folk worship experience with the exciting urban rhythms of jazz and classic blues. Sutherland describes the experience of "an extreme type of Holiness church" in Chicago: "Step into the Sunday morning services of a State Street store front to be greeted by the weird pleading of voices pitched to the tone of jubilee songs. Listen to the incessant clatter of tambourines. Watch the swaying of bodies and clapping of hands, the jerking and shouting, and dancing of spirit-filled souls. Hear the preacher raise his voice to an ever higher key as he hurries his prayers to the Lord in a jumble of syllables that man cannot hear."[68]

Music created by and for the congregation, and sometimes composed on the spot, was an essential component of the sanctified church service and the chief ingredient that caused many to slip over for a soul-stirring worship experience while maintaining their allegiance to the church of their baptism. The music of the sanctified church blended the indigenous and the urban, the traditional and contemporary. What became known as gospel was neither entirely progressive nor indigenous but an amalgam, an "expression developed from southern migrants' confrontation with the urban north."[69] It reflected their need to hang on to their southern roots while becoming thoroughly modern. The music gave the "evangelical revivalism" of southern religious practices an urban soundtrack drawn directly from the jazz and classic blues performed on The Stroll. Later, black Chicago disk jockeys would speak directly to this southernization of northern life in their on-air "street" patter. Before that, however, a community of gospel singers, musicians, and enthusiastic congregations developed and formed their own "fluid folk life" around the church and its new soundtrack of gospel music.

Conservative Protestants whose quest for more soul-stirring services outweighed apprehension and misunderstanding of the nontraditional sects found satisfaction at Pentecostal, Holiness, Spiritual, nondenominational, and other sanctified churches such as Elder Lucy Smith's All Nations Pentecostal, Bishop William Roberts's Roberts Temple Church of God in Christ, Rev. S. P. Dunn's Church of God, and Rev. Clarence Cobbs's First Church of Deliverance. One pastor of a church that embraced the religious practices of the South told Daniel: "There are persons whose churches have some very polished ministers, yet some steal away and come here. They say: 'I get my mental food all right yonder, but I can't get spiritual gems.' . . . In getting spiritual food, the people get to the state of ecstasy. They are taken away from the plane of domestic engagement and concern up to a spiritual plane."[70] Belonging to a church that felt like home and sounded like home, migrants not only could move "up to a spiritual plane" but also were able to establish a distinct identity and sense of belonging in the unfamiliar urban frontier where both identity and belonging were elusive.

On one hand, the proliferation of storefront and sanctified churches was welcomed by the deliberative Protestant churches because it helped ease overcrowding on Sundays. Besides, to the black bourgeoisie, migrants were seen as riffraff and impeded efforts at racial uplift. Nevertheless, extraordinary membership growth in the Old Landmarks meant the need for larger worship spaces. Fleeing Bronzeville in the wake of the Great Migration, white congregations sold their stone and brick churches and synagogues to the newcomers, but often at inflated prices. The ornate buildings communicated the churches' elevated status, but at the price of crippling debt service. Pastors groaning under the weight of heavy mortgages needed a concomitant amount of tithing to pay down the debt and maintain the church's other ministries. While there appeared to be sufficient numbers of black men and women in Chicago to help sustain the Old Landmarks, studies show that as the 1920s progressed, 75 percent of the five hundred churches located in Bronzeville were storefronts, each taking its share of potential membership from them.[71]

On top of this development, Chicago counted two hundred "jack-leg" preachers (ministers without a formal church congregation) who, depending on their oratory skills and personality, could attract a sizable following for their street-corner services.[72] Just as major churches often started as prayer bands, Bronzeville's up-and-coming church leaders, such as Elder Lucy Smith, Bishop A. A. Childs, and Rev. L. H. Ford, started their ministries by pitching revival tents in the city.

Pastors of established churches might have cast aspersions on the grow-ing number of storefronts, but they could not ignore them. St. Clair Drake and Horace Cayton contend that the denunciations of Spiritual and Holiness churches that pastors and members of deliberative congregations made indicate the pressure put on them to adapt to the migrant community.[73] Some of the larger churches began hosting revivals with old-fashioned singing and preach-ing to encourage newcomers to join, but contemporary accounts reveal that the revivals were "poorly attended" in comparison to their southern counter-parts.[74] As noted earlier, even as Old Landmark ministers incorporated fiery monologue into their sermons, their discouragement of overt emotionalism during Sunday services remained.[75]

The tension between the Old Settlers and the newcomers and their pre-ferred style of worship set the stage for an overall shift in the predominant preaching, singing, and worship style of the deliberative urban church. Gospel music would ultimately overturn Old World progressivism and become the predominant expression of sacred modernity in Chicago and throughout the nation.

A decade before Thomas Dorsey, Theodore Frye, Sallie Martin, and others introduced their version of indigenous, religious folk music into deliberative Protestant churches, first in the Midwest and then out to both coasts, the Pentecostal, Holiness, and Spiritual churches were already stirring souls with a musical soundtrack that set hymns, anthems, and new songs to a distinctly modern, urban beat. The influence of the sanctified churches in the develop-ment of gospel music cannot be overstated. Phonograph recordings during the 1920s and radio broadcasts of church services in the 1930s helped set the stage for the Dorsey revolution by disseminating the music of Pentecostal, Holiness, and Spiritual churches well beyond their walls.

CHAPTER 2

"When the Fire Fell"

The Sanctified Church Contribution to Chicago Gospel Music

Spontaneous in every sense of the word. No pianist, organist, or choir director interferes with the freedom. . . . A spiritual may be started any time in the service and by anyone who feels the urge to sing.

Robert Lee Sutherland, 1930

Chicago's Pentecostal, Holiness, Apostolic, and Spiritual churches—collectively referred to as the sanctified church—helped establish in the northern urban environment what historian Evelyn Brooks Higginbotham has called an "emotional folk orality." Working-class southern migrants brought their oral tradition, or "age of the voice," with them when they came north as part of the Great Migration.[1] But while the folk orators of the sanctified church sought to remain close to their southern roots, they also wanted to carve out their own position of power and influence among the city's African American cultural and political elite. By becoming "oral narrators of modernity," storefront preachers and evangelists—in person, on record, and on radio—could join their middle-class peers as thought leaders, standard-bearers, and morality enforcers for the new migrant community.[2]

Historians credit female evangelist Mattie L. Thornton as organizing the city's first sanctified church, the Holy Nazarene Tabernacle Apostolic Church, around 1908.[3] By 1919, approximately twenty Holiness churches had been founded in Chicago.[4] Like their Baptist and Methodist counterparts, sanctified churches often started as prayer bands—small, informal prayer groups that met in the home of a member—that typically consisted of the organizer and immediate family and friends. The groups would start by meeting regularly in the founder's living room. Once the flock grew in numbers, they traded up to a modest storefront along one of the city's main commercial avenues, such as Michigan Boulevard, State Street, Indiana Avenue, and South Parkway, now known as Dr. Martin Luther King Jr. Drive. The humble space was adorned with whatever furnishings the pastor and the members could afford at the time.

What Robert Austin Warner observed at a storefront church in New Haven, Connecticut, in 1934 could just as easily describe one in 1920s Chicago: "The essential fittings consisted of a pulpit; a Bible; some folding chairs, secondhand pews or benches; musical instruments such as a triangle, a tambourine, a pair of cymbals, or a battered piano; framed mottoes and a religious picture or two; and a dingy curtain shutting off a portion of the room behind the platform."[5] To this list one can add a comfortably appointed seat for the pastor and a pot-belly stove to warm the congregation during bone-chilling Chicago winters. The front window would be adorned with a hand-printed sign identifying the church and its founder and pastor, a favorite Bible passage or motto, times of service, and a welcome message.

Like brush arbor meetings or praise houses, the sanctuary's physical appearance was secondary to the reason for gathering: the preaching, praising, shouting, healing, breaking through, collection, and altar call. Every Sunday and selected weekday evenings, congregational singing and passionate oratory transformed humble Pentecostal and Holiness storefronts on Bronzeville and West Side thoroughfares into the urban manifestation of what Idella Johnson has referred to as the "visible counterparts of the antebellum 'invisible church,'" or what evangelist Mattie Poole describes as "Holy Ghost churches."[6] Through a dedication to spiritual purpose, seat-of-the-pants entrepreneurship, and irresistible preaching and singing, sanctified church leaders developed their storefronts into institutions that rivaled the Old Landmarks in membership, visibility, and financial sustainability. As such, notes Johnson, they "mirrored the past while simultaneously forecasting the future."[7]

"Soldiers in the Army": The Holiness and Pentecostal Movements

Of all the sanctified denominations with presences in Chicago, the Church of God in Christ (COGIC) played the most significant role in planting the seeds of gospel music. COGIC was established initially as a Holiness church in Lexington, Mississippi, by discontented Baptists Charles Price Jones and Charles Harrison Mason. Jones and Mason sought a religious experience that had as its foundation a commitment to purity and sanctification as the pathway to a state of true holiness. Their church's philosophy was challenged in 1907, when for five weeks, Mason attended Charles Seymour's Azusa revival in Los Angeles. The multicultural revival, which lasted from 1906 to 1915, was based on the principle that true holiness was achievable only through Holy Ghost possession and manifested by speaking in tongues, or glossolalia, a sound akin to an untranslatable foreign language.

COGIC historian Pastor Mack C. Mason describes the Azusa worship services and music as "holy disorder, spontaneous and unstructured."[8] The congregants did not use hymnals or instruments, nor did they rehearse, but they started songs as the spirit led them. Previously composed songs sung during the Azusa Street services included spirituals and revival hymns such as "Love Lifted Me," "Must Jesus Bear the Cross Alone," and "Heavenly Sunshine."[9] Some songs, however, were new creations, literally written on the spot, such as the music created by Jennie Moore, who demonstrated her newfound baptism by "singing in the spirit" and accompanying herself on piano, even though she had never taken a piano lesson.[10] The compositions, referred to at the time as "tongue-songs," were considered divinely inspired. Hymn scholar Jon Michael Spencer believes that tongue-songs were "one of the first and certainly one of the most theologically important forms of music manifested in primal Pentecostalism."[11] The spirit-led singing that filled Seymour's Azusa Street services was not only an evocation of West African traditions but also a precedent to the populism of gospel music in encouraging all congregants, regardless of musical ability, to participate in the music making.

Mason left the Azusa revival convinced that Seymour was right: speaking in tongues was the incontrovertible sign of spirit baptism. He brought the concept back to Lexington but found church leaders, including Jones, not persuaded by his argument. The debate split the denomination in 1907.[12] After a legal battle, Mason earned the right to use the name Church of God in Christ. Jones, meanwhile, named his community the Church of Christ Holiness. He remained in Lexington, while Mason moved COGIC headquarters to Wellington Street in Memphis. Here Mason met a shopkeeper, William Roberts, who would become one of his earliest assistants.

Bishop William Roberts and COGIC in Chicago

William Matthew Roberts was born in Okolona, Mississippi, on May 10, 1876, the fourth of thirteen children to former slaves Mr. and Mrs. Willie Roberts. William Matthew married Mamie Hill on November 19, 1899, and the couple moved to Memphis, where they opened a dry-goods store.[13] In 1904, Roberts heard Mason preaching on the streets of Memphis and joined his Church of

God in Christ. The couple even provided Mason with clothing from their store. Roberts had a reason to feel kinship with Mason. He, too, had participated in the Azusa Street Revival and witnessed firsthand the power of the nascent Pentecostal movement. So convinced was Roberts in glossolalia as a sign of spirit baptism that he was among the ministers who stood with Mason after the latter parted ways with Charles Price Jones. Roberts was named a deacon and later assistant pastor at the flagship COGIC church on Wellington Street.[14]

Around 1914, Mason developed a strategy for denominational growth that included planting COGIC churches in northern cities with significant numbers of new southern migrants. Chicago was on the short list. Immediately following Mason's directive, COGIC leaders Elder and Sister Bostic conducted a convocation in Chicago, but they decided not to remain in the city. An assemblage of other COGIC pastors also traveled to Chicago with hopes of planting churches, but they, too, forsook what they saw as a profoundly unsaved, perhaps unsavable, wide-open city on Lake Michigan with rampant crime, gambling, and prostitution.[15]

Undaunted, thirteen Chicago women, including Anna Davis, Mary Duncan Davis, and Lillian Coffey, organized a COGIC prayer group.[16] They held regular Bible study sessions in a member's home at Twenty-Ninth and LaSalle Streets. Since COGIC prohibits women from pastoring a church, they were unable to organize a formal congregation without a male leader. The women appealed to Bishop Mason to give Chicago another chance. They even had a potential pastor in mind: Mason's loyal associate, Elder William Roberts. The prayer group was so persistent that it raised and sent Roberts seventeen dollars for train fare from Memphis. Mason consented to the request, and Roberts embarked on an exploratory visit to Chicago.[17]

On Christmas Day, 1916, forty-year-old Roberts arrived in Chicago with his young son, Isaiah, in tow to consider the women's request. Years later, during an appearance on Isabel Joseph Johnson's *Rock of Ages* television program, Brother Isaiah Roberts told viewers that when he pressed his young face to the train's window screen, eager for his first eye-opening impression of the Promised Land of Chicago, he was sorely disappointed. The city was engulfed in smoke. There was so much soot on the window screen that Elder Roberts had to wipe the dust off his son's face with a handkerchief.[18]

After meeting with the women congregants, Roberts was persuaded that the partnership would work. He returned to Memphis, shuttered his dry-goods store, and in early 1917, relocated his family to Chicago. By this time, the family had added a second child, daughter Minnie Pearl. Roberts took a job in the stockyards to make ends meet as he led the city's first COGIC church, which moved out of the Davis home and into a commercial space at 3233 South State Street.

By 1919, the COGIC elders felt sufficiently confident with their new ministry to host the city's first Holy Convocation. It was a courageous decision, given that it occurred just days after the infamous Chicago Race Riot on July 27, 1919, which took the lives of thirty-eight, left hundreds injured, one thousand homeless, and exposed the city's undercurrent of poor interracial relations.

Not long after the convocation, Roberts moved his church west to Thirty-First and LaSalle. In 1920, it moved to Thirty-Seventh and Federal before settling in 1923 at 4021 South State Street, where the church remains to this day. Before rededication in 1953 as Roberts Temple COGIC, the church was known as "Fortieth," for its physical location at Fortieth and State Streets.[19]

What were the worship service and the music like at Fortieth during the 1920s? Perhaps not unlike what Sutherland found at an anonymous Chicago storefront Holiness service: "spontaneous in every sense of the word. No pianist, organist, or choir director interferes with the freedom. . . . A spiritual may be started any time in the service and by anyone who feels the urge to sing."[20] Sutherland added, "If the singing becomes over-enthusiastic the time is breathlessly rapid," and went on to describe a congregation that over the course of ten minutes sang and clapped faster and faster until it could no longer continue at the heightened tempo, at which time only the clapping continued, and then eventually stopped.[21]

Elder Eleazar Lenox and the Lenox Family

Like Roberts, Elder Eleazar Lenox was one of many leaders in Chicago's embryonic COGIC church community whose progeny would become important figures in gospel music. Lenox's son James, grandsons Kelvin and Lamont, granddaughter Annette "Queenie," and daughter-in-law Aldrea became internationally acclaimed gospel singers, musicians, songwriters, choir directors, and recording artists.

Born January 23, 1902, in Yazoo, Mississippi, Eleazar Lenox grew up on his family's farm in Terrell, Arkansas. In 1921, with no opportunities available for a sharecropper's son in the Jim Crow South, Lenox joined the exodus to Chicago. Upon arrival, he joined Bishop Roberts's Fortieth COGIC and served as its assistant pastor.[22] The following year, the remaining Lenox family in Terrell migrated to Chicago.[23] In 1925, twenty-three-year-old Eleazar accepted the pastorate of the small COGIC church at 1865 West Carroll Avenue when its founding minister, COGIC pastor Thomas Farley, retired. Carroll Avenue Church, as it was called, served migrants who had moved to the city's West Side to work in the nearby factories.

Lamont Lenox, current pastor of Carroll Avenue Church, now known as Greater Holy Temple COGIC, remembers his grandfather Eleazar as "a gentle man but a strong leader. He could say what he needed to say, he meant what he said, and you *did* what he said!" Lamont recalled Eleazar's particular penchant for preaching. "He knew the Word and he could preach a very, very long time. I remember when I was a kid, we probably stayed in [Sunday] service a good four hours. Stay in service four hours, go downstairs and eat something, get a little break, and then you are back at six o'clock for YPWW [Young People's Willing Workers]. And then an eight o'clock service!"[24]

By 1928, Eleazar Lenox had secured sufficient funds to move the Carroll congregation to a three-level building at 2673 West Lake Street. Doris Washington remembered that the newly relocated church, referred to either as Twenty-Six or Lake Street, was just east of Bethlehem Healing Temple, led by evangelists Mattie and Charles Poole. Bookended by two churches with equally spritely services, that section of Lake Street became known as "Blessed Street."[25] Lake Street, like Fortieth, was "a familiar setting, reminding the migrant members of their churches in the South, which were the organizing force for worship and a sacred place of acceptance, spiritual growth, and social networking."[26]

Those who attended services at Lake Street COGIC recall the music distinctly. Mary Lenox, the church's historian, wrote that musicians played "improvised and traditional instruments. Lucy Mallard played the cymbals, John Jackson played the guitar, and Ernestine Smith played the piano." The congregation sang gospel hymns such as "Savior Do Not Pass Me By," "I'm A Soldier in the Army of the Lord," "I'll Overcome Some Day," and "Peace Be Still."[27] Services included song, testimonies, a sermon, and healing. Both the Lake Street youth and adult choirs actively participated in the services.[28]

To COGIC members, or "saints," music was improvisational by definition. In step with the Azusa Street Revival, COGIC singing was inspired by the presence of the Holy Spirit and, like the Holy Spirit, could materialize at any time. Music represented both the manifestation of the Holy Spirit in the service and a divine gift to the musician or singer who played or sang it.[29] Singing and music making was participatory and central to the service. The musical component could extend for long periods, depending on the height of the spirit during the service. Everyone, regardless of musical talent, was encouraged to join in. In addition to piano, Pentecostal churches used what other denominations considered club or jazz instruments, including trombone, trumpet, cornet, saxophone, snare drum, mandolin, ukulele, triangle, harmonica, and tambourine. In other words, the worship service and music of the Church of God in Christ was lively, informal, and emotional, evoking the congregational spirit of southern church services, the spontaneity of Azusa, and West African religious traditions. At the same time, jazz instrumentation and its similarly improvised arrangements introduced the sound of the urban landscape into the church.

Elder P. R. Favors and the Sanctified Church on the West Side

Like Roberts and Lenox, Elder Peter R. Favors supported the early development of gospel music in Chicago. After being saved under Bishop Mason, Favors served as a deacon at the Church of God in Christ in Lexington, Mississippi, from 1916 to 1918, when he and his wife, Mother Pinkie Favors, and granddaughter Grace became part of the early wave of migrants to Chicago. By 1920, Favors was holding street-corner services in the Maxwell Street area on Chicago's near West Side. For decades, Maxwell Street was an open marketplace as well as a popular performance space for street-corner evangelists, blues singers, and blues musicians.

By autumn 1920, the Favors family and ten others had started a COGIC church in a basement at 1069 West Maxwell Street. When they could afford their own church home two years later, they moved to 1323 South Blue Island Avenue, where they rented a hall until spring 1929. On Sunday, June 2, 1929, the saints marched from Blue Island Avenue to their new church at 1319 West Thirteenth Street. Mildred L. Mondane, Favors's youngest granddaughter and one of the marchers, recalled the ceremony: "[We] marched, singing 'Praise God From Whom All Blessings Flow,' 'Praise The Lord Forever and Forever,' and 'When The Saints Go Marching In.' Eighty-five saints started in the march, and as latecomers and well wishers joined in, the group had increased to one hundred thirty-one when they arrived at the church and were counted. That Sunday service was blessed. Some of the Saints were praising God in the street."[30]

Thirteenth Street COGIC, nicknamed "the sanctified church of the West Side," would host some of the earliest COGIC revivalists, including Elder Utah Smith, Arizona Dranes, and Mother Katie Bell Nubin and her daughter Rosetta Tharpe. Among the products of Pastor Favors's church were Bishop Isaac and Mother Maggie Favors, whose son, Malachi Favors (1927—2004), was a jazz bassist who founded the Association for the Advancement of Creative Musicians (AACM) in 1965 and performed with the avant-garde Art Ensemble of Chicago. Mother Alva Johnson Roberts, who married Brother Isaiah Roberts of Fortieth COGIC, was an early member of Favors's church, as was Mother Fannie Gay and her family, including daughters Evelyn, Mildred, and Geraldine.

"Have Prayer Meetings at Home"

Until 1926, the only way to hear the music and preaching of Holy Ghost–inspired services in Chicago was to be a member of, or steal away to visit, a service at Lake Street, Fortieth, Thirteenth Street COGIC, or any other of the city's growing number of Pentecostal and Holiness churches. This would change in June 1926, when Arizona Juanita Dranes, a blind COGIC musician from Fort Worth, Texas, came to Chicago to make the first commercial recordings of the exuberant music of the Pentecostal Church.

The groundwork was laid a few years prior, when the recording industry noticed that the African American community was a fertile and largely untapped market for commercial recordings. In 1920, the General Phonograph Company released "That Thing Called Love" and "You Can't Keep a Good Man Down" by Mamie Smith and Her Jazz Hounds on its OKeh imprint. The *Defender* commented that the "unusual event" of "the release of a phonograph record made by a colored girl" was an opportunity for "those who desire to help in any advance of the Race . . . to buy this record as encouragement to the manufacturers for their liberal policy and to encourage other manufacturers who may not believe that the Race will buy records sung by its own singers."[31] Whether it was the *Defender*'s appeal, Smith's plaintive singing, Perry Bradford's jazzy orchestral accompaniment, or all three, people responded positively. Smith's follow-up selection, "Crazy Blues," often cited as the first classic blues record, sold seventy-five thousand copies within a month of its release.[32]

OKeh was the first record label to establish what was termed a "race series," a specially numbered catalog of records made by black artists for the black marketplace. The flurry of recording activity that followed "Crazy Blues" focused on female vocalists such as Mamie Smith and Gertrude "Ma" Rainey, who specialized in vaudeville, or classic, blues, which according to Jeff Todd Titon was "popular music, not folk music" and "ordinarily . . . composed by a Tin Pan Alley of professional black tunesmiths who wrote sophisticated songs and skits for stage reviews."[33] This was different from the rural sound of the downhome, or country, blues appearing later in the decade from singer-guitarists such as Blind Lemon Jefferson and Charley Patton.[34] By 1923, when Bessie Smith's Columbia recordings of classic blues comprised nearly one-fifth of all "race" record purchases that year, the profit potential in recording music by African Americans for the African American market was undisputed.[35]

Columbia's success with Bessie Smith notwithstanding, OKeh remained relatively unopposed in the race record market in the early 1920s, overcoming competition by Black Swan, a record company owned by an African American named Harry Pace. Black Swan had an impressive staff: its music director was classical composer William Grant Still and the recording manager was Harlem Renaissance bandleader and arranger Fletcher Henderson.[36] Black Swan pressed its records at Paramount Records' plant in Grafton, Wisconsin, which was also the location of the company's headquarters. This arrangement gave Paramount sales manager M. A. Supper an unimpeded view of the financial potential of recorded black music.[37] Supper had plenty of reason to be interested in a better product line because prior to summer 1922, Paramount's catalog was comprised of middleweight artists and milquetoast output. Record companies with better resources, such as Victor, Columbia, and Edison, had signed the top talents of the day and released better discs manufactured with superior sound fidelity. Paramount, on the other hand, used inferior material to manufacture its records, which resulted in a muddy sound reproduction.[38] When Black Swan went out of business in 1923, Paramount acquired its masters as payment of outstanding debt and began reissuing its catalog on the Paramount imprint, most notably discs by Black Swan's popular vaudeville blues sirens Alberta Hunter and Ethel Waters.[39] Paramount established a special 12000 numbering series for recordings aimed at the African American consumer.

In June 1923, the company experienced its first commercial success in selling black sacred music. The Norfolk Jubilee Quartette recorded the spiritual "My Lord's Gonna Move This Wicked Race" in Paramount's New York City studio.[40] The popularity of the disc confirmed Supper's intuition about the potential of black records, but it took J. Mayo "Ink" Williams, who understood the African American market, to make the 12000 series successful.

Born in Monmouth, Illinois in 1894, Ink Williams attended Brown University, where he was an All-American football star. After graduation, Williams moved to Chicago and joined the Hammond Pros, a pre-NFL football team based in northwest Indiana. From all accounts, Williams was an accidental record man. His fraternity brother, Joe Bibb, was the brother-in-law of Harry Pace and served as executive treasurer for Black Swan. Bibb hired Williams to serve as the collection agent for a Black Swan franchise.[41] When Black Swan went bankrupt, Williams approached Paramount about a job. He became the label's talent scout, the "first black to hold an executive position in a white recording company," although the honor was bittersweet: Williams was the only Paramount executive who had to use the freight elevator to get to company meetings held in Chicago's Palmer House hotel.[42]

Williams parlayed his position into one of prominence and power. He set up shop on the second floor of the Overton Building at Thirty-Sixth and State, in the midst of The Stroll and its supply of music talent. He hired classical pianist Aletha Dickerson as his assistant and began auditioning artists.[43] In addition to talent scouting, Williams supervised Paramount's Chicago-based race recording activity and operated its publishing arm, Chicago Music Publishing Company, the "earliest example of a record company publishing satellite." Through Chicago Music, Williams copyrighted song arrangements for Paramount, making the company the "most successful black publishing house of the era."[44] Under Williams, Paramount could find, sign, rehearse, and record the talent, press and sell the records, and profit from the publishing royalties.

One thing Paramount did not have was its own recording studio. It used as many as three different studios in the Wabash/Jackson/Adams section of Chicago's downtown Loop, including a studio at 218 South Wabash Avenue operated by white evangelist and songwriter Homer Rodeheaver. The Wiseman Sextette, the first black sacred group to record in Chicago for the Paramount label, recorded their discs in 1923 at Rodeheaver's studio.[45] Many Paramount releases were recorded at 218 South Wabash until April 1926. Williams also recorded artists at Orlando R. Marsh's Marsh Record Laboratories.

Williams paid performers a flat rate of twenty to fifty dollars per day to record as many songs as they could in the time allotted. Usually this produced between two and four marketable sides.[46] The masters were pressed at Paramount Records headquarters in Grafton, and the final product sold to black residents in Chicago and other northern cities. Railroad porters carried boxes of discs south and sold them "like door to door salesmen."[47] If a record sold more than ten thousand copies, the artist was called back for a follow-up session. If not, Paramount dropped the artist from the roster.[48] One estimate cited that of forty blues and sacred singers Williams recorded in Chicago between 1923 and 1927, only about half qualified for follow-up sessions.[49]

Under Williams's leadership, Paramount's Chicago satellite helped the company capture one-fifth of the market share of race recording. Its New York studios were eventually shuttered, and much of Paramount's race recording was moved to Chicago.[50] Despite Paramount's rising success, OKeh changed the sound of black sacred recording with its 1926 signing of Arizona Dranes.

Arizona Dranes: The First Gospel Recording Artist

It is not surprising that the earliest sanctified recording artist was a woman. During the 1920s, in denominations such as COGIC where only men were allowed to pastor churches, women had to be enterprising to carve their niche in the Pentecostal church. Some became teachers or evangelists. Others spread the good news by street singing or participating as vocalists for tent revivals. The main avenues and boulevards of Chicago's South and West Sides, and especially the storied Maxwell Street market, were mainstays of street-corner evangelism. Agnes Campbell told Jerma Jackson that she and her father, William Goodwin, held "street meetings" on Taylor Street, just north of Maxwell, where she would sing and her father would preach.[51] Likewise, when Katie Bell Nubin and her five-year-old daughter, Rosetta, arrived in Chicago from Cotton Plant, Arkansas, they joined Bishop Roberts's Fortieth COGIC but also held street meetings on Maxwell Street.[52] There, Rosetta sang and Katie played mandolin and delivered the Word. Eventually Rosetta picked up the guitar and, as Sister Rosetta Tharpe, parlayed her street-meeting experience into gospel music stardom.

The religious counterpart of street-corner bluesmen, evangelists ministered to passersby by singing and accompanying themselves on guitar, mandolin, or tambourine. They made up in enthusiasm and passion what they lacked in formal musical training. Street-corner evangelists who recorded in Chicago during the late 1920s included Sister Cally Fancy, Blind Joe Taggart, Blind Willie Davis, evangelist R. H. Harris, and William and Versey Smith.[53] Jerma Jackson suggests that guitar-toting evangelists, such as Tharpe and Blind Willie Johnson, learned their improvisational runs from country blues musicians with whom they shared performance space on commercial arteries in the heart of black urban America.[54] Social and cultural historian Adam Green adds that Paramount's success in selling records by country blues musicians such as Blind Lemon Jefferson may have enlightened company executives to consumer demand for vernacular music, including sanctified singing.[55]

The first African American religious folk artist to have a national impact through phonograph recordings was Arizona Dranes. Her recordings, made between 1926 and 1929, became a watershed for African American sacred music; anyone with access to a phonograph could hear sanctified music and preaching. Her discs not only represented the first time Pentecostal music was represented on record but also the first recorded examples of what would be termed gospel music. As such, Arizona Dranes qualifies not only as COGIC's first recording artist but also as the first gospel music recording artist.

Thanks to recent groundbreaking research by Michael Corcoran, we know more about Arizona Dranes than ever before. Arizona Drane—sometimes spelled Drain, and she added the s to her name after she left school—was born between 1889 and 1891 in Sherman, Texas. She was the youngest of three children born to Cora Jones and Milton Drane. Arizona, or Arazoni, as school enrollment records identified her, was born blind. To get an education and learn how to make a living as a sightless person, Dranes attended the Institute for Deaf, Dumb and Blind Colored Youths in Austin, Texas.[56]

From the moment she entered the institute, Dranes received classical training in piano and voice; by the time she was a preteen, she was singing arias. After graduation, she moved back to Sherman, where, according to the city directory, she plied her trade as an actress. Around 1922, Dranes moved to Wichita Falls, Texas, to live with Elve Doran, possibly a cousin. Here she met J. Austin Love, pastor of Wichita Falls' First Church of God in Christ. Corcoran suspects that it was at First COGIC where Dranes formally joined the COGIC church.[57] She followed Love to Fort Worth, where she played for the churches of two COGIC ministers: Emmet Morey Page in Dallas, and religious radio pioneer Bishop Samuel M. Crouch in Fort Worth.[58] She invigorated their services with her staccato piano style, changing riffs and tempos with the intuition of a silent film accompanist. As such, Dranes was an ideal musician for the effervescent and often unpredictable Pentecostal worship service. As Corcoran describes: "Under Dranes' playing hands the black and white keys became a symphony of harmony, rhythm, melody and tone, but mostly rhythm. Her left hand ostinato—constantly repeating a melodic fragment—was hypnotic."[59] In her dissertation on gospel piano style, Idella L. Johnson described Dranes's playing as "an amalgam of the Texas Barrelhouse tradition and Ragtime."[60]

Page, COGIC Overseer for Oklahoma, recruited Dranes to minister musically to churches throughout his jurisdiction. Between 1923 and 1926, she traveled from church to church, sharing her gift with the congregations and undoubtedly perfecting and expanding the arsenal of piano techniques that made her playing distinctive. She made a lasting impression on Helen Davis, who heard Dranes in Oklahoma City during the early 1920s: "She'd let the spirit overtake her. She'd jump up from that piano bench when [the spirit] hit her."[61] "She was a gifted piano player," Alva Johnson Roberts said. "It was just amazing. Whooo, she could play! I don't think I've ever heard anybody sound like her."[62] Alva's relative, Camille Roberts, remembered that Dranes would "get so good she'd just hit [the piano] with her elbows."[63]

Dranes also played around Dallas and at the annual COGIC Holy Convocation in Memphis. Reverend Crouch recommended the sightless musician to OKeh A&R man Richard M. Jones, who was looking for religious music talent to record for the label.[64] Elmer Fearn, president of Consolidated Music Publishing, was sufficiently intrigued to write Dranes through Crouch. His letter of May 4, 1926, states in part, "We have heard of you as a pianist and your excellent rendition of spiritual songs. We would like to hear from you as to whether or not you would entertain the idea or the possibility of coming to Chicago in connection with the recording of phonograph records." OKeh added one caveat: "We are bringing you to Chicago to make test records first. We do not guarantee to release them for sale."[65] Dranes replied by mail, seeking compensation based on "[their] best consideration" and explaining, "I am without sight, and playing music is my only way of making a support."[66]

Dranes arrived in Chicago from Fort Worth on Wednesday, June 16, 1926. The following day, accompanied by Jones and OKeh recording artist Sara Martin as her seeing companion for the visit, she sang and played in a south Loop studio. Jones engineered the session. Dranes made six sides that Thursday: two instrumentals and four vocals, for which she received $25 per side for a total of $150 and 25 percent royalties on songwriting—not an inconsequential sum for a sightless pianist making her living solely from church appearances.[67] The first two selections she recorded were "In That Day" and "It's All Right Now," the latter a hymn composed in 1909 by Benjamin Franklin Butts.[68] Dranes sang and played piano with urgency, but the tracks were unexceptional. Two other selections, "Crucifixion" and "Sweet Heaven Is My Home," were piano solos.

Johnson describes "Sweet Heaven" as "a good example of the Texas barrelhouse piano style," although it sounded cut off artificially at the end.[69] Given the time limitations of the 78 rpm disc, engineer Jones may have signaled Dranes to stop playing in mid-performance.

The next two sides established Arizona Dranes as the first gospel recording artist and ushered in an era of sanctified music on record. On "John Said He Saw a Number," Dranes banged the piano keys with wild abandon and sang in a loud, strident voice, while Jones and Martin responded antiphonally. "My Soul Is a Witness for My Lord," however, best captured the improvisational swing of the sanctified worship service. It contained several components that not only defined the verve of Pentecostal worship music but also laid the groundwork for gospel music. First, it included antiphonal, or call-and-response, singing. Dranes's exuberant lead singing style eschewed techniques associated with formal vocal training. Second, exclamations of "Amen" and "Hallelujah" punctuated the performance. Third, it incorporated a secular music style (barrelhouse piano). Fourth, it was a simple song and melody that any congregation could learn. The language came from, and spoke to, migrants whose vocabulary was limited. Johnson described Dranes's piano style on this selection as "intense perpetual motion" with "repetitive short, melodic phrases . . . conducive for 'shouting' or 'holy dancing'—hence the survival of dramatic Africanisms that maintain a predilection for *physical body motion*."[70] Three decades later, Dranes's muscular command of the keyboard and her physical transformation while playing in the spirit could be heard in the rock-and-roll riffs and performance techniques of Little Richard and Jerry Lee Lewis.

OKeh released four of the six sides in August 1926, and the two discs reportedly sold ten thousand copies each.[71] Not only was this sufficient for OKeh to schedule Dranes for a second recording session, but she toured the South on the strength of their sales. The follow-up session took place Monday, November 15, 1926. Despite a lingering illness, Dranes arrived in Chicago on November 6 so that she could earn extra money by performing in local COGIC churches two Sundays in a row.[72] Among the churches she may have visited while in Chicago were Lake Street COGIC, Thirteenth Street COGIC, and Fortieth COGIC. Indeed, writing about the musicians who visited Lake Street COGIC, Mary Lenox notes that "Sister Drain [*sic*], a blind woman, played the piano from time to time."[73] Since Dranes had met Rev. Ford Washington McGee on the church circuit around 1924, she might also have appeared at McGee's COGIC church at 3326 South Prairie Avenue.[74]

The November 1926 OKeh session—engineered by Tommy Rockwell, who replaced Jones when Columbia purchased OKeh that month—produced five additional titles, four of which were released: "I'm Going Home on the Morning Train" / "Lamb's Blood Has Washed Me Clean" (OKeh 8419) and "Bye and Bye

We're Going to See the King" / "I'm Glad My Lord Saved Me" (OKeh 8438).[75]
Dranes never recorded solo for OKeh again, so OKeh executives must have
felt that the ambience of a live congregation, provided by Jones and Martin
on Dranes's first release, was essential to future discs. This time, an authentic
flock—Reverend McGee and his Church of God in Christ Jubilee Singers—replaced Martin and Jones's makeshift congregation.[76]

McGee and his singers turned the OKeh studio into a revival. Dranes sang
herself nearly hoarse on "Lamb's Blood Has Washed Me Clean." During an
extraordinary piano solo on "I'm Glad My Lord Saved Me," she traded exhortations with McGee as if both were in the throes of spirit possession.

Still struggling with illness, Dranes returned to the Chicago studio for a
final session on July 3, 1928. She recorded six sides, and OKeh released four: "I
Shall Wear a Crown" / "I'll Go Where You Want Me to Go" (OKeh 8600) and
"Just Look" / "Don't You Want to Go?" (OKeh 8646). This time, the record
label identified the background vocalists only as a choir. For the first time on
a Dranes session, OKeh added a mandolin player. The mandolin/piano accompaniment and chugging rhythm on "I Shall Wear a Crown" gave the song
the energetic propulsion of a jug band without the jug. Two sides not released
at the time, "He Is My Story" (based on the revival song "Blessed Assurance")
and "God's Got a Crown," remained unissued for decades until they were discovered on test pressings and issued on albums for the collectors market.[77]

Although Dranes never recorded for OKeh after July 1928, prewar blues
and sacred music experts speculate that she is the piano accompanist on two
discs recorded in Dallas, Texas, in 1928 and 1929. Indeed, an accompanist with
a style much like Dranes's backs Laura Henton and the Texas Jubilee Singers
on their December 1928 disc for Columbia.[78] A year later, Rev. Joe Lenley's
sermons with congregational singing are accompanied by someone bearing
Dranes's signature staccato barrelhouse style, and a voice similar to Dranes's is
singing with the studio congregation.[79] Further, "Bye and Bye We're Going to
See the King," the song introducing Lenley's sermon, "Lord, Who Shall Abide
in Thy Tabernacle," was recorded for OKeh by Dranes.

Dranes may have become disillusioned with the record business because
she never made another commercial recording after 1930. For all the notoriety
the records gave her, they also provided headaches. For example, Dranes was
denied advance money that she needed, and she also encountered problems with
a musician who demanded payment from OKeh even though Dranes wrote the
company, "The money you gave for them, they got every dime of it. . . . I didn't
want you to think I would do any crooked work or tell a false about anything."[80]

Although she ceased recording, Dranes never stopped serving the COGIC
church. According to gospel scholar Anthony Heilbut and COGIC historian
Pastor Mack C. Mason, Dranes was an active volunteer for the denomination

and was often recruited to play for services and revivals.[81] She worked with Bishop Riley F. Williams, who planted COGIC churches in Alabama, Georgia, and Ohio.[82] Alva Johnson Roberts remembered hearing the sanctified pianist for the first time in Chicago during the 1930s. "I was a teenager at Pastor P. R. Favors's church when my mother and them moved to the West Side, and Arizona Dranes, yes, she came to that church several times in a revival."[83]

The last known public appearance of Arizona J. Dranes was in 1947 in Cleveland, where she was billed as the "Famous Blind Piano Player from Chicago." Dranes died of a stroke on July 27, 1963. At the time of her death, she was living in Los Angeles at 5219 McKinley Avenue and had joined Emmanuel COGIC, pastored by her longtime friend Bishop Crouch. The death certificate of gospel music's first recording artist listed her occupation as "missionary." She was buried at the Paradise Memorial Park in Santa Fe Springs, California.[84] Like blues singer-guitarist Robert Johnson, few photos exist of Arizona Dranes, which only adds to her mystique.

Recording Preachers in Chicago: Staid to Sanctified

Although Rev. W. D. Cook was the first Chicago pastor to appear on a commercial recording, the first Chicago minister to record a sermon commercially was Rev. William Arthur White. An advertisement in the September 26, 1925, *Defender* called White "Chicago's noted pastor" formerly known as the "Boy Evangelist" and later "Preacher White" as he toured the Midwest and the South.[85] White preached "Divine Relationship of Man to God" and "Prayer," which Paramount released in August 1925.[86] He delivered his message evenly, with a declarative but essentially emotionless voice and no studio congregation for exclamatory encouragement. The learned and staid message of Reverend White was evocative of what congregations heard in Bronzeville's Old Landmarks on Sunday mornings.

The tenor of recorded sermons changed when, in April 1926, Columbia Records recorded a series of impassioned sermonettes by Baptist minister Rev. J. M. Gates of Atlanta. Six months later, Columbia released a sermon called "The Downfall of Nebuchadnezzar" by the fiery Rev. J. C. Burnett, recorded originally for Meritt, a black-owned imprint from Kansas City.[87] When rerecorded for Columbia, with its estimable distribution system, the sermon became a runaway hit. Thus, if Paramount had sniffed out the potential for success in recording African American preachers, Columbia hit the rich vein of African American sacred oratory with its early discs of Burnett and Gates.[88]

Church leaders and singers were recognizing that phonograph records could serve as a national altar call, spreading their message beyond the confines of the church walls. By 1926, records were a popular form of entertainment in black households. In *Songsters and Saints*, Paul Oliver notes that although seventy-five cents per record was high in proportion to a working-class family's annual income, it was the working-class consumer who purchased race recordings. Jeff Titon reports that in the 1920s, as many as 20 percent of blacks owned phonographs.[89] Since sanctified churches were comprised mainly of working-class people, it is not surprising that sanctified singers were represented well in record catalogs.[90] Sanctified church leaders in Chicago had easy access to the recording medium because the city had become the center of black music publishing and recording, thanks largely to the efforts of Ink Williams of Paramount and Jack Kapp of Vocalion.

Rev. Ford Washington McGee

One of the most prolific recording preachers from Chicago's Pentecostal community was COGIC pastor Rev. Ford Washington McGee. Like William Roberts, Eleazar Lenox, and P. R. Favors, McGee was a migrant who had become an influential COGIC minister in the city. Unlike Roberts, Lenox, and Favors, McGee unleashed the potential of phonograph records early on to expand the scope of his ministry.

Born October 5, 1890, in Winchester, Tennessee, McGee was raised in Hillsboro, Texas. His parents were farmers, and his mother was reportedly a descendant of educator Booker T. Washington.[91] He married in 1910 and soon afterward moved to Oklahoma, where he became a schoolteacher and pastored a Methodist church.[92] In 1918, McGee joined the Church of God in Christ and ministered to congregations in Texas, Oklahoma City (possibly with the assistance of Arizona Dranes), and Des Moines, Iowa, where westward-moving southern migrants had settled. In 1921, McGee was named a COGIC Overseer.

Around 1925, McGee moved to Chicago and held Saturday outdoor worship services in the Maxwell Street area.[93] He eventually secured his own physical church structure on the South Side. After joining Arizona Dranes on one of her recording sessions, McGee was determined to launch his own recording career. His first recorded sermon, "Lion in the Tribe of Judah," was cut for OKeh in Chicago on May 6, 1927. The untested McGee must have seemed a bit of a risk for the company initially because they coupled his side with sanctified singer Jessie May Hill's "Earth Is No Resting Place," recorded the day before.[94] Like Dranes's recordings, "Lion in the Tribe of Judah" combined urban jazz with lyrics taken from the pages of Scripture. McGee shouted in a strident and raspy but tuneful voice and was backed by a barrelhouse piano (possibly Arizona Dranes), a trumpet, and a group of fervent female vocalists listed as the "Church of God in Christ Jubilee Singers"—probably the same group or some combination of the members who participated in Dranes's November 1926 session.[95]

The musicians could have been anyone; in 1964, McGee told researcher Bernie Klatzko that he used to invite guitarists and other instrumentalists hanging around his church to come in and accompany the singing.[96]

McGee's relationship with OKeh ended after the first disc, but his recording career was just beginning. A month later, he signed with Victor, and he cut his first two discs for the label on June 7, 1927. "Jonah in the Belly of the Whale," recorded at the end of this first session, became his biggest seller. It featured McGee's strident preaching and congregational response and concluded with exuberant singing and instrumental accompaniment, including trumpet.

On the flip side of "Jonah" was an up-tempo arrangement of "With His Stripes We Are Healed," set to the melody of "On a Hill Lone and Gray," a nineteenth-century hymn by Robert Carridine that had made its way into the Pentecostal repertory through its inclusion in revival songbooks. The release of "Jonah" and "With His Stripes" was feted with a public unveiling that pre-dated the record release party. The August 8, 1927, *Louisiana Weekly* reported:

> On last Wednesday and Friday nights mass meetings, attended by thousands, were held in the [COGIC] church, located at 3326 Prairie Avenue, Chicago, Ill., at which time the record of "With His Stripes We are Healed" was played for the congregation. The reception of this recording was the most genuine and spontaneous ever witnessed by this writer. Literally, hundreds of those attending were so impressed by what they heard that arrangements were immediately made whereby those wishing to were permitted to then and there place their order for one or more of this marvelous record.[97]

The success of "Jonah" encouraged Victor to release twenty-two discs featuring the preacher and his sanctified sound between June 1927 and July 1930.[98]

Much like McGee's lone OKeh release, the Victor recordings were characterized by the pastor's raspy, unfettered singing and occasional preaching accompanied by exhortations and background singing by the studio congregation. Various instrumental combinations included piano, guitar, mandolin, double bass, trumpet, trombone, tambourine, hand clapping, and drums.[99] McGee accompanied himself on piano. The double bass and guitar, coupled with piano and hand clapping, supported the steady rhythm. Like Dranes's recorded output, McGee's discs illustrated just how much the sanctified church, and specifically the Church of God in Christ, was laying the groundwork for the modern gospel music movement.

McGee's last Chicago recording session took place on October 23, 1929, five days before the Wall Street stock market crash. The preacher's relationship with Victor ended in 1930, and his last discs were made in New York City. The New York session produced one of McGee's finest selections, "Fifty Miles of Elbow Room." The rollicking recording opened with a clarion call on cornet and found McGee in superb vocal form. It also featured Arizona Dranes in her last known appearance on record.

Like Dranes, McGee ceased recording commercially after 1930, as the Great Depression caused record companies to falter, merge, or cut back on production, especially in its race series. McGee continued pastoring the McGee Temple COGIC, which moved to Vincennes Avenue.[100] One of his sons followed him in ministry. McGee died in Chicago on April 8, 1971.[101]

The Church of the Living God: Revs. D. C. Rice and Leora Ross

The Church of God in Christ was not the only denomination to pave the way for the gospel music movement. The Church of the Living God, Christian Workers for Fellowship (CWFF), also contributed to the recorded oeuvre of 1920s Chicago storefront religion. Like COGIC, the Church of the Living God was a growing denomination. In 1916, there were only 38 temples and 2,009 members, but a decade later, the U.S. Department of Commerce reported that the Church of the Living God had 81 congregations with 5,844 members. Around 1928, Sutherland identified 149 temples in the United States with 11,558 members—about 77 members per temple.[102]

Sutherland visited the Church of the Living God in Chicago, a congregation led by Rev. M. L. Gipson of Detroit that met in a basement apartment at 5608 Vernon Avenue.[103] He describes the service as ebullient: "Not one moment during the two hours and a half is there silence from the continuous singing, preaching, or testifying." The congregation sang "jubilee songs or spirituals, and revival songs," and Gipson welcomed quartets from outside the congregation to sing at the service.[104]

The denomination's most important recording artist of the 1920s was Rev. D. C. Rice. He was born in 1888 in Barbour County, Alabama, migrated to Chicago in the second decade of the twentieth century, and joined a Church of the Living God congregation pastored by Bishop Hill. When Hill died in 1920, Rice organized his own Church of the Living God congregation. Inspired by the growing popularity of recordings by Revs. J. M. Gates and McGee, Rice approached Jack Kapp of Vocalion Records. Kapp asked Rice to bring his congregation to the studio to make test pressings, but after they auditioned, he reportedly told Rice, "I wouldn't give you a nickel for your music." For whatever reason, Kapp did an about face the following Wednesday and offered the minister seventy-five dollars per side to make records for the company.[105] From 1928 to 1930, Rice and his congregation were exclusive Vocalion artists, cutting thirty-nine sides between March 1928 and July 1930, of which thirty were released.

The ad for Rice's "The Angels Rolled the Stone Away," posted in the June 23, 1928, *Defender*, proclaimed that the pastor "preaches and sings one of the best sermons ever heard," accompanied by piano, mandolin, and guitar.[106] Despite the ad's hyperbole about the sermon, the recording—like many Rice discs—was more about the singing than the spoken word. Many recording preachers of the 1920s used congregational singing to introduce their sermonic message, but Rice did the opposite. He opened recordings with a scriptural passage and a brief interpretation, and the remainder of the recordings featured exuberant congregational singing and instrumental accompaniment.

Rice told music historian Gayle Dean Wardlow that the Church of the Living God adapted its music from the COGIC church.[107] It is easy to see the similarity. The arrangements resemble the unfettered exuberance of Dranes and McGee, and the accompaniment consists of instruments such as trumpet, trombone, mandolin, tambourine, guitar, and triangle, all of which were welcomed in sanctified storefronts.[108]

The most noticeable distinction between Rice and McGee's recorded output, however, was a skillful trumpeter who participated on four of Rice's released sides. Oliver posits that the trumpeter was famed New Orleans jazz musician Punch Miller.[109] It has also been suggested that Rice, like McGee, pulled musicians off the street to play in his church, although if the trumpeter on the recordings is Punch Miller, it is likely that he was only a studio musician for Rice and his singers, not a church musician. Regardless, the trumpeter played boldly and with zest, clearly familiar with the fundamentals of a jazz solo. A female singer led Rice's most popular release, "I'm on the Battlefield for My Lord;" Heilbut believes that the singer may have been Sallie Martin, since she spoke of recording the song with a sanctified congregation.[110] A double bass propelled the performance, while the uncredited trumpeter punctuated the air with powerful improvisational lines. On the flipside, "He's Got His Eyes on You," the trumpeter played with brassy brightness, demonstrating that urban jazz not only had a tremendous influence on sanctified church music but was its first cousin.

Rice was the only recording preacher in Chicago during the 1920s to approximate McGee in terms of recording volume. He also purportedly broadcast his services on radio. If this was indeed the case, it would make him the first African American minister in Chicago to have a radio broadcast, because by 1932, two years before Elder Lucy Smith took her church services to the airwaves, Rice had left Chicago for Montgomery, Alabama.[111]

Although she was far less prolific than Rice, another member of Chicago's Church of the Living God, CWFF, Rev. Leora Ross (1900–ca. 1982), is no less important. One of the first black female ministers ever to record a sermon,

Ross made eight cuts for OKeh in 1927, of which four were released.[112] The record company ballyhooed the first of two releases, "Dry Bones in the Valley" / "A Gambler Broke in a Strange Land," with an ad boasting, "This record is as clear and powerful as if you were face to face with the preacher."[113]

The stylistic development of recorded sermons in the 1920s foreshadowed the stylistic evolution of sacred music in the 1930s black church. Sermons recorded prior to 1926 were formal and staid, in step with the march of the black middle-class to upward mobility and race pride. Similarly, black religious records made during the first half of the 1920s favored quartets, jubilee singers, and soloists rendering spirituals and hymns in a formal style. Black sacred composers, such as Tindley and Coleridge-Taylor, although intent on incorporating the black experience into their music, were educated and composed in the western European tradition. A review of appendix A, which lists black sacred recordings made in Chicago during the 1920s, testifies to the stylistic contrast between the formal music and sermons recorded prior to 1926 and the emotionally charged preaching and singing from 1926 onward. There were notable exceptions: Grace Outlaw's Paramount disc, recorded in Chicago with the Florida Jubilee Singers in 1926, was delivered in just as refined a style as her 1925 Paramount offering with the Sunset Four Jubilee Quartet.[114] Similarly, the Second Baptist Church Trio, a mixed group accompanied by piano who made one disc in Chicago around January 1927, sang "Just Want to Be There in Time" and "He'll Fix It All" in a formal, almost nineteenth-century parlor style, without a hint of grace notes, trills, runs, or blue notes.[115]

Still, after 1926, thanks in large part to the considerable output and popularity of Revs. Gates, Nix, Burnett, and McGee, impassioned, emotional preaching and singing was what consumers demanded and record companies supplied. By 1927, even the formerly staid Rev. William Arthur White turned up the intensity of his recorded sermons. It seemed as if each time he entered the studio, his pacing moved closer to those of Gates, Nix, and Burnett, whose prolific recording careers made them national celebrities among black churchgoers. On his final disc—"Many Rob God" and "Where Were You Job"—recorded in September, White opened with an energetically sung hymn and a message presented with greater gusto and a quicker tempo, though still lacking a studio congregation for demonstrable encouragement.

On September 13, 1930, twenty-six year-old Minnie Pearl Roberts, the second of William Roberts's nine children, cut two sides with her brother Willie and sister Gertrude, who accompanied on piano.[116] They called themselves Sister Minnie Pearl Roberts' Sanctified Singers and the two released sides were "Do

What My Lord Said Do" and "You Make Your Troubles So Hard." Roberts's singing was clear, melodic, and effervescent. Although her solo recording career was short, Minnie Pearl Roberts is reported to have organized "one of the earliest, if not the first" COGIC choirs and served as Fortieth COGIC's beloved radio broadcast announcer for many years. Gertrude Roberts married pioneer radio announcer Jack L. Cooper in 1938 and became one of the first female African American radio personalities.[117]

Sister Roberts's disc was released on Brunswick just as the Great Depression was taking its toll. By this time, Jack Kapp and his competitor, Ink Williams, had joined forces. In 1928, Williams was caught in an untenable rivalry with his white supervisor, Arthur Laibly. Williams resigned from Paramount and devoted time to building Black Patti, a label he began cultivating while at Paramount. The company, named after the legendary black soprano Sisserietta Jones, folded after releasing fifty records.[118] After Black Patti's failure, Kapp hired Williams to direct Brunswick and Vocalion's race series. Williams administered copyrights for Brunswick's State Street Music, two doors from his former Paramount office on State Street.[119] When the Great Depression put a temporary end to the black recording industry in Chicago, Williams moved to Atlanta and became the football coach for Morehouse College. He would be back in the record business by 1934.

Despite today's fascination with 1920s sanctified preaching, singing, and musicianship, the decade—in terms of recording volume, radio appearances, and popularity—belonged to a jubilee group from the city's fashionable suburb of Morgan Park. The Pace Jubilee Singers and their dynamic lead vocalist, Hattie Parker, blended the music of the Old Landmark churches with a touch of vaudeville blues popular with migrants to create something fresh and compelling.

CHAPTER 3

Sacred Music in Transition

Charles Henry Pace and the Pace Jubilee Singers

> Pace . . . never got the same note that Dorsey got, but he certainly by
> far was the better musician of the two.
>
> **Kenneth Morris**

The Pace Jubilee Singers, Charles Henry Pace's mixed vocal ensemble from
Beth Eden Baptist Church in Morgan Park, Illinois, represented an early, and
possibly deliberate, blending of the formal jubilee style enjoyed by the city's Old
Settlers with the urban vernacular popular music that appealed to the southern migrant. As such, the group is a fascinating example of African American sacred music in transition. While it did not resolve, or even necessarily
acknowledge, the tension inherent in its music, the Pace Jubilee Singers were
sufficiently popular to encourage record companies to dedicate more resources
to African American sacred music.

The Pace Jubilee Singers were among the city's first black religious artists
to perform on radio, broadcasting during the 1920s and early 1930s over radio
station WCBN and megawatt stations WLS and WGN, which carried their
music throughout the Midwest, the South, and even into portions of Canada,
securing for them a diverse following. The group was also among the first mixed
jubilee ensembles to feature a female soloist prominently.[1] Several of their more
than three dozen discs, recorded for companies such as Victor and Brunswick,
contained the first, or among the first, recorded examples of concert spirituals,
Baptist hymns, and revival songs, as well as compositions by pioneer African
American gospel hymnist Charles Albert Tindley.[2] The powerfully emotive,

ornamental contralto of the group's primary lead vocalist, Hattie Parker, may have influenced Mahalia Jackson's treatment of slower Baptist hymns.[3]

Charles Henry Pace was born to Charles and Frances (Daggar) Pace in Atlanta, Georgia, on August 4, 1886.[4] Like many migrant families, the Paces inched their way northward, settling first in Chattanooga, Cincinnati, and then St. Louis before planting roots in Chicago in 1899.[5] Their move to Chicago prior to 1900 placed them in the category of Old Settlers.

Young "Charlie" did not finish high school, but he did manage to acquire some formal music training on trumpet and piano.[6] Like fellow sacred songwriters Kenneth Morris and Thomas A. Dorsey, Pace cut his professional musical teeth on jazz and dance music. He secured his first orchestral assignment in 1910, at age twenty-four, conducting a dance band in Benton Harbor, Michigan. Pace began writing songs and established the first official headquarters of his publishing company, Pace Music House, while in Benton Harbor.[7] Around 1913, Pace's band was hired to perform in the fashionable spa resort town of French Lick, Indiana, and he moved his headquarters to that location.[8]

By 1915, Pace had moved back to the Chicago area and was operating the Pace Music House from his residence in Morgan Park. Initially using Otto Zimmerman & Son to print his sheet music, Pace eventually assumed all parts of the production process, from composition and printing to sales.[9] Unlike Morris and Dorsey, Pace created sheet music that was not a rough guide: it represented precisely the way he wanted his songs performed.

Pace composed ten secular songs between 1910 and 1929, but he considered himself primarily a religious songwriter. He referred to his religious material variously as "spiritual anthems," "spiritual medleys," and "gospel songs." Upon his return to Chicago, Pace worked as an arranger for Memphis migrant Lillian M. Bowles (Pannell) (ca. 1884–1949). Bowles was one of the first publishers of black religious music and specifically of the emerging gospel songs. While in her employ, Pace published two of Dorsey's earliest and most popular gospel songs, "If You See My Savior" and "How about You." He also arranged "This Little Light of Mine" for the company.[10]

In the mid-1920s, Pace augmented his own publishing concern and arranging duties for Bowles by becoming the choir director at Beth Eden Baptist Church in Morgan Park. He organized the Pace Jubilee Singers from members of the Beth Eden senior choir. One might surmise that he organized the group to promote his own song compositions, as did Sallie Martin and Roberta Martin. However, a review of the Pace Jubilee Singers' recorded repertoire suggests that his rationale for founding the group may have been to promote his printed arrangements of spirituals. Further supporting this hypothesis is the fact that Pace did not write many sacred songs during the ensemble's heyday (1926–31), and when he did publish a song folio in the early 1930s, it was called *Negro Spirituals Arranged by Chas. H. Pace as Sung by Pace Jubilee Singers.* According to Pearl Davis Jordan, whom Mary Ann Lancaster Tyler interviewed for her dissertation on Pace, two songs popular in the ensemble's repertory were "Lift Up Your Heads" and "Unfold All Ye Faithful," underscoring the group's commitment to classical material.[11]

The ensemble of seven to ten singers included contralto Hattie Parker, soprano Catherine Simpson, Mrs. Smith as soprano/alto, tenor Daniel M. Burke, Mr. Cassimere on baritone, and Mr. White as bass. Arlene Pace, Charles's second wife, sang in the group and helped manage the ensemble.[12] Other members throughout the Pace Jubilee Singers' brief tenure included Sarah Williams, Mrs. S. J. Johnson, Georgia B. Ford, and Wilfrid J. Spencer.[13] While the Pace Jubilee Singers performed frequently for audiences at Beth Eden and Arnett Chapel, they also are alleged to have sung at the opening of Chicago's Drake Hotel.

Pace did not sing in the group and may not have accompanied them either, at least not on record.[14] His youngest daughter, Frances Pace Barnes, remembered that her father preferred to remain behind the scenes, content to lead and compose. "He didn't sing," she said. "Never sang. He wasn't interested in singing. I don't think he ever considered himself an accomplished musician. He was the 'arranger.'"[15] Tyler reported that one of the Pace Jubilee Singers' early accompanists was Thomas A. Dorsey, who most likely took on the assignment while serving as music director for Morgan Park's New Hope Baptist Church, located near Beth Eden. The collaboration was brief: Josephine Consola Inniss reported that "a personality clash between Charles H. Pace and Thomas A. Dorsey led to Mr. Dorsey's departure from the group." Inniss, a well-respected music teacher and organist for Arnett Chapel AME in Morgan Park, had studied with Arlene Pace and succeeded Dorsey as accompanist.[16] Accomplished on piano and organ, Inniss was more attuned to the restraint of the jubilee style than to Dorsey's jaunty jazz riffs. It may well be Inniss, then, who accompanied the ensemble on piano for the recording sessions. If so, her assignment was to support the singers with fundamental chording and no improvisation.

Of all the members, Hattie Parker was the most prominent. At the time of the group's formation in 1925, Parker was labeled a gospel singer in *Defender* notices about her forthcoming church appearances. From Parker's ease in interpreting the Pace hymn repertory, Heilbut suggests that she specialized in Baptist hymns.[17] Although details on Parker's life are scarce, evidence indicates that she was Baptist, like her Beth Eden colleagues, and would indeed have been familiar with the songs Pace arranged. At the same time, it is unlikely that she was a member of the Beth Eden senior choir. More probable is that Pace knew her from the circle of music acquaintances he had developed through his publishing and arranging or through Lillian Bowles. Pace could not have helped but notice how her smoky coloration, dynamic phrasing, and vocal embellishments that hinted at a familiarity with the classic blues would give his amateur jubilee singers a sound unlike any other religious singing troupe in the city.

Parker's blues embellishments notwithstanding, the Pace Jubilee Singers reflected in repertory, dress, and comportment the middle-class social conservatism and emotional restraint of Beth Eden and Morgan Park. They dressed in formal concert attire: tuxedos and conservative dresses. Not only was this de rigueur for a jubilee group, but it also reflected Pace's own fastidiousness. Frances remembered that her father was meticulous about his personal grooming. "If he was doing some [music] printing in the back, he'd have on an apron and he'd roll up his sleeves, but he wore white shirts every day. And he wore a suit coat, even if he was just going from here to there. Once he got there, he took [the coat] off. But he wore a suit coat every day."[18]

Pace may have suspected that a mixed group singing religious songs led by strong female leads would be something of a novelty in the mid-1920s. At the time the first Pace recordings were made in September 1926, the predominant black female voice type on phonograph records was the classic blues siren. The Pace Jubilee Singers' other soprano lead, Catherine Simpson, possessed a big, soaring voice, equally suited to the stage as the altar, but it was Parker's plaintive, throaty, mysterious voice that gave the group its distinctive sound.[19]

The Pace Jubilee Singers signed with Victor Records and recorded for the first time in Chicago on September 13, 1926, in the Webster Hotel at Webster Avenue and what is now Lincoln Park West (future sessions would take place in the WGN studios in the Drake Hotel). The group waxed six initial sides for Victor that day: "You Gonna Reap Just What You Sow," "Everybody Got to Walk This Lonesome Valley," "My Lord, What a Morning," "My Lord Is Writin' All the Time," "I Do, Don't You," and "I'm Going through Jesus."[20]

The September 1926 session helped solidify the group's style, which Tyler describes as one of "asperity. . . . The voices had been trained to function as a unit but sounded individually untutored." This of course stemmed from the fact that the singing group was comprised of nonprofessional singers from Beth Eden's senior choir.[21] They employed simple harmonies, and on occasion the male singers added a rhythmic countermelody not unlike their quartet brethren. Parker articulated the melody and incorporated glides, scoops, grace notes, vocal interjections, and embellishments that were, as Tyler states, "among the liberties relished by the Pace Jubilee Singers."[22] In fact, as early as "I'm Going through Jesus," Parker demonstrated a keen sense of gospel timing. She knew instinctively when to build, when to moan, and when to accent a line with a muscular emphasis on the first syllable of the first word on a line. While Parker rolled her r's, she also displayed a hint of southern twang and gave a conversational rhythm to her singing that must have spoken to the migrants.

The first session for Victor produced the earliest commercial recording of the spiritual "My Lord What a Morning" and E. O. Excell's "I Do, Don't You," the song whose rendition by Rev. A. W. Nix in 1921 inspired Dorsey to write his first gospel song. The Pace Jubilee Singers introduced many more sacred songs to shellac. Gospel scholar David Evans notes, "In many cases, the Pace Jubilee Singers were the first African American group to record a standard Protestant hymn, always giving it a distinctive treatment that usually became the model for all other gospel versions."[23]

Between September 1926 and July 1929, the Pace Jubilee Singers recorded eighty-five sides, of which seventy-two were released by almost all the important labels that recorded black artists during the prewar era. With ten recording sessions, 1927 was the most prolific year. All the sessions took place in Chicago, including four mid-1927 sides produced by the Richmond, Indiana-based Gennett Records for Ink Williams's short-lived Black Patti imprint, which today represent the group's rarest discs. The March 5, 1927, session for Black Patti delivered the first commercial recording of the spiritual "Were You There When They Crucified My Lord." "Lawdy, Won't You Come by Here," recorded on Brunswick the following month, was among the group's most infectious sides, with the male singers taking more of a lead role than usual by offering a rhythmic descending countermelody.

The June 30, 1928, session produced the earliest recording of the hymn "What a Friend We Have in Jesus." Evans notes that "What A Friend" was the second hit for the group, "I'm Going through Jesus" being the first, and that its brilliance "has never been surpassed."[24] During that same session, the Pace Jubilee Singers made some of the earliest recordings of pioneer gospel hymnist Charles A. Tindley's "Stand by Me," "Nothing Between," and "Leave It There." "Seek and Ye Shall Find," also recorded that day, has a touch of polyrhythm in the group's mid-tempo singing.

"Stand by Me" could well be considered Parker's magnum opus because she delivered the song with such inner conviction, impeccable timing, and forceful articulation that it would have resonated with both the middle-class jubilee crowd as well as with those who preferred more emotional singing. By the January 1929 session for Victor, which produced eight sides (all released), Parker was the undisputed vocal leader of the Pace Jubilee Singers. On such selections as "The Haven of Rest," her explosively emotional delivery and vocal ornamentation provided a foretaste of what gospel singing in the 1930s and 1940s would become. Heilbut commented, "Parker is a fascinating cusp figure, but a cultured—perhaps trained—voice, obviously influenced by the vaudeville stage, who also exhibits the freedom of a Baptist hymn singer. Parker understands [the Baptist hymn style] extremely well, and particularly on her most soulful cuts, 'Walk with Me,' 'We Shall Walk through the Valley in Peace,' and 'Stand by Me,' she builds a song to what must have been ecstatic responses."[25]

Despite being a prominent artist who recorded prolifically and successfully with the Pace Jubilee Singers for some of the decade's major record labels and, on one occasion, by herself, Hattie Parker remains an enigmatic figure. She was a member of J. Wesley Jones's Progressive Choral Society and a popular gospel singer during the 1920s and 1930s, appearing regularly on church-sponsored programs throughout the South and West Sides.[26]

Parker's contribution to the Pace Jubilee Singers was not far removed from the vocal styles of the female classic blues singers of the day, particularly her liberal use of vocal slides and grace notes. Unlike the blues shouters, however, Parker was subtle and conservative in her use of vocal interjections, singing her top notes in a conservative manner.[27] Whereas a blues singer such as Bessie Smith would slide a note like a trombone, Parker's scoops were more like a grace note sounded on a trumpet. Heilbut noted that her short, croppy phrasing, "frequently at the expense of a more lyrical line," exhibits the "freedom of a Baptist hymn singer."[28] Samuel Charters, in *An Introduction to Gospel Song*, wrote that Parker's performance on "Leave It There" "shows already a greater expressiveness in her use of rhythm and vocal phrase, and represents the fullest use of the materials of the more Negroid [*sic*] tradition while retaining the quality of the trained choir group. Singers like Hattie Parker are an interesting anticipation of successful contemporary performers like Mahalia Jackson."[29]

The record companies, Pace himself, or both were in such awe of Parker's singing that many of the group's subsequent releases identified them as the "Pace Jubilee Singers with Hattie Parker." Some titles, including the ensemble's 1927 Vocalion recording of "We Will Walk through the Valley of Peace," even gave her top billing: "Hattie Parker with Pace Jubilee Singers." The accolades extended to print advertising. A Victor advertisement in the October 6, 1928, national edition of the *Defender* prefaced its introduction of the group's latest release, "Stand by Me" / "Leave It There" (Victor 21551), with "Hear the golden-voiced Pace Jubilee Singers with Hattie Parker." Other Pace Jubilee Singers contributed solos to the group's records and, presumably, to their live performances.[30]

Three months after her recording debut with the Pace Jubilee Singers, Parker made one classic blues disc as Eva Parker for Victor in Chicago. Accompanied by violin, piano, and guitar, she sang "You Got Another Woman, I'll Get Myself Another Man" and "I Seen My Pretty Papa Standing on the Hill."[31] The voice is unmistakably Hattie Parker's, and like Sam Cooke's brief dalliance as Dale Cook in the 1950s, the ruse probably fooled no one. One can only surmise that Victor wanted to try her out as a blues singer; changing her first name indicated that at least Parker understood the potential harm that singing blues could do to her religious singing career. Perhaps the record did not sell well enough for her to continue the experiment, for it took nearly two years for Hattie to record for Victor as Eva Parker again. In November 1928, she was accompanied by the Pace Jubilee Singers on "You're Going to Leave the Old Home, Jim" and "Careless Love."[32]

The Pace Jubilee Singers' final recording session for Victor occurred on Saturday, October 26, 1929, the weekend prior to Black Tuesday, when panic engulfed Wall Street.[33] In retrospect, some of the sides the Pace group recorded on the eve of the Great Depression seem prophetic, notably "Throw Out the Life Line," "Jesus Is a Rock in a Weary Land," and "You Got to Run, Run, Run."

The Pace Jubilee Singers on Radio

The Great Depression ended the Pace Jubilee Singers' recording career, but they continued their radio appearances. In early 1929, the ensemble secured a fifteen-minute program Sunday afternoons on WGN. According to an advertisement, the group was now a five-member ensemble.[34] As early as Sunday, November 17, 1929, and through December of that year, the Pace Jubilee Singers were part of an hour-long program on WGN called *Musical Melange*. In addition to Pace's group (now back to seven members according to an ad that featured a photo of the group), the variety broadcast featured an orchestra and classical singers, such as Walter Pontius, all broadcast in their own segments. In the embarrassingly condescending language of the time, the Pace Jubilee Singers were described in the *Chicago Tribune* ad for WGN radio programming as singing spirituals "in the exotic musical patterns characteristic of the Negro" and with "unrestrained rhythms."[35]

While their recorded repertory stuck to the sacred, on at least one occasion the Pace Jubilee Singers presented a radio program of secular material. On Friday, January 14, 1927, the group performed one hour of "southern melodies" on a WBCN radio program billed as *Way Down South in Dixie*. From 7:00 to 8:00 p.m., the group presented Stephen Foster songs to what must have been a largely white or mixed audience on the station owned by the *Southtown Economist* newspaper. An article in the newspaper stated that the Pace Jubilee Singers were well known in the United States and Canada for jubilee, quartet, and solo renditions of "plantation melodies."[36]

After the Pace Jubilee Singers disbanded, Parker continued soloing on local programs. Although recognized in a November 1935 program as a member of Liberty Baptist Church on the South Side, where Pace was music minister, she appears to have also devoted time to West Side churches.[37] For example, in 1936, she sang for a program at the Church of God at 2427 West Fulton. Others on the program included the Johnson Gospel Singers, with soloists Louise Lemon and Mahalia Jackson.[38] Parker also worked with Prince Johnson, the ensemble's director, who in the mid-1930s was director of the St. Stephens AME Gospel Choir on the West Side. She was featured on a St. Stephens program in January 1936. In August of that year, she directed an anniversary celebration of the Johnson Gospel Chorus at Fulton Street AME.[39] Given the comparisons that music scholars have made between the singing styles of Mahalia Jackson and Hattie Parker, the association Parker had with Prince Johnson and the Johnson Gospel Singers suggests that the two women probably knew each other, at least professionally. It is reasonable, therefore, to assume that the young Mahalia incorporated some aspects of Parker's singing style. Heilbut noted that "if you play [Mahalia's recordings of] 'My Task,' 'I've Done My Work,' and 'No Night There,' you can easily imagine Mahalia recalling Hattie Parker."[40]

If Parker had a gospel-singing male counterpart in 1920s Chicago, Heilbut believes it was Homer Quincy Smith. A nephew of W. C. Handy, as Heilbut discovered, Smith recorded two known commercial singles, the first for Paramount in Chicago in December 1926, three months after the Pace Jubilee Singers waxed their first discs.[41] The selections Smith sang at that session were the spirituals "I Want Jesus to Talk [Walk] with Me" and "Go Down Moses." Accompanied by J. Roy Terry's windy pump organ, Smith rendered the spirituals with the vocal enthusiasm, drama, and some of the embellishments that Parker employed. He even added falsetto for emphasis, holding the high notes in a demonstration of sacred showmanship. Heilbut suggests that Smith "probably had his own models, men who employed a semi-operatic falsetto to raise church members from their seats and out of their pews."[42] Smith reprised "I Want Jesus" as "Pilgrim's Journey" for Columbia in 1929, maintaining his falsetto but tossing in a few more vocal flowers than in the 1926 session. Heilbut posits that Smith could well be the first male gospel soloist. Most certainly, he was the first one to make commercial records.[43] Smith went on to become a member of the famous radio quartet, the Southernaires, joining William Edmondson, who was once a member of J. Wesley Jones's Metropolitan Community Church choir.[44]

During the 1930s, Victor determined that there was sufficient demand for the group's back catalog to reissue several songs on its Bluebird imprint. Titles selected for reissue suggest something of a Pace Jubilee Singers' greatest hits: "I'm Going through Jesus," "What a Friend We Have in Jesus," "Leave It There,"

"Old Time Religion," "When the Saints Go Marching In," "Everytime I Feel the Spirit," and "No Night There." That none of these recordings were coupled together originally suggests that Victor handpicked tracks that represented significant sales and generated the most consistent number of back-catalog inquiries. "Old Time Religion" was even pressed internationally. Parker's prominence as the group's featured vocalist was cemented further when one Pace Jubilee Singers Bluebird reissue, "Steal Away and Pray," was credited solely to "Hattie Parker, with Choir and Orchestration."

By 1934, Pace had parted ways with Lillian Bowles and was working as music director for Liberty Baptist Church. In 1935, he moved his Old Ship of Zion Publishing Company to 4550 South Michigan Avenue. The following year, Reverend Nix of Tabernacle Baptist Church in Pittsburgh asked Pace to serve as his music director and improve the church's music ministry. Pace accepted the responsibility in Pittsburgh and brought Old Ship of Zion Publishing with him. He established his enterprise at 2330 Centre Avenue in Pittsburgh.

Once settled in Pittsburgh, Pace formed a community choir called the Pace Choral Union. This new singing group was larger and more enduring than the Jubilee Singers. Since jubilee singing was becoming a thing of the past and robust choirs were gaining in popularity, the Pace Choral Union was more in step with the changing times. The choir grew from twenty-five to as many as three hundred voices; Pace's daughter Frances remembered a younger singing ensemble within the Choral Union.

Despite a 1940 flood that nearly destroyed his home and sheet-music enterprise, Pace continued writing and publishing sacred music, including gospel songs. His most popular gospel compositions were "Bread of Heaven," "Nobody but You, Lord," "I Shouted Joy, Joy, Joy," "Hide My Soul," and "After While It Will All Be Over." In 1951, he published a folio of songs for the Harmonizing Four of Richmond, Virginia, and provided rehearsal space for the young James Cleveland when the gospel singer was in town to appear at Olivet Baptist Church, just a few doors from the Old Ship of Zion. Pace even converted a standard typewriter into a sheet-music printing apparatus by swapping out letters for musical notes.[45] Since large publishing companies did not carry African American gospel songs, publishers such as Pace organized a national network of sales agents to sell his song sheets and folios. Roberta Martin, Theodore Frye, Thomas A. Dorsey, Lillian Bowles, and Martin and Morris sold his music in Chicago.[46] Likewise, he was an agent for out-of-town gospel publishers who wanted their music to be available in Pittsburgh.

Pace's music store was a favorite stopping point for gospel singers appearing in Pittsburgh. Frances Pace Barnes regularly met gospel stars, such as Philadelphia's Ward Singers and Singing Sammie Bryant of Detroit, as they came through the city to perform. She said, "[Artists] always stopped at the house to deal with my father because not only were they going to sell sheet music [at the musicals], they wanted to make sure that when they left, people who couldn't buy [the music] right then [could get it] at Pace's Music Store. They'd do commercials for him."[47]

Pace remained in touch with many musicians and singers whom he had met throughout his life. Family members recall that it was common for acquaintances from Pace's jazz and publishing days in Chicago, such as Louis Armstrong and W. C. Handy, to drop by their home for a visit.[48] By the 1950s, Pace had slowed his activities, preferring the quietude of the back of his store and his home studio to arrange music or help songwriters get their songs on paper and secure copyrights. While maintaining his meticulousness and hard work ethic, Pace "was a homebody," Frances Pace Barnes recalled. "When he relaxed, he liked boxing and basketball. That was his relaxation."[49]

Charles Henry Pace died in Pittsburgh on December 16, 1963. While Pace never considered himself an accomplished musician, fellow composer and publisher Kenneth Morris felt otherwise: "Pace . . . never got the same note that Dorsey got, but he certainly by far was the better musician of the two."[50] According to James Cleveland, "Pace wrote songs that were thirty to forty years ahead of his time."[51]

CHAPTER 4

Turn Your Radio On

Chicago Sacred Radio Broadcast Pioneers

As a youngster, I used to lie in my bed on Sunday nights listening to
this fantastic music.

**Joseph R. Washington Jr. on hearing the
First Church of Deliverance radio broadcast**

During the 1920s, several Chicago Pentecostal and Holiness church leaders
discovered that radio, like phonograph recordings, held the potential to trans-
mit their ministries to households throughout the city and beyond, touching
people they might never even meet. This deployment of a new medium for the
churches' message coincided with the overall entry of African Americans into
the radio industry.

African American entertainers appeared on Chicago radio from the earliest days of the medium—James Mundy's Choristers appeared on KYW in
1923 and the Umbrian Glee Club on WLS in 1924—but black-oriented radio
in Chicago as a cultural and economic phenomenon traces its origins to 1929
and the entrepreneurial efforts of Jack L. Cooper.[1] He is considered not only
Chicago's first black disk jockey but also the first in the United States.[2] Born
September 18, 1888, Cooper started his career as an amateur lightweight boxer
who was also skilled in baseball and billiards.[3] He worked as a vaudeville
singer, dancer, comedian, and ventriloquist. By 1925, he was submitting news
briefs from Washington, DC, for publication in the national edition of the
Chicago Defender when he was asked to write and perform in comedy skits
three times a week over DC radio station WCAP.[4] While WCAP provided him

with excellent radio training, it was also a constant reminder of the nation's condescending attitude toward African Americans. Not only were the skits in dialect, but Cooper had to ride the service elevator to get to the studio.[5]

Cooper moved to Chicago in 1926. His first job in the city was selling newspaper advertising.[6] He soon secured a spot on WWAE, where he hosted a radio broadcast for Welsh's Battery Service. Among the guests on Cooper's earliest Chicago broadcasts were recording artist Grace Outlaw and Norman McQueen's Optimistic Singers.[7] Cooper's radio career took off in 1929, when, "after 14 hectic months of trudging from station to station trying to sell the idea of an all-Negro hour to the owners and managers of the many broadcasting stations in and about Chicago," he found a sympathetic ear in Joseph Silverstein. Silverstein, considered Chicago's "father of ethnic radio," was the owner of 250-watt WSBC-AM (World's Storage and Battery Company), founded in 1928 as "Chicago's first southtown radio station."[8] According to *Defender* radio editor George Evans, Silverstein was impressed by Cooper and his idea for a radio broadcast that would "show the world that his people were capable of rendering just as good a musical program as were members of other groups."[9] Silverstein sold Cooper time on WSBC to produce the *All-Colored Hour*. The groundbreaking program, which showcased important black leaders and entertainers, debuted at 5:00 p.m. on Sunday, November 3, 1929.[10] Later, it aired from 9:00 to 10:00 p.m. Sundays from WSBC's South Side studio in the Metropolitan Funeral System building at 418 East Forty-Seventh Street. Cooper featured local quartets on his *All-Colored Hour*, mostly those under the tutelage of Alabama native and quartet trainer Norman McQueen, including the Southern Harmonizers, Harmony Queens, Humble Queens, and Optimistic Singers.

No stranger to sales, Cooper built a formidable and avid audience, and as producer and host of the *All-Colored Hour*, he amassed a stable of advertisers. Although WSBC was only a 250-watt station, its signal reached most black households in Chicago, making it attractive to businesses, including churches, seeking to serve the black community. Although WSBC originally used a white announcer to open and close the *All-Colored Hour*, a black announcer later assumed that duty.[11] To counter the racial stereotyping he encountered on WCAP as well as promote cultural assimilation, Cooper spoke in standard American English and a formal broadcast voice typical of the era's white announcers.[12]

Radio ministries had been in existence since the early days of the wireless. Chicago's WHT was among the first to feature religious programming.[13] In 1924, Rev. Samuel Crouch of the Wayside Church of God in Christ in Fort Worth, Texas, great uncle of gospel artist Andraé Crouch and associate of pianist Arizona Dranes, became the first black minister to broadcast on radio.[14] In Chicago, Rev. Preston Bradley was the first white preacher to use radio.

He broadcast his ministry from the People's Church on Lawrence Avenue in Chicago's Uptown neighborhood.

In Bronzeville, Elder Lucy Smith's All Nations Pentecostal Church and Rev. Clarence H. Cobbs's First Church of Deliverance were early adopters of radio for transmitting church services. Both Smith and Cobbs were working class and not part of the South Side church elite, but their radio presence transformed them into nationally recognized "oral narrators of modernity" and their churches into popular ministries whose membership and accounting ledgers competed with Bronzeville's Old Landmarks. By embracing the city's emerging gospel music singers, songwriters, and musicians and by transmitting their talent across the airwaves, All Nations Pentecostal Church and First Church of Deliverance ensured that gospel music was heard throughout the city, the Midwest, and, ultimately, the nation.

All Nations Pentecostal Church

Among black churches in 1920s Chicago, All Nations Pentecostal was the first to broadcast its worship services regularly on radio. Its founder, Elder Lucy Smith, was born on January 14, 1870, in Oglethorpe County, Georgia. She wrote in her autobiography: "I was born in a typical log cabin, about fifteen by twenty-five feet square. In this cabin I lived with my mother and sisters and brothers; one room was my home and my sisters and brothers and I would climb on a ladder and grasp it with a real grip and go up in the loft to sleep."

Lucy married William Smith around 1892. Their home had a dirt chimney and an open fireplace for cooking. The Smiths' first child was born two years after they married; Lucy gave birth to a total of nine children while on the farm. The family moved to Athens, Georgia, in 1908, but William subsequently disappeared. Smith shepherded her children to Atlanta and found work as a dressmaker.

Smith moved to Chicago in advance of the Great Migration and settled on the South Side on Sunday, May 1, 1910. She joined Olivet Baptist Church soon after her arrival. She switched her membership to Ebenezer Baptist Church two years later, then joined the Stone Church Assembly at Thirty-Seventh and Indiana, where she was baptized in 1914. William Smith later joined his wife in Chicago and stayed there until his death in 1938.

Sometime in 1916 or 1917, while at Stone Church, Smith participated in a prayer meeting during which blessings and healings occurred. From there she accepted the calling to start All Nations Pentecostal Church. She wrote:

> All Nations Pentecostal Church started as humbly as any other church of the time. In 1918 on New Year's Day, we had a meeting and we gave the visitors

chairs and we sat on the floor and stood around a wall. The Lord was trying to build up something but it was unknown to us. We continued praying, asking the Lord to give us some chairs, and the Lord sent a man and his wife to the prayer room. [The wife] looked in the paper and saw an advertisement for chairs . . . and bought them and gave them to us. In a week's time that set of chairs was filled and he answered and enabled us to get ninety-two dollars in a free will offering for [more] chairs. Then the place became too small and Brother William Smith tore down the partition. This place afterwards became too small.[15]

From June to October 1921, Smith held services under a tent at Thirty-Seventh and Vincennes. Of her earliest volunteers, only Brother and Sister Nealy and daughter Viola remained. The tent meetings were sufficiently successful that in October 1921, Smith and her congregation moved to the Star Theater building at Thirty-Eighth and State. Over the next couple of years, All Nations Pentecostal Church underwent a dizzying succession of moves in and out of buildings and tents throughout Bronzeville. Its members even worshipped in the Pekin, the city's first black-owned theater, at Twenty-Seventh and State. By 1926, the church had returned to Smith's home at 3733 South Vincennes.

It was at this point that Smith asserted her right to be the church's pastor. Prior to 1926, she was the congregation's leader in name only because in Pentecostal churches, women were prohibited from serving as pastor. She reported:

One Sunday morning at 3636 Cottage Grove Avenue the Lord said, "I want you to be the Pastor and I want you to get up and tell them, precious one." You know how embarrassing that was but I had to do it. You know some people don't care for a woman pastor and some do. We had a Saints March from my home at 3733 Vincennes to 3716–18–20 Langley Avenue to the Church, December 19, 1926. We went in there with out any doors, and we had to stop the crevices and openings with paper and rags to prevent the air from injuring our bodies and making it convenient. "Praise the Lord!" "Praise the Lord!" A-men to God! Now he has given me a Church, a house for all Nations.[16]

At 3716 Langley, Smith built the first of two churches for which she would oversee construction from the ground up. The All Nations Pentecostal Church membership was comprised of four women for each man, and pilgrims of all races sought refuge there because of Smith's reputation for physical healing. Crutches and canes discarded by those who were healed of their infirmities by Elder Smith festooned the church walls. Smith herself said in 1935: "This is not a colored church, but a church for all nations. . . . We has all kinds of people who comes here regularly. Swedes, Polish, Italians, just plain white folks, and Jews. . . . Everybody is welcome."[17] Romance Watson, a member of the Roberta Martin Singers, grew up in All Nations during the 1930s. He, too, remembered the church as having a diverse membership: "We had white members and members from the islands." Impoverished families received food, clothing, and other essentials from All Nations' social services. Smith herself referred to All Nations as the "friendly church in the heart of a friendly community."

The music was as bold, brassy, informal, and progressive as its founder. Smith herself described the music as having a "'swing' to it," explaining, "I want my people to swing out of themselves all the mis'ry and troubles that is heavy on their hearts. . . . What I like to see is to get them moving and singing so they'll forget their troubles."[18] The church assembled a band of musicians who produced jazzlike accompaniment to the congregational singing. Daisy Johnson directed the choir. James Austin, an accomplished trumpet player, was Johnson's assistant. Edgar G. Holly was pianist, pumping out "jazzy hymn playing." WPA worker Robert Lucas remarked about the services: "The interminable number of verses and choruses was accompanied first by the patting of feet, the clapping of hands, and then ecstatic shouts, shoulders twitching and bodies swaying. . . . Following a crescendo of music and voices, the members leaped to their feet, threw both hands high over their heads and shouted, 'Thank you Jesus' over and over."[19] All Nations member Gladys Beamon told Anthony Heilbut that the church's theme song was "The Fight Is On, Christian Soldiers," and that the congregation sang, marched, shouted, and often collapsed around the church. Another member, Floriene Watson Willis, said of the All Nations services: "You talk about a Holy Ghost time, we would have some church! A lot of people were healed during those services."[20]

Smith's radio program, *The Glorious Church of the Air*, was first broadcast on 5,000-watt WIND-AM 560 in early 1933. It was heard every Sunday at 11:00 p.m.[21] By 1935, the sixty-five-year-old founder and pastor of All Nations and her congregation could be heard as often as four times a week. WIND was sufficiently powerful for the signal to be picked up by listeners in several surrounding states. Smith later shifted her broadcast to WSBC and then to WCFL, but maintained her eleven o'clock to midnight slot.[22] By 1937, All Nations had secured sufficient contributions from radio listeners and congregants to build a fifty-thousand-dollar modern structure at 518 Oakwood Boulevard.

Some black Chicago residents, most notably those who saw urban life as an opportunity for racial uplift, were embarrassed by Elder Smith's services. In September 1934, Louis A. Dulaney wrote the *Defender* that the All Nations Pentecostal broadcast was an offense to black progress and an "insult to the Race." Calling Smith and her worshippers "ignorance personified," Dulaney criticized Smith's unschooled diction and turned his nose up at the church's music. "The solo, 'I Don't Know What I'd Do without My Lord' was a perfect number for some of the fan dancers or any cabaret," Dulaney wrote. "If that is their best effort for a hymn, Lord help them, I pray." A few weeks later, Lula

M. Cheek praised Dulaney's letter to the *Defender* as "wonderful," adding, "Certainly no one has the right to question the sincerity of the Christianity of [Smith], but the question of broadcasting to the world the most ignorant side of our people is the immediate problem for the better thinkers of our group."[23]

But seventy-two-year-old G. L. Pope shared another perspective with *Defender* readers: "I admit [Smith's] grammar was somewhat of a jolt, but I am sure anyone of a charitable nature would readily understand her aims. It does not always take a college degree to make one's self clear to the people." Ruth Wallace also leapt to Smith's defense: "No matter how crude it may seem, [Smith] is talking about God who truly understands her, and so do we." Wallace next addressed "educated ministers," taking them to task for their alleged unwillingness to "help fallen humanity . . . if it is going to cost a part of the receipts of the church." She added, "I asked one of our leading ministers why doesn't he broadcast and his reply was, 'Oh, it costs too much money.'"[24]

It would be unrealistic, however, to assume that all Old Settlers shied away from Elder Smith's services. Some attended Sunday morning services at an Old Landmark, such as Pilgrim, Ebenezer, or Olivet, but "stole away" to All Nations to enjoy its spirited Sunday evening or weekday services. They rejoiced in the healing services and sought Smith's anointed handkerchiefs. In the late 1930s, the pastor of an old-line church told researcher Miles Mark Fisher: "If you want to see my folks [members] on a Sunday night, go to Elder Lucy Smith's."[25] It is possible that All Nations was the "large Pentecostal church" that Vattel Elbert Daniel visited in the late 1930s "where from eight to nine hundred persons were present . . . [but] the church roll contained only one hundred and twenty-eight names. . . . Investigation revealed that the Sunday night congregation was made up mainly of persons from other churches."[26]

The potential that radio held for reaching mass audiences, building church membership, and saving souls was not lost on Smith or the new generation of bootstrapping pastors. Veteran radio producer and announcer Norman Spaulding observes that the high rate of illiteracy among southern black migrants between the ages of twenty-five and forty-five during that time was a significant factor in the growth of black radio as a popular medium in Chicago's black community.[27] According to Bradley S. Greenberg and Brenda Dervin, lower-income African Americans listened to radio more than any other socioeconomic group.[28] Radio therefore became a principal information resource, particularly for the unlettered. Radio also benefited from the primacy of orally transmitted information in black culture. Out of necessity, blacks passed news, stories, songs, history, and other information orally for centuries. Thus, while print media such as the *Chicago Defender* and the *Pittsburgh Courier* became essential means of communicating news and images throughout the U.S. black population, radio had a more extensive, diverse, and immediate following. Even regular *Defender* readers turned to radio for local and national news, athletic events, general information, and entertainment—so much so that by the mid-thirties, the *Defender* hosted a regular news broadcast on the radio.

In 1933, possibly following Elder Smith's lead, Rev. Sethard P. Dunn's Church of God at 4938 South Prairie Avenue became the second black church in Chicago to purchase broadcast time. Its service aired every Sunday on WSBC from 7:30 to 8:30 a.m.[29] Dunn's radio ministry, which continued well into the 1950s, earned him the nickname "The Radio Shepherd." His weekly *Evening Light Broadcast* featured the more restrained music consistent with this denomination.[30] Other Chicago church broadcast pioneers included Moses Temple at 4630 South Parkway, whose Sunday broadcast over WSBC also started around 1933.[31] In early 1937, Rev. C. E. Poole's All Nations Apostolic Church, located at 2204 West Washington Boulevard on Chicago's West Side, bought a half hour of broadcast time on WSBC to air its service on Thursdays at 11:30 p.m.[32]

But the Chicago church with the most influential and longest continuously running broadcast, one that had more to do than any other church in communicating the exuberance of gospel music nationwide, was First Church of Deliverance.

The First Church of Deliverance

It is fitting that Clarence Henry Cobbs, the founder and first pastor of the First Church of Deliverance, was born in Memphis on Leap Day, February 29, 1908. His unconventional birthdate suited this unconventional man. Growing up, Cobbs worshipped at St. Paul Baptist Church and attended Kortrecht High School, later renamed Booker T. Washington High School, where he studied in the classroom of gospel songwriter Lucie E. Campbell.[33] Cobbs traveled to Chicago during school vacations to visit his mother, Luella "Nana" Williams. Her home was at 3363 South Indiana, making her a near neighbor of Mahalia Jackson's aunts Hannah and Alice Clark. After he finished high school, Cobbs joined his mother in Chicago permanently. Together, they attended Pilgrim Baptist Church, which they could see from their doorstep.

Sometime between 1926 and early 1928, Cobbs met a woman who changed the trajectory of his life. "Mother" Della Hopkins Hedgepath was a fellow Tennessean, born in Nashville. She had migrated to Chicago via Indianapolis in 1905 and lived two blocks south of Cobbs at 3543 South Indiana. Although she, like Cobbs, was a registered member of a mainline denomination—Coppin Chapel AME—Hedgepath became a medium in 1909. In 1912, she began holding meetings and conducting lectures on spiritualism. She founded the Ladies Light House Mission, and her expertise was sought by so many that her lectures and meetings caused traffic snarls that required police intervention.[34]

The circumstances in which Cobbs met Mother Hedgepath are unknown, but she had a significant impact on his religious direction. The handsome, ambitious Cobbs, six feet tall and blessed with an expressive face and engaging smile, likely felt a personal kinship with a religion that was as flamboyant, eclectic, and focused as he on personal advancement. Ultimately, Cobbs's traditional Baptist upbringing gave way to the Spiritual church.

According to scholar Hans A. Baer, the Spiritual church in its early days "incorporated not only elements from black Protestantism but also Roman Catholicism and Voodoo, or at least its diluted magical form, hoodoo. . . . Some Spiritual churches added elements from other religious and esoteric traditions, including Islam, Judaism, New Thought, and astrology."[35] As a result, some members of conservative denominations viewed Spiritual churches with suspicion. "There were all these myths that ran amok in the 1920s, 1930s, and 1940s," said gospel historian L. Stanley Davis, "that these are candle burning people who talk to the dead. That's not true."[36]

Not long after Hedgepath's death on February 18, 1928, the twenty-year-old Cobbs sat on a Chicago city bus, lost in thought.[37] As his bus crossed Thirty-Fifth Street and Grand Boulevard, he heard a message that altered his destiny. Call it divine direction, a message from the dearly departed Mother Hedgepath, or a dream no longer deferred, the charge proffered to the young man on the bus was clear: start a Spiritual church in Chicago and name it "First Church of Deliverance."

The opportunity to establish a stronghold for the Spiritual church in Bronzeville was wide open. During his block-by-block assessment of African American churches on the South Side during the late 1920s, Robert Lee Sutherland counted only seventeen spiritual churches in a sea of traditional Protestant denominations.[38]

According to First Church of Deliverance's current pastor, Bishop Otto T. Houston III, the initial location of the First Church of Deliverance was Nana Williams's Indiana Avenue residence. He said that the members "used an ironing board for an altar and a Victrola as a lectern."[39] Cobbs's mother and his grandmother Maggie Drummond were two of the church's five charter members. The associate pastor was the soft-spoken and polished Mattie B. Thornton, nicknamed "Little Missionary."[40] Thornton became so intimately associated with First Church that until her death on May 31, 1964, she and Cobbs were affectionately known as Papa and Mama.[41]

While 1929 was a catastrophic year financially for the United States, it was a period of rapid growth for First Church. On May 8, Reverend Cobbs and his followers moved their services from Williams's living room to a rented storefront at 4155 South State Street. Three months later, First Church formally affiliated with the Metropolitan Spiritual Churches of Christ, the governing body of Spiritual churches around the country. The mother church of the denomination was Metropolitan Spiritual, founded in Kansas City, Missouri, by former Chicago residents Elder Leviticus Lee Boswell and Frank William Taylor. While in Chicago, Boswell and Taylor were members of the Metropolitan Community Church. When the two became disenchanted with the Chicago congregation, they moved to Kansas City and organized Metropolitan Spiritual Church of Christ.[42] In September, Cobbs and Thornton were ordained at Metropolitan during the denomination's first convention.[43]

First Church membership grew during 1929 and 1930 and required a larger facility, which Cobbs and his trustees found at 4633 South State Street. They held their first services there on Sunday, October 17, 1930. By 1933, this building was no longer sufficient for the increasing church membership, so Cobbs and his trustee board moved the church to a brick building on what would become the church's permanent site, 4315 South Wabash Avenue. On June 8, 1933, First Church held its first service in the new space.

Cobbs embodied in largesse and vision the modernistic mission of the First Church of Deliverance. "Preacher," as members referred to him, worked tirelessly to promote his church. He was a living witness to the church's acknowledgment that personal prosperity was important. A photograph taken at the time depicted Cobbs cutting a quintessentially cosmopolitan figure, adorned in a well-cut suit and a fashionable fedora, standing confidently next to a fine automobile: the Great Gatsby of Bronzeville. In *Black Metropolis*, a landmark study of Chicago's black community, social scientists St. Clair Drake and Horace Cayton observe, "[Cobbs] wears clothes of the latest cut, drives a flashy car, uses slang, and is considered a good sport. Such a preacher appeals to the younger lower-class people and to the 'sporting world'—he's regular."[44] Indeed, Cobbs was among the most cosmopolitan preachers of the era.

Cobbs could see that Elder Lucy Smith's church benefited from her regular radio broadcasts, and he subsequently brokered First Church's own weekly radio ministry. The popular broadcast of the church's services, complete with choir singing and Cobbs's sermon, debuted at 11:00 p.m. on November 10, 1935, on WSBC. The program started with the choir rendering Cobbs's arrangement of "How I Got Over."[45]

The First Church of Deliverance Choir was six years old when it debuted on radio. In fact, the group gathered for its first rehearsal on Tuesday, October 29, 1929, the day after Black Monday heralded the start of the Great Depression. Its first director, Robert L. (R. L.) Knowles (1915–71), was a Kansas City resident and a member of Boswell and Taylor's Metropolitan Spiritual Church. He came to Chicago as a teenager to assist First Church in organizing its choir and became its first soloist. Anthony Heilbut credits Knowles and another gospel singer,

Robert Anderson, with developing the improvisatory interaction that became one of gospel's most salient traits, during their years as a singing duo.[46]

Around this time, Julia Mae Kennedy also became part of the First Church music ministry. Kennedy was born circa 1887 or 1888 in Meridian, Mississippi, and attended Industrial High School in Birmingham. She was married briefly to Malachi Wilkerson, with whom she helped train young Birmingham students in the rudiments of singing. Around 1922, she toured with Williams's Jubilee Singers and then Mason's Jubilee Singers. In 1931, she joined Cobbs's First Church of Deliverance as its music director.[47] Although she spent a few interim years as music director at Morning Star Baptist Church, Kennedy returned to First Church and served in its music department until her death in 1981. She influenced many directors and musicians, including Charles Clency, who said he and his musician friends "would sneak over to [First Church]— [they] weren't supposed to go to First Church—because she was so tops." Clency recalled, "All of us tried to emulate her. I would go back to my church and try to do what we heard down at First Church. The music on the broadcast, their presentations at Easter, Christmas, it was tops. And everybody tried to imitate it, even the people who didn't really like them."[48]

Kennedy "was dynamic," recalled Bishop Jerry Goodloe, a member of the First Church choir from the mid-1950s to 1962. "She'd have Minister Ralph [GoodPasteur] up there directing the choir. Somebody would be off and she'd hear it. She'd stop them, come up and say, 'You're off!' She could tell that. She was just that good."[49]

"I call First Church the 'laboratory church,'" Davis said, "because all of the [gospel song] writers would try out their music on First Church. They would bring their music down to Julia Mae Kennedy and Kenneth Morris, and they would try the music out. The broadcast was a great mechanism for selling the music, because folks heard it."[50]

Davis considers First Church of Deliverance the originator of the hour-long radio service broadcast formula that many churches still follow today:

1. Church theme song, sung by the choir and congregation, opens the broadcast
2. Scripture reading
3. Singing of the Lord's Prayer
4. Evening or morning hymn
5. Congregational hymn
6. Twenty or twenty-three minutes of uninterrupted music (choir, guests)
7. Pastor's theme song, sung by the choir and congregation

8. Sermonette by the pastor
9. Church and community announcements, by the church's radio announcer
10. Prayer of faith
11. Song by choir or closing words from pastor[51]

The First Church of Deliverance choir performed anthems, hymns, revival songs, spirituals, and gospels in a spirited, sonorous manner, but without the unfettered emotional ebullience of the Pentecostal and Holiness churches. It is likely that the blend of enthusiasm and restraint came from the influence that Boswell's choral direction at Metropolitan in Kansas City had on Knowles.[52] Moreover, that influence may have originated in Chicago. In the early 1920s, Boswell served as assistant director of the Metropolitan Community Church choir under J. Wesley Jones. It is possible that Boswell took some of or all the techniques he had learned from Jones to Kansas City and applied them when organizing the Metropolitan Spiritual choir. If this is true, the dignified, majestic, and semiclassical sound of First Church's choirs is the indirect result of the music department of its neighbor, Metropolitan Community Church, through Boswell, who transferred his skills to Knowles.

Regardless of how the choir's anthemic sound came to be, it did not take long for the First Church broadcast to become a hit. In *Black Metropolis*, Drake and Cayton describe the broadcast as it sounded in the mid-1940s: "At eleven o'clock every Sunday evening a large segment of lower-class Bronzeville listens for [Cobbs's] radio theme song, 'Jesus Is the Light of the World,' sung by a well-trained but "swingy" choir to the accompaniment of two pianos, a pipe organ [*sic*], an electrical guitar, and several violins."[53]

Of the music and preaching he heard on the broadcast, Joseph R. Washington writes:

> Against the background of rollicking music and superb singing [Reverend Cobbs] comes on in a quiet manner as the counselor, addressing his audience in a unique way. As a youngster, I used to lie in my bed on Sunday nights listening to this fantastic music, puzzling over how it was possible for such a low-key preacher to be so successful. Most of all, it was this mystical note which he struck in contrast to the jubilant music that was fascinating. . . . I never could figure out the meaning of those mystery words repeated Sunday after Sunday— "It doesn't matter what you think about me, but it matters a lot what I think about you." Cobb [*sic*] made no pretension of being anything more than a religious leader who loved the ways of Black folk. He offered them his counsel and advice, allowing them to state the conditions of their life.[54]

Pastor Ray Allen Berryhill recalled the magic of actually *seeing* as well as hearing the First Church of Deliverance choir and worship service:

> About three minutes to eight [p.m.], Julia Mae Kennedy and the First Church of Deliverance choir came down that middle aisle. I had never seen anything like it. It was about two or three hundred of them. I'm sitting on the edge of the seat in the front, maybe the third row and I'm turning around because I had never seen a choir uniformed head to toe. These ladies, they had the same stockings, they had the same shoes, they had the same pump, the same dress, the same corsage. The men had the same suit, the same shoes, the same tie, the same shirt. They came down that aisle singing "Lead Me, Guide Me." I thought the heavens had opened up.[55]

Although First Church and All Nations Pentecostal occupied the same time slot on different stations, Sundays from eleven o'clock to midnight became synonymous with the First Church of Deliverance radio broadcast. Known as the "Midnight Broadcast," it became part of Bronzeville nightlife.[56] Celebrities showed up at the broadcast—Billie Holiday is alleged to have attended with her pet dog in her purse—and Chicago ministers endeavored to steer clear of that time slot when brokering their own church programming.

Even passersby could catch the Midnight Broadcast. "People didn't have air conditioners then in the summer," Davis explained, "so they would have the windows up and you could hear their radios. Everybody had on First Church of Deliverance. You could hear First Church's broadcast and never lose a beat!"[57] Goodloe added that by the 1950s, "the 11:00 [p.m.] service was so filled up, we'd get out of the 8:00 [p.m.] service, go for a break, and by the time we got back for the 11:00 [service], we'd have to weave our way in, there'd be so many people there."[58]

Radio introduced Chicago's white community to the sounds of sanctified singing and preaching. Individuals who never set foot in Bronzeville, let alone a black church, could tune their radios to WSBC and hear the impassioned preaching and singing at All Nations Pentecostal, Fortieth Church of God in Christ, and transcriptions of Elder Lightfoot Solomon Michaux's church services in Washington, DC. Charles Crockett of WAAF said of Rev. Louis Boddie's Greater Harvest Baptist Church broadcast: "I suspect that Boddie's listening audience must have been one-third white. At least, the mail and contributions that we received at the station had that percentage."[59] Gospel historian Alan Young concurred: "The airwaves were one area where Jim Crow's grip could be weakened. African-Americans could be denied access to America's democratic process and segregated as second-class citizens, but their music could be heard by anybody with a radio."[60]

Similarly, blacks raised as Baptists, Episcopalians, or Catholics could satisfy their curiosity about Pentecostalism, Holiness, or Spiritual churches by turning the radio dial to the far left or right to hear the singing and preaching. Gospel singers and musicians did not have to attend church programs or the National Convention of Gospel Choirs and Choruses confab to learn new songs and techniques: they were as close as the radio dial.

CHAPTER 5

"Someday, Somewhere"
The Formation of the Gospel Nexus

This is the way we sing down South!

Mahalia Jackson

Of those who played crucial roles in the development of gospel music in Chicago, Thomas Dorsey, Mahalia Jackson, Sallie Martin, Theodore Frye, and Magnolia Lewis Butts rank as the most significant. During the late 1920s and early 1930s, the five formed an informal nexus that spread the new gospel songs and gospel music style throughout Chicago and, ultimately, across the country.

Thomas Andrew Dorsey

A versatile pianist, composer, arranger, singer, and bandleader, Thomas Andrew Dorsey was pivotal in incorporating jazz and blues styles into gospel. He was born in Villa Rica, Georgia, the oldest of five children, to Etta Plant Dorsey and Thomas Madison Dorsey, on July 1, 1899. Thomas Madison, an 1894 graduate of Atlanta Baptist College (now Morehouse College), eschewed a formal church pulpit to serve as an itinerant preacher, supplementing his meager income from church donations by sharecropping.[1] The devoutly religious Etta Plant played the organ and sang hymns. Attending church as a youngster, Dorsey heard the hymn singing and moaning of the congregation. He also heard shape-note singing at Mount Prospect Baptist Church.[2] The emotional quality of both experiences left a lasting impression.

If Etta was the religious influence in Dorsey's life, Thomas Madison's ministerial practice gave him a feel for the importance of ritual. Even in his youth, Thomas Andrew was drawn to the spectacle, the "show." Underneath the porch of his home, he played church, hanging on the wall a child-sized cane that his parents bought for him, as he saw his father do in churches, and preaching to an invisible but undoubtedly enraptured congregation.[3]

During the agrarian depression of 1908, many rural blacks, including the Dorsey family, moved to southern cities in search of work. Atlanta was a prime intermediary destination, and the Dorseys made 84 Delta Place in that city their home. Etta took in laundry, and Thomas Madison tended gardens and preached whenever and wherever he could. Nine-year-old Thomas Andrew entered Carrie Steele Orphanage School, but because he had not spent much time in school, he was enrolled in first grade.[4] His parents' new status as laborers, coupled with his own demotion, made Dorsey feel like "a 'homely looking' piece of humanity."[5]

By age eleven, Dorsey had found work as a "butch boy," selling soda pop and candy at Atlanta's famed 81 Theater, a whistle-stop on the Theater Owners Booking Association's "chitlin' circuit."[6] During this time, he became enchanted with the sights and sounds of vaudeville life. Music historian Eileen Southern reports that around 1911, Dorsey also participated in a hastily assembled choir during "Colored Night" at a Homer Rodeheaver and Billy Sunday revival meeting.[7] Joining the volunteer choir was the latest episode in a series of musical epiphanies for the young Dorsey.

Dorsey dropped out of school at age thirteen, after completing only fourth grade, and focused on learning to play piano and read music from instruction books. He had an accurate ear for music and briefly took formal piano lessons from a Mrs. Graves.[8] By age fourteen, Dorsey was sufficiently competent on the piano to play for house parties and other venues throughout Atlanta. He developed a soft touch on the keyboard—a hushed barrelhouse technique developed deliberately to avoid disturbing neighbors during house parties.[9]

In July 1916, the promise of a better life and a chance to escape the demeaning social environment of Atlanta set Dorsey on a journey to Philadelphia to find work in the naval yards. En route to Philadelphia, he stopped in Chicago to visit relatives, including his uncle Joshua, a Bronzeville druggist. He decided to remain in Chicago because it would be better to have family around if hard times hit.[10]

Dorsey found work as a pianist in Bronzeville's buffet flats, which were unlicensed clubs that operated after hours and offered a variety of illicit entertainments, and soon gained local accolades as the "whispering piano player" for his soft touch. To avoid the draft, Dorsey labored in a steel mill, his only paid employment outside music. By 1920, he had joined Pilgrim Baptist Church and enrolled in the Chicago School of Composition and Arranging to take formal lessons in songwriting.[11] It was during this time, when Mamie Smith's "Crazy Blues" was fueling the classic blues phenomenon, that Dorsey copyrighted his first song: "If You Don't Believe I'm Leaving, You Can Count the Days I'm Gone." His father died that year, and as if following through on the declaration of his first song, Dorsey returned to Atlanta in October 1920, where he recovered from the first of several bouts of nervous exhaustion that plagued his early adulthood.[12]

After recuperating, Dorsey returned to Uncle Joshua's house in Bronzeville. In September, Joshua invited his young nephew to join him at the final Sunday session of the 1921 National Baptist Convention. Dorsey was initially reluctant but relented. The experience turned out to be life changing.

From September 7 to 12, 1921, the National Baptist Convention consumed Chicago's Eighth Regiment Armory at Thirty-Fifth Street and Giles. It was a study in kaleidoscopic contrast. Outside, distinguished men in "tuxedos, Prince Alberts and cutaways" and women in "laundered white" walked along Thirty-Fifth Street. Meanwhile, "low-rate" signs from local taxicabs vanished suddenly as drivers and the landlords to whom they dropped off their passengers increased prices to fleece the ten thousand faithful who traveled to Bronzeville for the annual confab. Inside, devout orations and sermons resounded off the walls. Junius Caesar Austin of Pittsburgh delivered the first sermon on the first evening of the convention. Austin, an "able preacher" and up-and-coming influential Baptist minister, so impressed the Chicago crowd that he would later be tapped to preside over Pilgrim Baptist Church. Working parallel to the sermons and the myriad committee meetings, minute taking, and devotional services, were "iron-throated vendors of the blathering of some puny scribbler in Massachusetts or Louisiana. . . . [They] tramped the aisles of the great hall, filching the pockets of the unsuspected of their money for a few dry and empty pages."[13]

One objective of the 1921 National Baptist Convention was to showcase *Gospel Pearls*, the Sunday School Publishing Board's new hymnbook. Among the 165 selections were spirituals, gospel hymns, and revival songs by black and white composers, standard Protestant hymns, and long-meter hymns. In the preface, the editors wrote that the new songbook would be "a boon to Gospel singers," making it clear that gospel singers existed at least as early as 1921.[14]

Naturally, the Sunday School Publishing Board wanted as many *Gospel Pearls* selections as possible sung during the convention. Rev. A. W. Nix, a director of the Sunday School Publishing Board, obliged the convention on Sunday morning, September 11, singing E. O. Excell's "I Do, Don't You" in front of the gathering.

Dorsey later recalled the transforming experience of hearing Nix sing "I Do, Don't You": "My inner-being was thrilled. My soul was a deluge of divine rapture; my emotions were aroused; my heart was inspired to become a great singer and worker in the Kingdom of the Lord—and impress people just as this great singer did that Sunday morning."[15]

What struck Dorsey most about Nix's performance was the way in which the preacher "worked the show," adding bent notes, slurs, and other vocal techniques to move a crowd. Nix could do with his voice what Dorsey could do on the piano. Dorsey could easily draw comparisons between Nix's performance and the artists he watched while selling candy at the 81 in Atlanta. Shortly thereafter, he wrote his first religious song. "If I Don't Get There" was an evangelistic song with conversational lyrics reminiscent of Charles A. Tindley's gospel hymns and a jaunty melody straight from Dorsey's house-party experience. It was the earliest example of his gospel song technique. Although the song never achieved the lasting popularity of some of Dorsey's later compositions, it was his first published religious song and was included in the late 1921 edition of *Gospel Pearls*. Dorsey was not paid for his contribution to the songbook, but nevertheless, many reprints later, "If I Don't Get There" remains no. 117 in *Gospel Pearls*.[16]

Dorsey continued his foray into sacred music by taking a job as music director of Morgan Park's New Hope Baptist Church. This employment lasted for only a few months, as the money was slim—"a donation every three or four weeks"—and if one could not make a living as a music minister in "dicty," or upper-class, Morgan Park, where could one work?[17]

Dorsey forsook the pinched-penny world of sacred music and spent his days at the House of Jazz Music Store, owned by recording artist Clarence Williams. Located just south of Thirty-First Street in the heart of The Stroll, the House of Jazz sold sheet music and served as an informal gathering site for black musicians living in or passing through Chicago. It was here that Dorsey met some of the decade's top performers, including Will Walker, director of a dance band called the Whispering Syncopators. Walker invited Dorsey to be the group's pianist. Dorsey worked with the Whispering Syncopators from 1922 to 1923. The gig ended abruptly when the group received an invitation to tour California from white pianist Ben R. Harney. The catch was that Harney, not Dorsey, would be the group's pianist in California.[18]

After severing ties with the Whispering Syncopators, Dorsey began writing and copyrighting classic blues songs. His career received its biggest boost to date when his 1923 "Riverside Blues" was recorded by Joe "King" Oliver's Creole Jazz Band for Paramount Records.[19] A year later, another Dorsey sacred composition, "We Will Meet Him in the Sweet By and By," was published in the *Baptist Hymnal*.[20]

In addition to composing, Dorsey went to work for Ink Williams and the Chicago Music Publishing Company, the publishing arm for Paramount Records' roster of black recording artists. Dorsey, who could read and write music, transcribed country blues singers' songs onto a lead sheet, wrote arrangements to the songs, copyrighted the arrangement, and even taught the artist how to perform for a recording. The attention to detail that marked Dorsey's music instruction during his more than sixty years in gospel was fashioned in part by his experience preparing bluesmen for the recording studio.

During his tenure with Williams, Dorsey rekindled his acquaintance with Gertrude "Ma" Rainey, whom he had heard initially at the 81.[21] Rainey needed a pianist, and Ink Williams recommended Dorsey. Rainey hired Dorsey to be her accompanist and lead her Wildcat Jazz Band, which included Albert Wynn, Fuller "Kid" Henderson, and Gabriel Washington. Dorsey debuted with Rainey in April 1924 at the Grand Theater at Thirty-Second and State Streets.[22] It was during this time that Dorsey developed the audience-pleasing technique of rising from the piano stool and, "in calculated abandon, kick[ing] it to the side, and play[ing] standing up."[23]

On August 1, 1925, after a protracted period of courting, Dorsey married Nettie Harper.[24] Nettie went on the road with her husband, serving as Rainey's personal wardrobe mistress. Dorsey held the position as the leader of the Wildcats until February 1926, when he was hospitalized for a second nervous breakdown.[25] While recuperating, Dorsey relinquished his Wildcat Jazz Band piano duties to Lillian Hardaway Henderson and band direction to her husband, cornet player "Kid" Henderson. Dorsey did not work with Rainey again until 1928.[26]

For two years, Dorsey battled a deep and physically disabling depression. The gray cloud of bleakness and despair did not subside until 1928, when, while visiting his sister-in-law's church, Dorsey was prayed over by Bishop H. H. Haley, who reportedly pulled a live serpent from Dorsey's throat. Dorsey saw this as a sign to return to religious music and attacked his work with newfound evangelistic fervor.

One product was his third sacred piece, "If You See My Savior," inspired by the sudden and inexplicable death of a neighbor.[27] In the first verse and chorus, Dorsey wrote:

I was standing by the bedside of a neighbor,
Who was just about to cross the swelling tide;
And I asked him if he would do me a favor,
Kindly take this message to the other side.

If you see my Savior, tell him that you saw me,
When you saw me I was on my way.
You may meet some old friend who may ask you for me,
Tell them I am coming home some day.

Dorsey used locally popular singers to introduce his religious songs to church congregations, but it was a difficult undertaking. Although he was the author of two gospel hymns published in Baptist hymnals, he could not persuade Chicago's premier black churches to introduce his blues- and jazz-flavored sacred songs into their sanctuaries. Dorsey even sent free samples of his compositions to more than one thousand ministers, a project he funded at considerable personal expense. In two years' time, however, all he had to show for it was a handful of modest orders.[28]

Frustrated and disillusioned by the cold shoulder of the church and needing to make a living to support Nettie, Dorsey returned to the world of blues, where he had had his only true success. He wasted little time. In August 1928, Dorsey copyrighted a sentimental pop number, "When You're in Love," and went to work as an arranger for Brunswick Records. Dorsey's association with Brunswick enabled him to make solo records.[29]

Later in 1928, Dorsey stumbled into a major critical and financial success. He had been performing with guitarist Hudson Whitaker, a southern migrant who went by the nom de plume of Tampa Red. Whitaker's forte was country blues. On September 6, 1928, Dorsey and Whitaker recorded three blues numbers of their own for Vocalion, but nothing clicked.[30] Over dinner one evening shortly afterward, Whitaker asked Dorsey if he would put music to some lyrics he had written for a composition called "It's Tight like That." Dorsey was initially reluctant. He had recommitted himself to the blues, but Whitaker's double entendre lyrics were a bit more risqué than the average blues. After some consideration, however, the need for financial stability won out, and Dorsey consented to set Whitaker's lyrics to music.[31] The duo took "It's Tight like That" into the recording studio on September 19 and again on October 8, but Vocalion was unimpressed. They tried again on Wednesday, October 24, and it finally came together.[32]

"It's Tight like That" was a commercial and artistic success. It pioneered the use of piano and guitar together in blues and also introduced a style of music called "hokum," an amalgam of country and city blues with suggestive lyrics and an infectious dance beat.[33] Between the fall of 1928 and 1932, Dorsey—either alone, with Whitaker, or with musicians such as Big Bill Broonzy and female vocalist Mozelle Alderson—recorded some sixty hokum recordings. Lester Melrose, supervisor of Vocalion's catalog of race releases and a pioneer producer of the Chicago style of blues, produced many of the duo's records. Recognizing the commercial appeal of songs such as "It's Tight like That," Melrose kept Dorsey and Whitaker, now known as the Famous Hokum Boys, busy in the recording studio.[34] However, the wave of success that Dorsey experienced with hokum did not curb his desire to promote his sacred songs. Whenever he and Whitaker traveled to New York to record, Dorsey visited local ministers to introduce and demonstrate his religious songs.

Interestingly, although Dorsey wrote his gospel songs for soloist and piano, the first sacred recording on which he was an active participant was a coupling of sanctified performances. "Hold to His Hand" and "Come and Go to That Land" were credited to the Gospel Camp Meeting Singers and released in 1929 on Vocalion 1283. Both sides were mid-tempo sanctified songs sung by a mixed group with piano and guitar accompaniment. Dorsey was given composer credit. The female singers are unknown, but Dorsey's soft but firm baritone is identifiable among the sonorous voices. A rhythmic piano (probably Dorsey) is joined by a strumming guitar (possibly Whitaker). The relative obscurity of this recording today suggests that it did not sell well, an outcome likely assisted by the lack of attention it received from Vocalion, which was busy promoting Leroy Carr, Reverend Nix, and the Famous Hokum Boys.[35] Dorsey is also presumed to be the piano accompanist for Sister Cally Fancy and Her Sanctified Singers' 1931 Vocalion release, "Death Is Riding through the Land."[36]

Dorsey decided that if selling sheet music to ministers was not working, perhaps demonstrating them to the general public would be a more successful endeavor. If the singer's interpretation of the song mattered more than the notes on the page—Nix's performance at the 1921 National Baptist Convention had proved that—a song demonstrator would be far more effective. But the soloists Dorsey used initially delivered mixed results. Louise Keller, daughter of Pilgrim Baptist Church assistant pastor Rev. Richard Keller, sang in a semiclassical style that did not match the music. Rebecca "Becky" Talbot, who would work with Dorsey later, had a low-down blues voice that was still too smooth to produce the desired effect. Not surprisingly, with Nix as the benchmark, Rev. E. H. Hall's voice suited Dorsey's needs perfectly.[37] Male preachers tended to mold their singing cadence and pacing after their pulpiteering. Dorsey heard this "preacher" quality in the voices of two others: Augustus "Gus" Evans and Rev. Luschaa Allen. Both Evans and Allen also helped Dorsey peddle his song sheets.

One Dorsey song demonstrator, however, was neither male nor a minster. She was a teenage migrant from New Orleans whose enormous voice was out of proportion to her diminutive frame and youthful innocence but clearly in line with her engaging personality.

Mahalia Jackson

Mahalia Jackson was born in humble circumstances in New Orleans to Charity Clark and Johnny Jackson Jr. She was named for her maternal aunt, Mahala, and added the "i" to her name later. According to her birth certificate, Jackson was born on October 26, 1911, but her aunts insisted the actual date was October 26, 1912, recollecting that Charity was pregnant with Mahalia during the May 1912 flood of the Atchafalaya River.[38] Charity and Johnny never married;

Jackson was raised by her mother and aunts in a section of New Orleans called Greenville, near Magazine and Walnut Streets, bookended by Audubon Park and the levee. The family attended Plymouth Rock Baptist Church, where the four-year-old Jackson made her public singing debut as a member of the children's choir.[39] Her slight frame belied the sonorous voice within as she led songs such as "Jesus Loves Me" and "Hand Me Down My Silver Trumpet, Gabriel."[40]

Charity died suddenly in June 1918 at age thirty. Jackson's namesake, Aunt Mahala, known as "Duke," assumed responsibility for raising the five-year-old girl and her half-brother, Peter.[41] Aunt Duke was a stern disciplinarian and threw Jackson out of the house on occasions when she did not follow orders. Jackson attended elementary school at McDonough 24 but dropped out in the eighth grade to work as a laundress. It was the last formal education that Jackson received and resulted in her championing academics throughout her adult life.

Although Jackson's classroom learning was short-lived, her musical education was not. She devoured the musical gumbo of New Orleans. Sacred music training came from participation in the choir at Mount Moriah Baptist Church on Millaudon Street, where Fletcher "Oozie" Robinson was the choir director.[42] Jackson credited the foot-tapping and hand-clapping congregational singing at Mount Moriah as a key ingredient giving her music its pulse or, as she called it, its "bounce." She also recalled the influence of the church's Baptist preacher: "It *is* the basic way I sing today, from hearing the way the preacher would sort of sing in a—I mean, would preach in a cry, in a moan, would shout sort of, like in a chant way—a groaning sound which would penetrate to my heart."[43]

The spontaneous and ecstatic singing of a sanctified church near Aunt Duke's also informed Jackson's performance style. In her 1966 autobiography, *Movin' On Up*, Jackson recalls listening to the saints as they worshiped with musical fervor to summon the Holy Ghost into their presence. "Everybody in there sang and they clapped and stomped their feet and sang with their whole bodies. They had a beat, a powerful beat, a rhythm we held onto from slavery days, and their music was so strong and expressive it used to bring the tears to my eyes."[44]

Jackson was also exposed to, fascinated by, and perhaps even a participant in the fabled second line of New Orleans's marching or funeral bands. Once mourners buried their dead, they gathered behind the marching band as a second line for the walk home. With the soul now at rest, the band literally changed its tune from sorrowful to joyful. "They would all get right into the jubilant feeling of this jazz music," Jackson remembered. "So that's how a lot of our songs that I sing today has that type of beat, because it's my inheritance, things that I've always been doing, born and raised-up and seen, that went on in New Orleans."[45]

The secular influences in her singing also came from accompanying her older cousin Fred Duskin to local dancehalls where jazz bands performed. "He loved music and he bought all the jazz and blues records he could," recalled Jackson.[46] "Aunt Duke never knew it, but when she was away at the white folks' house I played Fred's records all day long."[47] She heard King Oliver and his jazz band playing on the back of a flatbed truck as they advertised an upcoming dance.[48] She regaled playmates with renditions of "St. Louis Blues" and "My Blue Heaven" and incorporated into her singing the vocal scoops and plaintive moans of classic blues artist Bessie Smith. As a teen, Jackson was fond of Smith's mournful 1925 recording of "Careless Love."[49]

By the autumn of 1927, Jackson had grown weary of Aunt Duke's zero tolerance policies. After Duke put her out of the house for returning home after curfew, Jackson rented a house and tried living on her own. This lasted only a month, because when Aunt Hannah returned for Thanksgiving, she was persuaded to take Jackson back with her to Chicago. Together they boarded the Illinois Central for Chicago, where Jackson moved in with Hannah and Alice Clark at 3250 South Prairie Avenue, a red brick and white stone building a couple of blocks north of Pilgrim Baptist Church and east of The Stroll.[50]

In early December 1927, just a week after Jackson's arrival in Chicago, the sisters sought to cure their niece's homesickness by taking her to a Sunday-morning service at Greater Salem Baptist Church, at 3300 South LaSalle Street.[51] Jackson's first encounter with a deliberative worship service that December morning was a sonic clash of cultures. Standing up and giving her testimony at the 11:00 a.m. service, the fresh-faced migrant burst forth with her brassy, boisterous, New Orleans favorite, "Hand Me Down My Silver Trumpet, Gabriel." Her performance was met with an awkward silence from the congregation. Pastor C. C. Harper was stunned—Jackson at Greater Salem was like tangy barbecue at a tea party—but he and the music director astutely took note of the young woman with the big voice and invited her to join the choir. She did, but her voice was too big to blend with the choir, and she was limited to performing solos.[52]

At Greater Salem, Jackson met the Johnson brothers: Prince, Wilbur, and Robert. Together with Louise Lemon, they had recently formed a mixed quartet called the Johnson Singers and invited Jackson to join them. At first, the group performed exclusively for Greater Salem. With the musically talented Prince on piano, the troupe produced musical programs and religious plays. Jackson, her voice an aural postcard from down South, became the group's main attraction, and they were hired to perform at churches throughout Chicago. Dorsey recalled that the Johnson Singers "were really rocking them everywhere they went. Mahalia was with this group and was going and killing them off, I mean she was laying them out."[53] Although technically they were a quartet, the Johnson Singers are considered the first gospel group for their use of gospel techniques during performances.[54]

Word traveled about the young woman with the big voice. Jackson was invited to solo at sanctified church services, funerals, and tent revivals, such as those held by Rev. A. A. Childs, who built his Evangelist Temple at 3140 South Indiana but also held regular revival services in a tent at Thirty-Third and Giles.[55] In the 1930s, Reverend Childs made Jackson a regular attraction at his revivals, where her distinctive singing was celebrated for its ability to attract souls to Christ, members to the fold, and coins to the collection plate.[56] She sang at Pilgrim on Sunday nights, one of the only opportunities for demonstrative worship at the church prior to 1932.[57]

Those who saw Jackson perform in the early days recall her theatrical style. When the spirit moved her during a song, Jackson hunched down, lifted her dress slightly above her ankles, flashed the congregants a knowing smile, and launched into a lively two-step holy dance. Her physical performance and spontaneous hand claps exuded the unfettered freedom of expression that came straight from the sanctified church and the New Orleans second line, where the revelry released the tension and sorrow of the departed's home going. One could feel her physical movements in her breathless vocals. And when she was "in the spirit" or "got happy," Jackson peppered her songs with colorful vernacular interjections, such as "yeah, yeah, yeah," "Lord, have mercy," and other exclamations from black vernacular speech. New Orleans understood Jackson's holy dancing and her enthusiasts did, too, but conservative northern churchgoers sniffed. Some called her "snake hips," a reference to a popular dance of the time.[58] Once, she even had a toe-to-toe confrontation with a pastor who called her exuberant solo with the Johnson Singers "blasphemous." She retorted, "This is the way we sing down South."[59] Some ministers asked her to don a robe while singing to conceal her body movements from the congregants.[60]

While adjusting to life in Chicago, Jackson performed housework for a family on Hyde Park Boulevard, near the University of Chicago.[61] During this time, around 1928, she met Dorsey, who recalled Jackson as a "good mixer . . . and she loved everybody, at least she acted like she loved everybody. She called everybody 'baby, honey, darling.'"[62] In 1930, she accepted Dorsey's offer to demonstrate his songs. Standing on the sidewalk of busy Bronzeville streets and avenues, Jackson sang one Dorsey composition after another, attracting an audience that would be persuaded to purchase the sheet music for ten cents apiece.[63] Later in the 1930s, Jackson traveled the country with Dorsey as one of his chief demonstrators, but for now she was supplementing her income while taking domestic assignments and picking up an occasional singing job at a church or funeral as what she referred to as a "fish-and-bread" gospel singer.

Sallie Martin

Sallie Martin was another important Dorsey acquaintance who helped the struggling songwriter reap the financial and adulatory benefits of gospel music. She was born November 20, 1895, in rural Greene County, Georgia, east of Atlanta. Raised by her traveling musician mother and her maternal grandparents, Sallie was ambitious from an early age. She refused to live a sharecropper's life, telling oral historian Nathaniel C. Standifer: "I never liked any cotton picking and no kind of working in the fields."[64] She shared a similar sentiment with Anthony Heilbut: "I had a cousin with whom I played and I told her I would never live in the country when I grew up."[65]

At sixteen and with only an eighth-grade education, Sallie moved to Atlanta, where she took on a host of jobs, such as babysitting and laundry, to make ends meet. In Atlanta, she also met and married eighteen-year-old Wallace Martin. Like Jackson, the Baptist-born-and-bred Sallie also became enamored with the sanctified church. Unlike Jackson, Martin was saved at a Tuesday evening service at the local Fire Baptized Holiness Church. Throughout her life, she was at ease in any church, regardless of denomination.[66]

When a fire destroyed the Martins' Atlanta neighborhood on May 21, 1917, the couple migrated north to Cleveland. There she experienced "one of the coldest winters"; as she recalled, "[It] made me crazy momentarily." Around 1919, Sallie spent time in Chicago and found the weather there more acceptable. In Cleveland, "it was always cloudy, especially during the winter," she said. "When I came [to Chicago] . . . it was raining and as soon as the rain was over the sun came out. I said, 'This is the place for me.'"[67]

Sallie Martin may well be the only person in history to embrace Chicago for its clement weather, but she could not persuade Wallace to leave Cleveland. He did not believe that employment opportunities would be as plentiful in Chicago as in Cleveland, and consequently the couple did not move. Sallie worked at a school and sang in the church choir, while Wallace set up a hamburger stand in front of their home and was an usher in the church. By 1923, Sallie had had enough of cloudy Cleveland. Although Wallace still did not want to leave, she and her son, Joel, moved to Chicago without him. Before long, Wallace relented and joined them in the Windy City.

If the weather was better in Chicago, so was the fast life. It pulled Wallace into its vortex. "You know, he had a job and then when he finally got out of the job," Sallie reflected, "he just started where he'd have games and playing, men all in the house, drinking and would gamble all night. So finally it just came to a head." The saved and ambitious Sallie did not stand for nonsense, and the two had separated by the end of the decade.[68] Sallie took a job at the Chicago Municipal Contagious Hospital at Thirty-First and California on the city's Southwest Side, where the pay was low, but, as she later remarked, "at least I had my room and board."[69]

In 1929, Martin chanced to hear Dorsey's "How about You" performed at her church. She walked up to the soloist afterward and asked, "Girl, where did you get that number?" The soloist said, "Well I thought this was the old man who is on Fortieth Street." Old man? Dorsey was barely thirty years old. Martin explained, "You see, Mr. Dorsey's memory was kind of bad and . . . he had that old timey weird look on his face." She recounted: "So [the soloist] said, 'I'll tell you what to do. If you go to Fifty-Ninth and Wabash on a Saturday night, there's a lady there that's trying to teach you how to do gospel numbers and he comes in there with but few songs he has.' I said, 'All right.' I went over the next Saturday night."[70]

The singing teacher was Millie I. Dennis, and although Sallie attended the Saturday-night music class simply to obtain a copy of the song that had piqued her interest at church, Dennis's daughter encouraged her to sing for the assemblage. "But you see . . . I went to one of our [National Baptist] Conventions and I think I overstrained my voice trying to do some of that singing that I shouldn't have." Nevertheless, Sallie agreed to give it a try. True to the woman's word, Dorsey attended the session in time to hear the fellow Georgian in an impromptu recital.[71]

Dorsey was not terribly impressed by Martin's raspy contralto. He recalled that she "had not given much time and study to singing." However, he did give her sage advice: "The thing about it is you have to have somebody to play for you that can transpose. Because you'll never do that song in that key." Dorsey agreed to train her vocally. He invited her to stop by his uncle's house at Fortieth and South Parkway, where he was living, to join a group of female singers he was teaching, among them Dettie Gay and former show-business singer Rebecca Talbot.[72] Martin had entered Dorsey's orbit and was on her way to becoming a gospel singer.

The 1930 National Baptist Convention

The tipping point for Dorsey's gospel songwriting career, and the commencement of a gradual acceptance of gospel music by the established African American church, was the 1930 National Baptist Convention, back in Chicago for its Golden Jubilee celebration. Conventioneers enjoyed performances by a thousand-voice Golden Jubilee chorus, directed by George Garner, that sang every evening starting on August 15, while Chicago public school band director Captain Walter Dyett conducted a fifty-piece orchestra.[73] Recording preacher and delegate Rev. J. M. Gates was in town and took breaks from the convention to minister "to record-breaking audiences" at Friendship and Metropolitan

Baptist Churches.[74] Politically charged exchanges between Revs. J. C. Austin and L. K. Williams and discussions about the April shooting death of convention treasurer Edward Donahue occurred out of earshot of the rank-and-file delegates, who were eagerly "singing songs, praying and shouting out in the main body of the Coliseum."[75]

One of the rank-and-file delegates singing songs was Willie Mae Ford Smith. The soloist from St. Louis rendered Dorsey's "If You See My Savior" during the convention's morning devotions on August 23.[76] She sang it so convincingly that delegates wanted copies to take home. E. W. D. Isaacs asked Dorsey song demonstrator Rev. E. H. Hall to find the composer and bring him to the coliseum. Hall spent the next two days tracking Dorsey down. When he found him, Hall exclaimed, "It's a woman down there from . . . St. Louis, or Kansas City, somewhere in Missouri, man. She's got that 'If You See My Savior.' She's laying them out in the aisle and the folk are just jumping and going on."[77] Dorsey was initially reluctant and understandably so. Isaacs, director general of the Baptist Young People's Union, and pianist/composer Lucie E. Campbell exerted tremendous influence over which songs were sung at the convention and, by extension, in Baptist churches throughout the country. "Lucie Campbell and the music committee from the National Baptist Convention were the big thing," remarked gospel musician and arranger Kenneth Woods Jr. "If you could get your foot in that door, you had it made."[78]

Although Dorsey contributed one song each to *Gospel Pearls* and *Baptist Hymns*, Isaacs, Campbell, and the Sunday School Publishing Board failed to embrace his new gospel songs. Nevertheless, Hall's description of the conventioneers' enthusiastic response to the song was too much for Dorsey to ignore, and he accompanied Hall to the coliseum.[79]

Hall introduced Dorsey to Willie Mae Ford Smith at a rehearsal. Smith reprised her rendition of "If You See My Savior" for Dorsey, who was then asked to say a few words about his songs to the delegates at the rehearsal. His comments persuaded Isaacs to respond: "Go and bring your music down here and set you up a stand over there in the corner. . . . Bring some of—all your music."[80] Dorsey did so. Hall and Dorsey demonstrated the songs for the remainder of the convention and subsequently sold four thousand song sheets by its conclusion. Henceforward, Isaacs and Campbell assisted Dorsey in arranging concerts and programs to demonstrate his songs to Baptist audiences around the country.[81]

Theodore R. Frye

While selling his sheet music at the convention, Dorsey met another person who would become instrumental in his success. Theodore Frye had come to the convention to promote his singing ministry. Frye, who was born September 10,

1899, in Fayette, Mississippi, studied piano and voice as a child and as a young man served as a church choir director.[82] He attended Alcorn College (now Alcorn State University), the first state-supported college for African Americans. He also sang solos in local churches, especially at Vicksburg's King Solomon Baptist Church. In 1927, after the death of his stepfather, Silas B. Foster, Frye moved to Chicago to seek work as a church musician.

When it came to selling a song, Frye was as much a showman as Dorsey. His signature technique was to walk the church aisles while singing, a device that earned him the sobriquet of "The Walking Preacher." "[Frye] could tear up a church!" remembered Eugene Smith, who was recruited in 1933 for the Martin and Frye Quartette.[83] Many who knew Frye recalled his keen sense of humor and jovial personality, which undoubtedly added to his charismatic rapport with church congregations. Nephew Mack Marshall recalled that Frye could play piano as well as sing.[84]

Frye and Dorsey's meeting was one of those serendipitous moments in music history when two like-minded musicians join forces without any clear idea where their partnership would lead.[85] Just as Tampa Red was Dorsey's ideal blues partner, Dorsey and Frye were simpatico in gospel. During song demonstrations, Frye walked and Dorsey leapt from the piano bench, just as he did when accompanying Ma Rainey. Dorsey remembered that if Frye wasn't walking while singing, the crowd would yell out, "Walk, Frye, Walk!" He would "pound the beat out to [Frye's] marching steps. Frye would strut; women would fall out—don't know whether he looked good or they were just happy."[86]

Magnolia N. Lewis Butts

Also during the convention year, Dorsey "stumbled into a political meeting" at the Eighth Regiment Armory and heard "a slight, short brown-skinned woman" singing his composition "How about You" "with a big voice." The singer, Magnolia Lewis Butts, would also play a significant role in the dissemination of gospel music.

Classically trained Magnolia N. Lewis Butts was born in Tipton, Missouri, in 1896 or 1899. She studied music, graduated from Chriswell Delsartan School of Expression in Kansas City, and moved to Chicago in 1918. A *Chicago Defender* article from August of that year found her helping the war effort as secretary of Local [Draft] Board Number 5, whose chairman, Archibald Carey, was "the only person of our Race holding such a position in the country."[87] At the time of the 1920 U.S. Census, Butts was living with her widowed mother Alice at 3742 South Grand (later South Parkway) while working as a stenographer.[88]

Butts began a relationship with J. Wesley Jones that lasted for three decades when, as early as December 1919, she joined his Progressive Choral Society and served as its recording secretary.[89] In addition to her stenographic skills, Butts was a soprano singer who could be called upon to render a spiritual or a selection from Mendelssohn's *Elijah*. Her skill in the dramatic arts helped prepare the principal soloists for the Progressive Choral Club's 1920 presentation of *Esther*, which Jones directed.[90] In 1924, Jones and Butts were elected president and secretary, respectively, of the Chicago Music Association, Branch Number One of the National Association of Negro Musicians, an organization founded in 1919 to foster African American classical music performance and education.[91]

Sometime between 1921 and 1926, Butts joined the music department of Metropolitan Community Church, where Jones was the choir director. By 1926, she had become Jones's assistant director and among the choir's premier soloists. Butts also wrote and directed pageants for church members to perform. Additionally, she taught dramatic arts at Pauline Lee's Chicago University of Music, housed in a Michigan Avenue residence once owned by opera star Ernestine Schumann-Heink.[92]

Butts's singing and theatrical skills, her association with J. Wesley Jones and the Metropolitan Choir, and her willingness to volunteer her stenographic services as committee secretary secured her a premier position among black Chicago's classical music cognoscenti. Butts was even Metropolitan's chief stenographer. By 1935, she was drawing an annual salary from the church that surpassed Jones's by $260 because of her dual roles as stenographer ($720) and choir director ($140).[93]

In 1929, Rev. W. D. Cook, pastor of Metropolitan, asked Butts to organize a chorus to sing for funerals, "because the Senior Choir's repertoire wasn't funeral music."[94] Although in his studies Robert Lee Sutherland identified Metropolitan as a church that allowed some demonstrative expression during the worship service, it is probable that the music performed by Butts's new choir consisted of well-known spirituals and hymns because that was the type of music for which Metropolitan was known. When Cook died in Chicago on July 5, 1930, Butts's group renamed itself the W. D. Cook Singers in his memory. Sometime later, the group changed its name to the W. D. Cook Gospel Choir.

The group's reputation spread, and they began receiving invitations to sing at local churches. *Defender* columnist Maude Roberts George mentioned Butts's "gospel choir, full of religious fervor and well balanced tone" when reporting on a musical program at Institutional Baptist Church in August, 1931.[95] A year later, George said of Butts: "Her sincerity and love of the spirituals can always be felt by the audience, who respond with 'Amen' and words of praise."[96] Butts's choir also performed at Metropolitan's Friday night evangelistic service, called Fellowship Night, but not on Sundays—that was Jones's territory.[97] Regardless, Butts's reputation as a soloist at Metropolitan and in Bronzeville's classical music circle helped the group secure a following.

By 1930, the principal players in the gospel nexus—Dorsey, Frye, Martin, Jackson, and Butts—were in a position to transform African American sacred music, one church at a time. It would take another migrant, a pastor from Birmingham, Alabama, to provide the venue and visibility for gospel music to score its first major victory and gain a foothold—however tenuous—in the conservative African American church of the urban North.

CHAPTER 6

Sweeping through the City
Thomas A. Dorsey and the
Gospel Nexus (1932–1933)

The first Sunday that I came to Ebenezer, I joined Ebenezer. That beautiful gospel singing and those blue robes, I just went wild over those blue robes.

Alice Taylor

While Pilgrim Baptist Church is often cited as the birthplace of gospel music because Thomas Dorsey served as its music director, the creative spark propelling gospel to the forefront of black sacred music was actually struck two miles south of Pilgrim at Ebenezer Baptist Church. Ebenezer's leadership in the gospel chorus movement was a silver lining after two tumultuous years of political infighting that culminated in the resignation of its pastor. Out of the melee arose a new leader whose love for the soul-stirring religious songs he had heard in his native Alabama inaugurated a new epoch, not only in black sacred music but ultimately in American popular music.

"Let the Church Roll On"

In 1901, Civil War veteran Rev. John Frances Thomas walked out of Olivet Baptist Church after disagreeing with church leadership over a proposed purchase of property. Thirty members followed him. As the newly formed Ebenezer Baptist Church, Thomas and his followers worshipped at Arlington Hall for a year before purchasing a building at Thirty-Fifth and Dearborn Streets for

$11,500.[1] From humble beginnings, the congregation built Ebenezer into one of the largest black churches in Chicago.

But on August 26, 1920, at the height of Ebenezer's growth, Thomas succumbed to uremia. He died just as the church tendered its first payment to acquire Temple Isaiah, a Jewish synagogue designed by architect Dankmar Adler and located at 4501 South Vincennes Avenue.

Church leaders asked Rev. Charles H. Clark, pastor of the Mount Olive Baptist Church in Nashville, to be guest minister for the inaugural service in the new building after noting with approval how he had presided over Thomas's funeral.[2] By the time Clark preached at Ebenezer's opening service, he was the church's new pastor.[3] On October 30, 1921, with Clark in the pulpit, Ebenezer took possession of the large and austere Temple Isaiah, its home to this day.

For the next ten years, Clark built Ebenezer to more than three thousand members and raised sufficient funds to burn the mortgage three years ahead of schedule.[4] He was touted as a "dynamo" and "one of the greatest preachers and pulpit orators in the country," and further honored when, in 1923, he was named moderator of the General Missionary Baptist State Association. Noted as having an "international reputation" and being "a theologian without a peer," Clark was considered "the right man in the right place."[5] And he was, until 1930.

That was when rumors and hushed comments about the pastor's conduct developed into a political maelstrom. Several factors contributed to the strained relations between the sixty-one-year-old pastor and his flock. One was his marriage to twenty-seven-year-old Irma Mae Ramsey less than a year after his first wife's death. Another was the alleged extravagance of his salary—reportedly one hundred dollars per Sunday as well as the proceeds of a special weekly collection and as much food and clothing as the Pastor's Aid Club could supply.[6] Conspiracy theorists suggested there was a movement afoot within Ebenezer to replace Clark "with a pastor affiliated with the [Rev.] Lacey Kirk Williams [Olivet] faction of the National Baptist Convention, and who [would] consequently line up with Dr. Williams and . . . local Republicans."[7] Other church members felt that Clark had simply abused his pastoral authority because he "thought it was his right to rule the congregation as he saw fit."[8] In the church's Golden Jubilee Anniversary program, one member asserted that Clark was alienated from his flock because of "his dominant attitude, his policies, and his political affiliations."[9]

Tensions ultimately rose to the boiling point after Alford Hill, a member of Ebenezer, submitted an accusatory letter to the church's deacon board. The letter stated that during a June 30, 1930, business meeting, Clark took umbrage at Hill's unwillingness to provide him with a contribution and used "words unbecoming a pastor and a Christian."[10] The *Defender* reported that on Sunday, September 28, Hill was denied communion at Ebenezer because he was "out of harmony with Dr. Clark's program." Toward the end of the service, Clark reportedly announced that "all persons out of harmony with his administration and seeking to oust him were no longer wanted as members." He stated further, "I am here to stay until I die. You can't put me out. You must do as I say if you are to continue as a member of this church. If you don't want to do that, then go home."[11]

The church fell into an awkward silence. Clark's next words could well have echoed off the church walls. "There isn't anything wrong in that, is there?" The congregation answered with a resounding, "Yes! Yes! Yes!" Fearing that the Sunday service would turn ugly, Clark summoned the police, who happened to be stationed outside the church "as if by previous arrangement." The congregation settled down and the police did not need to intervene.[12]

In an interview with the *Defender* subsequent to the September 28 service, Clark denied making the comments attributed to him, stating that he simply pointed to a law that had been in the church's records since its founding, that "all disorderly cases [e.g., Hill's complaint] [were] to be settled by the deacon board and same reported to the church."[13] The Ebenezer case was settled in court, and on October 28, 1930, Clark tendered his resignation, pending payment of back wages and three months' severance.

Unfortunately, Ebenezer's woes did not end with Clark's departure. Rev. T. J. Jackson was prepared to step in as acting pastor, supported by a new slate of officers and deacons, but a restraining order secured by church members prevented the new leadership "from holding meetings or attempting to serve as officers."[14] One of Bronzeville's Old Landmarks was in crisis.

Hoping to find the right captain for the foundering ship, a group of Ebenezer trustees recommended Rev. Dr. James Howard Lorenzo Smith of Tabernacle Baptist Church in Birmingham, Alabama. Some members were not in favor of Smith because they believed the election had not been conducted according to the church bylaws. The *Defender* reported that Smith, still in Birmingham, had been served with a restraining order that forbade him to act as Ebenezer's pastor. This left Jackson in charge until the issue was settled in court.

Notwithstanding, Smith traveled to Chicago. On Sunday, April 12, 1931, his first service at Ebenezer was marred by a misunderstanding that turned violent. According to witnesses, Curly Beattie, a member who had opposed Smith's hire, left his seat during the service to go downstairs. Beattie's quick departure was misconstrued by a pro-Smith member as an act of protest. Fuming with indignation, the member smashed a chair over Beattie's head. Several women in the church piled on Beattie, and the congregation engaged in a "free-for-all scrap" that spilled out onto Vincennes Avenue. This time the police did intervene, while cars and taxis packed with gapers cruised the block to see what the buzz was about.[15]

Although tempers calmed and matters were once again settled in court, Smith decided to avoid the limelight. Instead, he made a series of friendly, informal visits to the church and eventually succeeded in endearing himself "to the members and friends of Ebenezer Baptist Church and to the community as well." Smith's former flock at Tabernacle Baptist contributed their endorsement by penning a proclamation that, among other plaudits, noted, "We congratulate [Ebenezer] upon the very great blessing that is yours in securing the services of this minister."[16] At last, on Sunday, August 9, 1931, "a capacity crowd of over 2,200 persons" greeted Smith with proper pageantry as Ebenezer's new pastor. His formal installation service was held the following October.[17]

The music program Smith inherited at Ebenezer followed the same classically oriented tradition flourishing at the city's other Old Landmarks. Its director, Mabel Sanford Lewis, was a classically trained musician, a pupil of renowned composer and spirituals expert Edward Boatner, and a beloved Chicago public school music teacher. She later produced a radio show, opened a music conservatory, and even performed at the Chicago Theater in a jazz version of Gilbert and Sullivan's *The Mikado*, called *The Mikado in Swing*.[18] Under Lewis's direction, Ebenezer's senior choir performed complex choral works fit for a Sunday afternoon musical, while "congregational singing was limited to familiar old songs."[19] With such a star at the helm of their music program, the congregants of Ebenezer must have been astonished when instead of embracing the church's erudite music programming, Smith declared publicly his preference for the "good old-fashioned songs that were born in the hearts of [their] forefathers down in the southland." Further, he wanted a singing group to lead it. In a suggestion that must have rankled Lewis and the senior choir, Smith wanted his indigenous sacred folk group to sit behind him in the pulpit—the coveted place of honor where the senior choir sat—not banished to the choir loft and out of sight.[20]

In Smith's mind, the natural leader of such a folk ensemble was Theodore Frye, who had already sung before the Ebenezer congregation during Smith's short tenure. Smith told Frye he was not satisfied with the occasional dose of old-fashioned singing. He wanted a permanent ensemble dedicated to singing the songs he remembered. He did not have any preconceived notion of what form the group should take; that was for Frye to decide. Upon accepting Smith's challenge, Frye called on Thomas A. Dorsey for assistance.[21]

The first gospel chorus rehearsal was held at Ebenezer on Sunday, October 11, 1931. Most of the men and women who comprised the one-hundred-voice chorus were recent migrants.[22] They were not required to audition or read music. They were expected to be loyal to the choir, attend church, and come to rehearsals regularly and on time. Most importantly, they were expected to live the life they sang about. By December 6, the group had rehearsed sufficiently for chorus advisor Deacon Samuel L. Reed to formally commission the chorus. "After giving us our commission," the Ebenezer history recounted, "[Reed] lifted his eyes toward Heaven, asking God's blessings upon us, and left the room."[23]

The primary appeal of the new chorus was its sound, but its appearance also resonated. Alice Taylor, an early member of the Ebenezer Gospel Chorus, recalled to Bernice Johnson Reagon: "The first Sunday that I came to Ebenezer, I joined Ebenezer. That beautiful gospel singing and those blue robes, I just went wild over those blue robes, they were homemade robes at that time, with big white collars, and I just fell in love with that singing."[24] Taylor also recalled, "If you was a gospel singer [at Ebenezer], no earrings, no paint on your cheeks, no lipstick on your lips. If you was a gospel singer you had to march down that aisle as a gospel singer, and I guess that meant you was closer to God, or you should have been."[25]

The songs that Dorsey and Frye taught the choir to sing were most likely a mixture of Dorsey's handful of sacred compositions, spirituals, and nineteenth- and early twentieth-century evangelistic songs published in *Gospel Pearls*. Dorsey and Frye even had to teach the members how to march.[26]

The Ebenezer Gospel Chorus debuted at the 11:00 a.m. worship service at Ebenezer on Sunday, January 10, 1932.[27] The skies were cloudy, the weather a frigid twenty-two degrees, but the church was filled to capacity. Nobody—not even Smith himself—knew what to expect, but the chorus did not disappoint. Along with their performance of sacred songs of the Southland, the group demonstrated a measured amount of theatricality, à la Dorsey and Frye. In his customary manner, Frye sang while walking up and down the aisles, rendering verses in his high baritone voice while the choir responded enthusiastically and antiphonally on the chorus. They sang in unison with rehearsed vocal scooping, hand clapping during verses to give the song momentum, and interjections of "Hallelujah" or "Amen" by individual members as the spirit moved them. After the second line of the chorus, accompanist Dorsey bolted upright from his piano bench and played standing up. It was rehearsed spontaneity, and while tame compared to the musical gymnastics that gospel choirs adopted later, the congregation at Ebenezer loved every second of it, even if some members of the senior choir were not entirely genuine in their platitudes.[28]

Smith got more than he asked for. While the singing of the Ebenezer Gospel Chorus came straight from the brush arbor and southern rural folk tradition, satisfying Smith's desire for southern-style church singing, the performance itself had an urban vibe, courtesy of Dorsey's club and vaudeville house experience. To ensure that the performance moved the congregation at Ebenezer, just as Ma Rainey moved the patrons at the Grand Theater, Dorsey and Frye infused indigenous religious singing with the urban sound of jazz and blues. Whereas the trained choirs emphasized the quality of the singing over the performance, the Dorsey-Frye gospel chorus made certain that the visual content was as important as the music and the message. The result was a captivating, rhythmic, emotionally charged, and eminently familiar religious experience. It was a sacred show for the eyes and ears.

Smith was delighted. He had something no other Baptist pastor in the city could claim, and he could not wait to show it off. He took the very first opportunity to do so—the following Sunday in another of black Chicago's Old Landmarks, and during nothing less than the pastor's anniversary, one of the church's most important annual events. If his gospel chorus could pass muster with the congregation of Pilgrim Baptist Church during the sixth anniversary of Rev. Junius Austin, it could make it just about anywhere in Bronzeville.

Pilgrim Baptist Church was founded on January 6, 1916, by Deacon John A. Finnie of Cincinnati and his wife, Juanita. The initial prayer group consisted of Mrs. Georgia Hansberry, Rev. S. S. Harkness, and a Mr. Bell. A total of five members met in the Finnie's home, but when the congregation grew beyond the confines of the living room, the members rented space at 4910 South Wentworth. The prayer group formally organized as Pilgrim Baptist Church on September 26, 1916, with Harkness as pastor. For the next few years, the church witnessed an array of temporary locations and a revolving door of pastors, including S. E. J. Watson. In 1922, Watson and the seven-hundred-member church purchased the Kehilath Anshe Ma'ariv synagogue at 3300 South Indiana Avenue for $125,000.[29] The synagogue was designed and built in 1890–91 by Chicago architect Louis H. Sullivan, with assistance from Dankmar Adler, who built Ebenezer's new quarters, Temple Isaiah.[30] When Watson died in 1926, Pilgrim selected as its new minister Rev. Junius C. Austin, the young man from Pittsburgh who had wowed the 1921 National Baptist Convention.

Reverend Austin was born in Buckingham County, Virginia, and educated in Lynchburg, Virginia. He graduated from Temple University and held pastorates in Virginia at Clifton Forge and Staunton before being selected, at age twenty-five, to head Ebenezer Baptist Church in Pittsburgh. Ebenezer was Pittsburgh's largest Baptist congregation, and Austin served eleven years as its pastor.[31] Pilgrim hired Austin away from Ebenezer in 1926, and one of the new pastor's first responsibilities was to deliver the eulogy at the funeral of Bessie Coleman, the first black female aviator.[32] His second was to erase Pilgrim's $100,000 of indebtedness, a task he accomplished with such acumen that other Chicago ministers attempted to replicate his financial strategy at their own churches.[33] Like Dorsey and Frye, Austin also had swagger. "He was an actor," historian Timuel Black told the *Chicago Tribune*. "He would strut up and down the pulpit and kind of talk about how well he was dressed, and he was. And how good looking he was, and he was. And people would be glad to go watch Rev. Austin, to hear his sermon, but also to watch him in action."[34]

Unlike Smith, Austin did not come to Chicago with a penchant for old-fashioned singing. He preferred the refined western European–influenced music prevalent in mainline Protestant churches, so much so that he recruited Edward Boatner away from Olivet to be Pilgrim's music director.[35] Boatner, an accomplished classical musician and scholar and arranger of spirituals, was also one of the city's finest baritone singers. Black musical society sought him as much as it did James Mundy and J. Wesley Jones. As director of the National Baptist Convention Chorus, Boatner had significant influence and a stellar reputation.

Pilgrim planned to celebrate Austin's sixth anniversary as pastor on Sunday, January 17, 1932. When the planning committee asked Smith to be the guest preacher for the occasion, it is unlikely it knew much, if anything, about Dorsey and Frye's gospel chorus. At the time, Smith himself was unaware how well the experiment would turn out, and since it was common for a pastor to bring his choir with him when visiting a church, he would likely have brought his senior choir. Thus Smith's selection of the gospel chorus instead undoubtedly did not sit well with senior choir members eager to participate in the anniversary celebration.

Nevertheless, Ebenezer's latest singing sensations accompanied their pastor to Pilgrim and performed rousing selections such as "I'm on the Battlefield for My Lord." Dorsey, Frye, and the chorus sang much as they had the previous week. Frye walked the aisles, and Dorsey accompanied the choir with his stride piano style, even though they risked facing a congregation that could have snickered or sat in silent embarrassment.[36] Instead, the Pilgrim congregation was appreciative and applauded the new group.

Austin, too, enjoyed the performance. In addition to acknowledging and commending the group's work before his congregation, the pastor joked, "Tell me this: What I want to know is where did you get that little black man [pointing to Dorsey] from?"[37] Whether Austin was joking or did not recognize one of his church members is unknown. But just as Rev. C. C. Harper invited Mahalia Jackson to join the Greater Salem Baptist Church choir, Austin was about to make a similarly significant offer.

Having won over the congregations of two of Chicago's most prominent main-line Protestant churches in as many weeks, the Ebenezer Baptist Church Gospel Chorus began to develop a word-of-mouth reputation throughout Bronzeville. Later that month, the "Radio Shepherd" Rev. Sethard P. Dunn, pastor of the Church of God at 4400 St. Lawrence Avenue, invited Smith's "gospel choir of 60 voices" to minister at his service.[38]

In March 1932, Austin sought out that "little black man" from his anniversary service and asked him to organize a gospel chorus at Pilgrim. As Dorsey remembered, "[Austin] sat onto the side of his desk and says, 'Brother Dorsey, I want you to do this for me.' I said, 'What is it?' 'I want you to get me together one of those things like Smith had down here.' He didn't say 'chorus.' He said, 'one of them things' that we had down here. I said, 'That was the Gospel Chorus.' 'All right, well and good. I want you to bring your gospel chorus.'"[39]

Austin's son, Rev. Junius C. Austin Jr., explained to Dorsey biographer Michael Harris why he believed his father wanted a gospel chorus at Pilgrim. "My dad could see times changing and people desiring another type of music. He tried [gospel music] in his church and, because of his preaching *and* the music, folk crowded out that church."[40] The fact that the accompanist was a member of Pilgrim may have given Austin sufficient confirmation that the decision was touched by God's providential hand.

The Pilgrim board of deacons consented to the addition of a gospel chorus and Dorsey as director as long as he was not compensated. They were already paying a handsome salary to Boatner, who was less than enthusiastic about this new addition. In fact, Boatner considered the gospel chorus's singing to be "degrading" and a "desecration." He resented Austin's suggestion that this chorus of "people who [hadn't] had any [musical] training" sit behind the pastor, as the group did at Ebenezer. Boatner intimated that he would resign his post if such a thing happened at Pilgrim. Thus, faced with the prospect of losing his star musician, Austin compromised, remanding the gospel chorus to the back of the church, where they stayed until Boatner left Pilgrim the following year.[41]

Boatner's expression of indignation was not surprising, given his musical upbringing and personal taste, but his reaction was ironic, maybe even slightly hypocritical. A similar salvo had been fired at him in 1928, when he was hired by Olivet Baptist Church to replace Alphonso W. Johnson, a well-known blind musician, as choirmaster. Johnson, director and organist at Olivet for twenty-two years, felt that he was being replaced by Boatner because the pastor, Rev. Lacey Kirk Williams, wanted to incorporate spirituals into the service, music Johnson steadfastly opposed and in which Boatner was an acknowledged expert. "I don't favor those slavery time songs because they are senseless and ridiculous," Johnson declared. "There is nothing in them but emotional sentiment." Johnson preferred anthems, but Williams felt anthems represented "white people's music."[42]

Despite Boatner's disdain, the choir's relegation to the back of the church, and the lack of financial compensation, Dorsey spent part of early 1932 organizing Pilgrim's first gospel chorus. Although his leadership of Ma Rainey's Wildcat Band and membership in the Whispering Syncopators had taught him to manage an ensemble of musicians, organizing a gospel chorus was new territory. After all, Frye directed the Ebenezer group; Dorsey was the accompanist and arranger. Plus, Dorsey did not initially envision his gospel songs for choruses but rather for soloists, such as Mahalia Jackson or Reverend Hall. Nevertheless, Dorsey borrowed Frye's techniques and applied them at Pilgrim. In the process, he established many rehearsal and performance techniques that remain staples of gospel choir protocol.

For example, if the chorus used sheet music at all, it was only for learning songs during rehearsal. Dorsey required his singers to memorize the music and lyrics. Not only did it look better to perform without sheet music, but memorization gave singers the freedom to clap and move in the spirit. It made the choir feel more relaxed and extemporaneous in its performance, not locked into a presentation of notated music that most members were unable to read anyway. Likewise, Dorsey directed the choir without referencing sheet music.

Just like the senior choir, the gospel chorus also learned to march ceremoniously from the back of the church to the front at the beginning of the Sunday service. Their footwork was in unison: in time to the music's 4/4 beat, members first stepped to the right and then brought their feet together, then stepped to the left and brought their feet together. They repeated this stepping until they entered the choir seats behind the pulpit.[43]

Perhaps the most significant decision that Dorsey made in organizing the Pilgrim gospel chorus was to emulate the Ebenezer formula by offering membership to anybody who wanted to be part of the new group. Choir members did not have to possess any special musical talent to join, nor did they have to audition. They were welcome as long as they were members of Pilgrim and abided by the tenets of Christianity. Dorsey handled the choir's musical training personally and taught supplemental courses on reading music.[44] In many respects, Dorsey's choir rehearsals were lessons in vocal training. Lena Johnson McLin, Dorsey's niece, recalled that he insisted members of the chorus clearly articulate each word in a song so that the listener could understand the message.[45] Chicago educator Juanita Tucker, who played organ and piano for Pilgrim services during the 1940s, remembered Dorsey fondly: "[Gospel music] had a beat, and, of course, there were some that resisted that beat, but

[Dorsey] did it with such style and such verve. . . . You know he had a habit of pointing his finger in a particular way when he was directing? Well, we all used to mimic him and that finger!"[46]

Making choir membership egalitarian had a sociological impact. It ensured that the gospel chorus was, like its music, for the masses. It was a club that members, especially new southern migrants, could call their own. As such, the gospel chorus served much the same purpose as the new storefront churches lining Bronzeville's main avenues. Both offered familiarity, commonality, and comfort to newcomers. Both were oases of belonging in a city where southern migrants were needed but not necessarily wanted. Thus, if Jones's Metropolitan Community Choir, with its classical repertory, was the pride of black middle-class society in Chicago, the gospel choruses, with their exuberant singing, were the pride of the new settlers. The gospel choruses also offered the migrants leadership opportunities by emulating the established church choir practice of forming a governing body.

During an interview by Bernice Johnson Reagon for her twenty-six-part radio series, *Wade in the Water*, Detroit gospel artist Donald Vails eloquently expressed how important gospel chorus membership was to the new migrants:

> I think about all these blue-collar people who had to deal with Jim Crow, meager salaries, and yet the maid who cleaned up somebody else's house all week long, the porter, the chauffeur, the gardener, the cook, were nobody. They had to sit in the back of the bus, they were denied their rights, but when they walked into their church on Sunday morning and put on a robe and went down that aisle and stood on that choir stand, the maid became a coloratura, and when she stood before her church of five hundred to a thousand, two thousand people, she knew she was somebody. And I think the choir meant so much to those people because for a few hours on Sunday, they were royalty.[47]

Royalty notwithstanding, in the early days, gospel choristers endured derision from some church folk, especially members of the senior choirs. June Levell, a member of the Ebenezer Gospel Chorus, said, "Sometimes you could hear [senior choir members] whispering, you know; they would grin at us, 'Oh, y'all just sing, y'all sure do.' But then we would hear what they was saying, you know: 'Old ignorant folks, wasn't singing nothing.' But whether they wanted it or not . . . the Senior Choir was in the balcony and the Gospel Chorus sits behind the Pastor."[48]

The gospel chorus celebrated, rather than disparaged, the migrants' southern roots. It offered newcomers an outlet for their frustrations, worries, and cares.[49] The chorus also gave members a vehicle for expressing their joy and happiness. The gospel chorus was *theirs*, and Bronzeville's Old Landmarks were taking notice.

Following its initial success, the Ebenezer Gospel Chorus continued its rise to prominence. It rehearsed every Monday evening at 7:30 p.m., except for Monday evening, February 8, 1932, when it hosted its first music festival at the church.[50] In a turnabout, the gospel chorus invited the senior choirs from Olivet and West Point, as well as its own senior choir, under the direction of J. T. Brock. An announcement in the *Defender* featured a prominent photograph of the Ebenezer Gospel Chorus with the caption "Ebenezer Boasts Largest Gospel Chorus."[51]

The Ebenezer and Pilgrim ensembles were turning heads, but they were by no means the first groups in the city to be called gospel choruses. Dorsey biographer Michael Harris notes that gospel choruses were in existence as early as the first part of the 1920s. Historians Lynn Abbott and Doug Seroff found even earlier references to gospel choirs in Chicago. For example, Walters AME Zion had a gospel choir in 1910, and a multi-church group called the Englewood Union Gospel Choir was also active in the same decade.[52] As early as 1913, Quinn Chapel, Chicago's first African American church, had a gospel choir that sang for a local revival.[53] In August 1927, St. Mark Methodist Episcopal advertised the first regular social meeting of its gospel chorus. Although traveling groups such as the Wise Singers of Philadelphia rendered evangelistic music for revivals, ministers understandably wanted their own singers and musicians to lead old-fashioned congregational hymn singing for funerals and revivals. Senior choirs lacked the size or repertory to accommodate such events. On the other hand, gospel choruses, made up of less-skilled singers, were ideally suited to perform simple, familiar gospel hymns and camp-meeting songs, though they did not employ the Dorsey-Frye techniques of hand clapping, spontaneous exhortations, jazz-influenced rhythms, and theatrical performance.

Although the gospel chorus movement began prior to April 1, 1932, according to a 1933 *Defender* article, Dorsey, Frye, and Magnolia Lewis Butts "launched a drive advocating a renaissance of gospel singing in the churches of Chicago" on this date.[54] April certainly witnessed a flurry of gospel chorus activity, starting with Morning Star Baptist Church, the church home of Mississippi migrants Lonnie and Susie Barrett and their ten children, one of whom, Delores, sang her first solo, "Jesus Love Bubbles Over in My Heart," for the congregation.[55] The church solicited Dorsey's services as gospel chorus organizer, "to help the regular choir in its work." The church reported that it "expected [the gospel chorus] to become one of the most popular organizations of the church."[56]

Because he was juggling responsibilities as director of the Pilgrim Gospel Chorus and accompanist of Ebenezer's Gospel Chorus, and also traveling to New York to record blues and hokum with Tampa Red, Kansas Joe McCoy, and Memphis Minnie, Dorsey could not give his undivided attention to the Morning

Star ensemble. He appointed Robert C. Cherry, a pianist and student at Wendell Phillips High School, to direct the choir in his absence. Under Cherry's direction and Dorsey's consultancy, Morning Star's Welcome Gospel Chorus grew to fifty voices and sang for both the 11:00 a.m. and the 7:30 p.m. services each Sunday.[57] Julia Mae Kennedy of First Church of Deliverance eventually succeeded Cherry, and Wiley C. Jackson replaced Kennedy at Morning Star when she returned to First Church, where she stayed for the remainder of her career.

Pianist and choir director Charles Clency recalled, "[Jackson] was of the likes of Julia Mae Kennedy, that old school, rich tradition, degreed or not degreed, still the same competency and stickler for quality, as were many of those guys during that time. All of them were highly competent."[58]

In 1932, Butts invited Dorsey to listen to her W. D. Cook Gospel Singers, which sang twice monthly at Metropolitan Community Church. Dorsey attended out of respect and curiosity, and perhaps also to generate sheet music sales. He discovered that the group had "a large crowd each time they sang."[59] Dorsey helped Butts's group inject more authenticity and showmanship into its performance style. But what the W. D. Cook Gospel Singers may have lacked in showmanship, they made up for in political clout. Having a local musical celebrity of Butts's stature as director and Metropolitan as sponsor, the Cook group sent a subtle but undeniable message to recalcitrant old-line ministers that gospel music merited more than a patronizing pat on the head. In fact, Butts's influence and reputation in the black community helped the Protestant church elite accept the new gospel chorus movement.

Recognizing that gospel music had the potential to attract new members and more revenue, African American churches of all sizes and denominations in the city organized gospel choruses and invited gospel choruses from other churches to sing for special worship services and musicals. The potential that gospel choruses held was especially vital for congregations that had purchased large churches at inflated sums. They were staggering under the weight of mortgages, and if indigenous folk music could help increase membership and tithing, it could not be ignored. Moreover, pastors preferred hosting musical programs in the church rather than losing members to tempting secular entertainments available throughout the South and West Sides.

Revivals also prompted deliberative Protestant church pastors to add permanent indigenous religious folk music groups to their music ministries. Revivals were held intermittently and over a period of several days, often in a tent, to simulate the nineteenth-century gospel camp-meeting experience with the objective of bringing souls to Christ. Not surprisingly, groups that sang in the rural southern tradition were in demand, because the success or failure of a revival depended on the power of the preacher's message and the soul-stirring music. Prince Johnson and the Johnson Gospel Singers, featuring Louise Lemon and Mahalia Jackson, was an especially popular quartet at Chicago revivals.

By May 1932, as many as twenty Chicago churches of various denominations had gospel choruses. In addition to Ebenezer, Pilgrim, Metropolitan, Monumental, and Morning Star Baptist Churches, traditionally more deliberative churches, such as Blackwell Memorial, St. Paul CME (Colored Methodist Episcopal, later changed to Christian Methodist Episcopal), and South Park ME (Methodist Episcopal), now also had indigenous singing groups in place.[60] Groups that sang old-fashioned songs in a vernacular style were even welcome in some of the city's African Methodist Episcopal (AME) churches, although their gospel choruses sang without the theatrical flair and emotionality of Dorsey-Frye ensembles.[61]

Additional signs that mainline Protestant churches were warming to the gospel chorus movement appeared in July 1932. The first was Dorsey's participation in the sixteenth annual session of the Baptist Young People's Union and the Sunday School Conventions of the Bethlehem District Association. Not only did Dorsey lead a song service during the conclave, which took place at Monumental Baptist Church, but he and Luschaa Allen were named music codirectors for the coming year. And on Sunday, July 31, Frye and the Ebenezer Gospel Chorus joined the stately senior choirs of Pilgrim, Metropolitan, and South Park ME in an afternoon "choir songfest" held at Metropolitan. Despite Pilgrim, Metropolitan, and South Park all having gospel choruses by this time, Ebenezer was the only gospel chorus invited to sing at the July 31 songfest.[62] The Ebenezer Gospel Chorus also held its own musicale that month. This time the wiry Dorsey was not at the piano. At the keyboard was an attractive young woman named Roberta Martin with charm school comportment, short-cropped hair, and a bright smile. She had just been hired to accompany Frye's Ebenezer Junior Chorus.

Roberta Evelyn Martin (née Winston) was born on February 14, 1907, in St. Francis, Arkansas, one of six children of William and Anna Eliza Clopton Winston.[63] Martin's father was a farmer and ran a grocery store. Anna stayed home to raise Roberta and her older brothers, William and James Hamilton (Anna's sons from a previous marriage), older sisters Legessa (nicknamed Jessie) and Beatrice, and younger brother Fontaine.[64]

Fontaine remembered Roberta as "kind of a tomboy." If Roberta was not doing schoolwork, helping in her father's store, or doing chores around the farm, she and Fontaine would ride horses "for half a day. She'd never get tired until I'd do something foolish. Then she'd want to go home."[65] At age six, Roberta, who had a keen ear, began taking piano lessons from a sister-in-law who taught music in the area, and she endeavored to learn standard western European classical repertory. Fontaine told doctoral student Irene V. Jackson that his sister's "biggest trouble during her childhood was getting away from the ear music and reading notes."[66] This trouble would later become a distinct advantage.

The Winston Family sent Roberta to Inter-State Academy, a private school near Helena. Around 1917, Anna took Roberta and Fontaine and moved north to Cairo, Illinois, to join one of the Winston daughters and her husband. Sometime around 1919 or 1920, Anna and the children moved again, this time to Chicago. William joined his family in Chicago about five or six years later. An experienced shopkeeper, he had little difficulty opening a neighborhood grocery store at Fifty-Seventh and Lafayette. Fontaine recalled that the family always had a baby grand piano in their home, suggesting the Winston family was better off financially than most migrants.[67] Heilbut noted that Martin was indeed living quite well, in terms of education and financial stability, when measured by the standards of a Mahalia Jackson, Rosetta Tharpe, or Marion Williams.[68]

While attending Chicago's Wendell Phillips High School, Roberta came under the tutelage of the school's choir director, Mildred Bryant Jones. Jones served as Roberta's piano teacher and taught her the rudiments of choral conducting. Martin's most intense period of musical study came at the age of fifteen, when she became seriously ill and was hospitalized several times. While recuperating, Martin turned to music to channel her energies and provide solace from her illness.

After graduating from high school, Martin set out to become a concert pianist. She attended Northwestern University to study music and completed two years but never earned her degree.[69] "The reason she said she didn't graduate," recalled Martin's adopted son, Leonard "Sonny" Austin, "was because she was too busy singing and performing."[70] Sometime during the late 1920s, Roberta married William "Bill" Martin. The couple lived in Morgan Park and stayed together for less than a year, but because Roberta was troubled by the notion of divorce, the two did not officially divorce until 1940 or 1941. She also retained her married surname for the rest of her life. By 1932, Roberta was the musician for Pilgrim Baptist Church's Sunday school as well as for Arnett Chapel AME in Morgan Park.[71]

In 1932, Roberta met Dorsey and Frye for the first time when she auditioned for the position of accompanist for Ebenezer's new junior chorus. They asked her to play a gospel song. Years later, she told historian Horace Clarence Boyer that she knew how to play only one gospel song at that time. Martin's one gospel song was sufficient to demonstrate her talent, and she got the job at Ebenezer, which paid five dollars a week.[72] Soon, Martin was assisting Frye in teaching four-part harmony to both the gospel and the junior choruses.[73]

An early recruit to the new junior chorus was a twelve-year-old boy from Salem Baptist Church named Eugene Smith. Smith was born in Chicago on April 22, 1921, the third of six children, to Eugenia and Scott Smith. In 1919 the family had moved from Mobile to Chicago, where they settled in Bronzeville and joined Salem. By age twelve, Smith, a gifted singer, was becoming a veteran of the church music circuit.[74] Salem's pastor, Rev. B. L. Rose, took Smith with him when he was asked to preach at the 1930 National Baptist Convention, the same Golden Anniversary convocation at which the organization's music department first demonstrated an interest in Dorsey's new gospel songs. Smith's performance so impressed attendees that he earned the nickname "Little Boy Wonder."

After his auspicious debut at the convention, Smith received invitations to sing at churches throughout the city, including one from Ebenezer's Rev. J. H. L. Smith (no relation). Eugene recalled the morning in 1933 when Anna Bryant took him to sing at Ebenezer, and he met Roberta Martin for the first time:

> I sang one Sunday morning at the Ebenezer Baptist Church. They gave me a seat down front. And I asked them, "Who's going to play [for me]?" There was a piano there, and there were three seats right there at the piano. Someone said, "That lady over there, that's Roberta Martin. She will accompany you." I went [over to her] and said, "I'm supposed to sing. Are you going to play for me?" She said, "Well, I can, yes. What are you going to sing?" "I Claim Jesus First and That's Enough for Me."[75] I said [to Miss Martin], "Do you know it?" She said, "No, but what key do you sing it in?" "I don't know what key!" She said, "I'll tell you what you do. Start it, and I'll get it."
>
> It was a good ten or fifteen minutes before they could get any kind of silence in that church. [Miss Martin] was so amazed she didn't know what to think. She said, "Little boy, where do you live?" I told her 3842 Langley. "Who do you live with, your parents?" I said, "Yeah." Do you know that before I could get home, because see I'm walking, and she's in the car, Roberta had been to my house to meet with my mother and father to ask them if I could join the Junior Chorus at Ebenezer that had just been organized. Well, my mother just thought it was wonderful, you know. I lived at Thirty-Eighth and Langley, and Ebenezer was at Forty-Fifth and Vincennes. I could walk! And that's where it started.[76]

The Ebenezer Junior Chorus sang a variety of songs, including Dorsey songs, as well as anthems, hymns, and revival songs. Martin recruited Johnnie E. Rogers Jr., a singer and colleague from Arnett Chapel, to help her arrange popular gospel hymns and spirituals, such as "Jesus' Love Bubbles Over," for the group. Eugene Smith said the junior chorus sang "whatever Roberta wrote or Mr. Dorsey wrote. She had her own arrangements on everything. She even took some of the old traditional hymns and made outstanding gospel music out of the hymns. 'What a Friend We Have in Jesus,' and oh, just many more."[77] Martin even introduced the youngsters—a photo of the three-hundred-voice Ebenezer Junior Chorus depicts members ranging from teenagers to toddlers— to a variety of classical choral literature. It was not unusual for early gospel choirs to perform classical pieces. For example, as director of the gospel chorus of Chicago's Greater Mount Olive Baptist Church in the mid-1930s, songwriter Eddie Clifford Davis taught his group to sing gospel songs, spirituals, as well as pieces by nineteenth-century French classical writer Charles Gounod.[78]

Although Dorsey and Frye hired Roberta Martin principally as an accompanist for the Ebenezer Junior Chorus, they also needed her as a substitute accompanist for the gospel chorus. Mable Sanford Lewis and Alice White had been assisting Frye as best they could, but they had their own responsibilities,[79] and it did not appear that Dorsey would be able to continue with Ebenezer. In addition to his duties at Pilgrim and Morning Star, he was receiving more invitations to participate in religious music events throughout the city.

Meanwhile, the number of churches adding gospel choruses continued unabated, even if the groups sang only one Sunday a month. Witnessing the activity, Butts suggested to Dorsey and Frye that Ebenezer, Pilgrim, and the W. D. Cook Gospel Singers combine to present a gospel musical.

The musical was held in August at Monumental Baptist Church. It was a bold move to use Monumental, as it was one of the most prestigious venues for highbrow Sunday musicals, but Butts had the political clout and Monumental had the space. The success of the first all-gospel chorus musicale prompted Butts to suggest an even bolder step: the formation of a bona fide gospel choral union.

A musicians' guild or union was not a novel concept. J. Wesley Jones had organized the city's Progressive Choral Club. Similarly, Alabama migrant Norman "Old Man" McQueen formed the Chicago Progressive Quartet Association. But Dorsey was skeptical about starting a union of gospel choruses and did not relish the amount of work it would require. He was already busy, and now his wife, Nettie, was expecting their first child. Dorsey told Butts that he did not consider the movement ready for such a step but agreed to try it.

On August 17, 1932, Dorsey, Butts, and Frye organized the Gospel Choral Union of Chicago with Dorsey as president—to his chagrin, initially, although he would remain its president for many years.[80] Butts served as secretary, and Henry J. Carruthers, organizer of St. Paul CME's gospel chorus, was chairman.

Carruthers hosted the debut performance of the Gospel Choral Union of Chicago at St. Paul CME, 4644 South Dearborn, on Monday, August 29. However well received the musical may have been, the performance was overshadowed by Dorsey's absence. A few days earlier, tragedy struck the Dorsey household, one that forever altered his music career and provided the inspiration for one of the most beloved gospel songs of all time.

As August drew to a close and Nettie Dorsey was about to give birth, Dorsey was invited to visit St. Louis, where Augustus A. Evans was successfully organizing gospel choruses and selling Dorsey sheet music. Despite the imminence of her delivery, Nettie encouraged her husband to make the trip, telling him she would have a "present" for him when he returned. Although he felt an inexplicable uneasiness, Dorsey set out for St. Louis by automobile to witness Evans's handiwork firsthand. Eddie Clifford Davis was his traveling companion.[81]

The two did not get far before Dorsey realized that he had left his briefcase full of music at home. They turned around and drove thirty miles back to Bronzeville. While retrieving his briefcase, Dorsey looked in on Nettie, who was asleep.[82] After Dorsey returned to the car, Davis told him he had forgotten about a previous engagement and couldn't break it. He would have to remain in Chicago, so Dorsey made the drive through the cornfields of Illinois to St. Louis alone.

On August 24, while in St. Louis for the gospel program, Dorsey mailed a postcard to Nettie, noting, "[I'm] having a pretty good time and success. I'll be home about the last of the week. Take care of yourself. Bee [sic] sweet. Ted."[83] He received a telegram back two days later with the news that Nettie's childbirth was not going well. He called home to see how things were proceeding and spoke to his uncle Joshua, who had the regrettable task of informing him that Nettie had died during childbirth that day. Upon hearing the news, Evans canceled the rest of the St. Louis concerts and drove Dorsey home to 448 East Fortieth Street. When he returned, Dorsey "just fell out of the car," entered his home, and fainted.[84]

Emotionally drained by the shock of his wife's death, Dorsey "struggled through the night," and upon waking, received more bad news from Joshua: Thomas Jr., though he had seemed healthy when Dorsey arrived, had not survived the night.[85] He was pronounced dead on Saturday, August 27.

The final rites for Nettie and Thomas Jr. were held at Pilgrim on Tuesday, August 30, with music rendered by the Chicago gospel chorus of three hundred voices, directed by Laconia Cornelius DeYamper. The three-hundred-voice choir most probably consisted of gospel choral union members, although representatives from other churches may have participated also. Regardless, the Dorsey funeral was likely the first church service to feature music by a gospel mass chorus.[86]

Dorsey's remembrance of the funeral service had a poetic poignancy: "I entered the Pilgrim Baptist Church and looked down that long aisle which led to the altar where my wife and baby lay in the same casket. I started the walk in the procession and the aisle grew longer and longer before me. My legs got weak, my knees would not work right, my eyes became blind with a flood of tears. There Nettie lay, cold, unmoving, unspeaking."[87]

After the funeral, Dorsey fell into deep despair. The following Saturday, September 3, Frye endeavored to pull Dorsey from his despondency by taking him out for the evening. They went to the Chicago branch of Poro College, a beauty school at 4415 South Parkway founded by Mrs. A. M. Malone, not far from Dorsey's home. More than a school, Poro served as a community and conference center for Bronzeville. Dorsey recalled it had a "beautiful and comfortable music room, well equipped, and a good piano."[88]

Not surprisingly, Dorsey found his way to the piano and fondled its keys, wandering to and eventually exploring the melody of "Must Jesus Bear the Cross Alone," a seventeenth-century hymn by Thomas Shepherd. The hymn declares that everyone has a cross to bear, a thought that could well have been in Dorsey's mind during this dark time.[89] But in addition to providing brief respite, the song inspired a new musical motif. Dorsey recalled:

> I called Mr. Frye. I said, "Come on, Frye! Listen to this. Come over here to this piano! I got this tune and I'm trying to put words with it." I played [it] for [Frye]. "What'd you think about it?"
>
> "It's all right, sounds good."
>
> I went over it again. He said, "No, man, no. Call him 'precious Lord'. Don't call him 'blessed Lord'; call him 'precious Lord'."
>
> "Why, why? He *is* a blessing."
>
> "Call him 'precious Lord'."
>
> And that thing like something hit me and went all over me, see. I said, "That does sound better! That's it!"[90]

Dorsey took his half-written composition home and completed the song that was destined to become his magnum opus:

Precious Lord, take my hand / Lead me on, let me stand,

I am tired, I am weak, I am worn;

Thru the storm, thru the night / Lead me on to the light,

Take my hand, precious Lord, lead me home.

Dorsey and Frye introduced "Take My Hand, Precious Lord" at Ebenezer on a Sunday that September. The response from the Ebenezer congregation was instantaneous, overwhelming, and to Dorsey confusing, given the extremely personal nature of the lyrics. "The folk went wild. They went wild," he recalled. "They broke up the church. Folk were shouting everywhere. I don't know what they were shouting for. I was the one who should be shouting . . . or sorry."[91]

In retrospect, the introduction of "Take My Hand, Precious Lord" at Ebenezer Baptist Church by Dorsey and Frye that Sunday in September 1932, and the congregation's reaction, was an even bigger highlight in the history of Dorsey's gospel songwriting than the events of the 1930 National Baptist Convention. Certainly, the gradual acceptance of gospel choruses by Chicago's most prominent Protestant churches provided the imprimatur that religious folk music needed to gain wider acceptance in the black community. But "Precious Lord" demonstrated that Dorsey's new sacred music could rouse deeply hidden emotions, or in the composer's own words, "prick the heart," without having to be played in double time. Gospel music could be just as effective, if not more so, as a slow, passionately sung ballad.

"Precious Lord" expressed a wellspring of emotion. It contained a more personal message than the songwriter's earlier, more didactic gospel songs. "If You See My Savior" did not have the same cathartic impact because Dorsey, as the song's narrator, was not immediately affected. In fact, Dorsey considered his neighbor, whose bedside he visited, an intermediary between him and the Lord. "Precious Lord," on the other hand, communicated a deep personal sadness, one that could be understood universally. Thus, when members of the Ebenezer congregation shouted, they did so out of empathy for Dorsey's loss but also out of their own deeply felt—and perhaps deeply hidden—feelings of loss, solitude, separation, indignation, poverty, and illness. After all, the migrants had their own wellspring of sadness. They were strangers in a strange land, having come up from the poverty-ridden, discriminatory, and dangerous South to a city that was as complicated and complex as the society they had left. They were recruited to fill jobs that had been abandoned, then reclaimed, by eastern Europeans who had fought in World War I. And then the Great Depression hit, making matters worse. Instead of finding a land of milk and honey, they were in a land of bread lines and unemployment. "Precious Lord" enabled migrants to grieve, to bare their souls through the communal catharsis of shared sadness. The haunting sound of "Precious Lord" that Ebenezer Baptist Church experienced that September Sunday altered the trajectory of Dorsey's career and African American religious folk music. Gospel music had its first major hit.

Dorsey's new song swept Bronzeville, crossed denominational boundaries, and found eager listeners in churches from Baptist to AME. It also moved across state lines. Songwriter and publisher Emma L. Jackson of Shreveport, Louisiana was credited with introducing the song to the National Baptist Convention.[92] On February 16, 1937, the Heavenly Gospel Singers made the first recording of "Precious Lord" for Victor's Bluebird subsidiary. The quartet used high and lonesome a cappella harmonies supported by steady vocal percussion, and at the conclusion, the lead vocalist launched into a mournful cry.[93] Heilbut notes that three months later, Elder Charles Beck, a COGIC singer, crooned a version for Decca like a big-band singer.[94]

Dorsey's struggle with his wife and son's death did not stop with music composition. In September, he asked the coroner to perform an autopsy on Nettie and brought medical malpractice charges against Illinois Research Clinic. Although the resolution of Dorsey's charges are unknown, the clinic told the *Defender* it would no longer accept "race patients."[95]

Shortly afterward, Dorsey's sister Bernice and her husband, Rev. Dr. Benjamin J. Johnson, allowed their four-year-old daughter Lena to move from Atlanta to Chicago to live with her uncle Thomas. Lena Johnson McLin said, "I didn't *move*! I was a little girl: I was *sent*! [Dorsey] told my mother that he couldn't find it to spend another year out of town, because he lost his son, he buried his son and the mother, and that was very rough for him. He wanted a child around him." McLin remembered her uncle as "soft-spoken, not loud at all, and very well dressed. He reminded me of my father: he always had a shirt and a tie and a suit, and he was always elegant, very mannerly, very nice. And he would sit at the piano and play something and say, 'that's good stuff!'"[96]

McLin heard her uncle's gospel chorus every Sunday morning at the 11:00 a.m. worship service at Pilgrim Baptist Church. "The gospel choir was very, very nice," she remembered. "Mr. [George] Gulatt and the [senior] choir, they were very good, and they were always first, they always sang first. And the gospel choir would sing. They always sang before Dr. Austin came out. [Austin] was powerful, very intellectual, very suave and that church would be packed at 10:30. You couldn't get a seat."[97]

Of all the accompanists Dorsey used for the gospel chorus, McLin's favorite was Charlena Willis. "She had a gorgeous technique. It was very becoming, very beautiful. She herself was very beautiful." To McLin, the group's articulate approach to the lyrics and melody, accompanied by pumping rhythm chords on the piano and a boogie-woogie riff tossed in for emphasis, was "very beautiful."[98]

McLin also came face-to-face with the unbridled spirit of religious musical fervor while at Pilgrim. One day when she was playing piano at the church, "this big round lady said, 'Play that piano, little girl,' and she started running down the aisle toward the piano." She recalled, "I knew she was headed for me and so I got up under the piano, right in church! I got scared and I got up under the piano. And it turned the church out! Folks stood up and applauded me!"[99]

A little more than a year after the establishment of the Ebenezer Gospel Chorus, enthusiasts had their pick of gospel programs. They could attend the debut performance of Greater Bethel AME's gospel chorus on Sunday, January 29, 1933; Mount Moriah's gospel chorus program on Monday, January 30; and enjoy the Gospel Choral Union of Chicago's musical at Blackwell Memorial AME on Tuesday the thirty-first. Meanwhile, the Gospel Choral Union met monthly at different churches and in one year's time grew in participation from six to twenty choirs. The mix of churches represented in the union "allayed denominational strife," notes Dorsey biographer Ruth A. Smith.[100]

Churches on the city's West Side also began adding gospel choruses to their music departments around 1933. Sometime prior to August, Eddie Clifford Davis became music director for the Greater Union Baptist Church on the West Side. Elder Eleazar Lenox's Lake Street COGIC organized a junior gospel chorus to render gospel songs, anthems, and perform dramatic readings.[101] Other notable West Side gospel choruses were organized by Fulton Street ME, Mount Zion Baptist Church, and Ter-Centenary AME.[102] The largest gospel chorus on the West Side during this time, however, was reported to be at Original Providence Baptist Church.[103]

Gospel choruses were even showing up in venues frequented by Chicago's white community. On March 5, 1933, the W. D. Cook Gospel Chorus, directed by Magnolia Lewis Butts, appeared at Orchestra Hall alongside Jones's Metropolitan Choir as part of the latter's annual music festival.[104] A month later, the Pilgrim Gospel Chorus was invited by the white Swedish Baptist Church on the North Side to participate in its thirty-eighth anniversary celebration.[105] Dorsey's Pilgrim ensemble would even appear at the 1933 World's Fair, providing music for A. Wayman Ward's July 14 program and address at the Hall of Religion.[106]

By the summer of 1933, the gospel choral union had grown from a handful of Chicago choirs to thirty-five hundred members in twenty-four states.[107] The union now had a formal name: the National Convention of Gospel Choirs and Choruses and Smaller Musical Groups, Inc. (NCGCC). Touted as the realization of "a new epoch in the musical world," the NCGCC held its first convention at Pilgrim Baptist Church from August 30 to September 1, 1933. Dorsey, the national president, and Butts, second vice president, presided over the event. The fifty-two delegates included those from Chicago, St. Louis, East St. Louis, Detroit, Philadelphia, Indianapolis, New York City, and Washington, D.C. Six hundred choristers enjoyed musical performances, lectures on spirituals and gospel songs, and general musical fellowship. Classically trained soloists, including Lawrence Evans, sang spirituals and hymns. Local politicians offered formal congratulations, and several ministers from Chicago churches with gospel choruses spoke before the conventioneers. Pilgrim's Austin preached the dedicatory sermon. J. Wesley Jones spoke, and while he complimented and encouraged the gospel singers, he did not miss the opportunity to "point out to them their defects and give them a remedy for them."[108]

The delegates formally recognized every Midwestern city with a developing gospel chorus community by electing a vice president for each. Gus Evans of St. Louis was named first vice president; Magnolia Lewis Butts (who married Jessie J. Butts on November 7) was second vice president; Artelia Hutchins of Detroit, third vice president; J. B. Harris of East St. Louis, fourth vice president; and J. E. McGavock of Indianapolis, fifth vice president.[109]

During the event, Dorsey recommended that "the gospel singers of this national convention have a home or headquarters, with departments to study, rehearse, and develop the highest type of gospel singing with the very best interpretation of the spirituals and heart songs. That the headquarters be a place for gospel singers to stop over when traveling through the city and that the place be kept free from any activity or doings unbecoming for a Christian home; a place to reach the young singer and help the older one to reach the highest accomplishment along this line."[110] The *Defender* declared the convention "an overwhelming success," and the NCGCC marked 1933 as the official year of its incorporation.[111]

Despite an increase in the number of gospel choruses in Chicago, gospel music and its fealty to secular sounds rankled H. B. P. Johnson, music director of the unincorporated National Baptist Convention. He addressed an "audience of music lovers" at Ebenezer, ground zero of the gospel chorus movement, on how the "jazz age was ruining church music."[112]

Francis Hatcher reported the story for the *Defender*: "[Johnson] charged that the gospel singer in his zeal to invoke the same kind of enthusiasm into his audience as 'the other fellow' will discharge an efficient accompanist who insists upon following his or her teaching by sticking to the printed page, and engage one who is able and willing to apply the jazz effects." Although endorsing highbrow music, Johnson acknowledged the dangers implicit in ignoring gospel music: "If we fail to give the fish some of the kind of bait he wants, he will seek it elsewhere." Rev. J. H. L. Smith of Ebenezer was in the audience. He "voiced his approval of accompanists employing methods which Professor Johnson classified as wrong and added that in his opinion emotion and spirit are so much akin that one could hardly be far removed from the other."[113]

By the end of 1933, fewer musicians and pastors were lining up with Johnson and more with Smith in their acceptance of gospel choruses. Dorsey was selling more sheet music, thanks to this greater acceptance as well as the salesman-ship of Augustus Evans and his new business partner, Sallie Martin. Small ensembles were also singing the new songs. Ebenezer once again served as a crucible, this time for one of the most influential gospel groups of all time, the Roberta Martin Singers.

The Roberta Martin Singers

In 1933, most Chicago residents were unaware of the inaugural National Con-vention of Gospel Choirs and Choruses. They had their sights set on another major city event: the 1933 World's Fair, known as the "Century of Progress Exposition." According to contemporary written reports, Pilgrim was the only gospel chorus at the 1933 World's Fair and only as an adjunct to A. Wayman Ward's scheduled presentation. Still, black contributions to classical music, jazz, and spirituals could be heard on the fairgrounds and in the city, with artists such as Percy Venable, Roland Hayes, and Chicago's twenty-year-old piano wunderkind Margaret Bonds performing as part of the five-month schedule of activities.[114]

The 1933 World's Fair was so popular that it reopened for several months in 1934. Those attending the fair on an unknown day in 1934 witnessed one of the first public performances of the Martin and Frye Quartette. Organized by Roberta Martin, the Martin and Frye Quartette was modeled in part after the vocal combination of Bertha Wise and the all-male Wise Singers of Philadel-phia, perennial favorites of the National Baptist Convention. Eugene Smith, a member of the Martin and Frye Quartette, recalled the day in 1933 that Roberta heard the Wise Singers at Ebenezer: "[The Wise Singers] were not gospel sing-ers; they sang the spirituals. And they came to Ebenezer. Bertha Wise played the piano and was a contralto singer. [The group was] all men, called the Wise Singers. They sang, 'I Can Tell the World.' They would get to the part where [Bertha] would take one note and hold it, 'I . . .' Then some of the fellows would [hold the note]. Roberta watched and listened [with astonished admiration and thought], 'I want to do that!'"[115]

Like Wise, Martin was a contralto and a piano accompanist and had al-ready organized a female quartet at Ebenezer called the Gospel Four.[116] Martin selected male singers from the Ebenezer Junior Chorus: fourteen-year-olds Robert Anderson and Willie Webb (who had migrated from Mississippi as a child), thirteen-year-old James Lawrence (who directed Ebenezer's Young Adult Choir in 1935), twelve-year-old Eugene Smith, and ten-year-old Norsa-lus McKissick.[117] Like Smith, McKissick was billed as a "wonder boy" singer.[118] Also like Smith, McKissick was discovered by Martin and invited to join the junior chorus. Martin first heard him while he was "sitting on a curb, singing 'Stormy Weather.'" He recalled, "I was seven years old. She went to my father and invited me to go to Ebenezer to sing a song, 'Old Ship of Zion.'"[119] Although Frye had little to do with the formation or training of the group, Martin named the group the Martin and Frye Quartette as a tribute to her employer.[120]

Like the Ebenezer Junior Chorus, the repertory of the Martin and Frye Quartette consisted largely of songs written or arranged by Martin, Frye, and Johnnie Rogers and published by Lillian Bowles. Bowles's new assistant, Kenneth Morris, helped with some of the arrangements. A list of Bowles's gospel music publications offers insight into the early repertories of the Martin and Frye Quartette and the Ebenezer Junior Gospel Chorus:

- "Jesus' Love Bubbles Over" (1934) arranged by Martin and Frye
- "Talk about a Chile That Do Love Jesus" (1934) words revised and music arranged by Martin and Frye
- "We Are Going Home to Glory Hallelu" (1935) by Martin and Rogers; arranged by Morris
- "Search My Heart" (1935) arranged by Martin and Rogers
- "There's a King of Kings Somewhere" (1935) words revised and music arranged by Martin and Frye
- "Go Shepherd, Feed My Sheep" (1936) by Martin and Frye; arranged by Morris
- "Didn't It Rain" (1939) a spiritual by Roberta Martin; arranged by Willie Webb[121]

In the beginning, the Martin and Frye Quartette sang principally for Ebenezer and other local churches. The World's Fair was a major exception. The invitation to sing at the event came from a Martin associate, classical vocalist James Oliver Willis. Smith explained: "By Roberta being in the classical [field], she played for a fellow by the name of James Oliver Willis. Roberta played for him. He had an hour and a half at the second meeting of the World's Fair [1934], and the Martin Singers had a half hour."[122]

In 1935, the Martin and Frye Quartette was renamed the Roberta Martin Singers.[123] Martin organized other small groups from the Ebenezer Junior Chorus, including the Stevens Singers, but none reached the renown or visibility of the Roberta Martin Singers.

Frye left Ebenezer in 1937 to organize a gospel chorus for Olivet Baptist Church, one of the city's most austere and politically connected Old Landmarks. Martin's leadership of the Roberta Martin Singers, now entertaining invitations to sing outside Chicago, as well as her work as head of the youth department of the NCGCC, left her little time to devote to the Ebenezer choruses. She departed Ebenezer in 1939. Johnnie Rogers replaced Frye as director of the gospel choruses. Willa Saunders Jones, who would organize the city's famous passion play, replaced Martin on piano, and B. Maye Whalum assumed organ duties.[124]

"This Is a Singing Age"

The appearance of the Pilgrim Gospel Chorus at Orchestra Hall and at the 1933 World's Fair, as well as the Martin and Frye Quartette's half-hour program at the World's Fair in 1934, demonstrated that gospel music had the potential to move beyond the confines of church sanctuaries and choir lofts and into environments reserved normally for secular entertainment. Congregation by congregation, the deliberative African American northern urban church was being transformed from a mainstay of western European classical music and conservative preaching to an aural postcard from home for southern migrants. By the end of the decade, pastors throughout northern urban cities who ignored the popularity of gospel music risked losing members, financial resources, and political clout to a new generation of populist church leaders who embraced the new sound. Dorsey told sociologist Vattel Elbert Daniel: "This is an age for this particular kind of music. The gospel song seems to have a soothing effect. Every song that I have written was born of a real condition. They are songs that come from the heart. This is a singing age. You may have a program of the choicest, most refined, most intelligent music, and the people will not respond as they will to gospel music. It began in Chicago."[125]

CHAPTER 7

Across This Land and Country

New Songs for a New Era (1933–1939)

The rhythm of the gospel song . . . takes the place of the rhythm of the spiritual.

Vattel Elbert Daniel, 1940

Despite the ardent efforts of conservative ministers to bar "jazzy hymns" from the church, a growing population of transplanted southern blacks and more than a few Old Settlers were thrilled by Dorsey and Frye's back-home sound. Ebenezer Baptist Church was filled to overflowing whenever its gospel chorus sang, whether for a Sunday-morning service or a special musical.[1] Migrants at other churches were eager to have gospel choruses of their own, and their influence was no longer insubstantial. Once the butt of jokes and subject to condescending social commentary, new settlers were growing in numbers and becoming an economic and political force. Sociologist Vattel Elbert Daniel considers semi-demonstrative churches such as Ebenezer and Pilgrim the "cultural descendents of the traditional Negro church" because they offered congregants an opportunity to participate in the worship service and express themselves with exclamations, shouts, and other public demonstrations of emotion when moved by the music, the preaching, or another part of the service. The semi-demonstratives, Daniel writes, were "especially effective in assisting migrants to become oriented to the city" because they provided familiarity for those with "a decided preference for the rhythm of the gospel songs rather than the more even tempo of the stately hymns and anthems." They were churches, he observes, where "the rhythm of the gospel song . . . takes the place of the rhythm of the spiritual." A migrant from Jackson, Mississippi, told Daniel: "That church I like better than any of the others that I have gone to, because the service there was more like the service that they had at home and I could enjoy it better."[2]

Competition among Chicago churches for members was great. Unlike the rural South, where only one or two churches might be within walking or riding distance, Chicagoans had hundreds of houses of worship from which to choose. By 1938, as many as 475 churches were located on Chicago's South Side, and 215 were Baptist.[3] Others joined or visited the Pentecostal and Holiness churches that had never abandoned the religious folk traditions practiced in the South. By the late 1930s, there were 107 Pentecostal and 51 Spiritual churches in Chicago; only the Baptist church surpassed them in the number of edifices.[4]

Whether or not they liked the new gospel music, church leaders had little choice but to respond to the requests of their members who did. The newcomers were, in fact, the answer to their prayers. Besides the evangelistic imperative to recruit new congregants and deliver souls to Christ, pastors needed additional income to relieve the weight of debt service on church mortgages. The more migrants who joined, the greater the tithing, and the sooner the mortgage could be burned.

Growth of the National Convention of Gospel Choirs and Choruses

By 1934, the growing number of gospel choruses in North and West Side churches was sufficient to start a second Chicago choral union as part of the National Convention of Gospel Choirs and Choruses (NCGCC). The North and Western Zone Choral Union tagged Prince Johnson of the Johnson Gospel Singers to be its music director. In addition to the Johnson group, members included the Union and Metropolitan Gospel Choruses and gospel choruses from Mount Hebron Baptist Church, Zion Travelers, and Mount Carmel.[5]

Thanks to the efforts of NCGCC leadership, especially Dorsey and Sallie Martin, the gospel chorus phenomenon was sweeping not only through Chicago but also through towns and cities across the Midwest. The gospel chorus community that Gus Evans established in St. Louis was early confirmation that Butts's argument for a national confab of gospel choirs and choruses was valid. With Dorsey as president, Sallie Martin as national organizer, and Roberta Martin as national supervisor of the Junior Department, the NCGCC was off and running.

The first NCGCC convention had been so well received that it became an annual pilgrimage of the faithful and newly converted. On July 24, 1934, no less than five busses and two automobiles carrying gospel singers representing the Chicago Gospel Choral Union and the North and Western Zone Choral Union traveled along the new Route 66 national highway to the First Baptist Church in St. Louis and the organization's second annual session. Evans, I. J. Johnson, and J. B. Harris led the organizing committee, and Ebenezer's J. H. L. Smith delivered the convention sermon. Delegates and approximately two hundred visiting singers heard lectures and plenty of singing, including performances by Artelia and Ruth Hutchins of Detroit, Magnolia Lewis Butts, Sallie Martin, Emma Jackson, and Roberta Martin. Gospel singers from several national chapters sang, as did a group from Chicago's Ebenezer called the Four Fryes.[6]

Around this time, Sallie noticed how informally Dorsey managed his publishing business. She recalled:

> When I would go to the rehearsals [at the Dorsey home], I would notice his uncle's wife's sister, she would do maybe the cooking and going to the store, while Mr. Dorsey had an old bag that you keep money in placed in a drawer. . . . I'd notice if she's going to the store, she'd go there and she would get her some money out and not make any record or nothing. . . . So after quite a few rehearsals, that was when I said to him, "You know, you have something here but you don't know what to do with it." He said, "What do you mean?" I said, "What I said." He said, "Can you do any better?" I said, "I think I can." He said, "Well, here it is." I said, "What are you going to pay me?" "Four dollars a week." I said, "All right."[7]

Sallie secured a three-dollar-a-week room at the Ritz Hotel at Oakwood and South Park, just a few doors down from the Dorsey home, and set out to show the songwriter how to sell his sheet music.[8]

Dorsey and Sallie Martin visited cities throughout the Midwest to organize gospel choruses and sell sheet music from Dorsey's song catalog to the newly minted ensembles. By 1934, Dorsey's portfolio of gospel compositions and arrangements was nearing one hundred in total.[9] His most popular releases were "How about You," "If You See My Savior," "Someday Somewhere," and "Take My Hand, Precious Lord." For a while, because most of the gospel songs sold to choruses and singers were Dorsey compositions, all gospel songs were called "Dorseys," whether or not Dorsey wrote them.

Regardless of the size of Dorsey's catalog, it was Sallie Martin's street-smart business acumen that transformed the songwriter's drawer full of dimes and lack of generally accepted accounting principles into a real enterprise. She also took her NCGCC national organizer role seriously, proving to be its most ardent ambassador and salesperson. During her 1934 Midwestern tour, for example,

Martin produced for the fledgling NCGCC eight new gospel choruses, two new choral unions, and untold amounts of sheet music sales for Dorsey.[10]

Martin was also a more than competent song demonstrator. Her alto voice was earthy and unpolished, but she could capture a house with her charismatic personality and delivery. In that regard, Martin was a perfect example of the populism that undergirded the gospel music movement. In gospel, vocal quality and training took a back seat to the religious conviction that could be felt, as well as heard, by the faithful. Nobody could deny that Sallie Martin had religious conviction in spades.

During the 1935 meeting in Cincinnati, the NCGCC resolved to start a scholarship fund drive and designated the fifth Sunday in June as the annual date when gospel choruses throughout the country would collect contributions for the fund and remit them to the NCGCC. Antonio R. Haskell of St. Louis was named chairman of the fund and H. J. Carruthers, director of the St. Paul CME Gospel Choir in Chicago, treasurer. The organization also decreed that each chapter would be required to establish an examining board of influential musicians, so that "before anyone [could] be admitted into [the NCGCC] as a director, he must be prepared by having a course of study and pass an examination set up by the board of examiners."[11] Gospel singers who wanted to be NCGCC soloists would be subject to the same process. In essence, if chorus membership was liberally bestowed, the business of operating the chorus ran along the same hard-and-fast principles as other church organizations.

At this time, Dorsey started "the first and only paper of its type ever published, *The Gospel Singer News*," to provide "needful advice and helpful hints" between events to the NCGCC membership, now comprised of 941 ensembles. The paper contained a catalog of songs, including Dorsey's, available for sale.[12] Dorsey also continued to hone his plans for the Gospel Singers Rest, a home "where people [would be] taught to excel along the lines of singing."[13]

Just how popular gospel music had become in a little more than three years was recognized formally on June 25, 1935. At the Third Annual Founder's Day Celebration of the Chicago Gospel Chorus Union, a group that now counted fifty-six choruses in its membership, Dorsey, Frye, and Butts were feted for their musical and organizing skills. The celebration, which drew more than a thousand attendees, was organized by Sallie Martin at Metropolitan Community Church. As the gospel nexus sat regally "on draped chairs on the pulpit," representatives of their respective churches recognized them for their individual and collective efforts, notably Rev. R. C. Keller of Pilgrim for Dorsey, Joseph Evans of Metropolitan for Butts, and Frank J. Hawkins of Ebenezer for Frye. Once again, Keller paid public tribute to gospel music, in comments noteworthy for their austerity: "Monuments over the graves of departed heroes cannot equal the tangible abiding merit in appreciative hearts for the solace in times of sorrow, the courage in moments of despair, and edification during the worship hour, brought in these songs written by Dorsey and used for the inspiration of countless millions of lives."[14]

Other highlights of the tribute included the performance of a mass chorus of more than six hundred choral union members, directed by music publisher Emma Jackson and accompanied by Pilgrim Gospel Chorus pianist Mabel Mitchell-Hamilton. At the conclusion, the three founders received large baskets of flowers.

Thus, as choir directors such as J. Wesley Jones and James Mundy sought to present music that demonstrated racial pride and the desire to assimilate into Chicago's broader middle-class society, Dorsey and the NCGCC presented music to promote racial pride and assimilation into the African American church community. Songwriter and choral director Dorsey, once an outsider, was now the spokesperson of a mass movement that was converting the avant-garde into the musical standard for black churches.

Religious Radio in the Early Gospel Era

Not only was NCGCC's earliest leadership culled primarily from the Midwest, but its earliest membership was overwhelmingly comprised of the mainline Protestant denominations, despite many instances of cross-denominational gospel music fellowship between Protestant and sanctified churches. Nevertheless, the Pentecostal, Holiness, and Spiritual churches had already discovered that phonograph records and radio were effective media to spread their message and music. In the mid-1930s, Chicagoans who wanted to hear an old-fashioned worship service on the radio had at least three options at 11:00 p.m. every Sunday evening: First Church of Deliverance on WIND, All Nations Pentecostal Church on WCFL, and Fortieth Church of God in Christ on WSBC.

Still, not everyone subscribed to swinging church choirs. A "Catholic housewife" quoted in *Black Metropolis* said, "I like good music, but I don't like the songs that these gospel choirs in the store-fronts sing—these jazz tunes."[15] Cleveland resident Gladstone Pulliam expressed more pointed outrage about jazz in churches when he wrote, "The preachers who permit jazz music in their churches or will allow their members to give jazz entertainments were not sent by God to preach. . . . [God] doesn't want us to be jazz band pilots or jazz babies and be filled with the devil's spirits. He wants us to be clean and holy and be filled with the Holy Ghost."[16] Ironically, it was precisely when congregants felt the presence of the Holy Ghost during a sanctified worship service that "jazzing of hymns" commenced in full force.

Despite such instances of public criticism, the First Church of Deliverance choir had built a solid enough reputation over the radio and in the community to receive invitations to perform at churches of all denominations throughout Chicago. A First Church bulletin from June 30, 1935, noted that the choir "under the direction of Mr. R. L. [Knowles] sang 'I'm Satisfied with Jesus'" at Canaan Baptist Church at Forty-Fifth and Wabash, where Rev. Louis Rawls was pastor.[17] By First Church's seventh anniversary celebration in 1936, which drew visitors from across the country, the church's official membership was cited as nearing three thousand persons, and the radio broadcast was hailed as appealing to "legions of eager listeners who are spiritually uplifted as [was] testified by the avalanche of fan mail which [was] received after each broadcast."[18]

Among the first radio shows to feature gospel choruses outside the worship service was *Quest for Choirs*. Debuting on WSBC in early 1937, the program was sponsored by Bob's Radio Store. Every Tuesday from 11:30 p.m. to midnight, it showcased "spiritual or gospel singing by choirs, glee clubs, quartets or jubilee groups" with the intention of selecting "the most popular group of colored singers in Chicago." The show, directed and announced by Jack and Gertrude Cooper, was broadcast from First Church of Deliverance. Employing a technique similar to the *Defender*'s annual "Mayor of Bronzeville" campaign, listeners were instructed to visit Bob's Radio Store at 540 East Forty-Seventh Street and vote for their favorite group from that week's episode. Store purchases entitled customers to more voting points, thus encouraging patrons to shop and support their favorite religious ensembles at the same time. By mid-1937, winners of the competition included gospel choirs from St. Minerva Spiritual Church, Galilee Baptist Church, Zion Hill Baptist Church, Progressive Community Church, and Fortieth Church of God in Christ. The All Nations Pentecostal and First Church of Deliverance choruses sang on the program, but as hosts, not as entrants.[19]

By 1939, thanks largely to the Coopers, WSBC was considered the "only all race-manned radio broadcasting studio in the country."[20] It was such a potent force that one of its sponsors, the B. Michelson Furniture Company, provided the station with a new broadcasting studio space atop its South Side retail store at 4237–43 Indiana Avenue. The new studio was wired with three microphones to accommodate live performances by as large as a 160-voice choir. Present at the formal dedication ceremony were Chicago Mayor Edward J. Kelly and "several hundred persons," including Thomas A. Dorsey, WSBC general manager Frank A. Stanford, Rev. William Roberts of the Church of God in Christ, and Harry Gray of Local 208 of the Musicians Union, the first and most powerful black musicians union in the country. All programming decisions for the South Side studio were in the capable hands of the Coopers.[21]

Although radio was transmitting gospel beyond church walls, sheet music remained an important way to get new gospel songs in the hands of singers. Gospel sheet music, however, was only a rough guide for the vocalist. First, most gospel singers could not read musical notation. Second, and more importantly, the composer or arranger, and the gospel music audience, expected the artist to make the song his or her own by improvising on the original composition. The improvisation produced a performance version of a composition that bore sufficient resemblance to the original for the listener to recognize the song, but with enough distinction that it seemed as if a new song were created in the moment. In other words, no two performances of a gospel song were exactly alike.

During the early- and mid-1930s, Dorsey, Lillian M. Bowles, and Charles H. Pace were the only gospel song publishers in Chicago. Memphian Bowles (1872–1945) was a songwriter, arranger, and publisher of sacred and secular music written by black composers and musicians. Located at 4640 South State, Bowles Music House was established in the late 1920s, at the height of black music publishing in Chicago. Charles H. Pace's Old Ship of Zion was one block south and two blocks west of Bowles's shop. He was also Bowles's house scribe and arranger, readying a song composition for publication by notating the vocal parts and accompaniment. When Pace left Bowles in 1934, his position was not vacant for long. Bowles learned about a seventeen-year-old jazz musician named Kenneth Morris who was looking for work.

Kenneth Morris was born August 28, 1917, in Jamaica, New York, to Ettuila and John Morris. An only child, Morris took piano lessons in grade school, served as a substitute accompanist for his Sunday school, and entered formal study at the Manhattan Conservatory of Music, where he learned composition, arranging, orchestration, and piano. Although a student of classical music, Morris enjoyed participating in impromptu jazz jam sessions with local teens. The sessions piqued his interest in the rhythms and melodies of jazz. After high school, Morris was determined to devote his music career to jazz and began performing professionally in various New York eateries and lounges.

Morris joined a jazz combo that never had a steady membership or even a formal name, though afterward it became known as the Kenneth Morris Band. In 1934, the group landed an opportunity to perform at the World's Fair in Chicago. They were thrilled that their first long-distance gig was at the year's biggest attraction. While at the fair, the teens performed day and night, often outdoors, where they were vulnerable to the meteorological extremes of the Chicago summer. The physical toll proved too much for Morris; he subsequently developed tuberculosis and ceased performing. When the gig was over, the other band members returned to New York, without their band's namesake, who remained in Chicago to recuperate.

Morris bided his time in the city by sitting in on informal sessions with other jazz musicians. Word traveled to Bowles that Morris would make an excellent replacement for Pace because, like Pace, he could read, write, and notate music. Bowles hired Morris as her new house arranger in 1934. Horace Clarence Boyer notes that although Morris was initially disappointed with Bowles's job offer because he would be transcribing the compositions of others, not composing his own songs, he remained her arranger for six years.[22] Otherwise, the job was ideal for Morris. The last thing his fragile health needed was more outdoor work or manual labor.

With Morris's capable assistance, Bowles's publishing catalog grew during the 1930s in tandem with the gospel music community. Among Morris's earliest arrangements for Bowles were Antonio Haskell's "God Shall Wipe All Tears Away," written originally in 1935; and Frye's 1937 adaptation of "I Am Sending My Timber Up to Heaven" and "God's Gonna Separate the Wheat from the Tares," recorded in Chicago in 1927 and again in 1934 by guitar evangelist Blind Joel Taggart.[23] Bowles's catalog included the earliest song compositions and arrangements of Theodore Frye, such as "There's a King of Kings Somewhere" (1935) and "Is Your All on the Altar" (1937). Roberta Martin's initial arrangements for Ebenezer's Young People's Choir, including "Jesus Love Just Bubbles Over in My Heart" (1934, with Theodore Frye) and "Go Shepherd, Feed My Sheep" (1936), an original Martin and Frye composition, were first made available in print by Bowles, as was Martin and Rogers's arrangements of "Search My Heart" (1935), and "Shall I Meet You Over Yonder" (1937).

Roberta Martin's reworking of the spiritual "Didn't It Rain" (1939), arranged by Willie Webb, first appeared in a Bowles song folio, or collection of songs.[24] Morris told Bernice Johnson Reagon that *Bowles Songbook*, no. 1, folio was his brainchild: "We were producing so many songs that weren't selling, so I said, why not put a cover over them and you could continue to sell them."[25] Bowles published a series of songbooks and the idea worked—packaging gospel songs as folios became an industry standard.

Eventually, Morris's desire to write and publish his own compositions was fulfilled. During a visit to the Bowles House of Music sometime in 1937, Rev. Clarence H. Cobbs met Morris and, after hearing him play piano, invited him to direct the First Church of Deliverance Choir. Morris accepted and that same year composed "Heaven Bells" for the choir. "Heaven Bells" was published not by Bowles but by First Church of Deliverance, which went on to establish its own music publishing and retail arm.

Gospel Records on the Decca 7000 Series

The Great Depression sucked the wind out of the sails of Chicago's black religious recording industry. Dozens of singers, quartets, and preachers made recordings in Chicago between 1926 and 1929, but as appendix B illustrates, only a handful did so between 1930 and 1939. The majority of black religious discs recorded in Chicago in the early 1930s appeared on Jack Kapp's Brunswick and Vocalion labels. In 1934, however, Kapp provided an enormous boost to gospel music recording when he organized the American Decca Records Company.[26] His commitment to lower-priced records in a wide variety of popular genres, as well as the popularity of Bing Crosby, the label's top seller, transformed Decca into one of the nation's most successful record companies by the end of the decade. Kapp named his former associate, Ink Williams, who had recently returned to Chicago, artist and repertoire (A&R) man for Decca's new 7000 Series, which meant that he was responsible for finding and recording black talent.[27] The 7000 series, variously called Decca's "race" or "sepia" series, was dedicated to commercially popular blues, jazz, and religious recordings made by African American artists. Decca's Chicago recording studio was located in the Furniture Mart at 666 North Lake Shore Drive, at the time one of the world's largest buildings.[28]

The first two religious releases in the Decca 7000 Series were recorded in Chicago on September 8, 1934, and featured a somewhat dated guitar-jug music duet by "Brownsville" Son Bonds and Tennessee bluesman Hammie Nixon.[29] Nevertheless, between 1935 and 1937, five artists incorporated new gospel songs into their Decca 7000 series recordings. First was the Four A Melody Men (Rudolph Allen, Frank Bass, Ernest Golden, and James Taylor), who were credited on record as the "Mound City Jubilee Quartette." On its February 25, 1935, Decca session, the quartet harmonized a cappella on "I'm a Pilgrim," "Old Ship Of Zion," "Lead Me to That Rock," and "If You See My Savior" (as "Standing by the Bedside of a Neighbor"). Its singing style clearly leaned toward the emerging gospel quartet tradition in its use of falsetto lead, polyrhythmic vocal percussion, and contrapuntal bass lines. The Mound City Jubilee Quartette also emulated the sound of their contemporaries. For example, the group's recording of "Sleep On Darling Mother" is a nearly note-for-note copy of the Silver Leaf Quartette of Norfolk's own version, recorded for OKeh in 1928, right down to the "clanka-lanka" vocal rhythm and prominent falsetto lead.[30] On "Standing by the Bedside of a Neighbor," the men borrowed liberally from the Five Blue Jays of Birmingham's 1932 disc, especially its pumping bass.[31]

Second, Professor Hull's Anthems of Joy, possibly with jazzman Punch Miller on trumpet, recorded eight sides for Decca on July 3, 1936, of which four were released on two discs. The band jazzed the hymns and spirituals, covering "My Lord's Gonna Move This Wicked Race" and "What a Friend We Have in Jesus" in a trumpet-led Dixieland jazz style.[32] "Love, Oh Love Divine" is done to the tune of "Careless Love," while "Sunshine and Shadows" is a peppy variation of "Heavenly Sunshine." Hull served as vocalist, and on one of the unissued tracks, "Everybody Talkin' 'Bout Heaven Ain't Goin' There," he parodied a preacher, though his speaking voice was more deliberate than those of the fiery recording preachers Gates, Rice, and McGee. The Anthems of Joy, without Hull, appeared on Chicago gospel programs well into the 1950s.

Third were the Golden Eagle Gospel Singers. Probable personnel on the Decca sides were Leandrew Wauford, M. Person, M. Mine, A. Thomas, and Hammie Nixon on harmonica.[33] In addition to the group incorporating the word "gospel" into its name, historian Ray Funk reports that an examination of the Golden Eagle Gospel Singers' recorded repertory suggests that they "were involved with the new gospel music publishing going on in Chicago at the time, rather than just relying on traditional spirituals."[34] Indeed, of the sixteen sides they recorded in Chicago for Decca between May 11, 1937, and June 4, 1940, the Golden Eagle Gospel Singers waxed standards such as "Gimme That Old Time Religion" and "The Old Ship of Zion," as well as new gospel compositions such as the Soul Stirrers' "He's My Rock."[35] Still, the group had more in common with sanctified singers than with gospel groups. The lead singer's raspy vocals, Nixon's bluesy harmonica, movable lyric couplets on "When Death Comes Creeping in Your Room," hand clapping and vocal interjections, and the group's overall country-church-style unison singing evoked southern traditions. On "A Warrior on the Battlefield," the group even emulated the sanctified sermon records popular during the late 1920s. Notices in the *Defender* suggest that the Golden Eagle Gospel Singers performed in local church programs at least through 1941. During the 1940s, Wauford secured a regular radio program and became a member of the Famous Blue Jays, which by then had moved its headquarters from Texas to Chicago.[36]

Fourth, the more conservative Goodwill Male Chorus recorded for Decca in Chicago on May 11, 1937.[37] Although their four sides were piano-led spirituals and the group sang in the jubilee quartet style, it is possible that the ensemble itself was an offshoot of the Metropolitan Baptist Church Goodwill Chorus, led at the time by Rev. Luschaa Allen. If this is so, these discs would constitute the first commercial recordings of a choir with direct links, via Allen, to Chicago's gospel chorus movement.

Thanks to Ink Williams, Decca amassed a significant catalog of black religious singing over four years. It tapped into the mother lode in October 1938, when young guitar evangelist Sister Rosetta Tharpe, the member of Fortieth COGIC who accompanied her mother, Katie Bell Nubin, at the Maxwell Street market, recorded Dorsey's "Hide Me in Thy Bosom" as "Rock Me." But a year prior to Tharpe's Decca debut, and just days after the Golden Eagle Gospel Singers and the Goodwill Male Chorus visited the Furniture Mart, the fifth important gospel artist to enter Decca's Chicago studio waxed her first commercial sides.

"Mahalie Is on the Box!"

Mahalia Jackson biographer Laurraine Goreau writes that Ink Williams learned of the twenty-five-year-old Jackson through Frank J. Hawkins, a local dentist, deacon, and fan. Hawkins ushered Williams to a funeral to hear Jackson and introduced them after the service. "I want to put you on records," Williams told Jackson. "You had all those people crying. I think we can do something with you."[38]

The next day, Jackson telephoned Williams to inquire how much it would cost to record. He told her, "Nothing; just come on down like we said." Jackson arrived at the Furniture Mart carrying a pint of whiskey and a box of cigars as gifts for Williams. She was joined by her accompanist, Estelle Allen, and Brother John Sellers, Jackson's teenaged protégé.[39] The four cuts Jackson recorded on Friday, May 15, 1937, were "God's Gonna Separate the Wheat from the Tares" and "God Shall Wipe All Tears Away," both from Bowles's catalog, as well as "Keep Me Every Day" and a Johnson Gospel Singers favorite, "Oh My Lord," also known as "Sing On, You Singers". On the two brisk-tempo songs— "God's Gonna Separate the Wheat from the Tares" and "Oh My Lord"—Jackson swung the sacred with youthful confidence.

For the two slow selections, "Keep Me Every Day" and "God Shall Wipe All Tears Away," Allen shifted from piano to an asthmatic pump organ. The slower tempo allowed Jackson to embellish the melodies and wring every ounce of emotion from the hymns. Although the quick-tempo songs were more infectious, the slow selections, especially "Keep Me Every Day," showcased Jackson as a singing star in the making. It was this somber sound that Williams had encountered at the funeral. Meanwhile, Allen's accompaniment, according to doctoral candidate Idella Johnson, drew on an "assortment of African-American pianistic styles—Blues, Ragtime, Boogie-Woogie, Stride, and Gospel."[40]

Decca was sufficiently satisfied with the recordings to release them as singles, but there was some question about whether Jackson herself was pleased. She did not tell her Chicago aunts or even her husband, Ike Hockenhull, about the session. She may have been disappointed with the results, or it may have been her preference for privacy—as Aunt Hannah suggested, "She always was one to keep her business to herself." Jackson did not breathe a word to her New Orleans kinfolk, either, but they learned about Jackson's records before the Chicagoans did. Coin-machine operators who knew of Jackson's

New Orleans roots wisely filled the Big Easy's jukeboxes with her records. It did not take long for word to reach the Clark family that "Mahalie is on the box!" The staunchly Baptist family found itself on unfamiliar territory—the Bumblebee tavern—listening to twenty-five-year-old Mahalia singing on a phonograph record.[41]

With the possible exceptions of the New Orleans and Chicago markets, the records did not sell well. Decca proposed to Jackson, via a reluctant Williams, that she turn her estimable talents to singing the blues. Jackson refused the company's offer and rejected similar requests from Louis Armstrong and Earl Hines, two artists she admired, to join their orchestras as a vocalist. Much to the chagrin of Hockenhull, Jackson even declined an opportunity to earn sixty dollars per week as part of the touring company of the *Hot Mikado*, a jazz version of the Gilbert and Sullivan musical.[42] Decca dropped Jackson.

Since being a "fish-and-bread singer" was not meeting household expenses, and Hockenhull's penchant for betting on horse races was not helping, Jackson sold cosmetics concocted at home from recipes that her mother-in-law provided. She quickly abandoned that enterprise to open a beauty shop in a storefront at 3252 South Indiana, one half-block north of Pilgrim Baptist Church. Given her need to be at the shop, Jackson limited her gospel singing to local appearances and weekend whistle-stop tours with Dorsey to help sell his sheet music.

Jackson's beauty shop became a fellowship hot spot for established gospel singers and aspiring talents. At any given time, Robert Anderson, Willie Webb, Myrtle Jackson, Myrtle Scott, Celeste Scott, Emma Jackson, and her protégé, teenaged Gwendolyn Cooper Lightner of Brookport, Illinois, could be found at 3252.[43] When in Chicago, Willie Mae Ford Smith and Rosetta Tharpe would stop by the salon.

The tight-knit group that gathered at Mahalia's Beauty Shop was an informal mélange of gospel artists with a shared commitment to sacred singing who formed a subset of the southern migrant population that had separated itself from the city's black bourgeois. The members of this community not only sustained gospel music in its embryonic days but became its first national stars. There were nonetheless individual preferences and rivalries among the first generation of gospel singers and enthusiasts. Dorsey has been quoted as saying, "There was more rivalry then among church singers than show folk."[44]

The fellowship also offered informal opportunities to perform. Gospel singers and musicians could and did fill in, often at a moment's notice, when another voice or instrumentalist was needed. For example, after Estelle Allen got a regular job and was not always available, Jackson could choose among other equally adept accompanists, such as Evelyn and Geraldine Gay, Robert Anderson, Willie Webb, Anna Crockett, New Orleans native James Lee, Pilgrim

Gospel Chorus accompanist Mabel Mitchell-Hamilton, Louise Overall Weaver, Roberta Martin, Gwendolyn Cooper Lightner, Mildred Carter Falls, and Ruth Jones (later known as Dinah Washington). Singer-publisher Emma Jackson had a reputation for knowing which accompanists were available.[45]

Accompanist availability was often a concern because musicians had to cobble together their income from a combination of day jobs, choir directing, and other church-sponsored performances. Sometimes the exact combination was unconfirmed until the hour of the program. It did not matter: the gospel community was sufficiently familiar with the oeuvre of newly composed songs, hymns, and anthems to play or sing at a moment's notice, even if that meant leaving one's seat during a program to fill in for a missing player.

From the Altar to the Auditorium

Although record companies and radio stations were spreading the new gospel music to a wider audience, the music was still by and large the exclusive asset of the African American church worship experience. Thus, when on February 3, 1938, Ebenezer Baptist Church's publicity committee experimented with making private recordings of "many outstanding gospel singers—individuals, groups and choruses," the result was not for national or local distribution but solely for the enjoyment of the church and the artists who made the discs.[46]

Things began to change in the mid- to late 1930s when some of the most influential Chicago gospel artists started staging programs beyond the church walls. In 1936, Dorsey organized the first gospel program to charge an admission fee instead of seeking a goodwill offering. It was advertised as a "song battle," or competition, between the two Martins: Sallie and Roberta. Who won is lost to time; the song-battle concept, originating in the competitions staged between quartets and choirs, was less a duel than a marketing tool. It was sufficiently successful, however, to encourage Pilgrim Baptist Church and First Church of Deliverance to sponsor another Sallie and Roberta Martin sing-off at DuSable High School in 1938, this time under the friendlier appellation of "gospel song recital."[47] Mahalia Jackson's first performance outside a church occurred in 1938, when she and Estelle Allen appeared before an audience of one thousand at DuSable on a program that included the city's famous Umbrian Glee Club and the Antioch Baptist Church gospel chorus.[48]

Presaging the rise of the major gospel program, Dorsey and the 150-voice Pilgrim Gospel Chorus joined forces with First Church of Deliverance's three-hundred-voice choir on Friday May 7, 1937, to present a "Gospel Song Feast." An audience of 2,500 filled DuSable's auditorium to enjoy the program. The *Defender*'s detailed report provides a glimpse into the content and presentation of early gospel concerts, which not only featured gospel singing but also spirituals, hymns, and other forms of entertainment, such as dramatic readings.

The program opened with the First Church and Pilgrim choruses joining forces on the former's theme, Cobbs's arrangement of "How I Got Over." The First Church's choir rendered Kenneth Morris's gospel song "Heaven Bells" and the spiritual "My Lord What a Morning." Next, Pilgrim Gospel Chorus accompanist Charlena Willis sang and accompanied herself on piano, joining University Radio Singers member Bertha Armstrong on "It's Jesus with You." Under the direction of Henry Markham, the Pilgrim Gospel Chorus performed "Go with Me" and "Jesus Lives in Me." Magnolia Lewis Butts delivered a dramatic reading. The first part concluded with selections by the University Radio Singers and the female chorus of First Church singing "Go Down Moses" and "King Jesus Is A-Listening."

The second half of the event featured Sallie Martin "doing her specialties, 'I'll Tell It [Wherever I Go]' and 'I'm Just a Sinner [Saved by Grace].'" Armstrong, Anna Ellis, and N. Calvin Delph sang next, and the program concluded with a presentation by a male chorus, though it is uncertain whether the men were part of the First Church or the Pilgrim aggregations, or both.

Additional insight into the stylistic diversity and formality of early gospel music programs can be gleaned from the "musical tea" sponsored by Olivet Baptist Church's new gospel chorus, directed by Ebenezer alumnus Theodore Frye, on February 13, 1938. The Sunday-afternoon musical opened with the congregation singing the black national anthem, "Lift Every Voice and Sing." Rev. John H. Branham, Olivet's associate pastor and master of ceremonies for the afternoon, delivered the prayer and invocation. A group called Webb's Quartette and individual soloists Geraldine Overstreet, W. O. Hoyle, and Frye offered one selection each. Following the music, Judge William H. Harrison introduced the keynote speaker, classical music maven Rebecca Stiles Taylor, whose presentation was followed by the Martin and Frye Quartette, a solo by "M. Jackson" (possibly Mahalia or Myrtle), the L. K. W. Singers (named after Olivet's pastor, Rev. Lacey Kirk Williams), and music (probably an organ solo) by Willie Webb.[49]

A Gospel Innovation at First Church of Deliverance

By the late 1930s, when First Church of Deliverance had outgrown the 4315 South Wabash building, Preacher Cobbs decided to raze the structure and build a new one in its place.[50] He commissioned African American architect Walter Thomas Bailey to design the new First Church of Deliverance, which he did, in the Art Moderne style. Bailey was born in Kewanee, Illinois, on

January 11, 1862, and in 1904 was the first African American to graduate with a bachelor of science in architectural engineering from the University of Illinois. He had prior experience in church design, having participated in the renovation of Pilgrim Baptist Church in 1937.[51] He completed First Church's new fifty-thousand-dollar structure in 1939.[52] The new altar and pulpit were perfect visual accompaniments to the First Church worship experience and the flamboyance of the music ministry. Curved dividers resembling a bandstand separated the altar below from the choir above. Two striking grand pianos bracketed the choir area to balance the sound. Rev. J. C. Austin delivered the sermon at the groundbreaking ceremony on Sunday, May 21.[53]

It was during this time that First Church of Deliverance's music director, Kenneth Morris, made his most significant contribution to the music department and to gospel music by introducing the Hammond organ. The chirping, warbling Hammond was one of gospel's first modern musical innovations. The organ's portability, combined with its uncanny ability to mimic the expressiveness of the human voice, made it the signature sound of black gospel music.

The Hammond organ was the brainchild of inventor and manufacturer Laurens Hammond, born in 1895 in Evanston, Illinois, a suburb north of Chicago. Hammond invented the organ not because he wanted to establish a new keyboard sound—he was tone-deaf—but because he wanted an electric instrument that could be mass-produced economically and in which there were "a relatively small number of parts, in which the various elements may be readily assembled." Further, Hammond believed that an instrument with a faster, more responsive keyboard than the pipe organ would be of interest to professional organists. At the time, the only electric organ on the market was the Wurlitzer, but it was bulky, heavy, expensive, and functioned like a pipe organ in its delayed keyboard action. Hammond drew up the engineering blueprints, filed a patent application for the Hammond organ on January 19, 1934, and on April 24 was awarded patent number 1,956,350.[54]

Hammond began turning out completed organs at a Chicago manufacturing plant he established at 4200 West Diversey Avenue. He designated the first version the Model A, which went on sale in 1935. Among the earliest adopters of the Model A, which cost $1,250 in the mid-1930s, were American composers George Gershwin and Sigmund Romberg as well as artists Lawrence Welk, Roger Wolfe Kahn, and Rudy Vallee.[55]

Soon after the instrument's introduction, Neota McCurdy Dyett (1898–1938), notable musician and ex-wife of the city's iconic high school band director Captain Walter Dyett, called Hammond's "pipeless organ" the most significant innovation "in the realm of art" in 1935. Although praising its practicality, affordability, and ability to produce "over a thousand effects," Dyett expressed concern "as to whether or not it will ever be accepted in the church" because "the tone [was] decidedly different from that of general church organs, being too 'eerie' in quality."[56]

Dyett's concern, though amusing in retrospect, was not without merit at the time. Although the Illinois College of Music, located in the Furniture Mart, offered Hammond organ lessons as early as 1935—Louise Overall Weaver was among the first African Americans to enroll—only one black church in Chicago, St. Edmond's Episcopal Church at 3831 South Indiana, reported having purchased one by April 1939. Around the same time, the William H. Leonard Funeral Home boasted of being the "only colored mortuary in Chicago equipped with a Hammond electric organ."[57]

Morris was intrigued by the new electric organ's versatility and fast action, as well as its ability to produce "over a thousand effects." An accomplished organist could make the Hammond shout for joy, keen in deepest mourning, hurl a crushing wave of sound to accompany an anthem, or bring a bright, pulsating swing to up-tempo arrangements. In other words, the Hammond was an ideal accompaniment for jazz and gospel.[58] The Hammond organ also offered the Wurlitzer's brightness of tone, and its relative affordability and portability were important to budget-conscious churches.[59] Ultimately, the Hammond responded to a singer's call like the bottleneck slide guitar answered the plaintive singing of itinerant evangelists.

When Cobbs decided to add an organ to the church in 1939, therefore, Morris knew what he wanted. "[Cobbs], of course, didn't have any musical knowledge," Morris told Horace Clarence Boyer, "but he loved music so [much that] he took me downtown to our largest music store to see about getting an organ."[60]

The "largest music store" was Lyon and Healy. Located at the corner of Wabash and Jackson in Chicago's downtown Loop district, Lyon and Healy was the city's music mecca. Records and sheet music were sold on the main floor, and a piano and organ showcase was on the second floor. Practice rooms for piano and organ students were rentable by the hour. Professionals and amateurs alike sampled and purchased instruments there, and if the instrument malfunctioned, the store repaired it. The Lyon and Healy Building was also the location of several recording studios.

Another important benefit not lost on the entrepreneurial Cobbs was that the Hammond Model A could make the First Church of Deliverance even more distinctive among its peers, including the musically inventive Pentecostal and Holiness churches, which made ample use of just about any instrument that could be plucked, banged, bowed, or blown. Morris said:

> I wanted nothing else. It sold itself. Reverend Clarence Cobbs was only too happy to get it because it did what he wanted [since] he wanted to use it for gospel purposes. . . . It was the most unusual thing you ever heard. People

came from all over just to hear me play that organ. Oh yes, it swept! It swept! Instantaneously! I kept experimenting with it, and I was getting all kinds of [sounds] out of it that had never been heard by anyone else before—so much so that Lyon and Healy hired me to exhibit the organ.[61]

Not only did the Hammond contribute to the popularity of the First Church radio broadcast, but the broadcast contributed to the popularity of the Hammond. Hammond's biographer indicates that more Hammond organs were sold in 1939 than all other organs combined.[62] But despite its many positive attributes, the Model A had a major disadvantage: the built-in Hammond tone box speaker produced what some musicians called a "dry tone," meaning it lacked the depth and warmth required to truly bring the new sounds out. This shortcoming was mended by Illinois-born Donald James Leslie.

A Los Angeles radio repairman, Leslie was born in Danville, Illinois, on April 13, 1911. An early adopter of the Hammond organ, Leslie believed its sound could be improved but was unsure how to do it. In 1937 or 1938, a pickup truck broadcasting from a large radio speaker on its roof passed by Leslie, and he realized that was it: incorporating the Doppler effect of sound into a speaker could give more fullness to the tone. He purchased a one-dollar speaker and mounted rotating metal horns eighteen inches in diameter onto a turntable. He installed the new tremulant apparatus in a large closet and covered the closet door with a grill. Sure enough, as the metal horns revolved, the organ's sound became warmer and richer. The tones were superior to those produced by the tremulant in the Hammond tone box. Leslie developed a special wooden cabinet so that the speaker would be as handsome and modern as the organ, and called the new amplifier the "Vibratone," or "Hollywood Speaker," after the location where it was manufactured. The wooden box with the rotary horn and bass reflector inside became known as the "Leslie speaker" and entered production in 1940.[63] The curious wooden box with slats became an instant companion to the Hammond organ. After the introduction of the Hammond B3 model in 1955, the Hammond B3 and model 122 Leslie speaker became synonymous with gospel music.[64]

The Hammond organ at First Church of Deliverance was a new injection of urbanity in sacred folk music. According to organist Kenneth Woods Jr., if Dorsey's piano technique incorporated the blues and ragtime popular in Chicago during the 1920s, Morris's Hammond organ technique was evocative of the swing bands popular at the time of the First Church organ purchase.[65] In other words, Morris contemporized gospel songs and spirituals by bringing them from the barrelhouse era to the swing era. Heilbut agrees: "Dorsey reflected the blues of his salad days, while Kenneth Morris was much more a product of the big band era."[66]

The Gospel Train Arrives

By the late 1930s, gospel music was sweeping through the city and leaving an impression on church congregations. Historian Davarian Baldwin writes that gospel music had become the "most notable indicator of black Protestant church life, with its own exclusionary rules and regulations of musical authority," and "Chicago served as the center of gospel music publishing and performance."[67] Nearly every black church in the city had a gospel chorus. Some of the singing groups possessed the theatricality of the Dorsey-Frye ensembles, and others were more formal and austere, but they all embraced the "gospel chorus" sobriquet.

After Frye became director of Olivet Baptist Church's gospel choir in October 1938, his Sunday-evening musicals at Olivet drew monthly attendances of two thousand. They became so popular that patrons were encouraged to arrive an hour early to secure a seat.[68] "At Olivet Baptist Church, at the evening program, the church would just go wild when [Uncle Teddy] would sing," reminisced Frye's nephew, Mack Marshall.[69]

While songs, hymns, or spirituals sung with gospel fervor were, as Vattel Daniel has noted, "introduced anywhere in the service and by anybody" in the Pentecostal and Holiness churches he researched, pastors of semi-deliberative churches discovered that gospel songs proved especially effective when rendered during the collection of tithes as well as during the "altar call," or public invitation to join the church.[70] The emotional fervor the song created helped achieve the desired response, whether to encourage giving or persuade congregants to formally accept Christ as their personal savior.[71] Daniel and his research team observed the following emotional responses to performances of gospel music, and of hymns and spirituals sung in a gospel style, in various semi-demonstrative Chicago churches in the late 1930s:

> "A frenzied gospel choir member is being fanned by a singing usher. Persons in the first few rows are jumping, yelling, and clapping."[72]

> "While the gospel song, 'Rock Me In The Cradle Of Thy Love' [Dorsey] is being sung, two persons become ecstatic, one of whom is a choir member. . . . One woman throws a pocketbook forward, and it strikes a front-seat worshipper in the head."[73]

> "[During the singing of "The Old Ship of Zion"—a Dorsey arrangement] A man in the choir shouts and suddenly jumps over the choir rail and upon the rostrum, and runs down the middle aisle into the vestibule. He then re-enters the auditorium through a side door of the vestibule and runs west into the ladies' rest room. After several minutes, he is revived and returned to the auditorium."[74]

Historian Timuel Black told the *Chicago Tribune* that because of Dorsey's choir and Austin's preaching, "people would be standing outside [Pilgrim] listening to the sermon on the megaphones because the inside was filled completely. They'd be standing near the windows peeking in."[75]

No musical program could have been more metaphorical in the transition of the sound of the African American church from restrained to enthusiastic than the December 31, 1939, Watch Night program at Pilgrim Baptist Church. The event brought the old guard and newcomers to African American sacred music together on one program, bringing to closure a decade that had witnessed a sea change in which songs would be sung, what musical accompaniment would be acceptable, and which choirs would sit behind the pastor during the Sunday-morning service.

Pilgrim was packed by patrons eager to hear the nationally famous Wings over Jordan, directed by Worth Kramer, sing spirituals as they did every Sunday morning over the CBS radio network. Alongside Wings over Jordan were Pilgrim's senior choir, directed by George Gullatt, and the gospel chorus, under Dorsey's direction. Sallie Martin and Roberta Martin each rendered a solo selection. Edward Boatner returned to Pilgrim to direct the senior choir in spirituals, and James Mundy conducted Handel's "Hallelujah Chorus." Reverend Austin's sermon was titled "A Forward Look," and at the end of the three-hour event, "blasting guns and shrieking whistles announce[d] the birth of the new year."[76]

The title of Austin's sermon could not have been more accurate. By Watch Night 1949, oratorios and classical music would be all but supplanted in many churches by the swing of gospel music. Singers and musicians predominantly from the migrant population became the oral folk authorities for a new generation.

Had Dorsey a moment to reflect on the significance of the 1939 Watch Night service, it might have seemed surreal. A decade earlier, the bluesman-turned-gospel-songwriter could not get a hearing from the pastors of Chicago's deliberative Protestant churches. Even storefront Baptist churches looked askance at his newfangled religious music. Now, on the precipice of a new decade, Dorsey was not only working alongside Chicago's black music cognoscenti; he was one of them. He went from being an audience member grateful to shake the hand of a celebrity director such as J. Wesley Jones to working alongside Jones in directing the one-thousand-voice choir for the annual American Negro Music Festivals.[77] He wrote "Does Anybody Here Know My Jesus?" for the 1937 Chicagoland Music Festival.[78]

If the Illinois Central station symbolized the coming of the migrants, the 1939 Watch Night service was their cotillion. Gospel was now on radio and available in sheet music, on records, and in programs that attracted thousands of paying patrons. Clarence Cobbs and Lucy Smith stood alongside A. Wayman Ward and Junius Austin as leaders of black Chicago. Thomas Dorsey, Sallie Martin, and Roberta Martin were celebrated church musicians. They and their migrant peers were the new voices of African American urban sacred modernity. The future was theirs.

CHAPTER 8

From Birmingham to Chicago

The Great Migration of the Gospel Quartet

Pick up four colored boys or young men anywhere and the chances are ninety out of a hundred that you will have a quartet.

James Weldon Johnson

The composer of "Lift Every Voice and Sing" may have exaggerated in his statement quoted in this epigraph, but he made a salient point: prior to the twentieth century, quartet singing was a popular and wholesome activity, especially for men, in the African American community.[1] Singing groups cultivated their sound in gathering spaces such as the barbershop, giving rise to the term "barbershop quartet."[2] Local quartets were invited to sing special numbers during church worship services and provide spiritual entertainment for church congregations.[3]

After 1870, black male quartets were invited to join professional traveling minstrel shows that, prior to the Civil War, had principally been all-white troupes performing in blackface. Further, by the 1890s, universities established to educate blacks, such as Fisk, Hampton, and Tuskegee, were organizing quartets out of their larger, mixed jubilee ensembles. The university groups possessed classical music training and sang a repertory of spirituals and secular songs in the formal Eurocentric style.[4] Among the first of the university-based quartets to record was the Dinwiddie Colored Quartette from the John A. Dix Industrial School in Dinwiddie, Virginia.[5] In 1902, Victor recorded the quartet singing six spiritual and secular songs, which it fit onto the company's one-sided seven- and ten-inch discs.[6]

The Fisk University Jubilee Quartette, however, was the most popular university quartet of the early twentieth century. John Work II organized this "second generation of Fisk Jubilee Singers," which Doug Seroff has described as "more serene and contemplative," emphasizing "proper diction and melodic precision."[7] The Fisk University Jubilee Quartette recorded many popular cylinders and discs for Columbia, Victor, and Edison that sold to both black and white consumers. Roland Hayes was a member before becoming an international opera star.

By the first decade of the twentieth century, Chicago's black community had a well-developed choral and part-singing community. Gospel music historians Lynn Abbott and Doug Seroff traced African American Chicago's rich vocal tradition to maestros such as Pedro T. Tinsley, who established the Chicago Choral Study Club in 1901 to foster the appreciation and performance of "the great choral compositions of the best masters."[8] Large ensembles, such as the Umbrian Glee Club, performed classical selections, anthems, hymns, and spirituals in churches and community auditoriums.

Quartet activity in Chicago prior to the Second World War can be divided into two distinct groups: jubilee quartets and gospel quartets. Jubilee quartets sang hymns, spirituals, and popular songs in the Eurocentric style of the Fisk University Jubilee Quartette. Gospel quartets, on the other hand, sang spirituals and newly composed gospel songs in a style influenced initially by quartet singers and trainers who migrated from the Virginia Tidewater area and Jefferson County, Alabama. Gospel music historian Kip Lornell describes the gospel quartet style as possessing a "rhythmic inventiveness, a strong sense of syncopation," accompanied by "growls, slurs and falsetto."[9]

Chicago Jubilee Quartets

Formed around 1890, the Standard Quartette was one of the first known quartets to headquarter in Chicago. Its members hailed from across the Midwest, and the group sang throughout the country, but Chicago was the quartet's base of operations.[10] Like most groups, the Standard Quartette's personnel changed over the years, but its main membership consisted of H. C. Williams, William Cottrell, Rufus L. Scott, and Ed DeMoss. DeMoss was the constant who stewarded the group's brand and sound.

The Standard Quartette was one of the first black singing groups to make commercial recordings. Its wax cylinder recordings, dating back to 1891, were essentially audio advertisements for its concerts, because they were placed in coin-operated phonographs in cities where the group was scheduled to perform.[11] In fall 1893, the Standard Quartette joined the cast of black impresario Billy McClain's *South before the War* traveling show. It was a national hit, depicting the romanticized, stereotypical vision of the antebellum South popular among whites around the turn of the century. With cast member Jessie Oliver, a white soprano, the Standard Quartette recorded songs they performed for the show, such as "My Old Kentucky Home" and "Old Folks at Home." According to early-recording historian Tim Brooks, their cylinders "may well represent the only surviving 'original cast recordings' from this popular show" and "apparently the first interracial recordings ever marketed."[12]

All told, the Standard Quartette recorded as many as thirty-two titles on cylinders between 1891 and 1897 for several enterprises, including the New York, Columbia, High Grade, and New Jersey Phonograph companies.[13] The Standard Quartette appears to have made only one cylinder in Chicago: an 1895 recording of "Swing Low, Sweet Chariot."[14] "Swing Low, Sweet Chariot" is known to have existed because it was listed in a cylinder sales catalog. The only two cylinders by the Standard Quartette that have been discovered to date, "Every Day'll Be Sunday Bye and Bye" and "Keep Movin'," were recorded around 1894 for Columbia in Washington, DC. These two performances captured a well-rehearsed a cappella group delivering crisply articulated harmonies, or "barbershop chords," in a loping rhythm. Brooks describes "Keep Movin'" as a seriocomic performance done in the style of a revival meeting.[15] "Apparently they were good sellers," he notes of the Standard Quartette's releases, "as stocks were quickly depleted."[16]

In 1898, toward the end of the Standard Quartette's popularity, Ed DeMoss was linked, at least on recordings, with the famed monologist and comedian Sam Cousins. As Cousins and DeMoss, the duo recorded both sacred and secular duets for the Berliner record company. To music historian David Giovannoni, Cousins and DeMoss recordings, such as "Poor Mourner" and "Who Broke the Lock," "exude the raucous enthusiasm of rock and roll" and presage gospel singing in their use of vocal interjections, fast-paced tempo, and polyrhythmic harmonies accentuated by banjo.[17] Indeed, these discs are strikingly different from "Every Day'll Be Sunday Bye and Bye" in their use of informal rhythmic freedom and vocal exuberance.

By the 1920s, dozens of amateur jubilee quartets sang throughout Chicago's South and West Sides for church services and musicals, political events, and occasions sponsored by a multitude of social clubs and associations. People packed churches and venues such as the Eighth Regiment Armory at Thirty-Fifth Street and Giles Avenue to hear nattily dressed male quartets sing music from the European masters, including Bach, Beethoven, Mozart, and Handel, as well as concert spirituals and compositions by black European composer Samuel Coleridge-Taylor. It also seemed as if every Chicago church of note had an in-house jubilee quartet. For example, Mount Olive Baptist had its Cross Bearing Four, and the Antioch Baptist Church made ample use of its Harmony Trio.[18] Lornell notes that churches formed their own quartets to sing for special worship services and programs, such as the pastor's or church's anniversary.[19]

The Sunset Four

Although Chicago's Pullman Porters Quartette, a jubilee quartet comprised of porters on passenger trains, debuted on radio station WBZ and made records for Paramount, the Sunset Four was the most popular Chicago-based jubilee quartet to follow the Standard Quartette.[20] The group was formed in 1923 by tenor Andy Bryant and bass William C. Buckner.[21] Buckner was with the group until 1924; in 1925, his life was cut tragically short when he was hit by a car and killed.[22] Other members were William "Hoss" Crawford, Leonard Burton, and Fred Vaughan. The Sunset Four toured and recorded prolifically in the early 1920s, singing on vaudeville and concert stages throughout the United States. A San Bernardino, California, newspaper reported that the quartet was "billed as eight hundred pounds of harmony" and "took several encores and could have taken more."[23]

Like other prewar quartets, the Sunset Four sang popular songs, such as "Carolina" and "Barnum's Steam Calliope," and spirituals, such as "Good News, Chariot's Coming," "Walk in Jerusalem Just like John," and "Wade in the Water."[24] "Barnum's Steam Calliope," an a cappella vocal imitation of a calliope, was the group's signature song. The *Greeley (CO) Tribune-Republican* called it a "genuine bit of novelty entertainment," noting that "this inimitable quartet illuminate[s] a melody with their shuffling feet, gesturing hands and the contortioning of their mobile faces."[25]

Although the Sunset Four appeared mostly in vaudeville houses, singing a mixture of popular and sacred songs, twelve of the fourteen sides they recorded in Chicago for Paramount Records between August 1924 and July 1925 were religious. On "You Must Come In at the Door," from an April 1925 session, the Sunset Four (billed as the Sunset Four Jubilee Quartette) sang bright harmonies in a call-and-response between lead and quartet, evoking the sound of their label mates, the Norfolk Jubilee Quartet, arguably the best-known recording black jubilee quartet after the Fisk group.[26] The Sunset Four's "Wade in the Water," also recorded in Chicago in April 1925, became the first commercially recorded example of this popular spiritual.[27] The men sang in

rhythmic harmony while one unidentified member interjected extemporaneous expressions such as "Amen" and "Hallelujah" in a style that borrowed as
much from the vaudeville stage as from the semi-demonstrative black church.

By 1926, the Sunset Four had taken on J. Nelson Andersen of the Georgia
Minstrels as its new bass singer.[28] A year later, Bryant died at his home in
Columbus, Ohio, after a protracted illness.[29] A newly staffed Sunset Four of
George Fugit, James Arnold, Irvie Richardson, and Robert L. Perry organized
to play the vaudeville circuit; they even performed in Honolulu for six weeks
in 1926. Nevertheless, the Sunset Four never recorded again.[30]

The Great Migration of the Gospel Quartet

The advent of gospel quartet singing in Chicago came about in the late 1920s,
when Norman McQueen, Charles Bridges, and other quartet trainers migrated
to Chicago from the South. These men introduced to Chicago groups a style of
part singing that was earthier and more vocally percussive than what jubilee
quartets were used to singing.

Gospel quartet singing had its origins in southern industrial and min-
ing centers such as Norfolk, Virginia, and Jefferson County, Alabama, which
included the cities of Birmingham and Bessemer. During Reconstruction,
men and women who earned degrees from historically black colleges, such
as Tuskegee Institute and Hampton Institute, were hired by rural schools in
the South and the Southeast to teach black youth. Both schools had celebrated
music departments, and their university-trained teachers were well versed in
the folk songs of African Americans. They taught their pupils to appreciate
the music of their shared heritage.

Vernon W. Barnett was one such instructor. A product of Tuskegee Institute,
Barnett was hired by the Charity High Industrial School in Lowndes County,
Alabama. He taught "voice culture" to his students, one of whom was R. C.
Foster. Foster later recalled that Barnett trained his class "to sing evenly, not
one higher than the others. You could hear the four voices [parts], but they
were so even that if you were sitting out there you couldn't hardly tell who
was singing what. . . . That's the way they learned it at Tuskegee." Foster also
described the quartet voicing as "one solid voice, and it sound just like a brass
band."[31] Another local quartet singer likened the closeness of the harmonies
to the sound production of a harmonica.[32]

Foster moved to Jefferson County, Alabama, in 1915 and organized the Foster
Singers, a quartet that Seroff calls "the first substantial, popular, and otherwise
significant black quartet active in Bessemer's industrial communities."[33] Foster
is considered the first quartet leader from Bessemer, Alabama. Drawing on
Barnett's tutelage, he taught three basic principles governing quality singing:

time (steady meter), harmony (chord structure), and articulation (distinct syllables, consonants, and vowels).

Service in World War I curtailed Foster's involvement with the Foster Singers, but he reorganized the group in 1919, when he returned home from active
duty. Its four members, all employees of Rick Woodward's Old Mine, were
Foster (tenor), Fletcher Fisher (baritone), Golius Grant (bass), and Norman
McQueen (lead singer).[34] McQueen sang with the Foster Singers until 1927,
when he migrated to Chicago and became the city's first, and one of its most
influential, quartet trainers.[35]

Norman McQueen

Norman "Old Man" McQueen was born March 29, 1899, in Hayneville, Alabama, and as an adult he worked in the local iron mines.[36] He married Corine,
born in Louisiana around 1902, and the couple resided in Lipscomb, Alabama.[37]

Shortly after migrating to Chicago in 1927, McQueen organized the Alabama
and Georgia Quartet. Seroff considers this group Chicago's "first important
community-based black religious quartet."[38] Besides McQueen, the members
were Davis Sorrell, Albert Fox, and Terry Austin. McQueen represented the
"Alabama" and Sorrell the "Georgia" components of the group's name.[39] The
Alabama and Georgia Quartet broadcast over WMAQ and WLS and were in
demand at quartet programs throughout the South and West Sides.[40] They did
not make any commercial recordings in their heyday, or at least none have been
discovered, but sometime in the 1950s or 1960s, Rev. Houston H. Harrington
released two Alabama and Georgia Quartet tracks on his Atomic-H label. "I
Want to Be Ready" and "He's So Good" sound as if they were dubbed from a
reel-to-reel tape recording made years earlier. Despite the audio limitations,
the disc spotlighted a finely tuned a cappella group that produced rich harmonies with a solid, confident underpinning by bass Ross Randall. The quartet
clearly operated within the Jefferson County principles of "time, harmony and
articulation," demonstrating successful tutelage by McQueen. Meanwhile, lead
vocalist W. Pratchett patterned his singing after a preacher's timing, demonstrating attentive listening to Rebert Harris of the Soul Stirrers.

Another Chicago quartet managed by McQueen during the 1930s was the
Southern Harmonizers, which included Colmon Pace, B. McAtee, Riley Chap-
pell, and Henry Redd.[41] The Southern Harmonizers and two other McQueen
groups, the Harmony Queens and the Humble Queens, appeared on Jack L.
Cooper's *All-Colored Hour* over WSBC as early as 1932.[42]

In March 1931, McQueen established the Chicago Progressive Quartet
Association, a consortium that served as a vehicle for organizing and promoting quartet programs.[43] Favorite venues for Chicago Progressive Quartet

Association programs included Mount Nebo Baptist Church at Twenty-Seventh and Dearborn, and the West Side Community Center at 1336 West Fourteenth Street.[44] Although McQueen's organization was short-lived, it gave dozens of local groups an opportunity to appear before large audiences.

McQueen and John Underwood founded the Optimistic Singers on November 6, 1932. Rev. Sterling Person joined the group in 1935 and Michael Bonaparte in 1936.[45] The Optimistic Singers appeared at churches throughout Chicago, the suburbs, and northwest Indiana, and eventually traveled throughout the Midwest. Every Sunday morning from 8:00 to 8:30 during the early to mid-1930s, the Optimistic Singers performed on the *All-Colored Hour*.[46] By 1937, the group had expanded to five members and had three weekly half-hour programs on WHFC—Sundays, Wednesdays, and Fridays at 10:30 p.m.—sponsored by South Side Fire Proof Storage.[47]

The Optimistic Singers suffered a tragic blow on September 22, 1941, when five of its members—Underwood, Person, Bonaparte, and two relatively new members, Arnett Muldrow and Eugene Wilson—were killed in an automobile accident outside Ann Arbor, Michigan. The singers were returning to Chicago from a Detroit program when their car, with Wilson at the wheel, collided with another car traveling "at a high rate of speed."[48] The impact flipped the Optimistic Singers' vehicle over. Wilson was killed instantly; the others were transported to a local hospital where they later succumbed.

McQueen, employed at the time as a janitor at Tilden Technical High School, did not participate in the fatal trip. He told the *Defender* that he had had a premonition about the journey when the brakes of his car "proved faulty during a test." "I was afraid then that something might happen, and then too, I wasn't so sure we could get back from Detroit in time for me to report to work."[49] WEDC dedicated a portion of its Sunday, September 27, morning radio time to the Optimistic Singers, filling the group's regular time slot with organ music.[50] A new Optimistic Singers was formed shortly thereafter, and the group resumed its weekly broadcasts.

McQueen remained active in the Chicago quartet community, becoming director of quartets for Jack L. Cooper Radio Presentations, which meant managing quartet programming for Cooper's many radio station customers around the city.[51] He also directed an organization called McQueen Quartettes and Society and managed and sang with the Golden Tones, a male quartet with whom he recorded one disc in 1952, for Art Sheridan's Chance label.[52]

Two other quartets influenced by the Jefferson County singing style migrated to Chicago and became the city's first professional gospel quartets with a national reputation: the Famous Blue Jay Singers of Birmingham and the Soul Stirrers of Houston.

Charles Bridges and the Famous
Blue Jay Singers of Birmingham

Like Norman McQueen, Charles Bridges (1901–89) started as a Jefferson County quartet singer and trainer and became a pivotal figure in the prewar gospel quartet movement in Chicago. Abbott and Seroff credit Bridges's commitment to quality quartet singing as "nothing less than the underpinnings of the gospel quartet singing movement."[53] During the early 1920s, Bridges sang with a relatively short-lived group called the Dolomite Jubilee Singers. Foster recalled that Bridges had the gospel feeling in his baritone voice even then. In 1925, Bridges organized the Birmingham Jubilee Quartet, the first Jefferson County quartet to gain a national reputation through touring, radio broadcasts, and professional recordings. The group, which included Bridges, Leo "Lot" Key, Dave Ausbrooks, and Ed Sherrill, was influenced by the sound of the Foster Singers.[54] Seroff cites the Birmingham Jubilee Quartet's varied and complex singing devices as preeminent examples of "much of what is great and distinctive about the Birmingham quartet style."[55] Bridges's reputation as a quartet trainer who instructed groups on the primacy of "time, harmony and articulation" can be heard on the Birmingham Jubilee Quartet's 1926 and 1927 recordings. Issued by Columbia, with its muscular distribution and superior pressing capability, these records are considered the first to expose a national audience to this regional style of quartet singing.

The Birmingham Jubilee Quartet was the ensemble to emulate but also to try to defeat at local and regional singing contests. One group that challenged the Birmingham Jubilee Quartet was the Famous Blue Jay Singers of Birmingham. Considered "the most important quartet that ever came out of Jefferson County," they were organized in 1926 by Clarence "Tooter" Parnell with thirteen-year-old Silas Steele as lead singer. Other founding members included Jimmie Hollingsworth and Charlie Beal. The Blue Jays' emotional performances, fueled by Steele's impassioned vocal delivery, as well as no small amount of showmanship, gave the group a distinct advantage over their rivals' "meticulous, classic approach."[56]

Eventually the Blue Jays were afforded national recognition through a schedule of multicity tours and recordings, including the very first record of Thomas A. Dorsey's "If You See My Savior," as "Standing at the Bedside of a Neighbor," recorded in January 1932 for Paramount.[57] Abbott and Seroff note that the quartet's Paramount disks, and particularly "Neighbor" and "Clanka A Lanka" (aka "Sleep On, Mother") "give the clearest depiction available of the historical transition from spiritual to gospel quartet mode" in part because of Steele's fiery lead singing.[58] When the Birmingham Jubilee Singers disbanded during the Depression, Bridges moved on to sing with, and teach, other quartets. He joined the Blue Jays in 1940, after the death of Tooter Parnell.

Although it retained "Birmingham" in its name, the Blue Jays moved its base of operations to Dallas. With the Kings of Harmony of Bessemer now in Houston, it seemed as if the Alabama quartet movement had migrated to Texas. By relocating, the Blue Jays and the Kings of Harmony brought Jefferson County's vocal percussion and the region's cardinal rules of singing—time, harmony, and articulation—to a new community of regional quartets. One group that learned from them was the Five Soul Stirrers of Houston.

The Five Soul Stirrers of Houston, Texas

The Soul Stirrers were not organized in Chicago, their founding members were not born in Chicago, and their first recordings were made in Texas and California. Nevertheless, the Soul Stirrers became associated with the Windy City after migrating there about a decade after being founded by teenager Senior Roy Crain.

Crain was born June 7, 1911, in San Augustine, a small East Texas town.[59] He organized the Soul Stirrers at Mount Pilgrim Baptist Church in Trinity, Texas, around 1926. The other charter members were Reed Love, Bennie Albott, and Lloyd Bailey. Later, El Connie Davis replaced Albott. According to Crain, the group earned its name when "a member of the audience came forward to compliment them on how much they had stirred his soul." The group's tight harmonies and formal dress and comportment were patterned after the Fisk University Jubilee Quartette. The original aggregation of Soul Stirrers sang together until 1930, when the Great Depression shut down Trinity's lumber mills and scattered the singers throughout the Lone Star State in search of new employment.[60]

In 1931 or 1932, Crain moved to Houston, where he found work in the rice mills.[61] There he encountered many gospel quartets, none better, in his opinion, than the New Pleasant Grove Gospel Singers, founded in 1928 by tenor Rev. Walter LeBeaux and named for the group's home church, New Pleasant Grove Baptist. When the quartet's baritone died, Crain was exactly the person the group needed to fill the harmonic void. Crain negotiated his membership under the condition that the group assume the name of his original quartet, the Soul Stirrers. They agreed to this condition, and Crain joined.[62]

The newly minted Five Soul Stirrers of Houston included LeBeaux as first tenor, Crain as utility singer, Ernest R. Rundless as second tenor, A. L. Johnson as baritone, and O. W. Thomas as bass. It was this roster that recorded for Alan Lomax on February 12, 1936. Lomax was making field recordings for the Library of Congress and captured the group singing "Lordy, Lordy," "John the

Revelator," "How Did You Feel When You Come out of the Wilderness," and Dorsey's "Standing by the Bedside of a Neighbor."[63] To Lomax, the Five Soul Stirrers sang "the most incredible polyrhythmic stuff you've ever heard."[64] Anthony Heilbut has noted that the Stirrers sounded like the early Blue Jays on these recordings, an aural indication of the Birmingham group's profound influence on the Texas aggregation.[65]

The Five Soul Stirrers came into their own during a particularly heady time for vocal harmony groups. Quartet singing was gaining ground in churches and in clubs. The Mills Brothers were delighting audiences with vocal imper-sonations of jazz instruments. The Ink Spots were dazzling with falsetto leads and high harmonies, and sacred groups were securing national reputations through radio broadcasts and recordings. In the early 1930s, the Southernaires were the first African American quartet to host a coast-to-coast network radio broadcast. Other groups to hold down regular radio broadcasts on powerful stations included the Heavenly Gospel Singers, the Golden Gate Quartet, and the Fairfield Four. The Golden Gate Quartet in particular augmented the en-tertainment quotient of gospel quartets with their infectious percussive vocal line, dapper uniforms, and audience-pleasing choreography. The Gates' jump jubilee style, which combined the Baptist moan and the intensity and drive of the Pentecostal and Holiness churches with biblical storytelling, was the product of their experience singing for congregations of many religious de-nominations. It made for an exciting aural and visual style.[66] The polyrhythmic singing, the uniforms, the traveling, the show, the adoring audiences, to say nothing of doing what they loved—singing for the Lord—gave quartets such as the Soul Stirrers newfound ambitions.

By 1937 the Stirrers had added bass singer Jesse James Farley, and they soon made another important acquisition in Rebert H. Harris. Harris was born on a Texas farm March 23, 1916, to a family of Methodist "common farmers" who were members of Harris Chapel CME. Harris said he learned to sing by listening to the warble of the birds. "I became the first male ever to sing falsetto . . . even women didn't sing falsetto in church back then."[67] Together with some of his brothers and cousins, Harris formed a singing group called the Friendly Five. After high school, Harris entered Mary Allen Seminary in Crockett, Texas, but when he was eighteen, the Soul Stirrers invited him to join. "I always did have a traveling mind," he told Heilbut, "though I want you to know that [the Soul Stirrers] had to get sole permission from my parents for me to leave the house."[68]

The Stirrers lineup of Harris, Farley, Crain, and baritones Thomas Bruster, James Medlock, and R. B. Robinson migrated to Chicago in 1937.[69] The group began adding more newly composed gospel songs to its repertory, though not without criticism. Farley told Anthony Heilbut that some "didn't think a quartet should sing church songs."[70] But the Soul Stirrers were innovators. Among the performance techniques the quartet introduced was the "switch lead," in which two strong vocalists passed lead singing responsibilities back and forth to heighten the performance's emotional pitch.[71] When Harris joined the group, he traded leads with Medlock, but when the group acquired Paul Foster from Oakland, California, the Harris-Foster combination proved more flammable because of the striking contrast between Harris's chirping falsetto and Foster's take-no-prisoners vocal vigor.

Despite any misgivings about singing gospel songs in church, the Stirrers garnered sufficient popularity by 1938 to headline a November 4 program at Olivet Baptist Church, where the guests of honor were champion prizefighter Joe Louis and his wife, Chicago-born Marva.[72] After a four-month national tour, the Stirrers returned to Chicago to sing at a March 28, 1939, program at Progressive Community Church, then headed west to California.[73]

While in California in June 1939, the Stirrers—now Harris, Crain, Farley, Mozel Franklin, and Rundless, who had returned to the group—recorded their first four commercial sides for Leroy Hurte's Bronze Records. Bronze was the second black-owned independent label in Los Angeles and a precursor to the independent record-label movement that transformed the music business after the Second World War. The quartet recorded "Freedom after Awhile," a rhythmic version of Dorsey's "Precious Lord," "He's My Rock," and "Walk Around."[74]

Originally titled "I Want Jesus to Walk around My Bedside," "Walk Around" was written by Harris in the early 1920s, and he considered it to be the first modern gospel composition. Whether or not it was the first gospel song, "Walk Around" was the finest of the four cuts and one of the best Soul Stirrers recordings of all time. It showcased a group whose vocal engine was purring at optimal performance. Harris chirped a steady, birdlike falsetto with blue yodels for accents as the quartet chanted the refrain, "Walk around, walk around," in the "clanka lanka" vocal percussion technique popular among Virginia and Alabama gospel quartets. "Walk Around" was the Five Soul Stirrers' calling card to churchgoers not exposed to the gospel-quartet style. Kenneth Morris and Lillian Bowles arranged and published the song, and the Stirrers dedicated it to Morris and Theodore Frye. Frye likely orchestrated the quartet's November 1938 appearance at Olivet Baptist Church.[75]

The Famous Blue Jays followed the Soul Stirrers north to Chicago sometime around 1941.[76] Once settled, the group recruited Nathaniel Edmonds as bass and Rev. John R. Kellum as manager. Silas Steele did not like living in Chicago, and sometime in the late 1940s or early 1950s, he moved to Memphis, where he joined the Spirit of Memphis Quartet and became the group's lead singer.[77]

Both the Soul Stirrers and the Blue Jays had regular Sunday-morning radio programs. Radio appearances cost money, but they provided greater exposure and higher status, both of which could lead to additional performing opportunities. Before phonograph record sales became the measuring stick of popularity, a regular radio broadcast was a badge of honor. Being a radio quartet separated a group from its amateur competitors. The Stirrers held down a fifteen-minute broadcast on WIND at 7:45 a.m. starting in 1940, and the Blue Jays sang over WEDC at 8:45 a.m., immediately following the Optimistic Singers, who came on at 8:30.[78] Leander Wafford—a member of the Golden Eagle Gospel Singers who joined the Blue Jays—was on WSBC at 8:00 a.m.[79] The Blue Jays later joined the Stirrers on WIND, singing from 7:15 to 7:30 a.m. on Sundays, though by mid-1944, their fifteen-minute time slot had been shifted to 8:15 a.m.[80] The Stirrers and the Blue Jays maintained their Sunday-morning broadcasts on WIND into 1946.[81]

By the Second World War, the Soul Stirrers and the Blue Jays were the most popular professional quartets headquartered in Chicago. Together, they stimulated a vibrant quartet community in the city and further fueled a national passion for gospel quartet singing.[82] Heilbut has noted that the Five Blind Boys of Mississippi and Carey Bradley of the Kings of Harmony came up to Chicago to soak up the Stirrers' style.[83] Despite the accolades, the groups needed side businesses to cover living expenses. To supplement his income when not traveling with the Blue Jays, Hollingsworth opened Blue Jay Music Studio at 3609 Cottage Grove, a record store that also served as the quartet's official headquarters.[84] According to Bridges, the studio sold records, "along with candies and peanuts and potato chips and different things."[85] The Stirrers established the Soul Stirrers Cleaning and Pressing Shop at 657 East Forty-Seventh Street, though their official headquarters in the early 1940s was at 4533 South Prairie.[86]

Other Chicago Gospel Quartets

For every Soul Stirrers or Blue Jays, there were dozens of semiprofessional and amateur quartets working in Chicago during the pre–World War II years. Church free-will offerings were insufficient to raise a family, so the groups limited their appearances to weeknights and weekends, when they could travel short distances and return to punch the time clock Monday morning. Almost nothing beyond the fact that they existed is known about most of the city's prewar amateur groups. One exception is the Windy City Four. Formed in August 1929 by J. W. Floyd, the Windy City Four never reached the height of national popularity of the Stirrers or the Blue Jays, but the quartet was popular locally and had secured a Sunday-morning radio program on WHIP by 1940.[87] They made their first records during the 1960s and 1970s. On "Deep River," the sole single from an otherwise unissued 1961 Checker album, the group sang a cappella with rich, robust bass tones, an anachronism in the era of the electric bass guitar. Original member Cornelius Worlds was still with the group in the 1970s, when they recorded *Don't Let the Devil Ride* for Sound-O-Rama's Peace label. By then, the Windy City Four had followed the lead of other gospel quartets by adding musicians to their lineup. Besides Worlds, other members at the time of the Peace Records session included manager Townzy Booker, Cleveland Ficklen, Robert Johnson, Earl Leggan, Nelson Larkins, Michael Adams, and Michael Bector.[88] The Windy City Four performed, albeit with personnel changes, into the 1980s.

Local groups relished the chance to appear on a gospel program with the Soul Stirrers or the Famous Blue Jays. Although they were not paid, the exposure was important, and it was an honor to share the spotlight with quartets they admired. By 1942, there were so many active quartets in Chicago that the Soul Stirrers organized a special program called "Quartets on Parade." The event, which included an appearance by the Roberta Martin Singers, was held March 20, 1942, in the DuSable High School auditorium, a space that became synonymous with Soul Stirrers gospel spectaculars.[89] Six months later, on September 20, Tabernacle Baptist Church held a musical for which twenty-five different quartets were scheduled to perform.[90] Chicago had quartet fever.

Female Quartets in Chicago

While the Chicago gospel quartet community was predominantly male, there were numerous female quartets in the city, including the Four Harmony Queens, the Crooning Sisters, the Golden Tone Female Quartet, the Four Loving Sisters, and the Jubilee Four Female Quartet. Norman McQueen has been credited as championing the cause of female gospel quartets in Chicago.[91] From contemporary reports, the Four Loving Sisters were more active than many other Chicago-based amateur female quartets. Members of Ebenezer Baptist Church, the Loving Sisters appeared on programs with the Windy City Four and the Soul Stirrers in the early 1940s. As of 1942–43, the Four Loving Sisters consisted of R. Johnson, J. S. Hamilton, M. Worlds, E. L. Williams, and M. Randall.[92] They remained active in the city for decades.

The Golden Harps Quartette, organized in Chicago in 1933, was one of the city's most popular prewar female quartets. The a cappella ensemble from Liberty Baptist Church hit its stride in 1940 after adding twenty-year-old Virginia migrant Jeanette Price to its roster, which included Ann Harris, Irene Williams, Betty Weathers, Lucille Henderson, and Gussie Henderson Wilson. For the next twenty years, they wrecked churches with their highly charged interplay between lead and quartet. Heilbut called Price one of the most significant female quartet singers in the history of gospel and noted her influence on Dorothy Love Coates and Mavis Staples.[93] The Golden Harps' 1951 debut on Peacock Records, especially the two-part "Any Stars in My Crown," testified to the quartet's capacity to eke every ounce of drama out of an a cappella performance. The Golden Harps and the Soul Stirrers appeared on programs together during the 1940s and 1950s. A July 7, 1946, program even pitted the two groups in a musical battle, which may have been one of the first examples of a battle of the sexes in gospel music.[94] One difference, Heilbut notes, is that while R. H. Harris sang flatfooted in place, "Jet" Harris walked the aisles while singing.[95]

The Golden Harps' popularity was such that they secured a fifteen-minute radio broadcast on WIND as early as 1948, singing at 7:05 a.m. on Sundays.[96] During their career, the group also sang over WBEE, WEAW, and WTAQ, and in 1955 took first place in a competition among gospel groups.[97] They were among the first to record "I Call Jesus My Rock," written by Virginia Davis, a prominent gospel song arranger who was Theodore Frye's assistant director at Olivet Baptist Church and principal soloist of the Chicagoland Music Festival during the 1950s and 1960s. The Harps also introduced Kenneth Morris's "Jesus Steps Right In Just When I Need Him Most" in 1945, a song the Davis Sisters of Philadelphia made popular in the 1950s. Price and R. H. Harris, by now gospel quartet royalty, married in Chicago on June 24, 1948.[98] Their marriage lasted until 1960. Sometime in the 1960s, Jeanette left the Harps to care for her four children. The Golden Harps recorded an album for Checker in 1965 and continued performing long after Harris's departure.

The Southern Echoes were another popular Chicago female quartet. The group was organized in 1937 and eight years later made Greater Harvest Baptist Church its home.[99] Members of the group over time included Annie Mae Washington, Mary Simmons, Alberta Roberson, Lucille Henderson, Hattie Boyd, Ozella Grant, Lillie Mae Williams, and Pearl Tolbert. Tolbert, whose straightforward, deliberate singing was emblematic of the era, came from El Bethel Baptist Church's a cappella group, the Illinois Spiritual Singers, which included Hattie Redman, Nellie Oden, Johnnie May Warden, and Myrtle McLain. Like the Golden Harps, the Southern Echoes also toured outside Chicago, but as part of the healing ministry of William Roberts, founder of the Universal Community Church.[100] The Southern Echoes' responsibility was to compliment Roberts's healing services by demonstrating the "healing power of spiritual and gospel songs."[101]

The Southern Echoes made their first recording in 1950 for the Gotham label, "Blessed Be the Name" / "I Want to See Jesus." "Blessed Be the Name" showcased no-nonsense gospel singing cut squarely from the Soul Stirrers–Blue Jays mold: fiery lead trading backed by harmonic and metronomic repetition of the song's title. The Echoes continued to record intermittently throughout the 1950s and early 1960s, including for Al Benson's short-lived Divine Grace imprint.[102] "Seeking for Me," from the Benson sessions but released on Checker, featured a hypnotic extended vamp that mimicked the repetitive congregational singing of the Pentecostal and Holiness churches as popularized by quartets such as the Swan Silvertones and the Dixie Hummingbirds.

By December 1941, when the United States entered the Second World War, the formal a cappella jubilee style was losing ground to the vocally percussive and emotionally demonstrative quartet style. It was the quartet sound that propelled gospel to the apex of national popularity. Along with Mahalia Jackson and Sister Rosetta Tharpe, professional quartets introduced the nation to the new gospel music and, in doing so, struck a deal with commerce that had a profound influence on gospel's future prospects.

PART TWO

Branches

CHAPTER 9

Sing a Gospel Song
The 1940s, Part One

The sermons are more political and less spiritual than they used to be. The gospel songs make up what people have lost from sermons.

Senior choir member, Chicago, late 1930s

Migration from the South continued unabated into the 1940s, with as many as two thousand African Americans moving to Chicago each month.[1] Church congregations swelled with newcomers, and the boundaries of Bronzeville extended further south, past Sixty-Third Street and deep into the Southwest and West Sides. Seeking better housing, African American families integrated formerly white neighborhoods. Physical violence and property damage met them initially. Then they watched their white neighbors disappear to other neighborhoods and the suburbs.

Likewise, gospel singers and musicians were popping up on the South and West Sides like dandelions in springtime. Like the group that assembled at Mahalia's Beauty Shop, they bonded out of a shared hunger for religious and social continuity with their southern roots. As gospel music gained a greater foothold in the church, the community expanded into a significant subculture. Providing some of the social betterment that migrants sought in coming to Chicago, the "fluid folk life" of the gospel music community offered familiarity, comfort, fellowship, an alternative diversion for young churchgoers, and, above all, spiritual satisfaction.

An indication of the ascendancy of gospel music in Chicago was rising popularity of the church-sponsored gospel musical. In the early 1930s, the musical was dominated by classical singers and musicians. A decade later, usher boards, women's clubs, choirs, and other church organizations vied to book the city's most popular gospel stars. If the sponsoring church was too small to accommodate the audience anticipated for such popular draws as the Roberta Martin Singers or Mahalia Jackson, it rented a larger church or an auditorium. Advertising a gospel program, however, meant relying to a great extent on oral communication, a folk tradition just as important in Bronzeville as in Bessemer. Although some of the more significant musical programs were advertised with flyers and placards or an announcement in the *Defender*, enthusiasts often learned about gospel artist appearances from church bulletins, radio broadcasts of church services, or word on the street.

Nevertheless, before the heyday of commercial recordings, gospel radio programs, and television shows, the church-sponsored musical was where one heard the latest gospel artists and songs. The events provided the devout with a diversion from daily duties. Attendees spent several hours in fellowship while listening to inspiring music that lifted their anxieties and emboldened them to face the coming week, and its insidious indignities, with greater resolve.

In addition to offering wholesome entertainment and spiritual uplift, gospel programs served as classrooms for emerging singers and musicians. While sheet music of the latest gospel songs was often available for sale at musical programs, gospel singers and musicians were typically self-taught. They learned to play or sing by ear and were more skilled at learning songs by attending gospel programs or listening to radio broadcasts of church services than by interpreting sheet music. This was especially true for singers and accompanists from traditions such as the Church of God in Christ, where there was no hymnbook and church music was learned by rote. Artists and audiences alike applauded a singer's distinctive vocal techniques in the same way that jazz fans marveled at the musical permutations of accomplished soloists.

Rev. Dr. Issac Whittmon, pastor of Chicago's Greater Metropolitan Church of Christ and lifetime board member of the Gospel Music Workshop of America, confirmed the value that he received from attending gospel programs. "There was no school for gospel music when I came up, so what I did was use programs for schooling. I watched everything. I was like a sponge. I watched signals. I watched how they would move from one song to the other song. I learned that when they had two mikes, the lead singer always had the best mike, and the background group circled around the other mike!"[2]

Music historian Eileen Southern has noted that a gospel pianist could develop his skills "by attending concerts of the celebrated pianists he wanted to emulate."[3] Classically trained Rev. Charles Walker, who accompanied the Fellowship Missionary Baptist Church choir in the early 1960s, told doctoral candidate Idella Lulumae Johnson what he learned by watching Willie Webb during gospel programs. "His organ playing was smooth," Walker said. "It was a beautiful style with flair and harmonically well thought out—cerebral without losing soul. . . . Whenever he played, you knew that there was a strong mind, a genius mind behind the things he did—and he did it almost effortless[ly]."[4]

Church programs and radio broadcasts thus became the first lecture halls of what would be called the Chicago School of Gospel, a music curriculum that combined the latest gospel songs and arrangements from writers such as Thomas A. Dorsey, Roberta Martin, and Kenneth Morris with performance techniques by such singers and musicians as Mahalia Jackson, Robert Anderson, DeLois Barrett Campbell, and Willie Webb.

The Fertile Field of First Church of Deliverance

One Chicago church that overflowed with gospel talent during the 1940s and 1950s was First Church of Deliverance. Every Sunday evening at 11:00, 5,000-watt WIND beamed the church's famed midnight broadcast into tens of thousands of living rooms. Because radio waves travel greater distances at night, the broadcast could be heard throughout several states. *Ebony* named Reverend Cobbs "the most popular Negro radio minister in the U.S.," estimating that as many as one million listeners nationally heard his church's weekly broadcasts.[5]

The First Church of Deliverance music department was anchored by Julia Mae Kennedy and organist Kenneth Heitz, both of whom had served the church almost from its inception.[6] Maurice E. McGehee, director of the Sharps and Flats chorus, directed First Church choirs from time to time during the early to mid-1940s.[7] The department was later fortified by "Uncle" Ralph GoodPasteur (1923–96), who had come to Chicago from Los Angeles in 1948 at the urging of Sallie Martin and organized the church's music publishing company, the only African American church in the city to have an in-house music publishing and printing enterprise. Other organists at First Church included David Weston, Joseph Henderson (of Greater Harvest Baptist Church), Charles Miller, Fred Nelson Jr., and his son, Fred Nelson III.

Many popular female gospel soloists got their start singing at First Church, most notably Myrtle Jackson, Irma Gwynn, Edna Mae Quarles, and Elizabeth Hall. Myrtle Jackson was among the first female gospel singers from First Church of Deliverance to launch a solo career. Dubbed "the singing lady from the south,"[8] Jackson came from a musically gifted family. She began singing at age eleven, and although she intended initially to focus on classical repertory, her religious roots won out.[9] She joined First Church of Deliverance and parlayed her popularity as a soloist on the midnight broadcasts into invitations to sing throughout the city, especially at other Spiritual churches. For example, during the mid-1940s, Jackson soloed on the By Way of the Cross Spiritual Church's broadcasts on WSBC and may also have directed and accompanied its radio choir.[10]

Jackson recorded twenty sides for Brunswick/Coral between 1949 and 1953, and in 1963 she released an album on Savoy Records. She wrote popular gospel songs such as "But This I Pray, Oh Lord, Remember Me" and "Christ My Hope," delivering them with polish and just the right amount of emotion. "During the time when I was coming up [the 1940s and early 1950s]," recalled Chicago gospel singer Aldrea Sanford Lenox, "you had to have that smooth, mellow, good sounding voice. Myrtle's voice was a phenomenon."[11] Jackson later entered the religious ministry, joining Bishop James L. Anderson's Redeeming Church of Christ, another Spiritual church, as assistant minister and featured soloist.

Irma Gwynn (1925–2006) also called First Church of Deliverance her church home. Like Jackson, Gwynn was capable of rendering classical as well as gospel songs. Since Cobbs appreciated cultured voices, she was an ideal soloist for First Church.[12] Gwynn was also a charter member of Robert Anderson's Good Shepherd Singers.

Although not as well known outside Chicago as Jackson and Gwynn, Edna Mae Quarles was a popular First Church soloist. Stricken with infantile paralysis that left her with a limp, Quarles was encouraged by her mother, Mary Morris, to play piano and sing.[13] Besides soloing with her vocal group, the Quarlettes, she accompanied First Church choirs from time to time. One of Quarles's signature songs was "When the Roll Is Called in Heaven." Even her young daughter Rose Mary—a gospel version of Shirley Temple—got into the act, stirring the First Church congregation and radio listeners during the early 1940s with Kenneth Morris's "Jesus Will Be with Me in My Dying Hour." During 1940 and 1941, Quarles directed the gospel choir at Rev. Keller's Beth Eden Baptist Church in Morgan Park. She was so beloved at Beth Eden that in December 1941, the congregation purchased an automobile for her.[14] By 1947, Quarles was also assisting the music department at Tabernacle Baptist Church. That same year, *Chicago Defender* reporter Marian Downer praised Quarles: "Edna Mae has latent ability that has never been tapped. From the very first time I heard her sing and play gospel songs in First Deliverance, I've been one of her most ardent admirers."[15]

Elizabeth Hall was another legendary gospel soloist from First Church of Deliverance. Like Mahalia Jackson, Hall was from New Orleans and, according to Anthony Heilbut, "had more volume and stamina than Mahalia, though she was circumscribed by the church's stringent demands."[16] Every gospel singer had at least one signature number, and for Hall, it was Anna Shepherd's "Only a Look," which became a national hit later in the decade when the Roberta Martin Singers recorded it.[17]

Not only women but also male soloists made their initial mark at First Church. R. L. Knowles, who was responsible for organizing the church's choir in the late 1920s, remained active there as a soloist. Knowles was a handsome man with a pencil mustache who resembled silver screen swashbuckler Errol Flynn. His signature selection was "Take My Hand, Precious Lord." He joined Robert Anderson in 1939 to form a singing duo. For two years, the Knowles and Anderson Singers were among the city's most popular gospel attractions. They were also sufficiently well known outside Chicago to embark on a successful tour of the West Coast, during which Anderson is reported to have secured a walk-on role as an extra in the film *Gone with the Wind*.[18]

By 1941, the two men had dismantled their group, in part because Anderson's gospel solo career was gaining traction. Born March 21, 1919, in Anguila, Mississippi, Anderson possessed a smoky baritone that earned him accolades as the "Black Bing Crosby" and made him one of the decade's most popular male gospel singers.[19] "When I used to sing, people would sit so still you could hear a pin drop," Anderson told Heilbut.[20] Anderson could also play piano and for a time served as Mahalia Jackson's road accompanist, although his tardiness drove her to bouts of apoplexy.[21] In 1943, he rejoined the Roberta Martin Singers, but when the ensemble began touring more frequently and for longer stretches, Anderson chose to remain in Chicago. He gathered Irma Gwynn and other female singers he knew from Chicago and northwest Indiana to form his background group, the Good Shepherd Singers.

While First Church of Deliverance had a robust team of soloists, it did not have the patent on gospel singers. Cora Winters Swift Ashton, whom Eugene Smith called a "charming contralto," hailed from Progressive Community Church, where her father was the pastor.[22] In the early 1940s, Swift sang over WHIP Wednesday afternoons, directed the Swift Spiritual Singers, and was a regular on local gospel programs. Although James Francis and Willie Webb were her usual accompanists, for an October 21, 1940, recital, Swift selected young Ruth Jones to accompany her.[23] Not long afterward, Jones transformed her music persona into blues vocalist Dinah Washington.[24]

Other gospel singers active during the war years included Sadie Durrah, director of the New Mount Olive Baptist Church Gospel Chorus and briefly a member of the Roberta Martin Singers.[25] Mahalia Jackson told Heilbut that Durrah had once been a vaudevillian.[26] Kenneth Woods Jr. remembered Durrah as possibly a bit older than Martin, with "beautiful, gray hair. A wonderful contralto, a good singer." Along with Viola Dickinson Bates, Durrah was part of the Bowles Singers, an ensemble organized by publisher Lillian Bowles to advertise her song catalog.[27]

A singer with great longevity, Vernon Oliver Price emerged during the 1940s and continued to sing well into the twenty-first century. She was born in Chicago on December 1, 1929. Her mother, Maudell Connor Oliver, was a singer and missionary who worked with COGIC founder and Senior Bishop C. H. Mason as well as Bishop William Roberts at Fortieth. She and her family—including sister Loretta, who also gained prominence for her commanding singing—were members of Fortieth. It was here that, at age three, Vernon was placed atop a table to sing her first public solo. She remembered: "I never sang like a kid. Everybody said I sounded like a grown woman because of the way I sang, the way the Lord gave it to me to sing."[28] Vernon joined St. Paul COGIC in 1943, when its pastor, Rev. Louis Henry Ford, invited her to sing for his church congregation. Recognizing that St. Paul would afford her more singing opportunities, she became an active member of its music department and directed its choir for many years.

Born in 1924, Princess Theodosia Stewart Asbury, better known as Princess Stewart, emerged on the gospel scene in the early 1940s and enjoyed a long and productive music career. The sightless daughter of Ethiopian lecturer Prince Kololozeeze, Stewart studied classical music and opera at the Illinois State School for the Blind in Jacksonville. After Jack L. Cooper heard her perform, he arranged for her to host a Sunday-morning radio program on WSBC. She also served as a radio announcer for other WSBC programs. Despite her handicap, Princess Stewart joined the gospel circuit and toured with Mahalia Jackson, Alex Bradford, and the Willie Webb Singers.[29] In 1946, she placed second, behind Louise Lemon of the Johnson Gospel Singers, in a citywide competition for the best singer of Dorsey's "Precious Lord."[30]

Like other gospel singers, Stewart patched together a music career by accepting several assignments. She directed the Commonwealth Community Church Choir at 18 East Garfield Boulevard and was a member of actor and musician Dorothy Herron O'Bryant's female ensemble, the Harmonettes.[31] The Harmonettes were stylish singers, their only known commercial recordings being Christmas songs for J. Mayo Williams's Ebony Records. Also like many other gospel soloists, Stewart had backup singers to accompany her.[32] According to Rev. Dr. Stanley Keeble, who was one of Stewart's accompanists, she ran her hands over the front of her musicians' clothing prior to a program to ensure they were properly dressed.

Song Battles and Candle Lighting Services

Dorsey's decision in 1936 to move gospel from the altar to the auditorium and sell tickets, rather than continue to take chances with freewill offerings, became de rigueur shortly thereafter. Admission fees to gospel concerts were typically $1.00 to $1.25 if purchased in advance from music stores or participants and

$1.25 to $1.50 if purchased at the door. The better known the artists and the bigger the venue, the greater the potential for financial profit.

Eventually, even churches charged admission fees. Touted at the time as the largest black church in the country, Rev. Dr. Louis Rawls's Tabernacle Baptist Church was also one of the largest South Side locations for paid and freewill gospel programs. According to Rev. Clay Evans, Tabernacle was "the first megachurch that would hold better than two thousand people on the South Side."[33] By the 1950s, Tabernacle's membership exceeded seven thousand.[34] In addition to Tabernacle, other venues large enough to handle bigger programs were the auditoriums at DuSable and Wendell Phillips High Schools. They were especially popular jousting grounds for quartets. Other South Side venues that seated thousands for gospel spectaculars were the Chicago Coliseum, the Eighth Regiment Armory, and Metropolitan Community Church.

Because gospel music aficionados demonstrated as much loyalty to their favorite singers and groups as sports enthusiasts did to professional athletes, promoters and sponsors began branding some programs "gospel song battles." The friendly competitions occurred between two or more quartets, groups, or singers, with the audience choosing the victor. There were so many song battles in Chicago during the 1940s and 1950s, it could have seemed to the uninitiated that the gospel community was in a perpetual civil war.

Quartets, who had staged song battles and competitions for decades, led the way in the use of this marketing strategy. The Soul Stirrers dared other quartets to compete against them regularly. They battled fellow WIND radio broadcasters the Famous Blue Jays as well as Detroit's Evangelist Singers and Flying Clouds, Los Angeles's Pilgrim Travelers, and Cleveland's Friendly Gospel Singers and Shields Brothers. On the female side, the Golden Harps took on their local rivals, the Southern Echoes.

Song battles were also staged by gospel singers and groups. On May 12, 1946, Mahalia Jackson battled her friend, Sister Rosetta Tharpe, at the Eighth Regiment Armory with the formidable Greater Harvest Radio Choir and Jackson's own St. Luke Baptist Church Choir on the program.[35] Three months later, on August 18, Jackson squared off against Roberta Martin at Tabernacle Baptist Church with Myrtle Scott, Sallie Martin, and Robert Anderson as special musical guests.[36] Some song battles pitted the sexes against each other. On July 7, 1946, R. H. Harris led his Soul Stirrers against the Golden Harps, fronted by his bride-to-be, Jeanette Price.[37] There was even a West Side versus South Side singing bout. On March 26, 1947, Tabernacle Baptist Church witnessed Mollie Mae Gates's South Side team, including James Lee and the Martin Singers (it is unclear whether this was Roberta's or Sallie's aggregation), versus Rosetta Alexander's West Side team, bolstered by the Shaw Brothers and the Gibson

Singers.[38] City battled city: on April 6, 1948, Vernon Oliver Price and her trio from St. Paul COGIC took on St. Louis's Martha Bass, though not on neutral territory: the musical scuffle was held at St. Paul.[39]

The always-innovative First Church of Deliverance upped the ante on gospel spectaculars when it organized the Candle Lighting Service and Gospel Music Festival. More than six thousand attended the inaugural Candle Lighting event at the American Giants Park September 18, 1938, where the church's choir joined soloists Myrtle Jackson, R. L. Knowles, Sallie Martin, and Edna Mae Quarles on the program.[40] The Chicago Coliseum was the venue for the fourth annual festival on November 26, 1941, and starred the church's two-hundred-voice radio choir.[41] An audience of approximately seven thousand heard the choir perform a combination of gospel and spiritual songs, including "Just a Closer Walk with Thee," "Trampin'," and "I Know the Lord Will Make a Way." Sallie Martin led the choir in "I Can't Turn Around." Kenneth Morris played the organ and directed the choir, assisted by Kenneth Heitz and Opal Moore. But despite the richness of the talent assembled for the program, R. L. Knowles was the evening's highlight performer for his rendition of "He Knows How Much I Can Bear." Not surprised, Heilbut commented that the recently introduced song "was probably the most intricate gospel ballad to date, one perfectly suited to a big band singer manqué like Knowles."[42] Interestingly, a reporter noted that "quite one-fifth of the audience was composed of white people."[43] The multicultural audience suggested that Cobbs's midnight broadcasts were popular beyond the African American community.

The Candle Lighting Service and Gospel Music Festival became a popular annual event on the Bronzeville social calendar. So many people sought to attend the festival that First Church of Deliverance moved the venue to Comiskey Park, the stadium of the Chicago White Sox baseball team, at Thirty-Fifth and Ellis Streets. Approximately twenty-five thousand were expected to attend the 1944 festival, held at Comiskey Park on Saturday, September 16, at which the Roberta Martin Singers and Mahalia Jackson were the headliners.[44] Illinois state senator Ethel Alexander, a longtime member of First Church of Deliverance, recalled one year when inclement weather threatened to cancel the outdoor Candle Lighting Service: "The rain was pouring, the heavens opened, [but] Preacher [Cobbs] told the choir to walk down on the field in the rain and pray, and it stopped raining."[45]

"She's the Empress! The Empress!"

Of all the Chicago singers appearing on weekly gospel programs, none was busier than Mahalia Jackson. When she and Dorsey were not traveling on weekends to peddle his songs, Jackson was in Chicago, singing at church programs.[46]

Denomination did not matter to Jackson. She was the living embodiment of gospel music's ecumenism and was welcomed everywhere, especially at Gammon Memorial Methodist Church on the West Side, where Robert T. Johnson, her former Johnson Singers colleague, directed the gospel chorus.[47]

A Jackson program at Morning Star Baptist Church in 1940 was especially notable for providing the singer with an unexpected coronation. As the day of the musical neared, Jackson was bereft of her usual accompanists. In a pinch, she asked Dorsey to be her pianist for the program. With Dorsey at the piano, Jackson wrecked the church with his arrangement of "The Day Is Past and Gone." Even mild-mannered Dorsey felt the spirit surge. Leaping from his piano bench, he cried out: "Mahalia Jackson's the Empress of Gospel Singers! She's the Empress! The Empress!"[48] Henceforward, Jackson was the "Empress of Gospel" and then the first "Queen of Gospel."[49]

Jackson, too, was forced to cobble together a living in the early 1940s. In addition to operating her beauty shop, she directed the choir at St. Luke Baptist Church and purchased an apartment building at 3726–3728 South Prairie, where she lived and paid the mortgage by collecting rent.[50] Later, she sold the beauty shop and started a florist service.

Things were looking up for Jackson financially, but artistically, she learned firsthand that an innocently mistaken circumstance could tarnish a gospel singer's reputation and career. In April 1944, Rosetta Tharpe was starring in a musical revue at the Regal Theater on Forty-Seventh and South Parkway. Jackson jumped at the chance to invite her famous friend to perform at a benefit musical for St. Luke Baptist Church. In gratitude for her appearance, Jackson—sporting a borrowed silver fox stole—treated the equally fashionably dressed Tharpe to dinner at Morris's Eat Shop, a popular Bronzeville dining spot on Forty-Seventh Street. A photographer snapped the women as they chatted outside the restaurant, next door to the Rhumboogie night club. When their photo appeared in the April 15, 1944, *Chicago Defender*, the headline read: "At Boogie Opening." The caption noted erroneously that the ladies "were among the first nighters of the opening of a new Rhumboogie show Thursday night."[51]

A significant mandate in the gospel music community, especially at that time, was not to "backslide," or cross over from a clean lifestyle to a sinful life, which included attending nightclubs, with their attendant drinking and suggestive floor shows. Brother John Sellers told Jackson biographer Laurraine Goreau that when that photo and caption appeared in the newspaper, Jackson "liked to fainted."[52] While Tharpe was already known to blur the line between the music of Saturday night and Sunday morning, Jackson was perceived as without blemish. Some pastors no longer wanted her to sing in their church. An erratum was printed in the following week's paper, but the rumor mill was in full swing. The damage was done.

Not all church leaders were scandalized. The first to come to Jackson's rescue, Sellers reported, was "a little old lady who pastored a Spiritualist storefront, but was on radio."[53] The "little old lady" was Rev. Mildred Barnes of By Way of the Cross Spiritual Church. Jackson was invited to sing on her radio program and chose an appropriate title: "I'm Gonna Tell God All about It When I Get Home." The song would become Jackson's first postwar single.

Goreau's biography suggests that Jackson regained her stature among the church set by going on a revival tour of the South, but the storm did not take long to pass over. Jackson was scheduled to appear at Carey Temple AME on Sunday, April 30, 1943, two weeks after the photo brouhaha. On June 4, 1943, she celebrated her eighteenth anniversary as a gospel singer at a special program held at the DuSable High School auditorium. Among the singers scheduled to appear were her friend Robert Anderson, Edna Mae Quarles, John Davis, and the Simmons Singers of Detroit.[54] Even if the Carey Temple AME program was cancelled due to the misunderstanding, and there is no indication that it was, the June 4 program demonstrated that if Jackson was barred from churches, the community of singers and musicians would rally to her side.

Popular Chicago Gospel Groups in the 1940s

Of the Chicago-based groups that plied their singing trade during and immediately after the war years, three in particular stood out: the Roberta Martin Singers, the Lux Singers, and the Gay Sisters. The Martin Singers and the Gay Sisters were considered "sweet singers," or groups that harmonized without exuberant shouting. The Lux Singers, on the other hand, were far more energetic in their gospel music performance.

The Roberta Martin Singers

Initially, Roberta Martin was the lone female member of the group that bore her name. This changed in 1939, when Bessie Folk of the Stepney Five, a female gospel group, joined Martin's troupe. "I was the shortest and the fattest in the group," Folk joked at a 1981 Smithsonian conference on Roberta Martin. "They used to call me Little Miss Five by Five. I used to get kind of peeved, you know, but then I got used to it."[55] The Roberta Martin Singers discovered Folk at a 1939 Stepney Five performance at Liberty Baptist Church. Satisfied that the young woman had vocal talent, Roberta secured approval from Folk's mother to teach her daughter the Roberta Martin Singers repertory. After a month of rehearsal, Martin took Folk to Baltimore to link up with the rest of the group, currently on tour. Folk recalled: "Miss Martin drove to Baltimore with me and Eugene [Smith], Willie Webb, Robert [Anderson] and Norsalus [McKissick] like to have died! 'Miss Martin, we don't want no girl! I'm just not going to sing.' Miss Martin said, 'I tell you this. If Bessie doesn't sing tonight, then I'm going home.' Just like that. So that's how I became the first girl of the Roberta Martin Singers."[56]

The transformation of the Roberta Martin Singers from an all-male to a mixed ensemble was so successful that in 1944, the formerly skeptical McKissick delivered another young woman to Miss Martin: seventeen-year-old Englewood High School soprano Delores Barrett.

Born March 12, 1926, Delores Barrett (her husband later encouraged her to stylize her first name as DeLois) was the seventh of ten children born to Lonnie and Susie Barrett, Mississippi migrants who had settled in the Englewood community. Six-year-old DeLois sang her first solo, "Jesus Love Bubbles Over," at Morning Star Baptist Church, where her aunt directed the choir. Young DeLois and sister Billie formed the Barrett and Hudson Singers with a cousin, Johnnie Mae Hudson. After Hudson died at the age of eighteen or nineteen, the Barretts' baby sister, Rodessa, began to sing with the ensemble, and they became the Barrett Sisters. DeLois recalled how she met Roberta Martin:

> Norsalus McKissick directed a youth chorus at Central Baptist Church on State Street on the South Side of Chicago. We had a monthly musical, and he directed the choir. I was in the choir, and he and I used to sing a duet, "Will the Lord Remember Me?" He would lead a verse, and I would lead a verse. So by him being one of the Roberta Martin Singers, he told Miss Martin to come over and hear me sing. She came, and after she heard me sing, she said that I had an unusual voice. She asked me did I want to be a Roberta Martin Singer when I finished school? And I told her yes! At Ebenezer Baptist Church, where I'd first heard the Roberta Martin Singers when I was just a teenager, I used to sit way up in the balcony, and I said I'm going to sing with that group someday. I never dreamed that I would.[57]

When Barrett graduated from Englewood High in 1944, she was ready to tour with the Roberta Martin Singers, but she needed her parents' permission:

> My dad didn't really want me to [join] because he was a very strict man. He did not want me to travel. In fact, we didn't even spend a night away from home, only when my mother was having a baby. But he became very fond of Miss Martin. She came over and asked him if I could go, and he said yes. [Martin] took me under her wing and just everywhere she went, I went. Of course, I couldn't go if Miss Martin didn't go. My dad was very strict about that, about their being boys in the group.[58]

The Roberta Martin Singers soon put Barrett in charge of starting their musical performances. Barrett recalled: "I was the youngest of the group and I had sort of like an operatic voice, a very high voice. And at that time there were a lot of churches that didn't want no clapping and no dancing like they do now. We didn't have that. So I was kind of a strict singer, stand flatfooted and sing, so [Martin] always put me up first and then Bessie, then Norsalus, then Webb, and then Eugene. Eugene was the emcee most of the time."[59]

The Roberta Martin Singers' touring schedule was an annual ritual. The group left Chicago shortly after New Year's Day to travel the country, hitting certain cities at the same time of year. For example, Palm Sunday to Easter Sunday found the ensemble at Mount Carmel Baptist Church in Philadelphia. The singers returned to Chicago in June and spent the summer performing and rehearsing in the city. Rehearsals were held around the mahogany spinet piano at Martin's studio. Then, from Labor Day to Christmas, the group returned to the road for more fixed dates.[60] Gospel historian L. Stanley Davis eagerly awaited the group's annual visit to his native Baltimore, where they would hold revival at Shiloh Baptist Church from December 26 to New Year's Eve.[61] By 1945, the Roberta Martin Singers were so popular they commanded a salary of three thousand dollars for a weeklong revival in California.[62]

Besides being a singer, songwriter, pianist, and director, Roberta Martin was also a teacher. Romance Watson told Idella Johnson: "She taught us how to breathe. . . . She taught us how to present our songs. . . . She always said, 'Be sure that you enunciate so that people will know what you're singing about along with that gorgeous voice that you have. So you can get your song across.' . . . She taught us stage presence. She just taught us everything."[63] Archie Dennis said to Johnson: "The Martin Singers taught you a way of life—how to be a Martin Singer. You were carrying her name. There were certain things you just don't do. You never smoked in public, if you smoked. . . . If you drank or tasted, you had to be sure of the person that you did it around."[64] Martin flatly declined when Eugene Smith suggested the group play the Apollo Theater in New York. She said he was welcome to organize the Eugene Smith Singers and appear at the Apollo, but her name would never appear on a theater marquee.

"Roberta Martin was one of the great artists who influenced my career," commented Rev. Harold Bailey, leader of the Harold Bailey Singers. "She was not only a woman who could play piano; she was a woman of grace. When she sat at the keyboard, you knew her feelings were going to her fingers. When she would smile, all was well."[65] Rev. Charles Walker told Idella Johnson: "I think with Roberta Martin, gospel music playing began to really crystallize its own style. When you heard Thomas Dorsey, you knew that was honky-tonk, that was the blues. But with Roberta Martin, we have the beginnings of a distinctive gospel idiom."[66] Roberta Martin transformed Dorsey's gospel music into an art form.

The Lux Singers

"Those aren't children—those are midgets!"[67] Mahalia Jackson's backhanded compliment of the energetic and mature-sounding Lux Singers was telling. The ensemble blended Pentecostal and Holiness exuberance with piano-accompanied gospel singing and performance before it became the standard in gospel music. For all their innovation, however, the Lux Singers are not as well known today because they did not make commercial recordings or have their own radio broadcast. Still, for more than a decade, the group sang in and around Chicago; was a regular guest on church radio broadcasts; appeared alongside the city's best-known gospel soloists, groups, and quartets; and even staged its own gospel music programs with headliners.

Beautician Beatrice Lux organized the Lux Singers in 1937, a year before she graduated from the Lamb School of Beauty Culture. A member of Progressive Community Church, Lux was dissatisfied with the lack of emotional content in the church's music offerings. She stole away whenever possible to sing at nearby Galilee Baptist Church, where she found the gospel music ministry more moving.

The Lux Singers consisted primarily of young vocalists. Bertha Burley Melson (b. March 4, 1933, Chicago), who joined the group as a teenager, described their performance style as "unorthodox." "Back then," she said, "Folks sang real nice and smooth and slow, like any minute they were going to fall out and die! And us, we would jump around and sing."[68] Melson recalled Florence Strutters and Margaret White as among the early members. Published reports note that the group sang every second Sunday evening at Sacred Heart Church at Forty-Seventh and State.[69] Vernon Oliver Price recalled that in the mid-1940s, when she was with the Emma Jackson Singers, they rehearsed at a studio at Forty-Third and Michigan where the Lux Singers rehearsed.[70] Melson, however, remembered rehearsals taking place at Lux's beauty salon at 5040 South Calumet, where there was a piano in the back.

Over the years, the Lux Singers included Ida Mae Davis, James Whitehurst, Imogene Greene, and Jerome Burks.[71] More than anything, however, the Lux Singers are notable for introducing two future gospel music stars: Clay Evans and James Cleveland.

Cleveland was born in Chicago on December 5, 1931, to Ben L. and Rosie Lee Brooks Cleveland. Ben was born in Macon, Georgia, and had migrated to Chicago; he eventually joined the armed forces and retired as a sergeant from the United States Army after thirty-five years of service. Rosie Lee was born in Chicago. Both encouraged their young son's musical ambitions.[72]

Cleveland's grandmother was a member of Pilgrim Baptist Church, and he accompanied her to choir rehearsals. When Thomas A. Dorsey heard the boy's clear soprano, he perched him atop a box to sing "All I Need Is Jesus" in front of the Pilgrim congregation.[73] It was Cleveland's first official church solo.

Cleveland enjoyed piano as much as he did singing and credited Roberta Martin as an early influence. Because Cleveland's parents were unable to afford a piano, James improvised creatively. "I used to practice each night right there on the windowsill. I took those wedges and crevices and made me black and white keys. And, baby, I played just like Roberta."[74]

Cleveland admired the singing of Myrtle Scott, Eugene Smith, and Robert Anderson, who would serve as one of his mentors.[75] He was also enthralled by Mahalia Jackson. As the Empress of Gospel's paperboy, he would listen at her door to catch an earful of her singing. He joined Thorne's Gospel Crusaders, a fifty-member chorus of youth between the ages of ten and fourteen, sponsored by a Mrs. Thorne who operated a music studio at 3305 South Michigan.[76]

In Cleveland's early teens, his boy soprano changed to a preacher's raspy baritone.[77] He turned to the piano and accompanied a young woman named Imogene Greene whom he met in school.[78] Floriene Watson Willis, who attended Wendell Phillips High School with Cleveland, remembered that he would play piano for the school's annual spring gospel festival.[79] Cleveland, his sister Iris, and Greene joined the Lux Singers. James sang and accompanied the group on piano. Assessing James's nascent keyboard skills, Clay Evans laughed that Cleveland "wasn't big enough to get up on the piano stool [at that time], but he had a lot of showmanship."[80]

Clay Evans was born June 23, 1925, in Brownsville, Tennessee, to Henry Clay and Estanauly Evans. He attended Woodlawn Baptist Church and sang in the church choir. The young Clay migrated to Chicago at the age of twenty-one, "looking for better opportunities." For him, that meant becoming an undertaker. "That was the most successful thing in Brownsville," he said. "There were no professional folks, doctors and lawyers and so forth." Mortuary school, however, cost a thousand dollars, and Evans acknowledged ruefully that he "didn't have a dime." He joined Tabernacle Baptist Church at Forty-First Street and Indiana Avenue and worked at the Brass Rail, a cocktail lounge downtown at 52 West Randolph.[81] It was during his Brass Rail days that Evans discovered he could sing and imagined himself as a big band vocalist. He recalled:

> Back at that time, there was [Cab] Calloway, there was Duke Ellington, there was any number of big bands that were being featured at that time, and I saw myself as being on the stage there. I even asked Lionel Hampton to play for me. I worked at the Brass Rail downtown. The Brass Rail was a cocktail lounge, and he was the band for the week. I spoke to him about an audition, because he was auditioning people, and he told me to come back, [because] he was busy then. And between there and going back, something told me not to go back. I had a voice like Cab Calloway, but the Lord had something else for me to do.[82]

Meanwhile, Evans sang with a local quartet called the Soul Revivers, as well as for Tabernacle. It was while at Tabernacle that he was invited to join the Lux Singers. "Some people hear you [singing and] say come join us," Evans recalled of the impromptu introduction.[83] It is possible the introduction occurred during a June 1946 program at Pastor P. R. Favors's COGIC Church on Thirty-Ninth Street, where the Lux Singers and Evans were guests on a gospel program.[84] Chicago's gospel singing community was so tight, it was not uncommon for singing unions to occur informally or for artists from one group to fill temporary vacancies in another group.

That Evans's voice was suited to big-band singing as well as gospel was not unusual because swing was the predominant sound of 1940s African American popular music. Heilbut has pointed out that many Chicago gospel men, such as R. L. Knowles, Jerry Bratton, James Lenox, Norsalus McKissick, and Robert Anderson, sounded like big-band vocalists, noting, "The parallels [between gospel] and jazz and light classical music are almost as significant as those with the blues, which many fans have chosen to emphasize."[85] Evans sang with the Lux Singers until 1950, when that something else the Lord had in store for him was to organize a church.

The Lux Singers' repertory included "Will the Lord Remember Me," the Blue Jays' "I'm Bound for Canaan Land," "The Lord Will Make a Way," "I'm Sealed until the Day of Redemption," Evelyn Gay's "That's What I Like about Jesus," and "By and By," written by Clay Evans while he worked at the Brass Rail: "I wrote it on a cocktail napkin, there, in the bar, early in the morning."[86] Starting slow and concluding at breakneck pace, "By and By" became one of the group's most popular songs and Melson's signature performance.[87] Melson said: "Miss Lux had a little gimmick. If she wanted to really sound good, she let James start the song, and I would finish it. And I'd sing, 'cause I like to see them shout, I love to see folks shout, and I would sing and they would shout! We would have good church!"[88]

"By and By" was so popular that the Chicago Youth Union choir sang it at the 1949 NCGCC Convention in Los Angeles, with Evans as soloist.[89] In the early 1950s, the Davis Sisters of Philadelphia recorded "By and By" in two parts, slow and fast, offering what may be the only commercially recorded example of the Lux Singers' performance "gimmick."

Lux Singer Jerome Burks (born July 14, 1933 in Chicago) recalled the group's sound as "really traditional. There wasn't any contemporary, nothing like that. Miss Lux was a traditional singer." Burks's signature song with the group was Dorothy Love Coates and the Gospel Harmonettes' energetic arrangement of "Get Away Jordan," while Ida Mae Davis was known for her version of the Angelic Gospel Singers' "Touch Me Lord Jesus."[90]

The Lux Singers were as much a mainstay of the Chicago gospel circuit as any popular singer or group of the day. For example, on October 12, 1941, they were featured in a song battle, pitched against Mahalia Jackson, the Roberta Martin Singers, and Cora Winters Swift.[91] On April 8, 1942, the Lux Singers presented Martin and her group, along with Theodore Frye, at the YMCA at

Thirty-Eighth and State.[92] On October 28, 1945, the Lux Singers were at Peter's Rock Baptist Church, down the block from the YMCA, engaged in a song battle with an equally youthful gospel group, the Gay Sisters.[93]

The Lux Singers slowed when members began going their separate ways. "You know how it is with a branch," Jerome Burks explained. "You have everybody branch out on their own, like James Cleveland. James Whitehurst went out on his own. Clay Evans went out on his own. But they all stemmed from the Lux Singers."[94]

At that point, Burks, Ida Mae Davis, and Bertha Melson joined Johneron Davis, Rev. Jerome Goodloe, and Isabel Gamble in the Haynes Singers. Burks and Goodloe also sang with Rev. Maceo Woods in the Heaven Bound Trio. Despite everything, Burks added, the Lux Singers "really never broke up. Whenever [Miss Lux] needed us, wherever we were, we would come together. We all loved her, so if she had a program, she'd get on the phone and we would come as the Lux Singers, no matter what other work we were doing."[95]

The Gay Sisters

The Gay Family of Chicago, Anthony Heilbut observes, "provides in microcosm a history of black migrants."[96] Mother Fannie Parthenia Gay and Jerry Gay migrated from Georgia and settled on Chicago's West Side. They had five surviving children, who each had a keen musical talent. Robert, the oldest son, was a gifted trumpeter and flautist who worked with such iconic jazz musicians as Dizzy Gillespie and Sonny Rollins. Evelyn was a contralto who, like DeLois Barrett Campbell and Hulah Gene Dunklin Hurley of Detroit, had the capacity to add coloratura passages to her performances. Mildred and Geraldine sang in, and Geraldine accompanied, Mother Gay's choir at Elder P. R. Favors's Church of God in Christ on the West Side. Youngest brother Donald developed a baritone that, like Clay Evans, would have been welcome in any jazz band of the era—Heilbut contends that he would later be compared to jazz singer Joe Williams—but his knack for oratory as early as age three earned him the sobriquet "Boy Preacher." At age six, he became the first African American child to be a successful contestant on Joe Kelly's popular *Quiz Kids* television program.[97]

In addition to her directing skills, Mother Fannie Gay was, like Katie Bell Nubin, a sought-after evangelist. Someone in need of prayer and divine intercession simply sent for Mother Gay. Mahalia Jackson relied on Mother Gay's wisdom and prayer, especially in 1952, when she was invited to tour Europe for the first time but was so ill she did not think she could fulfill the engagement. At this and other times, Mother Gay prayed with, or over, Jackson, and the Queen of Gospel would emerge reinvigorated.[98]

While Evelyn took piano lessons and could read and write music, it was baby sister Geraldine who was the most gifted pianist. Geraldine suspected Nubin had something to do with this in utero:

> [Mother Bell] came to the church where we lived, over on the West Side. At the time, she didn't have a place to lay her head. My dad told my mother, "Get Mother Bell and bring her home with you, Fannie." She brought Mother Bell home to live with us. My mother was expecting me at the time, and she said, "Mother Bell, would you please pray for me that I'll have a gifted child like Rosetta?" [Mother Bell] said, "Oh, Mother Gay, I'll be very happy to pray for you." She put her hand on her stomach, she laid hands on her and prayed that the child that would be born would be gifted.[99]

Geraldine's talent at a young age seemed to confirm Mother Bell's prophesy. "Evelyn would be playing the piano, taking lessons from a little lady named Mrs. Clark," Geraldine said. "I would listen to [Evelyn] play the piano and every song that she played, I would be able to sit down at the piano and play."[100] Geraldine's teachers at St. Joseph Catholic Elementary School wanted to send her to Julliard to study music, but the family decided against it. Eventually both Evelyn and Geraldine joined the ranks of the city's go-to gospel accompanists. Said Donald: "One of the great things about Evelyn and Geraldine, they could play for anybody. They could hear you talk and they knew what key you sang in."[101]

Elder Lucy Smith of All Nations Pentecostal Church was among the Gay Family's circle of friends and acquaintances. Mildred and Evelyn sang with Elder Smith's granddaughter, Little Lucy Smith, in the All Nations church choir. Through Fannie's intercession, six-year-old Geraldine made her public debut as a pianist in front of the All Nations congregation during one of its Sunday evening radio broadcasts over WCFL. Geraldine recalled: "The people were elated to see such a little girl play the piano. [They] were screaming and hollering . . . and scared me to death! I looked and saw where my father was, and I got down off of the stool and ran into my dad's arms, because I was frightened! Why wouldn't I be frightened? I was only six!"[102]

Mildred, Evelyn, and Geraldine formed a gospel group called the Gay Sisters.[103] Donald called the Gay Sisters "the first authentic sister group to originate from the Church of God in Christ."[104] Their tight harmonies, stage presence, classy outfits, and elegantly coiffed hair and sophistication defied the prevailing stereotype of the sanctified singer. Commented Donald: "The Holiness Church was thought of as people, when you said 'holy rollers,' [that meant] uncultured, no dignity, kind of rough around the edges. But here's a sister group that was polished, they had a presence, they could walk, they could talk, they could tell you their names, addresses, things of that sort! And they had come from a solid family, and they were from the Holiness church."[105]

Evelyn composed and arranged the songs, Mildred was the featured vocalist, and Geraldine—nicknamed the "Erroll Garner of Gospel" for her fluid and distinctively jazz-influenced style of piano—accompanied.[106] Evelyn called Geraldine "Miss Intro" for her ability to write the ideal keyboard introduction to a new song. "[Evelyn] said I could give a song an intro and the intro was actually the part that sold the song," said Geraldine.[107]

In 1946, the Gay Sisters toured New York and New Jersey.[108] While in Brooklyn, the trio met J. Earle Hines, popular vocalist for the National Baptist Convention and leader of the convention's Goodwill Singers. He encouraged the sisters to move to Los Angeles, where he was working with the Echoes of Eden Choir at St. Paul Baptist Church. While they did not relocate to the West Coast, the Gay Sisters, with Mother Gay as chaperone, did attend the Baptist Alliance and Ministerial Alliance meetings in Los Angeles, where they were regularly asked to minister in song. While in town, they met John Dolphin, music store proprietor and owner of the Dolphin's of Hollywood label. In 1949, Dolphin issued the Roberta Martin Singers' independently recorded "Jesus" and "Only a Look" to meet the demand for the group's records during its visits to Los Angeles. Perhaps he saw the same opportunity with this other Chicago-based gospel group, because in 1950 the Gay Sisters cut their first record, "Old Rugged Cross" and "Have a Little Talk with Jesus." Although the Dolphin's disc sold poorly, a Gay Sisters' release for another label the following year would make them the darlings of the national gospel circuit.

As the number of gospel singers crisscrossing the country increased, so did the demand for new songs as well as interest in professionally publishing one's own musical handiwork. Until 1940, however, there were very few publishers of gospel sheet music. Bronzeville, already a pioneer in the gospel chorus movement, would lead the way once more, this time as the nation's fertile crescent of gospel music publishing.

CHAPTER 10

"If It's in Music—
We Have It"

The Fertile Crescent of
Gospel Music Publishing

In the 1930s, gospel singers, groups, quartets, and choirs plied their trade singing Dorsey songs, using *Gospel Pearls*, and rendering spirituals, hymns, and nineteenth-century revival songs that were arranged, or "gospelized." Charles Pace and Lillian Bowles were the city's only music publishers, besides Dorsey, who handled sheet music of gospel songs in the 1930s. Since Dorsey published his own work, Pace and Bowles published the songs of other gospel composers and arrangers. Then Pace moved to Pittsburgh in 1936, leaving Bowles and Dorsey to satisfy the demand for gospel sheet music in Chicago.

As gospel music became more accepted in the church, the demand for new songs and arrangements increased. If the gospelization of spirituals and hymns represented the 1930s—Dorsey originals notwithstanding—the 1940s represented a renaissance of more-sophisticated gospel songwriting. The new songs were prayers and sermonettes set to music, sung with piano or organ accompaniment, and delivered with a preacher's force and conviction or a poor pilgrim's supplication. The song structure of verse and chorus was borrowed from the standard hymn, but the vernacular lyrics spoke the language and articulated the worldview of disenfranchised African Americans throughout the nation.

By writing, publishing, and performing the new songs, Dorsey, Roberta Martin, Theodore Frye, Kenneth Morris, and Sallie Martin established what historians call the Chicago School of Gospel. Together, they transformed Bronzeville into the "fertile crescent" of gospel sheet music publishing, sales, and distribution for the entire nation. The substance and style of their compositions became the benchmark for gospel music in what Anthony Heilbut has termed its Golden Age: 1945 to 1960.[1]

Thomas A. Dorsey: "Songs That Carry a Message"

From 1932 to 1939, Dorsey worked through the emotional pain of losing his wife and infant son by writing songs, directing the one-hundred-voice Pilgrim Baptist Church Gospel Choir, and pouring energy into expanding the National Convention of Gospel Choirs and Choruses.[2] He also organized the Thomas A. Dorsey Gospel Singers, an ensemble consisting of Solomon Green (bass), Cecelia Mason (soprano), Ernest Brown (baritone), Gayle Little (lyric soprano), and Bertha Armstrong (contralto). Armstrong was the veteran, having been a member of Dorsey's University Radio Singers who sang over WCFL during the 1930s.[3]

In terms of gospel songwriting, it was the beginning of Dorsey's most creative and inspired period. A number of his compositions during these eight years became gospel standards: "Take My Hand, Precious Lord" (1932), "Watching and Waiting" (1935), "My Desire" (1937), "I'm Just a Sinner Saved by Grace" (1937), "I'll Tell It Wherever I Go" (1938), "It Is Thy Servant's Prayer, Amen" (1938), "Jesus Is the Light of the World" (1938), "There'll Be Peace in the Valley for Me" (1939), "Hide Me in Thy Bosom" (1939), "Remember Me" (1939), "Today" (1939), and "When I've Done My Best" (1939).

The 1940s found Dorsey implementing his long-held dream to establish a school and home for gospel singers. In late 1945, he purchased a twenty-six-room house at 4048 South Lake Park Avenue for twenty-two thousand dollars. The mortgage burning took a year of fund-raising and was assisted greatly by a four-thousand-dollar contribution from Kenneth Morris.[4] At the 1946 NCGCC convention in Chicago, Dorsey proclaimed that the organization would take occupancy of the home in the coming year, though the facility did not open until April 1948.[5] The official grand opening occurred in October 1949. The Gospel Singers Home and School was a meeting place for gospel singers but also a South Side community center in the manner of the Poro Beauty School, offering rental space for "teas, recitals, weddings, and club meetings."[6]

Among the better-known gospel songs that Dorsey wrote or copyrighted in the early 1940s were more soon-to-be gospel chestnuts: "Walking Up the King's Highway (1940), "Someday Somewhere" (1941), "I'm Going to Live the Life I Sing about in My Song" (1941), "I Don't Know Why I Have to Cry Sometime"

(1942), "If We Never Needed the Lord Before, We Sure Do Need Him Now" (1943), and "The Lord Will Make a Way Somehow" (1943).[7]

As a songwriter, observes Horace Clarence Boyer, Dorsey "was able to take the anxieties, joys, and aspirations of the poor, rejected, and often uneducated African American population and express them in lyrics that not only captured the very essence of the Christian movement but also spoke for each Christian as if he or she were making a personal statement."[8] Dorsey biographer Ruth Smith writes that his gospel compositions "went not above the people but into their hearts."[9] Indeed, the messages of Dorsey's songs were so memorable that some titles became part of the church lexicon. For example, commenting on the war, segregation, lynching, poor housing, or unemployment, someone could sum up his feelings by quoting a Dorsey song title: "If we never needed the Lord before, we sure do need him now" or "The Lord will make a way somehow." A church member could respond to a greeting of "How are you?" with "I'm just a sinner saved by grace."

Dorsey's melodies were as accessible as his lyrics. A church musician with only a rudimentary understanding of music could interpret his arrangements without difficulty. The key signature was within the singing range of the average soloist or chorister. He sometimes employed a 2/4 beat, or stomp, a traditional jazz technique that Mahalia Jackson used on up-tempo songs, such as "Power of the Holy Ghost." In other instances, he recalled his experience with ragtime syncopation, and yet other times injected the "gospel waltz" or "rocking chair" tempo of 12/8. Boyer pointed out that in the latter instance, Dorsey taught choirs the songs in 4/4 but played them in 12/8.[10] Dorsey's rhythms tended to evoke the "natural flow of African American speech," and the 12/8 tempo became as linked to gospel music as the Hammond Organ and the Leslie speaker.[11]

Although gospel songwriters such as Dorsey were profiting on sheet music sales, they were missing out on royalties from public performances of their songs or placement on phonograph records, called mechanical royalties. Music publishing brothers Julian and Jean Aberbach of Hill and Range Songs noticed this and in February 1951 persuaded Dorsey to let their company promote and administer three of his most important compositions, "How about You," "Want to Go to Heaven When I Die," and "Take My Hand, Precious Lord." Later, he allowed Hill and Range to handle more of his works, including "Peace in the Valley," which, like "Precious Lord," was popular with black and white audiences. The royalties Dorsey realized as a result of this partnership were reportedly the first he had ever earned.[12] It was another example of gospel music's growth from a religious expression of the migrant experience into a commercial enterprise with vast potential.

The Roberta Martin Studio of Music

Roberta Martin joined Dorsey and Bowles by starting her own music publishing studio in 1938. She opened her business in the basement of her home at 432 Bowen Avenue and subsequently rented a storefront at 69 East Forty-Third.[13] Martin's mission was to publish and print songs that the Roberta Martin Singers performed. These included her own compositions and arrangements and expanded to include early works by Lucy Smith (Matthews), Willie Webb, Alex Bradford, and James Cleveland. Among Martin's first self-published pieces were arrangements of "In That Great Get'n Up Morning Fare You Well," as sung by the Ebenezer Baptist Church Gospel Chorus, and "When We Get Over Yonder," a revival song with the steady rock of a spiritual cowritten with Johnnie Rogers and dedicated to Bishop William Roberts and Fortieth COGIC. Four early releases from the Roberta Martin Studio of Music remained in the group's repertory throughout its tenure: "God's Amazing Grace" (1938), reworkings of the spiritual "Didn't It Rain" (1939) and "The Unclouded Day" (1942), and a gospel blues, "I Know the Lord Will Make a Way, Oh Yes He Will" (1941).[14]

In 1944, Martin set the music to Myrtle Jackson's lyrics for "But This I Pray, Oh Lord, Remember Me," an early hit for the Soul Stirrers. She also added music to "Each Day (I Grow a Little Nearer)," a 1948 composition by Louise King that became Sister Wynona Carr's first disc in 1949. Martin used the pseudonym Faye Brown for songs she published for which the composer did not want credit, such as "I'm Just Waiting on the Lord."[15] Like Dorsey's songs, Martin's music was accessible to anyone, regardless of musical ability. She also made her music affordable, especially for churches that needed a hundred or more copies to teach their choirs.[16]

On December 30, 1947, a month after the Roberta Martin Singers held their anniversary program in the Chicago Coliseum, before ten thousand fans, Martin married Leonard Austin in a private ceremony in her home at Fifty-Fourth and Michigan Avenue.[17] Austin was the trumpeter for All Nations Pentecostal Church and Little Lucy's stepfather. The Austins adopted a son, Leonard "Sonny," and by 1948, Martin had left the road to raise her son and focus on her publishing business.[18] She put Eugene Smith in charge of national booking and touring.

Martin's steadfast belief that gospel music and the secular world should not mix, best exemplified by her unwillingness to allow the Roberta Martin Singers to appear at the Apollo Theater in New York, extended also to her song compositions. Sonny recalled that one day before he turned sixteen, "somebody came to [Roberta] to buy [her publishing company], and they offered her fifty thousand dollars. At that time, fifty thousand dollars was probably the equivalent today to somewhere like two million dollars. [She told me] 'I'm not going to do it, I'm not going to do it, because they'll take my music and they'll have it in taverns and juke joints and all the places that I don't want it.'"[19]

Theodore R. Frye Publishers

Theodore Frye's experience composing and arranging gospel songs in the 1930s, notably "There's a Great Change in Me" and "Talk about a Chile That Do Love Jesus" (with Roberta Martin), led him to hang his publishing shingle at 1507 East Fifty-Fifth Street in the early 1940s. His influence as organizer of the one-thousand-voice National Baptist Convention mass choir and cofounder and president of the National Baptist Convention's Music Convention enabled him to compile and publish a series of song folios titled *Frye's Echoes*. However, his best-known work was a 1947 revision and arrangement of the Coleman Brothers' "I'm Going to Walk That Milky White Way," recorded by several artists, from the CBS Trumpeteers to Elvis Presley.[20]

Theodore R. Frye Publishers was aided greatly by Virginia Davis, assistant director of the Olivet gospel chorus starting in 1942 who was promoted to choir director in 1948.[21] She also served as one of Frye's assistant directors of the one-thousand-voice National Baptist Convention choir in 1943. Davis not only was a talented choir director, but she also could write and arrange music. Her best-known works included "He Knows the Depths of My Soul" (1946), "He's So Wonderful" (1952), and "I Have a Friend above All Others" (1946), but none became as instantly popular as "I Call Him Jesus, My Rock" (1950). The up-tempo composition was an instant hit with the gospel music community and recorded soon after its introduction by the Golden Harps, Myrtle Jackson, the Swan Silvertones, and the Sensational Nightingales. Dedicated to songwriter Sylvia Boddie, wife of Pastor Louis Boddie of Greater Harvest Baptist Church, "I Call Him Jesus, My Rock" became Greater Harvest's motto.

As a lyric soprano, Davis "electrified the [1943] National Baptist Convention musicale" with her performance.[22] Frye and Davis appeared together in a June 1945 preconvention musical called *Rolling Along in Negro Song* for the National Baptist Sunday School and Baptist Training Union Congress confab in St. Louis.[23] Her Virginia Davis Singers, including Marion Fornby, Natie Jones, Fannie McGru, and Ester Goodman, appeared on gospel music programs into the 1950s and even toured the South. In 1948, Davis married Edgar L. Marshall of Boston, and by 1949 she had joined the staff of the National University of Music as an instructor "in interpretation of gospel songs and spirituals."[24] In 1950, Davis resigned her position at Olivet to serve as music director for Chicago's Second Timothy Baptist Church and was a featured soloist at the annual Chicagoland Music Festival.[25]

"If It's In Music—We Have It":
The Martin and Morris Music Studio

Of all the publishing entities sprouting up in Bronzeville, the Martin and Morris Music Studio was the most successful and longest lived. It evolved from the dissolution of two publishing partnerships—Thomas Dorsey and Sallie Martin, and Lillian Bowles and Kenneth Morris. Martin, an indefatigable manager and saleswoman for Dorsey, was angered at what she perceived to be his unwillingness to acknowledge publicly her contributions to the success of his enterprise. The conflict ended with Martin resigning from the Thomas A. Dorsey Publishing Company. The two maintained a cordial and professional relationship for decades through their mutual association with the NCGCC, but Martin would never work for Dorsey again. She would not need to. As her own boss, Sallie Martin became one of the most financially successful African American businesswomen of her generation.

Sometime just before or after the split with Dorsey, Martin told Reverend Cobbs, whose First Church of Deliverance she attended and in whose radio choir she was a member, about her idea to open a music studio. She reasoned accurately that the demand for gospel sheet music was greater than the current publishers could supply, but she needed someone who could write and transcribe music. Cobbs had the perfect solution: Kenneth Morris, who since 1937 had been First Church's organist and assistant in the music department. He had experience in the publishing business through his tenure with Bowles, but he had become increasingly unhappy about his pay. Matchmaker Cobbs brought the two together.[26]

Funding was another stumbling block. According to one report, all Sallie could contribute to the business was thirty-five dollars and her car.[27] Cobbs came to the rescue again. He had just finished building a brand-new church for fifty thousand dollars, but money continued to flow into First Church coffers, due largely to the popularity of the weekly midnight broadcast. He gave Martin and Morris the seed money to start their business.[28] In 1940, they rented a storefront at 4315 South Indiana Avenue, two blocks east of First Church. Eventually, the studio moved to the other side of Indiana Avenue at 4312–4314. The business's original name, Martin and Morris Music Studio Teaching School, was later shortened to Martin and Morris Music Studio. A sign that hung in the front window said it all: "If It's In Music—We Have It."

Sallie Martin's job description was much the same as it was with Dorsey. She demonstrated and sold the studio's catalog of songs locally, regionally, and nationally. When someone asked Martin about publishing, she referred them to Morris, who handled the management, retail, and publishing side of the enterprise.

The fledgling enterprise began generating orders in its first week of operation, using Rayner, Dalheim and Company, at 2801 West Forty-Seventh Street,
to print its music. According to company ledgers, Roberta Martin was Martin
and Morris's first customer.[29] Other early customers included associates, such
as Willie Mae Ford Smith, Beatrice Brown, Emma Jackson, Clarence E. Hatcher,
Rev. A. A. Peters, A. B. Windom, and Henri Lawson. Martin and Morris even
received orders from the influential E. W. D. Isaacs of the National Baptist
Convention Publishing Board.[30] Business records further indicate that Dorsey,
Bowles, Roberta Martin, and Charles Pace sold their sheet music through
Martin and Morris's retail store.

Martin and Morris was ideally located. Churches of all sizes bracketed
Indiana Avenue from one end of Bronzeville to the other. Other busy avenues
with churches, such as State, Michigan, Cottage Grove, and South Parkway,
were a quick streetcar ride away. The store became as much a gathering place
for gospel singers and musicians as Mahalia Jackson's beauty salon. Martin
and Morris stayed open late to accommodate the flow of gospel enthusiasts
seeking sheet music copies of the songs just performed at gospel musicals and
on late-night broadcasts. According to ethnographer Richard Waterman, by
1951, even South Side churches were selling gospel sheet music in their en-
tranceways to make it easier for patrons of services and musicals to purchase
it as they exited.[31]

The two also took a page from Dorsey and Roberta Martin's playbooks and
assembled a singing group to demonstrate their catalog aurally. The Martin
and Morris Singers, sometimes known as the Sallie Martin Gospel Singers,
was organized in 1940. At one time or another, the group consisted of Martin, Dorothy Simmons, Sarah Daniels, Cora Brewer (whom Sallie would later
adopt), Charlie Mae Lomax, Julia Mae Smith, and, intermittently until 1943,
Ruth (Dinah Washington) Jones on piano.[32] During a visit to California, the
Martin and Morris Singers recorded four known sides for the Bronze label, the
same imprint that had released the Soul Stirrers' first commercial recordings.
Of the four cuts, one was an old standard, "Traveling on the Jericho Road,"
while "Must Be Jesus' Love Divine" and "I'm Walking with My Jesus" were
Kenneth Morris compositions.[33] Just as Roberta Martin recorded her singers
on her private label, the Martin and Morris Singers released at least two cuts
on their own Martin and Morris imprint: "I'm Going to Bury Myself in Jesus'
Arms" and "Joy in My Soul."

In 1941, Sallie Martin established a Martin and Morris branch in Los Angeles and began traveling between the West Coast and her Chicago home at
409 East Oakwood Boulevard. Los Angeles singer-songwriter Doris Akers was
an early client of the West Coast office. By the decade's end, Martin had made
the West Coast her second home. There she managed the company's branch

office and assisted former Chicago minister Rev. J. H. Branham in establishing a gospel radio choir for St. Paul Baptist Church, where he was pastor.[34]

Martin and Morris developed such a strong reputation in the gospel community that songwriters—amateur and professional alike—approached them about publishing and selling their compositions. The Martin and Morris Songwriters Service was born.[35]

The Songwriters Service was as egalitarian as Dorsey's gospel choruses. For twenty dollars, anyone could hire Kenneth Morris to set a song poem (lyric) to music, score it, and print five hundred copies in the sheet music industry's standard octavo, or ten by seven inch, format. Clients ordering a double-sheet copy could have a photo on the front cover. Martin and Morris typically printed one thousand copies of each scored piece: five hundred for the client, who could sell the inventory at a markup, and five hundred to sell at the retail store or through the nationwide network of sales representatives. During the 1940s and 1950s, five thousand to ten thousand of Martin and Morris's most popular sellers were printed and sold in Chicago, Los Angeles, and via 326 music agents spread throughout the country.[36]

Morris wrote a staggering number of melodies for song poems. Sometimes his workload was so overwhelming that the lag time for setting a new text might run two months or more. If he was booked, Morris referred business to Dorsey.[37] But for an amateur lyricist to have a song poem distributed by Martin and Morris, with Kenneth Morris as cowriter or arranger, was the equivalent of an amateur pop songwriter having a Tin Pan Alley specialist set his poem to music. On the other hand, it benefited Martin and Morris to retain partial ownership of any gospel song with the potential to be successful. Compositions that Morris felt held great promise or sold well were candidates for inclusion in a Martin and Morris song folio, modeled after the booklets that Morris developed for Lillian Bowles.

Martin and Morris song folios, each with as many as sixty-four pages, offered examples of the most popular gospel tunes of the day. The company even created entire folios dedicated to artists such as the Soul Stirrers, the Caravans, the Argo Singers, Brother Joe May, and the Pilgrim Travelers, who sang material from its catalog. Morris recalled that, all told, the studio's annual revenues went from between $70,000 and $100,000 in its first few years to as high as $200,000 at the company's peak period of 1944–54.[38]

In addition to working with amateur songwriters, Morris also assisted Rev. William H. Brewster, pastor of East Trigg Baptist Church in Memphis, who was a professional songwriter at the level of Lucie Campbell or Thomas Dorsey. Among Brewster's most popular compositions were "Let Us All Go Back to the Old Land Mark," "Surely God Is Able," "How I Got Over," and "Move On Up a Little Higher." Morris listened to a member of the Brewsteraires ensemble sing a song, transcribed what he heard, and arranged it later.[39] A letter from Brewster to Morris, dated September 28, 1945, suggests that Morris had an ongoing engagement to score music for the Memphian.[40]

Kenneth Morris: The Dean of Gospel Songwriters

Kenneth Morris wrote and published approximately three hundred compositions in his lifetime. The volume, quality, and consistency of Morris's output place him in the company of such gospel songwriters as Campbell, Dorsey, Charles Tindley, and Charles Price Jones. Morris's words transformed African American working-class expressions of sorrow and joy, humiliation and victory, and frustration and hope into works of art with rhythm and melody. In their lyric as well as in their musical and performance context, his songs expressed the emotions of a people struggling under the weight of poverty, Jim Crow, disenfranchisement, lynching, Ku Klux Klan terrorism, and stereotyped depictions on radio, film, and advertising.

Morris's first published gospel song was "Heaven Bells" (1937), which he wrote for the First Church of Deliverance choir. The song that earned him national attention, however, was "I'll Be a Servant for the Lord" (1940) because it was sung by the Wings over Jordan Choir, who broadcast coast-to-coast over the CBS radio network every Sunday morning.[41]

Boyer wrote that the popularity of Morris's songs was due in part to the songwriter's penchant for crafting lyrics in the problem-resolution style. That is, Morris stated the earthly problem or challenge in the first part of the verse and resolved it either in the second part or in the chorus. He introduced the resolution with a literal or inferred "but," meaning that no matter what the challenges were, a steadfast reliance on divine intervention, or faith and hope in a loving God, would solve them. For example, his "Yes, God Is Real" (1944) contains the verse:

> *There are some things I may not know*
> *There are some places I can't go.*
> *But I am sure of this one thing*
> *My God is real, for I can feel him deep in my soul.*[42]

In a stanza, Morris expresses frustration with discrimination and confirmed a faith in God that was greater than any earthly challenge. Similarly, in "Christ Is All," Morris states:

> *I don't possess houses or lands, fine clothes or jewelry,*
> *Sorrows and cares in this old world my lot seems to be.*

But I have a Christ who paid the price way back on Calv'ry,

And Christ is all, all and all this world to me.[43]

Some of Morris's lyrics were inspired by his recovery from a devastating illness, possibly his mid-1930s bout with tuberculosis. About "He's a Friend of Mine," Morris states, "While I was invalided in my bed, my friends' visits became less frequent and they disappeared one by one; but I had this consolation, I had a friend who wouldn't forsake me and whenever I was lonesome I could call on Him and He never failed to hear my cry."[44] Similarly, about his 1943 composition "Does Jesus Care," Morris recalls, "Often, as I lay on my bed of affliction, I wondered whether the Lord hadn't forgotten me and I asked myself, 'Does Jesus really care?'"[45] "My Life Will Be Sweeter Someday" was a song of hope after "the doctors had just pronounced [him] 'incurable' and didn't give [him] long to live."[46]

Like Dorsey, Morris wrote with a keen understanding of the technical limitations of the singers and musicians who were his customers. He set songs in keys that were closer to a speaking tone and therefore easier to sing. He used simple melodies and arrangements that could be performed by artists with little or no ability to sight-read and interpret complex harmonies or lyric lines.[47]

As is customary in gospel music, Morris also sought inspiration from the Bible. For example, in "Eyes Have Not Seen," Morris placed the premise of 1 Corinthians 2:9 ("Eye has not seen, nor ear heard, nor have entered into the heart of man the things which God has prepared for those who love him") into a workingman's vocabulary:

When those around you prosper

Even though they are in the wrong;

Why must you be discouraged?

Why must you be alarmed?

You don't have to worry,

Just remain steadfast and true;

Eyes have not seen, ears have not heard

What the Lord has in store for you.

That Morris's compositions are still sung today is a testament to their timelessness and universality. Among the more popular titles Morris wrote and/or copyrighted during the war years were "I'll Be a Servant for the Lord" (1940), "I'll Let Nothing Separate Me from His Love" (1940), "My Life Will Be Sweeter Someday" (1940), "I Can Put My Trust in Jesus" (1941), "He's a Burden Bearer, Yes I Know" (1942), "If I Can Just Make It In" (1942), "Is It Well with Your Soul?"

(1944), "King Jesus Will Roll All Burdens Away" (1944), "Does Jesus Care?" (1944), "Yes God Is Real" (1944), "I Must Tell Jesus" (1944), "Eyes Have Not Seen" (1945), and "Jesus Steps Right In Just When I Need Him Most" (1945).

"Just a Closer Walk with Thee"

The song that literally put Martin and Morris "on the map" was "Just a Closer Walk with Thee."[48] There are several versions of how the company became the first to publish one of the world's most beloved gospel hymns. In a 1987 interview, Morris told gospel historian Bernice Johnson Reagon that he had heard a choir sing the song when he was in Kansas City for a conference. Morris asked the choir director, William R. Hurse, where he had originally learned it. Hurse said he had heard the song his entire life. Believing it to be a plantation melody or spiritual, Morris brought the song back to Chicago and arranged and printed it.[49]

A second variation, related by Horace Clarence Boyer, is that Morris was aboard a train from Kansas City to Chicago when he heard a railroad porter singing "Just a Closer Walk with Thee." Morris was so enchanted by the song that he hopped off the train at the next stop and boarded another train to return to the station where he had heard the song. He found the porter, asked him to sing the song again, jotted down the words and melody, added a few lines of his own, and published it.[50]

Yet another version of the story places Morris nowhere near the scene. Eugene Smith insisted that Robert Anderson and R. L. Knowles heard "Just a Closer Walk with Thee" while in Kansas City during their 1939 western singing tour and brought it to Morris for publication.[51] The original published sheet music offers no clues and in fact complicates matters. The song was published as dedicated to William Hurse and to Anderson and Knowles "upon their return from California."[52]

Morris admitted to Reagon that the firm ultimately lost the rights to the song because it was careless in registering the copyright. Although the song sheet carried a 1940 copyright notice, the company never registered the song with the U.S. Copyright Office. A larger publisher discovered the discrepancy and secured the official rights.

Nevertheless, "Just a Closer Walk with Thee" was a hit out of the gate. The Selah Jubilee Singers recorded it on Decca in October 1941, and two months later, Sister Rosetta Tharpe recorded her version, also for Decca.[53] The Martin and Morris Singers introduced the song at the 1944 National Baptist Convention. "Just a Closer Walk with Thee" went on to became a jazz band favorite and a staple for black and white church congregations, singers, groups, and quartets.

Despite the advances that gospel music made in the African American church during the 1930s and 1940s, it still existed on the periphery of American society. Gospel music was almost unknown by the white community, although exceptions included Chicago journalists Studs Terkel and Irving Kupcinet, music impresario John Hammond, and a handful of jazz aficionados such as semanticist, professor, and regular *Defender* columnist S. I. "Doc" Hayakawa, who heard the jazz influences in gospel, as well as the curious who tuned into the Sunday church broadcasts of First Church of Deliverance or All Nations Pentecostal.[54] This situation changed in 1947 when records by a Chicago artist introduced an international audience to gospel and confirmed the genre's potential to make cash registers ring.

CHAPTER 11

"Move On Up a Little Higher"

The 1940s, Part Two

There's a woman, my friends, I've seen and heard, who sings like the great blues singer, Bessie Smith, only Mahalia Jackson of the South Side doesn't sing the blues. She sings what is known in her church as "the gospel."

Studs Terkel

The U.S. record industry experienced an explosion of entrepreneurship after the American Federation of Musicians recording ban was lifted in 1944 and the Second World War ended the following year. Independent labels, or "indies," set out to grab their share of the record market. Fledgling companies such as Apollo, Coleman, Hub, and Joe Davis featured the latest blues, rhythm and blues, jazz, and gospel (classified as "spirituals") in their catalogs. Newark, New Jersey's Savoy Records dedicated its 5000 series to spiritual releases, and King Records in Cincinnati added gospel to its flagship label as well as to its Queen subsidiary.

One of the first Chicago gospel singers to record for an indie label in the immediate postwar period was Mahalia Jackson's protégé, Brother John Sellers. Although by June 1944 Sellers had signed a five-year contract with the Coleman Brothers of Newark and moved to New York, he cut his first records in Chicago in March 1945.[1] The discs were released by Black and White Records, a Los Angeles imprint organized by Lillian and Paul Reiner that same year. Accompanied by pianist Howard Wilson, Sellers covered two songs from Jackson's repertory, "God's Gonna Separate the Wheat from the Tares" and "You Sing On," selections she recorded for Decca in May 1937. On these sides, Sellers imitated his idol with as much vocal bounce as he could muster.

During the same period, Sellers made records for Mayo Williams's new Southern and Chicago imprints. The jazzy backup provided by Sister Anne C. Graham and her trio provided Sellers the rhythmic propulsion he needed for his gospel songs. In late 1946, Sellers moved to Lee Egalnick's fledgling Chicago independent, Miracle Records, for which he cut several sides, including the first commercial recording of Brewster's "Move On Up a Little Higher."[2] Sellers benefited again from a small jazz combo for accompaniment, this one consisting of Floyd Hunt, Clarence Hall, and Al McDonald.[3]

About the time Sellers was returning to Chicago from New York to make records for Miracle, his mentor, Mahalia Jackson, was traveling from Chicago to New York to record for Apollo Records. Apollo was organized in New York in 1944 by Ike and Bess Berman, Hy Siegel, and Sam Schneider.[4] Advertising itself as "first with hits by popular colored artists," Apollo released discs by artists such as Charlie Barnet and Dinah Washington. The label entered gospel music with several selections by Clara Hudmon, the "Georgia Peach," and former Decca recording artists the Dixie Hummingbirds.

Jackson came to Bess Berman's attention after appearing on a gospel extravaganza at New York's Golden Gate Auditorium. Organized by gospel promoter Johnny Meyers, the program paid Jackson one thousand dollars, her biggest one-night payday to that point. Her performance so impressed Meyers that he recommended that Berman meet the Chicago singer. Meyers and Jackson met with Berman and Apollo A&R director Art Freeman at the label's office on Forty-Fifth Street in Manhattan. They agreed to record four sides.[5]

On October 3, 1946, Jackson and her accompanist Rosalie McKenny cut "(I'm Going to) Wait until My Change Comes," "I'm Going to Tell God," "I Want to Rest," and "He Knows My Heart." Mail-order record companies advertised "I Want to Rest," but none of the sides went far commercially. Berman wanted to end the agreement, but Freeman persuaded her to give Jackson one more chance. He was interested in recording her singing a song she used for a vocal warm-up. It was the song Sellers had just recorded: "Move On Up a Little Higher."[6] Freeman persuaded Berman by telling her he would record Jackson in Chicago, thereby saving the cost—and time, too, since Jackson was afraid to fly—of bringing the singer and her accompanist to New York.

Jackson's biggest concern was finding a musician for the Chicago recording session. McKenny had moved back to Buffalo, New York, to get married. Jackson found fellow New Orleans migrant James Lee, accompanist for Bishop A. A. Childs's Evangelistic Temple COGIC and, according to Heilbut, "gospel's first male soprano."[7] Rev. Charles Walker told Idella Johnson that Lee was on his honeymoon at the time of the recording session, but "Mahalia called saying, 'now James, we've got to go down here and make a record,' and he left his wife (laugh)!"[8]

Wanting to combine piano and Hammond organ to strengthen the background, Jackson secured organist Blind James Francis, another New Orleans native. The three met Freeman following a marathon rehearsal of the song at St. Luke Baptist Church at Thirty-Sixth and Indiana, where Jackson was choir director. In the early morning hours of September 12, 1947, Freeman recorded the song in two parts to capture Jackson's ability to build the emotional tension of a gospel song. Freeman returned to Manhattan with at least two acceptable takes of each side on tape. In early 1948, Apollo issued "Move On Up a Little Higher" as a two-sided single.[9]

Evoking a reunion "with all God's sons and daughters" in the hereafter, "Higher" was Jackson in full "Nawlins" second-line strut, punching out lyrics timed to get the church to shouting:

"I'm goin' out sight-seeing in Beulah,

March all around God's altar;

Walk, never tire,

Lord, never falter;

Move on up a little higher,

Meet with ol' man Daniel;

Move on up a little higher,

Meet my loving mother;

Move on up a little higher, Lord,

Meet that Lily of the Valley;

Meet with the Rose of Sharon,

And it will be always howdy, howdy;

It will be always howdy, howdy,

It will be always howdy, howdy, Lord, and never goodbye."

"Move On Up a Little Higher" was not only Jackson's breakout recording—the hit she had hoped for since May 1937—but it also became gospel music's hottest record to date, reportedly selling more than two million copies.[10] Jules Schwerin reported that Jackson's royalties exceeded three hundred thousand dollars in the record's first year.[11] Although the song was written by Brewster, Frye copyrighted and printed Jackson's arrangement.[12]

Her follow up single, "Even Me," also recorded during the early-morning session in September, was purported to have sold a million copies.[13] By August 1948, Apollo had proclaimed Mahalia Jackson to be "one of the top disc sellers during the first half" of the year, with her latest effort, "Dig a Little Deeper," "topping sales of her previous platters."[14] As the year ended, Jackson signed a three-year contract with Apollo and was crowned official soloist of the National Baptist Convention.[15] It seemed as if Jackson's "fish-and-bread" singing days were finally over. It had taken two decades, but the migrant from "back a' town" New Orleans was gospel's latest overnight success.

Despite the success of "Move On Up," it was "I'm Going to Tell God" that got the attention of Chicago disk jockey and raconteur Louis "Studs" Terkel. He was so taken with the voice leaping off the grooves of the Apollo 78 he heard in a local record shop that he programmed it on his *Wax Museum* program on WENR. "There's a woman, my friends, I've seen and heard, who sings like the great blues singer, Bessie Smith, only Mahalia Jackson of the South Side doesn't sing the blues. She sings what is known in her church as 'the gospel.'" Terkel then played her record and eventually interviewed Jackson on his radio show. It was the beginning of a lifelong friendship and Jackson's introduction to the larger Chicago community.[16]

Apollo Records and the (G)old Ship of Zion

Jackson's success encouraged Berman to add more Chicago gospel artists to the Apollo roster. Signed in 1949, the Roberta Martin Singers became Apollo's next major acquisition.[17] The Roberta Martin Singers were no strangers to recording: in 1945, Roberta recorded and released at least four discs on her own label, Roberta Martin Studio of Music, including "Jesus" / "Only a Look" and "No, No, Nothing Can Change Me" / "Oh Say So." She pressed five hundred copies of each record and sold them for one dollar each at live programs and, presumably, at her retail store.[18] Two years later, Detroit-based Religious Recordings issued some 78s on the ensemble.[19] The big seller, however, was the July 1949 Apollo release of "Old Ship of Zion," recorded during the Roberta Martin Singers' first session for Apollo. From Martin's trademark piano introduction and Norsalus McKissick's bluesy baritone to the group's tight vocal blend that moved from hushed legato to demonstrative staccato, "Old Ship of Zion" was the quintessential demonstration of the group's style. In truth, the ensemble's more than forty released sides for Apollo between 1949 and 1953 not only defined the Roberta Martin sound but inspired countless other groups across the country to follow in their stylistic footsteps.

The Roberta Martin Singers were successful because Martin selected singers who could blend their voices into a crisp ensemble sound and also were talented soloists with the ability to move a church congregation to fits and tears. For example, "Come into My Heart, Lord Jesus" ranks among gospel's finest recorded moments because of the richness and color of DeLois Barrett Campbell's tone and the earnestness of her delivery. Eugene Smith underscored critical verses in "I'm Saved" with dramatic leaps in volume, while McKissick employed his smoky baritone to render "Let God Abide" with the practiced rhythm of a preacher. Martin herself possessed a lovely, straightforward tone, but it was her conviction that endeared her to an audience, especially when she sang her favorite hymn, "What a Friend We Have in Jesus." Leona Price recalled that during song battles, all Roberta had to do was start with "What a . . ." and the house was hers. She also remembered a program "at Progressive Baptist Church . . . the group was up singing and some man just got up and started shouting and went over the seats. [Martin] was just that powerful."[20] No less a superstar than Aretha Franklin idolized Martin's singing and, as Heilbut wrote, emulated her in "demonstrating soulfulness by singing softly."[21]

Pearl Williams-Jones described Martin's piano style—a style that Little Lucy learned and perpetuated after Martin no longer toured extensively with the group—as "an integral and integrating force in the performance, supplying accompaniment, rhythm, and effects. Her style is characterized by improvisatory fills, a rhythmic bass line and colorful and complex chord structures."[22] New York disk jockey and promoter Joe Bostic called the Roberta Martin sound "rich, restful, and righteous." Gospel groups and singers, most notably James Cleveland, adopted Martin's keyboard technique and replicated her flowery but understated and instantly recognizable song introductions, melodic embellishments and fills during natural rests in the music, and concluding arpeggios. Said Rev. Charles Walker, "Her playing was always refined, always contoured."[23] This style, with Martin on piano and Lucy Smith on organ, literally defined the gospel sound during the 1940s through the 1960s as much as did the Hammond B3 and the Leslie speaker. Martin took Dorsey's gospel music and made it an art form.

Besides "Old Ship of Zion," other popular Apollo singles by the Roberta Martin Singers included "I'm Saved," "Come in the Room," "Since I Met Jesus," "Come into My Heart, Lord Jesus," "He's My Light," and "I Know the Lord Will Make a Way, Oh Yes He Will."[24] *Billboard* called the Roberta Martin Singers a "first rate chorus" for their work on "Only a Look," and Roberta Martin to be "one of the finest spiritual voices around" on "He Knows How Much We Can Bear."[25] In 1952, Martin received a gold record from Apollo records "in recognition of the hundreds of thousands of Martin records which ha[d] been sold."[26]

Roberta Martin alumni also found recording homes on Apollo. McKissick and Folk left the Roberta Martin Singers briefly to join James Cleveland in his short-lived group, the Gospelaires. Between October 1950 and January 1951, the Gospelaires recorded three singles for Apollo, with "Oh What a Time" representing Cleveland's debut as a lead vocalist on a commercial record.[27] In 1954 and 1955, Robert Anderson recorded a handful of Apollo sides, including his trademark "Oh Lord Is It I," accompanied by Martin on piano and Wooten Chorale Ensemble founder Robert Wooten Sr. on organ.[28] Cleveland returned to Apollo in 1953, this time with the Gospel All Stars, which included his high school pal Imogene Greene.[29] Cleveland's tender duet with Greene on "Lord Remember Me" gave listeners an aural glimpse of two major gospel stars as works in progress.

Though not for Apollo, Roberta Martin Singers alumnus Willie Webb secured a recording contract for his own gospel group. The Willie Webb Singers was a piano- and organ-accompanied ensemble based at Rev. Elijah Thurston's Forty-Fourth Street Baptist Church, where Webb was music minister. Like most gospel groups, its membership was fluid—Romance Watson was a member from 1946 to 1949, before he was recruited by Roberta Martin for her group—but those participating in the group's first commercial recording date, a September 1950 session for Irving Ballin's Philadelphia-based Gotham, were Allen McClinton, Ozella Weber, Edna Coles, Elizabeth Mitchell, Ora Lee Hopkins, and Alex Bradford.

Known as the "Singing Rage of the Gospel Age," Alex Bradford was born in Bessemer, Alabama, on January 23, 1927.[30] His mother was a cook and beautician, and his father was an ore miner. Drawn to the theater at an early age, Bradford took dance lessons and performed on the vaudeville stage at four years old. He was fascinated by the musical and theatrical flamboyance of Prophet Jones, founder of the Triumph the King of Christ Universal Dominion Kingdom of God and Temple of Christ.[31] Bradford was drawn to the sanctified church in general and attempted to join, but his staunch Baptist mother kept him seated firmly in the pews of the Baptist church.

At age thirteen, Bradford joined a children's choir called the Protective Harmoneers and took jazz piano lessons from Mildred Belle Hall. After his discharge from the army, Bradford moved to Chicago in hopes of securing a position with the Roberta Martin Singers, but there was no slot available. There was room in Mahalia Jackson's ever-expanding coterie, however, and Bradford became her personal secretary. While working for Jackson, Bradford received a call from Webb regarding a vacancy in his ensemble. It wasn't the Roberta Martin Singers, but was Bradford interested?

Bradford joined the Willie Webb Singers as they were about to record for Gotham. He led three of the group's six cuts for Gotham. His lead vocal on "Every Day and Every Hour," from September 1950, demonstrated his ability to punctuate vocal lines with soaring falsetto notes like a male Marion Williams.[32]

If Robert Anderson was sacred and suave, Bradford was sanctified and flamboyant. After participating in one more Gotham session in March 1951, soloing on Kenneth Morris's "Eyes Have Not Seen," Bradford formed his own ensemble, the Bradford Singers. After signing with Apollo, probably because of Roberta Martin or Mahalia Jackson's endorsement, the Bradford Singers cut thirteen sides between August 1951 and September 1952. Berman released all but one as singles.[33]

Since recording, performing, and touring were not paying all his expenses, Bradford joined former Willie Webb Singers colleague Ozella Weber in the music department of Second Timothy Baptist Church, where Rev. J. M. Stone was pastor, sometime in late 1951.[34] By March of the following year, as Bradford and his singers prepared to tour the East and the South, he left Second Timothy to be choir director and pianist for Prophet L. A. Wheeler's Universal Church of Science at 5056 South State Street.[35]

Bradford was an equally gifted songwriter. He penned several songs for his Apollo sessions, including "He's So Good to Me," "Turn Away from Sin," "Who Can I Blame," "He'll Be There," "Do You Know Jesus," and "He's a Wonder." He also wrote some of the Roberta Martin Singers' popular Apollo singles, such as "Come On in The Room" and the bluesy "Too Close to Heaven." Recorded under the title "I'm Too Close," Bradford's composition proved successful for Martin, but it was his own version, recorded for Specialty in 1953, that became a smash hit, a timeless classic, and made Bradford a national gospel star.

Independent Chicago-Based Record Companies

Several Chicago-based indie record labels released discs by local gospel artists during the 1940s and 1950s. Besides Ink Williams's Southern/Chicago labels, among the first to do so in the postwar period were Miracle, Premium, and Hy-Tone Records.

Although only lasting from 1946 to 1950, Lee Egalnick's Chicago-based Miracle Records was responsible not only for Brother John Sellers's early discs but also for the first recordings by St. Louis singer and preacher Cleophus Robinson. But Sellers and Robinson did not make Egalnick's cash register ring like Robert Anderson did. Miracle signed the popular crooner and put significant muscle into promoting him as "America's Foremost Gospel Singer."

Anderson's pop-inflected and thoughtful baritone evoked the era's top R&B crooners Charles Brown, Roy Milton, and hometown hero Nat Cole. In November 1949, Egalnick presented Anderson with the Miracle Trophy at a gospel music spectacular held at Tabernacle Baptist Church. The program drew a capacity crowd of 3,400 patrons and, according to press reports, 2,500 more were turned away at the church door.[36] That same month, Miracle placed a prominent ad in the *Defender*, soliciting "suggestions for songs YOU would like recorded by Mr. Anderson."[37] The songs Anderson and his Good Shepherd Singers brought to the January 1950 session were sufficiently popular that they may well have been fan recommendations: "Do You Know Him," "The Last Mile," "God Answers Prayers," and "He Lives in Me." But by the time "Do You Know Him" hit stores, Miracle was out of business.

Miracle vanished, but Egalnick did not. He opened Premium Records and rereleased several Anderson and Good Shepherd Singers sides from Miracle. In June 1950, he produced new discs by the group and issued one disc by the Holy Wonders, a quartet from Greater Harvest Baptist Church that included then-unknown Spencer Taylor. Premium lasted until 1951, when it, too, shut its doors.[38] By this point, Anderson was so popular that the Dorie Miller Foundation declared February 20, 1951, Robert Anderson Day and held another gospel program at Tabernacle in his honor, where more than 3,500 people showed up.[39] Leonard Allen, owner of the United and States labels, astutely picked up Anderson's contract from Egalnick. The Good Shepherds were part of the deal and, it turned out, become the golden egg Allen was looking for.

Anderson's former singing mate, R. L. Knowles, recorded for Hy-Tone, a product of Chicago bandleader Freddie Williams and jukebox operator Nathan Rothner. Rothner told music historian Robert Pruter: "I heard [Knowles] singing one of his spirituals and I thought it was great. So we decided to record him." The five known Knowles discs were the only gospel output in Hy-Tone's catalog during its existence from 1945 to 1948.[40] Accompanied by pianist James Miller, Knowles performed songs such as "Lord I've Tried" and one of his personal favorites, "Precious Lord," for the recordings. In Knowles's "Precious Lord," one hears Mahalia Jackson's plaintive reading, especially on its opening lines, and Thomas Dorsey's meticulous enunciation on "When my life grows drear / Precious Lord linger near." Sadly, Knowles's Hy-Tone discs did not capture the vocal prowess of the performer proclaimed to have outsung everyone at First Church of Deliverance's Candle Lighting service.

If by 1950 local labels were failing to achieve the success enjoyed by Apollo with Mahalia Jackson and Roberta Martin, it was not for lack of superior recording studios. Many Chicago indie labels relied on Universal Recording Studios, founded in 1946 by Bill Putnam, Bernie Clapper, and Bob Weber. The studio's first location was atop the Civic Opera Building at 20 North Wacker Drive. By 1954, it moved to 111 East Ontario, and in 1956, to 46 East Walton. The first studio to feature an echo chamber—by placing a microphone and a receiver in the women's restroom—Universal had become by the 1950s the city's most popular recording studio for indie labels with jazz, blues, R&B, doo-wop, soul, pop, and gospel catalogs.[41]

"Reverend Cobbs of the West" and the Echoes of Eden

While Chicago gospel soloists, groups, and quartets were tapping the power of phonograph records, the Chicago gospel chorus sound had yet to be captured on commercial disc. This changed when Rev. John Branham assumed the pastorate of St. Paul Baptist Church in Los Angeles. He helped St. Paul's chorus become a West Coast version of the Chicago gospel chorus. By securing a recording contract with a major label, Branham put the St. Paul Baptist Church and its gospel chorus on the musical map.

John Branham came from a well-respected Chicago church family. His father, Rev. J. H. Branham Sr., served as associate pastor at Olivet Baptist Church for twenty-three years until his death on January 21, 1942.[42] His two sons, Joseph Jr. and John, followed him into the family business. Joseph Jr. ministered at a Waukegan, Illinois, church before becoming pastor of Chicago's South Shore Baptist Church at Sixtieth and Champlain. John was ordained at Olivet in 1937 and a year later assumed duties at Calvary Baptist Church in San Diego, California, where he met Ethel Ellis Carter. The two were married in February 1940.

When Olivet's pastor, the National Baptist Convention leader Rev. Lacey Kirk Williams, died in an airplane crash in 1940, John resigned his position at Calvary and returned to Olivet to assist his father, who was in failing health and unable to assume the leadership responsibilities of the church on his own. On October 5, 1943, after stints at Pilgrim Baptist Church in South Bend, Indiana, and Greater Bethesda Baptist in Chicago, John left to lead St. Paul Baptist Church of Los Angeles at Twenty-First and Naomi.[43] Raising funds to modernize the church facility was one of his first tasks.[44] Starting a regular Sunday evening radio broadcast for the church earned him the sobriquet "Rev. Cobbs of the West."[45] The radio station was KOWL, and the announcer, Joe Adams, the "Mayor of Melody," would announce: "Swing it away, Echoes of Eden Choir!"[46]

"John Branham took the [gospel] style of Chicago to California," Eugene Smith declared, "and the people went wild. It was hopping here, but it wasn't out there. He was among the first churches in Los Angeles to go on the air because he took it from here."[47] Ineze Caston concurred, telling the Los Angeles Times in 1994, "The fur did fly when I organized a gospel choir at [my husband's] Trinity Baptist [Church]. Gospel hadn't come to the West Coast. It was the late '40s. They were still singing hymns from Europe."[48]

The 170-voice Echoes of Eden, as the St. Paul Baptist Church Choir was called, was aided greatly by the direction of J. Earle Hines. A muscular bass-baritone singer, Hines was a stalwart of the National Baptist Convention. His traveling ensemble, the Goodwill Singers, were the organization's musical ambassadors. As director of St. Paul's Echoes of Eden, Hines was instrumental in helping one of its youngest members, Jamesetta Hawkins, develop her singing style, one she later perfected as R&B singer Etta "Miss Peaches" James.[49]

"We had one of the biggest, baddest, hippest choirs anywhere," James writes in her autobiography, *Rage to Survive*. "The music was thunder and joy, lightning bolts of happiness and praise, foot-stomping, dance-shouting, good-feeling singing from the soul." As a young girl, James absorbed the singing of artists such as the Sallie Martin Singers and Sister Rosetta Tharpe.[50] But for her, it was all about J. Earle Hines, her musical mentor. She wanted to sing just like him. "All that spill-your-guts-out power. . . . When he sang, the saints would faint; nurses were always standing by with smelling salts." James took voice lessons from Hines and piano lessons from his wife, and sang solos at St. Paul on Sundays.[51]

The popularity of the Echoes of Eden on St. Paul's broadcast helped the group secure a record deal with Hollywood-based Capitol Records. There was sufficient artistic input from Chicago gospel personnel that one could argue that Capitol recordings of the St. Paul Baptist Church of Los Angeles made during church services on Sunday, May 25, 1947, were the first commercial discs to capture a Dorsey-Frye gospel chorus in live performance. For example, Sallie Martin, her Chicago-born adopted daughter, Cora Brewer, and organist Gwendolyn Cooper—"she's the one who put the 'ump' in gospel playing," gospel artist Richard Smallwood told Idella Johnson—all assisted with the choir.[52] It has also been suggested that Theodore Frye visited Los Angeles to teach the Echoes of Eden the techniques of practiced informality and exuberance and vocal articulation. Given Branham's close association with Olivet Baptist Church, where Frye was choir director, the presumption is not far-fetched.[53]

Even the first single that the Echoes of Eden recorded on May 25 had Chicago provenance. "I'm So Glad Jesus Lifted Me" was credited to Reverend Cobbs and first popularized by First Church of Deliverance. Backed by Cooper on piano and rhythmic hand clapping from the choir, Hines shouted bluesy exhortations of "I'm so glad" as the choir enthusiastically sang "Jesus lifted me" in response. The Echoes of Eden's theme song was on the flip side: Dorsey and Detroit choir organizer Artelia Hutchins's "God Be with You until We Meet Again." Hines led in his throaty tone—his live performance was superior to his studio discs with the Goodwill Singers—and the choir alternated between well-articulated staccato and legato responses. "Walking with My Jesus" contained residue from the shape-note singing style in the construction of its verses and harmony. Choristers and congregants shouted and clapped in joyous approval during this cut as well as on Dorsey's "What Could I Do," led by the ebullient Erie Gladney. Cora Martin's conversational, demonstrative lead on Roberta Martin's "Didn't It Rain," and especially her extended notes over the choir's chanting of "listen to the rain," stimulated hearty support from the choristers in the form of exhortations and hand claps.

Between 1947 and 1950, the St. Paul Echoes of Eden made thirty-three sides for Capitol, of which thirty-one were released as 78s, 45s, or compiled for the group's sole LP, *On Revival Day*.[54] It was not only the first time that the electricity generated by a church-based gospel chorus was captured on record, but the choir's recorded repertory also served as a collection of Chicago gospel's greatest hits of the 1930s and 1940s. In addition to singing Dorsey, Cobbs, and Roberta Martin compositions, the choir recorded Kenneth Morris's "Look for Me in Heaven (I'll Be There)"—Hines's hard singing on the song produced screams from more than one female in the church—and Myrtle Jackson's "But This I Pray, Oh Lord, Remember Me." Sallie Martin, who led the last verse of the choir's rendition of "Just a Closer Walk with Thee," served as choir director for St. Paul during 1948. In February, the Sallie Martin Singers joined the choir for one of Sallie's trademark songs and another Morris copyright: "Dig a Little Deeper in God's Love."

The St. Paul Baptist Church of Los Angeles Choir became one of Capitol's best sellers in the sacred field.[55] The choir's rendition of "Search Me Lord" in 1949 moved a *Billboard* reviewer to comment that the "magnificent spirit and rhythm of spiritual and gospel music has rarely been performed and captured so successfully on record."[56] Anthony Heilbut asserts that the Echoes of Eden "usher[ed] in the modern choir sound" and were responsible for "as far as [he could] tell, the first live postwar recording to capture the gospel drama."[57]

Sallie Martin and Capitol Records

An October 15, 1949 *Billboard* article announced that "rhythmic sacred singer" Sallie Martin was joining Capitol Records. Perhaps it was her involvement with the Echoes of Eden that helped her secure the contract, but for Capitol it was a calculated risk. The Sallie Martin Singers recorded lackluster discs for Bronze in 1944 and for Aladdin in 1947 as Sallie Martin and her Singers of Joy. A *Billboard* reviewer found Martin's first Aladdin release, "Four and Twenty Elders," to be "fair," and the flip, Morris's "Jesus Steps Right In," stronger but still underwhelming.[58] These and two more sides recorded for Dolphin's of Hollywood in 1949 fell quietly into obscurity.

"You had to see [Sallie] sing to appreciate her," explained her accompanist, Kenneth Woods Jr. Martin's voice was not the most beautiful pipe in the organ, but what she lacked in vocal beauty she made up for in conviction, personality, and showmanship. Watching Sallie Martin sing was like watching the stern church mother get happy. Woods recalled that the Sallie Martin Singers "tore the house up" when they introduced "Dig a Little Deeper" at the 1948 NCGCC, because during the performance, Sallie grabbed the microphone stand and pantomimed the act of digging. While appearing on a boat cruise in Washington, DC, Martin broke into "Move On Up a Little Higher." Her no-nonsense delivery of Reverend Brewster's lyrics, combined with her self-imitative stage personality, brought the partygoers to fever pitch. Woods laughed: "I thought folk were going to jump off the boat and into the Potomac!"[59]

Martin recorded four solo sides for Capitol during 1949, but a hit record remained elusive.[60] *Billboard* found one of the releases, Dorsey's "The Little Wooden Church on the Hill," to have a "rhythm gospel beat but not much else that is spirited."[61] Nevertheless, in 1950, Dave Dexter, head of Capitol's Rhythm & Blues Department, re-signed Martin and added Cora for the expressed purpose of "mother-daughter duets."[62] Recording with Cora and a jazz combo comprised of bassist Leonard Bibb, drummer Zutty Singleton, and guitarist Nappy Lamare, who picked staccato notes like Rosetta Tharpe, Sallie produced two fine singles. On "I'm Going to Follow Jesus," from the March 10, 1950, session, Cora sang with crystalline power, while Sallie answered Cora's calls and interjected with the gumption of a Holiness singer.[63] Their rendition of "Do You Know Him" was equally energetic.

By mid-1950, Martin had left Capitol for Art Rupe's Specialty Records, also based in Hollywood. Specialty had become a powerhouse in the gospel field on the strength of hits by the Pilgrim Travelers and the newly signed Soul Stirrers. Martin's two-year relationship with Specialty produced eight released sides and more than a dozen unreleased cuts that represented Sallie's finest recorded work to date.[64]

"Jesus Never Fails": Rev. Louis Henry Ford and Chicago's St. Paul Choir

Perhaps it was the success of the St. Paul Baptist Church Echoes of Eden recordings that prompted Black and White Records of Los Angeles to be the first to put a Chicago gospel chorus on wax. It was not the company's first foray into gospel, as it had released Brother John Sellers's first discs, nor was it their premier venture into black choirs, for it had produced several discs by Los Angeles's famed McNeil Jubilee Choir. In January 1948, Black and White recorded four sides by the St. Paul Church of God in Christ Choir of Chicago. The choir sang "Why Should I Worry," "I'll Never Turn Back," "Amen," and "Somebody's Knocking." In the tradition of Rev. Glenn T. Settle and Wings over Jordan, St. Paul's founder and pastor, Rev. Louis Henry Ford, introduced the songs with a brief narrative while the choir hummed quietly behind him before launching into thunderous singing.[65]

Ford was an enterprising young pastor who parlayed his ministry into a political and social force for Chicago's African Americans. Ford was born in Clarksdale, Mississippi, on May 23, 1914, and began preaching at age thirteen. He was educated at the Saints Industrial and Literary School in Lexington, Mississippi, and became a junior minister for the COGIC church in Lexington. He migrated to Chicago in 1933 with, as he liked to say, "twenty-five cents in my pocket." Ford ministered at a church in Evanston, married Margaret Little, and was ordained by Bishop William Roberts. Subsequently, he moved his ministry to Bronzeville street corners, and in 1936 he started St. Paul COGIC with two members.[66] Eventually the congregation grew so much that the church needed a permanent space, and Ford rented a storefront at 4618 South State.[67] Within six years, St. Paul COGIC, whose motto was "Jesus Never Fails," was believed to have the "second largest membership of its denomination in the city.[68] Anna Broy Crockett directed the radio chorus, and Vernon Oliver Price was a regular soloist.[69] At this time Ford secured for St. Paul a Sunday-evening radio broadcast on WSBC.[70] What was originally to be a three-month stint for the *Old Fashioned Camp Meeting Revival* became one of the most popular church services on Chicago radio.

Not long afterward, St. Paul moved its worship services to a tent at 5049 South Wabash, where it remained until 1946, when the congregation, by now three thousand members strong, raised the funds to build a new church structure. Located at 4528 South Wabash and costing thirty-five thousand dollars, St. Paul COGIC was next door to the oldest remaining private residence in Chicago, which it later purchased and restored.[71]

It is uncertain how, or through whom, St. Paul and Black and White Records met and inked a partnership. Nevertheless, the St. Paul radio chorus's identification on the record label as simply the "St. Paul Choir," along with Black and White being a Los Angeles–based company, may have caused confusion among record purchasers who thought they were obtaining new singles by the better-known Los Angeles aggregation. Whether the tactic was an intentional deceit on the part of Black and White or an innocent coincidence is lost to time. Interestingly, on record, the Baptist Echoes of Eden were more spontaneous and demonstrative than St. Paul COGIC's chorus, which delivered powerful but tightly arranged gospels.

No further Black and White recording sessions for St. Paul COGIC took place after the January 1948 session. By October 1949, the company was out of business. Owner Paul Reiner sold the masters after offering Black and White artists the right to purchase them first.[72] For a decade, the St. Paul COGIC Choir did not record at all, and when it finally did, it was for the denomination's Central Illinois Music Department (CIMUDE) imprint.

Nevertheless, for St. Paul COGIC to be one of the first gospel choirs on record was a feather—one of many—in Reverend Ford's cap. His local campaign to turn out the vote for Harry S. Truman as president earned him an invitation to the inauguration. In 1949, Illinois governor Stevenson appointed Ford a delegate to the National Freedom Day Celebration.[73] Ford was elevated to bishop on August 19, 1954, and eventually assumed the rank of presiding bishop, the highest level of leadership in the Church of God in Christ.[74]

Move On Up a Little Higher . . . on the Radio

By the mid-1940s, Pentecostal, Holiness, and Spiritual churches were joined on the radio by a legion of semi-demonstrative Protestant denominations—predominantly, though not exclusively, Baptist churches. Not all broadcasts attained the multistate listenership of a First Church of Deliverance, All Nations Pentecostal, or St. Paul COGIC, but several established significant and regular followings. Among the two most important Baptist church broadcasts to start in the 1940s were those of the Greater Harvest and Forty-Fourth Street Baptist Churches.

Greater Harvest Baptist Church

Rev. Louis Boddie, born September 16, 1878, in Nesbitt, Mississippi, organized Greater Harvest Baptist Church in 1912 and remained its pastor until his death in 1965. The musical accompaniment to the church's Sunday-afternoon broadcasts on WAAF, which started as early as 1945, was provided by the Greater Harvest Radio Choir, directed by Ethel Hampton Eaton and, later, by Robert Anderson and Robert Wooten. Sylvia Boddie, the pastor's wife and a talented songwriter, accompanied on piano.[75] Gary, Indiana, music critic Charles Hopkins remarked in 1952 that the Greater Harvest choir "swings in the best tradition of jazz." He added, "[the] best illustration of the relationship of jazz and spiritual music can be heard when the pianist on Rev. Bodie's [sic] Sunday afternoon program begins to move."[76]

Like First Church of Deliverance, Greater Harvest was blessed with superb gospel musicians. One was Edward Robinson. Born May 10, 1933, in Birmingham, Robinson taught himself to play piano at age thirteen. He and his siblings migrated to Chicago in 1949 after his mother, evangelist Althea Robinson, moved to the city and established a place to live. Boddie hired him to play organ at Greater Harvest, and he held the position for twenty-five years. It was at Greater Harvest in the mid-1950s that Robinson met Mahalia Jackson; he subsequently became one of her accompanists and toured with her nationally and internationally.[77] Another was Robert Wooten, who directed the Greater Harvest Choir and played organ alongside Robinson.[78] Renowned organist Joe Henderson was once in the Greater Harvest music department. The Holy Wonders and Southern Echoes quartets called the church their home base.

Yet another was Mollie Mae Gates, who started her gospel music career in 1945 and shortly afterward was recorded by Ink Williams on his Harlem label. In their accompaniment and song selection, Gates's four sides for Harlem could not have represented 1940s Chicago gospel better. She sang Sylvia Boddie's "Now Lord" to the accompaniment of Louise Overall Weaver on piano and Willie Webb on Hammond organ.[79] In June 1954, the same month and year that she debuted as a guitarist at a Metropolitan Community Church program, Gates received an honorary doctorate from Providence Baptist Theological Seminary in Los Angeles.[80] By decade's end, she was director of Greater Harvest's Victory Choir and toured the West Coast as a singer and guitarist in the early part of 1959.[81] Gates also made robes for gospel singers and choirs. "Seven to ten dollars [per robe], that's all she would charge," Aldrea Lenox remembered.[82]

Forty-Fourth Street Baptist Church

Rev. Elijah Thurston organized Forty-Fourth Street Baptist Church in 1934. Located at 735 East Forty-Fourth Street, the church started its radio broadcast in 1944 and, like Greater Harvest, was heard Sunday afternoons on WAAF. During the mid-1940s, the Forty-Fourth Street choirs were directed by Willie Webb and Louise Overall Weaver.[83] At one time or another, Robert Anderson and Alex Bradford also directed the Forty-Fourth Street choir.[84]

One of the church's most celebrated musicians was Louise Rochelle Overall Weaver. Weaver was born April 13, 1915, to Monroe Overall and Mary Ramsey Overall, pastor of True Vine All Nations Spiritual Church.[85] Born an invalid, Weaver was spared life in a wheelchair when thirty operations restored her legs to full strength. She began playing piano at age five and in 1932 was hired by Friendship Baptist Church, but to play its pipe organ. A six-hour lesson gave her what she needed to transpose her keyboard skills to pipe organ. Three years later, she and Clarice Saunders became the first African American women to learn the new Hammond organ, taking lessons at the Illinois College of Music in the Furniture Mart.[86] Weaver accompanied a mixed group called the Douglas Singers on piano around 1936 and from 1939 to 1943 played for Metropolitan Baptist Church. Reverend Thurston hired her for Forty-Fourth Street, and her first performance was on Sunday, February 4, 1945, at a dedication service for their new Hammond organ.[87] Idella Johnson notes that Weaver's previous experience playing the pipe organ "brought a smooth and sophisticated classicism to the Hammond organ." Rev. Charles Walker commented, "She was graceful too in her playing and she was cute—she was so short! She wasn't much taller than the organ. And she'd get up there and she was masterful."[88]

During the late 1940s and 1950s, Forty-Fourth Street Baptist Church was a major hub of gospel music activity in Chicago. In addition to Weaver, Forty-Fourth Street benefited from the piano accompaniment of classically trained

Sylvia Watson Hoston, sister to Floriene and Romance Watson.[89] Besides its cadre of house singers, such as Ozella Weber and other members of the Willie Webb Singers, Forty-Fourth Street was host to a passing parade of local and national gospel artists who ministered to the congregation. Eventually, Forty-Fourth Street outgrew its namesake facility and moved to Seventy-Seventh Street and became New Covenant Baptist Church. In April 1953, the church moved its broadcast to WGES, where it secured the coveted Sunday 11:00 p.m. slot.[90]

Notwithstanding the new competition, Chicago's church broadcast pioneers remained active. By the mid-1940s, All Nations Pentecostal had moved from WCFL to WGES. The broadcasts featured the Lucy Smith Trio, comprised of Elder Smith's granddaughter Lucy, Gladys Beamon, and Floriene Watson.[91] For a brief period, All Nations produced transcription discs of the live services, which were replayed on at least four other radio stations elsewhere in the country, making it the "first colored church to have a radio program and sermon heard throughout the nation and across the sea."[92]

WCFL lost All Nations to WGES but picked up First Church of Deliverance in 1950 from WIND when things were not well between the church and its longtime radio host. The station argued that listenership for Reverend Cobbs's 11:00 p.m. broadcast was falling off and proposed to shorten the hour-long program to thirty minutes "until there was an appreciable increase in air patrons."[93] On November 9, 1950, Cobbs inked a deal with WCFL instead. First Church debuted on WCFL Sunday, November 25 at 11:30 p.m. WIND's listenership concerns notwithstanding, WCFL reported that First Church's midnight broadcast reached seventy-five thousand households.[94] Regardless, the broadcast atmosphere was exciting for choristers and congregation. Bishop Jerry Goodloe, a member of the First Church choir, remembered the magic of watching the broadcast light go from red to green. "That meant we were on the air," he said.[95]

Bishop William Roberts, whose Fortieth COGIC was now considered the largest Pentecostal church in the country, had secured time from his son-in-law Jack L. Cooper on WSBC. The broadcast was a family affair. Gertrude Roberts Cooper accompanied the radio choir, and Sister Minnie Pearl Roberts was the radio announcer. Delores "Honey" Sykes grew up at Fortieth and remembered Minnie Pearl Roberts with great affection. "She gave everybody a chance. If you didn't have a great voice and cracked every note, you were still her precious child. 'Come on and sing for Auntie Minnie.' She put us on the radio at three o'clock in the afternoon, the *Just Jesus* [radio] hour."[96] In addition to singing in the choir, Sykes played alto in the Fortieth band, which included Isaac Grover, who played the electric guitar with the proto-rock intensity of fellow Pentecostal musician, Elder Utah Smith.[97]

Bishop Roberts gave Jack Cooper cause for apoplexy on at least one occasion. Sykes recalled:

Poppa [Roberts] was so comical. He had a habit over the radio calling people "jackass." "You're nothing but a jackass!" [Jack L. Cooper] called him and told him, "Poppa, you'll have us thrown off the air! You can't say that on the radio, live, like that!" He said, "Why?" "Because it's just not allowed. It's federal law." So the next Sunday we didn't know what on earth would happen. Poppa was preaching, and his regular words were coming out, and all of a sudden he took the mike and covered it, and he said, "You jackass," and they didn't hear most of it. He let it go right quick, and said, "That's how I have to say it. I can't say it over the radio!" The church started laughing. That's just the kind of personality he had.[98]

Fortieth was just one of Jack and Gertrude Cooper's many radio clients. By 1949, Jack L. Cooper Productions held more than fifty contracts of brokered airtime representing approximately forty hours of programming on WSBC, WHFC, WAAF, and WBEE.[99] Jack, as managing director, produced his own broadcasts over a leased wire transmitter from his home in Morgan Park.[100] Gertrude was the company's musical director and secretary, and her brother, Isaiah Roberts, was director of religious programming.

Gertrude was also the first black female radio announcer in Chicago, having started as early as 1938 by hosting a homemaker program.[101] A February 5, 1950, *Defender* advertisement announced that she kicked off Sunday mornings on WSBC with her 6:00 a.m. *Songs by Request*. In 1949, Isaiah, who three years earlier began serving as unofficial ombudsman for Black Chicago as host of WSBC's phone-in show *May I Help You?*, launched a gospel music record show on the station called *Songs of Zion: Brother Isaiah's Church of the Air*.[102] Sponsored by Pekin Cleaners, the program aired Sundays at 10:30 a.m.

Alabaman quartet trainer Norman McQueen was responsible for quartet programming on Cooper's stations. In 1950, his *Quartets on Parade* aired Sundays at 8:30 a.m. and Mondays through Fridays at 11:00 p.m. on WEDC and WSBC. He offered quartets such as the Alabama and Georgia Singers, the Western Harmonizers, and Jeannette Tall Sims's Victorettes fifteen minutes to a half-hour of singing time.[103] Later in the decade, McQueen hosted *McQueen's Reminiscent Hour* from 6:00 to 7:15 a.m. Sundays on Evanston, Illinois–based WEAW. The station, established in 1947 by Edward A. Wheeler, broadcast at 1330 AM as well as at 105 FM, potentially making McQueen one of the first in the nation to broadcast African American sacred music on FM.[104]

Around 1954, beautician and salon owner Isabel Joseph Johnson helped found the Religious Radio Announcers Guild. Its mission was to support radio announcers—the men and women who served as radio emcees for the broadcasts—and "boost civic and religious organizations." Early guild members besides Johnson, who was guild president, were Argo Singer Lorenza Brown Porter and Rev. Consuella York, a pioneer in prison ministry who brought the Fellowship Baptist Church radio broadcast on the air every Sunday.[105]

Move On Up a Little Higher . . . in The National Baptist Convention

As late as 1948, the National Convention of Gospel Choirs and Choruses was the only national organization dedicated exclusively to serving the nascent gospel music industry. Theodore Frye, who had been directing National Baptist Convention choruses since at least 1943, decided to make music an even more integral ingredient of the annual confab by organizing a music convention as an auxiliary unit. Modeled after NCGCC, the music convention was divided into divisions for senior choirs, gospel choruses, youth choirs, songwriters, recording artists, musicians, and choir directors.[106] As music convention president, Frye secured Georgiana Rose as secretary, Mahalia Jackson as treasurer, William McDowell as chairman of the advisory board, and Kenneth Morris as Illinois State president.

The first National Baptist Music Convention was held in Houston, Texas, from September 8 to 12, 1948.[107] Kenneth Woods Jr. recalled that the music convention had an area where sheet music vendors rented concession booths to sell their songs. Songwriters and publishers also introduced their latest compositions to large audiences by petitioning the National Baptist Convention Music Department to allow an artist or group to sing their songs on one of the big nights of the convention. "Once you got in the door with the big time preachers [and] they knew you could produce vocally," Woods said, "then you had your way made."[108]

Short-lived, the music convention offered impressive presentations while it lasted. If the September 6–13, 1953, gathering in Miami is any indication of the variety and scope of talent that participated, Frye and his organizing committee of Sallie Jones, Alice Jones Adams, and Celeste Scott treated attendees to sermons and presentations from Rev. O. M. Hoover of Cleveland and Chicago's Rev. J. C. Austin. A consecration service featured religious singers from all over the country, and musicals starred artists such as Myrtle Jackson, the Roberta Martin Singers, Mollie Mae Gates, Robert Anderson, and Singing Sammie Bryant from Detroit. Lucie Campbell delivered the keynote address.[109]

Move On Up a Little Higher . . . to Carnegie Hall

The growing popularity of gospel music encouraged prominent promoter and radio announcer Joe Bostic (1909–88) to present the new music in its most austere venue to date: New York's Carnegie Hall. Carnegie Hall was opened in 1891, and in its first few decades, it had witnessed debuts and performances by the crème de la crème of the classical music community. But classical performers were not the only artists to grace the Carnegie Hall stage. On January 16, 1938, Benny Goodman's racially mixed swing band made its Carnegie Hall debut, securing critical respect for its passionate style of jazz. Later that year, on December 23, John Hammond presented "From Spirituals to Swing" in the storied auditorium, introducing a wider audience to religious artists Sister Rosetta Tharpe and Mitchell's Christian Singers.[110] Duke Ellington, Woody Herman, Dizzy Gillespie, Charlie Parker, Ella Fitzgerald, Billie Holiday, and even the Grand Ole Opry stars from Nashville's WSM radio appeared at Carnegie Hall. Why not a gospel music program?

Declaring it the First Annual Negro Gospel Music Festival, Bostic knew who he wanted to headline. He visited Mahalia Jackson, who, with Blind Francis, was in the Apollo studio cutting her newest single, "Just over the Hill." When the session concluded and Bostic had a chance to propose his idea to the singer, he received a curt reply: "You must be some kind of a fool, mister." Bostic was relentless, even finding accommodations for Jackson at the Dawn Hotel, where he worked persistently to persuade her. Around 5:00 a.m., she agreed.[111]

The date was set for October 1, 1950. An estimated three thousand people attended the performance, which featured nearly two dozen religious music artists and personalities.[112] Rev. Adam Clayton Powell Jr. of Harlem's Abyssinian Baptist Church opened the program with an invocation. Several local quartets sang one number each. Popular Chicago baritone Lorenzo Stalling performed "Sweet Hour of Prayer." The program also featured the Belleville A Cappella Choir of Belleville, Virginia; the Angel Lites of Brooklyn (an "unusually brilliant kiddie gospel troupe," the program declared); the Cornerstone Baptist Church Gospel Chorus of Brooklyn; the all-black cast of the WLIB radio program, *The Negro Sings*; Bill Landford and the Landfordaires; Mother McClease; the Music Harps; and the Gospel Clefs.[113]

Although the Ward Singers were to perform a medley of their current gospel hits, "Each Day," "Come Ye Disconsolate," and "Stretch Out," Anthony Heilbut has noted that they added "Surely God Is Able." "Marion ran those aisles," he said. "The people went crazy!"[114]

Through Jackson's persuasion, Bostic added Mildred and Evelyn Gay and their brother Donald to the program. The Gays came on just before Jackson. Donald vividly remembered the event sixty years later: "Evelyn played the piano and we took a tambourine on stage with us. We sang 'I'm a Soldier in the Army of the Lord.' And we all just had a good old time; we were having church! Right there in Carnegie Hall!"[115]

While the Gays were turning the hall into a revival, Jackson was backstage, wrestling with abnormally severe preconcert jitters. Jackson's intestinal butterflies are often attributed to singing in such an intimidating venue as Carnegie Hall, but Heilbut has posited that they may also have been stimulated by the Wards taking the house from her with their impromptu "Surely God Is Able." Nevertheless, Donald Gay, who "had a chance to see all of the nervousness that each person had," recalled: "Mahalia's getting ready and they said, 'You're next.' And she went in her dressing room and started screaming at the top of her voice. 'Oh! Oh!' She just went into convulsions. I was standing there as a kid; I didn't know what was going on. Evelyn and Mildred went in and held her hand and had prayer with her, and she regained her composure. And came back and did a magnificent job."[116]

Jackson entered the stage and sang a medley including "City Called Heaven," her signature concert opus "In My Home Over There," and "Prayer Changes Things." Louise Overall Weaver accompanied her on Hammond organ—brought in especially for the concert—and Mildred Falls played a nine-foot Steinway grand piano.[117] The audience was so taken that the troupe was called back for three encores, during which Jackson sang "It Pays to Serve Jesus," "The Last Mile of the Way," and "Amazing Grace." She came back at the conclusion of the program to sing a medley of requested songs—"I Do, Don't You," "Move On Up a Little Higher," and "Just over the Hill."[118]

Critics lavished praise on Jackson. One called her "a truly great artist in her field." Nora Holt of the *Amsterdam News* dubbed Jackson "the diva of all gospel singers" and "a genius unspoiled." Another reporter said she nearly "turned the afternoon into a revival meeting."[119] Francis D. Perkins of the *New York Herald Tribune* wrote that Jackson "displayed a voice of range and timbre well suited to the character of her music."[120] John Hammond wrote in the *Daily Compass* that Jackson had "a voice of enormous power, range and flexibility, and she used these with reckless abandon."[121] The gossip mill churned with rumors that Jackson's next conquest would be to present gospel music in Europe.[122] Elated, Bostic announced that the festival would become an annual event. It did, with Jackson as permanent headliner.

Carnegie Hall paved the way for another first, for both gospel music and Jackson: a scholarly analysis at the Music Inn in Lenox, Massachusetts. The musicology program, held from August 26 to September 3, 1951, was organized by the Institute of Jazz Studies. The new entity was led by Marshall Stearns, a professor at Hunter College who was awarded a Guggenheim Fellowship to study jazz. John Hammond assisted Stearns in the venture.[123]

Jackson sang for the Music Inn audience's meticulous analysis and everlasting enjoyment. Stearns was impressed by her "blue tonality" and ability to "add embellishments that take your breath away." He added, "[She] breaks every rule of concert singing . . . but the full-throated feeling and expression are seraphic."[124] Anthony Heilbut's *How Sweet It Was: The Sights and Sounds of Gospel's Golden Age,* an anthology of gospel performances, contains a rare audio recording of Jackson at the Music Inn rendering Roberta Martin's "Didn't It Rain." She sang with such abandon it left her nearly breathless.

"God Will Take Care of You"

A month after the Carnegie Hall program, *Billboard* reported that Apollo Records had signed the Gay Sisters, but nothing materialized from this partnership.[125] Meanwhile, the trio—Evelyn, Mildred, and Geraldine—was appearing at a Brooklyn church when they met Herman Lubinsky of Savoy Records. Lubinsky had started Savoy in 1942, and while the Newark, New Jersey, company focused initially on jazz, it had been enjoying success with its release of recordings by the Ward Singers. The label owner was sufficiently impressed with the Gay Sisters to sign them to a contract.[126]

On March 21, 1951, the Gay Sisters became the first of several Chicago gospel groups to record for Savoy. They reprised their Carnegie Hall selection, "I'm a Soldier," in the studio, tambourine and all. However, it was their arrangement of the hymn "God Will Take Care of You" that became their biggest hit, reportedly selling a million copies.[127] "A lot of people sang 'God Will Take Care of You,'" Geraldine Gay Hambric said, "but they didn't sing it like the Gay family. Evelyn wrote the staccato rhythm. The intro really doesn't sound right unless you play that little staccato beat."[128]

The Gay Sisters toured on the strength of "God Will Take Care of You." In August 1951, the trio embarked on a "six-day tour of auditoriums and churches in New Orleans," followed by an August 12 program at the Atlanta Auditorium, where the ladies shared the bill with the Davis Sisters, the Gospel Twins, and steel guitarist and singer Willie Eason.[129] Although Lubinsky did not release "God Will Take Care of You" until the end of June, he must have heard something in that first session that foreshadowed the single's success, because he arranged two more recording dates, May 30 and July 6, for the group.

The Argo Singers

If the Gay Sisters were considered sweet singers because of their close harmonies, the Argo Singers were another story altogether. Although the female gospel group started out as a close-harmony group akin to a quartet, they eventually became a hard-singing gospel group to rival the Davis Sisters and Dorothy Love Coates and the Gospel Harmonettes.

The Argo Singers were formed in 1937 from members of the Antioch Baptist Church Choir of Argo, Illinois, a town southwest of Chicago named for Argo cornstarch, where its producer, Corn Products Company, had a factory.

The original lineup consisted of Mildred Thomas, Tlithia Irons, and Minnie Colbert. Colbert's brother, Rev. T. E. Weems, was Antioch's pastor. When a minister from Evanston, Illinois, told the ensemble that they were good enough to move beyond Antioch, they decided to intensify their singing schedule. Adding Willa Murphy, Ruby Roberts, and Thelma Speed, the group toured the southeastern United States.[130]

Born in Marietta, Arkansas, Lorenza Brown Porter migrated with her family to Chicago at age seven. They first settled at Forty-Seventh and South Langley, then moved into the Ida B. Wells Homes and attended Rev. T. E. Brown's Progressive Baptist Church. Around this time, Porter's mother met a young female gospel group called the Over Coming Four. Porter said that her mother simply informed the group, "'My daughter's going to sing with you.' She didn't ask them, she just told them!" Renamed the Over Coming Five, the group received an invitation by an Elder Brown to sing in Argo. There Porter met Elder Brown's son, Dorsey, and the two were married. After moving to Argo, she joined Antioch Baptist Church and sang in the choir, where she met Thomas, Irons, and Colbert. When two of the original Argo Singers were no longer able to travel, the group invited Porter to take their place.[131] Porter's muscular soprano was distinctive because she could hit high notes but also get deep like a quartet lead.

By 1950, the Argo Singers were Thomas, Irons, Colbert, Murphy, Brown, Louise Rhodes, and Willella Burrell. They appeared on the same gospel programs as other top Chicago groups, singers, and quartets of the day and also had a regular Sunday morning broadcast on WTAQ in LaGrange, Illinois.[132] Their recording career began when they shared a program with the Southern Sons from Jackson, Mississippi.[133]

The Southern Sons were signed to Lillian McMurry's Jackson-based Trumpet label. One of the Sons was Roscoe Robinson, a young singer from Gary, Indiana's Royal Quartet. Because the Argo Singers and the Southern Sons blended well in live performance, McMurry decided that they should record together. In January 1951, the Argo Singers and the Southern Sons recorded "Whisper a Prayer" and "Jesus Will Make Things Alright" at Chicago's RCA Victor studios at 445 North Lake Shore Drive. The organ-piano combination supporting the vocalists was more evocative of traditional gospel group accompaniment than the a cappella quartet vibe of the Southern Sons. Nevertheless, the lead trading between Lorenza Brown and James Walker (who would later join the Dixie Hummingbirds) was powerful. Each group maintained its respective singing style: the Argos disciplined and melodic and the Southern Sons harmonic with flights of vocal virtuosity.

In November 1951, the Argo Singers and the Southern Sons combined forces for McMurry once again, this time at Chicago's Universal. "Near the Cross" and

"Going Home" were the second and final product of the Southern Sons–Argo Singers collaboration.[134] "Near the Cross" became an Argo Singers staple, and the group rerecorded the hymn at its first session for Vee Jay Records on March 9, 1956.[135]

Gospel Singing on Billiken Day

On Saturday, August 11, 1951, nearly twenty years after Dorsey and Frye began rehearsing the first Ebenezer Baptist Church Gospel Chorus, thousands surrounded a makeshift bandstand in Chicago's Washington Park, site of the 1893 Columbian Exposition, to hear the debut of an all-star gospel extravaganza. Brainchild of female evangelist Z. Hawkes Broomfield of Watley Temple COGIC, the Religious Festival of Song was part of the city's annual Bud Billiken Parade. Named for a character invented by David Kellum of the *Chicago Defender* to interest young people in reading the newspaper, the parade was a South Side summer treat for children and adults and featured a full day's worth of festivities bracketing the main event. Each year, a national television, radio, film, or sports personality served as parade marshal, and a local vendor supplied free ice cream to youngsters.

Alongside Broomfield, St. Paul COGIC's Anna Broy Crockett and Father R. O. Brown of Boys' Town directed the inaugural Religious Festival of Song. Willie Webb and Louise Overall Weaver assisted on organ. Scheduled to appear on the bandstand was a representation of the city's most popular gospel artists, including the Greater Harvest Baptist Church Radio Choir with Robert Anderson directing, the Roberta Martin Singers, the South Park Baptist Church Youth Choir (under Martin's baton), the Gay Sisters, Rev. Clay Evans, Ora Lee Hopkins, Princess Stewart, the Thompson Community Singers, the Crockett Jubilee Singers, James Whitehurst, the Willie Webb Singers, DeLois Barrett Campbell, and Rev. Luschaa Allen's Versatile A Cappella Singers. Virginia Davis Marshall and Celeste Scott performed a duet. The Meatchemaires of Morning Star Institutional Baptist Church, led by youth advocate Mother Rose Meatchem, were also slated to appear. Though not as well represented on the debut program, quartets included the Spiritual Five, the Gibson Harmoneers, and the Campbell Jubilee Harmonizers.[136] The religious music program was such a success that the organizers made it a regular part of the annual Billiken Day festivities.[137]

If the Billiken program demonstrated how ecumenical and popular gospel music had become by the early 1950s, a program at Tabernacle Baptist Church the following Tuesday, August 14, further blurred the line between sacred and secular. To celebrate the fourth anniversary of his group, Willie Webb brought Dinah Washington "back to the church." The former Ruth Jones, who started her career in gospel as an accompanist and member of the Sallie Martin Singers, was now queen of the jukebox. "Hey Good Looking," her duet with the Ravens, was charting well. On the program with Washington and the Willie Webb Singers were the Davis Sisters of Philadelphia, Martha Bass of St. Louis, the Roberta Martin Singers, Robert Anderson, the Forty-Fourth Street Baptist Church Choir, the Greater Harvest Radio Choir, and the Haynes Singers. The first two hundred patrons to arrive received a free Willie Webb record.[138]

The Wooten Chorale Ensemble, organized by Robert Wooten in 1949 at Beth Eden Baptist Church in Morgan Park, was also invited to participate. Wooten recalled:

> My cousin, Louise Overall Weaver, was the organist at Forty-Fourth Street Baptist Church. I knew Webb from there, and he asked me, "Why don't you bring your group [Wooten Chorale Ensemble] on over?" So I figured you're not going to get on that kind of a bill, so I went on over there. We were just going to be one of those thrown in the pot with the rest of them, but the Lord saw fit to deliver us in another way.
>
> I was nervous, but we got there and we sang. They were trying to get somebody to get a hold of the house, and I went up there and we did a number titled "I Heard the Voice of Jesus Say." That just tore [up] the house! Mahalia was the emcee and she tried to pick it up, and Louise Overall Weaver was on the organ. The rhythm was a little odd, and they tried to carry it on. Somebody said [to me], "Go on back on!" I said, "No, no, no, let well enough alone!" I sat down, because my legs were just shaking![139]

Although some members of the African American church criticized gospel's dalliance with the business world, it offered a level of financial security that migrants such as Tharpe and Mahalia Jackson had once felt was forever out of reach. In April 1951, Rev. Clarence Cobbs vacated his 5139 South Michigan home for a twenty-room, four-car garage mansion at 4801 South Woodlawn Avenue that he purchased for fifty thousand dollars.[140] Cobbs also bought a vacation home in Cedar Crest, Michigan.[141] Dorsey, who enjoyed fishing and the outdoors in his spare time, purchased his vacation home in Three Oaks, Michigan. Roberta Martin and her family, who had moved to a similarly sized mansion one block south of Cobbs, at 4901 South Woodlawn Avenue, also became a Michigan property owner. She purchased a former motel, complete with cabins, in the southwestern part of the state. Martin's son, Leonard "Sonny" Austin, recalled that the property, known formerly as Rustic Cabins, was located about twenty-five miles west of Kalamazoo. Austin explained, "[It consisted of] a little motel, but it had a little house and about six little cabins. We never rented them out, [Roberta] just, whenever she had company up there, they would stay in the little cabins." Austin said that she "just loved to go up there, because she was away from everybody, except her family, and she could just be herself."[142]

Times were changing. Emblematic of the change was the death of a member of the original gospel nexus. Fifty-five-year-old Magnolia Lewis Butts suffered a heart attack shortly after fellowship services at Metropolitan Community on Friday, December 9, 1949. She was taken immediately to her home at 6037 South Parkway, where she suffered a further setback on Saturday, and efforts to revive her proved futile.[143] She died on December 10.[144] Despite Butts's many contributions as a classical and gospel singer, songwriter—she is credited with writing the congregational favorite "I Know It Was the Blood" with Georgia Jones—director, dramatist, orator, and organizer, the *Defender*'s report of her death was brief and relegated to page seventeen.[145]

Nevertheless, Dorsey dedicated his *Songs with a Message No. 1* song folio to Butts, declaring her the "Mother of the Convention." During the opening program of the April 1950 Board Meeting of the NCGCC, held at Pilgrim Baptist Church, the mass choir dedicated their singing of "Let Mount Zion Rejoice" to her.[146] The following Wednesday, Dorsey and Anna C. Edge unveiled a portrait of Butts, painted by artist Joseph Evans, and by the end of the Board Meeting, a motion carried to place a plaque memorializing the convention's first vice president in the Gospel Singers Home and School.[147] There may have been some concern about the future of the NCGCC without Butts, however. According to the 1950 board meeting minutes, Rev. D. N. Byrd "wanted to see Dr. Dorsey and Mr. Theodore R. Frye shake hands and let the convention know they [would] walk together and lead these people on to greater achievements." The two men shook hands, "and the holy spirit sanctioned their union."[148]

CHAPTER 12

Postwar Gospel Quartets
"Rock Stars of Religious Music"

Chicago was the Promised Land. . . . If you could make it to Chicago, you had it made.

Cleave Graham, Pilgrim Jubilee Singers

After risking their lives to emancipate Europe from the Axis terror, southern black soldiers returned home from the Second World War to find conditions in their communities just as perilous as the ones they had left. Jim Crow laws, lynching, and other forms of brutality at the hands of southern whites were as present in 1945 as they had been in 1941. Lacking access to the voting booth, blacks were unable to unseat southern lawmakers who supported the status quo. These conditions, plus a phasing out of the sharecropper system of farming and the demand for industrial workers in a surging postwar economy, resulted in a continued mass exodus of African Americans to Chicago. The University of Chicago reported that the city's nonwhite population increased 42 percent between 1940 and 1949; Chicago's black population grew to 813,000 the following decade, when more than 2,000 southern black migrants poured into Chicago every week.[1] By 1960, Chicago claimed 500,000 more black residents than in 1940.[2] There were so many migrants from Mississippi that singer Otis Clay joked that Mississippi was a Chicago suburb.

The city's West Side became a significant port of entry for many southern migrants who arrived after 1945. African Americans had been living on the West Side since the 1830s, first settling near Lake and Kinzie Streets, but by 1960, the new wave of migration had increased the black population on the West

Side to 68,146.[3] The area was attractive because Bronzeville was overcrowded. Attempts to integrate neighborhoods beyond Bronzeville's south and southwest borders met with resistance, including both restrictive covenants, which limited where black people could live, and violence, such as broken windows and firebombed homes. There was so much turmoil surrounding the 1953–54 integration of the city's Trumbull Park housing development in the South Deering neighborhood that it appeared as if a portion of the city was embroiled in civil war.

The postwar migration coincided with the rise to national prominence of the male gospel quartet. By the late 1940s and early 1950s, quartets such as the Soul Stirrers, the Pilgrim Travelers, both Blind Boys aggregations (Alabama and Mississippi), the Fairfield Four, the Harmonizing Four, and the Swanee Quintet had gone pro. Hailed as the "rock stars of religious music" by music historian Al Young, quartets packed auditoriums, sang on hundreds of radio stations, and sold records by the tens of thousands.[4] They electrified radio airwaves with their muscular harmonies, hard-singing lead vocalists, and polished showmanship. Sporting matching suits, shirts, and ties—called uniforms— quartets delivered exciting live performances to match their vocal prowess.

The hard-singing quartets were a response to audiences that, as Abbott and Seroff put it, "demanded something more emotionally compelling than simply perfect, 'flat-footed' harmony singing."[5] The adulation that gospel quartets received in the postwar period, coupled with their commitment to religious ministry, led many young Christian men to organize their own quartets. After moving to Chicago from Arkansas, Mississippi, or Louisiana, singers brought their groups to the North, joined quartets already active in the city's gospel network, or started new aggregations. The proliferation of 1950s gospel quartets paralleled the rise in vocal harmony groups organized in the wake of the success of the Ink Spots, the Ravens, the Orioles, and the Four Tunes.

To their elders' fiats of time, harmony, and articulation, Chicago's second-generation quartets, such as the Highway QCs, the Pilgrim Jubilee Singers, and the Kelly Brothers, added lead singers with youthful brilliance, the unbridled passion of the Baptist preacher, or both. Audiences, and particularly female enthusiasts, clamored to hear charismatic Chicago singers such as Sam Cooke, Johnnie Taylor, Lou Rawls, Roscoe Robinson, and James Phelps—who all ultimately entered the popular music world—as well as Spencer Taylor, Leroy Taylor, Cleave and Clay Graham, and Cleve Minter, who did not.

Perhaps most importantly, a quartet that was well respected on the gospel circuit bestowed on its members a badge of honor that was nearly as important as earning a title in the church. Quartet membership offered a measure of status in a society that implicitly and explicitly kept African Americans, and particularly African American men, on the lowest rung of the economic and social ladder.[6] Further, the newfound fame of quartets and their lead singers further blurred the line between church music and big business. The question of what it meant to be black, religious, and cosmopolitan was tested once again.

"Them Soul Stirrers Was Bad!"

Of all first-generation Chicago quartets, none was as formidable as the Soul Stirrers. They were regulars on radio, received top billing at live appearances, and were ready to make a national impact on record. After cutting sides that appeared on Irving Ballin's Gotham and 20th Century labels, and Ink Williams's Harlem imprint, the Stirrers launched a successful run of nearly two dozen singles for Eddie, Leo, and Ira Mesner's Aladdin Records.

The Soul Stirrers lineup during its Aladdin era, May 1946–December 1948, was among its most inspired. It featured R. H. "Pop" Harris, James Medlock, Senior Roy Crain, Thomas L. Bruster, R. B. Robinson, and Jesse James Farley.[7] The quartet's first Aladdin single, released in late June or early July 1946, coupled the spiritual "Steal Away" with the Roberta Martin Singers' "The Lord Will Make a Way." Released simultaneously, the second single, "Remember Me," featured crescendos of resplendent harmonies underpinning Harris's pleading tenor.

The quartet could not have had a more auspicious debut on Aladdin than these two singles. *Billboard* extended its congratulations to the new partnership, commenting, "The diskery has done well to put this vocal quintet on wax."[8] By November 1946, Aladdin was advertising the Stirrers' output alongside records by its top sellers in other categories, including Lester Young in jazz, and Wynonie "Mr. Blues" Harris and Amos Milburn in R&B.[9]

During 1946 and 1947, Medlock and Harris were the Stirrers' main lead singers. Their lead trading was well choreographed—Medlock stated a song's motif in his rich, resonant baritone and then passed the microphone to Harris, who raised the intensity with blue notes and falsetto leaps that evoked the Texas songbirds that he claimed to be his earliest inspirations. After Harris finished his section, Medlock returned, amplifying the emotionality with an even more deliberate delivery. This set up Harris to push the passion to the near-breaking point.

Leroy Taylor joined the Stirrers in 1948 as an alternate baritone lead partner for Harris.[10] Taylor—R. H. Harris told Anthony Heilbut that he was the best gospel singer the group ever had—arrived from the Norfolk Singers, one of Chicago's most revered early quartets.[11] Next they needed a hard-shouting singer. Beginning around 1946 or 1947, both Blind Boys quartets and the Spirit of Memphis were stunning audiences with lead vocalists whose unfettered vocal power evoked a demonstrative preacher at his emotional apex. Thus, in late 1949 or early 1950, when Medlock and Taylor departed the group, the Stirrers acquired Paul Foster, a hard-singing lead who had been working with several West Coast quartets.

Aladdin Records offered the Soul Stirrers six hundred dollars per session, which was decent money for a gospel group at that time, but the quartet often had trouble collecting payment. Art Rupe's Specialty Records, on the other hand, was prepared to offer the quartet the same session rate plus a penny per side in royalties.[12] Further, Specialty had the Pilgrim Travelers, an a cappella quartet famous for their walking rhythm. Thus, as Aladdin promoted the Stirrers' latest release, "Seek and Ye Shall Find" and "One of These Days," in *Billboard* ads as the "gospel hit of the year," the group was in the studio cutting its first sides for Specialty.[13] The first session, held February 24, 1950, produced several selections, including the Stirrers' magnum opus, the two-part "By and By." On "By and By," Harris and Foster traded ever-intensifying leads in a quartet tour de force that moved Anthony Heilbut to remark that the single was "art almost immune to criticism."[14] Although the Pilgrim Travelers were Specialty's top quartet in terms of record sales, *Ebony* dubbed the Soul Stirrers "the top gospel group in the country."[15]

Just as the Soul Stirrers were experiencing great success, Pop Harris opted to leave the group. He wanted to get off the road and spend more time with his family, especially with his infant daughter, but he also had concerns that the gospel highway was becoming morally treacherous. Some of his contemporaries, however, felt Harris knew his value to the Stirrers and was "pulling a power play" to get more of his financial share.[16] Nevertheless, Harris made his departure official at the conclusion of the Stirrers' September 24, 1950, program at DuSable.[17]

Pop Harris would be hard to replace—he was indeed as much a draw as the Stirrers—but R. B. Robinson had an idea. The person he had in mind was not the most conventional choice to fill Harris's shoes, but he was convinced it would work.

Along the 3800–4100 blocks of South State Street could be heard some of the finest gospel quartet singing the city had to offer during the 1940s and 1950s. Several churches and venues on this four-block stretch were notable for programs, musicals, and singing competitions featuring local and traveling quartets. One was Peter's Rock Church at 3839 South State, where former Soul Stirrer Rev. E. A. Rundless was pastor. Travelers Rest Spiritual Church, two blocks south of Peter's Rock at 4014 South State Street, also sponsored regular programs of local talent such as the Willing Four, the Links of Harmony, the Comet Star Gospel Singers, the Southern Faith Singers, the Teenage Kings of

Harmony, the Rising Star Spiritual Singers, and the venerable Alabama and Georgia Singers.[18] Listeners citywide could enjoy the Travelers Rest quartet musicals on its Friday broadcasts over WHFC.[19]

Rose of Sharon Baptist Church, at 3825 State, was an early headquarters for the Quartet Union of Chicago. The Chicago Union was one of the first chapters chartered by the National Quartet Convention, an organization formed sometime after 1945 by Harris of the Soul Stirrers, Charles Bridges of the Blue Jays, and Abraham Battle. Feeling that the principles of time, harmony, and articulation had been all but forsaken, the trio felt that the convention would teach fundamentals and professionalize quartet singing. Harris said, "[Quartets weren't] being accepted by the public because of their language, their pronunciation, their diction—all of that was completely out of order."[20] The union held its first confab at Rev. L. H. Ford's St. Paul COGIC, and among its first order of business was the chartering of individual unions for seven states.[21]

Like Dorsey's National Convention of Gospel Choirs and Choruses, the National Quartet Convention held annual confabs in a different host city each year. Member Flozell Leland told historian Kip Lornell that union activities taught quartet singers "how to meet people, how to address an audience, how to perform, how to dress, and, really, how to sing."[22] For local quartets, it was not only an honor to be selected to represent its city or union at the annual convention, but it also represented abundant opportunities for national exposure.

The local quartet union also functioned like the musician's union in finding performance opportunities for members and was a welcome wagon for traveling groups seeking performance opportunities in town. The Chicago union's Thursday-night quartet battles at the YMCA auditorium at 3838 South State were legendary.[23] With a maximum capacity of two hundred listeners, 3838 State became ground zero for friendly competition between established quartets and newcomers.[24] Quartets that won song battles at 3838 State, especially if they upended a more formidable foe, wore their victory as a badge of honor.

Among the younger groups to participate in 3838 State song battles were the Highway QCs. The original group consisted of brothers Lee and Jake Richardson, Gus Treadwell, Creadell Copeland, and Marvin Jones, whose uncle was Eugene Smith of the Roberta Martin Singers.[25] Because the Highway QCs were trained by R. B. Robinson, employed the Soul Stirrers vocal techniques, and sometimes filled in for the elder quartet on its weekly radio program, the QCs were referred to as the Soul Stirrers Juniors. There is agreement that the Highway portion of the quartet's name was a tribute to Highway Baptist Church on Thirty-Third Street, where several members attended services. The QC portion, however, remains shrouded in mystery. In *Dream Boogie*, Peter Guralnick reports that Copeland's father suggested QC thinking erroneously—and to his son's mortification—that it stood for Quiz Kids, the name of Joe Kelly's popular program.[26] Spencer Taylor, who became a QC in the mid-1950s, believed that the two letters referred to a school that some of the members attended. Regardless of the name's provenance, the most remarkable member of the Highway QCs was Mississippi migrant Sam Cook.

Cook—he added the *e* to his surname after becoming a pop singer—was born in Clarksdale, Mississippi, on January 22, 1931, the fourth of eight children to Rev. Charles and Annie May Cook.[27] Charles was a minister in the Church of Christ Holiness, the denomination organized by Charles Price Jones after his split with C. H. Mason. Cook brought his family to Chicago in the mid-1930s and supported them by working in the stockyards and as assistant pastor of Christ Temple Cathedral at Forty-Fourth and St. Lawrence. The family first settled in an apartment at 3527 South Cottage Grove, near West Point Baptist Church, and later moved around the corner, to 724 East Thirty-Sixth Street.

Like many gospel singers, Cook first performed with his siblings. He, his brothers Charles and L. C., and sisters Mary and Hattie were advertised as the Singing Children. Reverend Cook took the troupe with him whenever he was a guest minister at a church, but the youngsters also sang before the West Point congregation. They impressed West Point member Albertina Walker, who found them to be more than a cute novelty group: "They all *could* sing," she said.[28] They became so popular that David Peale, a friend of their father's, managed their growing number of paid engagements.[29] The group disbanded when the Cook children got older and assumed other responsibilities. Sam subsequently sang spare change off streetcar passengers at Thirty-Fifth and Cottage Grove, crooning "South of the Border" and selections from the Ink Spots catalog.[30]

In 1947, Lee and Jake Richardson happened upon Cook serenading a female admirer and persuaded him to join their Highway QCs. The quartet's big break came when they appeared on a September 26, 1948, program at Wendell Phillips High School with the Fairfield Four, the Flying Clouds of Detroit, and the Soul Stirrers, as well as other national heavyweights. Undaunted in their blue uniforms with matching white pocket handkerchiefs, the QCs hit harmonies like their idols.[31] They impressed Louis Tate, a Gary steelworker from Louisiana who was in the audience. He had experience managing quartets and offered to be their manager.[32]

Under Tate, the QCs hit the gospel highway, traveling to cities such as Detroit, where they caught the ear of Rev. C. L. Franklin. In Memphis, bluesman-turned-preacher-turned-radio personality Rev. Dwight "Gatemouth" Moore invited them to perform on his program on 50,000-watt WDIA. They secured their own fifteen-minute radio program Sunday mornings on WIND, coming on the air with their theme song, "When We Bow in the Evening at the Altar."[33] Tate produced homemade acetates of the QCs but could not secure a recording contract for the youngsters. The labels he pitched felt the quartet sounded too much like the Soul Stirrers, or their voices would soon change and the novelty would be gone.[34]

Nevertheless, Sam Cook's warm smile, personality, and relaxed way of singing—Heilbut has noted that Robert Anderson was one of Cook's influences—gave the QCs their advantage live.[35] But in 1950, the group's similarity to the Soul Stirrers took a heartbreaking turn when they, too, lost their lead singer.

Depending on whose story you believe, replacing R. H. Harris with nineteen-year-old Sam Cook was either R. B. Robinson's idea or S. R. Crain's.[36] Robinson trained Cook and the Highway QCs, and was convinced that the young man's smooth voice and likeable personality would be a great addition to the Stirrers. On the other hand, Crain was the Stirrers' manager and responsible for approving new members. The rest of the Stirrers were not concerned with Cook's singing ability—they heard him with the QCs and knew what he could do. They were worried about how national audiences would respond to replacing Harris with a relatively unknown teenager.[37] Nevertheless, Cook auditioned by singing Reverend Brewster's "How Far Am I from Canaan," and after securing Tate's permission and his fellow QCs' reluctant blessing, Cook became a Soul Stirrer.[38]

Fortunately, the first test of the substitution occurred on friendly territory: the auditorium of Cook's alma mater, Wendell Phillips High School. During a program there, the Stirrers launched into "How Far Am I from Canaan," and as Cook assumed the lead, a young female fan jumped up and shouted, "That's my baby! Sing, baby!" Henceforward, the program belonged to Cook.[39]

The hometown crowd was supportive, but the group was right: pleasing the gospel highway would take some doing. Cook was what the quartets referred to as a "pretty" singer, a pop crooner like Roy Hamilton or Tommy Edwards. He did not have the gut-wrenching vocal power to outsing legendary church-wreckers Archie Brownlee of the Original Five Blind Boys, Sam McCrary of the Fairfield Four, or Kylo Turner of the Pilgrim Travelers. Instead, it was Cook's charisma that initially charmed quartet fans, especially women. Crain noticed it almost immediately. "They're not around Archie; they wasn't around Turner; they wasn't around Sam McCrary," he said. "They was around Sam Cook: leader of the Soul Stirrers!"[40] Still, some promoters were reticent to book the Stirrers without Harris, regardless of whether the new kid could sing. The quartet needed a hit record to change their minds.

The Soul Stirrers' first recording session with Cook happened at Universal Recorders in Hollywood on March 1, 1951. Until he arrived at the studio that day, Art Rupe did not know that Harris had left the group. He was understandably vexed; after all, Harris was the star, but studio time was ticking away and the Pilgrim Travelers' J. W. Alexander, present for the session, vouched for Cook and his singing ability. The quartet ran through their numbers, including "Canaan" and "Peace in the Valley," on which an aurally uneasy Cook traded leads with the thrilling Foster. The quartet's decision to record "Jesus Gave Me Water" that day became another thorn in Rupe's side. The Pilgrim Travelers had released the song on Specialty just two years prior, but the Stirrers assured Rupe that Cook sang it differently.[41] If Cook was somewhat tentative on "Peace," he came into his own on "Water." His voice danced gracefully along the melody line. Rupe need not have worried. Within two months after its April 21, 1951, debut, "Jesus Gave Me Water," coupled with "Peace in the Valley," sold 17,000 copies. Daniel Wolff contends that the disc "single-handedly made Sam Cook's reputation and started the group on its most profitable period."[42]

For the next few years, the Sam Cook–Paul Foster combination was unstoppable. A recording of Cook and Foster sharing lead duties on "Be with Me Jesus" at a July 22, 1955, Stirrers performance at Los Angeles' Shrine Auditorium demonstrated the intensity these two singers generated. During the song's extended vamp, Foster shouted exhortations like a hellfire-and-brimstone preacher, and Cook echoed with passionate responses. Cook took the lead on "Nearer to Thee," and when Foster stormed in with passionate interjections, one female audience member lofted a blood-curdling scream that echoed off the Shrine Auditorium walls.

Sam Cook's brother Charles remembered the impact that the Soul Stirrers had on their audience. "Them Soul Stirrers was bad! Could beat anything else we'd ever heard. . . . When they announce the Soul Stirrers, Sam would be standing at the back of the church, and they'd come down the aisle, and, man, people would just start in to shouting when they'd start singing their theme song. The house would almost come down then, just by them walking in. Them young girls, man. It was quite a scene when Sam would get to town."[43]

In addition to touring, recording, and radio, the Stirrers and their new singer hosted major gospel programs in Chicago. Chief among these events was their annual Mother's Day musical, held at DuSable High School's auditorium. For an admission price of $1.25 in advance or $1.50 at the door, gospel enthusiasts enjoyed an annual who's who of gospel music. Among the featured artists on Stirrers' Mother's Day programs in the 1950s were the Pilgrim Travelers, the CBS Trumpeteers, the Swanee Quintet, the Swan Silvertones, the Dixie Hummingbirds, and the Original Five Blind Boys. To drum up attendance, guest quartets sang on the Stirrers' weekly radio program, which by 1952 was heard Sunday mornings at 9:00 on WAIT.[44]

Hosting an anniversary program was another way for quartets to attract audiences. On October 14, 1955, the Soul Stirrers celebrated their twenty-first anniversary by hosting their largest promotion ever. Titled the *World Series of Gospel*, the musical featured several major gospel artists of the day, including both Blind Boys quartets—Alabama and Mississippi—the Pilgrim Travelers, the Harmonizing Four, the Ward Singers, Dorothy Love Coates and the Gospel Harmonettes, the Willie Webb Singers, and Brother Joe May.[45]

Seeing gospel audiences growing, Specialty's publicity director Lillian Cumber devised the idea of packaging gospel groups and quartets to tour nationally. A September 7, 1952, Herald Attractions program in Albany, Georgia, featuring the Soul Stirrers and Pilgrim Travelers, pulled in more than twenty thousand persons.[46] In New York, radio announcers Thermon Ruth of the Selah Jubilee Singers and the duo of Doc Wheeler and Fred Barr were booking quartets and gospel groups in major venues such as the Apollo. Citing the successes of the Pilgrim Travelers and Mahalia Jackson in broadening the base of gospel music beyond the church walls, reporter Lawrence LaMar opined in 1954 that gospel had the potential to revive all of show business.[47]

With performance opportunities for quartets abounding, R. H. Harris could not stay away from the gospel highway for long. A year after leaving the Stirrers, he organized the Christland Singers with George Croffet from the Norfolk Singers and Stirrers alumni James Medlock and Leroy Taylor. Given its personnel, it was not surprising that the Christland Singers sounded exactly like the pre-Cook Soul Stirrers. Also like the Stirrers, the quartet hosted a radio program—the *Christ Land Broadcast*—over WIND on Sundays at 6:45 a.m.[48] The Christland Singers even sponsored gospel extravaganzas featuring major artists. At their first musical, held May 6, 1951, the quartet presented Charles Watkins, a gospel crooner in the Robert Anderson tradition, who was touring on the strength of his debut single, "Up in My Heavenly Home."[49]

The Christland Singers recorded its first two discs at Universal in Chicago in October 1951.[50] "Let Me Tell You about My Jesus," one of four sides cut that day, reprised the Harris-Medlock duets of the Aladdin era.[51] The recordings were released on Don Robey's Houston-based Peacock Records, whose success with the Original Five Blind Boys of Mississippi and the Bells of Joy made it the premier label for quartets seeking national exposure.

Either the same day or immediately afterward, Harris's wife, Jeanette, brought her Golden Harp Gospel Singers, who had been singing over WIND every Sunday at 7:05 a.m., to Universal to make their debut records for Peacock.[52] At the time of the recording session, the group consisted of Harris, Ann Grant, Irene Williams, Gussie Walton, and Betty Weathers. The first of their two singles was the two-part "Any Stars in My Crown." With drums as their only accompaniment—Robey claimed to be the first to add drums to gospel records to accentuate the rhythm—the Golden Harps chanted in metronomic rhythm while Price intensified the drama steadily throughout the two-part single.[53] The women also recorded "I'll Make It Somehow" and Virginia Davis Marshall's "I Call Him Jesus, My Rock," but neither selection topped the unfettered power of "Any Stars."[54]

While the Golden Harps did not record again until the 1960s, the Christland Singers completed additional sessions for Peacock in August 1953 and April 1955. The dynamic duo of Harris and Taylor traded leads on "I Am Too Close" and "Someday, Somewhere."[55] The group later moved from Peacock to Nashboro, where its "Where Could I Go (but to the Lord)" offered an excellent example of the Harris-Taylor vocal interplay. Supported by energetic harmonizing by the quartet, Taylor burrowed his resonant voice deep into the microphone. When it was his turn, Harris performed a tour de force of falsetto leaps and yodels.

"Music in the Air"

With gospel groups performing with piano and organ, and small combo rhythm and blues groups dominating black radio and jukeboxes, a cappella quartet singing was fast falling from fashion. Unaccompanied quartets, or those that only featured acoustic guitar for rhythm, could not afford to lose performance dates or record deals because promoters or A&R men thought they sounded anachronistic. Around 1952 and 1953, therefore, quartets started adding "music," or instrumental accompaniment. The most common addition would be the electric guitar, but some groups also added drums, piano, and organ.

The innovative Soul Stirrers may have persuaded gospel quartets to move beyond acoustic guitar when they added the Hammond organ to their February 27, 1953, recording session. The accompaniment gave mid-tempo songs such as the joyous "He'll Welcome Me (to My Home)" heightened rhythmic force. The session also introduced the record-buying public to Cook's gospel yodel. The possible origin of Cook's vocal trademark was a California program just prior to the recording date. Cook attempted but failed to hit a high note just out of reach and recovered by improvising a melismatic line—Crain called it "floating under." The result sounded like *whoa-a-oh*.[56] In the studio, Cook debuted his yodel on "End of My Journey," a rearrangement of Lucie Campbell's "He'll Understand, He'll Say Well Done," which the Stirrers recorded in 1948 with Harris and Farley on lead.[57] The vocal riff became so much a part of Cook's vocal technique that on his breakout pop single, "You Send Me," his flirty *whoa-a-oh-a-oh-a-oh* helped the disc soar to number one on the pop chart.

Cook's charm and youthful vigor brought freshness to the sound of the Soul Stirrers and introduced a pop sensibility to the gospel quartet. "Jesus, I'll

Never Forget"—a song one *Billboard* reviewer called "one of their best records" of 1954—and "Nearer to Thee," as well as Virginia Davis Marshall's "Wonderful" and Cook's "Touch the Hem of His Garment," were as melodically and rhythmically infectious as anything on radio.[58] Cook embellished melodies with a vocal arsenal of grace notes, yodels, and raspy turns. The soundtrack of African American sacred modernity was being rewritten by a new generation of youth.

The next young adult added to the Soul Stirrers roster was singer and electric guitarist Leroy Crume. He was born in Swift, Missouri, the eighth of eleven children to Mississippians Dillard and Lonia Crume.[59] The Crumes migrated to Chicago around 1943; they settled first on the South Side and eventually moved to 607 West Division on the North Side.[60] Leroy purchased his first guitar on layaway with eighteen dollars he earned as a *Chicago Sun-Times* paperboy. In the late 1940s, he joined his brothers Amos, Rayfield, Arthur, Willie Peter, and Dillard in organizing a gospel quartet. Except for Leroy's electric guitar, the Crume Brothers' style was consistent with the Highway QCs and the Soul Stirrers.[61] According to Arthur, local churches had to adjust to hearing an electric guitar accompany a gospel quartet. Jack L. Cooper also became apoplectic when Leroy accompanied his brothers on a Cooper-brokered radio program. Musicians were not allowed to play on radio unless they were members of the musicians union, and Cooper doubted Leroy was a member. Leroy assured Cooper that he had a union card to prove his membership, but that presented Cooper with another conundrum: he was unprepared to pay union scale to a musician on a broadcast scheduled for a cappella quartet singing.[62]

Leroy and his eighteen-dollar guitar left the Crume Brothers in the early 1950s to accompany R. H. Harris and the Christland Singers, who recorded "Sell Out to the Master" and "You Got to Be Born Again" in 1956 with organ as well as guitar.[63] By spring of that year, Leroy became the Soul Stirrers' guitarist, replacing Bob King of the Southern Tones and the Bells of Joy.[64]

On February 16, 1955, the Stirrers upped the ante by deciding not to record in Hollywood, as had been their annual ritual, but at Universal in Chicago with musicians specifically associated with gospel groups and soloists. "Art [Rupe] was always sticking his one, five, and ten cents in," Crain explained to Cook biographer Wolff: "We didn't want Art Rupe hanging around. We didn't want nobody but us. We wanted to see how good we were."[65] With Willie Webb on organ and Eddie Robinson on piano, the quartet recorded "Nearer to Thee" and "One More River" with Cook as the sole lead, and "Be with Me Jesus" and "I'm So Glad (Trouble Don't Last Always)" with Cook and Foster trading leads.[66] The sales ledger was proof of the session's success; released around April 1955, "Nearer to Thee" sold twenty-five thousand copies in three months and forty-three thousand copies by year-end. Rupe dropped "One

More River" in June, and it sold twenty-two thousand copies in six months, thereby marking the first time that the Soul Stirrers outsold their Specialty label mates, the Pilgrim Travelers.[67]

Meanwhile, Sammy Mitchell, Lee and Charles Richardson, and Creadell Copeland of the Highway QCs watched their friend Sam's star rise with a mixture of admiration and disappointment. Their lead singer was on his way to fame and fortune and they had no suitable replacement. Fortunately, they found a Sam Cook soundalike named Johnnie Taylor. Born in Crawfordsville, Arkansas, on May 5, 1937, Taylor had been with the Five Echoes, a Chicago vocal harmony group. With Taylor in the lineup, the QCs secured a deal with Vee Jay Records and completed their first session at Universal on May 22, 1955. One of the songs the quartet waxed that day was "Somewhere to Lay My Head," which Taylor wrote especially for the group. With the organist, probably Vee Jay session musician Maceo Woods, providing not so much a beat but a pulse, the QCs with Johnnie Taylor made a record that sounded every bit like a Soul Stirrers production. Taylor yodeled and juggled bent notes just like Cook to the quartet's close harmonies. With Taylor and Lee Richardson as the group's lead singers, the QCs followed "Somewhere" with "Pray"—a song they had learned from the Southern Sons—the buoyant "I Dreamed Heaven Was Like This," "I'll Trust His Word," and "He Lifted My Burdens."[68] "Somewhere to Lay My Head" became so popular that the Sensational Nightingales quickened the tempo and released their own version immediately.

By early 1956, the QCs had added another Taylor to its ranks. Spencer Taylor (no relation to Johnnie) turned out to be a fortuitous acquisition because he would lead them into the twenty-first century. Born March 6, 1928, in Indianola, Mississippi, Taylor migrated to Chicago around 1947 and began attending Greater Harvest Baptist Church, where he met the Holy Wonders. Organized the year Taylor migrated, the Holy Wonders at one time or another included Robert Clay, James Walker, Chris Flowers, Sam Cook's brother L. C. Cook, John Edwards, Alonzo Price, James Phelps, and Lou Rawls.[69] In 1948, the Holy Wonders were looking for a new lead singer and recruited Taylor. Two years later, they made one recording for the Premium label.[70] The group never recorded again or sought the national spotlight because its members had work and family responsibilities; they limited themselves to performing in cities such as Detroit, from where they could return to Chicago in time for work on Monday morning.

Taylor left the Holy Wonders when he entered the service and did not rejoin them when he returned to civilian life. Instead, in late 1955, he was recruited by the Highway QCs. "I knew the QCs, we all came up together," Taylor said. "Sam Cook, all of us, we used to sing together occasionally. We were very familiar with one another. [The] QCs needed a lead singer, and they came looking for me. Johnnie [Taylor] was a very good singer, but they thought they needed somebody else and I was the guy they were looking for."[71] His recruitment underscored the influence of Chicago's informal gospel network, one more powerful than the musicians union, and even the National Quartette Convention, in providing singers and instrumentalists for one program, one season, or for the length of a career.

Like the Holy Wonders, some of the charter QCs eventually left the gospel highway to focus on family and work responsibilities. In 1957, Spencer Taylor recruited former Holy Wonders singers James Walker and Chris Flowers to fill the gaps.[72] The new iteration of QCs became nearly as popular as the Soul Stirrers. With Spencer Taylor on lead and the addition of guitarist Arthur Crume from the Swan Silvertones, the QCs released a string of hits for Vee Jay during the 1950s and 1960s, including "He Said" (1960), "Do You Love Him" (1961), and "All Men Are Made by God" (1962)." The QCs relied on Vee Jay's studio band of Maceo Woods on organ, Al Duncan on drums, and occasionally jazz artist Walter Perkins on drums.[73] The group stayed with Vee Jay until the company went bankrupt in 1966, and they then moved to Peacock. In 1963, Ray Crume left the QCs to organize the Bells of Zion in Miami.

Despite their success, the Highway QCs must have felt like the Soul Stirrers' farm team when in 1957, Johnnie Taylor was recruited by the Stirrers to replace Sam Cook, who was heading into the popular music world.[74]

Sam Cook's last recording session as a Soul Stirrer took place on April 19, 1957. A host of Chicago residents accompanied the quartet, including Evelyn Gay on piano, Willie Webb on organ, L. C. Cook on drums, and Leroy Crume on guitar. The session produced the inspirational "That's Heaven to Me." Like many of its predecessors, "Heaven" had the feel of a pop song with religious lyrics. Two days later, Cook joined the Stirrers on stage for the final time.

The church community was understandably disappointed when Sam Cooke departed for pop stardom, but nobody could deny the economic impetus of his decision. As a teenager, gospel singer Betty Lester enjoyed seeing the Highway QCs perform at Rising Sun Baptist Church in South Chicago. She said, "I was coming back from Florida [in 1957] and I heard this voice [on the radio]: 'Darling, you send me.' I knew it was Sam Cooke. Oh, my goodness! Oh no! I was so hurt that he had switched over, but as I got older, I began thinking, well, he has a family to support."[75] Indeed, Cooke was reportedly making $400 per week with the Soul Stirrers, which was considered "a top figure for the church circuit." After six months in the pop arena, however, Cooke was poised to earn $100,000, and pundits at the time anticipated his earnings would reach $250,000 by 1958.[76] "There were a lot of things I wanted to do," Cooke reported. "I wanted to do things for my family, and I wanted nice things for my own. Making a living was good enough, but what's wrong with doing better than that?"[77]

On March 4, 1958, as Cooke's latest pop single, "You Were Made for Me," was emanating from transistor radios, the Soul Stirrers went into the studio with Cooke's replacement, Johnnie Taylor. Taylor led a song he wrote called "The Love of God." He evoked Cooke's smooth sincerity as he had done many times with the Highway QCs. Taylor and the Stirrers' final recording session for Specialty occurred in February 1959, producing a handful of tracks, including "When the Gates Swing Open."[78] A year later, Rupe, exhausted from the record business, ceased operations on Specialty Records.

Meanwhile, James Cleveland recorded "The Love of God" with Detroit's Voices of Tabernacle Choir in 1959. Ironically, it was Taylor's intensely spiritual quartet song sung by the Voices of Tabernacle that signaled the decline of quartet dominance in gospel music.

James Phelps, the Gospel Songbirds, and the Clefs of Calvary

Johnnie Taylor was not the only quartet lead to incorporate Sam Cooke's melodic vocal flourishes into his singing. James Phelps sounded so much like Cooke that Chess Records thought he just might be the next singer to cross over successfully from gospel to soul.

Born in Shreveport, Louisiana, Phelps sang in a local quartet called the Spiritual Five before migrating to Chicago around 1949.[79] With unfulfilled hopes of becoming a Soul Stirrer, Phelps joined Greater Harvest Baptist Church, where he sang in the choir, directed by Robert Anderson.[80] At Greater Harvest, Phelps met and joined the Holy Wonders, whose personnel included then-unknown Lou Rawls.[81] He eventually switched to the Gospel Songbirds, where he led "When They Ring Those Golden Bells" and "God's Creation" for the quartet's debut single on C. H. Brewer.[82]

In 1960, Phelps joined yet another Chicago quartet, the Clefs of Calvary. Led by Phelps's Cooke-inspired vocals, the Clefs of Calvary captured the Soul Stirrers' sound so well that the Stirrers were mistakenly asked to sing Clefs of Calvary songs during their live performances.

Around that time, Shirley Caesar introduced the Clefs to Ozzie Cadena, who recorded the quartet at Rudy Van Gelder's famous studios. Phelps told Chicago radio announcer Bob Abrahamian that one of the cuts, "Standing

Where Jesus Stood," not only became the quartet's biggest gospel hit; it also entered the R&B charts and landed the Clefs on *American Bandstand*.[83]

Phelps's desire to be a Soul Stirrer was granted in 1964 when he filled in for lead vocalist Jimmy Outler on an engagement in Michigan. Phelps moved the audience so thoroughly that he was invited to join the Stirrers, where he remained for a year, including a Madison Square Garden performance where he and Cooke sang a duet on "Trouble in the Land." Phelps was also featured on some of the group's appearances on Sid Ordower's *Jubilee Showcase* television program, singing such songs as "Mother Don't Worry about Me" and "Must Jesus Bear the Cross Alone." The Clefs of Calvary replaced Phelps with Roscoe Robinson.

After hearing Phelps at the Michigan program, Roebuck Staples was worried that Phelps might follow Cooke's lead: out of the Stirrers and into the pop world. His hunch turned out to be correct. Chess Records persuaded Phelps to make secular recordings, thinking he could be the next Sam Cooke. Chess producer Gene Barge wrote Phelps's breakout soul single, "Love Is a Five Letter Word." Released on Chess's Argo subsidiary in 1965, the song hit the top of the R&B charts and enjoyed a seven-week run.[84] Other singles followed, but none equaled "Love" in success. By 1972, Phelps had grown weary of the vicissitudes of the music business. He moved to California and became an entrepreneur until his death in 2010 at age seventy-eight.[85]

The Emergence of Roscoe Robinson

Like Sam Cooke, Johnnie Taylor, Lou Rawls, and James Phelps, Roscoe Robinson left gospel, where he had honed his craft in some of the era's most popular quartets, to sing pop music. Unlike the others, however, Robinson eventually returned to gospel music full-time.

Born May 22, 1928, in Dermott, Arkansas, Roscoe Robinson migrated to Chicago with his mother after his father's death. He sang briefly with the Kelly Brothers, but when his mother moved to nearby Gary, Indiana, Robinson moved with her.[86] He soon entered Gary's robust quartet community, singing with Joiner's Five Trumpets and the Royal Quartet, a group he called "about the biggest thing in Gary" at the time.[87]

Probably named for its radio sponsor, the Royal Barber Shop, the Royal Quartet was indeed one of the most prestigious Gary-based gospel quartets of the early 1950s. At the time, the group consisted of Robinson, manager Joseph Dishman, Clifford Thomas, Alvin Dixon, Lindsey Davis, John Whitfield, and S. W. Smith.[88] Their Sunday-morning radio show on WJOB was so popular that they joined the Echoes of Eden, one of Northwest Indiana's best-known female gospel quartets, on a November 1950 citywide salute to popular DJ Eddie Honesty.[89]

Robinson first met Cooke when the Royal Quartet and the Highway QCs participated in a Chicago Quartet Union monthly musical. Soon afterward, the QCs appeared with the Southern Sons in Little Rock, Arkansas. The Sons wanted Cooke to join them, but Cooke convinced them that "'Scoe is the guy you need." The Southern Sons met Robinson at a Gary restaurant and, going completely on Cooke's recommendation, asked Robinson to audition for them.

Robinson sang with the Southern Sons briefly in 1951 and then entered the army. After his discharge in 1953, he met the Silver Quintette's Huey Lee Brown, who informed Robinson that Nashville's Fairfield Four was breaking up. Some members, including bass singer Isaac "Dickie" Freeman, were forming a new group called the Skylarks. Brown persuaded Robinson to contact Fairfield Four manager Sam McCrary and suggest that he and the Silver Quintette join McCrary as a reconstituted version of the Fairfield Four. McCrary consented, and with Robinson and Joe "Snap Your Fingers" Henderson, the Silver Quintette became the Fairfield Four at live appearances, although not for recordings.

A performance deal gone sour led Robinson to discontinue his association with the Fairfield Four. He linked up with Ernest James of the Sensational Nightingales, who brought him into his new quartet, the Gospel Jays. While performing with the Jays in California, Robinson ran into Archie Brownlee, lead singer of the Original Five Blind Boys of Mississippi.

For some time, Brownlee had been trying to get Robinson to join the Blind Boys, but Robinson forever declined. "I have to be honest with you," Robinson said, "at the time, I was afraid of blind people."[90] He finally overcame his phobia of the sightless and capitulated to Brownlee's persuasiveness. But Brownlee had bigger plans for the Gary resident than singing in the background. Robinson recalled:

[Brownlee said,] "They want to put me into the hospital." I said, "Hey, man, who gonna sing [lead]?" He said, "You." I said, "Man, I can't even." He said, "Yes you can." I said, "No, I can't." Then, what really made me do it, he said, "Why you think I been sitting up late at night giving you pointers and singing with you?" That's what he told me. I said, "Well, I guess you're trying to help me." He said, "I *was* trying to help you. You're qualified. Take the group until I come back, man."[91]

Brownlee entered Charity Hospital in New Orleans in early 1960. "We were in Baton Rouge, Louisiana," Robinson said, "and Lloyd Woodard called to check on Archie. They told him he had passed." Robinson assumed responsibility for the group's leads thereafter.

Brownlee's confidence in Robinson was well founded. He proved himself a soulful messenger of a gospel song, as demonstrated on "Weeping for a Mighty Long Time" and "The World Is Full of Sin," both recorded for Checker, and

"Sending Up My Timber" on Peacock. But when Peacock owner Don Robey wanted the Blind Boys to sign a predated contract that suggested to Leonard and Phil Chess that the quartet had recorded their Checker album while still under contract to Peacock, Robinson and Lawrence "Shorty" Abrams refused to sign. The issue ballooned into a legal matter. In Bil Carpenter's *Uncloudy Days*, Robinson is quoted as saying, "It was hard for me to get a job with another gospel group because they made it look like I had left the Blind Boys for the white man. They didn't get it how it should have been that I left because I was trying to do the right thing. People believed it, so promoters wanted no part of me."[92] In her history of Chess Records, *Spinning Blues into Gold*, Nadine Cohodas reports that the complaint between Chess and Peacock was so entangled that the FBI investigated the matter. In 1963, Judge J. Samuel Perry found in favor of Peacock, but the Chess brothers appealed. Subsequently, other Blind Boys spoke out about the altered agreement. Perry was criticized by the appeals court for "a failure to exercise sound legal discretion" in his earlier ruling, and the matter was remanded to his court. Perry again found in favor of Peacock, and the case dragged on until 1970, when the appeals court threw out Perry's judgment, nearly a decade after the initial complaint.[93]

Meanwhile, Robinson and Abrams organized the Blind Boys of Ohio and cut one single for Constellation Records, "Sell Out to the Master." Unable to get their music played on the radio, Robinson became disillusioned with gospel and shared his concern with producer Gene Barge. Barge wrote his friend a secular song, "That's Enough," and Robinson recorded it for his own Gerri label, named for his second wife. Ernie Leaner of United Distributors got the disc into the hands of Scepter Records. Scepter rereleased the song nationally, and it became a top-ten R&B hit.[94]

"Ernie Leaner made me in the R&B field," Robinson said. "He was the one who took my record and made sure it was played in Chicago, and it got big enough, and then he put out the feelers for me at different labels."[95] Robinson has since returned to gospel quartet singing and organized a new aggregation, the Birmingham Blind Boys, in 2012.

The Soul Stirrers and Highway QCs were Chicago's top quartets in a city teeming with groups. Some, such as the Holy Wonders, had more modest aspirations, limiting their singing to weekends or to their home church. Other quartets, such as the Southern Faith Singers, the Faithful Wonders, and the Chicago Travelers, built strong reputations in the Midwest but did not record until later in their career. Others, such as the Kelly Brothers, the Pilgrim Jubilee Singers, and the Willing Four, pursued a national audience through live performances and recordings, as did the Silver Stars, the Spiritual Five, the Kingdom Bound

Singers, and the Kindly Shepherds. Although the history of Chicago gospel quartet singing merits its own book-length examination, the Pilgrim Jubilee Singers, the Kelly Brothers, and the Norfleet Brothers are three examples of quartets that formed in the South, migrated to Chicago, and became nationally recognized artists.

The Pilgrim Jubilee Singers

Two of thirteen children born to farmers Columbus and Josephine Chandler Graham, Cleave (b. January 8, 1928) and Clay (b. August 26, 1936) Graham started singing in an informal family group with their brothers, Theophilus "Hoppy" (1914–84), Elgie C. B. (1920–85), cousin Monroe Hatchett, and cousins-in-law Willis Johnson and Alfred Brownlee. From Houston, Mississippi, the Pilgrim Jubilee Singers—C.B. is credited with suggesting the name—organized officially around 1944, when Cleave replaced Brownlee and the group began singing for the family's home church, New Zion Missionary Baptist, as well as at other local venues.[96]

Seeking more than a life of farming, Hoppy joined the postwar migration to Chicago in 1947 and settled on the city's Near West Side. "Chicago was the promised land," Cleave commented. "To most of us black in southern states, if you could get to Chicago, you had it made."[97]

In Chicago, Hoppy met Major Roberson, a fellow Mississippi migrant born in Gunnison on June 11, 1925. The two sang in a local quartet called the Bells of Zion, but in 1949 Roberson joined the Pilgrim Harmonizers, a quartet comprised largely of members from Greater Whitestone Missionary Baptist Church on the West Side.[98] Cleave and Elgie eventually joined Hoppy in Chicago, and in 1952 they brought on Monroe Hatchett and reorganized the Pilgrim Jubilee Singers, known colloquially as the "Jubes." Teenaged Clay had just migrated to Chicago and at first sang with the group only on occasion. Then Roberson left the Pilgrim Harmonizers; he joined the Jubes, bringing along one of the quartet's popular songs, "Life's Evening Sun."[99] In 1953, the Jubes—with Roberson and bass singer Kenny Madden but without Hoppy—made their first recording. Roberson told Young: "We heard about this Chance Records—that they would do you a session, then charge you so much for so many records. You would pay it and take your records and go on about your business. So that's the way it was. We weren't contracted, we paid them. Then we carried them around in our arms and sold them on the programs."[100]

The group recalled selling between five hundred and one thousand copies of their Chance disc, which contained a cappella versions of "Happy in the Service of the Lord" and "Just a Closer Walk with Thee."[101] In late 1953, the Jubes, with Arthur Crume on guitar, made a second self-financed record, this time for the Northern Brightrecord Corporation, a short-lived Chicago label run by C. H. Brewer. It was the first Jubes disc to feature an original song, "Angel," written by Roberson.[102]

In 1954, while Roberson was recuperating from tuberculosis, Roy Harris, the former manager of the Norfolk Singers, took over management of the Pilgrim Jubilee Singers.[103] The group purchased time on WSBC, sharing the cost (forty-five dollars) and time (fifteen minutes) with the Spiritual Five, a Chicago quartet that consisted of Silas Washington, Lee Toussaint, and Marshall Jackson. Purchasing radio time was a good investment for quartets because a popular broadcast could lead to paid engagements.

R. H. Harris, who Heilbut said credited the Jubes with a unique time sense, paid the Jubes an even higher compliment by nominating them to represent the Chicago Quartet Union at the 1955 National Quartet Convention in Oakland.[104] There the group met S. R. Crain of the Soul Stirrers, who introduced them to Art Rupe in hopes that he would sign them to Specialty Records. On Crain's recommendation, Rupe recorded the quartet singing several selections, but no recordings were released.[105] J. W. Alexander of the Pilgrim Travelers was concerned that the groups' similar names would confuse the public. Rupe told the Jubes that he would keep them on contract if they changed their name, but they declined.[106]

The group's next opportunity to release records on a major gospel label came when the Spiritual Five introduced them to Ernie Young of Nashboro Records, for whom they began recording in 1955.[107] Released in 1959, the Jubes' third record for Nashboro, "River of Jordan," and "Father, I'm Coming Home," became their most successful disc to date and helped open up national doors.[108]

The first open door led to Barney Parks. The husband and manager of national recording artist Edna Gallmon Cooke was in a quandary because Cooke was ill and unable to fulfill a handful of upcoming singing engagements. He needed a group to fill the dates, heard and liked the Jubes' Nashboro record, and offered them the job.[109] The Jubes not only completed the Cooke engagements, but along the way they received additional invitations to sing.

Ironically, the second door opened by "River of Jordan" paved the way for the Pilgrim Jubilees to leave Nashboro Records and sign with Peacock. The quartet was to appear on a major gospel program at Atlanta's City Auditorium. Dining alone across the street from the Atlanta hotel where the quartet was staying, Cleave saw an automobile roll past the restaurant, advertising the City Auditorium program by blaring "River of Jordan" over an external loudspeaker attached to the roof. Hearing his group's music played over a loudspeaker was exciting to Cleave, but he was not the only one in the restaurant who took notice. Dave Clark, Peacock's A&R man, happened to be sitting at another table. He wanted to know the name of the group being broadcast over the loudspeaker. Cleave said: "People [in the restaurant] told him it was one of the groups that would be on the program tomorrow. I said, 'That's the Pilgrim Jubilees, that's my group!' Peacock was the boss recording company back then, especially [for] quartet[s]." Clark gave Cleave his business card and met with the Jubes at their hotel, but nobody in the group believed Clark actually represented Peacock until they got the formal recording contract in the mail.[110]

The Jubes' first session for Peacock took place in late 1959 at Universal in Chicago, with Willie Dixon as producer. The group planned to record "Stretch Out," a variation on the Roberta Martin Singers' 1957 "Dark Hours," and "Evening Sun," the song Roberson brought from the Pilgrim Harmonizers. What the group did not know was that their bass singer, Kenny Madden, was not planning to attend the session. Cleave said:

> We had that recording session set up for Universal Recording Company, down there on the Gold Coast. And my bass singer decided he wasn't going to record. In fact, we didn't know he wasn't going to be there until we were at the studio. We didn't have that bass to do the boom-boom-boom. Major saw a big upright bass sitting in the studio and asked Willie Dixon, "Who does this instrument belong to?" Willie said, "That's mine." He said, "You can play it?" He says, "Sure I can play it. Let's try it." We got on it right quick and bam! Man, ["Stretch Out"] came out with that bass guitar going, and people started calling us the Rock and Roll Jubilees. Then they started calling us the "Stretch Out" boys. It just changed the whole quartet [sound]. You talk about quartets firing bass singers! Boy, I know [bass singers] didn't like us too well![111]

Willie Dixon had played double bass behind gospel artists before, most notably in 1955 backing COGIC pianist Rev. Robert Ballinger on his Chess recording of "This Train." Unlike Ballinger's disc, "Stretch Out" became a national hit. It set the Pilgrim Jubilee Singers on a path to prominence. Afterward, Peacock began recording other gospel artists, including Ballinger, at Universal, with Dixon's bass providing the propulsive rhythm.[112]

Over the course of more than a decade, the Pilgrim Jubilee Singers recorded several hits for Peacock, including "Old Ship of Zion," "Wonderful," "Too Close," and "True Story." Recorded in 1963, "True Story" was based on a conversation Clay had with a North Side man who was beaten down by life and wondered whether the Lord would forget him when he died. The song inaugurated the Jubes' practice of including sermonettes, or story songs, in their live and recorded performances.[113]

The Kelly Brothers

The Kelly Brothers, another important Chicago gospel quartet during the 1950s and early 1960s, was first known as the Little Delta Big Four when brothers Andrew (1935–2005), Curtis (b. 1937), and Robert (b. 1939) Kelly began singing with cousin Robert Pittman at Pleasant Valley Church in Alligator, Mississippi.

Mattie Deere of the *Clarksdale (MS) Daily Press* was sufficiently impressed with the young quartet to become its manager and book appearances for them at churches around Clarksdale, Mississippi, and in Arkansas. In the late 1940s, the Kelly Family moved to Chicago. There, in 1951, the youths met William Adair, who persuaded them to reorganize their gospel quartet.[114] With Adair as manager, the quartet called itself the Kelly Brothers. The name came about, Robert told music journalist Martin Goggin, because "there was a lot of 'family' groups in gospel and we would do gospel programs at churches with groups like the Crume Brothers and the McCauley Sisters."[115] Adair also sang lead until Offe Reese joined the group in 1952. Reese, born June 9, 1928, in Hernando, Mississippi, knew the Kellys before they migrated north.[116]

While singing for local churches, the Kelly Brothers met C. H. Brewer who introduced them to an up-and-coming record man named Ewart Abner, who was working for Art Sheridan at Chance Records. The quartet recorded "Let Me Fly" and "God Laid His Hands on Me" for Chance in 1954. The disc was never released, suggesting that it was not a self-financed record such as the Pilgrim Jubilee Singers' effort but rather a session requested by Abner and Sheridan.[117] Sometime after T. C. "Charles" Lee joined the quartet, Brewer persuaded the group to record for his own label. The Kelly Brothers returned to the studio to wax "Prayer for Tomorrow" and "God Said He Is Coming Back Again" for C. H. Brewer Records. The quartet had better luck this time; the C. H. Brewer release became the group's first commercial disc.[118] The Reese-led "Prayer for Tomorrow" came to the group from James Walker of the Dixie Humming-birds. Roscoe Robinson, who sang with the Kelly Brothers from time to time and briefly worked with Walker in the Southern Sons, introduced Walker to the Kellys.[119]

Reese became the group's manager in 1955 and secured appearances for them in churches, auditoriums, and other venues throughout the city, the country, and into Canada. The Kelly Brothers sang regularly over local radio stations WOPA and WSBC to promote their live appearances. Reese sought new recording deals, too, inking one in 1956 with Abner, who by then had left Chance to work for Vee Jay Records. In September 1956, the Kelly Brothers rerecorded their two C. H. Brewer sides for Vee Jay. Curtis Kelly told Goggin: "Having a record on Vee Jay was a big deal back then. [Promoters] looked at us in a different light, because the only other Chicago groups we knew that were recording were the Soul Stirrers and Highway QCs."[120] When Vee Jay dropped the Kelly Brothers, Reese went to Nashboro, where the Spiritual Five, the Pilgrim Jubilees, the Christland Singers, and the Kindly Shepherds, a local group that signed with Nashboro as early as 1952, had enjoyed success. The Kelly Brothers recorded for Nashboro, but the deal ended in 1959, after two years and two singles.

In 1960, the group met with Alphonso "Sonny" Thompson (1916–89), King Records' A&R man, at his office at Twenty-First and Michigan in Chicago. Thompson, a recording artist, had held the A&R position since the late 1950s, succeeding Ralph Bass, who had moved to Chess.[121] Thompson was not interested in recording the quartet initially but later reconsidered and signed them to Federal, a King subsidiary. On June 1, 1960, the Kelly Brothers cut eight sides, all of which were released. Both sides of the group's third single, "He's Alright" and "He's the Same Today," became radio hits.[122] The discs showcased the group's churchy, vocally intense, guitar-driven approach, a style that was prevalent among gospel quartets during the early 1960s. The Kelly Brothers recorded another eight sides in February 1962, and Thompson was sufficiently confident of the quartet's sales potential to package most of their singles on an LP called *The Kelly Brothers Sing a Page of Songs from the Good Book*.[123]

By 1963, the group was not making enough money from the gospel highway to care for their families, so they heeded Thompson's recommendation that they sing soul music. Thompson renamed the group the King Pins, and they waxed several sides for Federal, even while still performing on gospel programs as the Kelly Brothers. Dual identities posed a problem; during a Huntsville, Alabama, concert, one attendee exclaimed, "That ain't no King Pins. I saw them last month, that's the Kelly Brothers!"[124]

Ironically, the King Pins' breakout hit for Federal, "It Won't Be This Way Always," was the secularization of a gospel song. It hit number thirteen on the R&B chart in 1963. While King released more singles by the group, none achieved the impact of "It Won't Be This Way Always." After a few more years on the soul circuit and some releases for Nashville-based Sims Records, where they worked with fellow Chicago residents Dillard and Rufus Crume, the Kelly Brothers returned to their gospel roots. In 1970, the group recorded for Creed and then for Reese's indie imprint, One Way.[125]

The Norfleet Brothers

Organized in 1946, the Norfleet Brothers were a quartet that, like the Harmonizing Four and the Radio Four, held fast to the sweet, jubilee-style harmonies made popular by their favorite group, the Golden Gate Quartet, even though quartet singing had transitioned toward a harder, sanctified sound by the time they migrated to Chicago.[126]

Consisting of fifteen children—ten sons and five daughters—the Norfleet Family originated in Marion, Alabama, not far from Selma.[127] The family worshipped at Oak Grove Methodist Church, where some of the children sang in the choir. Joe Norfleet told gospel music historian Opal Nations that a senior member of the family named Moses, nicknamed Mose, organized the first iteration of Norfleet Brothers when his brothers returned from active duty in World War II. The liner notes to the group's debut album for Checker suggest that several of the brothers were harmonizing informally prior to the war, and the *Chicago Defender* noted that Pete and Arthur began as a duet at age ten and twelve, respectively.[128]

The Norfleets migrated to the Chicago area in 1948, and during the early 1950s, Joseph, Junious, Arthur, Peter, and Nathaniel Norfleet began making the rounds of quartet programs. Their straightforward, uncomplicated singing, without vocal melisma or shouting, evoked the family's musically conservative Methodist upbringing. In 1957, with cousin George Taylor singing bass, the Norfleets made their first commercial recording, "None but the Righteous," for JOB, a label founded in July 1949 by Joe Brown and James "St. Louis Jimmy" Oden.[129] The group recorded again in late 1958 or early 1959 for Al Benson's Divine Grace imprint, but nothing was released from that session.[130] Meanwhile, with Robert Bonner on guitar, the quartet was steadily building a national reputation and landed weekly radio assignments on WBEE and WSBC.[131] The brothers also recorded radio commercials for American Family Detergent, Aunt Jemima Self-Rising Flour, and Al Abrams Pontiac.[132]

By 1960, the Norfleet Brothers were operating out of the Second Baptist Church of Harvey and had signed with Violet Muszynski's Chicago-based Jerico Road label, where they cut an EP called *Songs of Faith and Praise*.[133] Like the JOB disc, the EP showcased the quartet's sweet jubilee singing with rhythm guitar accompaniment. Cuts such as "Jonah" and "Shadrack" paid tribute to the Golden Gate Quartet, a favorite of the Norfleets since their Alabama days. Although their 1961 tribute to Rev. Dr. Martin Luther King Jr., recorded for Henry Rush's eponymously named label, was a local favorite, the Norfleet Brothers became most associated with "Shadrack," a jubilee-style number that evoked the Golden Gate Quartet's technique of telling a Bible story in rhythm.

Sherman Abrams of Al Abrams Pontiac took a special interest in the group and had them perform on his gospel program that broadcast over WBEE from his dealership's showroom. When in 1963 the *Jubilee Showcase* television program debuted on WBKB, the Norfleets sang the opening theme song and were regulars on the program. "Shadrack" and their *Jubilee Showcase* appearances earned them a recording contract for Checker, where their first album, recorded in 1963, was predictably titled *Shadrack*.

Traveling the Gospel Highway

Deacon Reuben Burton of the Victory Travelers noted that many quartets may have wanted to record but did not know how to go about it.[134] On the other hand, groups that signed with a major label—gospel or otherwise—had to tour to promote the record. Not all groups had an appetite for such a commitment. Those unwilling or unable to tour were passed over in favor of quartets that were willing to ride the gospel highway, no matter how treacherous it was.

Quartets that took to the road to promote their records discovered how harrowing touring could be. Driving hundreds of miles through the early morning hours to get from program to program was arduous and stressful. Rev. Cleve Minter explained: "At that time, wasn't no money being made. We weren't making *no* money. Sometimes we didn't make enough for car fare! It was just one of the things, but we loved singing. So we sacrificed. There were times when we would take off our jobs, we'd leave here Friday, get back in early Monday morning in time enough to go to work. But we loved it. Anytime you love something, you're going to sacrifice to do it."[135]

"You had to be dedicated and really want to do it," said Robert Dixon of the Salem Travelers, "because the average guy went on the road for six or seven years. Some of them left good jobs. Some lost their wives and stuff, because that happens when you're gone a lot. So it had to be something you made up your mind, this is really what I want to do and I'm going to do it. There wasn't anything given to you."[136]

A passion for singing notwithstanding, quartets often participated unwillingly in highway drama such as poor weather conditions, dangerous mistakes by fellow motorists, and mechanical failures of their autos and busses. Henry Sutton, manager of Chicago's Willing Four, recalled the quartet's most frightening automobile accident: "We were coming out of Detroit, and a fruit truck hit us on the side and knocked us all the way across the road. Knocked one of the guys out of the van. The door came open and he flew out of the van. About all he could see was that truck coming back at him. And he got up and rolled out of the way. I think all of us went to the hospital. It totaled that van."[137] Not only the van, but the accident also damaged some of the musicians' instruments, including Arthur Sutton's Rickenbacher electric bass guitar.

The Pilgrim Jubilees recalled a similarly harrowing incident from the 1950s. Cleave told Jubes biographer Young: "We were doing eighty-five miles an hour. We went into a low place in the highway, where it was shady, and it wasn't nothing but black ice. The minute we hit that ice, the car swerved. We were going so fast it was going sideways. And when it switched back around, it came up on the dry pavement, and that flipped it. But God blessed us . . . There was five or six of us in there, one man had a little scratch on his leg."[138] Roberson added that "the car was on its side, so we had to reach up to open the door—and just like little bugs, we came out."[139]

Even a minor road breakdown could become dangerous, explained Zadella "Mama" Curtis, a former choir director who became an ardent promoter of quartet music. "If their car broke down on the road, they pushed the car, because if a truck came by with a white person, they were so afraid that the truck was coming back and it was going to be with people with bats and the hoods. They were coming to kill them, so they had no alternative."[140]

Minter remembered such an engagement in Shula, Mississippi: "In those days, segregation was heavy down [in Mississippi]. I learned after we had gotten out of town there was some people came looking for us to 'sing for them.' They weren't quartet lovers!" Luckily, by the time the people got to where the quartet had been staying, "we were well out of the state of Mississippi."[141]

Even in the best of driving conditions, traveling through the segregated South meant not being served at restaurants and being barred from staying in hotels or using public restrooms at gas stations. "Quartets didn't have the luxury of buses and vans," Curtis said. "They were piled up in the car. Everybody tells the story of sitting in the back seat—four, five, six in the back seat—everybody sleeps the same way, and the first one to wake up and wants to turn, you've got to wake everybody up so everybody can turn at the same time."[142]

Despite the drawbacks, the gospel highway also provided memorable anecdotes. Willing Four bass player Arthur Sutton recalled a time when their lead singer, Isaiah Beene, was "working the crowd. He was going up and down the aisles, and he went into a squall. He threw his head like this, he sings, 'Waaahhh,' and his [false] teeth came out of his mouth! Hit the floor and rolled up the aisle! He went and grabbed them and kept on to the back of the church, came back around, kept on singing. Man, I had to turn my head, I was so tickled I didn't know what to do!"[143]

Robert Dixon remembered a time when the Salem Travelers experienced a wardrobe malfunction. "Chester Feemster was five-five, and I'm five-seven. We wanted to buy a Nehru, this long coat, but Chester was short. He told me that's not for short guys, but the majority won so they decided to go ahead and get it. Chester, he went and had his [coat] tailored so it wouldn't be so long. When it came time to go on stage, everybody put the coats on, and [he] put [my] coat on by accident. When he came on stage, I looked at him and said, 'It looks like you've got a robe on!' He looked down, looked at me. He started to go off, but then he came back. We laughed about that for years!"[144]

A storefront Church of God in Christ in Chicago.
(Russell Lee; photo courtesy of Library of Congress, Prints and Photographs Division)

Chicago COGIC pioneers Bishop William and Mrs. Mamie Roberts.
(Photo courtesy of Ronald and Ramona Branch)

The first gospel record:
Arizona Dranes on OKeh,
1926.
(Author's collection)

Pace Jubilee Singers; Charles H. Pace is in the back row, far left.
(Author's collection)

Pioneering radio minister Elder Lucy Smith.

(Lucy Collier Papers, courtesy of the Vivian G. Harsh Research Collection of Afro-American History and Literature, Chicago Public Library)

Rev. Clarence H. Cobbs (right, in robe) with members of the First Church of Deliverance.
(Photo courtesy of First Church of Deliverance)

First Church of Deliverance Choir.
(Photo courtesy of First Church of Deliverance)

Thomas A. Dorsey, circa 1935.
(Author's collection)

Left to right: Necie Morris, Kenneth Morris, Sallie Martin, unknown date.
(Photo courtesy of Kenneth Woods Jr.)

Early promotional photo of
Mahalia Jackson.
(Author's collection)

A young Theodore R. Frye.
(Ebenezer Missionary Baptist
Church Papers, courtesy of
the Vivian G. Harsh Research
Collection of Afro-American
History and Literature, Chicago
Public Library)

Magnolia Lewis Butts,
Mother of the Convention.
(Photo courtesy of Kenneth
Woods Jr.)

The first Ebenezer Baptist Church Gospel Chorus, 1932.
(Ebenezer Missionary Baptist Church Papers, courtesy of the Vivian G. Harsh Research
Collection of Afro-American History and Literature, Chicago Public Library)

Luschaa Allen and the Versatile A Cappella Chorus, 1951.
(Louise Overall Weaver Papers [1946–84], courtesy of Chicago History Museum, ICHi-67661)

Sallie Martin and her Singers of Joy, circa late 1940s. Left to right: Dorothy Simmons, Melva Williams, Sallie Martin, Julia Smith, Cora Brewer Martin.
(Photo courtesy of Kenneth Woods Jr.)

Roberta Martin Singers, circa 1939. Left to right: Eugene Smith, Norsalus McKissick, Willie Webb, Roberta Martin, Robert Anderson; James Lawrence (inset).

(Group photo from author's collection; Lawrence photo from Lucy Collier Papers, courtesy of Vivian G. Harsh Research Collection of Afro-American History and Literature, Chicago Public Library)

Soul Stirrers, 1950s. Sam Cooke is front, center.

(Author's collection)

Louise Overall Weaver, 1949.
(Louise Overall Weaver Papers [1946–84], courtesy of Chicago History Museum, ICHi-50029)

Loving Sisters.
(Photo courtesy of Roberts
Temple Church of God in Christ)

Martin and Morris Music Studio at Forty-Third Street and Indiana Avenue.
(Photo courtesy of Martin and Morris Music Company Records, Archives Center,
National Museum of American History, Smithsonian Institution)

Robert Anderson.
(Photo courtesy of Fisk University, John Hope and Aurelia E. Franklin Library, Special Collections, Thomas A. Dorsey Collection, box 11, folder 9)

Roberta Martin.
(Photo courtesy of Fisk University, John Hope and Aurelia E. Franklin Library, Special Collections, Thomas A. Dorsey Collection, box 11, folder 7)

The Gay Sisters' first record: Dolphin's of Hollywood, 1949.
(Author's collection)

Pilgrim Jubilee Singers, circa 1961.
(Photo courtesy of Alan R. Young)

Holy Wonders, 1951; Spencer Taylor, far right.
(Louise Overall Weaver Papers [1946–84],
courtesy of Chicago History Museum; ICHi-50028)

Gospel Songbirds.
(Photo courtesy of Robert Pruter)

Norfleet Brothers.
(Lucy Collier Papers, courtesy of Vivian G. Harsh Research Collection
of Afro-American History and Literature, Chicago Public Library)

Isabel Joseph Johnson, host
of TV's *Rock of Ages.*
(Author's collection)

Roberta Martin (far right) with Philadelphia gospel singer
Mary Johnson Davis (on her right); others unknown.
(Photo courtesy of Romance Watson)

The Barrett Sisters, the "Sweet Sisters of Zion." Top to bottom: Rodessa Barrett Porter, DeLois Barrett Campbell, Billie Barrett GreenBey.
(Author's collection)

The Caravans with James Cleveland, mid-1950s.
(Author's collection)

Albertina Walker singing at an annual testimonial service honoring
Rev. John L. Thurston, New Covenant Baptist Church, 1956.
(Louise Overall Weaver Papers [1946–84], courtesy of Chicago History Museum, ICHi-67659)

Lucy Smith Singers, mid-1950s. Clockwise from top: Sarah McKissick, Little Lucy Smith Collier, Gladys Beamon Gregory, Catherine Campbell.
(Lucy Collier Papers, courtesy of Vivian G. Harsh Research Collection of Afro-American History and Literature, Chicago Public Library)

Maceo Woods Singers, circa 1952. Maceo Woods is front, center.
(Author's collection)

The Duncanaires.
(Photo courtesy of Delores "Honey" Sykes)

Staple Singers, circa 1954. Left to right: Pervis, Roebuck "Pops," Cleotha, and Mavis Staples.
(Photo courtesy of Robert Pruter)

Wooten Choral Ensemble.
(Photo courtesy of Bobby
Wooten)

Robert Wooten (front row center, in dark robe) and Maceo Woods (to his right).
(Photo courtesy of Bobby Wooten)

Helen Robinson Youth Chorus.
(Author's collection)

Charles G. Hayes, Founder, Cosmopolitan
Church of Prayer.
(Author's collection)

Bishop James L. Anderson, Founder, Redeeming Church of Christ, at New Covenant Missionary Baptist Church.

(Louise Overall Weaver Papers [1946–84], courtesy of Chicago History Museum, ICHi-67660)

Jessy Dixon.

(Author's collection)

Left to right: Mahalia Jackson, Robert Miller, Rev. John Thurston,
Louise Overall Weaver at New Covenant Baptist Church, 1965.
(Louise Overall Weaver Papers [1946–84], courtesy of Chicago History Museum, ICHi-67662)

Sallie Martin Singers, 1960s. Standing: Sallie Martin, Eugene Burke,
Bessie Folk, Shirley Bell; Seated at piano: Kenneth Woods Jr.
(Photo courtesy of Kenneth Woods Jr.)

CHAPTER 13

The Gospel Caravan
Midcentury Melodies

Chicago was the best place to be on Sundays, because of all the wonderful music that you would get to hear.

Archie Dennis

By the 1950s, gospel music, once disparaged as "jazzing the hymns," had all but supplanted the highbrow oratorios and anthems as the predominant sound of the semi-demonstrative, as well as some deliberative, or sermon-centered, African American churches in the urban North.[1] Gospel songs and choirs had also swept the country. Bernice Johnson Reagon writes: "By midcentury, gospel was completing a circle of sorts, as the old home country churches [of the South] whose families had been impacted by migration to the north began to organize their gospel choirs."[2]

Joel Friedman commented on the growing potential of gospel music as entertainment in the February 4, 1956, issue of *Billboard*: "Spiritual artists are now prospering more than ever before, with bookings opening up to them that never before existed. Radio stations are devoting more time to the broadcast of spiritual and gospel music, and accordingly the record companies are servicing these stations in greater numbers." Friedman quoted Lillian Cumber of Specialty's Herald Attractions, who reported that "ball parks, auditoriums and arenas which wouldn't book a spiritual show years ago have found the business to be quite lucrative today."[3]

Few gospel artists of the era better understood the financial upside of gospel music in postwar America than Sister Rosetta Tharpe. Jerma Jackson has posited that the shift from church to commerce started with Tharpe's appearance, singing and playing her National resonating guitar, in the 1938 and 1939 reviews at New York's fashionable Cotton Club.[4] But early criticism of gospel music's commercial leanings came from two of its early innovators: Thomas Dorsey and Kenneth Morris. In his 1949 book *Improving the Music in the Church*, Kenneth Morris railed against gospel singers who were "in it for 'what they [could] get out of it' or for purely commercial reasons."[5] Meanwhile, Dorsey took aim at gospel songwriters "who [took] old songs out of books that were written by other writers more than thirty years ago; re-print[ed] them and [put] their names on them as the writer and composer." He opined, "I think it is very low to take another man's song over which he has worked hard, publish it, leave his name off the copy and place another's name there who never wrote a note."[6] Dorsey's diatribe was undoubtedly stimulated, at least in part, by Tharpe's 1939 rearrangement of his "Hide Me in Thy Bosom" as the swinging "Rock Me," for which she was given composer credit on the record label.

Nevertheless, the enthusiasm Tharpe generated caught the attention of key figures in the rapidly consolidating American music business—men who converted enthusiasm for blues and jazz into cash. Tharpe's appeal suggested that black sacred music, too, might ultimately prove lucrative.[7] "Eager to capitalize on the music's commercial possibilities," Jackson observes, "a group of powerful men inadvertently forged a place for gospel in mainstream popular culture."[8] In Chicago, the "group of powerful men" who sought to commodify gospel music for mass consumption were independent record company owners, religious disk jockeys, and promoters. Some, such as Vivian Carter and Al Benson, occupied all three categories.

Prior to 1945, most gospel artists, with the exception of quartets, did not consider recording essential to their ministry. For artists interested in moving beyond the local church circuit, participation in national church conventions and radio broadcasts was sufficient. After the Second World War, however, records became the predominant measuring stick of success. Adam Green notes that this ascendancy was due in part to the establishment in 1940 of the performing rights organization Broadcast Music Incorporated (BMI). A competitor to the American Society of Composers, Authors and Publishers (ASCAP), BMI fostered inclusivity of genres and artists that had previously been ignored by ASCAP. It gave black musicians and entrepreneurial record men—at the time, the industry was almost entirely dominated by men—greater access to the marketplace.[9]

One Chicago record man who traded in African American popular music was policeman and tailor Leonard Allen (1899–1985). In July 1951, Allen organized United Record Company and its subsidiary, States, with assistance from Lew Simpkins (1918–53), who had been with Lee Egalnick's Miracle and

Premium Records. Robert Anderson and his female background vocalists, the Good Shepherd Singers, were among the artists Simpkins brought to United from Miracle, and the first gospel artists to record for United and States.[10] In 1952, the Good Shepherds became the Caravans. They would go on to be one of the most popular female gospel groups of all time.

Robert Anderson and the Gospel Caravan

Like most gospel groups, the Good Shepherds' personnel changed periodically. For example, Gary vocalist Betty Jones, an early member of the Good Shepherds, left prior to the United sessions.[11] Ann Rhodes Yancy was also a member of the group. The iteration that Anderson took to Universal in December 1951 to record their first disc for United, however, was Irma Gwynn, Nellie Grace Daniels, Elyse Yancey, and Ora Lee Hopkins.

An accomplished singer, pianist, and organist, Nellie Grace Daniels was born November 27, 1926, in East Chicago, Indiana. She graduated from Washington High School and attended the Chicago Conservatory of Music at 410 South Michigan. She first met Anderson around 1946 through a mutual friend, George Upshaw. Upshaw "took me to Gary," Daniels recalled, "to Robert Anderson's record shop, and he introduced me to Robert. Robert wanted me to sing with his younger group."[12] Anderson soon promoted Daniels to the Good Shepherds.

Not long after Daniels joined Anderson's group, Willie Cook, a high school chum, suggested that she audition for a vocalist opening with the Duke Ellington Orchestra. Daniels auditioned at Chicago's Blue Note, where Ellington and his orchestra were appearing. The bandleader was interested in hiring her, but she decided not to break her prior commitment to Anderson.[13]

Elyse Yancey was the oldest member of the Good Shepherds. "Robert would listen to her," Daniels said, "because she was the oldest of the group, and she was the first in the group."[14]

Ora Lee Hopkins was born in Baton Rouge on March 26, 1929, to Rev. John E. and Fannie Hopkins. She began singing publicly at Rising Sun Baptist Church in Baton Rouge, where her family attended services. The Hopkins family migrated to Chicago in 1936. John got the call to become a minister in 1939 but served first as a deacon at Forty-Fourth Street Baptist Church, under Rev. Elijah Thurston, before founding New Nazareth Baptist Church on the South Side. Ora Lee married Thurston's son John and sang in the Forty-Fourth Street choir before joining the Good Shepherds.[15]

Hopkins's son, Rev. Darryl Reed, said that his mother was not a showman but stood in one spot, flatfooted, to deliver her song.[16] Pastor Ray Allen Berryhill concurred: "Ora Lee would stand and sing and would not stop until she wrecked the whole church. She would do it week after week, just demolish a church. When you talk about Chicago style, I can't help but think of an Ora Lee Hopkins, who was a phenomenal singer."[17]

"Ora Lee was a humble person," added Chicago-based gospel singer Betty Lester. "She would tell me about how she'd made some missteps in her life, and how her father would put her out of the church and she'd come back and apologize, and he would take her back. I really admired how she could sing. She had such a voice, such a beautiful voice. I haven't heard a voice like hers since."[18]

Born on the South Side to Marcella and Arthur Gwynn, Irma Gwynn joined First Church of Deliverance when she was five. Her father was a pianist and became a trustee of First Church, while Marcella sang in the choir. Irma received as much formal classical training as her parents could afford, then picked up additional music instruction from singing in the DuSable High School glee club under Bryant Jones and performing in Captain Walter Dyett's fabled *High Jinks* variety shows. "I played different parts and learned to sing some of the blues there," she said.[19]

Gwynn learned gospel technique as part of First Church's music department, under the tutelage of Julia Mae Kennedy. Gwynn sang alongside and even toured with First Church singing stars R. L. Knowles and Edna Mae Quarles and soloed on the church's weekly radio broadcasts. She appeared as a soloist on a myriad of local church programs and joined Maurice McGehee's Sharps and Flats, a choral group from Chicago whose repertory included a variety of song styles. Anderson was aware of Gwynn from First Church and received permission from her parents to bring her into the Good Shepherds. Gwynn traveled with the group and participated in Anderson's 1949 Miracle sessions, the first discs to feature the Good Shepherds.[20]

Anderson and the Good Shepherds sang in and around Chicago but also hit the gospel highway. Reverend Reed said that Ora Lee recalled when the group traveled "and they wouldn't have much gas, they would cut the car [engine] and let it coast."[21] Daniels recalled a more dramatic encounter that happened during a stay in Birmingham:

> We were supposed to sing at the city auditorium but that Saturday, it got hot. We knew we couldn't sing in robes. So we went to downtown Birmingham, into a great big department store. We had no knowledge if the dresses were going to fit, so we told the girl that [we tried them on but] we couldn't buy them. We didn't know that [in the South] we had to buy them because we had tried them on. The girl called the manager, the manager came up there, and said, "You n——, you're going to have to buy these clothes because you tried them on." Elyse [Yancey] told him, "Who are you calling n——? We're not going to buy these clothes." He said, "Then I'm going to throw you all out of this window."

We were up on the second floor. Elyse wasn't afraid of anything. She said, "Well, you're going out right behind us!"[22]

After Gwynn married, she left the group to raise a family. Anderson had the choice to fill the vacancy with Gladys Beamon of the Lucy Smith Singers or Albertina Walker, a young artist currently with the Willie Webb Singers. He chose Walker, and the group formally voted her into the Good Shepherds. Shortly after Walker joined, the Good Shepherd Singers were re-christened the Gospel Caravan.[23]

Albertina Walker, who would be crowned Queen of Gospel after the death of Mahalia Jackson in 1972, was born in Chicago on August 28, 1929, to Reubin and Cammila Walker.[24] The couple migrated to Chicago from Macon, Georgia, sometime between 1915 and 1920.[25] At the time of the 1930 U.S. Census, the Walkers were residing with their five daughters and four sons at 747 East Forty-First Street. Walker's father worked as a car washer for the Pullman Railway Car Company, and Cammila stayed home to raise the children.[26] The family attended West Point Baptist Church, and at age four, Walker began singing in the children's choir, directed by Pete Williams, who tapped Walker to perform with his Williams Singers.[27] By age thirteen, she was determined to meet her idol, Mahalia Jackson. "I thought there was nobody like Mahalia Jackson," Walker told Jackson biographer Laurraine Goreau. "When I was a little girl, Mahalia used to come sing at our church; all of her programs that I could go to, I would. So now I'd just show up at her house, and she'd kid me. 'Girl, you just got so much nerves, and you even come up to my house and I ain't even invited you and you just *refuse* to leave! Well, I can afford you because you re-mind me so much of myself when I was coming up.'"[28] Jackson became Walker's unofficial singing mentor. "Then I started singing with Robert Anderson and Willie Webb, so I really *did* get to be a part, because of the programs."[29]

Although Walker's singing career started in the church, she experimented briefly with secular music. In her video autobiography, Walker recalled how Rev. Elijah Thurston once spotted her singing in a local nightclub.[30] "Albertina had sung in a couple of little night clubs, lounges—secular music," Walker's housekeeper and friend Ethel Harris explained, "and [Thurston] told her this is really not what God called you for. He tried to talk to her until finally he came and pulled her out of one of those places, and really gave her a talking to. He told her you need to search your heart because this is not what you should be doing."[31] Walker subsequently recommitted herself to singing only gospel.

Around 1949, Walker joined the Melody of Zion Gospel Singers, a female gospel group that included Ozella Weber and Louise Overall Weaver. A year later, she joined Weber in the Willie Webb Singers and by 1951 had become a member of the Good Shepherds.

With two United discs already on the street, Anderson and the Gospel Caravan of Hopkins, Yancey, Daniels, and Walker entered Universal on April 18, 1952, to record four more sides for United: "Come in the Room," "O Lord, Is It I," "How Could It Be," and "He's Pleading in Glory for Me." Louise Overall Weaver served as session organist and Eddie Robinson as piano accompanist.[32]

After the four songs were committed to tape, the Caravans recorded two tracks without Anderson. Whether the group-only tracks were preplanned is speculative. Various stories abound about what happened between the leader and his group that day. Some suggest there was a rift between the group and Anderson. Daniels recalled no animosity whatsoever; she said that Anderson's name was on the April 18 recording contract, so their first single was recorded essentially under his sponsorship.[33] It is also possible that the suggestion came from Allen and Simpkins, who could not have been unaware of the growing national popularity of other female gospel groups such as the Ward Singers, the Angelic Gospel Singers, and the Davis Sisters.

However it came about, the Caravans were no longer relegated to a supporting role, and, with Weaver and Robinson as accompanists, claimed their own musical territory on "Think of His Goodness to You," and "Tell the Angels." Walker led on both sides, offering an especially bluesy reading on "Tell the Angels" until the ladies quickened the pace on the final chorus.

As an ensemble, the Caravans pounced on vocal lines with church-wrecking power and precision, filling each lyric line and the pauses between them with intense emotional conviction. Their tight, intense harmonies, dynamic ebbs and flows, and staccato attack of the verses were straight out of the church. James William Herndon, who joined the Caravans in the late 1950s, agreed that the singers' deep church roots were the genesis of their sound. "Albertina had grown up in West Point and a lot of the other churches, you know, because she fellowshipped with everybody in Chicago. They just had these strong roots, and that would come out. Man, when it did, those women were a hard act to follow!"[34] Herndon added: "The Caravans had a marvelous ability to feed off each other. They could practically feel each other. Tina could support you in the background. She could push you, she'd make you sing! And man, she was the best person in the world that I've ever known for supporting a lead singer. She'd make you sing your heart out, and she could do it just standing in the background."[35]

Allen released the songs on the United subsidiary States as by the Caravans, and thanks to Daniels's persistence, the company listed each member's name on the record label. Subsequently, Allen turned his attention from the smooth-voiced Anderson to the Caravans and released fourteen singles on States between 1952 and 1956.

Meanwhile, Mahalia Jackson came to her friend Anderson's rescue by persuading Bess Berman of Apollo to sign him. She reportedly oversaw his first recording session herself.[36] Aldrea Lenox laughed that Anderson and Jackson were such tight friends, they would sometimes work hand in hand to gauge the size of audiences for their performances. "Dr. A. A. Childs had Sunday afternoon tent musicals once a month for fifty cents," Lenox said. "Robert Anderson and Mahalia were the two top singers in the city, and they'd ride around to see who's coming to the musical. They'd ride around about four or five times, and if it didn't fill up, they'd just keep on going!"[37]

Walker became the Caravans' business manager and its main soloist, but like the Roberta Martin Singers, the group was an assemblage of soloists. Historian Sherry Sherrod DuPree believes that the Caravans produced "more gospel vocal stars than any other gospel group."[38] Herndon agreed. "The Caravans had one profound distinction: they are the only group that has ever traveled professionally that had every member of the group as a standalone artist. I give Walker credit because a lot of people—especially being the manager—would have been so busy promoting themselves, they would not have allowed the other members of the group to have as much out-front recognition as she did. But she didn't have to worry about it, because she could do it whether she was in the background or whether she was leading."[39]

As the Caravans' popularity soared, their schedule ballooned with dates outside Chicago. Ironically, it was success that spelled the end of the original Caravans. Most of the charter members had outside responsibilities that precluded them from maintaining a heightened level of commitment. They began to go their separate ways. Yancey returned to northwest Indiana, where by 1956, she was assisting Gary's premier female gospel group, the Echoes of Eden. Daniels now had a young daughter, Bernadette, and could no longer travel at will. She returned to singing for her East Chicago church as well as a brief stint with the Echoes of Eden.[40] Hopkins stayed behind to direct the one-hundred-voice choir at her father's New Nazareth Baptist Church.[41] Iris Humble, another early Caravan, moved back to her native New Orleans.[42]

To fill the vacancies, Walker recruited Bessie Griffin and Gloria Griffin (no relation). Born in New Orleans to Enoch and Victoria Broil on July 6, 1922, Arlette Broil became Bessie Griffin after schoolmates persisted in teasing her about her first name. Orphaned at age five, Griffin was raised by her mother's cousin, Lucy Narcisse, a relative of the famous Spiritual minister King Louis H. Narcisse.[43] For ten years, Griffin, a contralto, sang with the Southern Harps, a female a cappella quartet. Accompanied by bluesman Brownie McGhee on acoustic guitar, she cut some solo discs in 1948 for Bob Shad's Sittin' In With label.[44]

Griffin turned eight thousand heads during her October 19, 1951, appearance on Mahalia Jackson's twenty-fifth anniversary program at the Chicago Coliseum.[45] She told Heilbut that after she sang "Come Ye Disconsolate" and "How I Got Over," even the honoree could not top it.[46] Chicago singer, director, and keyboardist Rev. Stanley Keeble recalled the first time he saw Griffin perform. "She sang, 'I'm Too Close,' and the folks probably shouted two hours. She was not a mover; she'd stand in one spot. Maybe she'd take a step or two, but would just slay everybody in the building. I consider Bessie Griffin one of the greatest gospel singers that ever lived."[47]

Griffin stayed with the Caravans until 1955, eventually moved back to New Orleans, and signed with Specialty around 1956.[48] She and the Consolators, a group that included her husband, Spencer Jackson, released two singles with Specialty, including the mid-tempo "Whosoever Will."[49] By 1960, she had relocated to Los Angeles and organized a new group, the Gospel Pearls. The group's 1959 performance in Langston Hughes's stage play, *Portraits in Bronze* was, according to Heilbut, "the first move of gospel into clubs and coffeehouses."[50]

Gloria Griffin was born in Mississippi on December 15, 1933, but was raised in St. Louis. As a young girl, she sang with the Haynes Singers of East St. Louis, Illinois, but moved to New York City at age sixteen to work with former Chicago resident Bishop Alvin A. Childs, who was pastoring the city's Faith Temple Church. She spent time in the Ward Singers and became a Caravan in 1954.[51] She was present for an October 5 recording session but did not lead any of the songs. Griffin is better known for her tenure with the Roberta Martin Singers, where her performances of "God Specializes," "God Is Still on the Throne," and "I'm Grateful" became gospel classics. She, too, pursued a solo career during the 1960s and 1970s.

By 1954, Walker was the only Caravan remaining from the April 1952 roster. She recruited James Cleveland as the musician, and singers Johneron Davis and Cassietta George.

Cleveland was already well known in Chicago as a passionate singer, an indefatigable music entrepreneur, and a piano accompanist influenced by Roberta Martin and Little Lucy Smith, whose style was "more aggressive than Roberta's," Rev. Charles Walker told Idella Johnson.[52] Detroit keyboardist Herbert "Pee Wee" Pickard told author Aaron Cohen, "James was hard on that instrument. . . . I seen him press the pedals so hard, they'd break underneath the keyboard."[53] "He could take hold of an auditorium and rock the chairs loose from their nuts and bolts," adds Rev. Harold Bailey of Chicago's Harold Bailey Singers.[54]

Cleveland was also a budding songwriter and began publishing his songs through Roberta Martin's publishing concern. Among his earliest compositions was "Grace Is Sufficient." In Bil Carpenter's *Uncloudy Days*, Cleveland admitted,

"I sold all of those tunes to Miss Martin for little or nothing. Of course, she made fabulous sums of money off of them, but that wasn't my interest at the time. My mother was still doing day work for eight hours a day and sometimes she would come home and I'd have the money there in my hand—more money than she was making as a grown woman—and it was a big deal."[55]

After his stint with the Lux Singers, Cleveland formed the Gospelaires with Roberta Martin Singers Norsalus McKissick and Bessie Folk, then joined Imogene Greene in Charles Taylor's Gospel All-Stars. Almond Dawson, an accompanist for the Gospel All-Stars, called Greene "a consummate gospel singer. . . . I called her the 'creeping' gospel singer. When she sang, she would go down in the audience and work the floor. She'd hold the back of the benches as she sang, and she would squall during her renditions. She would sing until overcome by the spirit. I had to watch her all the time because I never knew what she was going to do. I was always amazed by her. She was so creative!"[56]

After running into Cleveland at Mahalia Jackson's home, Albertina Walker asked him if he wanted the job as Caravans chief musician, since John Burns was no longer working with them. Cleveland assented, and together they visited Universal on October 5, 1954, to record "What Kind of Man Is This" and "This Man Jesus."[57] The release earned a coveted spotlight review in the February 5, 1955, issue of *Billboard*.[58] Cleveland's prayerfully intoned call and the women's response on the follow-up, "The Solid Rock," was so popular that the Dixie Hummingbirds parodied it on their novelty "Let's Go Out to the Program, No. 2."

Johneron Davis was born April 12, 1929, and sang with the Caravans from 1953 to 1962. "Johneron was just as sweet as she could be," recalled James Herndon, "but she was straightforward. She would say what she thought, how she felt about a thing, whether you liked it or not. And she didn't mean it offensively, she was just being frank. But the way she could do that sometimes, a lot of people would have fallen out with her altogether."[59] Johneron's friend Aldrea Lenox remembered her as a "sweetheart": "Her mother owned a restaurant on Sixteenth Street, and she'd pick me up and take me to the concerts."[60] Davis married, becoming Johneron Austin, and died of cancer on August 4, 1965, at the age of thirty-six.[61] "Johneron was one of the greatest fans the Caravans ever had," Herndon said, "because even after she left, the Caravans were the center of her heart."[62]

Cassietta Baker George was a Caravans acquisition from Memphis. Born January 23, 1929, George began singing as a preschooler in her father's church. In the early 1950s, she formed the Songbirds of the South, a female a cappella quartet. When she came to Chicago, she joined Fellowship Baptist Church, where the Caravans first heard her. They invited her to join them in 1954. George wrote several of the group's songs and first led a Caravans recording in October 1954.

George's church background—her father was a minister—was telling. "We were in Shreveport, Louisiana," said Herndon. "Louisiana, that's basically quartet territory, and we had sung, and the people had enjoyed it, and somewhere out of the clear blue, Cassietta decided she wanted to sing, 'Guide Me, O Thou Great Jehovah,' that great hymn. And man, she tore that place all to pieces! That's what I remember as being one of our best services."[63]

Critical acclaim notwithstanding, record sales were dipping in 1955, while personal appearances were increasing in number and financial return. The Caravans recognized that signing with Lil Cumber's Herald Attractions would help them reap their share of the financial rewards.[64] The group thus withdrew from a scheduled tour with the Robert Anderson Singers to sign with Herald and embarked on a tour of Ohio, Tennessee, Georgia, and the Carolinas with Brother Joe May and his sister, Annette; the Soul Stirrers; the Pilgrim Travelers; Dorothy Love Coates and the Gospel Harmonettes; and Ethel Davenport.[65] By that time, the Caravans consisted of Walker, Cleveland, George, Davis, Griffin, and Louise McDowell, a first soprano whom Herndon remembered as also "a dynamite piano player. She could kick a piano to death!"[66]

The Herald Attractions gospel caravan arrived on the West Coast for the First Annual Mid-Summer Festival of Gospel Music. Held at Los Angeles's Shrine Auditorium on July 22, 1955, the program was preserved on tape by Specialty and when released in 1993 on compact disc, offered the most complete aural portrait of a golden age gospel program.[67] It included two Caravans selections, "What Kind of Man Is This," led by Cleveland, and "Since I Met Jesus" with Walker substituting for Bessie Griffin, who carried the original recording. Roberta Martin's influence on Cleveland's piano accompaniment was telling, from the flowery introduction to the fills between chords. Cleveland quickened the tempo for "What Kind of Man Is This," and the audience clapped along as the Caravans responded antiphonally to Cleveland's raspy lead vocals.

Five months later, on December 16, 1955, the Caravans, along with their fellow Herald travelers, and Alex Bradford and the Original Five Blind Boys played New York's Apollo Theater. The event was heralded as "unprecedented in the annals of show business" because it put gospel music on the same entertainment plane as the major R&B package shows.[68]

Following the Herald tour of 1955, the Caravans signed three new singers: Inez Andrews, Dorothy Norwood, and Shirley Caesar. Like Bessie and Gloria Griffin, Andrews, Norwood, and Caesar were southern acquisitions.

Born May 29, 1935, in Atlanta, Dorothy Norwood toured in the early 1940s with her family group, the Norwood Gospel Singers, then made her way to Chicago with the aspiration to become a nationally known gospel singer. She got her wish when Walker heard her sing "Low Is the Way" on a 1956 Fellowship Baptist Church radio broadcast and invited her to join the Caravans.[69]

Norwood's first lead on a Caravans record was 1956's "Standing in the Need of Prayer."[70]

Not long after the recording session, Norwood's mother fell ill, and she returned to Atlanta to care for her. When she came back to Chicago, she did not rejoin the Caravans but linked up instead with the Gospel Chimes, James Cleveland's latest group, which showcased the vocal talents of Imogene Greene, Jessy Dixon, Claude Timmons, and Lee Charles Neely. By 1963, Norwood had organized her own group. Her first single for Savoy, a sermonette called "Johnny and Jesus," established her reputation as "The Storyteller." The LP of the same name earned a gold record.[71]

Born Inez McConico in Birmingham, Alabama, on April 14, 1929, Inez Andrews was a toddler when her mother died, leaving her father and other relatives to raise her. She was married briefly at age eighteen and worked as a domestic to support her two daughters. She met James Cleveland on a Nashville program while substituting for Dorothy Love Coates in Birmingham's Gospel Harmonettes. Cleveland told Walker about the demonstrative singer he witnessed whose "Soldiers in the Army" sent shockwaves through the audience. Walker recruited Andrews to the Caravans in 1957.[72]

That same year, Andrews recorded her first lead with the Caravans, trading vocal lines with Dorothy Norwood on "Come on Jesus." She also led "I'm Not Tired Yet," "Hold to God's Unchanging Hands," and the explosive "Mary, Don't You Weep." In performance, during the "Mary, Don't You Weep" extended vamp, Andrews walked the aisles of churches and auditoriums, peering off in the distance and calling for Mary. The song became her calling card.

Andrews stayed with the Caravans until 1962, when she acquired the personnel of a Long Island, New York, female gospel group and renamed them the Andrewettes. Peacock chief Don Robey nicknamed Andrews the "Song Bird," inspiring the name for Peacock's subsidiary label, on which the Andrewettes recorded. In addition to "Mary, Don't You Weep," Andrews is best known for her 1972 solo hit, "Lord, Don't Move That Mountain." A Doris Akers composition propelled by Gene Barge's soulful production, "Mountain" crossed over from the gospel to the R&B charts, introducing Andrews to a wider audience.[73]

Shirley Caesar was the third acquisition. She was born in Durham, North Carolina, on October 13, 1938, to James "Big Jim" and Hallie Martin Caesar.[74] Big Jim sang with a local a cappella quartet called the Just Come Four; his premature death, however, left Shirley to care for her semi-disabled mother. Along the way, Caesar sang in a choir called the Charity Singers and traveled with her pastor, Bishop Yelverton, singing to accompany his preaching. She also worked with evangelist "One Leg" Leroy Johnson, John Landers, and blind evangelist Thelma Bumpess, whose singing group, the Royalettes, she joined around 1950.[75] In October 1951, the preteen Caesar—nicknamed "Baby Shirley" for her diminutive size—made her first record. Released on Federal, the disc coupled two duets with Bumpess: "Every Hour, Every Day" and "Sweeping through the City." A month later, Federal released Caesar's first solo disc, "I'd Rather Serve Jesus" and "I Know Jesus Will Save." By age thirteen, Caesar had three single releases to her credit.

"I used to try to imitate Sam Cooke and Mahalia Jackson and Edna Gallmon Cooke," Caesar told doctoral candidate Brooksie Harrington. "When I just stand flat-footed and just sing a song, now I got that from Albertina Walker."[76]

Caesar told Harrington that she met the Caravans at a program in Kinston, North Carolina. She wrote a note, "Please ask Sister Shirley Caesar to sing a solo," and gave it to the emcee. Her request was granted, and the teenager sang Dorsey's "The Lord Will Make a Way Somehow" at the program as the Caravans listened.[77] She told the Caravans' accompanist, Eddie Williams, who had replaced James Cleveland as musician, how much she wanted to sing with the group. Williams interceded on her behalf, and upon approval from Caesar's mother, the Caravans took the teenager with them. Caesar remained with the Caravans from 1957 to approximately 1966.

Right when the Caravans were being celebrated as one of the most popular female gospel groups, Leonard Allen's diskery foundered, United and States Records were no more, and the group's contract was up for grabs. Their new signing was contentious. Herman Lubinsky reported to *Billboard* that he had signed the Caravans to Savoy Records in early October 1958. Don Robey riposted that he had not only signed the group to Peacock but produced a recording session with them as well.[78] He released a statement that he had received an oral commitment from Walker and was assured that the documentation was in the process of being signed. "I am forced to assume," Robey concluded, "that the confusion came as a by-product of another of Mr. Lubinsky's 'low blows.'" To which Lubinsky countered: "It's sour grapes, that's all. He's just a poor loser."[79]

Victorious, Savoy placed the Caravans on its Sharp and Gospel subsidiaries and reissued most of the group's approximately four dozen issued and unissued States sides. The initial recording session for Gospel, held October 9, 1958, produced two of the group's most enduring hits: "You Can't Beat God's Giving" and "I'm Not Tired Yet." It also included Caesar's first recorded lead vocal with the group, a duet with Walker on "Swing Low."[80]

In 1958, the Caravans added Delores Washington. Hailing from Robbins, a far south suburb of Chicago, Delores was born to Evelyn and Robert Washington and began her singing career as an entrant in a talent competition called "Artists of Tomorrow." She was awarded a scholarship to the Chicago Conservatory of Music, where she received classical training before joining the Caravans.[81] Washington became known as the Gospel Princess for her youthful vibrancy and trained soprano voice.

This latest iteration of the Caravans—Walker, Andrews, Caesar, Washington, and Davis—was among its most memorable. Carpenter writes: "The combination of Caesar's youthful energy and squalling soprano, Andrews's shrieking high-Cs, Washington's sweet high notes, and Walker's crusty rasp made for a delicious listening experience."[82] This combination made famous songs such as "I'm Not Tired Yet," Eddie Williams's "Lord Keep Me Day by Day," and Andrews's two-part masterpiece, "Mary Don't You Weep." When "Mary" became a huge hit, Caesar suggested that the group raise its performance fee. She told Harrington, "We were the hottest group out there. Why go and sing for $200 or $125? So I asked Tina to let me do the booking for them, and when I started booking them, I raised their prices."[83]

The Caravans recruited Josephine Howard to fill Davis's space when she left the group around 1962. Howard had just left Inez Andrews's Andrewettes, so the Caravans knew what she was capable of contributing. "She had basically the same second soprano range that Johneron had," Herndon explained, "except she was more of a lead singer, where Johneron was not. [Howard] could contribute both to the background and to the lead."[84]

Eddie Williams departed the group in 1959, leaving the Caravans once again without an accompanist. Caesar knew what to do. She called her friend and schoolmate James Herndon. Born March 30, 1938, in Wake County, North Carolina, James Herndon was steeped in Durham's Baptist and Holiness communities. A self-taught piano player from age twelve, he knew Caesar well but never expected her telephone call that day in 1959. "I mean just totally out of the clear blue, it just blew me away," he said. "I was shocked. I had been a follower of [the Caravans] for years."[85] Herndon moved to Chicago to rehearse with the group in preparation for his first program with them, at the Wheat Street Baptist Church in Atlanta. Herndon recalled his earliest performances with the Caravans as "intimidating":

> When we were singing in these auditoriums with three thousand folk, four thousand folk, the piano was the only instrument. I had to somehow try and maintain the tempo, regardless of all the other people in there. That took some doing, because people are clapping their hands in different sections of the place. Well, they hear the music just a fraction of a second after we might have sung it, depending on how large the auditorium is. Sometimes that can affect the tempo of your song very badly, and if a song is supposed to be up-tempo, you can lose it, if it gets too slow. For the first year, my fingers were just blistered! We didn't have any drums, any bass guitars, anything like that to help us. We

just had the piano. To this day, I stomp my foot very loud because that was my drum. That was my time piece![86]

Herndon eventually added more than piano; like Cleveland and Williams, he also wrote some of the Caravans' most popular songs, such as "I Won't Be Back," "No Coward Soldier," and "Where Is Your Faith in God." He stayed with the group until the mid-1960s. By then he was so fatigued from the constant traveling that he left to form the James Herndon Singers, with two former Caravans, Delores Washington and Josephine Howard. He also added Louella Hunt and Roxie Bibbs, an alumna of the Helen Robinson Youth Chorus and the Dorothy Norwood Singers.[87] In 1969, the Washington-led "Oh Lord Have Mercy" was reported to have been one of the best-selling gospel records of the year.[88]

After recording more than a dozen sides for Apollo, Alex Bradford signed with Specialty on the recommendation of Sam Cooke, whose Soul Stirrers were riding high as the label's top gospel hit maker.[89] "Too Close To Heaven" was one of the first compositions Bradford brought to Specialty. It was the second song that he and his Bradford Specials—James Brandon, Charles Campbell, Louis Gibson, Billy Harper, and Jonathan Jackson—recorded during their first recording session for Specialty on June 19, 1953.[90] Art Rupe released it as the group's debut single around the same time as the final Bradford Singers' release for Apollo, "Turn Away from Sin" and "Who Can I Blame," saw the light of day. Bradford's bluesy baritone and piano, and the Specials' intense response, propelled "Too Close" beyond earlier recorded versions by the Roberta Martin Singers and the Davis Sisters. It became one of the biggest selling gospel records of 1953 and the biggest for Specialty since the Pilgrim Travelers' "Mother Bowed" in 1948.[91] A year later, Bob Rolontz of *Billboard* noted that "Too Close" was one of the three best-selling gospel records, according to dealers and distributers specializing in R&B and gospel music.[92] It catapulted Bradford to the A-list in gospel promotion and touring.

The Bradford Specials were more than the newest stars on the gospel music circuit. Unlike male quartets that performed in matching suits, ties, and pocket handkerchiefs, the group dressed in choir robes.[93] Also unlike male quartets, they were early adopters of piano and organ accompaniment and emulated the highly charged, flamboyant performance style of female gospel groups such as the Gospel Harmonettes and the Ward Singers. Male groups such as the Raymond Rasberry Singers of Cleveland and the Gospel Clefs of Newark patterned their attire and performance techniques after the Bradford Specials.

Bradford himself was effervescent, alternating between rollicking, sanctified performances and raspy-voiced gospel ballads. It is not unrealistic to draw a direct line between Bradford's kinetic stage presence and falsetto leaps to his equally explosive label mate, Little Richard, who Heilbut asserts emulated the high soprano notes rocketed by the Ward Singers' Marion Williams.

Willie James McPhatter of Buffalo, New York, whose cousin, Clyde, was basking in international fame as the dynamic lead singer of the Dominoes and the Drifters, became a Bradford Special around 1956. Bradford first approached Willie James about joining his group in 1954, after hearing him play during a Bradford Specials appearance in Buffalo. McPhatter, who had already organized several gospel groups of his own, initially declined Bradford's proposal. After recognizing that joining Bradford offered the possibility of writing, singing, recording, and traveling, McPhatter reconsidered.

"Bradford always loved company," McPhatter recalled. "He never liked being alone. He'd make jokes but he was serious about his music. He could sit at a piano and start writing a song, in the studio! We wouldn't get done with rehearsal until two in the morning, then sleep, then get up and rehearse again. If you didn't get it right, you had to go over and over again until you got it right. [Bradford also] liked to record late at night. He never liked recording during the daytime, because any time after midnight, your voice is open and he could get the sound he wanted."[94]

But even a group as popular as the Bradford Singers was not immune to the disappointments of the gospel highway. McPhatter recalled a particularly anxious trip:

> We were going from New York to Jacksonville, Florida, and when we got there, the lady had cancelled the program. Here we go, with seven folks in one car, all the way from New York to Florida. No program. So we had to leave from there and go to Los Angeles. We went from Florida to Los Angeles on a bushel of peaches. [Later] Bradford went to the telephone booth and called a friend in Alabama, and in that booth, he found a wallet with 300 dollars. Took us all the way! There was no name, no nothing, it was just a wallet with 300 dollars. We could not find out who owned the wallet, there was nothing in it. We were blessed that time![95]

Bradford's relationship with Specialty lasted from 1953 until Rupe shuttered the label at the end of the 1950s. In addition to "Too Close to Heaven," this fruitful six-year period produced classics such as "Lord! Lord! Lord!," "He'll Wash You Whiter Than Snow," "Somebody Touched Me," "Holy Ghost," and the plaintive "If Mother Knew," recorded in New Orleans in October 1956. After Specialty, Bradford followed the Caravans to Savoy Records, where he recorded for its Gospel subsidiary.

The Maceo Woods Singers

The Maceo Woods Singers were another popular Chicago-based male gospel group. Maceo Len Woods was born April 23, 1932, to Fred and Rosa Anna Anderson Woods, who had migrated from Mississippi to Morgan Park.[96] By age twelve, Maceo was serving as organist for Mount Calvary Baptist Church in Morgan Park, where his family was a member. Initially drawn to a career in medicine, Woods became more interested in music. While attending Shoop Elementary School, he became friends with other aspiring keyboardists, notably Robert Wooten, Harold Freeman, Leon Oliver, and Leon's brother Milton. In the 1940s, no Morgan Park church had a Hammond organ, so Woods, Wooten, Leon Oliver, and their pals Bob Wesby, Joe Henderson, and Fred Nelson Jr., traveled downtown to Lyon and Healy. There a musician could rent a practice room with a Hammond organ. "We had to scrape our little fifty cents together, and we'd go down to Lyon and Healy," remembered Wooten. "We'd go up there and we'd eat our sandwiches; it was quite an experience!"[97] Woods recalled that if he and his friends lacked the rental fee, they waited patiently until a customer left a room with time to spare, and they would run in and play the Hammond until time ran out.[98] "Many times, I know we overstayed our time," added Wooten, "because that was our only opportunity to play the Hammond organ."[99]

Woods organized his first singing group, the Maceo Woods Male Chorus, at Mount Calvary.[100] Woods's godfather, Eugene Smith of the Roberta Martin Singers, suggested that the young man condense his fifty-voice chorus into a smaller aggregation so it could travel more cost-effectively. Woods heeded Smith's advice and in 1952 formed the Maceo Woods Singers. The group emulated the techniques of the Roberta Martin Singers and Alex Bradford Singers in the use of high harmonies, deft piano and organ accompaniment, and quality soloists. Original members were Melvin Gunnerson, Cleodorus Kimbrough, John Wesley Moore, Thomas Parker, Clarence Tate, Ben Turner, Donald Smith, and Norman Murchison and his brother Ira, a world-champion sprinter.[101]

Smith and Bradford helped the Maceo Woods Singers strike their first recording deal with Apollo Records.[102] Bradford's pianist, Joe Washington, even accompanied the ensemble on its sole Apollo session in October 1952.[103] The group's only Apollo single, "Witness" and "He Brought Joy to My Soul," was released in February 1953. Written by Woods, "Witness" became a gospel radio hit and a favorite of that year's National Baptist Convention. The First Church of Deliverance Choir performed "Witness" on its midnight broadcasts for eighteen consecutive weeks.[104] The song must have been in the group's repertory well before the recording date, because the Caravans released a quicker-tempo version for States earlier in the year, with Ora Lee Hopkins on lead. Nevertheless, the Maceo Woods Singers version did well enough to get the attention of Gary disk jockey Vivian Carter, who signed them to her fledgling Vee Jay Records.

Vivian Carter's family moved to Gary when she was three years old. She graduated from Gary Roosevelt High School in 1939 and started her career with the Signal Corps. In 1943, she opened a cleaning and shoeshine business in Gary, but a local strike "cleaned [her] for every dime [she had] saved, scraped, and borrowed." In 1947, she ventured to Washington, DC, to be a clerk-typist for the quartermaster general's office but after six months sought a transfer back to Gary.[105]

Carter's radio career began in 1948, when she won a disk jockey contest sponsored by Al Benson. The prize was an opportunity to work as a "satellite jock" for Benson's program on WGES, a labor she shared with Sid McCoy, another aspiring radio personality.[106] Carter soon moved to WJOB in Hammond, Indiana, where she assisted Eddie Honesty with his *Rockin' in Rhythm* radio program. She parlayed this experience into two shows of her own on Gary's WGRY. On *The Vivian Carter Show*, she played blues, jazz, R&B, and gospel weekdays from 9:30 to 11:30 a.m. Carter greeted her WGRY listeners as "your radio hostess that loves you the mostess."[107] Her all-religious music show, *Vivian's Spiritual Hour*, aired Sunday mornings from 9:00 to 10:00.[108]

In 1950, Carter expanded her enterprise by opening Vivian's Record Shop. The store was located first at Eighteenth and Massachusetts in Gary and later moved to 1640 Broadway, Gary's main commercial artery. Three years later, she landed a spot on WWCA, where she hosted *Living with Vivian*. Also in 1953, she founded Vee Jay Records with her brother Calvin and Kansas City native James Bracken.[109] Vee Jay, named for Vivian (Vee) and Jimmy (Jay), functioned initially out of the record store. On December 16, 1953, Vivian and James were wed at United Record Distributors in Chicago.[110]

The Maceo Woods Singers' first session for Vee Jay took place at Universal and produced the label's first gospel single, "Keep Trusting," a mid-tempo song led by Murchison. The flip side, "Run to Jesus," featured lead vocals by tenor Samuel Lee "Billy" Kyles, a new member of the group.[111] Donald Smith led "Garden of Prayer," also from that session, and it became the group's first radio hit on Vee Jay.

In addition to recording and performing with his group, Woods was also the organist in Vee Jay's house band, led by Al Smith. This assignment resulted in "a lot of overnight sessions with other Vee Jay artists at Universal Studio on Ontario Street," Woods told gospel music historian Opal Nations. "It was much cheaper to record at night, and we'd try to cram in as many acts as possible into one all-night session."[112] For example, Vee Jay brought several groups to Universal on Palm Sunday, April 11, 1954, where they recorded nearly a year's worth of gospel releases. Later that week, the Maceo Woods Singers, now consisting of Woods, Parker, Kyles, Tate, and Norman Murchison, recorded four more sides. One, "Never Grow Old," garnered a favorable review from *Billboard*. Heilbut credited the Kyles-led performance to be the inspiration behind Aretha Franklin's version of "Never Grow Old," recorded two years later in her father's Detroit church.[113]

In summer 1954, Vivian Carter was searching for a theme song to accompany her religious program on WWCA. Woods recalled:

> We were both down in the radio station one day. Vivian had finished her show and it was getting close to three in the morning. In a casual way, Vivian suggested I try to come up with an organ instrumental to open her program. I fooled around with a few spiritual standards, including "Amazing Grace." Unbeknownst to me, Vivian had passed word to the engineer to tape my impromptu session. Vivian took to my on-the-spot, ad-lib, once through version of "Amazing Grace" and wanted to try it on her audience on her next program. That was it. The hymn clicked immediately. It was this rough, unpolished version of the hymn that got released in January 1955.[114]

Despite *Billboard*'s middling review of "Amazing Grace" as a "good organ performance . . . that should get spins on many religious shows," Vee Jay believed it had a hit and advertised the single alongside "You Don't Have to Go," the latest release by its best-selling artist, bluesman Jimmy Reed.[115] The public agreed with Vee Jay: "Amazing Grace" went on to become the best-selling gospel instrumental of all time, reportedly selling two hundred thousand copies in its first year of release.[116] Idella Johnson considers "Amazing Grace" "one of the most soulful soundscapes of the African-American church."[117]

The instrumental single sparked greater interest in the Maceo Woods Singers, and the ensemble embarked on the national gospel highway. In his autobiography, *A Graceful Journey*, Woods recalled that in live performances, his signature move was to appear in a white suit and, after playing the final chord, get up and walk around the organ, dusting it with his white handkerchief, as the tonic chord hung heavy in the air.[118]

Sid McCoy was another radio announcer who found Woods's organ technique appealing. A World War II veteran who served with the Army Corps of Engineers, McCoy had graduated from Englewood High School and served as the road manager for jazz pianist Earl "Fatha" Hines while also conducting the Contemporary Jazz Seminar at Lake Forest College in Lake Forest, Illinois. McCoy's first radio job was in 1948, narrating a program called *Destination Freedom* on WMAQ.[119] Like Vivian Carter Bracken, McCoy honed his radio skills at the feet of Al Benson, parlaying that experience into a 12:00 midnight to 2:00 a.m. program on WGES.[120] In 1958, he was tapped to host *Sunday Morning.* Touted as "America's only national Negro radio program," the half-hour show aired from the Chess Records studios and featured music by the top gospel artists of the day, including the Roberta Martin Singers, the Dixie Hummingbirds, the Staple Singers, the Ward Singers, the Highway QCs, and the Davis Sisters.[121] The program aired on sixty-six stations in more than forty states and was heard in Chicago over WBEE at 9:30 Sunday mornings.[122] Pet Milk Company, the national sponsor of *Sunday Morning,* hired Woods to be the show's organist. Woods also accompanied McCoy reciting sacred poems for a Vee Jay various-artists compilation based on the broadcast.[123]

Although Woods's relationship with Vee Jay spanned the length and breadth of the record company's existence, the Maceo Woods Singers stopped recording around 1956. "Our experience with Vee Jay records was a very good experience, to a degree," remarked Donald Smith. "[But] after a while, they started focusing their attention on the Highway QCs."[124] Meanwhile, Woods recorded organ solos for Vee Jay and brought his Christian Tabernacle Ensemble to the label in the 1960s.

In the mid-1950s, Woods augmented his music portfolio by producing live gospel music programs. His first "Spiritual Cavalcade," later to be called "Gospel Supreme," was held at his home church of Mount Calvary, where Willie Webb, Robert Anderson, James Lee, and Rev. Dwight "Gatemouth" Moore were special guests.[125] Eventually, Woods's programs became so popular that he hosted his 1956 "Spiritual Cavalcade" at the larger Tabernacle Baptist Church. This event earned Woods a ministerial award "for his service to Christianity."[126] In 1957, Woods's program, again held at Tabernacle, brought the Davis Sisters and the Gospel Harmonettes to town, with R. L. Knowles as guest soloist and Sallie Martin as emcee.[127] It was the start of a string of annual "Gospel Supreme" musical extravaganzas that have continued well into the twenty-first century.

The Staple Singers: Gospel's First Family

The Staple Singers were among Vee Jay's most successful signings in any genre. The group was formed by family patriarch Roebuck "Pops" Staples—he dropped the "s" from their last name for professional purposes—who was born on a Winona, Mississippi, plantation December 28, 1915. When not picking cotton, Staples absorbed the sound of local bluesmen and the spirituals his grandfather taught him.[128] In 1931, Staples began accompanying a local quartet, the Golden Trumpets, on guitar. He married Osceola Ware (b. September 10, 1917) in Drew, Mississippi, in 1933. Two years later, with one-year-old Cleotha (b. April 11, 1934) in tow, the Staples migrated to Chicago.[129] They initially boarded with

Roebuck's brother, Chester, until they found a place of their own.[130] Roebuck worked in the city's stockyards, steel mills, and construction sites but continued to accompany quartets, using his sixty-five-dollar pawnshop guitar to back the Trumpet Jubilees. Osceola worked downtown at the Morrison Hotel. The couple had four more children: Pervis (b. November 18, 1936), Yvonne (b. October 23, 1937), Mavis (b. July 10, 1939), and Cynthia (1941–73).[131]

Although Roebuck taught his children to harmonize on the hymns and spirituals he had learned in Mississippi, the seeds of their professional singing career were sown in 1948, when Roebuck's sister Katie invited them to appear at her church.[132] The congregation responded so positively that Staples decided they could supplement their income by singing in public. As early as 1951, Roebuck, Mavis, Cleotha, and Purvis appeared on musicals at Mount Olivet Baptist Church and St. Philip AME, while Osceola stayed home to care for Cynthia.

Like other gospel artists of the era, Roebuck turned to radio and records for further promotion. He brokered fifteen minutes on WTAQ in suburban La Grange and, in 1953, pressed a vanity recording. "Faith and Grace" and "These Are They" were released on Staples's homemade Royal imprint; the family sold the disc at their live programs.[133] These may be the songs Roebuck referred to when he told a reporter that they only had two prepared numbers at first: "one for performance and the other for encore."[134] Heilbut believes that the Staples' "These Are They" was influenced by the Gospel Harmonettes' interpretation of Reverend Brewster's composition.[135]

Evelyn Gay introduced Roebuck to Leonard Allen of United Records. With Gay on piano, the Staple Singers cut nine known sides in two sessions, September 7, 1953, and October 5, 1954.[136] The only single released at the time coupled "It Rained Children" with "Won't You Sit Down" (aka "Sit Down Servant").[137] *Billboard* rated the disc as excellent, but Allen preferred that the Staple Singers consider singing popular material.[138] When Roebuck refused, the association with United ended.

Maceo Woods introduced the Staples to Vee Jay Records in October 1955.[139] "[The Maceo Woods Singers] worked with the Staple Singers," Donald Smith said. "We used to put [Mavis] up on chairs so that she could be seen when we were in places where there were large crowds."[140] The family quartet's first record for the Brackens, "If I Could Hear My Mother Pray" and "God's Wonderful Love," recorded on November 1, reportedly sold only three hundred copies.[141] No one could blame Roebuck for doubting the efficacy of commercial recording at that juncture.

Hoping their luck would improve, the group returned to Universal on September 11, 1956, to record four more sides for Vee Jay.[142] Mavis had the flu and did not feel like going anywhere, but when her father said they were going downtown to record, she mustered sufficient energy to join them.[143] One of the sides the group completed that day was an arrangement of the hymn "The Unclouded Day," later known as "Uncloudy Day." "Uncloudy Day" benefited from the family's tight harmonies, the thick tremolo from Roebuck's electric guitar, as well as Mavis's husky contralto—lower, no doubt, because of her illness. The record was their breakthrough, initially selling thirty-six thousand copies and going on to sell a reported half million copies.[144] It established the Staples as the latest gospel sensation and, ultimately, earned them the title "First Family of Gospel."

From there, the Staple Singers produced one popular single after another for Vee Jay. They all featured the group's distinctive down-home quartet harmonies, Roebuck's guitar tremolo, and Mavis's deep, resonant lead vocals. Among their biggest hits during the 1950s were "Will the Circle Be Unbroken," "Pray On," "Don't Knock," a new version of "Low Is the Way" with Roebuck's guitar as lead instrument, and "This May Be the Last Time," covered a decade later by the Rolling Stones.

Vee Jay Records continued to dominate the gospel music field during the 1950s, securing the Original Five Blind Boys of Mississippi with Archie Brownlee from Peacock. The company signed the Highway QCs and other local groups such as the Argo Singers, whose "Near the Cross" was a gospel radio favorite. It also signed the Knowles and Jackson Sextet, organized by Sallie Martin's accompanist, Kenneth Woods Jr., and featuring First Church of Deliverance alumni R. L. Knowles and Myrtle Jackson.

In late January 1962, Vee Jay hired Atlantic Records' public relations man Gary Kramer to serve as "executive consultant and talent scout" for its gospel division.[145] Under Kramer, Vee Jay signed the stars of Langston Hughes's critically acclaimed gospel musical, *Black Nativity*: Alex Bradford and the Bradford Singers, Princess Stewart, Marion Williams and the Stars of Faith, and the Patterson Singers.

Hughes and Kramer were inspired to create *Black Nativity*, a musical retelling of the birth of Jesus, in part upon hearing the Christmas album that Marion Williams and the Stars of Faith released on Savoy in 1959.[146] When the musical premiered at New York's Forty-First Street Theater in December 1961, reviews focused not on the acting or the staging but on the music. One reviewer noted, "The voices plunge into sudden dark growls like muted trombones and soar in ecstatic squeals and frantic clarinets."[147] *Black Nativity* headed to Europe in 1962; among its stops was the famed Spoleto Festival of Two Worlds in Italy. The following Christmas, the original cast played New

York City's Philharmonic Hall at the same time that Vee Jay Records released the original-cast soundtrack album. The year 1963 meant another trip to Europe followed by a forty-one-week tour of the United States.[148] Miraculously, a portion of Princess Stewart's eyesight was restored after she was injured in an auto accident during one of the troupe's European tours.

By the end of 1962, Vee Jay completed yet another prominent acquisition when it signed the Caravans, now featuring Albertina Walker, Cassietta George, Shirley Caesar, Delores Washington, Josephine Howard, and James Herndon as vocalist and pianist. They produced several hits for the company, notably Walker leading "Amazing Grace," Washington on "Seek Ye the Lord," and Shirley Caesar singing Herndon's "No Coward Soldier."

Around this time, gospel singer Gene Viale witnessed his first Caravans concert at the arena side of the Oakland Auditorium: "One by one, the managers or one of the singers from each group would make their way to the microphone and announce to the crowd, 'Please make sure that you get one of our latest albums. . . . They are just $3.00 each.'"[149] Then he caught his first glimpse of Albertina Walker. "She entered the auditorium from the front entrance and walked the full length of the auditorium as thousands of fans looked on. She had such a presence. She was wearing a knee length black dress with thin shoulder straps and had record albums under her right arm. Large, dark sunglasses obscured her beautiful full face, but the crowd, including me, knew exactly who she was."[150]

The Caravans struck Viale as strong and confident, and "each one of them was a soloist in her own right." Walker stood and sang "Lord Keep Me Day by Day," and George followed with "Remember Me, Oh Lord," walking through the audience as she sang. Caesar, "about four foot eleven and a half and just a young girl then, ran through the audience, kicking off her shoes as she went," singing "I Won't Be Back."[151] Rev. Walter J. Butts, another Caravans enthusiast, agreed: "They just sang, and man, you knew you'd been to church!"[152]

The group's affiliation with Vee Jay produced many other gospel classics, not the least of which was Cassietta George's haunting solo "Walk around Heaven All Day." The song became George's all-time signature piece. According to Heilbut, the song was based on Aretha Franklin's Columbia Records rendition of "That Lucky Old Sun"—not much of a reach to go from "roll around Heaven all day" to "walk around Heaven all day." Notwithstanding the obvious heist, Heilbut considers the Caravans' "Walk around Heaven All Day" to be "one of the last hits of gospel's golden age."[153]

When Vee Jay went broke in 1966, the Caravans returned to Savoy Records and its Gospel subsidiary, where they stayed until 1967 or 1968. By then, Walker had recruited new members, including the effervescent Loleatta Holloway, Julia Price-Williams, Gwen Morgan, and Willie James McPhatter, to replace James

Herndon, Inez Andrews, and Shirley Caesar, who had moved on to pursue successful careers as soloists and group leaders.[154]

"The Gospel Wonders of the Midwest"

Like the Gay Sisters, the Duncanaires were another gospel group from Chicago's Church of God in Christ tradition. Billed as the "Gospel Wonders of the Midwest," the Duncanaires organized at Bishop William Roberts' Fortieth COGIC on Easter Sunday, April 13, 1952.[155] Charter member Dolores "Honey" Sykes explained how the group came to be:

> One day we were fooling around at [Fortieth] in the back, where the piano was, and we started singing. One of our members, we call her the founder, Alva Lou Duncan Weaver, she was married to Elder [Edgar J.] Duncan's nephew. We were singing, and all of a sudden [Weaver] says, "Let's form a group now, and we'll ask Duncan if we can call ourselves the Duncanaires after him." [Duncan] said he'd be delighted, thrilled, and honored for us to be named after him. We started singing from then on. Matter of fact, Duncan put us right up to sing. We did our debut, and we sounded pretty good to everybody.[156]

The Duncanaires were regulars on Roberts Temple's weekly radio broadcast. "We would sing on the live broadcast every Sunday at 11:00," Sykes said. "We had special seats up in the pulpit. Once the public heard the Duncanaires, they were there every Sunday night. We stuck to straight old-time music."[157]

Besides Sykes and Alva Weaver, other members of the original Duncanaires were James Hopkins, Ralph Adams, Catherine Maloy, pianist Bobby Bolden, and Claude Timmons. Geraldine Gay accompanied the group for a short time, and Loretta Oliver, sister of Vernon Oliver Price, became a member later. The Duncanaires' first musician was Alva Lou's sister, Louise Lindsey. Lindsey was killed in 1953 when the group had an automobile accident en route to St. Louis for a program. Lindsey, the driver, and one other person were killed; Timmons, Weaver, and a couple of others, including Maloy, were in serious condition but survived. Timmons left the group in the late 1950s to join James Cleveland and Jessy Dixon in the Gospel Chimes.[158]

The local popularity of their "Lead Me, Guide Me" brought the Duncanaires close to starting their recording career in the mid-1950s, with Vee Jay Records, but nothing came of it. The Duncanaires were poised to move from Vee Jay to Savoy Records when Roebuck Staples convinced them they would do better financially by signing with Riverside, where the Staple Singers had been recording since leaving Vee Jay in 1962. The group took Staples's advice and their first commercially released single, "One Day Closer" and "Breathe on Me," was recorded at Universal. It earned a four-star rating from *Billboard* upon its release in the fall of 1963.[159] The group at this time consisted of Sykes, Oliver, Maloy, and pianist Eddie Williams. *Lead Me, Guide Me*, the group's second full-length album, was one of the first three releases that Orrin Keepnews issued on his Mainstream label in 1966.[160] Riverside promoted the Duncanaires' sound as modern and different, largely because the group wrapped its traditional gospel style with more complex harmonies and pop-flavored arrangements. In short, despite their commitment to "straight old time music," the Duncanaires were actually pushing the gospel envelope before other innovative COGIC groups, such as Andraé Crouch and the Disciples, the Hawkins Family, the Winans, and the Clark Sisters, would do so.

The Little Lucy Smith Singers

The Little Lucy Smith Singers—Lucy Smith, Gladys Beamon, and Floriene Watson—were organized in 1944 as the Lucy Smith Trio of All Nations Pentecostal Church.[161] They sang for the church's weekly radio broadcast on WGES and WCFL and, thanks to recorded transcriptions of the live broadcast, were heard nationally over four radio stations.[162] The trio was also a favorite participant on local gospel programs.

Born in Chicago in 1928, "Little Lucy" Smith was tinkering with the piano at age four and singing for her grandmother's broadcasts as a five-year-old. By age twelve, she was All Nations' organist.[163] Her talent was not lost on Roberta Martin, who retained her as the Roberta Martin Singers' musician. Charles Clency and DeLois Barrett Campbell called Lucy Smith the best pianist of her generation.[164] "Little Lucy did not get the credit as the best musician, or pianist, at that time," Clency recalled. "There were folk around who got more credit than she got, but in terms of proficiency, piano agility, being able to handle herself well at the piano and play anything, any style, she was the one."[165]

Floriene Watson acquired her early musical experience with the Watson Family Singers, a gospel group that included her brothers Romance and Irvin, father Amos, and sisters Vivienne and Sylvia. They sang at Forty-Fourth Street Baptist Church, where Sylvia served in the music department, and at All Nations Pentecostal, the Watson family's home church. She met Little Lucy and Gladys Beamon at All Nations, and together they formed the Lucy Smith Trio, with Smith on alto, Beamon on soprano, and Watson on tenor. They sang gospel songs such as "How I Got Over" for the church's radio broadcasts. When Floriene soloed, her signature song was "Just Tell Jesus, Tell Him All." "People used to call in and request for us to sing different songs," Watson recalled.[166] Floriene was often requested to sing "Never Grow Old." In addition to their regular spot on the All Nations radio broadcast, the Lucy Smith Singers appeared on programs around the city and would sometimes travel with the Roberta Martin Singers.

Watson left the group when she moved to California, and Catherine Campbell and Sarah Scott McKissick took her place. Campbell was a recruit from All Nations, while McKissick was an Atlanta native who married Roberta Martin Singer Norsalus McKissick in 1951. Doris Sykes and Gloria Griffin also sang with the Little Lucy Singers for a short while, but the most important singer in the group was Gladys Beamon.[167] Born Gladys Allbritton in 1925, Beamon had the potential to become a star in the secular music world when in 1947 she was a finalist on WBBM radio's "Radio Star Quest" talent contest. The contest offered the winner a contract to perform over WBBM for thirteen weeks. Although she did not win, Beamon was complimented for selling a song like "another Ethel Waters."[168]

Smith, Campbell, Beamon, and McKissick made a handful of recordings for Leonard Allen's States label between 1955 and 1956, with Little Lucy on organ and Kenneth Woods Jr. on piano. Beamon led five of the eight released sides. Among the group's recorded highlights were "Hold the Light," which concluded with a playful vocal interchange between Beamon and the ensemble designed to lift an audience to its feet. A local gospel hit, the doo-wop-inspired arrangement of "Somebody Bigger Than You and I" caused *Billboard* to gush that Beamon was "blessed with a big voice and using a style reminiscent of Mahalia Jackson."[169] At their second and final session for United on June 22, 1956, the Little Lucy Smith Singers remained in the Universal studio to sing background for Sammy Lewis's "The Man behind the Clouds." Written by Lewis, "Clouds" had a syrupy country-ballad feel that paled in comparison to the high energy, organ and boogie-woogie-fueled flipside, "I'm Heaven Bound," but it allegedly became the first African American gospel song featured on the television program *Your Hit Parade*.[170]

The Little Lucy Smith Singers' limited recording output, at a time when recordings had surpassed radio as a primary marketing tool, is why the group never attained the widespread, lasting popularity of the Caravans or Argo Singers. Nevertheless, the group was a superb representation of the churchy sound of Chicago gospel. Heilbut, who produced several projects on Chicago gospel legends, commented: "Lucy and Gladys were the most talented and versatile singers I recorded in Chicago. Both could have ascended to the level of their pal, Dinah Washington. The trio must have been staggering back in the day."[171]

The First Crown Prince of Gospel: Singing Sammy Lewis

Born in 1925 to Montgomery and Lucinda Lewis, Sammy began singing gospel in 1930 and was a member of the Roberta Martin Singers for seventeen years, though he never recorded with them.[172] Martin, in fact, bestowed the nickname "Singing Sammy" on him in 1934 after the nine-year-old soloist brought down the house at an Ebenezer gospel program.[173] Bishop Isaiah Roberts of Roberts

Temple COGIC is credited with giving Lewis the added moniker of "Crown Prince of Gospel." Lewis attended Chicago Music College and commenced his recording career in July 1949 by waxing Lucie Campbell's "Something within Me" and a Mahalia Jackson standard, Antonio Haskell's "God Shall Wipe All Tears Away," for Leonard Chess's Aristocrat Records. At an April 7, 1952, program at St. Luke Baptist Church, Jackson named Lewis the "most outstanding gospel singer" of 1951.[174]

In addition to soloing, Lewis directed the All Nations Pentecostal Church choir and, by the mid-1950s, was minister of music at Mount Eagle Baptist Church, under the pastorship of Rev. C. J. Rodgers.[175] He signed with Vee Jay Records in 1954, and his first release, "Lord Will I Find Peace Someday," with Eddie Robinson on piano, was cited as *Cash Box* magazine's number one religious record for four months.[176] After the aforementioned disc for United in 1956, Lewis ceased recording until around 1962, when he reappeared on Henry Rush's eponymously named imprint. By this point, Lewis had entered the religious ministry and was pastoring New St. Paul Baptist Church on Chicago's South Side. Rush released a two-sided 45 of Lewis singing "What Is This," written by Willie Morganfield, a relative of Chicago bluesman Muddy Waters. Accompanied on piano by Almazita Clay, New St. Paul's first minister of music, Lewis infused "What Is This" with the raw bluesiness of Morganfield's original.[177] The single was reported to have held the number one position for gospel songs in Chicago for eight consecutive weeks.[178]

Pastor Ray Allen Berryhill, minister of music under Lewis at New Hope Baptist Church at 647 West Division, said, "Singing Sammy Lewis was the icon, the star of the North Side, if you will. He came and took a church that was struggling, maybe had fifty people, but he took it and put it on the map. He was a member of Fellowship, and so Reverend Clay Evans would come over to help him and bring Lou Della [Evans Reid] and the choir over."[179] A 1963 automobile accident nearly took Lewis's life, but he returned to his pulpit that October to resume his ministry.[180] In the mid-1960s Lewis brought his penchant for intensely hard gospel singing to Chess/Checker and continued recording well into the 1970s.

Mahalia Jackson: "The World's Greatest Gospel Singer"

In a city bursting with titled gospel singers, Mahalia Jackson was the undisputed queen. She returned triumphantly to a sold-out Carnegie Hall on October 7, 1951, for Joe Bostic's Second Annual Negro Gospel and Religious Music Festival, sharing the stage with James Cleveland's Gospelaires.[181] After Carnegie Hall, Jackson appeared on Ed Sullivan's nationally televised *Toast of the Town* and was preparing to become the first gospel singer to tour Europe. But just prior to the October 1952 tour, Jackson learned that she had sarcoidosis, a disease affecting the lymph glands that she might have contracted as early as childhood.[182] Her illness threatened to derail the European trip, but Mother Fannie Gay's prayerful intercession gave Jackson sufficient assurance that she was ready to go.[183] Nevertheless, to arrive in France on time, Jackson had to swallow her fear of flying and cross the Atlantic by air.

Upon arrival on European soil, the singer was welcomed as royalty and delighted audiences and reporters in France, England, and Denmark. Exclaimed reporter Max Jones: "When she dances those little church steps at the end of a rocking number, you need a heart of stone to remain unsmiling."[184] But as she was returning to Paris, with Italy ahead, Jackson was too ill to continue and was flown home. So many in Chicago were worried about her health that Rev. Clarence Cobbs went on the radio to tell people to give the Queen of Gospel some space and let her rest.[185] Jackson had conquered as much of Europe as her health permitted but in the end traveling had taken its toll. She would battle sarcoidosis for the rest of her life.

In 1954, Jackson pioneered again, becoming the first solo gospel singer to sign in the postwar era with Columbia Records, the major label of major labels. Because Jackson's Apollo contract appeared to be up for renewal at the conclusion of 1953, Columbia talent chief Mitch Miller believed she was open to sign with the company in 1954.[186] He offered her a fifty-thousand-dollar-per-year guarantee for four years, during which she would record four times per year. Miller explained that Columbia would expand her recorded repertory, but Jackson would hear none of that: it was gospel or nothing. Miller capitulated.

By then, Jackson was prepared to leave Apollo Records. She and Bess Berman had had their share of dustups over money. And while Jackson's Apollo contract was up for renewal at the end of every calendar year, Berman retained the right of first refusal. As well as Jackson's records were doing in the marketplace, Berman could be expected to renew her contract for 1954.[187] Columbia moved forward, nevertheless, presenting their new prospect at the 1954 Music Operators Association Convention, held March 8–10 at Chicago's Palmer House. Jackson's performance was so powerful she was deemed the star of the confab.[188] Meanwhile, Berman affirmed that her contract with Jackson had not lapsed. As a riposte, she ran an ad in *Billboard* in which Jackson thanked the Convention "for the way you received me"—identified as an Apollo recording artist.[189]

Columbia pressed on, preparing *The Mahalia Jackson Show* for its debut on the CBS radio network.[190] The half-hour radio program would make her the first African American gospel singer with a sustaining program on CBS network radio.[191] One wrinkle still needed ironing: Jackson insisted that her friend and loyal fan, Studs Terkel, be the show's chief writer. Terkel, however, would not sign any document stating that he had never been, and was not currently, a Communist. As a result, CBS did not want to use him, but Jackson put her foot down again. This time, CBS met the artist only halfway. Network executives agreed that Terkel could write the program as long as he was not recognized in the credits or in advertising.[192]

Taped in Chicago's historic Wrigley Building, *The Mahalia Jackson Show* debuted September 26, 1954. Each weekly half-hour program featured Jackson singing four or five gospel tunes and spirituals, as well as an assortment of inspirational songs such as "Summertime," "Danny Boy," and "Brahms' Lullaby."[193] *The Mahalia Jackson Show* helped expose the singer, and gospel music, to a wider and more diverse audience, but after just seventeen weeks, the show was shortened to ten minutes. On February 6, 1955, after twenty episodes, the program was cancelled for lack of a national sponsor.[194] In Jim Crow America, prospective sponsors feared offending southern white customers by sponsoring a program starring a black woman, even if she was singing religious music.[195]

With the Apollo contract tussle finally resolved, Columbia ushered its new star into the studio on November 22, 1954, and subsequently released "Rusty Old Halo" as the first single. *Billboard* called the song a "'semi-spiritual' that should appeal in both the spiritual and pop field [*sic*]."[196] The reviewer had harsher words for the second single, "Walk All Over God's Heaven." He liked Jackson's treatment but felt "the disc suffer[ed] from a pop-styled, affected backing," adding, "It is doubtful if this platter will be appreciated by her followers."[197] Since "Rusty Old Halo" was written by theatrical and novelty hit songwriter Bob Merrill, while "Walk All Over God's Heaven" was written specifically for Mahalia by her friend and former employer, Thomas A. Dorsey, one can infer that the reviewer was perplexed that two songs with vastly different provenances received similarly syrupy arrangements. A *Billboard* reviewer shared the same sentiment about the flipside to "Walk," "Jesus Met the Woman at the Well," a song popular with gospel quartets from the Pilgrim Travelers to the Fairfield Four. Nevertheless, by early 1955, "Walk" was reported to have sold a quarter of a million copies.[198] The third single, "You'll Never Walk Alone," from Rogers and Hammerstein's *Carousel*, was not gospel at all, though Jackson wrapped her soulful voice around it.[199] Columbia was clearly searching for loopholes within its "religious songs only" commitment to make Jackson a pop singer palatable to a mainstream audience that, in 1955, put Patti Page, Teresa Brewer, and Rosemary Clooney on top of the charts.

Billboard's commentary about the consequences of commercializing Mahalia Jackson and gospel music was telling. In January 1955, Steve Schickel reported that, among other things, a "12-city survey conducted by Specialty Records" uncovered a "strong resentment . . . against the commercialization of religion. Avid gospel devotees feel there is no connection between their music and any other kind of music . . . [and] want no association with these other fields." Their resentment extended to disk jockeys who programmed gospel alongside R&B and jazz.[200]

Nevertheless, Jackson's debut LP, *The World's Greatest Gospel Singer*, drew a five-star rating from the jazz magazine *Downbeat*.[201] It secured the singer top billing on the *Chicago Tribune*'s prestigious Chicagoland Music Festival, where she and teen heartthrob Eddie Fisher appeared in front of a packed Soldier Field.[202] Joel Friedman wrote that Jackson's signing to Columbia "caused a general resurgence throughout the whole [gospel] field and resulted in a period of extremely high sales for all firms in the business."[203] The album also provided Theodore Frye with an unanticipated windfall. The songs on Jackson's LP published by Frye persuaded Jean and Julian Aberbach of Hill & Range Music to purchase the performance rights to Frye's catalog, "considered one of the important ones in the field from the standpoint of performances, sheet music and mechanicals."[204]

In April 1956, amid her rising fame and fortune, Jackson purchased a ranch-style home at 8328 South Indiana for forty thousand dollars, only to have her front window riddled with bullets by toughs who did not want black homeowners in the predominantly white Chatham Village neighborhood. A woman who ladled out homespun wisdom as often as her famous gumbo, Jackson reflected: "When I go to New York City and sing at Madison Square Garden and at Carnegie Hall, I feel like a peacock with all my feathers spread out; but when I get back to Sixty-Third Street in Chicago and look down at my feet, all the feathers disappear."[205]

Jackson's personal relationship with Chicago mayor Richard J. Daley ensured that her home received heightened security following the shooting incident. CBS television journalist Edward R. Morrow was so disturbed over the shooting that he broadcast an episode of his *Person To Person* television program, during which he interviewed famous people in their home, featuring Jackson. A camera was set up in Jackson's living room, and Morrow interviewed her from New York.[206] Thereafter, several white neighbors greeted Jackson, wanting to do whatever they could to help, although "For Sale" signs began to pop up on lawns along Indiana Avenue.[207]

"The Helen Hayes of Gospel"

In late January 1957, the Roberta Martin Singers left Apollo Records to sign with Savoy.[208] Herman Lubinsky did not waste a moment. In one year, the ensemble visited the studio three times to record eighteen sides. At the time of the signing, the group consisted of Martin, Lucy Smith, DeLois Barrett Campbell, Norsalus McKissick, Eugene Smith, Gloria Griffin, and Romance Watson.

Watson was not only the latest acquisition of the Roberta Martin Singers, but he was also one of its youngest members. Born on January 4, 1930, Watson was, like sister Floriene, a member of the Watson Family Singers. As youngsters, Romance and his sisters, Floriene, Sylvia, and Vivienne, learned gospel songs at the feet of Sallie Martin and Thomas Dorsey. He recalled: "Sallie Martin would teach us various songs, and before you know it, [Dorsey]'d sneak up behind us with his accordion and scare the devil out of us! Oh, it was such a wonderful group! But [Elder Lucy Smith] put a stop to our being with Thomas A. Dorsey and Sallie Martin. She told my parents that these children need to be in their own church; they don't need to be out there singing with these other folk. They need to be up here in this choir."[209] Elder Smith's influence had no bearing on Watson's decision to become a Roberta Martin Singer; he was overjoyed to receive the invitation. "We held Sister Roberta Martin in such high esteem," Watson said. "She was first class."[210]

Martin even managed to charm Lubinsky, who dubbed her the "Helen Hayes of Gospel" for her genteel manner.[211] Recalled Savoy producer Lawrence Roberts: "Miss Martin was the only artist who could go into [Lubinsky's] office, along with Mr. Fred Mendelsohn and myself, say a very few words, flash her famous smile, and get Lubinsky to pull out the checkbook and begin to write. Sometimes two days later, he would say affectionately, 'Roberts, how much did I give her?'"[212] Nevertheless, with the Roberta Martin Singers, the Ward Singers, and the Davis Sisters on Savoy and ringing cash registers, Lubinsky gushed to *Billboard*: "It's a great day for the sanctified beat."[213]

It *was* a great day for the sanctified beat. Throughout the 1950s, African American popular artists were gradually incorporating gospel music techniques into their singing and performing. Since the early 1950s, Willie James McPhatter's cousin Clyde had parlayed his church training into melismatic lead singing for the Dominoes and the Drifters, and at midcentury, Little Richard Penniman shouted and leaped into falsetto on "Good Golly Miss Molly" and "Tutti Frutti." Etta James's gutsy, passionate singing and lyric timing were the fruits of her gospel training under J. Earle Hines. Former quartet member James Brown and his Famous Flames burst onto the R&B music scene in 1956 with a stage show that mimicked the sweaty intensity of the Holiness worship service. Jackie Wilson painted early soul hits such as 1958's "Lonely Teardrops," written by pre-Motown Berry Gordy Jr., with gospel melisma and wordless vocal fills. Ray Charles's churchy workout "What I Say" and the Isley Brothers' "Shout," which Heilbut reported was done in homage to Marion Williams and her high "whooos," were released the following year.[214]

Gospel was coming full circle: borne out of African American popular music, it was now influencing the future direction of pop music. In Chicago, an early significant partnership between sacred and secular occurred in 1958, when Jerry Butler and the Impressions recorded the haunting slow-dance ballad "For Your Precious Love." The song, which Calvin Carter of Vee Jay Records remembered the Impressions referring to as "that spiritual thing we worked out" and that sold nearly a million copies in its first issue, is considered by many to be Chicago's first soul record.[215] If so, the gospel music education that Butler and fellow Impressions member Curtis Mayfield received as members of the Northern Jubilee Gospel Singers from Chicago's Traveling Souls Spiritualist Church provided most of the musical underpinning.[216]

By the end of the 1950s, Chicago had further anchored its primacy in gospel music by being home base for most of the major gospel publishing houses as well as gospel artists of national stature. Record companies—Vee Jay in particular—were pumping out gospel releases. Nearly every nonliturgical church had a gospel choir, and many broadcast their music-filled services over radio. But a tsunami of change was charging westward from Detroit. It arrived on the South Side in 1959, altering the sound of the Chicago gospel chorus forever.

CHAPTER 14

"He Could Just Put a Song on His Fingers"

Second-Generation Gospel Choirs

Detroit came to Chicago and that changed everybody. That changed gospel music, period.

Charles Clency

Like a forest fire, word traveled through the Chicago gospel community about a choir with a huge sound that James Cleveland had brought from Detroit to Chicago to appear at True Light Baptist Church. Since many gospel music devotees missed the initial program, a second musical was scheduled for July 6, 1959, this time at the larger First Church of Deliverance. Robert Anderson and Eddie Robinson sponsored the July 6 "Mountain of Gospel Music," starring James Cleveland and the choir that had stirred such curiosity—the Voices of Tabernacle from Detroit's Prayer Tabernacle Church.[1]

"You could not get near First Church," said gospel musician Charles Clency, who attended the July 1959 program. "The church was jam-packed, standing room only."[2]

The Voices of Tabernacle was James Cleveland's latest in a nonstop string of projects. In the late 1950s, Cleveland parted ways with the Caravans, relinquished his music post at Rev. B. F. Paxton's True Light Baptist Church, and set off for Detroit. He worked briefly with Ernestine Rundless and the Meditation Singers, directed the choir at Rev. C. L. Franklin's New Bethel Baptist Church, and taught Franklin's daughter Aretha to play piano.[3] When in 1958

Rev. Charles Craig left his music position at Rev. James Lofton's Church of Our Prayer to found his own Spiritual church, Prayer Tabernacle, he asked Cleveland to be the minister of music. This included directing the church's house choir, the Voices of Tabernacle. Under Cleveland's direction, the Voices of Tabernacle bowled over one Detroiter in particular: beautician and House of Beauty owner Carmen Caver Murphy. Murphy cobbled together the funds to record and release an album of the ensemble on her own imprint, HOB. The gamble paid off. *The Love of God*, taken from the album's title track, an arrangement of Johnnie Taylor's Soul Stirrers hit from 1958, was hugely successful and influential. *Billboard* called the 125-voice choir "one of the great spiritual choruses performing today."[4] The album introduced several important soloists, including Hulah Gene Dunklin Hurley, Louise McCord, and Richard Roquemore, to the larger gospel music community.

"Before Detroit," Clency explained, "the sound of gospel was the groups. It was the Caravans, the Maceo Woods Singers, the Willie Webb Singers, the Roberta Martin Singers, a lot of singers. It was that tight, four, five singers to a part, with regular gospel chords, the I-IV-V that made gospel *gospel*. And the sound was not big because it was just four or five people to a part. But when Detroit came, everything became choirs."[5] Gospel singer Rev. Walter J. Butts agreed. "Chicago had that churchy sound, that gutsy churchy sound, down to earth, the type of music that just comes from your soul. The Detroit sound was more of a contemporary sound."[6]

First Church of Deliverance was filled to bursting on July 6, as program attendees waited eagerly to hear the Voices of Tabernacle, the group that had, according to the publicity, "won such hearty public support" at True Light that this second program was scheduled "in response to a popular demand."[7] The ensemble did not disappoint.

Clency, who attended the program, said that the impact of the Voices that night was "indescribable."

I heard sounds I never heard before in gospel. I could not believe what I was hearing; none of us could. It wasn't just gospel. They showcased gospel—gospel was their thing—but they did everything else! They did Beethoven. They had an organ, piano, directors, they had about one hundred singers, and they sang everything, with music and without music. The organ and piano were unbelievable in terms of balance, quality, expertise, dynamics, soft, loud, spirituals, gospels, anthems. The musicians were trained musicians. Alfred Bolden was on the organ, and Herbert "Pee Wee" Pickard was on the piano. Alonzo Atkins and Reverend Leslie Bush assisted with the directing chores.

Charles Craig and James Cleveland came out with a completely brand new idea of all kinds of contemporary chords, extended chords, chord alterations.

Things the organ would do, the piano would answer, and vice versa. And a lot of jazz rhythms, where you had sevenths and ninths and thirteenths—Charles Craig could hear all that and incorporated it into his music, along with Beethoven, Mozart, a lot of the masters. Everything in music changed after that, across the country, to a point that no longer was it just the verse and the chorus, and maybe an extended chorus, and foot-patting and basic chords. It became extremely contemporary—it was a completely new sound. The gospel sound after 1960 became all choirs and big. The Voices of this, the Voices of that, the Voices of Tabernacle, my group was the Voices of Melody, you had the Voices of Cosmopolitan. Everybody had to be the "Voices of" because everybody was trying to be like the big choir from Detroit.[8]

Barry C. Johnson Sr. states that Cleveland's triumph with the Voices of Tabernacle turned him from "years of struggling" into "a major gospel attraction. The choir directors began copying his unconventional time signatures, which allowed for large sections of rubato to be utilized during improvisatory, narration, and preaching during the performances. The 'back-home' choruses who were used to hymns and Dorsey retired from the spotlight, and young people's choirs that could keep up with Cleveland's changes became the rage."[9]

"James Cleveland had an uncanny knack for putting people together and putting songs together with people," former Cleveland Singer Gene Viale reflects. "It was natural for him to hear a singer and automatically retain the singer's sound and ability in his mind."[10] "James Cleveland always had soulfulness," said Clency. "He was the Ray Charles of gospel. But Charles Craig was the one who had the innovation and the musicianship."[11]

The Community Choirs

Because membership in a church choir was reserved for members of that church, community choirs formed to enable people from various churches and denominations, and especially youth, to sing together. Community choirs also offered a positive social outlet for the rising number of Christian teens, an alternative to the rising tide of juvenile delinquency and gang membership. Anyone could audition for the community choir, and singers could belong to both a community choir and a church choir, with their pastor's approval.

Civil rights leader Addie L. Wyatt of the Vernon Park Church of God organized the Wyatt Choral Ensemble in Chicago's Altgeld Gardens housing project as early as 1947, but the Thompson Community Singers, founded the following year, are typically cited as Chicago's first community gospel choir.[12] They set a musical standard for community gospel choruses everywhere.

Thompson Community Singers

In 1948, nineteen-year-old Milton Brunson organized the Thompson Community Singers in the basement of St. Stephen AME Church at 2000 West Washington Boulevard. He named the choir in honor of St. Stephen's pastor, Rev. Eugene Thompson. Although the original forty choir members consisted of Brunson's schoolmates at McKinley High School, L. Stanley Davis recalled that Brunson did not accept members younger than fifteen years old.[13] The group rehearsed every Tuesday evening and appeared at St. Stephen every third Sunday afternoon.[14] "We wanted to get together and sing spirituals and everything else," Brunson told *Totally Gospel* magazine. "We just wanted to sing."[15] Original member Leon Bailey told the *Chicago Defender* in 2009 that the group originally sang spirituals and show tunes. "We didn't start singing gospel until we left St. Stephen."[16]

For his part, Reverend Thompson introduced the Thompson Community Singers, nicknamed the Tommies, to other churches on the city's West and South Sides, and soon the group was a regular attraction at gospel programs. The choir even traveled to Detroit, where Aretha Franklin sang with them during an appearance at her father's church.[17] By 1952, the group had 135 voices, and a year later included as many as 250 voices.[18] The group's chief accompanists were Metropolitan Baptist Church musicians Dolores Mercer Chandler (organ) and Robert Williams (piano).[19]

"I never heard a choir sound like that," said Delores "Honey" Sykes, upon hearing the Tommies at All Nations Pentecostal around 1949. She joined the Tommies, even though it meant pulling a double shift singing for her own church, Roberts Temple COGIC, and then "sneaking out and going over" to sing with the Tommies.[20] Delecta Clark, who in the late 1950s emerged as R&B star Dee Clark ("Raindrops," "Hey Little Girl,"), indicated that he received early musical training as a member of the Tommies.[21] Vernon Oliver Price, soloist from St. Paul COGIC, was a member of the Tommies in the 1950s, as was her sister, Loretta Oliver. "Before I started singing with them," Price said, "I used to go and listen to them rehearse. At that time, I had children and so I just sat there, but then I decided to join because they had discipline."[22]

If discipline was a Tommies performance objective, a civic objective was to raise funds to establish an educational, recreational, and social community space for West Side youth. The plan succeeded: an eleven-room center at Millard and Ogden Avenues opened February 2, 1960.[23] Two years later, Brunson entered the ministry and in 1964 became pastor of Christ Tabernacle Missionary Baptist Church. Initially meeting at the A. R. Rayner Funeral Home, Christ Tabernacle secured a site at 4244 West Madison Avenue and began broadcasting its worship services on radio at 11:00 p.m. on Sundays.[24]

In addition to Sykes, Price, and Oliver, other gospel artists who joined the Thompson Community Singers and went on to solo fame included Billy Kyles, Leanne Faine, Kim McFarland, George Mayes, and Aldrea Sanford Lenox and James Lenox of Greater Holy Temple COGIC. Singer-songwriter Darius Brooks and producer Percy Bady were also products of the Tommies. James Lenox's experience in the Tommies inspired him to form the Chicago Pentecostal Choir, a community choir specifically for Pentecostal church musical fellowship.

The Tommies did not record until the early 1960s, when Richard Simpson produced their first two albums, *Yes Jesus Loves Me* and *The Soul of the Thompson Community Singers*, issued by Vee Jay in 1963 and 1964, respectively. *Yes Jesus Loves Me* featured songs by James Cleveland and Kenneth Woods Jr., as well as modern arrangements of traditional hymns and spirituals. Listeners were treated to a sonorously strong ensemble with powerful lead vocalists, including Vernon Oliver Price and Loretta Oliver. Brunson narrated and sang, his coarse baritone evocative of James Cleveland. The Tommies sounded like a young choir with an old soul, infusing contemporary songs, such as Cleveland's "Beyond the Dark Clouds," with a soaring vocal line reminiscent of the pop classic "Harbor Lights." "Old Ship of Zion" elicited shouts from a chorister, caught up in the spirit.

Taking more musical liberties, 1964's *The Soul of the Thompson Community Singers* featured songs and arrangements from newcomer Jessy Dixon. For example, Dixon infused the spiritual "Motherless Child" with an Asian rhythm and melody, not unlike the experimental music of the Gospel Clefs of Newark, New Jersey. The album's sole single, "Soldier in God's Army," was the Pentecostal favorite set to a march tempo. On the other hand, "I've Come a Long Way" was pure gospel blues.

Born March 12, 1938, in San Antonio, Texas, Jessy Dixon was one of the most important musicians to work with the Tommies. He studied classical piano and as a teenager began singing at the local Refuge Church of Our Lord Jesus Christ. He earned a scholarship to attend a Catholic college but abandoned his studies to become a professional musician, working at one point at Antioch Baptist Church in San Antonio. James Cleveland saw him perform in San Antonio in 1959 and invited the young man to succeed him as music minister for True Light Baptist Church.[25] Dixon also joined the Gospel Chimes, the vocal group Cleveland organized in fall 1957 that included, at one time or another, Lee Charles Neely, Claude Timmons, Dorothy Norwood, and Imogene Greene.

Dixon was as fine a songwriter and arranger as he was a musician. He authored more than two hundred songs, including standards such as "God Can Do Anything but Fail," "I Love to Praise His Name," "Hello Sunshine," and "The Wicked Shall Cease from Troubling" (aka "Sit at His Feet and Be Blessed").[26] Inspired by the Voices of Tabernacle, Dixon endeavored to incorporate their sound into his organ playing and the choirs he directed, such as at Omega Baptist Church, under the leadership of radio and recording pastor Rev. Edmund Blair, where he was also minister of music. In 1963, Dixon joined the Thompson Community Singers and led the Chicago Community Choir, an ensemble of younger Tommies members. Dixon's single with the Chicago Community Choir, "Got to See My Lord," earned a four-star rating from *Billboard* in 1965.[27] The group's rendition of "Hello Sunshine" earned a Grammy nomination in 1971 for Best Soul Gospel Performance.[28] Dixon also formed the Jessy Dixon Singers, which included Chicago powerhouse singers Aldrea Lenox and Ethel Holloway. The Jessy Dixon Singers served as background vocalists for Gene Viale on his 1968 solo album for Checker, *What Color Is God*, and beginning in 1973, for pop star Paul Simon.[29]

The Tommies' biggest hit came in 1969, after they signed with HOB Records. "I'll Trade a Lifetime," with its moving solo by fifteen-year-old Maggie Bell Childs, was popular on soul music radio and gospel broadcasts.[30] The Tommies went on to record a string of popular LPs for HOB during the 1970s. Church musicians eagerly embraced each successive album because it contained songs they could teach their choirs and groups to sing.

Wooten Choral Ensemble

The city's second community gospel choir, the Wooten Choral Ensemble, was named after its founder, Robert Eugene Wooten. The choir reflected Wooten's knowledge of, and appreciation for, classical music, choral literature, and formal training, blending gospel chorus and senior chorus techniques.

Considered a musical prodigy on piano and organ, Wooten was born in Morgan Park to Flora and John Henry.[31] He founded the Morgan Park Crusaders in 1945 and the Wooten Choral Ensemble out of Beth Eden Baptist Church in Morgan Park in July 1949.[32] Wooten said the two pioneer community choirs often fellowshipped together in the early days: "When they used to be at St. Stephen's Church every third Sunday, we would go over there, and sometimes [Brunson would] put us on his program, and they'd come out when we did our big services down here [at Beth Eden]."[33]

Wooten juggled many music assignments. He managed the Wooten Choral Ensemble, took music lessons at the American Conservatory of Music, directed the Greater Harvest Baptist Church radio and youth choirs, and taught high school music. On Sundays, Rev. Louis Boddie of Greater Harvest and Rev. Richard C. Keller of Beth Eden had to share Wooten. "The first and third Sundays were the heaviest Sundays at Beth Eden, so I would be at Beth Eden," Wooten said. "Second and fourth Sundays, I would be at Greater Harvest for the afternoon broadcast."[34]

If Wooten's group was not Chicago's first community gospel choir, it was the first to record. In 1953, the choir self-produced "The Hand of God" and "I

Heard the Voice of Jesus," the song that had brought down the house at Willie Webb's 1951 anniversary program at Tabernacle. Lawrence Evans, grandson of Pastor Joseph Evans of Metropolitan Community Church, led "The Hand of God." Art Sheridan released the vanity disc on Chance, but it sold only modestly.

The choir recorded again a decade later, this time releasing a full-length album, *Altar Stairs of Song*, on Vee Jay. Wooten picked selections that his pastor Keller liked.[35] "I knew what [Keller] liked, and it was in tune with the kind of thing I liked, too," Wooten recalled.[36] Most were spirituals, such as "Ride the Chariot," "Over My Head," and "Down by the Riverside," which stayed in the ensemble's repertory for fifty years.

The Wooten Choral Ensemble continued recording through into the twenty-first century, releasing products privately. When Wooten died on March 27, 2008, his son Bobby took over management of the group, which still performs actively.

Youth Federation of South Chicago

The Youth Federation of South Chicago was another early community choir designed to give the city's young people a positive outlet. It was organized in 1950 by Almond Dawson Jr. after he and his family moved from the Ida B. Wells Homes in Bronzeville to the city's far South Side. Dawson, born in Chicago on April 13, 1932, to Quitman, Mississippi, migrants Luzella and Almond Dawson Sr., grew up admiring the deft choral direction of Arthur Logan. His parents were members of Logan's Goodwill Spiritual Singers at Monumental Baptist Church, but because Almond Sr. was a Pullman porter and traveled for weeks at a time, Almond Jr. often accompanied his mother to choir rehearsal.[37] "I would take my homework with me and listen to them rehearse," Dawson said. "Logan was influenced by a cappella groups like Wings over Jordan, and he did not use music. He would pick out the parts on piano and create distinct harmonies."[38]

Betty Lester, one of the Youth Federation's principal soloists, was hesitant to join the choir initially; her sights were set on becoming a blues singer. "I just thought it was a glamorous life, being a blues singer," Lester reflected. "I would come home from school every day, get in the mirror, and I would practice singing the blues I heard on the radio."[39] Nevertheless, once she joined the Youth Federation, she was hooked. "We would [rehearse] wherever someone had a piano. We would go around to different churches on Sundays and sing, because all the churches had musicals. Because we were kids, they'd let us sing."[40]

The group lasted until 1954, when the Dawson family moved from the area. Two years later, Dawson left Chicago to accompany the Wilson and Watson Singers on tour and afterward accompanied the Gospel All Stars. In 1962, Dawson organized the female Inspirational Singers. Their poignant "God's Ever Near," recorded for both St. Lawrence and Checker, was their signature song.

South Side Community Singers

Willie Webb organized the South Side Community Singers in 1954. He trained the group and turned directing responsibilities over to Eugene Gibson and Doris Sykes. "We started out rehearsing at Fellowship," Sykes recalled, "because that's where Webb was playing. People from different churches started coming together. That's the way it started. We traveled, and we had a radio show with Big Bill Hill on the West Side every Sunday morning at 5:00."[41]

Born in St. Louis and raised by an aunt and an uncle who was pastor of a Baptist church, Doris Sykes had a naturally distinctive high soprano range and acquired the poise of an opera singer. Willie Mae Ford Smith was a cousin. Sykes first sang for the public at her uncle's church. "We used to have musicals," she said, "and I used to write my dad notes, 'Please let Doris Sykes sing.' He knew it was my writing!"[42] The family moved to the Chicago area when Sykes's uncle became pastor of Antioch Baptist Church in East Chicago, Indiana.[43] New Covenant singer Devella Norton Tuck became one of Sykes's musical inspirations.

By 1955, the South Side Community Choir numbered approximately two hundred voices, and Sykes recalled that at one point it grew to as many as five hundred singers. Stanley Keeble was one of its accompanists. In 1957, the choir recorded a vanity disc with the South Side Recording Company, coupling "Somebody Touched Me" and "Great Is the Lord."[44] The group was said to have "more male soloists . . . than any other Chicago choir."[45] Several of the choir's male soloists, including Melvin Smothers, Woodrow Walker, Karl Tarleton, Willie Shepard, and Rev. Dr. Issac Whittmon, became renowned gospel soloists in the 1960s and 1970s.

The Helen Robinson Youth Choir

The Helen Robinson Youth Choir was the city's most popular youth community choir of the late 1950s and the 1960s and ultimately gained a major record label deal. The choir was the brainchild of Helen Robinson, born Helen Albertha Evans in New Orleans on January 31, 1915. Robinson migrated to Chicago in 1933 and settled in Morgan Park. She married Robert Robinson Sr. in 1934. Their marriage produced seven children: Robertine, Robert Jr., Raymond, Jerome, Jeanette, Julean, and Bernardine. The family moved from Morgan Park to a two-story apartment building at 3232 South Wentworth Avenue. The Robinsons converted the first floor into a grocery and lived on the second floor.[46]

Robert Sr. died in 1946, leaving Robinson a widow with seven children. She sold the store and took a job with the YMCA College. In 1949, while serving as president of the Webster Elementary School PTA, Robinson organized the mothers into a singing group.[47] Two years later, she assembled her children and thirteen youth from the neighborhood into the Junior Robinsons and later changed the name to the Helen Robinson Youth Choir. Robinson's daughter Jeanette, who became the choir's chief soloist, said that her mother founded the choir to give local youth a constructive outlet. "Our neighborhood wasn't a bad neighborhood, because we all knew each other," she said. "There just wasn't a whole lot for us to do."[48]

Soon more children began joining the choir, and by 1955, it claimed one hundred voices and had a regular Sunday morning radio broadcast on WTAQ.[49] The chorus also substituted for the Christland Singers when the quartet was on tour and unable to fulfill its radio date.[50]

The choir's first recording deal came through Argo Singer Lorenza Brown Porter, who introduced Robinson to Vee Jay's Vivian Carter and James Bracken. Their single, "Time Is Winding Up," written by member Aubrey Pettis, was recorded at Universal on September 11, 1956, the same day and same studio where the Staple Singers cut "Uncloudy Day." James Cleveland produced the Robinson single. Nearly fifty years after the recording date, the choristers still recalled how perfectionist Cleveland was persistent in getting the sound just right, as well as the anticipation of dining at Ronny's Steak House after the session concluded.[51]

The Helen Robinson Youth Choir was back at Universal in 1959 to record sides for Specialty, but Art Rupe shuttered the label before the Robinson discs were released. The choir's next recording break came around 1962, when they produced several singles and an album for Chicago songwriters, publishers, and record-company owners Margaret Aikens and Ollie Lafayette. The two women attended Morgan Park Assembly, a Pentecostal church. "Aunt Margaret," as the Helen Robinson Youth Choir called her, wrote many of the group's songs.

Aikens was born Margaret Melton in Lexington, Mississippi, on May 14, 1925, to a black mother, Marie Cengella Melton, and a white father, Joel Bryant Melton.[52] She began composing songs as a young girl. "I was about seven, eight years old," she recalled. "I would wake up and hear music. I could hear songs just ringing in me. I would be writing and hiding them away."[53] Her sister Ora taught her to play piano. She sang with her sister Celeste Scott, who became an officer in the National Baptist Convention Music Convention and secretary to Mahalia Jackson. Jackson nicknamed Aikens "Little Missionary" because she took after her mother, a locally known prayer warrior. "My mother was a praying missionary," Aikens recalled. "If [anyone in the neighborhood] got sick or anything, Mama would go, run down, and pray . . . she prayed for so many people."[54] Jackson recorded some of Aikens's songs, most notably "The Only Hope We Have" and "Brighter Day Ahead."

In her thirties, Aikens and Lafayette, along with several other local singers, formed the Mel-Tones, a gospel group whose name was a play on Margaret's maiden name, Melton. It is probable that Charles Walker played piano and Joseph Henderson of Greater Harvest was organist on some or all of the Mel-Tones' recordings.[55] The songs were released on the women's Mag-Oll Records, the name created from the first letters of the first names of the women and their husbands: *M*argaret *a*nd *G*abe and *O*llie and *L*ouis *L*afayette. Aikens and Lafayette Publishing published the songs.[56] The label lasted until Aikens and Scott moved to California in the mid-1960s, where they formed the Ladies of Song with Rodena Preston, Gwen Smith, and organist Billy Preston's mother, Robbie Williams Preston.

On Mag-Oll, Aikens and Lafayette produced a handful of singles and one album, *Inspirations from Heaven*, for the Helen Robinson Youth Choir. Sallie Martin's accompanist, Kenneth Woods Jr., arranged many of Aikens's songs for sheet music sales. Aikens's gospel ballads, such as "The Only Hope We Have" and "Thy Grace Is Sufficient for Me," featured the plaintive lead singing of Jeanette Robinson. Robinson's melancholy voice and serious performance demeanor were so distinctive they drew James Cleveland's attention. He invited the young soloist to join his Cleveland Singers, but she declined. As a consolation, Cleveland added "The Only Hope We Have" to his repertory.[57]

Richard Simpson recorded the group again in 1967 for Atlantic Records. The album *Joy* featured arrangements by Pettis and the choir's longtime pianist, Ethel Brooks Campbell, mother of Tommies member and gospel soloist and songwriter Darius Brooks. The single "I'm Happy with Jesus Alone" was a Jeanette solo in the plaintive style of "The Only Hope We Have." WBEE parlayed it into a minor hit, and the Voices of Nashville covered it in the 1970s.

By the time Atlantic's Cotillion subsidiary rereleased *Joy* in 1972 on the gospel series of its Cotillion subsidiary, the Helen Robinson Youth Choir was running out of steam. Members were now adults, married with children—several choristers married fellow choir members—and working full-time. Helen Robinson continued doing community service until her death on June 17, 1993.

Treadwell Community Singers

Willie A. Treadwell was born the youngest of three children to David and Lemmar Treadwell in Anniston, Alabama, on February 28, 1931. The family moved to Chicago in 1948 and settled on the West Side. Willie attended Wells High School and the National College of Chiropractic Medicine. After serving in the U. S. Army from 1952 to 1955, where he advanced to the rank of sergeant, Treadwell returned to the West Side.[58] In 1955, he and Frankie Powell, a member of the Tommies, organized the Treadwell Community Singers from a group of West Side youth and young adults between fifteen and twenty-seven years of age.[59] Willie directed and Frankie accompanied. The two were married a year later.

The ensemble's style was similar to the Tommies in its sonority and rhythmic spirit. For a 1964 appearance on *Jubilee Showcase*, the group performed vigorous versions of "Jesus' Love Bubbles Over in My Heart" and "I Can Depend on Him." "Now to me, the Treadwells were the singers," said Zadella "Mama" Curtis, "because they sang a cappella. Treadwell brought the element of surprise. They would come in and sit all over the church. Frankie would sit at the piano, hit the chord, and the Treadwells would start singing 'Where He Leads Me, I Will Follow,' or 'Heaven in My View.' They knew what part of the song to get up on, and they would start walking to the choir stand."[60]

The group recorded its first album, *Heaven in My View*, for Harold Freeman's Michael imprint, but by the time Chicago soul musician Monk Higgins produced the choir's 1967 sophomore album for Checker, *Love Is a Three Letter Word: GOD*, the group's sound was no longer a cappella but bass-driven rhythms and arrangements with as much soul as the latest radio hits. Even "Heaven in My View," with its extended quartet-like vamp, had a funky underpinning. The lyrics were evocative of the times and specifically of Ralph Bass and Checker's penchant for material about peace and amity, a style that became known as gos-pop. Later recordings of the Treadwell ensemble, without the gos-pop treatment, showcased a group closer in vocal and musical pedigree to the Tommies.

Like Brunson, Treadwell entered the ministry. He was ordained a deacon in 1959 and in 1969 became pastor of Union Missionary Baptist Church in Robbins, Illinois. Two years later, Treadwell founded United Faith Tabernacle Church on the West Side, where he ascended to the level of bishop and remained until his retirement from daily church activities in 2003.[61]

Two years after the Treadwells' founding, True Light Baptist Church awarded the Helen Robinson Youth Choir as well as the Tommies, the South Side Community Singers, and the Treadwell Community Singers a gold cup for being "outstanding youth groups that have helped in curbing juvenile delinquency."[62] In 1961, the Helen Robinson Youth Choir received the Mahalia Jackson Award of New York's Fourth Annual World Gospel Festival.[63]

Other community choirs followed. Rose Meatchem—known as Mother Meatchem—formed a youth chorus as part of a youth club that by 1953 was meeting regularly at 10 West Forty-Third Street.[64] In the 1960s, Andrew Jackson and Larry Woods organized the Community Youth Choir, to provide local adolescents with a positive out-of-school activity. Charles Geiger's Emanon Choral Ensemble, featuring soloist Lorraine Powell, performed in the contemporary style of the Wooten Choral Ensemble and Charles Clency's Voices of Melody.

The Emanon Choral Ensemble was just as comfortable singing the Lutheran stalwart "A Mighty Fortress Is Our God" as the latest gospel choir composition.

Second-Generation Church Choirs

After the war, many newly formed Chicago church choirs became just as popular as the first-generation gospel choruses of Ebenezer, Pilgrim, First Church of Deliverance, St. Paul COGIC, Forty-Fourth Street, and Greater Harvest. These "second-generation" gospel choirs represented newly established churches such as Fellowship, True Light, and Omega Baptist Churches; Hyde Park Bible Church; Redeeming Church of Christ; and Cosmopolitan Church of Prayer. Through live programs, radio, records, and television, these aggregations fostered the talents of many emerging gospel luminaries.

Times had changed, however. While the gospel choir's music still spoke to the person in the street, choir membership became stricter. Bishop Jerry Goodloe said that when he joined Liberty Baptist Church's choir in 1946, "They didn't just let anybody in the choir. You had to audition, find out what voice you sang, and if you were a lead singer or a background singer."[65] This added layer of selectivity may well have helped second-generation choirs become more musically proficient than their predecessors.

Fellowship Missionary Baptist Church

Among second-generation church choirs, the ensemble at Fellowship Missionary Baptist Church—fondly known as "The Ship"—was in a class of its own. Rev. Clay Evans organized the church choir on September 15, 1950, one week after he founded the church itself. His brother Pharis, who established Clark Road Missionary Baptist Church in Gary eleven years later, directed the eight-member choir. Their sister, Lou Della, accompanied on piano and eventually became the church's choir director and minister of music.

Lou Della Evans was born in Brownsville, Tennessee, on July 7, 1930. She took music lessons from Kate Evans and accompanied the junior choir at the family's home church, Woodlawn Baptist. After graduating from high school in 1949, she married Robert Louis Reid and planned to become a nurse. After migrating to Chicago the following year, Reid became the first woman to join her brother Clay's church and recommended its original name, Hickory Grove Baptist.[66]

The choir's first radio broadcast was on WWCA from 9:00 to 10:00 p.m. on Sunday, October 19, 1952. Later, the broadcast moved to WGES, where it could be heard from 4:00 to 5:00 on Sunday afternoons. Organist Rev. Stanley Keeble, who joined Fellowship's Music Department in the late 1950s, described what he considered the best Fellowship radio broadcast in which he participated:

We came on with "What a Fellowship." Reverend Consuella York was our announcer on the radio. She announced the church information, and we were
going to do "The Lord's Prayer." We did "The Lord's Prayer," and as soon as we
got through, the organist went right back to "What a Fellowship!" Every time
it would get to the end and Reverend Evans would go to the pulpit to say something, they'd break out again. We sang "What a Fellowship" almost an hour. But
it was so phenomenal—it looked like everybody in the building was shouting![67]

During the 1950s and early 1960s, Fellowship could boast of having one
of the richest church music departments in the city. Willie Webb was music
minister for a short period in Fellowship's early years. Robert Anderson directed the radio choir in 1956. Evans secured A. A. Goodson from Los Angeles, where he had been responsible for the Voices of Victory Choir at Victory
Baptist Church, under the pastorate of Rev. Arthur Atlas Peters.[68] Goodson
was Fellowship's music director from 1955 to 1961.[69] Rev. Milton Brunson was
a Fellowship soloist, and civil rights leader and presidential hopeful Rev. Jesse
Jackson was an assistant pastor. Early on, Evans asked Floriene Watson of the
Lucy Smith Trio to accompany the church choir. She declined because she was
a member of a Holiness church and Fellowship was Baptist. "You know how
they were back in that day," she said, but rued, "I sure regret it now!"[70]

Evans, who regularly brought classical artists to perform for special events
at Fellowship, secured classically trained Charles Walker as the church's organist in 1961. A keyboard prodigy, Walker was pianist for Bishop A. A. Childs's
Evangelistic Temple, earning ten dollars every Sunday. He served the Providence Baptist Church Choir in the same manner.[71] Walker began formal music
studies in 1948, but rheumatic fever forced him to put his lessons on hold. After
graduating from high school, Walker earned bachelor's and master's degrees in
music from DePaul University and became the first African American to head
a DePaul fraternity.[72] Thanks to scholarships and funding from his aunt, Mahalia Jackson, Walker studied in Paris and throughout Europe. He integrated
his classical training into his keyboard technique and served as Fellowship's
organist until 1965.[73]

The choir had several top vocalists, including Woodrow Walker (no relation) of the South Side Community Choir. A strong vocalist who rolled his Rs
like Dorsey, Walker introduced the church's theme, Stuart Hamblin's "It Is No
Secret," on its weekly radio broadcast. "Woodrow was phenomenal, absolutely
phenomenal," Keeble recalled. "He had been a Willie Webb Singer, and that's
how he got introduced to Fellowship. He sang in a rich baritone voice. It was
something."[74]

When in 1962 the choir decided to make its first record, Evans chose Idessa
Malone to manufacture its albums. Formerly associated with King Records,

Malone specialized in publishing songs, copyrighting music, setting "your words to music," and making on-site recordings "at any speed" for churches to sell to the community or as fund-raisers.[75] Although many of Malone's recordings were released on her Staff label, the two Fellowship albums, recorded at Universal in 1962 and 1963, were cut for Fellowship Records. The discs showcased the Fellowship Choir in its musical prime. They included the church's popular radio songs, the up-tempo and effervescent "Leaning on the Everlasting Arms" as "What a Fellowship," and "It Is No Secret," with Woodrow Walker.

True Light Baptist Church

While not as well known today among gospel music enthusiasts as other Chicago choruses, the radio choir of Pastor B. F. Paxton's True Light Baptist Church at 4527 South Dearborn was notable for a music department that had, at one time or another, Willie Webb, James Cleveland, Jessy Dixon, George Jordan, Doris Sykes, and Rev. Dr. Issac Whittmon.

Organized in 1923, True Light was led during the late 1930s by Rev. E. J. Coles, whose son, Nat "King" Cole, played piano for the services. Paxton became pastor of True Light in 1944 and served in that capacity for nearly forty years. It was during his watch that the church inaugurated its live radio broadcast. From 1950 until 1963, the True Light broadcast aired Sunday evenings from 6:00 to 7:00 on WAIT.[76]

James Cleveland served in the True Light music department during the 1950s and brought Jessy Dixon in 1959 to replace him. When Dixon entered military service, he was replaced by George Jordan, who went on to work with the Harold Smith Majestics chorus of Detroit.[77] In 1956, Willie Webb was minister of music, and Doris Sykes, who directed the choir at Watley Temple COGIC after her tenure with the South Side Community Singers, became True Light's choir director.[78] "She was a showman directress, I mean she was just dynamite," recalled Rev. Dr. Issac Whittmon, who also spent time at True Light.[79] After her tenure at True Light, Sykes went to Hyde Park Bible Church, where Willie Webb was minister of music.[80] Willie Webb was kind of like the pied piper," noted Keeble. "The folk that were associated with Webb followed Webb."[81]

Hyde Park Bible Church

Bishop Chester M. Batey founded Hyde Park Bible Church on the South Side around 1957. Batey was the former proprietor of Mr. B.'s Record Mart at 3947 South Parkway and an alleged policy king who was converted and became an elder in the Church of God in Christ.[82] Hyde Park began broadcasting Sunday services over WOPA while temporarily headquartered at the Temple of Brotherly Love at 6250 South Cottage Grove. Its first radio broadcast took place on January 19, 1958, from 10:00 to 11:00 p.m., with Willie Webb as music minister and chief soloists Herbert Williams, Rev. Dr. Issac Whittmon, and Melvin Smothers.[83] April 1958 witnessed Batey's elevation to bishop and his church's lease of the former Willard Theater, a twelve-hundred-seat auditorium, at 340 East Fifty-First Street. By then the congregation numbered three hundred.[84]

When Webb left Hyde Park in late 1958, Batey named Maceo Woods minister of music and director of the seventy-five-voice Hyde Park Bible Church choir. Whittmon recalled that Woods made significant changes when he arrived at Hyde Park, changes no doubt inspired by his burgeoning experience producing gospel spectaculars.

> Maceo came and reorganized everything. He put pride in the choir. He put us in very nice robes. Hyde Park Bible Church had a big screen, and when service started, he would have the screen go up and the lights come on, like theater. He dimmed the auditorium, put the spotlights on us, and it became a wonderful church, a showplace, really.
>
> [The church] seated fifteen hundred people, but if you didn't get there early, you didn't get a seat. It was a great choir. Doris Sykes was there. Willie Webb was the organist. James McCray was the organist. We had another organist, Sharon Robinson. Herman Ludlow, he was there. But [Smothers] was *the* singer. And then there was a young man called Clay Wilbourn. He followed in [Sykes's] footsteps in terms of being that type of a director. He could just put a song on his fingers and have the audience up.[85]

By the time Woods assumed leadership of the choir, Hyde Park had switched its broadcast to WHFC, though maintaining the 10:00 to 11:00 Sunday evening time frame.[86] On a self-produced single, released around 1960, the Hyde Park Bible Church Choir sang "Holy Ghost Fire," an uncomplicated, spirited selection with rhythmic organ supporting a hand-clapping chorus.[87] Cassietta George of the Caravans is reported to be the female soloist on the B-side, "I'm Ready." In the 1960s, Jessie Birden (Woods), another lead singer and choir director for Hyde Park Bible Church, sang and recorded with the Kayvetts, a female vocal group later known as the Tears.[88]

Redeeming Church of Christ

Redeeming Church of Christ, a Spiritual church, was established by Bishop James L. Anderson, once a member of the Katherine Dunham Dancers.[89] Redeeming moved from 3554 South Vincennes to 3559 South Cottage Grove around March 1959 and opened its Sunday afternoon broadcasts on WBEE with its theme, "I'll Overcome."[90] Gene Viale, who sang on Redeeming Church radio broadcasts in the mid-1960s, remembered Anderson as "perfection. His grooming, clothing, speech—everything. He was class all the way."[91]

Musicians and future pastors who worked at Redeeming included Charles G. Hayes, Rev. Dr. Issac Whittmon, Kenneth Clark of the Rasberry Singers, and Myrtle Jackson, the soloist from First Church of Deliverance. Jackson not only served as a principal soloist, but she also became an associate minister under Anderson. Redeeming made a full-length album in the 1970s, but by then the group reflected the stylistic changes that had taken place in gospel, especially those that arose from the famed Detroit Invasion of 1959.

Cosmopolitan Church of Prayer

One of the first Chicago churches to adopt the new Detroit gospel choral style was Cosmopolitan Church of Prayer. The church was organized by Charles G. Hayes, born in Verbena, Alabama, on December 10, 1937, to Mamie Lee and Will Hayes. The family attended Mount Olive Baptist Church in Keystone, Alabama where, in 1947, ten-year-old Charles made his public debut, singing "Move On Up a Little Higher."

Inspired by fellow Alabaman natives Dorothy Love Coates and Alex Bradford, the teenaged Hayes played piano for a quartet called the Original Golden Voices of Birmingham, Alabama. He visited Chicago for the first time in 1955, when the Golden Voices were hired to appear on a gospel program in the city. The appearances were the Golden Voices' last. The quartet disbanded and returned to Birmingham, somehow leaving their teenaged pianist stranded on the South Side. Through the courtesy of a passerby, Hayes found temporary quarters with Bishop Anderson at Redeeming Church of Prayer before returning to Alabama.[92]

Hayes graduated from high school in 1956, studied for the ministry in Atlanta, and returned to Chicago on August 31, 1957. Straightaway, he became the accompanist for Redeeming Church and served in this capacity until April 28, 1959, when he founded Tabernacle Church of Prayer at 634 East Woodland Park, in the basement of the home of Mr. and Mrs. Morris E. Jackson. Subsequently, the church moved to a storefront at 4213 South Cottage Grove.

Hayes started the choir on October 25, 1959, with a handful of church members. "I started playing the piano," Hayes remembered, "and they started singing. I said, 'Well, this is going to be our first choir.' It was made up of the Avant family, the Williams family, and the McElroy family. We had robes, we'd jump, do all that stuff. We had it down pat."[93]

By 1961, the newly christened Universal Kingdom of Christ had moved into a former Illinois Bell Telephone building on 842 East Forty-Third Street. As the membership grew to approximately five hundred, Hayes and his assistant pastor, Rev. Napoleon Payne, moved the church to larger quarters at 6315 South

Langley.[94] Although the church was prospering and even had a Sunday after-noon radio broadcast on WHFC, Hayes was not welcomed by everyone. Some did not want a black church in a white neighborhood, while others harbored suspicions about Hayes's promotion of the Kingdom Gospel. Hayes said:

> They set the church on fire three times over there on Langley. They didn't want us in the neighborhood. We don't know if it was the Caucasians or if it was the blacks. Three doors down from the church on Langley was a man who didn't like me. He called me a moron. He said I wasn't good for the young folk. At that time the street gangs—the Disciples and the Black Stone Rangers—were very much alive. In our church, I had families that were parents to those children, and they made those children come to church. I got to know them, I got to know both sides, because they would come over into the Disciples territory for church, although they lived in the Black Stone Rangers' [territory]. When [the Disciples] found out they were coming to church, they didn't bother them.[95]

It was at the Langley address in 1965 that Charles Clency joined the church as minister of music. Clency had been working since 1962 at Antioch Baptist Church, where Kenneth Morris also served in the music department, but frustration with the pay drove the young accompanist to seek greener pastures. Hayes just happened to be looking for a music director and hired Clency. "Whatever I gave them, they did," Clency said, "and [Hayes] supported it. He didn't stop me; he was my best supporter. We did portions from Handel's *Messiah*. We did songs with a washboard, we did from A to Z, because when you're young, you're willing to do anything. There was no restriction. By the time I'd been there maybe a year or two, you could not get near the place. The church started filling up from week to week to week. By 10:40, for the radio broadcast, the church was full. It got to where people were standing around the block."[96]

As a teenager, Dennis Cole, president emeritus of the Chicago Area Gospel Announcers Guild, made his first visit to the Universal Kingdom of Prayer radio broadcast. "It was a thrill. The atmosphere was like a nightclub. It was blue lights, and it had gospel music, and Reverend Hayes burned incense. It was just something different."[97]

In addition to setting the mood for the broadcast service, Hayes also handled the technical aspects of the broadcast himself. "Back then, when they did [radio] broadcasts," Cole explained, "they always had a technical person that came to the church to set the mikes up, set the boxes up. Dr. Hayes never wanted that. He wanted to do it himself. Dr. Hayes was very disciplined."[98] Clency, who worked for the church for eleven years, added that Hayes "ran the thing tight. He sat at the door and took attendance."[99] Hayes even unselfishly shared

Clency with Mahalia Jackson, whom he served as organist on recordings and at national and international programs. Often, Clency would fly back from a Jackson program just in time to handle the music for the church's 11:00 p.m. Sunday radio broadcast.[100]

Clency created the distinctive sound of the Universal Kingdom of Christ choir by integrating lessons from Julia Mae Kennedy at First Church of Deliverance, Wiley C. Jackson at Morning Star, and the Voices of Tabernacle. He also emulated Harold Smith's Majestics, a Detroit choir founded in 1963. Smith, who was once a musician at First Church of Deliverance, wrote "Come On Children, Let's Sing," a song that exemplified the easy swing of the First Church choir and was made famous by Mahalia Jackson. "Nobody else in Chicago would touch that sound from Detroit but me," Clency recalled. "I was just totally mesmerized by the arrangements, the creativity. Chicago had its own energy—it was great—but not that quality, that Detroit sound. [Universal Kingdom] was the first group to imitate that sound. In a very short time, the church was jam packed because they were hearing Charles Craig all over again."[101] The product was a sonorous choir that was one-half Detroit innovation and one-half Chicago gospel swing.

The Universal Kingdom of Christ recorded an album for Checker, though the only commercially released product of the evening session was "Tell Me How Did You Feel." Nevertheless, the two-part single provided ample demonstration of the Universal Kingdom choir as redefined by Clency. Hayes introduced the song, and Cynthia Price handled the lead as the choristers clapped along enthusiastically to an up-tempo beat propelled by organ and piano. "[The song] was popular before we recorded it," remembered Chedwick Allen Cathey, a chorister present for the recording who succeeded Clency as music director. "Every week we would get seven, eight, ten calls from people asking could [Cynthia] sing that song!"[102]

Besides Price, the choir was fortunate to have a long list of soloists, among them Herbert Williams (formerly of Hyde Park Bible Church), Michele Brown, Sammy Jeter, and arguably its most famous soloist, Dianne Williams. Among its musicians were Shelby Wills and Marion Gaines, who later moved to Detroit and formed the Marion Gaines Singers. The omnipresent Willie Webb also accompanied the choir on organ in a pinch.[103]

By the late 1960s, the church had changed its name to Cosmopolitan Church of Prayer. It pressed its own recordings as well as recorded for Harold Freeman's Righteous Records, Offe Reese's One-Way imprint, and HOB, but its first national recording success came on Savoy with the hit "Jesus Can Work It Out," written by George Jordan and first recorded in 1974 by Rev. Maceo Woods's Christian Tabernacle Choir.

Rev. Maceo Woods and the Christian Tabernacle Concert Choir

In 1959, Woods was at the top of his game. A songwriter, recording artist, and gospel program impresario, the twenty-something Woods had just wowed New York's Apollo Theater audience when Bishop Batey relieved him of his music position at Hyde Park Bible Church. Blindsided and disheartened, Woods commiserated with friends and colleagues Doris Sykes and Charles Clency at Gladys's Restaurant, and together they tried to untangle what had just happened.[104] After the Hyde Park Bible Church choristers got word of Woods's dismissal, many were so upset that they vowed not to return.[105] On December 14, 1959, Woods received the calling to ministry and founded Christian Tabernacle Church in the home of a friend. There were eleven members at the start, including Sykes, Melvin Smothers, Pearl McCombs, Eugene Borden, and William Kidd. In February 1960, Woods secured space for his church in the Public Theater at 4712 South Prairie. Built in 1913, the building had a seating capacity of seven hundred but had fallen into disrepair and disrepute, as it was now home to a gambling operation.[106] Undaunted, Woods and his team ordered the gamblers out and transformed the theater into a church. Woods converted the projectionist booth into a temporary personal living space.[107] By October 1960, Christian Tabernacle counted 814 members, 92 percent under the age of thirty-seven.[108]

Sykes, Smothers, McCombs, and Borden organized themselves into the Christian Tabernacle Ensemble to sing for services. Over time, the group grew to include Lawrence Ester, Alfreda Burton, Nelson Dupree, and George Jordan. Woods leveraged his relationship with Vee Jay Records to secure a recording contract for the Christian Tabernacle Ensemble. Recorded in June 1961 but not released until 1963, *Messages of Hope* showcased the ensemble's superb soloists—Sykes, Smothers, McCombs, Borden, and Dupree—on classic songs, including "Do You Know Him" and "Christ Is All," as well as on new compositions such as Woods's "Come On Up to Bright Glory."[109] Each vocalist lent a distinct color to the ensemble's sound. Doris Sykes was a coloratura soprano similar to DeLois Barrett Campbell. Pearl McCombs was a bluesy, fiery shouter in the mode of Dorothy Love Coates. Melvin Smothers was the high tenor capable of weaving intricate vocal runs. Nelson Dupree had a warm, smooth delivery that could evolve into intense shouting for heightened emotional impact. One of the album's highlights was Willie Webb's "He Is All I Need." Sykes led the song's deliberate first half, but McCombs jumped in when the tempo quickened, growling while Sykes punctuated the performance with chirps of high soprano. Woods handled organ duties on all twelve tracks.

"Do You Know Him" and "He Is All I Need" were the singles chosen from the album, and they earned a "Special Merit Pick" in the June 15, 1963, issue of *Billboard*, meaning they were "of outstanding merit which deserve[s] exposure and could have commercial success." The reviewer called the group "a splendid choir of five separate soloists, each of whom knows how to put out the message. The presence of this recording is such that the listener is virtually in the church, so clean-cut is the mastering."[110]

The Christian Tabernacle Ensemble evolved into the Christian Tabernacle Concert Choir with about thirty members. Around this time, George Jordan was discharged from the military, and although he returned to live in Detroit for a time, he eventually came back to Christian Tabernacle and was named the church's minster of music.[111] The choir's first significant commercial recording was "Hello Sunshine," written by Jessy Dixon, who had recorded the song initially with the Chicago Community Choir. An album of the same name by the Christian Tabernacle Baptist Church Choir was recorded on September 29, 1969, at Chicago's Auditorium Theater, albeit without any aural indication of an audience, and was originally released on Righteous Records.[112] Righteous released "Sunshine" as a single, and it garnered so many spins on WBEE by announcer Rev. Dwight "Gatemouth" Moore that Ernie Leaner of United Distributors felt national distribution was in order. He put Woods together with Al Bell at Stax Records in Memphis, and *Hello Sunshine* was reissued on Volt.[113] Henceforward, the Christian Tabernacle Concert Choir enjoyed a string of albums and singles with Gospel Truth, the gospel subsidiary of Stax in Memphis. The original "Jesus Can Work It Out," written by George Jordan, made its debut for Gospel Truth, and it was re-recorded when the group switched to Savoy Records. Later the choir recorded for Woods's own imprint, Gospel Supreme, named for the annual gospel music extravaganza that he started in 1963 and produced well into the twenty-first century.

Broadcast Hopping

On Sundays, Chicago-area radio stations such as WSBC, WEDC, WGES, WBEE, WTAQ, and WVON devoted most of their airtime to paid religious broadcasting, including live church services. Remote equipment operated by radio-station personnel transmitted the music, preaching, prayers, and announcements directly from the church to the station. During the 1950s and 1960s, Fellowship, True Light, Omega, Hyde Park Bible, Redeeming Church of Christ, Cosmopolitan Church of Prayer, and other churches broadcast their services on radio. By the mid-1960s, so many churches aired over WVON that listeners could leave the radio tuned to this station all afternoon and evening and catch one church broadcast after another. The number of South and West Side churches with Sunday radio programs sparked a phenomenon called "broadcast hopping." It was a journey that gospel music enthusiasts made on Sundays to be present for as many live radio broadcast services as possible.

Doris Sykes described the broadcast hop that she and her friends made: "[Start] at Greater Harvest, go to Fellowship, go to Omega, come to True Light, go to Bishop Anderson's [Redeeming Church of Christ], and go to First Deliverance. We'd eat dinner at Gladys's. And we would walk! You could walk in those days; you weren't scared."[114] As a teenager, Dennis Cole traversed a similar trail: "We would get out of church and go eat, then we'd go to Greater Harvest. We would go to Hyde Park Bible Church, then we'd either get something to eat or run down to Shiloh [Baptist Church], which was on Wabash, around the corner. Then we'd wind up at Omega, try to sneak out and go to Fellowship, and then over to Bishop Anderson's."[115] Allen Cathey cited New Nazareth, Shiloh, Faith Temple, Redeeming, and Omega as part of his weekly broadcast route, which he navigated around his responsibilities for Cosmopolitan and its radio broadcast.

Broadcast hopping could potentially become a nine-hour affair, according to Almond Dawson. The first stop was 3:00 p.m. at Greater Harvest, 4:00 p.m. at New Nazareth, 5:00 p.m. at Hyde Park Bible Church, 6:00 p.m. at Mother Meatchem's church, 7:00 p.m. at Shiloh, 8:00 p.m. at Omega, 9:00 p.m. at Fellowship or Cosmopolitan, 10:00 p.m. at Redeeming, and 11:00 at First Church of Deliverance.[116] "You could go to a broadcast from eleven a.m. in the morning until twelve midnight," said gospel music historian L. Stanley Davis.[117] This process became another way for musicians and singers to learn the latest gospel songs and techniques.

No matter the broadcast hopping route, "Chicago was the best place to be on Sundays," Archie Dennis told Idella Lulumae Johnson, "because of all the wonderful music that you would get to hear."[118]

Chicago gospel artists had come a long way by the 1960s. Artists were appearing with regularity on major stages both nationally and internationally. Gospel records were selling steadily, and radio broadcasts of worship services could be heard just about every hour on Sundays. Mahalia Jackson, the global ambassador for gospel music, was appearing on television frequently. Still, prior to late 1962, pop singers had *Your Hit Parade* and rock had *American Bandstand*, but there was no television program dedicated exclusively to gospel music. In other words, one could hear gospel music through a variety of media but to see performances required attendance at gospel programs and church services. That changed with the advent of *TV Gospel Time* and Chicago's longest-running gospel music television program, *Jubilee Showcase*.

CHAPTER 15

"God's Got a Television"

Gospel Music Comes to the Living Room

Songs truly American . . . music that both entertains and inspires.

Sid Ordower, host, *Jubilee Showcase*

The June 1950 *Ebony* had hopeful news. Television, albeit still in its infancy as a communication medium, held the potential to provide better performance opportunities for African Americans. "Negro footlight favorites are cast in every conceivable type of TV act—musical, dramatic, comedy. Yet rarely have they had to stoop to the Uncle Tom pattern which is usually the Negro thespian's lot on radio shows and in Hollywood movies."[1] Indeed, in April 1949, black radio pioneer Jack L. Cooper became "the first Negro in America to carry a regular weekly television feature." *The Jack L. Cooper Revue* piloted May 6, 1949, and aired Friday evenings on Chicago's WENR-TV. Among Cooper's musical guests were the Optimistic Jubilee Singers, the quartet he featured faithfully on the *All-Colored Hour*.[2] The revue spotlighted "outstanding Negro talent throughout America," inspiring a soft-drink company to consider sponsoring another Cooper concept: a television show about black youth.[3]

Five years later, in May 1954, radio innovator Rev. Clarence H. Cobbs celebrated the twenty-fifth anniversary of First Church of Deliverance by presiding over the "first television service presented by any Negro church in the country without commercial sponsorship." The show premiered its weekly telecasts on WBKB-TV (ABC) on Holy Saturday, April 17, 1954. In keeping with its legendary midnight broadcast, the program aired at 11:30 p.m. Those with television sets organized "TV clubs" of friends and neighbors so that they could watch the First Church service together.[4]

Mahalia Jackson was the first gospel artist to attract significant attention from television studios. As early as Christmas Eve in 1951, Jackson appeared on Studs Terkel's *Studs' Place* telecast.[5] Ed Sullivan invited Jackson to be a guest on the January 20, 1952, episode of his nationally televised *Toast of the Town*.[6] On August 21, 1952, Jackson appeared on Chicago host Irv Kupcinet's program, which aired locally on WBKB-TV.[7]

In 1955, after the cancellation of her network radio show, Jackson secured a local television program on CBS affiliate WBBM. Taped at the Garrick Television Center at 64 West Randolph, *Mahalia Jackson Sings* premiered at 10:15 p.m. Sunday, March 13, 1955, with Mildred Falls and Ralph Jones accompanying her and the Jack Halloran Quartet performing on its own segments. Terkel, still a lightning rod of criticism for Communist baiters, provided the narration and asked Jackson about her songs, but as a disembodied voice.[8] Jackson sang selections from her Columbia album debut, including "Didn't It Rain," "The Lord's Prayer," "His Eye Is on the Sparrow," and the secular/sacred combo "Summertime" and "Sometimes I Feel like a Motherless Child." The show was sponsored by local automotive dealer Martin J. Kelly.[9] The program had garnered enough attention by April for there to be talk that CBS would make it available networkwide.[10] But Mahalia needed gallbladder surgery in December, and by the time she recovered, the sponsor had walked and the TV show was canceled.[11]

Jackson's appearance on the June 1, 1958, episode of NBC's *The Dinah Shore Show* was noteworthy because it was heralded as "the first time a Sepia has been seen on the program."[12] "I wanted her because I liked her, and because it would be a milestone for me," Shore is reported to have said. "I thought it might just lay one little brick in the cornerstone of television. . . . I thought it was *terribly* important at that point."[13] Accompanied by Mildred Falls and a pared-down studio orchestra, Jackson sang "He's Got the Whole World in His Hands," then joined Shore on a rousing "Down by the Riverside."[14] Shore told Jackson biographer Laurraine Goreau, "All the incredible shows we did in the years of that whole series, the one that people single out to talk about today is that one we did with Mahalia."[15] Jackson was invited for return appearances on the November 16, 1958, and December 6, 1959, episodes.[16]

By 1961, Jackson had her own television program once again, also called *Mahalia Jackson Sings*. It was a series of five minute music videos—and this time it was syndicated nationally. Harold Goldman, president of Television Enterprises Corp., was in charge of the project, while Jackson owned a majority interest in Songs of Praise, Inc., the series producer.

Taping eighty-two five-minute *Mahalia Jackson Sings* television segments in black and white began in June 1961 and concluded the following month.

Larry Peerce, son of opera star Jan Peerce, directed the programs, which were filmed on Melrose Boulevard at a Hollywood studio leased from Paramount. The musicians were well-known jazz session players Barney Kessel on guitar, Red Mitchell on bass, and Shelly Manne on drums. Louise Overall Weaver played the Hammond B3, while Mildred Falls and Eddie Robinson took turns on piano. Background vocalists, when needed, were members of local church choirs recruited by gospel singer–songwriter Doris Akers, Gwen Cooper Lightner, and Dorothy Simmons. Simmons, a former Sallie Martin Singer, served as a body double for Jackson during some of the silhouette shots.[17]

The finest *Mahalia Jackson Sings* episodes featured Jackson singing loosely and confidently inside the circle of jazz musicians. She plunged body and soul into New Orleans favorites, such as "When the Saints Go Marching In," punctuating the performance with emphatic hand claps.[18] Among the first stations to air *Mahalia Jackson Sings* was Chicago's WBKB, which programmed three five-minute segments every day for several weeks.[19] *Mahalia Jackson Sings* earned the Silver Dove Award from the International Catholic Association for Broadcasting and Television for "doing the most good at international understanding."[20]

Jackson was not the only gospel pioneer to work in early television. Her former employer and mentor, Thomas A. Dorsey, wrote music for *Ordeal by Fire*, a program about the Civil War, which aired in late 1959 on WTTW, Chicago's public television station. Arthur Logan, director of the Goodwill Spiritual Singers, was in charge of the background music.[21] The following year, Dorsey wrote and directed two shows for WTTW's *Time for Religion* television series. *The Little Wooden Church on the Hill* aired July 20, 1960, and *The Amen Corner* on July 27. One or both programs featured J. C. Austin, Dorsey's Pilgrim Baptist Church Gospel Chorus, Sallie Martin, and the Celestial Trio with Julia Mae Smith, who had been singing with Dorsey since the early 1930s. Jim McFarland and William Friedkin produced the programs.[22] In 1961, WTTW honored Dorsey, Pilgrim, the Celestial Choir, and the Halo Gospel Singers on a July 20 program called *Songs with a Message*, coincidentally the title of a Dorsey song folio series.[23]

TV Gospel Time

Despite the inroads made on television by Mahalia Jackson and Thomas A. Dorsey, gospel music did not have its own variety program until the advent of *TV Gospel Time* in 1962. Howard Schwartz's Allied Productions produced the thirty-minute program, securing Pharmaco Products as the sole sponsor. Pharmaco manufactured the chewable laxative Feen-A-Mint and sold hair and skin products such as Sulfur-8 and Artra Skin Cream targeting the African American marketplace.[24] But *TV Gospel Time* had higher aspirations than featuring gospel music and selling hair products. "There is no continuous television programming directed toward the Negro market," Alan Cowley, Artra's advertising manager told Dave Hepburn of the *New York Amsterdam News.* "By offering a program of gospel music which has many values beyond simple entertainment, we hope to give the nation a chance to sample the wealth of Negro culture." The show was touted as the first time "Negro talent [would] be seen doing a series of commercials."[25]

Taping commenced in fall 1962 with plans for the first *TV Gospel Time* episode to pilot in New York; Washington, DC; Charleston, South Carolina; and the Georgia cities of Macon, Augusta, and Columbus.[26] The first episode, taped at Rev. F. D. Washington's Washington Temple COGIC in Brooklyn, premiered on New York's WOR-TV on September 30, 1962.[27] The Singing Angels, Nancy McNeil, and James Hayward performed on the opening program. Washington's wife, noted gospel singer Ernestine Washington, soloed.

The first thirteen episodes were sufficiently well received for *TV Gospel Time* to expand to more than twenty-four different U.S. stations, including Chicago's WBKB-TV, where the show aired Sunday mornings at 10:00 a.m. starting in late January or early February 1963.[28]

Soon afterward, *TV Gospel Time* began taping in other cities so that local groups, especially large choirs, could perform on the program without the expense of traveling to New York. The producers also recognized that focusing on regional artists would all but guarantee increased viewership in the area, while a handful of headliners would deliver the national audience. For example, when the *TV Gospel Time* crew came to Memphis in February 1963, it taped the Pentecostal Temple Choir, directed by COGIC Bishop J. O. Patterson's wife, Deborah, as well as the Soul Stirrers, the Highway QCs, and the Caravans of Chicago. On October 10, 1964, *TV Gospel Time* came to the WMAQ television studio in Chicago's Merchandise Mart to record episodes with the Thompson Community Singers, Jessy Dixon and the Chicago Community Choir, Inez Andrews and the Andrewettes, Bessie Griffin, the Helen Robinson Youth Chorus, the Omega Baptist Church Chorus, and other local talent.[29] Robert Anderson was emcee of one of the Chicago episodes.[30]

After its first year of broadcast, *TV Gospel Time* reported strong ratings, and Schwartz indicated that after the Pharmaco contract ran out, he would go "the station-by-station route rather than with a single sponsor."[31] But by October 1964, *TV Gospel Time* was no longer being broadcast on WBKB. By 1965, the pioneering gospel television show vanished entirely, but not before laying the groundwork for Chicago's *Jubilee Showcase.*

Jubilee Showcase

Prior to BET's *Bobby Jones Gospel*, *Jubilee Showcase* was the longest running gospel television show. Debuting on Chicago's WBKB in February 1963, it ran for twenty-one years.

The seed for *Jubilee Showcase* came from a live gospel-music radio show that Sherman Abrams began broadcasting in 1959 from the showroom of Al Abrams Pontiac at 1110 East Forty-Seventh Street. "He thought it would be a good idea to have people come in and see a gospel show, bring people into the dealership," recalled Myrna Ordower, widow of the show's longtime host, Sid Ordower.[32] Sid Ordower, who hosted the radio program, had the idea to take the show to television from the start, so once *TV Gospel Time* hit the airwaves, he and Abrams decided it was time to pitch WBKB. The concept was uncomplicated: present new talent and the best gospel music in a dignified manner and be educational.[33] Station management gave the project a green light and signed on for twenty-six episodes.

Donald Gay posits that *Jubilee Showcase* may also have had its origins in another radio broadcast. Ozie Vincent, president of the United Packinghouse Workers Union Local 10, began broadcasting the *Ozie Vincent Spiritual Hour* on WBEE around May 1961. The show aired from the Packinghouse Workers Community Center at 4859 South Wabash. Among the artists who appeared on Vincent's program were R. H. Harris and the Gospel Paraders, the Kingdom Bound Singers, the Thompson Community Singers, and the Gay Family.[34]

Vincent hired Evelyn Gay to assist him with the weekly radio broadcast. Donald said, "Ozie and Evelyn had the idea that there could be a television program that could come about. They pitched the idea to Sherman Abrams. [Abrams thinks] the idea is good, they make the contract, they are going to go with it, and Ozie Vincent is killed."[35] Donald said that when Vincent died, so did the concept. "During the interim, the idea kind of lingered there. Sid already had a radio program on Sunday mornings where all the quartets would always come and sing. The guy who was the main man on the mike was a guy by the name of Rev. Bud Riley—Elder Bud Riley, they called him. So they moved Bud out, and Sid took over the mike doing the radio program. But Evelyn and Ozie, they were the guys that brought the idea to Sherman."[36]

The show's origins notwithstanding, the television version of *Jubilee Showcase*, hailed as "the city's most successful gospel radio program," was sponsored by Al Abrams Pontiac. Initial indications were that Abrams and Ordower would cohost, leaning "heavily on the talent developed in the successful gospel radio programs of the past."[37] Ultimately, Ordower became sole on-air host.

Sidney Ordower was not a Johnny-come-lately. He had a long relationship with the city's African American community and the civil rights movement.

Born January 11, 1919, in Quincy, Massachusetts, Ordower attended Syracuse University and the American Academy of Dramatic Arts in New York. He was a World War II veteran who had served in the European theater, participating in six major battles and five major invasions.[38] Whether he was born with a social conscience, developed it as a result of the war, or both, Ordower became active with the Progressive Party. A member of the Metropolitan Chamber of Commerce, he promoted economic growth for the South Side. He also fought for human rights, trade unionists' rights, and open housing for blacks in Chicago.[39]

In the early 1950s, Ordower traveled to Mississippi to speak on behalf of a black man accused of raping a white woman. "He was warned not to go," his son, Steven, said, "but he went down there with other civil rights leaders. When he got off the plane, there were a lot of people who said some pretty nasty things, and then he got beat up with brass knuckles. I think he was threatened to be thrown in front of a train."[40] Although he was Jewish, Ordower "spent more time in churches than in synagogues," Steven said. "He was a very tough guy, but he had the soul of one of the most spiritually enlightened and kind people you'd ever want to meet."[41]

Ordower was untested on television, but he was familiar with radio and had training in the dramatic arts. In addition to the *Jubilee Showcase* radio show, he had hosted a program on WJJD called *Chicago Speaks*, on which he debated political issues with guests. As such, Ordower's on-air voice was clear and articulate, exhibiting professional training and experience.

The first talent coordinator for *Jubilee Showcase* was Katie Davis. She had gotten her start in radio in 1958 working for a local disk jockey as cashier, telephone operator, and assistant announcer. Al Abrams Pontiac hired her in April 1962 to be an announcer and engineer for its gospel radio program, and Abrams was so pleased with her work that she was given the talent coordinator position for the television version. "I'm what you call a back pusher," she told the *Defender*. "One who stands in the background and pushes others to the front. The singers kid me about this quite a bit. They say that I should sing sometimes. Trouble is—I can't sing."[42]

The Norfleet Brothers, the Gospel Songbirds, and the Hutchinson Sunbeams headlined the debut episode of *Jubilee Showcase*, which aired on WBKB-TV at 9:00 a.m. Sunday, February 24, 1963.[43] The Norfleets sang "Shadrack," the Gospel Songbirds did "When I Was Baptized" and "When the Saints Go Marchin' In," and the Hutchinson Sunbeams performed "Joshua."[44]

A preteen gospel group, the Hutchinson Sunbeams were sisters Jeannette, Wanda, and Sheila Hutchinson. Their father, Joe, accompanied on guitar.[45] The group was cut from somewhat of the same cloth as the Staple Singers— father on electric guitar accompanying his young children singing in close harmony—but their sound contained none of the Staples' folk overtones. Joe, who wrote original songs and arrangements for the group, played a straight-forward rhythm that served as accompaniment but not an additional voice, as Roebuck Staples' reverberating guitar strumming was for his ensemble. Performing soul and disco music as the Emotions, Sheila and Wanda scored a major hit in 1977, and a Grammy Award, for "Best of My Love."

The Hutchinson Sunbeams and DeLois Barrett Campbell's six first-season appearances notwithstanding, several of the earliest *Jubilee Showcase* episodes were dedicated to Chicago quartets. Episode 2, for example, featured "Somebody" by R. H. Harris and the Gospel Paraders, recently signed to Sam Cooke's SAR label. The Norfleets did "Rock of Ages," and the Salem Travelers sang "I'm Tired."[46] On March 10, the female Golden Harps sang "I Know the Lord Will Make a Way" and the Kindly Shepherds did "Die Easy." The Faithful Wonders were paired with the Norfleets and Josh White Jr. on episode 4.[47]

The *Jubilee Showcase* format that evolved during the first season remained steady in successive years. Episodes typically opened with the Norfleet Brothers, alone or with guest artists, singing the show's theme—"Jubilee! Jubilee! Jubilee!"—in an ascending do-mi-so chord. From there, either the Norfleets transitioned into "Shadrack" or the studio musicians launched into an invigorating gospel instrumental while the guest artists and audience clapped along. As the music continued in the background, Ordower offered a brief greeting and introduction of the guest performers and cued the opening artist's first song. He introduced each guest by providing a short history and mentioning the artist's most recent achievements. The artist performed at least two songs during the twenty-four-to-twenty-five-minute program, which left a few minutes for commercial breaks. At or near the conclusion, Ordower provided a brief inspirational message that typically invoked peace and understanding among people. The guest artists joined on a final, rousing selection as the credits rolled.

Jubilee Showcase was "like church before church," said Steven Ordower.

> [My father] wanted to present gospel music as an art form in the most respectful way he could, and let it speak for itself, and that's what he did. He never spoke more than a minute or two minutes when he did an intro. And at the end of shows—I don't want to say he was preaching or anything—but he would talk specifically about how love for one another can overcome our fear of one another. Then we can actually start to get along, and things of this nature. He would slip in these moral messages, but not overdone or over the top at all. He never wanted to be the focus, ever.[48]

Jubilee Showcase differed from *TV Gospel Time* in several ways: *Jubilee Showcase* used one permanent host (Ordower) instead of several rotating guest hosts. It was taped at one studio (WBKB/ABC, Chicago) instead of several regional locations. Ordower did not pitch advertisers' products, whereas on *TV*

Gospel Time the host sometimes spoke about the sponsor's product. Finally, while both programs had studio audiences, the *TV Gospel Time* audience was heard and not seen, but on *Jubilee Showcase*, the audience was visible and clapped politely after each song.

While *Jubilee Showcase* received a favorable response in its inaugural season, it did not escape minor criticism. Etta Moten Barnett chided Abrams and Ordower for encouraging the live audience to applaud between songs because it was contrary to church etiquette. The two responded that their intention was to create not a church atmosphere but rather "meaningful entertainment with religious overtones."[49] In fact, several artists who appeared on the first season of *Jubilee Showcase*, namely, the McLin Ensemble, folksingers Inman and Ira, and Oscar Brown Jr., were not gospel singers or groups. When asked why Mahalia Jackson had not yet appeared, Ordower replied, "We tried to get [Jackson] but [she] is in a high income bracket and her price is far more than what we are able to pay."[50] Nevertheless, artists were paid for their appearance. "He worked with AFTRA [American Federation of Television and Radio Artists] very closely, and he followed all the rules," Ordower's widow, Myrna, said, "because he was a stickler that it had to be done perfectly. He was very principled; he would have taken it out of his own pocket. Never wanted a word said, so he paid, it wasn't wild money but he paid the standard rates."[51]

Ordower was a stickler for orderliness. "Perfectionist is the word," said Myrna. "If you didn't come up to that, you would hear about it. There were no swear words, nothing of that sort, but you would know that you had been bullet ridden. He wanted dignity for the show. He wanted it perfect."[52] Steven concurred. "It's not like you are going to bring your B game to a Sid Ordower production. You bring your A game, or you don't step on the court."[53]

Perhaps the biggest heartache of the first season was that the first thirteen episodes were erased by the production crew to conserve tape usage. "Sid was sick about that," Myrna said, "because of the historical content of it."[54] Scouring the *Defender's TV Fare* magazine and articles in its daily edition provides a list of artists appearing on the thirteen erased episodes:

Episode 1: February 24, 1963: Norfleet Brothers, Gospel Songbirds, Hutchinson Sunbeams

Episode 2: March 3, 1963: Norfleet Brothers, Gospel Paraders, Salem Travelers

Episode 3: March 10, 1963: Norfleet Brothers, Golden Harps, Kindly Shepherds

Episode 4: March 17, 1963: Norfleet Brothers, Faithful Wonders, Josh White Jr.

Episode 5: March 24, 1963: Norfleet Brothers, Supreme Councils featuring Evelyn Gay on piano

Episode 6: March 31, 1963: Norfleet Brothers, True Believers,
   Christland Singers

Episode 7: April 7, 1963: Norfleet Brothers, Gospel Songbirds,
   Golden Tones

Episode 8: April 14, 1963: Norfleet Brothers, Staple Singers,
   Hutchinson Sunbeams, Louise Overall Weaver

Episode 9: April 21, 1963: Norfleet Brothers, Kindly Shepherds,
   Kingdom Bound Singers, Louise Overall Weaver

Episode 10: April 28, 1963: Norfleet Brothers, DeLois Barrett Campbell
   featuring Roberta Martin on piano, Houk Singers of Gary

Episode 11: May 5, 1963: Norfleet Brothers, Royal Jubilee Singers

Episode 12: May 12, 1963: Norfleet Brothers, Oscar Brown Jr. and the
   Floyd Morris Trio, Louise Overall Weaver

Episode 13: May 19, 1963: Norfleet Brothers, Inman and Ira,
   Louise Overall Weaver

The Caravans made their *Jubilee Showcase* debut on the June 9, 1963, program. The Silver Stars, the Harold Bailey Singers, the Sallie Martin Singers, the Traveling Kings, the Heavenly Kings, and the Five Blind Boys all appeared on the program during June and July 1963.

WBKB was sufficiently impressed with the twenty-six-episode first season that it signed *Jubilee Showcase* for another thirty-nine weeks of half-hour programs for 1963–64.[55] The Norfleet Brothers and Louise Overall Weaver, who debuted on the April 14 episode, became regulars. Weaver accompanied many of the show's featured artists on organ, while the Norfleets opened, closed, and performed during episodes for many years.

After season 1, *Jubilee Showcase* expanded from a focus on quartets to gospel artists of all configurations. The March 29, 1964, episode, for example, focused on the city's Fellowship and Greater Bethesda church choirs, singing alongside Arluster Westbrooks and the Ladies of Harmony.[56] Early broadcasts included nonsinging guests; civil rights and civic leaders joined Ordower in the studio from time to time. For example, Rev. Jesse Jackson of Operation Breadbasket (later Operation PUSH: People United to Serve Humanity) recited poetry on the show.[57] When comedian and activist Dick Gregory appeared on a late 1964 episode, Ordower encouraged viewers to support Gregory's "Christmas for Mississippi" food drive. Al Abrams Pontiac presented Gregory with its own contribution to the fund-raiser.[58]

Sometimes, Ordower centered the show on a specific theme. For the December 22, 1963, program, *Jubilee Showcase* presented the original cast of the gospel musical *Black Nativity*, in town for a seven-week run at the Civic Opera House at the time of the telecast.[59] Alex Bradford and the Bradford Singers, Marion Williams and the Stars of Faith, and Princess Stewart, whom *Chicago*

Tribune drama critic Claudia Cassidy proclaimed "the Ethel Barrymore of song," provided the audience with samples from the musical.[60] By 1964, *Black Nativity* had played to more than three million people in the United States and overseas.[61] Bradford told Ordower on a 1965 episode of *Jubilee Showcase* that the troupe had performed *Black Nativity* in twenty-eight countries, including Australia, where their performance before an audience of fifty thousand included a symphony orchestra and was simulcast on radio and television.[62] All the artists in the cast gained from the play's reputation, but perhaps none more than Alex Bradford and one of his singers, Madeline Bell. Bell relocated to London and become a prolific lead vocalist and background singer.[63] The show inspired Bradford's involvement with musical theatre.

The concluding moments of *Jubilee Showcase* often offered viewers a chance to see and hear rare combinations of artists. While opportunities to hear multiple artist collaborations were commonplace in gospel programs, by being televised and preserved, *Jubilee Showcase* became the repository of the only surviving examples of many of these magical moments. For example, a 1966 episode combined DeLois Barrett Campbell, the Staple Singers, and the Arthur Logan Singers on "Just a Closer Walk with Thee," while Willie Dixon, who appeared as a *Jubilee Showcase* musician on multiple occasions, played upright bass. The following year, Brother John Sellers, the Norfleet Brothers, and the Hutchinson Sunbeams closed the program with a spirited "He's Got the Whole World in His Hands," with Dixon on bass and LeRoy Crume on guitar. On a 1964 broadcast, the Norfleets, Sallie Martin and her Singers of Joy, and the Barrett Sisters gathered in a circle and traded leads on the spirited "Come and Go with Me to My Father's House," while Roberta Martin accompanied on piano and Weaver on organ. Similarly, a 1965 program ended with the Swanee Quintet, the Jessy Dixon Singers, and the Frost Brothers, a white quartet from Nashville, joining their voices on "Glory, Hallelujah."

One episode of special historical interest was taped February 9, 1964. Along with show regulars the Norfleet Brothers singing "Shadrack" with Louise Overall Weaver on organ, the program featured Brother John Sellers performing "Coming Back Home to Live with Jesus," accompanied by Dixon on upright bass and Thomas A. Dorsey playing boogie-woogie piano. The polished female Shekinah Trio of Ebenezer AME Church in Evanston, Illinois, sang Dorsey's "If I Can Help Somebody" while the sixty-four-year-old Father of Gospel Music sat motionless at the back of the set, listening intently.

The *Jubilee Showcase* live audience was comprised mostly of family and friends of the performing artists. Women wore hats and men wore suits, just as they would to a church service or gospel program. Small children, also dressed in their Sunday best, sat fidgeting quietly. Sometimes the scheduled artists sat among the audience, and other times they sat behind the performers, as had been the custom for 1940s and 1950s gospel programs. However, while audience members often clapped along to the rhythmic music, they were either too keenly aware of the glare of the television cameras to shout or admonished not to do so by studio personnel. This bewildered L. Stanley Davis. He recalled that some artists preparing to perform on the show got nervous "because back then, the audiences didn't shout. This did not typify a typical church audience." He commented, "I don't know whether it was fear that it was coming into homes on Sunday morning, and how people would view it, but everybody was just sitting there. I became a talent coordinator of the show in its latter years because [Sid] said, 'Well, *if* you think you can do a better job, then you do it.' So I did!"[64]

Nevertheless, gospel singers such as Mavis Staples and Shirley Caesar found ways to interact with the audience. In 1964, Staples shouted like a Baptist preacher on the vamp of "Help Me, Jesus," shaking hands with the front row of the audience, as was her tradition, converting the chilly television studio into a mini-revival. Caesar walked among the studio audience in 1972 while singing "God Is Not Dead."

Inspired by the popularity of *Jubilee Showcase*, Yusim Chrysler-Plymouth began broadcasting *American Gospel Jamboree*, a radio equivalent to the television program, over radio station WBEE from its dealership at 930 East Forty-Seventh Street. With Ordower as host, Katie Davis as talent coordinator, and Stanley Keeble as organist, the show debuted September 26, 1965, and aired Sunday mornings from 10:30 to 11:30.[65]

Reported to have had a weekly viewership of 250,000 by 1969, *Jubilee Showcase* never compromised its commitment to providing a dignified setting for gospel music, but it did adapt to the changing times.[66] For example, in keeping with the funkier sounds favored by musicians during the late 1960s and early 1970s, the set became more colorful, and the technical direction somewhat psychedelic.

The program was unceremoniously cancelled in 1984; Sid Ordower died January 4, 2002, a week shy of his eighty-third birthday.[67] During its twenty-one-year run, *Jubilee Showcase* became an institution in Chicago. It was awarded an Emmy in 1966 by the Chicago Chapter of the National Academy of Television Arts and Sciences for "a pioneer project with the widest variety of gospel, spiritual, and jubilee music."[68] The approximately one hundred episodes available at the Chicago Public Library represent some of the only video of gospel groups such as the Harold Bailey Singers and the Hutchinson Sunbeams in performance. Another assortment of *Jubilee Showcase* shows is housed at the Center for Black Music Research, Columbia College Chicago. Sid Ordower donated this collection at the urging of L. Stanley Davis.

"I appreciated Sid Ordower," Vernon Oliver Price reflected, "because he took me and did things that other people should have done. I've been out here for years, I've been singing since I was three. I appreciate him to this day."[69]

The Barrett Sisters: "The Sweet Sisters of Zion"

In many ways, the career trajectory of the Barrett Sisters rose parallel to *Jubilee Showcase*. Although the trio of DeLois Barrett Campbell, Rodessa Porter, and Billie GreenBey sang publicly even before DeLois joined the Roberta Martin Singers—"this was a little side thing we did; we just went around to churches and sang," Campbell remarked—the group came into its own as a gospel group around 1962.[70] "[The Roberta Martin Singers] were always coming off the road in the summer months," recalled Campbell. "During the summer, [the Barrett Sisters] kind of worked around the city. Then after a while, I asked Miss Martin if she would ask Savoy to record us, so in [1964] they recorded the Barrett Sisters. Miss Martin played the piano."[71]

The Barrett Sisters were nicknamed the "Sweet Sisters of Zion" for their Baptist soulfulness and concert decorum. Each of the women had formal music training: Campbell with the Roberta Martin Singers, Porter as director of the Galilee Baptist Church Choir, and GreenBey as a student at the American Conservatory of Music. The trio was in demand at local gospel programs, church and artist anniversaries, and funerals. DeLois received so many requests to sing for funerals that she kiddingly called herself the "national funeral singer."[72]

With their cultured singing, sweet harmonies, refined performance technique, and elegant style of dress, the Barrett Sisters were cut from the Roberta Martin School of Music mold. On their debut album, *Jesus Loves Me*, the trio's crystal-clear treble harmonies floated atop Martin's trademark piano riffs and a gently purring organ. The title track was a contemporary arrangement of the perennial Sunday-school favorite and became the group's first single. DeLois was principal soloist on Little Lucy Smith's "He's My Light," but she also shared the spotlight with her sisters as they interjected lyrical snippets like vamping jazz brass players. They also lent their tight arrangement and harmonies to "You'll Never Walk Alone," officially gospelized by Mahalia Jackson in 1954, and "Somebody Bigger than You and I," tagged for gospel by the Little Lucy Smith Singers in 1955. The title track of the Barrett Sisters' similarly styled follow-up album, *I'll Fly Away*, became one of the trio's most enduring requests.

Gospel in the Ballroom

Perhaps gospel's added exposure on television, and the success of shows at the Apollo Theater in New York prompted Chicago secular entertainment venues to host multiartist gospel extravaganzas. On September 11, 1964, the Regal Theater held the All-American Gospel Spectacular of 1964 with the Five Blind Boys of Alabama, the Mighty Clouds of Joy, the Swan Silvertones, the Swanee Quintet, the Loving Sisters of Arkansas, and the Staple Singers. Not everyone, however, appreciated the sound of gospel music in the early 1960s. After attending the Regal program and suffering its "clash" of vocal harmony and "hectic rhythmic beat," Earl Calloway, a well-regarded music columnist for the *Defender*, echoed the severe criticism of AME Bishop Daniel Payne about demonstrative worship when he wrote:

> It is impossible to believe that the human voice could stand such punishment as hollering, screaming, with jumping and all manners of contortions. . . . Through all this it was impossible to clearly understand the message these actors were endeavoring to convey. One performer remarked, "If you can 'rock and roll' for the devil, I can do the 'Mashed Potato for God.'" When Thomas A. Dorsey introduced gospel music as we know it, he did so with a sincere religious sense of spiritual value. Although its texture was a mix of the blues and jazz, that was the way he could best express himself and the music became useful in evangelistic meetings. I would prefer to hear a good dance band well performed than to sit in the midst of such a program of so-called gospel music as the singers presented at the Regal Gospel Revue.[73]

Calloway was not alone. A South Side organist with a doctorate wrote to the *Defender* under the nom de plume of "A Disgraced Music Lover": "I was so ashamed of the entire program. I never expected to hear rock-and-roll at a religious service. We must be real and stop playing with God."[74] On the other hand, Mrs. L. Hudson retorted: "I have never enjoyed anything in my life as much as I enjoyed that [Regal] show. We need more programs like that in our community. We should have had a program like that years ago. I hope in the future we will have some place to go besides church—not that there is anything wrong with church, but it gives us older people somewhere to go one night a week."[75]

Criticism notwithstanding, a month later, the *Defender* hosted a gospel festival at the Trianon Ballroom as part of its annual Home Service Show. Organized by DeLois Barrett Campbell, Isabel Joseph Johnson, and Sid Ordower, the October 18 program drew five thousand attendees to hear local favorites such as the Norfleet Brothers, the Silver Stars, Vernon Oliver Price, and Stevie Hawkins of Cleveland, recently signed to Checker Records. A highlight of the show was the Barrett Sisters performing their current single, "Jesus Loves Me."[76]

Rock of Ages

Next to *Jubilee Showcase*, Chicago gospel aficionados cite Isabel Joseph Johnson's *Rock of Ages* as a seminal local gospel music television program. A native of New Orleans, Johnson was radio announcer for South Park Baptist Church, a beauty salon entrepreneur, a religious programmer for WVON radio, and an indefatigable emcee. Debuting on WCIU Channel 26 in 1969, *Rock of Ages* differed from *Jubilee Showcase* in that it was taped live, was one hour instead of thirty minutes, and aired Saturday evenings at 7:30 instead of Sunday morning.[77] With Willie Webb as music director, *Rock of Ages* had the informality of gospel radio, whereas Ordower's show was taped and edited before it hit the airwaves.[78] Gene Viale recalls vividly his first appearance on *Rock of Ages*:

> It was produced downtown in the Loop area in an old multi-floored building. Ms. Johnson would sit at a desk and singers, groups, soloists, and choirs would come in from all around the area by her invitation. She would announce the upcoming local gospel concerts. Many times groups, choirs, and solo artists from outside the Chicago area who may be in Chicago for a concert the next day would come up that long steep stairway after traveling up a number of floors by elevator. They would sometimes stand for quite a while on those stairs until it was their time to sing. The [broadcast] room was extremely small and warm. As the singers completed their song or songs, if Isabel didn't begin to speak to them, they were free to leave.[79]

In addition to Chicago artists, Johnson brought in guests from Detroit, St. Louis, and Los Angeles. She featured local church and youth choirs, including the chorus from her church home, South Park Baptist, and presented top-shelf artists such as Gloria Griffin and the Roberta Martin Singers, Rev. Sammy Lewis, Willie Webb's South Side Community Choir, and Father Hayes and the Cosmopolitan Church of Prayer Choir.[80]

Reflecting on the program's tenth anniversary in 1979, production member Frank J. Chambers, Jr., wrote:

> Isabel also hosted a similarly named show on Sunday mornings on WVON-AM. Both shows featured local talent from churches all around Chicago. *Rock of Ages*, in its original format, was a live 90 minute show with the first half hour featuring live commercials for a local furniture store. The show was later cut back to an hour when they lost the sponsor.
>
> It was a logistical miracle. There were nights when several hundred people were on the shows. Mostly choirs, but some nights would have three or four of them. Mixed in between them would be smaller groups. You would have to see a map of Channel 26's studio back then to appreciate how well run this show was, and how well behaved the choirs and groups had to be to make this work. As mentioned, it was a live show and during the breaks we would often be resetting the entire musical set from a choir to a soloist with a piano while an interview was going on just a few feet away.[81]

The program even performed an act of civic duty when it came to the rescue of Omega Baptist Church. On April 27, 1970, Omega's roof caved in. By flashing on the bottom of the screen a telephone number to call with gifts and pledges, Johnson helped Omega's pastor, Rev. Edmund Blair, raise the money to cover repair costs until the insurance company paid.[82] Johnson also sponsored an annual Choir Jubilee, which awarded prizes to youth community choirs and junior choruses from local churches. She rounded up celebrity judges such as Rev. Milton Brunson of the Tommies and Devella Norton Tuck, minister of music at New Covenant.[83]

"She didn't mind boosting your talent if she thought you had talent," said Rev. Walter Butts, whose Butts Singers sang on Johnson's radio and television programs. "She would make you feel so good, as young people, because she was promoting you out there."[84]

Although *TV Gospel Time*, *Jubilee Showcase*, and *Rock of Ages* were the premiere gospel telecasts for Chicagoans, other gospel-focused TV programs came and went during the 1960s and early 1970s. In 1968, Rev. Dwight "Gatemouth" Moore, now Bishop Moore, secured a television program on WCIU-TV, the same station that aired *Rock of Ages*. Although it featured a variety of guests, *The Gatemouth Moore Show* included gospel groups such as Almond Dawson's Inspirational Singers on its Wednesday night at 10:10 time slot. Elder Samuel Patterson, guitar player and leader in the Church of God in Christ, also hosted a gospel music television program on Channel 26 called *Gospel Train*.[85] Other cities added gospel television programs. For example, the Jubilee Hummingbirds performed on a half-hour telecast on Memphis's WREG-TV, and Rev. Cleophus Robinson preached and sang on television in St. Louis.[86]

By the end of the decade, gospel music was considered a sizable enough draw for ABC-TV to air a taping of the Folk Gospel Music Festival on prime time television. The open-air festival, held in Harlem's Mount Morris Park, New York City, on Sunday, July 13, 1969, was part of the Harlem Cultural Festival, organized by nightclub and film star Tony Lawrence. Mahalia Jackson, the Staple Singers, Ben Branch and the Operation Breadbasket Band, Clara Walker and the Gospel Redeemers, Professor Herman Stevens and the Voices of Faith, and Professor Caldwell and the Mighty Mellowtones were among the performers. Rev. Jesse Jackson of Operation Breadbasket and promoter Joe Bostic were also part of the program. Some seventy thousand people attended the festival, which ABC broadcast on Tuesday, September 16, 1969.[87]

The Folk Gospel Music Festival was a product of its time. It was no coincidence that the Operation Breadbasket Band performed "Hard Times" and "Motherless Child," the Staples sang "Give a Damn," and the Mellowtones concluded with "We Shall Overcome." *Ebony*'s prediction in 1950 that television would play a pivotal role in the defeat of Jim Crow became a reality in the 1960s. American viewers watched in horror as African Americans, and predominantly youth, were beaten, attacked by dogs, and had pressurized water from fire hoses turned on them in their pursuit of basic human rights. Gospel songs and spirituals buoyed spirits weary from marching and sitting in jail. Radios crackled with songs protesting U.S. involvement in the Vietnam conflict. Many gospel singers and musicians who migrated to Chicago to escape the brutality of the South—and experienced it all over again while traveling through southern states—turned their attention from their personal challenges to the emerging civil rights movement. To paraphrase Lucie Campbell's "He'll Understand, He'll Say Well Done," it was time for gospel singers to give the best of their service.

CHAPTER 16

"Tell It Like It Is"

Songs of Social Significance

It's time Negroes stop waiting on the Lord for help and start helping himself. They are turning dogs and water hoses on our people in the South. We must do something about it.

Mahalia Jackson

By the mid-1950s, Mahalia Jackson had racked up a few million selling singles and had conquered Carnegie Hall, Music Inn, Europe, radio, and television in the name of gospel. She was the newest star in the Columbia Records galaxy of artists. But none of that made any difference as she stood nervously on the side of a lonesome Louisiana highway, a hapless victim of two overzealous state troopers.

In *Got to Tell It*, Jules Schwerin describes the time when Jackson was pulled over by the Louisiana State Police en route from Chicago to New Orleans. It was the middle of the night. Two officers slowly circled Jackson's car, demanding to know why she was driving a Cadillac. "Ain't yours, for sure," one sneered. They ordered her out of the car, made her remove her shoes and dump the contents of her handbag on the ground. When several hundred dollars tumbled out—Jackson preferred that performance money be paid in cash—the officers assumed she had stolen it. Transporting her to the home of a local judge, the police hardly had to relate a story. The sleepy-eyed judge fined her $250 for speeding. Jackson knew the police had also helped themselves to some of the loose currency that fell from her purse. "One of those bastards lifted two hundred, somehow, somewhere, in between," she told a shocked Schwerin, "and they damn well knew who I was!" She added, "They would have just as soon put me in the pokey, if they had found all that money I was carrying in my bra and other places."[1]

Encounters with racism on the gospel highway were almost unavoidable if you were black and drove a luxury automobile. While touring the South in the early 1960s, the Staple Singers stopped at a filling station just outside West Memphis, Arkansas. After the attendant fueled up their Cadillac, Mavis Staples asked for a receipt so that the group could use it for tax purposes. The attendant had the receipt in his hand but told Staples if she wanted it, she would have to accompany him into the station to get it. When Roebuck "Pops" Staples asked why this was necessary, the attendant responded with "abusive language" and by "contemptuously making references to the Cadillac that they drove." The man "reminded them that they were not in Illinois but in the South, where the white man's word was law." Roebuck told the attendant that his comments were unwarranted and grabbed the receipt from his hand. The attendant swung at Roebuck, but Pervis intervened and knocked the man to the ground.

The Staples jumped in the car and sped away but soon found themselves pursued by three cars full of police, shotguns, and dogs. They pulled over to the side of the road, and the police began searching each member of the family. One ordered Roebuck to open the trunk of the car. Upon seeing copies of Staple Singers records and glossy photographs, the police captain recognized the group, apologized profusely, sought forgiveness for mistakenly believing they had fled the filling station without paying for gas, and even requested some of the group's phonograph records.[2]

Even when not subject to the direct scrutiny of police, touring in the Jim Crow South "was a nightmare," Jackson told Schwerin. "There was no place for us to eat or sleep along the major highways. The restaurants wouldn't serve us . . . some gasoline stations didn't want to sell us gas or oil. Some told us no restrooms were available. The looks of anger at the sight of us colored folks sitting in a nice car were frightening to see. . . . It got so we were living on bags of fresh fruit during the day and driving half the night, and I was so exhausted by the time I was supposed to sing, I was almost dizzy."[3]

Gene Viale, a member of the Cleveland Singers in the mid-1960s and of Puerto Rican heritage, also experienced prejudice on the gospel highway. "You would have had to have traveled the road with us to fully understand the danger, the pressure, the hours upon hours of driving, the lack of places to stay, the lack of places where kind faces would greet us."[4]

Whether from personal experience or from hearing the tales of physical and emotional injury, gospel artists could not help but be swept up into the civil rights movement. Although only a handful of singers, such as Jackson, the Staples, Inez Andrews, and the Gospel Harmonettes' Dorothy Love Coates, were Christian soldiers on active duty for the movement, most artists recognized the importance of lifting their voices in song to help the cause. This included participating in gospel programs that raised funds for civil rights organizations, writing odes to the movement, or singing songs that expressed displeasure with the way black people were treated everywhere—not just in the South but up North as well. If, as doctoral candidate Brooksie Harrington writes, "gospel reflects the conditions and consciousness of its audience," gospel songs of the 1960s could be expected to resound with cries for freedom.[5]

Of all Chicago-based gospel singers, Mahalia Jackson was the most ardent activist of the civil rights movement and passionate believer in its leader, Rev. Dr. Martin Luther King Jr. Her involvement with the movement began in 1956, when Rev. Ralph David Abernathy invited her to sing for an event to stimulate financial and moral support for the Montgomery bus boycott. The boycott began on December 1, 1955, when seamstress and NAACP member Rosa Parks was arrested for refusing to relinquish her seat to a white passenger on a Montgomery, Alabama, bus. An assemblage of local African American leaders, including King, newly appointed pastor of the Dexter Avenue Baptist Church, organized the Montgomery Improvement Association (MIA) to boycott the city's bus line. The boycott forced most African Americans to walk to work. As the months rolled on and the miles began mounting, MIA leaders felt the boycotters needed some cheerful encouragement by way of a special program. Jackson consented to sing for the program, and when asked her fee, she replied, "I don't charge the walking people." She became deeply involved in the cause and developed close friendships with King and his willing workers.[6]

Jackson assisted King again on May 17, 1957, when she sang "I've Been 'Buked and I've Been Scorned" for the Prayer Pilgrimage for Freedom.[7] The noon gathering, held on the steps of the Lincoln Memorial in Washington, DC, featured King's clarion call to the president and Congress to guarantee blacks suffrage. Although overall turnout was about half of the seventy-five thousand anticipated, King's oration on the importance of voting rights prompted New York's *Amsterdam News* to call him "the number one leader of sixteen million Negroes in the United States."[8]

While Chicago churches were passively supportive of late 1950s activities to promote freedom and equality in the South, they became more active after watching brutality leveled at young people as they staged sit-ins and at the Freedom Riders as they traveled the South by bus, challenging states to uphold the Supreme Court's prohibition of segregation in interstate transportation. In *Just My Soul Responding,* music historian Brian Ward notes that even northern blacks who did not participate directly in sit-ins or protests could not help but be inspired every time King and the Southern Christian Leadership Conference (SCLC), which coordinated civil rights activity throughout the country, chipped away at the wall of segregation.[9] In response, organizations in northern cities held sympathy demonstrations and musical programs to raise money for, and awareness of, the cause. For example, on Sunday afternoon, October 21, 1962, the Student Nonviolent Coordinating Committee (SNCC) held the "Gospel for Freedom" program at Chicago's McCormick Place. Featured gospel artists were James Cleveland, the Caravans, the Highway QCs, and the Helen Robinson Youth Choir, which sang "Democracy Is Meant for Me."[10] A "Freedom Chorus" of students who had participated in the sit-ins was a special added attraction.[11]

King and the SCLC used nonviolent resistance in 1963 to battle long-standing segregation in Birmingham. During April and May, Birmingham police commissioner Eugene "Bull" Connor gave approval to police to use high-pressure fire hoses on the protesters, threaten them with dogs, and fill the prison to capacity with marchers. Arrested with them, King wrote his *Letter from a Birmingham Jail* while behind bars. Network television news captured the inhumanity of the police response to the protests, especially the injury of black schoolchildren. The world was outraged.

"It's time Negroes stop waiting on the Lord for help and start helping himself," Mahalia Jackson told reporters. "They are turning dogs and water hoses on our people in the South. We must do something about it."[12] Committed to helping the SCLC replenish its coffers after covering bail-bond payouts, Jackson organized a May 27 benefit at Arie Crown Theater in McCormick Place. Her goal was to raise fifty thousand dollars. Disk jockey Al Benson pledged one thousand dollars and airtime to the cause. Several prominent Baptist pastors pitched in, including Rev. Clay Evans of Fellowship, Rev. W. N. Daniel of Antioch, Rev. Louis Boddie of Greater Harvest, Detroit's Rev. C. L. Franklin, and local SCLC director John Thurston of New Covenant. King, along with Ralph Abernathy and Wyatt Tee Walker, attended the event, which drew better than five thousand to hear Dinah Washington, Eartha Kitt, Aretha Franklin, Louis Jordan, Gloria Lynne, Wade Flemons, the Red Saunders Orchestra, and comedian Dick Gregory. Chicago journalist Irv Kupcinet was emcee. Studs Terkel introduced King, who addressed those seated and hundreds more in the lobby. The event met the organizers' fifty-thousand-dollar goal.[13]

On the front line, things were going from bad to worse. On June 11, Medgar Evers, field secretary for the Mississippi NAACP, was murdered in his driveway by Byron de la Beckwith. Ten days later, Jackson returned to Carnegie Hall, the site of her 1950 success, to headline a June 21 program to benefit SNCC. In Chicago, the Wooten Choral Ensemble participated in an October 25 benefit for the Congress of Racial Equality (CORE).[14] Even the cast of *Black Nativity* did its part, headlining a December benefit at the South Side Community Art Center for Protest at the Polls, a group whose aim was "to solidify the Negro ballot into a more powerful voting bloc."[15]

After participating in a building-fund benefit for Fellowship Baptist, Jackson headed east to be on the main program for the historic March on Washington.[16] The march, scheduled for August 28, 1963, became, according to historian Taylor Branch, "a transcendent ritual of American identity."[17] It was the brainchild of Asa Philip Randolph, international president of the Brotherhood of Sleeping Car Porters. He, Mary McLeod Bethune, and NAACP executive secretary Walter White, threatened a march on Washington as early as 1941, but President Roosevelt signed Executive Order 8802, creating the Fair Employment Practices Committee (FEPC), without the need for a formal protest event.

With the support of the NAACP, CORE, the SCLC, SNCC, and the Urban League, Randolph donned the mantle of march organizer once again and named Bayard Rustin deputy director in charge of event logistics.[18] Anticipating the possibility of a riot, the city all but evacuated in preparation for the march. Jackson is reported to have said: "Driving into Washington the night before the march, it looked to me like we were entering a city about to be captured by an enemy army. Houses were dark and the streets were deserted. There were so many police patrols and soldiers around, you'd have thought the Russians were coming."[19]

Yet as late as 9:30 on the morning of the twenty-eighth, organizers remained concerned that march participation would not meet expectations. Then a traffic snarl suddenly broke open, and the space between the Washington and Lincoln Monuments filled with more than 250,000 people of all races and walks of life.

Nestled among the day's speakers were several musical guests. Opera star Marian Anderson was scheduled to open the formal program with the national anthem, but had difficulty making her way through the throng to the dais and had yet to appear. Camilla Williams, another opera singer, performed in her stead (Anderson sang "He's Got the Whole World in His Hands" later in the program).[20] Odetta; Josh White; Joan Baez; Bob Dylan; Peter, Paul and Mary; and the SNCC Freedom Singers sang folk songs prior to the formal program.[21]

Jackson was slated to sing "Take My Hand, Precious Lord" just prior to remarks by American Jewish Congress president Rabbi Joachim Prinz and King's keynote presentation. As she was about to perform, King asked Jackson to replace "Precious Lord," his favorite gospel song, with "I've Been 'Buked and I've Been Scorned," the spiritual she sang at the 1957 Prayer Pilgrimage for Freedom. Jackson started the spiritual slowly, but the vast crowd began to energize Jackson like a Chicago church audience. She told Schwerin: "I heard a great murmur come rolling back to me from the multitude below, and I sensed I had reached out and touched a chord. I was moved to shout for joy, and I did! I lifted the rhythm to a gospel beat. The great crowd began singing and clapping, and joy overflowed."[22]

Although Jackson was to sing only one selection, the crowd shouted for more, so she did "How I Got Over" as an encore. In the tradition of the gospel singer setting the tone for the minister's sermon, Jackson readied the crowd for King's "I Have a Dream" speech, considered by many the greatest address of the twentieth century. Jackson may even have prompted King to incorporate the dream motif, which he had used in prior presentations, when she shouted to King to "tell 'em about the dream, Martin."[23]

Terkel described to Schwerin his personal experience of the moment:

> By God, there was a great rolling murmur from the crowds! But at that moment, during the singing, there was an airplane buzzing . . . and it was a noise that was quite disturbing . . . you might say, impiously buzzing. And she looked up. I knew what she was going to do. She just looked up at the plane, but she *sang* up to the plane. And, so help me, her voice drowned out the buzz! At that moment, the scores of thousands around the pool took out their white handkerchiefs and waved them as a wave of banners of triumph, for it was! She outsang, she, the human, had outsung the flying machine![24]

The euphoric sense of hope engendered by the March on Washington evaporated on Sunday, September 15, 1963, when dynamite planted beneath the stairs of Birmingham's Sixteenth Street Baptist Church—a headquarters for the Birmingham civil rights campaign—blew a hole in the church, killing four young girls and injuring many other churchgoers. A bystander summed it up: "My God, we're not even safe in church."[25]

The tragedy stunned the nation and hung thickly in the air four days later, on Thursday, September 19, as James Cleveland and the Savoy recording team gathered at Trinity Temple Seventh Day Adventist Church in Newark, New Jersey.[26] Rev. Lawrence Roberts, responsible for gospel production at Savoy Records, where Cleveland was under contract, was also the pastor of First Baptist Church in Nutley, New Jersey. Roberts was in favor of live recordings: not only had he captured the Roberta Martin Singers in live performance at First Baptist in March of that year, he had also persuaded Cleveland to perform with his Angelic Choir for two live albums in 1962. The albums had sold so well that they scheduled a third session for September 19.

One of the selections readied for the recording was an arrangement, attributed to George Jordan, of "Peace Be Still," a hymn about Jesus calming a storm, based on Mark 4:39: "And he arose, and rebuked the wind, and said to the sea, 'Peace, be still.' And the wind ceased, and there was a great calm."[27] As lead singer, Cleveland assumed the character of one of Jesus's disciples, invoking his Lord as cymbals evoked crashing waves. It was as if he was leading community prayer about the Birmingham bombing and the rest of the year's injustices in beseeching God to calm the raging waters of American injustice and brutality.

"Master," Cleveland sang plainly. Then he unleashed the full, seething authority of his raspy baritone: "The tempest is raging!" The formidable power of Cleveland's entreaty prompted several choristers to shout, "Sing, James!" He continued:

> *The billows are tossing high.*
> *The sky is o'er shadowed with blackness;*
> *No shelter or help is nigh.*
> *Carest Thou not that we perish?*
> *How canst Thou lie asleep,*
> *When each moment so madly is threatening*
> *A grave in the angry deep?*

The Angelic Choir, directed by Roberts, joined in the hushed chorus:

> *The winds and the waves shall obey Thy will;*
> *Peace! Be still.*

Cleveland interjected, "Get up, Jesus!" as the choir chanted "Peace! Be still," their voices swelling and ebbing, awakening more shouts.

Rev. Dr. Stefanie Minatee, Roberts's niece and leader of the gospel group Rev. Stef and Jubilation, was five years old at the time of the recording, but she remembers the session vividly:

> I can remember sitting in the church, excited and eager to experience the music ministry of Rev. James Cleveland and the Angelic Choir. I loved to hear the Angelic Choir sing! You could feel the excitement in the air! I remember watching my mother, Pearl, a charter member of the choir, and others, scurry around the building in preparation for the recording. The building was packed to capacity! Once the session began, every song recorded was a worship experience. I recall Pastor Roberts and Rev. Cleveland tag-teaming the congregation with words of encouragement, faith and liberation. The church was on holy ghost fire![28]

The album became one of Savoy's biggest sellers. The two-part single of "Peace Be Still" and the LP occupied *Billboard*'s Top Spirituals Singles and

Albums lists, respectively, for two years after their release. In March 1966, Fred Mendelsohn of Savoy Records reported that the company had already sold more than three hundred thousand copies of the album.[29] The disc ultimately sold more than a million units and helped usher in the era of live gospel recordings.

While Jackson and Cleveland were tackling prejudice in action and song, other black artists were accused of not doing enough. In 1964, Rev. Sammy Lewis riposted accusations of his lack of activity, noting that he had been "working actively . . . with the NAACP and other civic groups" since 1952. He noted his participation in local boycotts and demonstrations and said that he had offered assistance to Rev. Carl Fuqua, executive secretary of the NAACP in Chicago, but had yet to receive a response. "I am not a publicity seeker and I do not run over people to get my picture taken for notice in the rights movement like many others," he declared. "Because of this, I am criticized. I defy those who even hint that I have not aided this great movement."[30]

The March 7, 1965, mass march from Selma to Montgomery became another rallying point for the gospel music community. After a series of brutally repressed and failed attempts by the Alabama city's blacks to register to vote, a march was staged from Selma to Montgomery to protest in front of the state capitol. As the marchers crossed Selma's Edmund Pettis Bridge to begin their trek eastward along US Highway 80 to the steps of the capitol building, they were met with a wall of state troopers with nightsticks and tear gas. The event came to be called "Bloody Sunday" for the ensuing violence that left many marchers beaten and bloodied. Finally, on March 24, with King and Abernathy in the front row, the marchers successfully completed their historic journey to the state capitol.

In support, Rev. W. N. Daniel pledged the use of Antioch Baptist Church for a March 29, 1965, musical to benefit the SCLC. Ushers gathered a freewill offering from attendees who came to hear Almond Dawson's Inspirational Singers, the Gospel Songbirds, the Gospel Sensationals, and the Salem Travelers.[31]

If the SCLC and SNCC had made progress in the South and helped stimulate the passing of the 1964 Civil Rights Act and 1965 Voting Rights Bill, blacks in northern urban areas still suffered from slum living conditions, inequity in public schooling, and high unemployment rates. Support for the movement among Chicago clergy and gospel artists intensified in 1966, when the SCLC decided to make the city the site of its first northern campaign. The SCLC aligned with Al Raby's Coordinating Council of Community Organizations (CCCO), a coalition of civil rights groups, to form the Chicago Freedom Movement.[32] Dr. King outlined the movement's position in Chicago as "directed against public and private institutions which over the years, [had] created in-famous slum conditions directly responsible for the involuntary enslavement of millions of black men, women and children." On education, he declared: "Educational facilities, while an improvement over Mississippi, are hardly adequate to prepare Negroes for Metropolitan Life." Further, "[a] labor force of some 300,000 [had] found little beyond low-paying service occupations open to them." Reflecting on the promises of Chicago that encouraged masses of blacks to uproot their southern lives and move North, King said, "It was the promised land for thousands who sought to escape the cruelties of Alabama, Mississippi and Tennessee. Yet, now, in the year 1966, the cycle has almost reversed. Factories moving south, employment and opportunities on the increase, and recent civil rights legislation are rapidly disintegrating the cruelties of segregation. . . . Those who generations ago sang 'Going to Chicago, Sorry But I Can't Take You' now sink into the depths of despair."[33] To further fix the national spotlight on local conditions, King moved into an apartment at 1550 South Hamlin on the city's West Side.

One of the most important mass marches in Chicago that year took place on July 10. Some thirty thousand people took part in Freedom Sunday, which opened with a rally at Soldier Field and, despite sweltering summer conditions, concluded with a mass march to City Hall, where the assembly petitioned Mayor Richard J. Daley to address discriminatory real estate practices, police brutality, and other inequities for the city's black residents.[34]

Still, neither the rally nor the Chicago campaign was wholly embraced by the city's African American leadership, prime among them Rev. J. H. Jackson, pastor of Olivet Baptist Church. Jackson, president of the five-million-member National Baptist Convention, would not support the rally because he considered the SCLC's Chicago campaign unnecessary and ineffective and believed that nonviolence led ultimately to violence.[35] Jackson's lack of support for King's strategies had drawn criticism three years earlier, when the pastor was booed during a July 4 NAACP rally in Chicago's Grant Park. Mahalia Jackson's influence was essential in bypassing Reverend Jackson and rallying the local African American church community directly.

King needed as much support in Chicago as possible. Two days after the rally, police and residents on the city's West Side tussled over an open fire hydrant that children were using to cool off from the sweltering temperatures. When tempers boiled, residents were beaten and Molotov cocktails were thrown at police.[36] An August 5 march around Marquette Park to protest the Southwest Side's recalcitrant stance against blacks living in the community was met by an angry white mob. They taunted the marchers and tossed bottles and rocks at them. King was struck in the head with a brick. "I've never seen anything like it," he said later. "I've been in many demonstrations all across the south, but I can say that I have never seen—even in Mississippi and Alabama—mobs as hostile and as hate filled as I've seen in Chicago."[37]

Rev. Clay Evans supported King as staunchly as Mahalia Jackson did. On September 16, his Fellowship Baptist Church held a Gospel Festival Spectacular at the Arie Crown Theater. The program, also a fund-raiser to benefit the church's building fund, featured King as keynote speaker.[38] Gospel artists who joined Evans and the 150-voice Fellowship Choir for the program were the James Cleveland Singers, the Staple Singers, the Soul Stirrers, the Faithful Wonders, and Jeanette Robinson Jones of the Helen Robinson Youth Choir. Rev. Jesse Jackson, Sid Ordower, and WVON gospel announcer Bill "Doc" Lee also assisted with the program.

The presence of the Staple Singers on the 1966 program was fitting because they had been lending their talent to civil and human rights causes for several years. Their recordings for Orrin Keepnews's Riverside label blended the sounds of folk, blues, and gospel with lyrics that were more socially significant than their recordings for United or Vee Jay. With Riverside, they became the first gospel group to record Bob Dylan's "Blowin' in the Wind" and "Masters of War." Civil rights workers sang the Staples' version of "This May Be My Last Time" as a sobering reminder of the potential dangers ahead.[39] The Staples anticipated gospel's wider embrace of the folk repertory by the end of the decade.

Following the collapse of Riverside, Columbia signed the Staples to its Epic subsidiary, placing Nashville A&R man Billy Sherrill in charge of recording the group in Chicago.[40] Sherrill worked fast. *Amen* was recorded at the end of October 1964. One of the tracks was a rerecording of a Staples' Riverside single, "More Than a Hammer and Nail," a mid-tempo paean to familial love and commitment. With Epic's distribution muscle behind it, the song occupied the top five on *Billboard*'s Hot Spiritual Singles Chart well into mid-1965, sharing space with James Cleveland and the Angelic Choir's "Peace Be Still," the Consolers' "Waiting for My Child," and the Caravans' "Walk around Heaven All Day." Likewise, *Amen* landed on *Billboard*'s top five Hot Spiritual Albums, solidifying the Staple Singers' position among gospel's royalty.

Roebuck wrote the title track of *Freedom Highway*, their second Epic album and first live project for the label, in tribute to the 1965 Selma to Montgomery march. Although not a huge leap from the mother wit of "Hammer and Nail" and their repertory of Woody Guthrie and Bob Dylan songs, "Freedom Highway" was the group's first originally composed message song. The album was recorded in April 1965 at Rev. John Hopkins's New Nazareth Baptist Church in Chicago. Although the congregants responded warmly to the Staples' version of "We Shall Overcome," their up-tempo "Help Me Jesus," with Mavis on lead, turned the Baptist assembly into an old-fashioned church service. *Billboard* agreed, saying the album "contains all the fever and tense excitement of an honest-to-goodness revival meeting."[41]

If "Freedom Highway" signaled the Staples' growing commitment to songs of social significance, 1966's "Why (Am I Treated So Bad)" confirmed it. Pops opened the bluesy title track of their follow-up album to *Freedom Highway* with a narrative about children prohibited from riding a school bus. From there the group harmonized on the title's rhetorical question. Pops's story would have been recognizable to southern blacks, but the Staples' Chicago fan base would also have shouted in assent, having spent several years fighting de facto racial segregation in the Chicago Public Schools. The song entered the civil rights lexicon and became one of King's favorites. "Step Aside" brought biblical pilgrims to an allegorical vision of Birmingham, Selma, or Chicago. The following year, the Staples scored another hit with a cover of Stephen Stills's protest song "For What It's Worth." *What the World Needs Now* (1968) included the iconic Dylan ballad, "A Hard Rain's A-Gonna Fall," Curtis Mayfield's "People Get Ready," and the freedom song "Don't Let Nobody Turn You Around."[42]

The Staples' performance of "The Ghetto" on a *Jubilee Showcase* episode that year was one of the program's most poignant moments. Mavis led the solemn song about the travails of living in poverty, concluding that in a New Jerusalem, "there will be no more ghetto." It blended the premise of the Golden Gate Quartet's brisk "No Segregation in Heaven" with the melancholy of "Walk around Heaven All Day." The studio audience continued applauding well after Roebuck started to introduce their next number.

The August 10, 1968, *Billboard* announced the Staples' move to Memphis-based Stax Records.[43] Although this move represented an intentional shift from gospel to soul, the group's social conscience remained intact with selections such as "Respect Yourself" and "I'll Take You There," the latter analogous lyrically to "Move On Up a Little Higher" with explicitly incisive, politically relevant imagery. Instead of moving to a heavenly place where "it is always howdy, howdy," Mavis envisioned a place on earth where nobody was crying, or worried, and there were "no more smiling faces / Lying to the races."

As the Staples' "More Than a Hammer and Nail" took up residence on *Billboard*'s Hot Spiritual Singles List, Sam Cooke's "A Change Is Gonna Come" was listed in the January 30, 1965, issue as a "Breakout Single." Recorded in early 1964 as an album track, the song included an indictment of Jim Crow: "I'd go to the movie and I'd go downtown / Somebody keeps telling me, don't hang around." Tagged onto the flipside of the soul dancer "Shake," albeit without the controversial verse, "A Change Is Gonna Come" debuted on the Hot 100 Singles chart at number 70 and peaked at 31.

Cooke never had a chance to witness the song become a hit. He was killed in the early morning hours of Friday, December 11, 1964, at the Hacienda Motel in Los Angeles's Watts community.

The circumstances of Cooke's death engendered nearly as many conspiracy theories as the assassination of President John F. Kennedy a year earlier. What all parties could agree on was that Cooke and a female companion named Lisa Boyer had rented a room at the Hacienda, that Boyer had run off with Cooke's clothes and wallet, and that the enraged and embarrassed singer had confronted the manager of the Hacienda, Bertha Franklin, about Boyer's whereabouts. When the conversation became heated, Franklin shot and killed Cooke with a pistol.

Cooke was waked from 3:00 to 7:00 p.m. on Thursday, December 17, at Chicago's A. R. Leak Funeral Home.[44] He had been a member of Fellowship Baptist, but it was not big enough, so the funeral service was held at Tabernacle. "They had to block off Indiana Avenue from Forty-Third all the way down to Forty-First," said Rev. John Wesley Moore, present for what he called the largest funeral in Tabernacle's history. "I was talking to one of the officers when C. L. Franklin, Aretha Franklin's father, came through there. [The police] didn't want to let him through, and I had to go and talk to them to let him through, because there were so many people. I understand they had over nine thousand people attend that funeral."[45] Rev. Clay Evans delivered the eulogy, and the Staple Singers and the Soul Stirrers sang. Original Highway QCs Creadell Copeland and Charles, Lee, and Curtis Richardson were pallbearers.[46]

The Soul Stirrers' S. R. Crain sponsored a memorial program for his friend and business associate at the Arie Crown Theater in McCormick Place on February 15, 1965. In tribute to Cooke's dual affections for soul and gospel, Crain dedicated half of the program to gospel and half to soul music. Rev. C. L. Franklin emceed the gospel portion, which featured the Soul Stirrers and the Highway QCs, as well as SAR Records artists R. H. Harris and the Gospel Paraders and the Meditation Singers. E. Rodney Jones of WVON hosted the second portion of the program, which included Jerry Butler, the Impressions, and the Valentinos, a group consisting of the Womack Brothers, whom Cooke first met when they were young children. Sam's brother, L. C. Cooke, was also slated to sing. Proceeds went to Reverend Evans for the Fellowship Building Fund.[47]

Dolores "Honey" Sykes of the Duncanaires remembered the last time she saw Cooke alive. "Sam was very close to us," she said. "We were very good friends. The last time we got to see him was really strange. The Duncanaires were [in Hollywood] for a gig. We had been out shopping at Hollywood and

Vine, and Sam Cooke passed us. He looked and turned around. We looked and turned around, because we thought that's who we saw. He said, 'Duncanaires!' We said, 'Sam Cooke!' What a reunion! We hugged and kissed, because we loved him so much."[48]

By their very nature, gospels, spirituals, and jubilee songs are freedom and protest songs. Spirituals are said to have contained coded messages that steered enslaved African Americans to brush arbor worship services and directed their safe passage to freedom in the North. Even a casual listener could recognize the implicit judgment in the jubilee quartet standard, "My Lord's Gonna Move This Wicked Race." Rev. Charles A. Tindley's gospel hymn "I Will Overcome Someday" was converted into the civil rights anthem, "We Shall Overcome."

Gospel artists recorded songs with explicit social messages prior to the 1960s, although radio stations, especially in the South, were hesitant to program them. These included the Golden Gate Quartet's "No Segregation in Heaven" (1942) and the Capitol City Quartette's similarly titled "No Jim Crow in Heaven" (1950). Gospel announcer and promoter Otis Jackson wrote and recorded story songs—ballads in the truest sense—about African American heroes Dorie Miller, Mary McLeod Bethune, and the NAACP.

"The Story of Martin Luther King" by the Norfleet Brothers (1961) was among the first songs by a Chicago gospel group to pay homage to the civil rights leader. The A-side recounted King's organization of the Montgomery bus boycott, while the flipside told of the September 20, 1958, assassination attempt on King. It concluded with a brief description of King's October 1960 arrest for participating in Atlanta sit-ins.[49] The Norfleets further confirmed their commitment to message songs when they performed a nearly note-for-note cover of the Golden Gate Quartet's "No Segregation in Heaven" on a 1964 episode of *Jubilee Showcase*.

The Salem Travelers made message songs their trademark in the 1960s. The Chicago quartet was organized by Chester Feemster at Mahalia Jackson's home church, Greater Salem Baptist, in 1957. During the early 1960s, when they made their debut appearance on the second episode of *Jubilee Showcase*, the Salem Travelers consisted of Feemster, Arthur Davis, Timothy Bailey, James Morris, Samuel Hatchett, Tolman Thomas, and Bill Farel.[50] Their single "The Children Goin' Astray," written and led by Davis and released on Halo Records, a subsidiary of the soul label One-Derful, was the first of their socially relevant oeuvre. With the assistance of respected Chicago soul musician-songwriter-producer Milton Bland, aka Monk Higgins, this diatribe about children forsaking the church and turning to disruptive behavior was released in 1965. It became the quartet's first hit and initial calling card. Halo's release of the Golden Tones' "Why Can't We Love Our Fellow Man" shortly afterward was likely in response to the success of the Salem Travelers' disc.

Robert Dixon, who became the Salem Travelers' lead singer and longest lasting member, joined the quartet after the release of "Children."[51] Born in Memphis on May 19, 1941, Dixon moved to Arkansas after completing high school and migrated to Chicago in 1962, where he connected with two cousins who sang with the Spiritual Jubilaires quartet. Dixon stayed with the Jubilaires from 1962 to 1966, then joined the Clefs of Calvary, replacing James Phelps when he became a Soul Stirrer.

Dixon became a Salem Traveler in 1967. "Arthur Davis was the lead singer with the Salem Travelers before I got with them," Dixon reminisced, "and he was talking about going solo. The Salem Travelers talked to me about coming in to replace him, but he didn't leave. He stayed there and we all sang together."[52] Two years later, Dixon took over managing duties from Davis and henceforward handled the group's booking.

Besides Vee Jay, the Chicago record company with the largest catalog of gospel recordings during the golden age was Chess/Checker. Chess's most significant religious recording artist of the 1950s and 1960s was Rev. C. L. Franklin. The label not only reissued Franklin's vast collection of sermons, recorded live in Detroit by Joe Von Battle, it also reissued Von Battle's first disc of Franklin's teenaged daughter, Aretha. When Von Battle recorded sermons by Chicago pastor H. R. Jelks of Mount Pleasant Baptist Church, Chess issued those, too. Chess/Checker was the home of the Christland Singers, the Golden Harps, Sammy Lewis, Martha Bass, Harold Smith's Majestics, and the electric-guitar-toting evangelist, Elder Utah Smith of New Orleans, who recorded his famous theme, "Two Wings," for Checker in July 1953 while in Chicago to appear on a gospel program.

Veteran record man Ralph Bass joined Chess Records in 1959 after a successful seven-year run with Federal Records, a King Records subsidiary. He started his career with the Los Angeles–based Black & White Records in 1945, the label that produced the first discs by the St. Paul COGIC Choir of Chicago. He joined Savoy Records in 1948 and moved to Federal in 1951, where he helped launch the careers of stars such as the Platters, the Dominoes, James Brown, and "Baby Shirley" Caesar. A falling out with King's founder Syd Nathan brought him to the doorstep of Chess.[53] As A&R man for the Checker subsidiary, Bass was eager to inject a youthful groove into gospel. Since quartets and groups such as the Violinaires, the Meditation Singers, the Soul Stirrers, and the Salem Travelers already had a propensity for soulful and sonorous instrumentation, bass-driven rhythmic drive, and hard singing, Bass focused his attention on them.

The musical blending of gospel, R&B, and soul with lyrics that replaced the theme of people's relationship to God with their relationship to their brothers and sisters became known as gos-pop. "The message of gos-pop," Bass told *Billboard*, "is that there is more to gospel than just finding solace in the church. This follows the same message of Martin King, who was fighting for a new way of life. Kids are tired of hearing 'Jesus Give Us Help.' They want a positive message. Gos-pop teaches a way of life." For Checker's part, Bass said, "I'm using horns and an r&b sound in gospel recordings. We have no charts. All the musicians are given the chord changes. I want the cats to think when we're cutting. I want spontaneity, and that's what we're getting."[54]

The Salem Travelers signed with Checker and recorded their first album in February 1968. The quartet's decision to incorporate songs of social significance into their repertory "was conscious," Dixon said. "And then Chess Records, the producers, wanted us to do that. They said we had that kind of style that we could sing that kind of stuff."[55] What the Chess team of Gene Barge, Sonny Thompson, and Ralph Bass heard and augmented was the soulful, hard-driving vocal delivery and musical combination of drums, electric guitar, and electric bass assembled by Monk Higgins at Halo. By the mid-1960s, this instrumental combination was de rigueur in African American sacred and secular music. Slowly but perceptibly, the musicians started to assert themselves from the background to near-equal footing with the vocalists.

One selection from the Salem Travelers' initial session for Chess, "Give Me Liberty or Give Me Death," was an Arthur Davis tribute to the "young men and young women" working for freedom. Set to an urgent, aggressive march tempo, it was an example of Bass's music vision. Davis sang:

They learned that the word freedom,

They've learned it is not just a word.

They've been run over by horses and bit by dogs.

Davis saved the declamatory call to action for the chorus: "Give us liberty or give us death."[56]

Gos-pop fueled the Salem Travelers appearance on the heralded stage of New York's Apollo Theater as part of George Hudson's Gospel USA tour, which included James Cleveland and the Cleveland Singers, the Mighty Clouds of Joy, the Violinaires, the Pilgrim Jubilees, and Rev. Claude Jeter of the Swan Silvertones.[57] "We were singing in the Apollo Theater when Martin Luther King got killed," Dixon said. "Arthur Davis sang ['Give Me Liberty or Give Me Death']. We were supposed to be there ten days; I think we were there about seven. They had to close everything down because of the riots."[58]

On Thursday afternoon, April 4, 1968, King, Ralph Abernathy, Rev. Jesse Jackson, and former Maceo Woods Singer Rev. Billy Kyles were gathered at the Lorraine Motel in Memphis. They were preparing to drive to Kyles's Memphis home for dinner, then to Mason Hall for a rally in support of the striking garbage collectors. Jackson introduced King to saxophonist and singer Ben Branch. An employee of Lyon & Healy's organ sales department and an artist under contract to Chess Records, Branch was also a member of Jackson's twenty-piece Operation Breadbasket Orchestra, in Memphis to perform at the rally. King leaned over the iron railing and said to Branch, "Ben, I want you to sing 'Precious Lord' for me tonight like you never sung it before. Want you to sing it *real* pretty." "Ok, Doc, I will," Branch responded.[59]

As the group waited for Abernathy, who had gone back into room 306 to slap on some aftershave, King's driver, Solomon Jones, advised King to don a coat because the weather was getting chilly. The next thing the group heard was a rifle clap. King lay on the balcony walkway, his head shrouded in blood.[60] Kyles and Abernathy rushed to his side, and Kyles covered him with a bedspread. An ambulance sped King to the Emergency Room of St. Joseph's Hospital, where he was pronounced dead at 7:05 p.m.[61]

Betty Washington reported for the *Defender* that the first prayer vigil took place in Chicago at Liberty Baptist Church. The fifteen-hundred-seat church was already filled to brimming as Rev. Clay Evans approached the pulpit and tried to calm the crowd, especially the younger members who were shouting, "Black Power!" and "Damn the honkies!" "This is a time for us to be united," Evans declared. "Dr. King would not want violence. He was a non-violent man." One youth said, "Martin Luther King warned that there was going to be violence this summer, and there is going to be violence this summer." Evans appealed, "Please, can we go on with the service we have planned tonight? A vigil and prayer meeting. We'll stay here all night." At that point, Liberty's pastor, Rev. A. P. Jackson, stepped forward. "I have no reason to doubt the feelings all of us have about the dastardly act that took place in the Lorraine Motel in Memphis. . . . We are determined that his death will not be unavenged. We are not going to take this lying down."[62]

The seething anger and grief could not be assuaged. From Friday afternoon, April 5, through Palm Sunday, April 7, Chicago's West Side was engulfed in flames from rioting. One observer described sections of Madison Street and Roosevelt Road as resembling "the war torn cities of World War II."[63] In the aftermath of King's death, 110 U.S. cities experienced riots that left thirty-nine dead, mostly African Americans.[64]

The first portion of King's funeral took place at Ebenezer Baptist Church in Atlanta. Some eight hundred family, friends, and associates were allowed into the church, while between sixty thousand and eighty thousand mourned outside on the sidewalk and street.[65] A procession, with the casket in a wagon pulled by a mule, moved toward Morehouse College, his alma mater, where his body lay in state outside Harkness Hall. Mahalia Jackson, in Los Angeles recording her latest album, *A Mighty Fortress*, came immediately to the funeral. At Morehouse, she sang "Take My Hand, Precious Lord." Michael Kiliana, reporting in the *Chicago Tribune*, called her singing at Morehouse "the most sacred moment" of the funeral. "Mahalia Jackson sang ['Precious Lord'], her eyes closed, her face upturned. There was a long silence afterward."[66]

King's assassination spawned several tribute recordings. Nina Simone, who had performed at the 1965 Selma to Montgomery march, recorded the somber "Why (the King of Love Is Dead)" at the Westbury Music Fair twenty-four hours after King's death.[67] Artists such as the Loving Sisters of Arkansas and the Swan Silvertones' Rev. Claude Jeter expressed their sorrows on disc, just as gospel singers did following the assassination of President John F. Kennedy in November 1963.

The first recorded King tribute from Chicago was *The Last Request*. Recorded April 17 and 18, 1968, the album-length salute was in posthumous fulfillment of King's request for Branch to perform "Take My Hand, Precious Lord," at the April 4 rally. Rev. Clay Evans sang "Motherless Child." On the nine-minute "Take My Hand, Precious Lord," Branch wailed mournful sobs on the saxophone, with "beauty and power," according to *Billboard*.[68] Rev. Sammy Lewis, undoubtedly vindicated after earlier attacks on his alleged lack of participation in the movement, performed "Yield Not to Temptation." The Operation Breadbasket choir also sang.[69] Among the musicians accompanying Branch were bassist Phil Upchurch, Leonard Caston on piano and organ, and Charles Stepney on organ for "Hard Times." Chess promoted the album vigorously, and royalties were to be contributed in King's memory to Operation Breadbasket, the economic arm of the SCLC led by Rev. Jesse Jackson.[70] Meanwhile, Columbia compiled a handful of previously recorded Mahalia Jackson songs, including "We Shall Overcome," "How I Got Over," and the 1956 recording of "Precious Lord," and released them as *Sings the Best-Loved Hymns of Dr. Martin Luther King, Jr.* sometime in late May or early June 1968.[71]

Shirley Wahls was another Chicago resident who paid her respects to King on vinyl. By 1968, Wahls was a vocal group veteran, having spent the better part of the 1960s as a member of the Argo Singers, the Gertrude Ward Singers, and the Dorothy Norwood Singers. In the 1970s, Minnie Riperton referred Wahls to Stepney, who selected her for membership in the Rotary Connection, an innovative soul/jazz ensemble. Wahls also did background vocals for many recordings, including Garland Green's "Jealous Kind of Fella," and in 1968 was writing and recording with Jo Armstead at Mercury and Giant Records. With Armstead's blessing, Wahls wrote and performed "We've Got to Keep Movin'

On" for the Mercury subsidiary Smash, and donated the proceeds to Operation Breadbasket.[72] Bathed in a Motown-esque soul sensibility, "Moving" was Wahls's plea to not forget King's dream of unity. She sang: "All of you young still in school, / Let his dream be your golden rule" and "We've got to reach the top of the mountain / Follow his dream and move along." In 1976, Wahls also recorded "Remember Martin Luther King" for Blue Candle Records with pianist, arranger, and producer Tom Washington, known for his work with the Esquires, Gene Chandler, and the Chi-Lites. "When we lost Martin, the world lost a friend," Wahls wailed on the single. "But don't worry, Martin, I'll see you again."[73]

The Salem Travelers did not record again until several months after King's death. Among their first recordings, in August 1968, was a tune for a Checker Christmas collection, where the group contributed "A Letter for Christmas." It was an incisive protest against the horrors of the Vietnam War, in which the singer receives a letter from his brother fighting in Vietnam. Although the brother wants to come home for Christmas, it is evident that he wants to come home, period. "It's bad living here," the letter reads. "Everyday you're living in fear. Knowing when you lay down at night, / In the morning you might not be here." The letter concludes: "This is between you and I, / I might not see the family again, / If I don't, tell them I said goodbye."

Other socially relevant Salem Travelers songs included "These Are Trying Times" (1968), "Keep On Holding On" (1969), "What You Gonna Do (1970)" "Troubles of This World" (1970), and "Tell It Like It Is (1968)."[74] On "Tell It Like It Is," Dixon lamented that those who are criticized and scorned were "sick and tired of waiting for something to be done." To stinging psychedelic guitar riffs, Dixon declared: "Don't you bite your tongue / Don't be afraid to speak" and "There's gonna be a brighter day." Dixon appeared to be echoing the frustrations of the Black Power movement, whose youth were growing disillusioned with the promise of a nonviolent multicultural solution. On the other hand, his conclusion—"The black and white should take a stand and rid this hate"—sympathized with King's integrationist stance and Wahls's message of unity on "We've Got to Keep Movin' On." Similarly, during a 1969 episode of *Jubilee Showcase*, the Emanon Choral Ensemble, a contemporary community choir led by Chicago-born director Charles Geiger, presented a complex but heartwarmingly rendered ode to tranquility called "Peace, Brother, Peace."

On Easter Sunday, April 6, 1969, on the one-year anniversary of King's assassination, Sid Ordower dedicated an entire episode of *Jubilee Showcase* to the fallen leader. On hand to pay tribute were DeLois Barrett Campbell, Rev. Clay Evans, Rev. Jesse Jackson, and the Operation Breadbasket Choir, codirected by Frederick Young and Billy Jones. To Dorsey's "Take My Hand, Precious Lord," sung by the choir with organ and piano accompaniment, Jackson reflected on King's final days and moments. He concluded, "It is significant to me that [King] went through this trauma en route to his own crucifixion for the sake of peace in the world, but that he went with the conviction that he was not alone. And he asked the Lord to take his hand. . . . And it is so fitting that he went out asking the precious Lord to lead his hand."[75] The program was so popular with audiences that ABC rebroadcast the episode on the two subsequent Easter Sundays.[76]

In late 1968, Ralph Bass reported before a committee of the National Association of Television and Radio Artists (NATRA) that "several [radio] stations received tremendous audience ratings after the death of Dr. Martin Luther King when these outlets were programming gospel exclusively." He believed that professionally produced commercials featuring the music of top gospel artists could be a boon to their careers.[77]

Daniel Goldberg reported in the August 16, 1969, issue of *Billboard* that Ralph Bass "believes that people now have the need for the kind of spiritual message that gospel provides, and that if presented correctly, gospel offers a great appeal for the mass market."[78] Songs such as "Give Me Liberty or Death," "Tell It Like It Is," and the Meditations' "Stand Up and Be Counted" and "It's Wrong to Fight," fit snugly within the oeuvre of socially conscious R&B songs with insistent rhythm sections.

In other words, gospel groups were taking up a "new walk," a musical swagger that articulated the self-assuredness of the latent black pride movement. One of these groups was the Lucy Rodgers Singers. The daughter-in-law of Rev. C. J. Rodgers, a recording preacher and pastor of Mount Eagle Baptist Church, Lucy was Mount Eagle's minister of music. As of the mid-1960s, the personnel in her all-female group included Edna Thomas, Virginia Riley, and Geneva Dudley.[79] In August 1966, her group released the apocryphal "I'm Fighting for My Rights" on Saint Lawrence, a local label whose stable of gospel artists included groups that had, or would, record for Checker. Monk Higgins produced and cowrote "Fighting," which found Rodgers cloaked as a Christian soldier, sword and shield in hand, fighting to earn her final reward, all to a loping I–IV–V–IV boogie-woogie arrangement. Although the "soldier in the army of the Lord" theme was common in gospel music, especially among Pentecostal churches, the use of "rights" in the song title linked the purpose of Rodgers's battle implicitly with the freedom movement. Further, Rodgers's line, "I was injured," must have resonated with movement workers who endured physical and psychological abuse on the journey to freedom. Rodgers rerecorded the song a year later for a Checker album, accompanied by Mount Eagle's Angelic Choir and Higgins as producer. Her bluesy Baptist shout and improvisational abilities, notably on "Sign My Name," attested to her nickname, "Sister Soul."

If, as Brian Ward suggests, the gospel ingredient in the work of soul stars such as Ray Charles and James Brown reflected and stimulated the black pride movement, it was a two-way street—young gospel artists of the late 1960s absorbed the arrangements, musicianship, and self-confident lyrics of soul.[80] Even some groups' performance attire reflected the more flamboyant fashions found on the streets of African American neighborhoods in large cities. Ironically, the gos-pop sound honed in Chicago inspired the contemporary gospel sound that ultimately shifted the locus of power away from the Windy City. The dominant "sacred expression of black modernity" in the 1970s would come from the West Coast.

CHAPTER 17

One of These Mornings
Chicago Gospel at the Crossroads

One of these mornings, it won't be very long,
You'll look for me, and I'll be gone.

**"Walk around Heaven All Day," as sung by Cassietta George
and credited to the Caravans**

In September 1968, the Roberta Martin Singers entered the studio to record *Praise God*, their first album in two years and, as it turned out, their last. With Rev. Lawrence Roberts at the helm, *Praise God* contained new songs as well as nearly note-for-note retreads of Apollo-era hits, such as Norsalus McKissick's "Saved" and DeLois Barrett Campbell's "Come into My Heart, Lord Jesus." The main difference was the inclusion of drums, which gave the group's classic sound enough of a contemporary vibe to attract younger gospel enthusiasts. According to Savoy's publicity department, *Praise God* was the release that prompted Joe Bostic to comment: "That's the Roberta Martin sound as only they can do it: rich, restful, and righteous."[1]

Martin's final solo recording, "I Have Hope," provided aural testimony to the remaining strength in her voice, if not her body, as she sang with more diaphragmatic power than usual. "I hope you understand what I meant by that song," she told her husband after she learned that her cancer was terminal. "'I Have Hope,' a beautiful hope of the future, you know it was Christ, not hope of getting well."[2] She died Monday, January 13, 1969, one month short of her sixty-second birthday.[3]

Martin's funeral was held Sunday, January 19, at Mount Pisgah Baptist Church at Forty-Sixth Street and King Drive, where she had served as music director from 1956 to 1968. The funeral was reported to have attracted more than fifty thousand mourners, the largest for an African American celebrity in the city's history—more than clogged the South Side's arterials in 1952 for Elder Lucy Smith or in 1964 for Sam Cooke.[4]

Martin's son, Leonard Austin, recalled the service. "I went in and I sat down next to my dad. I was there about twenty minutes, and I kept hearing all these people behind me. I looked, and there was no place in the church for nothing but air. There was no room for another human being to get in that church. Not a place, not a spot could you find in that church, and [Mount Pisgah] is a big church."[5]

Rev. Joseph Wells delivered the eulogy. A cavalcade of gospel singers, including DeLois Barrett Campbell and Lucy Rodgers, sang their final farewells to their beloved Miss Martin, who was interred the following morning in Burr Oak Cemetery, near other family members.[6] "When we got to the cemetery, her grave wasn't dug," Leonard said. "They dug the grave with the same [model] tractor we had up in Michigan, and I just freaked, I just freaked."[7] Martin's marker was a standard flat rectangle stone, barely visible above the grass. The "Helen Hayes of Gospel" was unpretentious and humble, even in death. Norsalus McKissick and the Barrett Sisters saluted Martin by singing "Old Ship of Zion" and "Grace" on an October 1969 episode of *Jubilee Showcase*. An admirable effort was made to keep the Roberta Martin Singers going after its leader's death, but by the end of 1970, the group had disbanded, thirty-seven years after its formation.

"Listen, there has never been, and never will be, another Roberta Martin," remarked Eugene Smith.[8] "I have said many times if Miss Martin didn't make it in [heaven], then everybody else ought to stop and forget it."[9]

Mahalia Jackson was the next major Chicago gospel singer to cross from labor to reward. After becoming ill while touring in Europe, the Queen of Gospel was flown home from Germany and arrived in Chicago on October 23, 1971. The diagnosis was coronary artery disease or sarcoidosis, depending on the consulting doctor.[10] Jackson never regained her full strength and was admitted to Little Company of Mary in Oak Lawn, Illinois, on Wednesday, January 19, 1972. She entered surgery on Monday, January 24, and, despite a brief resurgence of postsurgical energy, suffered a heart seizure and died Thursday, January 27.[11]

The Queen of Gospel received no less than three funeral services. The first, on January 31, was held at her home church, Greater Salem Baptist, now on

Seventy-First Street. Despite bitter Chicago winter winds, the mourners' line began forming the night before. The next day, more than forty thousand processed past Jackson's casket.[12] Jules Schwerin described the deceased as "dressed in a long blue gown with golden threads. . . . Her hands, encased in white gloves, held a large Bible opened to the 20th Psalm of David."[13] Sallie Martin paid tribute to her longtime associate by singing Dorsey's "It Don't Cost Very Much," and Clara Ward sang "Beams of Heaven."[14]

To accommodate the multitudes who were unable to squeeze into Greater Salem, Chicago mayor Richard J. Daley organized a second funeral service at Arie Crown Theater on February 1.[15] Ella Fitzgerald, Coretta Scott King, Ray Charles, Pearl Bailey, Studs Terkel, Berry Gordy, and Ralph Abernathy were among the six thousand seated. Two thousand additional mourners were turned away.[16] Daley and Illinois governor Richard Ogilvie attended the service, and Sammy Davis Jr. represented President Richard M. Nixon. Sallie Martin, Thomas Dorsey, Albertina Walker, the Gay Sisters, Eugene Smith, and the Staple Singers were among the Chicago gospel community present to remember one of their own.[17] Mildred Falls accompanied Robert Anderson, who sang "Move On Up a Little Higher." DeLois Barrett Campbell sang "Until Then;" Anthony Heilbut notes that when J. Robert "Mr. Baptist" Bradley sang "I'll Fly Away" as "a slow, emotionally devastating funeral dirge," Jackson's former accompanist James Lee "wound up collapsed on the floor."[18] When at the conclusion, Aretha Franklin rendered "Precious Lord," two teenaged mourners were carried out.[19] Coretta Scott King received a five-minute standing ovation; she said, weeping, "She's not dead. She lives in the hearts and souls of each one of us."

Forty-five years after arriving in Chicago in a dingy, dusty section of a passenger train, Jackson returned to New Orleans aboard an airplane. Upon arrival, a funeral cortege collected her casket and then wound its way to the downtown area, passing crowds who had gathered to remember the woman who introduced gospel music to the entire world.[20] The cortege stopped at the Rivergate Convention Hall, where sixty thousand mourners processed past her casket.[21] Some five thousand attended her funeral service at the convention hall, but the day was not without controversy. Rev. Simmi Harbey, pastor of Jackson's childhood church, Mount Moriah, told reporters, "When Mahalia was here last year to bury her niece, she told me that if anything happened to her she wanted to come back to Mount Moriah." He said Jackson's nephew, Allen Clark, had helped him with the arrangements, but a last-minute change moved the services to the convention center. Harbey was told it was a family decision, but he considered it "political maneuvering." He added: "I was asked by several people after the change was announced not to let Mahalia down. . . . Now I don't know what's going to happen."[22]

What happened was the Rivergate program went on as planned. Bessie Griffin paid tribute to her fellow New Orleans sister with "Move On Up a Little Higher."[23] On February 4, 1972, Jackson was buried in Providence Memorial Park in nearby Metairie, Louisiana.[24] In contrast to Roberta Martin's humble marker, Mahalia Jackson's headstone was enormous, fit for a queen.

"Gonna Be Some Changes Made"

Jules Schwerin has called Mahalia Jackson's death the "eclipse of gospel's golden age," but Roberta Martin's passing three years earlier was also emblematic of the fading of the traditional sound.[25] To what extent gospel was changing became supremely evident in 1968, when a track from a privately recorded album by a California youth choir became a Top 40 pop hit.

In the early 1960s, Edwin Hawkins and Betty Watson of Oakland, California, formed the Northern California State Youth Choir of the Church of God in Christ. In 1968, they wanted to record the choir and hired Lamont Bench to engineer a custom pressing, released on the aptly titled Custom label. Five hundred copies of *Let Us Go into the House of the Lord* were pressed, and five hundred sold. That might have been the end of the story, but a disk jockey at San Francisco's KSAN began playing one of the album's selections, "Oh Happy Day," on his radio show. It was a soulfully mellow arrangement of an old hymn with lead singer Dorothy Morrison accenting the choir's dynamic ebbs and flows with gospel runs and trills. WVON broke "Oh Happy Day" in Chicago and other cities followed suit. Major record companies entered into a bidding war for the record, and Neil Bogart's Buddah Records scored the winning offer. "Oh Happy Day," by the renamed Edwin Hawkins Singers, became a Top 40 hit.[26] The smooth contemporary sound dominated gospel music on record, radio, and television for the next two decades.

The overwhelming success of "Oh Happy Day" was the natural culmination of an incremental transition in the gospel music field that began even before the 1959 Detroit Invasion. During the late 1950s, Leon Lumpkins and the Gospel Clefs of Newark displayed a flair for complex arrangements and distinctive melodies that predicted, and perhaps stimulated, departures from the standard gospel sound. Other early contemporary gospel composers included Bernard Upshaw and the Psalmeneers, and Andraé and Sandra Crouch and the Disciples. At the same time that the Hawkins Family was gaining widespread acceptance, the Rance Allen Group—COGIC youth Rance, Steve, and Tom Allen of Monroe, Michigan—were injecting inspirational music with the energy and excitement of soul and funk.

Youth have always been at the forefront of musical change, and gospel was no different. Noted Guthrie Ramsey: "While church leadership has generally guarded and cherished the notions of tradition and convention, forces from within the church (more often than not the younger generation) have defied the older heads . . . and claimed stylistic change as an artistic priority."[27] It even impacted *Jubilee Showcase*. On a 1969 episode, Sid Ordower announced that they were adding "folk and inspirational" music to the show's regular helping of gospel, jubilee, and spirituals.

Was Chicago's churchy traditional sound antiquated against this new sacred backdrop? Aretha Franklin was among the first to say no. The Queen of Soul had just made her acting debut, playing a gospel singer on the TV sitcom *Room 222*, and was about to celebrate her Baptist upbringing on record.[28] She joined Rev. James Cleveland and his Southern California Community Choir at New Temple Missionary Baptist Church in the Watts section of Los Angeles on January 13, 1972, for two days of live recording for her first gospel album, the double album *Amazing Grace*. The Franklin-Cleveland combination made sense. Franklin was Cleveland's artistic protégé during his days in Detroit, when she was young and learning. He was now a pastor of a Southern California church, training and promoting gospel choirs with the evangelistic fervor of Dorsey and Martin in the 1930s.

In *Amazing Grace*, the first book-length exploration of Franklin's monumental gospel album, *Downbeat* assistant editor Aaron Cohen notes that Franklin could just as easily have included original songs or reworked hymns in the fashion of the Edwin Hawkins Singers or the gos-pop of Ralph Bass and Monk Higgins. Instead, she drew from the golden age of gospel canon.[29] Giving them her own touch, Franklin rendered gospel songs and hymns such as "God Will Take Care of You," "Precious Lord," "How I Got Over," "Mary, Don't You Weep," and the version of "Never Grow Old" learned from Billy Kyles and the Maceo Woods Singers. Twenty years after its release, *Amazing Grace* was certified Double Platinum by the Recording Industry Association of America (RIAA), meaning it had sold two million copies.[30] It became Franklin's bestselling album, demonstrating the power of traditional gospel to transcend changes in music styles.

Meanwhile, in Memphis, Stax Records created the Gospel Truth subsidiary to release the Rance Allen Group's bold inspirational music but also signed Rev. Maceo Woods's more traditional Christian Tabernacle Concert Choir. Former Peacock A&R man Dave Clark, who directed the new label, echoed the music marketing philosophy of Ralph Bass when he called Gospel Truth a melding of "truth lyrics" with contemporary sounds. Youth interest in gospel, Clark told *Billboard* in 1972, had "never been higher," noting, "We have also seen that more kids are attending gospel concerts—it's no longer a strictly middle-aged audience."[31]

Like Christian Tabernacle, the Thompson Community Singers extended and broadened their reputation well into the 1980s. Church music ministers awaited each new Tommies release with eager anticipation, knowing it would provide new songs and arrangements to teach their church and community choirs. Like Christian Tabernacle, Reverend Brunson's community choir remained a strong presence on *Billboard*'s Top Gospel Albums charts and garnered several hit singles. It also earned a Grammy Award, multiple Stellar Awards (the highest award in gospel music), and was inducted into the Gospel Music Hall of Fame in 1998. Six years later, Tommies alumni Darius Brooks and Percy Bady reunited other former members and released an album of the choir's best-known selections.

In 1971, Rev. Clay Evans inked a deal to record the Fellowship Missionary Baptist Church Choir on Stan Lewis's Shreveport, Louisiana-based Jewel Records.[32] With Lou Della Evans Reid as director and featuring vocalists such as Jeanette Robinson Jones of the Helen Robinson Youth Chorus, the choir's Jewel albums delivered enough gospel singles and albums to merit a best of collection in 1980.

Charles G. Hayes's Cosmopolitan Church of Prayer Choir, with Allen Cathey as music minister, released a stream of double albums on Savoy Records that expanded on Charles Clency's churchy vibe and musical innovation. Lead singers such as Dianne Williams, Michele Brown, and Herbert Williams led high-octane performances that earned the group the nickname "The Warriors." Cathey recalled the circumstances behind the Warriors' smash hit, George Jordan's "Jesus Can Work It Out:"

> At first, Herbert Williams was singing it. It didn't work right with him, so I suggested to Shelby [Wills], "Why don't you try Diane [Williams] on 'Jesus Can Work It Out'?" We got in rehearsal, Diane sang it, but on the night of the recording, we did not know that she was going to put in all that she did. She started talking about baby needs shoes, and I said, "What is this girl talking about?" She was like rapping. I said, "Oh God, this girl has messed up the record! These people are going to boo us!" In a church, rapping? No churches were doing stuff like that in those days. I was scared, I was mad at her for doing that but it worked out.[33]

Not only did "Jesus Can Work It Out" become the Warriors' signature song; it also signaled gospel's continued distinction as a music of the here and now. In the vamp, Williams let loose with a litany of specific economic woes that Jesus could fix, including needing money to buy shoes for the baby, pay utility expenses, and cancel the telephone disconnect notice. The litany struck a chord with those in the audience who could relate to never-ending financial challenges.

Of all Chicago residents who contributed to the expansion of the gospel chorus, James Cleveland deserves the greatest credit. In 1967, he organized the

Gospel Music Workshop of America (GMWA) to foster greater collaboration among gospel artists and provide an alternative confab to the National Convention of Gospel Choirs and Choruses for singers and musicians to learn from one another. Further, the *James Cleveland Presents* series on Savoy Records helped many church choirs receive national recognition. Los Angeles gospel choir director Alexander Hamilton told Aaron Cohen, "I think [Cleveland] had eight, ten albums a year he had to do. Way it worked was all he had to do was have his name on it and [sing] one song to get paid. . . . He would look around to the good groups and say, 'I'm James Cleveland and will get you on Savoy.' We'd do one marathon, six, seven hour session and the album would be done. It would be 'James Cleveland Presents . . .' and he became known as the Star Maker . . . That made him rich."[34] The Chicago choirs that recorded on Savoy through Cleveland's intervention included Christian Tabernacle, Cosmopolitan Church of Prayer, New Friendship Baptist—the pastor, Rev. Harold Freeman, was an early member of the GMWA Board—and Bishop Jerry Goodloe's Lighthouse Baptist Church, where in 1981 Albertina Walker led the choir on Calvin Bridges's hand-clapping "I Can Go to God in Prayer."

Greater Metropolitan Church of Christ, founded by Rev. Dr. Issac Whittmon, a longtime associate of Cleveland, was another beneficiary of *James Cleveland Presents*. The series' *The Lord Is My Light*, which featured a Cleveland and Whittmon duet on the title track, garnered a Grammy nomination in 1977.[35]

Although gospel music was moving forward, Chicago's gospel pioneers were getting long-overdue accolades. George Nierenberg's 1980 documentary film, *Say Amen, Somebody*, featured classic footage of gospel pioneers Dorsey, Sallie Martin, the Barrett Sisters, and Willie Mae Ford Smith at the National Convention of Gospel Choirs and Choruses convocation in St. Louis. The Barrett Sisters' heartwarming and soul-stirring performances, and the documentary's reception by the press—film critic Roger Ebert called it "one of the most joyful movies I've ever seen"—turned the sisters into national celebrities. They appeared on *The Tonight Show, Starring Johnny Carson* and *The Oprah Winfrey Show*, sang at folk festivals, and toured the world. They were the only gospel group invited to participate in the Black Music Seminar at the Kennedy Center.

In 1981, historians Pearl Williams-Jones and Bernice Johnson Reagon, along with the Smithsonian Division of Performing Arts, Program in African American Culture, organized a conference to honor pioneering composers of gospel music. Dorsey, Kenneth Morris, and Roberta Martin were among those celebrated. The centerpiece of the first conference, which honored Martin, featured a reunion of nine members of the Roberta Martin Singers. The group sang songs from the Martin catalog and participated in a roundtable discussion on the significance of their mentor, whom Reagon called "the dean of the ensemble sound of classic gospel performance."[36]

The Gospel Arts Workshop created the first known modern gospel festival when it presented "O for a Thousand Tongues to Sing" at the James C. Petrillo Bandshell in Chicago's Grant Park on Saturday, June 14, 1980. The festival, which attracted 12,700 attendees and honored gospel pioneers Thomas Dorsey, Sallie Martin, and Julia Mae Kennedy, featured a 350-voice mass choir and twenty-seven musicians along with the First Church of Deliverance Choir. California-based recording artist Tramaine Hawkins of the Hawkins Family was the special guest on a program that included many of the Chicago gospel community's crème de la crème, such as Robert Anderson, DeLois Barrett Campbell and the Barrett Sisters, Albertina Walker, Jessy Dixon, and Sara Jordan Powell. Two years later, in June 1982, L. Stanley Davis and the Gospel Arts Workshop produced the second gospel festival, which provided an audience of 27,000 a program by the 350-voice mass choir and special guests Walter Hawkins and the Hawkins Family.

On June 15, 1985, a group including L. Stanley Davis, Frederick Young, and Lena McLin, staged Chicago's third modern gospel festival. Held at the South Side Country Club, the free-admission Thomas A. Dorsey Gospel Fest evoked the Billiken Gospel Festivals of the 1950s and 1960s, attracting a variety of top local and national talent, such as the Rance Allen Group, Andraé Crouch, Al Green, Albertina Walker, and the Norfleet Brothers. A tribute choir paid homage to the festival's namesake. Later, Sasha Daltonn took the program back to Grant Park.[37] The Mayor's Office of Special Events once again assumed responsibility for the festival, and gospel announcer Pam Morris directed the festivities until her retirement in the late 2000s. Billed as the world's largest free outdoor gospel festival, and drawing as many as 260,000 attendees, Chicago Gospel Fest continues to attract the genre's top stars alongside local favorites and, depending on the year, has included a quartet stage, youth tents, and special tributes to gospel music's legends, especially those from the Windy City.

The 1980s and 1990s witnessed the rise of new Chicago community choirs, such as Walt Whitman and the Soul Children, Dan Willis and the Pentecostals of Chicago, and Ricky Dillard and the New Generation Chorale. Dillard's "More Abundantly," with its cascading parts, became a gospel choir standard. In 1971, while in high school, James C. Chambers organized the Ecclesiastes Community Choir (ECC). It became the Chicago Mass Choir in 1988 and has since traveled the world and been nominated for ten Stellar Awards and two Grammy Awards. Feranda Williamson, alumna of the ECC and the Christian Tabernacle Concert Choir, is now president and CEO of the Chicago Mass Choir.

In addition to new chorales, long-standing groups such as the Wooten Choral Ensemble continue to attract crowds. Gospel choirs representing Trinity United Church of Christ, Apostolic Church of God, and Christ Universal Temple have performed at nontraditional venues such as Orchestra Hall and the Ravinia Festival. Meanwhile, entrepreneur Willie Wilson's *Singsation*, a television program once hosted by Vickie Winans, has continued *Jubilee Showcase*'s legacy of providing local gospel talent with another vehicle for exposure.

In 1985, Chicago-based television producer Don Jackson, whose Central City Productions made its name televising the annual Bud Billiken Parade, staged the first Stellar Gospel Music Awards at the Arie Crown Theater. Today, the Stellar Awards is the top awards program for African American gospel artists, and the main event—considered the biggest night for gospel music—is televised across the country.

All the while, the roster of living gospel pioneers was shrinking. Sallie Martin died in Chicago on June 18, 1988. Three years later, on February 9, 1991, James Cleveland died. Thomas Dorsey succumbed in Chicago on January 23, 1993. In tribute, Anthony Heilbut gathered a few of the remaining faithful to produce *The Soul of Chicago*. Akin to a gospel jam session, the recording at Paul Serrano's P. S. Studios was a reunion of the city's sacred music stalwarts, including Robert Anderson, the Golden Harps, the Gay Sisters, Eugene Smith, DeLois Barrett Campbell, Lucy Smith Collier, Irma Gwynn, Gladys Beamon Gregory, Bessie Folk, Vernon Oliver Price, and guitarist Rev. Sammy Patterson. Musicians such as Nash Shaffer, Charles Pikes, and Jonathan DuBose accompanied the artists in an informal, dignified, and ultimately joyous celebration of the uniquely American art form as it was born and fostered in Chicago.

On July 15, 1998, Roberta Martin, Mahalia Jackson, Sister Rosetta Tharpe, and Clara Ward were honored by the United States Postal Service (USPS) as part of its commemorative stamp series, "Legends of American Music." Four thirty-two-cent stamps, designed by Gary Kelley, featured their likenesses. The unveiling ceremony took place at the New Orleans Superdome during the Full Gospel Baptist Church Fellowship Conference.[38] The previous year, Illinois congressman Danny Davis introduced a bill to redesignate the Post Office branch at 324 North Laramie Street in Chicago in memory of Rev. Milton Brunson, who died April 1, 1997, at age sixty-seven.[39] The Reverend Milton R. Brunson Post Office building was dedicated in 1998. "He set high standards," Davis told Congress, "and thus his choir turned out members who would go on to become lawyers, doctors, teachers, judges, and gospel singers, as well as other productive citizens in society."[40]

Davis's remarks echoed Donald Vails's own when, in 1986, the Detroit gospel singer-songwriter summarized the generational changes that had taken place since gospel music began. "The grandchildren of the maids, the janitors, the cooks, now hold PhDs," he wrote. "They're now computer analysts and programmers, attorneys and physicians. They're the principals and superintendents of schools their forebears couldn't attend. Some now live in houses where once they could only have been servants. God has allowed them to exchange mules for Cadillacs, riding streetcars for Mercedes." He added, "Although our journey has been a long one, we 'still have miles to go before we sleep.'"[41]

Although current gospel stars such as Kirk Franklin, Mary Mary, and Marvin Sapp dominate gospel radio, television, and recordings, traditional sightings in Chicago are still possible. On many weekends during the year, especially on the West Side, quartet enthusiasts can enjoy programs featuring Deacon Reuben Burton and the Victory Travelers—now the city's hottest quartet—the Pilgrim Jubilees, the Willing Four, the Stars of Heaven, the Mixon Singers, the Douglas Singers, and many other locally popular groups. Golden-age gospel singers Vernon Oliver Price, Dolores "Honey" Sykes, Doris Sykes, Lorenza Brown Porter, Bertha Melson, Catherine Austin Baymon, and Dolores Washington continue to make the rounds of churches, anniversary celebrations, and funerals. Frequently, Stanley Keeble or Richard Gibbs Jr. are their accompanists, sometimes on the spur of the moment. Kenneth Woods Jr. and Charles Clency are active choir directors. While none have achieved the monetary gains their talent deserved, they press on, propelled by their abiding faith and because the local gospel music community is a family. In that family is a new generation of soloists, such as Lemmie Battles, Angela Spivey, LaVarnga Hubbard, Queenie Lenox, LuVonia Whittley, Debbie Orange, Shirley Bell, Leanne Faine, and Malcolm Williams. They look to the legends for inspiration.

Their numbers have diminished, but first- and second-generation gospel singers still turn out for tribute programs and artist anniversaries. So many gospel artists honored Delores "Honey" Sykes of the Duncanaires on October 22, 2005, that the group photo was the Chicago gospel equivalent of the iconic jazz photograph, *A Great Day in Harlem*. On March 15, 2009, the believers celebrated Geraldine Gay Hambric's birthday at the family's small South Side church, Prayer Center COGIC. Lorenza Brown Porter of the Argo Singers and Bertha Melson of the Lux Singers each sang. Jessy Dixon joined Pastor Donald Gay at the altar. Eugene Smith did not sing but spoke passionately about the history of gospel music.

A year later, Eugene Smith was dead. DeLois Barrett Campbell and the Barrett Sisters sang at his funeral service. Although DeLois's husky soprano was hushed to a whisper from a long illness, her smile was as illuminating as ever. Then she, too, was gone. Geraldine Gay Hambric died. In rapid succession, the Chicago gospel community lost many more artists, including Inez Andrews, Little Lucy Smith, Jessy Dixon, Ethel Holloway, Gladys Beamon Gregory, George Jordan, and the Queen of Gospel, Albertina Walker, who died on October 8, 2010. The year 2014 saw the passing of Charles G. Hayes and

Nash Shaffer, among others. Ruminating on the thinning ranks of the genre's pioneers and legends, Kenneth Woods Jr. remarked: "I think about people and I want to ask them questions, but I can't. They're all gone."[42]

Although it lost its preeminence in gospel music to California in the 1970s, Chicago gospel is showing signs of recapturing its sacred music supremacy. Singer, songwriter, and producer VaShawn Mitchell, who grew up on the city's far South Side, is among a new crop of gospel artists representing Chicago. Multiple award–winning singer-songwriter and producer Donald Lawrence works in Chicago. Grammy winners Pastor Smokie Norful and Heather Headley call Chicagoland home. Anita Wilson from Fellowship Missionary Baptist Church garnered a 2013 Grammy nomination for her debut solo album, *Worship Soul.* Gospel artist Mark Hubbard champions the genre for the Chicago Chapter of the Recording Academy. Apostle Donald L. Alford welcomes new gospel artists to his Progressive Life-Giving Word Cathedral in Hillside, Illinois. Brian Courtney Wilson grew up in nearby Maywood. Shekinah Glory Ministry and worship leader Phil Tarver from south suburban Valley Kingdom Ministries have won multiple Stellar Awards with their multisensory brand of sacred music known as "praise and worship." Continuing the tradition of the Barrett Sisters, the Brown Sisters of Chicago are sharing their energetic blend of gospel and praise-and-worship style with audiences around the world. DeAndre Patterson channels Eugene Smith in his work as emcee and gospel singer.

In January 2013, Pastor Charles Jenkins and the Fellowship Missionary Baptist Church Choir captured five Stellar Awards, including best song, "Awesome," and best album, *The Best of Both Worlds*, which opened with a tribute medley to old-school Fellowship classics, such as the church theme, "What a Fellowship." That same weekend, evangelist Delores Diggs, longtime leader in the Church of God in Christ Music Department, was presented with a Chicago Music Award.

Familial links to the founding fathers and mothers of Chicago gospel include Bryant Jones and Bobby Wooten, who carry on the tradition of their famous parents, Rev. Billy Jones and Jeanette Robinson, and Robert Wooten Sr., respectively. Former child prodigy Fred Nelson III keeps his family's music history alive. The Acme Missionary Baptist Church Choir, led by Pastor Bernard Sutton, a member of the Willing Four, was the first to win Verizon's "How Sweet the Sound" competition for the best church choir in America. Pastor Ray Allen Berryhill, who worked under Sammy Lewis, led his multicultural Evangel Celebration Chorale to a near victory in Verizon's second annual competition. Dexter Walker and the Zion Movement Chorale brought the honor back to Chicago in 2013.

The Gospel Music according to Chicago (GMAC) Choir, a large ensemble of veteran singers and young choristers who enjoy the traditional sound, performs several times a year. It made a special appearance at the Gospel Music Workshop of America and recorded an album of Chicago classics. On June 4, 2010, the executive board of GMAC, including Dennis Cole, L. Stanley Davis, and Nash Shaffer, inducted twenty-five of the city's pioneers and legends, deceased and living, into its hall of fame during a ceremony at Rev. Dr. Johnnie Colemon's Christ Universal Temple. A 2012 documentary by Regina Rene saluted DeLois Barrett Campbell and the Barrett Sisters.[43]

But whether or not Chicago gospel music recaptures the primacy it held in the early days, the emotional and spiritual impact of the Chicago School of Gospel prevails. Before her own passing, DeLois Barrett Campbell reflected: "I sang for Mahalia Jackson's funeral. I sang for Thomas A. Dorsey's funeral. I sang for Roberta's funeral—of course the group did for Roberta. I sang for Sallie Martin's funeral. Theodore Frye. All of these are great writers and singers, and I had the privilege of singing for them—and just to think that at this age, eighty-one, I still love to sing a good old gospel song. . . . In gospel, you don't make a lot of money. You don't get rich, but I can say the Lord has provided for me all that I needed."[44]

"Really, that's all black people had," explained Betty Lester.

That's all we had. In the traditional gospel song, you're asking God for his help, and you're praising him. And this is what got you through; otherwise you would have just lost your mind, some of the things that you had to go through. You really would have just said, "Forget it, I'm out of here." But because you could come to church and fellowship with the body of Christ, it gave you hope that it's going to be a better day, that things are not always going to stay the same, if you just keep trusting in God. And it has gotten better.[45]

Yet as gospel, spiritual, and jubilee songs have stressed for decades, the final freedom beckons from the other side of the Jordan River. Ethel Harris, Albertina Walker's housekeeper at the time she died, described a special visitation:

I'm a spiritual person, I come from a Spiritual church—First Church of Deliverance—and so I believe in the spirit. [Tina] came back to me. I was dead asleep, and in the dream was Albertina Walker. She was young, and she had on a jump suit. I'd never seen Albertina in pants! I was amazed, and I found myself saying, "She's so young and pretty." She leaned over, as if she was suspended at the end of my bed, and said, "I'm okay, baby." She said, "I am all right, I am fine," with that big old beautiful smile. That was her spiritual sign telling me she was okay. She just leaned over and said, "I'm okay. I'm better now."[46]

One can imagine Albertina Walker entering heaven's gates, walking the streets of gold to the jaunty rhythm of "Move On Up a Little Higher," among all of God's sons and daughters, where it is always howdy, howdy—howdy to Magnolia, Roberta, Sallie, Dorsey, Frye, Mahalia, James Cleveland, Robert Anderson, Elyse, Johneron, Ora Lee, all of them, shed of their old form and robed in glory, in the Promised Land at last. Shouting, troubles over.

1920s African American Sacred Music Recordings Made in Chicago

Artist	Style	Recording dates	Label
Wiseman Sextette	Jubilee singing	ca. July 1923	Pm
Sunset Four	Quartet singing	ca. August 1924–July 1925	Pm
C. A. Tindley Bible Class Gospel Singers	Quartet singing	ca. May 1925–May 1926	Pm
Grace Outlaw	Quartet singing	ca. July 1925–October 1926	Pm, Her
Rev. W. A. White	Sermons	ca. August 1925–September 1927	Pm
Mme. Mae Frierson Moore	Spirituals	ca. September 1925	Pm
Rev. Cook w/Community Chorus	Sermon with choir	ca. September 1925	Pm
Deacon L. J. Bates (Blind Lemon Jefferson)	Guitar evangelist	ca. December 1925–January 1926	Pm, Her
Hermes Zimmerman	Gospel singing	April 1926	Vo
Arizona Dranes	Singing with piano	June 1926–July 1928	OK
Pace Jubilee Singers	Jubilee singing	September 1926–October 1929	Vi, Br, Vo, BP, Ge
Rev. Mose Doolittle	Sermons with singing	September 1926	Vi

Artist	Style	Recording dates	Label
Second Baptist Church Trio	Quartet Singing	ca. November 1926	OK
Mount Vernon Choir	Choir	ca. November 1926	OK
Paramount Ladies Four	Female quartet singing	ca. November 1926	Her, Pm
Homer Quincy Smith	Hymns	December 1926	Pm
Rev. J. M. Gates	Sermons with singing	December 1926	Vi, BB, Sr, MW
Deacon A. Wilson	Singing with choir	December 1926–October 1927	Vi, Br
Rev. James Beard	Sermons with singing	January 1927	Pm
Rev. Sister Mary Nelson	Songs	February–April 1927	Vo
Evangelist R. H. Harris	Sanctified singing	March 1927	Ge
Willie Packard	Song	March 1927	BP uniss
Ernia Mae Cunningham	Songs	April 1927	Pm
Sister O. F. Franklin	Sanctified singing	April 1927	Br
T.C.I. Women's Four	Fem. Quartet singing	ca. April 1927	Pm
Rev. T. T. Rose and Singers	Sermons with singing	April–November 1927	Pm
Rev. A. W. Nix	Sermons with singing	April 1927–March 1931	Vo
Mississippi Jubilee Singers	Quartet singing	May 1927	Pm
Rev. Leora Ross	Sermons with singing	May–December 1927	OK
Jessie May Hill	Sanctified singing	May–December 1927	OK
Rev. F. W. McGee and Congregation	Sermons with singing	May 1927–July 1930	OK, Vi
Rev. W. M. Clark and Congregation	Sermons with singing	Mid-1927	Pm, BP
Blind Connie Rosemond	Gospel songs	June 1927	Pm
Blind Joe Taggart	Guitar evangelist	June 1927–December 1928	Vo, Pm, Her, Me
Williams Black Patti Jubilee Singers	Jubilee singing	July 1927–September 1930	BP, Br
Famous Jubilee Singers	Jubilee singing	August 1927	Pm
William and Versey Smith	Sanctified singing	August 1927	Pm
Rev. Johnnie Blakey	Sermons with singing	September 1927–December 1928	Pm, OK
Rev. M. L. Gipson	Sermons with singing	September 1927–August 1929	Pm
Cotton Belt Quartet	Quartet singing	ca. October 1927	Pm
Katie Daniels	Songs	ca. October 1927	Pm

Artist	Style	Recording dates	Label
Rev. [James Morris] Webb	Sermons	ca. November 1927	Pm
Pullman Porters Quartette	Quartet singing	ca. November–December 1927	Pm
Blind Willie Davis	Guitar evangelist	ca. January–December 1928	Pm, Her
Rev. R. M. Massey	Sermons with singing	ca. January 1928	Pm
Rev. Moses Mason	Sermons with singing	ca. January 1928	Pm
Winkfield Sentiment Singers	Quartet Singing	ca. March–April 1928	Pm
Rev. D. C. Rice and Congregation	Sermons with singing	March 1928–July 1930	Vo
Daniel Brown	Sanctified singing	May 1928	Pm
Rev. T. N. T. Burton	Sermons	May 1928	Pm
Famous Myers Jubilee Singers	Jubilee singing	May 1928	Pm
Novelty Four Quartet	Quartet singing	July 1928	Vo
Rev. Frank Cotton	Sermons	ca. August 1928	Pm
Southern Plantation Singers	Jubilee singing	September 1928	Vo
Evangelist Anna Perry	Sermons with singing	October 1928	Vo uniss
Lucy Smith Jubilee Singers	Jubilee singing	October 1928	Vo
Shands Superior Jubilee Singers	Jubilee singing	October–November 1928	Vo
Handy's Sacred Singers	Jubilee singing	ca. October 1928–January 1929	Pm
Jessie Austin (Sanctified Trio)	Sanctified singing	November 1928	Vo uniss
Elders McIntorsh and Edwards	Sanctified singing	December 1928	OK
Lulu Jackson	Sacred singing	December 1928	Vo uniss
Rev. P. W. Williams	Sermons with singing	ca. December 1928	Pm
Cotton Top Mountain Sanctified Singers	Sanctified singing	February–August 1929	Br
Southern Sanctified Singers	Sanctified Singing	March–April 1929	Br
Bethlehem Four	Quartet singing	April 1929	Vo uniss
Gospel Camp Meeting Singers	Sanctified singing	May 1929	Vo
Gospel Sanctified Singers	Sanctified singing	August 1929	Br uniss

Artist	Style	Recording dates	Label
Sister Cally Fancy's Sanctified Singers	Sanctified singing	August 1929– October 1931	Br, Vo
Rev. Jim Beal	Sermons	August 1929	Br
Rev. P. C. Edmonds	Sermons with response	August 1929	Pm
Frank Palmes	Songs	ca. September 1929	Pm, Her
Cotton Pickers Quartet	Quartet Singing	December 1929	Vi, BB, Sr

Key

uniss   unissued

Record Labels

BB   Bluebird
BP   Black Patti
Br   Brunswick
Ge   Gennett
Her   Herwin
Me   Melotone
MW   Montgomery Ward
OK   OKeh
Pm   Paramount
Sr   Supertone
Vi   Victor
Vo   Vocalion

African American Sacred Music Recordings Made in Chicago, 1930–1941

Artist	Style	Recording dates	Label
Mother McCollum	Sanctified singing	ca. June 1930	Vo
Minnie Pearl Roberts Sanctified Singers	Sanctified singing	September 1930	Br
Rev. J. L. Hendrix	Sermons with singing	ca. October 1930–March 1931	Vo, Br
Southern Wonders	Quartet singing	November 1930–January 1931	Vo, Me
Thomas A. Dorsey and Singers	Gospel singing	March 1932, March 1934	Vo
Corbett Chandler Jubilee Singers	Jubilee singing	ca. September 1934	Decca uniss
Blind Joe Taggart	Guitar evangelist	September 1934	Decca
Brother Son Bonds	Guitar evangelist	September 1934	Decca
Southern Jubilee Singers of Chicago	Jubilee singing	ca. 1935	Mildmay (*UK*)
Gospel (Memphis) Minnie	Gospel singing	January 1935	Decca
Hallelujah Joe (McCoy) and Congregation	Sermons with singing	January–May 1935	Decca
Uncle Joe Dobson	Sanctified singing	February 1935	Decca

Artist	Style	Recording dates	Label
Mound City Jubilee Quartette	Quartet singing	February 1935	Decca
Blind Willie McTell	Guitar evangelist	April 1935	Decca
Fisk Jubilee Singers	Jubilee singing	ca. April 1935	Rainbow
Clara Bolton and William Henry Smith's Singers	Jubilee singing	May 1935	Decca
Chicago Sanctified Singers	Sanctified singing	July 1935	ARC, Cq
Rev. Nathan Smith	Sermons with singing	August–September 1935	Decca
William H. Smith's Jubilee Singers	Jubilee singing	May 1935	Decca, Ch
Professor Hull's Anthems of Joy	Gospel instrumentals	July 1936	Decca
Lula Duncan	Gospel singing	September 1935	Decca uniss
Goodwill Male Chorus	Jubilee singing	May 1937	Decca
Mahalia Jackson	Gospel singing	May 1937	Decca
Martin and Morris Singers	Gospel singing	ca. 1940	Bronze (*LA*)
Mitchell's Christian Singers	Quartet singing	August 1940	OK, Cq, Co
Brother George and Sanctified Singers (aka Blind Boy Fuller)	Gospel singing	June 1940–May 1941	OK, Co
Rev. W. M. Chambers and Congregation	Sermons with singing	May 1941	OK, Cq

Key

uniss	unissued
LA	Los Angeles
UK	United Kingdom

Record Labels

ARC	American Record Company
Br	Brunswick
Bronze	
Ch	Champion
Co	Columbia
Cq	Conqueror
Decca	
Me	Melotone
Mildmay	
OK	OKeh
Rainbow	
Vo	Vocalion

NOTES

Introduction

1. Boyer, *How Sweet the Sound*, 50, emphasis in original.
2. Special thanks to Ronald Weber, retired professor at the University of Notre Dame, for the use of his freedom from/for construct.
3. For more on the definition of gospel music, see Williams-Jones, "Afro-American Gospel Music," 376–78; Boyer, *How Sweet the Sound*, 9, 49; and Southern, *Music of Black Americans*, 459–60.
4. Martin and Morris, *Twelve Gospel Song "Hits."*
5. Morris, *Improving the Music*, 47.
6. Quoted in Dyja, *Third Coast*, 143.
7. Sutherland, "Analysis of Negro Churches," 115–16.
8. Ibid., 124.
9. Green, *Selling the Race*, 66–68.
10. Ibid., 69.
11. Morris, *Improving the Music*, 47.

Chapter 1. Got On My Traveling Shoes: Black Sacred Music and the Great Migration

The section title "How Shall We Sing the Lord's Song in a Strange Land?" is taken from Psalm 137:4 (King James Version).

1. Marks, *Farewell—We're Good and Gone*, 36.
2. Drake and Cayton. *Black Metropolis*, 602.
3. Rev. Dr. Wealthy Mobley, interview with author, April 10, 2010.
4. Sernett, *Bound for the Promised Land*, 154–55.
5. Sutherland, "Analysis of Negro Churches," 14.
6. Marks, *Farewell—We're Good and Gone*, 20.
7. Ibid., 17.
8. Sutherland, "Analysis of Negro Churches," 16.
9. Ibid., 16.
10. Drake and Cayton, *Black Metropolis*, 79.
11. Sutherland, "Analysis of Negro Churches," 34.

12. Drake and Cayton, *Black Metropolis*, 73.

13. *Chicago Defender*, October 2, 1925, I5.

14. Grossman, *Land of Hope*, 129–32.

15. Best, *Passionately Human*, 2.

16. Williams-Jones, "Afro-American Gospel Music," 379.

17. Jon Michael Spencer, "The Rhythms of Black Folks," in Johnson and Jersild, *Ain't Gonna Lay My 'Ligion Down*, 43.

18. Kempton, *Boogaloo*, 9; Pitts, *Old Ship of Zion*, 65, 72–73.

19. Pitts, *Old Ship of Zion*, 65.

20. Alonzo Johnson, "Pray's House Spirit," in Johnson and Jersild, *Ain't Gonna Lay My 'Ligion Down*, 16–17.

21. "I Love the Lord, He Heard My Cry" is an example of a long meter hymn still sung in churches.

22. Pitts, *Old Ship of Zion*, 66–67.

23. I. L. Johnson, "Development of African American Gospel Piano Style," 76.

24. Ibid., 83.

25. Bliss and Sankey, *Gospel Hymns and Sacred Songs*; Bliss and Sankey, *Gospel Hymns No. 2*.

26. Pitts quoted in I. L. Johnson, "Development of African American Gospel Piano Style," 79.

27. Woodson, *Rural Negro*, 155.

28. Quoted in I. L. Johnson, "Development of African American Gospel Piano Style," 64.

29. Maultsby, "Music of Northern Independent Black Churches," 416.

30. Baldwin, *Chicago's New Negroes*, 159.

31. Quoted in Higginbotham, "Rethinking Vernacular Culture," 225.

32. Maultsby, "Music of Northern Independent Black Churches," 410–11.

33. Sutherland, "Analysis of Negro Churches," 6, 100. There were enough of this type of church for Sutherland to assign it one of his five types. A decade later, sociologist Vattel Elbert Daniel called this church type "semi-demonstrative" ("Ritual in Chicago's South Side Churches").

34. Harris, *Rise of Gospel Blues*, 122.

35. Daniel, "Ritual in Chicago's South Side Churches," 2.

36. Kempton, *Boogaloo*, 36–37.

37. Baldwin, *Chicago's New Negroes*, 59.

38. Harris, *Rise of Gospel Blues*, 111.

39. Ibid., 107.

40. *Chicago Defender*, November 2, 1935, 5, 7; January 8, 1927, I8.

41. Harris, *Rise of Gospel Blues*, 109.

42. Ibid., 115; Kempton, *Boogaloo*, 38.

43. Harris, *Rise of Gospel Blues*, 117.

44. Grossman, *Land of Hope*, 156.

45. Rev. Dr. Wealthy L. Mobley, interview with author, April 10, 2010.

46. Sernett, *Bound for the Promised Land*, 246; Woodson, *Rural Negro*, 160.

47. Baldwin, *Chicago's New Negroes*, 166.

48. R. A. Smith, *Life and Works of Thomas Andrew Dorsey*, 46.

49. Grossman, *Land of Hope*, 157.

50. Drake and Cayton, *Black Metropolis*, 649.

51. Reproduced in Seroff's liner notes to *There Breathes a Hope*, 87.

52. Best, *Passionately Human*, 63–65.

53. Ibid., 52; Grossman, *Land of Hope*, 158.

54. Sernett, *Bound for the Promised Land*, 161; Daniel, "Ritual in Chicago's South Side Churches," 13.

55. Sutherland, "Analysis of Negro Churches," 44.

56. Harris, *Rise of Gospel Blues*, 120.

57. Quoted in Sernett, *Bound for the Promised Land*, 163.

58. Sernett, *Bound for the Promised Land*, 193.

59. Grossman, *Land of Hope*, 131.

60. Sutherland, "Analysis of Negro Churches," 49.

61. Sernett, *Bound for the Promised Land*, 7, 200, 202.

62. Drake and Cayton, *Black Metropolis*, 633–34.

63. Ibid., 628.

64. Schwerin, *Got to Tell It*, 166.

65. Sernett, *Bound for the Promised Land*, 191.

66. Sutherland, "Analysis of Negro Churches," 57.

67. Rev. Dr. Wealthy L. Mobley, interview with author, April 10, 2010.

68. Sutherland, "Analysis of Negro Churches," 79.

69. Best, *Passionately Human*, 2.

70. Daniel, "Ritual in Chicago's South Side Churches," 126.

71. Drake and Cayton, *Black Metropolis*, 412, 415.

72. Ibid., 629.

73. Ibid., 646.

74. Ibid., 618.

75. Harris, *Rise of Gospel Blues*, 122–23.

Chapter 2. "When the Fire Fell": The Sanctified Church Contribution to Chicago Gospel Music

The chapter title refers to the gospel song "When the Fire Fell," from the Church of God in Christ repertory. The subsection title "Soldiers in the Army" is taken from the song "I'm a Soldier in the Army of the Lord." The subsection title "Have Prayer Meetings at Home" is taken from an OKeh Records advertisement in the *Chicago Defender* (national ed.), September 11, 1926, I6.

1. Higginbotham, "Rethinking Vernacular Culture," 227.

2. Ibid., 228, 230.

3. Oliver, *Songsters and Saints*, 186; DuPree, *African-American Holiness Pentecostal*

Movement, 260; Baldwin, *Chicago's New Negroes*, 166. This is not the same Mattie Thornton who assisted Rev. Clarence H. Cobbs in developing the First Church of Deliverance.

4. Grossman, *Land of Hope*, 158.

5. Quoted in Sernett, *Bound for the Promised Land*, 190.

6. I. L. Johnson, "Development of African American Gospel Piano Style," 88; liner notes, *Mattie B. Poole Memorial Album*. Poole was cofounder with her husband of Chicago's Bethlehem Healing Temple.

7. I. L. Johnson, "Development of African American Gospel Piano Style," 88.

8. Mason, *Make Room for the Holy Ghost*, 22.

9. Ibid.

10. Spencer, *Black Hymnody*, 142.

11. Ibid.

12. Mason, *Make Room for the Holy Ghost*, 23; Spencer, *Black Hymnody*, 140–41.

13. *Chicago Defender*, November 26, 1949, 3.

14. Roberts, *My Life with Brother Isaiah*, 22.

15. Ibid., 22–23.

16. Lillian Brooks Coffey became the International Supervisor of Women for the COGIC denomination.

17. Elder Mack C. Mason, interview with author, March 5, 2007; Roberts, *My Life with Brother Isaiah*, 23.

18. Roberts, *My Life with Brother Isaiah*, 23–4.

19. Elder Mack C. Mason, interview with author, March 5, 2007. It was commonplace in those days to identify COGIC churches by their street address.

20. Sutherland, "Analysis of Negro Churches," 89.

21. Ibid., 90.

22. Elder Lamont Lenox, interview with author, March 24, 2010.

23. Lenox, *Living in Faith*, 18–19.

24. Elder Lamont Lenox, interview with author, March 24, 2010.

25. Lenox, *Living in Faith*, 23.

26. Ibid.

27. Ibid., 29–30.

28. Ibid.

29. J. A. Jackson, *Singing in My Soul*, 38.

30. This quote, and all information on the early history of Elder P. R. Favors, comes from a typewritten remembrance written on March 15, 1982, by Mildred Mondane, granddaughter to Elder Favors, and forwarded to the author.

31. *Chicago Defender* (national ed.), July 31, 1920, 4.

32. J. A. Jackson, *Singing in My Soul*, 41.

33. Titon, *Early Downhome Blues*, xv.

34. Lieb, *Mother of the Blues*, xiii; see Titon, *Early Downhome Blues*, for the distinction between classic, or vaudeville blues, and downhome, or country, blues, xv.

35. Harris, "Conflict and Resolution," 176.

36. I. L. Johnson, "Development of African American Gospel Piano Style," 113n.

37. Calt, "Anatomy of a 'Race' Label," 11.

38. Kennedy and McNutt, *Little Labels—Big Sound*, 25.

39. Calt, "Anatomy of a 'Race' Label," 12.

40. Ibid.

41. Weusi, "Rise and Fall."

42. Calt, "Anatomy of a 'Race' Label," 12–14, 28.

43. Ibid., 16.; According to Dixon, Godrich, and Rye, Aletha Dickerson accompanied blues singer Marie Grinter on a June 1926 session for OKeh; see *Blues and Gospel Records*, 332. Dickerson, however, did not hide her disdain for blues music.

44. Calt, "Anatomy of a 'Race' Label," 17.

45. Lewis, "Rainbow Records Discography," 71–72.

46. Kennedy and McNutt, *Little Labels—Big Sound*, 27.

47. Ibid., 29.

48. Calt, "Anatomy of a 'Race' Label," 20.

49. Ibid.

50. Ibid., 14.

51. J. A. Jackson, *Singing in My Soul*, 37.

52. Heilbut, *Fan Who Knew Too Much*, 104.

53. The R. H. Harris referenced here was a female evangelist, not the Soul Stirrers' male lead singer, Rebert H. Harris.

54. J. A. Jackson, *Singing in My Soul*, 40.

55. Green, *Selling the Race*, 54–55.

56. Most of Dranes's pre-recording history comes from Corcoran, liner notes to *He Is My Story*.

57. Ibid., 17.

58. In *Songsters and Saints*, Oliver gives Dranes's birth year as 1905 (188). Bishop Crouch is the great uncle of gospel singer-songwriter Andraé Crouch.

59. Corcoran, liner notes to *He Is My Story*, 19.

60. I. L. Johnson, "Development of African American Gospel Piano Style," 265.

61. Corcoran, liner notes to *He Is My Story*, 25.

62. Alva Roberts, interview with author, March 5, 2007.

63. Corcoran, liner notes to *He Is My Story*, 6.

64. Ibid., 20.

65. Ibid., 3.

66. M. Shaw, "Arizona Dranes and OKeh," 85.

67. Ibid., 85–86; Corcoran, liner notes to *He Is My Story*, 31.

68. Oliver, *Songsters and Saints*, 188; Dixon, Godrich, and Rye, *Blues and Gospel Records*, 226.

69. I. L. Johnson, "Development of African American Gospel Piano Style," 226.

70. Ibid., 241.

71. Corcoran, liner notes to *He Is My Story*, 25.

72. M. Shaw, "Arizona Dranes and OKeh," 86; Dixon, Godrich, and Rye, *Blues and Gospel Records*, 226.

73. Lenox, *Living in Faith,* 29.

74. Corcoran, liner notes to *He Is My Story*, 26; Lenox, *Living In Faith*, 29; Alva Roberts, interview with author, March 5, 2007.

75. Corcoran, liner notes to *He Is My Story*, 25.

76. The Jubilee Singers were probably members of McGee's church choir. See M. Shaw, "Arizona Dranes and OKeh," 86; Dixon, Godrich, and Rye, *Blues and Gospel Records*, 226.

77. M. Shaw, "Arizona Dranes and OKeh," 89; Dixon, Godrich, and Rye, *Blues and Gospel Records*, 226; the tracks can be heard on Document DOCD-5186 and Tompkins Square's *He Is My Story*.

78. Dixon, Godrich, and Rye, *Blues and Gospel Records*, 910.

79. Ibid., 537.

80. Corcoran, liner notes to *He Is My Story*, 28.

81. Anthony Heilbut, telephone interview with author, January 2011; Mack Mason, email communication with author, February 2012.

82. Corcoran, liner notes to *He Is My Story*, 4.

83. Alva Roberts, interview with author, March 5, 2007.

84. Corcoran, liner notes to *He Is My Story*, 42–43.

85. Romanowski, liner notes to *Preachers and Congregations*.

86. Dixon, Godrich, and Rye, *Blues and Gospel Records*, 1024.

87. Ibid., 123, 287.

88. Burnett stayed with Columbia until 1929, when he moved to Decca. Gates, on the other hand, recorded for just about every major record label and subsidiary in existence from 1926 to 1941.

89. Jeff Titon cited in I. L. Johnson, "Development of African American Gospel Piano Style," 114.

90. Oliver, *Songsters and Saints*, 198.

91. I. L. Johnson, "Development of African American Gospel Piano Style," 134n.

92. Ankeny, "Rev. F. W. McGee."

93. Mason, *Saints in the Land of Lincoln*, 92–93.

94. Dixon, Godrich, and Rye, *Blues and Gospel Records*, 576, 396.

95. Ibid., 576.

96. Klatzko, liner notes to *Memphis Sanctified Jug Bands*.

97. *Louisiana Weekly*, August 8, 1927, reported by Abbott, *I Got Two Wings*, 17.

98. Dixon, Godrich, and Rye, *Blues and Gospel Records*, 576–77.

99. Ibid., 576–77; *Rev. F. W. McGee* (Eden LP ELE 1–200).

100. *Chicago Defender*, December 30, 1939.

101. Oliver, Harrison, and Bolcom, *New Grove Gospel, Blues and Jazz*, 198.

102. *Chicago Defender* (national ed.), January 21, 1928, A1; Sutherland, "Analysis of Negro Churches," 72.

103. Sutherland, "Analysis of Negro Churches," 8.

104. Ibid., 81, 88.

105. Brennan, "Rev. D. C. Rice"; Misiewicz, *Rev. D. C. Rice*. For his source material, Misiewicz used Gayle Dean Wardlow's interview with Reverend Rice published in *Storyville* 23, June–July 1969.

106. *Chicago Defender,* June 23, 1928, 6.

107. Klatzko, liner notes to *Memphis Sanctified Jug Bands.*

108. Dixon, Godrich, and Rye, *Blues and Gospel Records,* 753–54, 845.

109. Oliver, *Songsters and Saints,* 180.

110. Anthony Heilbut, email communication with author, September 6, 2012.

111. Brennan, "Rev. D. C. Rice"; Misiewicz, *Rev. D. C. Rice.*

112. Simmons and Thomas, *Preaching with Sacred Fire,* 903.

113. *Chicago Defender,* August 27, 1927, 3.

114. Dixon, Godrich, and Rye, *Blues and Gospel Records,* 695.

115. Although unconfirmed, this group may have been from the historic Second Baptist Church, a church founded in the 1870s in Evanston, Illinois, a suburb immediately north of Chicago.

116. Personnel identified by Elder Mack C. Mason.

117. Sissieretta Jones was often compared to the opera singer Adelina Patti, thus earning her the sobriquet of "Black Patti."

118. Calt and Wardlow, "Paramount Part 4," 15–17.

119. Ibid., 18.

Chapter 3. Sacred Music in Transition: Charles Henry Pace and the Pace Jubilee Singers

1. Broughton, *Black Gospel,* 30.

2. Robert Darden, "Charles Pace and the Pace Jubilee Singers," in McNeil, *Encyclopedia of American Gospel Music,* 289.

3. Anthony Heilbut, email communication with author, September 6, 2012.

4. Tyler, "Music of Charles Henry Pace," 10, 225. The author is indebted to Tyler, whose research contributed immeasurably to the composition of this chapter.

5. Ibid., 10, 225.

6. Ibid., 225–26.

7. Ibid., 131.

8. Ibid.

9. Ibid., 4.

10. In the 1930s, Pace's arrangement of "This Little Light of Mine" was compiled, with revisions, for *Bowles Favorite Frye's Special Gospel Song Book No. 6.*

11. Tyler, "Music of Charles Henry Pace," 147.

12. Ibid., 143–44.

13. Dixon, Godrich, and Rye. *Blues and Gospel Records,* 698–701.

14. Tyler, "Music of Charles Henry Pace," 13.

15. Frances Pace Barnes, interview with author, October 15, 2010.

16. Tyler, "Music of Charles Henry Pace," 144.

17. Anthony Heilbut, interview with author, September 12, 2012.

18. Frances Pace Barnes, interview with author, October 15, 2010.

19. The record companies described Parker as a soprano, but Anthony Heilbut has aurally identified her as a contralto.

20. Dixon, Godrich, and Rye, *Blues and Gospel Records*, 698.

21. Tyler, "Music of Charles Henry Pace," 148.

22. Ibid., 148, 156.

23. Evans, liner notes to *Pace Jubilee Singers*, vol. 1.

24. Evans, liner notes to *Pace Jubilee Singers*, vol. 2.

25. Anthony Heilbut, interview with author, September 12, 2012.

26. Regarding the Progressive Choral Society, see Abbott and Seroff, *To Do This*, 255.

27. Anthony Heilbut, email communication with author, September 6, 2012.

28. Anthony Heilbut, interview with author, September 12, 2012.

29. Quoted in Tyler, "Music of Charles Henry Pace," 146.

30. Dixon, Godrich, and Rye, *Blues and Gospel Records*, 698–701.

31. Ibid., 706.

32. Ibid. Tyler also suggests that Eva Parker and Hattie Parker were the same person ("Music of Charles Henry Pace," 146).

33. Dixon, Godrich, and Rye, *Blues and Gospel Records*, 701.

34. *Chicago Tribune*, March 3, 1929, I8; March 17, 1929, I10.

35. Ibid., November 24, 1929, I6; December 29, 1929, B4.

36. *Southtown Economist*, January 11, 1927, 12.

37. Tyler, "Music of Charles Henry Pace," 9; *Chicago Defender*, October 26, 1935, 22.

38. *Chicago Defender*, October 31, 1936, 7.

39. Ibid., January 18, 1936; 6; August 29, 1936, 17.

40. Anthony Heilbut, interview with author, September 12, 2012.

41. Anthony Heilbut, email communication with author, September 6, 2012.

42. Heilbut, *Fan Who Knew Too Much*, 255.

43. Ibid., 255–56; Dixon, Godrich, and Rye, *Blues and Gospel Records*, 822.

44. Heilbut, *Fan Who Knew Too Much*, 255; Abbott and Seroff, *To Do This*, 225.

45. Tyler "Music of Charles Henry Pace," 1, 226.

46. Ibid., 135.

47. Frances Pace Barnes, interview with author, October 15, 2010.

48. Ibid. Barnes confirmed that her father was friends with Armstrong and Handy. She met both men personally when they visited the family home in Pittsburgh.

49. Frances Pace Barnes, interview with author, October 15, 2010.

50. Boyer, "Kenneth Morris," 310.

51. Quoted in Tyler, "Music of Charles Henry Pace," 162.

Chapter 4. Turn Your Radio On:
Chicago Sacred Radio Broadcast Pioneers

1. Spaulding, "History of Black Oriented Radio," 33; Abbott and Seroff, *To Do This*, 230.

2. *Chicago Defender*, July 5, 1947, 10.

3. Ibid., March 5, 1949, 4; May 28, 1949, 35.

4. Ibid. (national ed.), February 14, 1925, A7; Barlow, *Voice Over*, 51–52.

5. Barlow, *Voice Over*, 52.

6. Spaulding, "History of Black Oriented Radio," 71.

7. *Chicago Defender*, March 5, 1949, 4; May 28, 1949, 35.

8. Ibid., November 11, 1939, 19; Barlow, *Voice Over*, 52.

9. *Chicago Defender*, October 21, 1933, 33.

10. Barlow, *Voice Over*, 53.

11. *Chicago Defender*, October 21, 1933, 33; November 11, 1933, 17. According to George Evans, the *Defender*'s radio columnist at the time, WSBC's main offices and studio were located at Thirteenth and Michigan Boulevard (Avenue). Gene Dyer owned and operated WSBC at that time.

12. Barlow, *Voice Over*, 51.

13. Samuelson and Peters, "Landmarks of Blues and Gospel," 11.

14. Spaulding, "History of Black Oriented Radio," 101.

15. Smith, *Biography of Lucy Smith*, 3.

16. Ibid., 4.

17. Best, *Passionately Human*, 174.

18. Drake and Cayton, *Black Metropolis*, 644, 648.

19. Best, *Passionately Human*, 173.

20. Floriene Watson Willis, interview with author, July 5, 2013.

21. Late-night air time was less expensive; see Best, *Passionately Human*, 116. A *Chicago Defender* article from May 26, 1951, 40, cites Elder Lucy Smith's twenty-fifth year on radio, which would have put her broadcast debut in 1926.

22. *Chicago Defender*, July 24, 1937, 4; July 31, 1937, 7.

23. Ibid., September 1, 1934; September 22, 1934.

24. Ibid., October 27, 1934; November 24, 1934.

25. Cited in Best, *Passionately Human*, 177.

26. Daniel, "Ritual in Chicago's South Side Churches," 135. An endnote to the quoted citation demonstrates corroboration by Miles Mark Fisher, who told Daniel on August 5, 1938, that "members of the more formal Baptist and Methodist churches are often found at Cobbs' or at Elder Lucy Smith's on Sunday Nights."

27. Spaulding, "History of Black Oriented Radio," 43.

28. Greenberg and Dervin cited in I. L. Johnson, "Development of African American Gospel Piano Style," 119n.

29. *Chicago Defender*, May 6, 1933, 7; June 16, 1933, 6.

30. Ibid., April 19, 1947, 12; November 16, 1946, 27.

31. Ibid., July 8, 1933. The *Defender* reports that Moses Temple's broadcast was heard on WSBC Sunday evenings from 9:00 to 10:00, which is confusing, since this was the same time as Cooper's *All-Colored Hour*.

32. Ibid., March 20, 1937, 12.

33. Walker, *Miss Lucie*, 27–28. Lucie Campbell confirmed that Cobbs was in her class when she attended a celebration in his honor and told the assemblage that she had taught him. See *Chicago Defender*, January 17, 1959, 5.

34. *Chicago Defender* (national ed.), February 25, 1928, A7; July 11, 1936, 8.

35. Baer, "Metropolitan Spiritual Churches," 141.

36. L. Stanley Davis, interview with author, March 1, 2007.

37. For Hedgepath's death, see *Chicago Defender*, February 25, 1928, 7.

38. Sutherland, "Analysis of Negro Churches," 38.

39. Bishop Otto T. Houston III, interview with author, January 2007; see also *Chicago Defender* (national ed.), June 4, 1938, 23; Oliver, *Songsters and Saints*, 186.

40. Bishop Otto T. Houston III, interview with author, January 2007.

41. Baer, "Metropolitan Spiritual Churches," 143.

42. Ibid., 142.

43. First Church of Deliverance website, www.firstchurchofdeliverance.org/Our _Church.htm, accessed May 4, 2007.

44. Drake and Cayton, *Black Metropolis*, 646.

45. *Chicago Defender*, November 16, 1935, 25. According to Anthony Heilbut, "How I Got Over" is Cobbs's arrangement, not his composition. Anthony Heilbut, email communication with author, September 6, 2012.

46. Heilbut, liner notes to *The Great Gospel Men*; Anthony Heilbut, email communication with author, September 6, 2012.

47. Abbott and Seroff, *To Do This*, 116–17.

48. Charles Clency, interview with author, December 3, 2012.

49. Bishop Jerry L. Goodloe, interview with author, September 26, 2013.

50. L. Stanley Davis, interview with author, March 1, 2007.

51. Ibid.

52. Bishop Otto T. Houston III, interview with author, January 2007.

53. Drake and Cayton, *Black Metropolis*, 646. In those days, it was not necessarily the modus operandi of Spiritual ministers to "shout the congregation."

54. Washington, *Black Sects and Cults*, 114, quoted in Spaulding, "History of Black Oriented Radio," 170.

55. Pastor Ray Allen Berryhill, interview with author, April 8, 2010.

56. Best, *Passionately Human*, 117.

57. L. Stanley Davis, interview with author, March 1, 2007.

58. Bishop Jerry L. Goodloe, interview with author, September 26, 2013.

59. Quoted in Spaulding, "History of Black Oriented Radio," 102.

60. Young, *Woke Me Up This Morning*, 144.

Chapter 5. "Someday, Somewhere": The Formation of the Gospel Nexus

1. Harris, *Rise of Gospel Blues*, 12, 15.

2. Harris, "Conflict and Resolution," 166.

3. Harris, *Rise of Gospel Blues*, 17–18.

4. Ibid., 26; Kempton, *Boogaloo*, 10.

5. Harris, *Rise of Gospel Blues*, 27.

6. Ibid., 31; Boyer, *How Sweet the Sound*, 58.

7. Southern, *Music of Black Americans*, 453.

8. Harris, "Conflict and Resolution," 171.

9. Kempton, *Boogaloo*, 12.

10. Ibid., 13; Harris, *Rise of Gospel Blues*, 48.

11. Smith, *Life and Works*, 16–17; Kempton, *Boogaloo*, 15.

12. Kempton, *Boogaloo*, 18; Harris, "Conflict and Resolution," 172; Smith, *Life and Works*, 26.

13. *Chicago Defender*, September 17, 1921, 3.

14. Southern, *Music of Black Americans,* 458; *Gospel Pearls*.

15. Harris, *Rise of Gospel Blues*, 68.

16. Boyer, *How Sweet the Sound*, 59; Kempton, *Boogaloo*, 18–19; *Gospel Pearls*, 117.

17. Harris, *Rise of Gospel Blues*, 75–77.

18. Ibid., 77–78.

19. Ibid., 81, 84.

20. Ibid., 128.

21. Ibid., 86–87; Kempton, *Boogaloo*, 22–23.

22. Harris, *Rise of Gospel Blues*, 88.

23. Kempton, *Boogaloo*, 25.

24. Smith, *Life and Words*, 17.

25. Lieb, *Mother of the Blues*, 28, 36–37.

26. Ibid., 40.

27. Harris, *Rise of Gospel Blues*, 95–96; Kempton, *Boogaloo*, 26.

28. Harris, "Conflict and Resolution," 179.

29. Ibid.

30. Dixon, Godrich, and Rye, *Blues and Gospel Records*, 222.

31. Harris, *Rise of Gospel Blues*, 148.

32. Dixon, Godrich, and Rye, *Blues and Gospel Records*, 222, 881.

33. Harris, *Rise of Gospel Blues*, 149.

34. Kempton, *Boogaloo*, 33.

35. Later that year, Tampa Red recorded an accomplished rhythmic slide guitar solo on "You Got to Reap Just What You Sow," perhaps inspired by the many guitar evangelists who recorded during the 1920s.

36. Dixon, Godrich, and Rye, *Blues and Gospel Records*, 256.

37. Harris, *Rise of Gospel Blues*, 171.

38. The Mississippi River flooded the New Orleans area in May 1912, and the Atchafalaya levee was breached. It did not happen in May 1911. See Brown, "Mississippi River Flood of 1912," 645–57.

39. Goreau, *Just Mahalia, Baby*, 13.

40. Ibid., 13.

41. Ibid., 14–16.

42. Ibid., 19, 27.

43. Schwerin, *Got to Tell It*, 35, emphasis in the original.

44. Jackson and Wylie, *Movin' On Up*, 32–33.

45. Schwerin, *Got to Tell It*, 25.

46. Jackson, *Movin' On Up*, 33.

47. Ibid., 34.

48. Schwerin, *Got to Tell It*, 32–33.

49. Ibid., 24; Goreau, *Just Mahalia, Baby*, 24.

50. Goreau, *Just Mahalia, Baby*, 48–51. The building survived urban renewal and regentrification and still stands.

51. Greater Salem later moved to its present location at 215 W. 71st Street in Chicago.

52. Ibid., 52–53.

53. Harris, *Rise of Gospel Blues*, 258.

54. In a January 10, 2008, interview with the author, Eugene Smith referred to the Johnson Singers as a quartet. In *Just Mahalia, Baby*, Brother John Sellers and Laurraine Goreau also refer to the group as a quartet (54, 73).

55. Goreau, *Just Mahalia, Baby*, 54.

56. Ibid., 57.

57. Ibid., 54.

58. Ibid., 57.

59. Ibid., 55.

60. Schwerin, *Got to Tell It*, 61.

61. Goreau, *Just Mahalia, Baby*, 53.

62. Harris, *Rise of Gospel Blues*, 258.

63. Goreau, *Just Mahalia, Baby*, 56. Mahalia told Alfred Duckett of the *Chicago Defender* that she worked "selling ten cent sheet music by singing the songs for people passing by." *Chicago Defender*, June 23, 1956, 27.

64. Sallie Martin, interview with James Standifer, September 19, 1981.

65. Heilbut, *Gospel Sound*, 5.

66. Carpenter, *Uncloudy Days*, 265; Emmitt Price, "Sallie Martin," in McNeil, *Encyclopedia of American Gospel Music*, 243; Sallie Martin, interview with James Standifer.

67. Sallie Martin, interview with James Standifer.

68. Ibid. Wallace Martin died sometime prior to 1935.

69. Heilbut, *Gospel Sound*, 7.

70. Sallie Martin, interview with James Standifer.

71. Ibid.

72. Heilbut, *Gospel Sound*, 7. During the 1981 James Standifer interview, Sallie Martin mentioned Dettie Gay as being part of the group.

73. *Chicago Defender*, August 16, 1930, 22; August 23, 1930, 1.

74. Ibid., August 30, 1930, 13.

75. Ibid., April 26, 1930, 1; May 3, 1930, 6; July 5, 1930, 1; September 20, 1930, 1.

76. Michael Harris, "Thomas A. Dorsey," in Reagon, *We'll Understand It Better*, 180; Harris, *Rise of Gospel Blues*, 175. Michael Harris cites Saturday, August 23, as the morning when Smith sang "If You See My Savior," but the remaining details of Dorsey's participation in the convention bring the accuracy of this date into question. If, according to Dorsey, it took Reverend Hall two days to track him down, the convention would have been over by the time Hall and Dorsey went to the coliseum, because it concluded on the twenty-fifth. Even if Hall located Dorsey on the twenty-third, it seems unlikely that all the events subsequent to Dorsey's introduction to the convention—meeting Smith and E. W. D. Isaacs at the rehearsal, collecting his music and setting up a table to sell the sheets, generating sales of four thousand copies,

and hearing Frye sing—could have taken place within the time frame of two days. This would have been especially difficult because concluding ceremonies took place at Olivet Baptist Church, not at the Coliseum. It is more likely that Smith sang the Dorsey composition earlier in the week.

77. Harris, *Rise of Gospel Blues*, 176.

78. Kenneth Woods Jr., interview with author, February 19, 2007.

79. Harris, *Rise of Gospel Blues*, 175–78.

80. Ibid., 178.

81. Ibid.

82. Boyer, *How Sweet the Sound*, 64.

83. Eugene Smith, interview with author, January 10, 2008.

84. Mr. and Mrs. Mack Marshall, interview with author, May 28, 2010.

85. The initial meeting of the Beatles' Paul McCartney and John Lennon is another example.

86. Harris, *Rise of Gospel Blues*, 194.

87. *Chicago Defender* (national ed.), August 10, 1918, 1.

88. 1920 U.S. Federal Census, database available online at http://www.ancestry.com.

89. *Chicago Defender* (national ed.), December 27, 1919, 13.

90. Ibid., June 5, 1920, 10.

91. Ibid., April 12, 1924, 8.

92. Ibid., August 5, 1922, 15.

93. From 1935 Metropolitan Community Church *Annual Report*, Save the Met papers, Vivian Harsh Collection, Chicago Public Library.

94. Harris, *Rise of Gospel Blues*, 187; Piper, *Handbook*, 7.

95. *Chicago Defender*, August 29, 1931.

96. Ibid. (national ed.), October 22, 1932, 15.

97. Ibid., December 17, 1949; Harris, *Rise of Gospel Blues*, 187.

Chapter 6. Sweeping through the City: Thomas A. Dorsey and the Gospel Nexus (1932–1933)

The section title "Let the Church Roll On" is the title of a popular jubilee song sung by many artists, including Chicago's Eureka Jubilee Singers.

1. *Chicago Defender*, December 6, 1952, 33.

2. Ibid. (national ed.), September 4, 1920. 1.

3. Ibid., October 29, 1921, 4.

4. Ibid., January 13, 1923, 5.

5. Ibid., June 2, 1923, 5.

6. Ibid., February 28, 1931, 4.

7. Ibid., November 1, 1930, 1.

8. Ibid., February 28, 1931, 4.

9. *From a Rough Stone.*

10. *Chicago Defender* (national ed.), October 4, 1930, 1.

11. Ibid.

12. Ibid.

13. Ibid.

14. Ibid., December 6, 1930, 13.

15. Ibid., April 18, 1931, 1.

16. Ibid., August 15, 1931, 4.

17. Ibid., October 17, 1931, 20.

18. Ibid., November 19, 1928, 6; April 8, 1939, 10. Mable Sanford Lewis played Katisha. The show attempted unsuccessfully to tour beyond Chicago and eventually closed.

19. Harris, *Rise of Gospel Blues*, 191.

20. Ibid., 192.

21. Ibid., 193–95.

22. Harris, "Conflict and Resolution," 181.

23. *From A Rough Stone.*

24. *Wade in the Water*, episode 25.

25. Ibid.

26. *From A Rough Stone.*

27. Ibid.

28. Harris, *Rise of Gospel Blues*, 195–96.

29. *Chicago Defender*, April 1, 1939, 11.

30. Best, *Passionately Human*, 46–47; *Chicago Defender*, September 21, 1935, 11.

31. *Chicago Defender*, July 2, 1938, 10.

32. Ibid. (national ed.), May 15, 1926, 2.

33. Ibid., April 1, 1939, 11.

34. *Chicago Tribune*, January 7, 2006, 1.1.

35. Harris, *Rise of Gospel Blues*, 107.

36. Ibid., 196. Dorsey places the date of the Pilgrim performance in February 1932, but according to the *Chicago Defender* (January 16, 1932, 4), Austin's sixth anniversary was to be held Sunday afternoon, January 17, 1932.

37. Harris, *Rise of Gospel Blues*, 196.

38. *Chicago Defender*, January 30, 1932, 4.

39. Harris, *Rise of Gospel Blues*, 201.

40. Ibid., 198–99, emphasis in original.

41. Harris, *Rise of Gospel Blues*, 198.

42. *Chicago Defender* (national ed.), March 10, 1928, I2.

43. I. V. Jackson, "Afro-American Gospel Music," 49.

44. Harris, *Rise of Gospel Blues*, 266.

45. Lena Johnson McLin, interview with author, June 15, 2007.

46. Black, *Bridges of Memory* (2005), 229.

47. *Wade in the Water*, episode 25.

48. Harris, *Rise of Gospel Blues*, 195.

49. *Chicago Defender*, February 8, 1941, 4.

50. The rehearsal time was noted in the church's weekly bulletin, *Ebenezer Reminder*.

51. *Chicago Defender*, March 19, 1932, photo page.

52. Abbott and Seroff, *To Do This*, 252–53.

53. Ibid.

54. *Chicago Defender*, August 19, 1933, A1. Although the movement technically began in January 1932, it was formalized in April.

55. DeLois Barrett Campbell, interview with author, March 22, 2007. Delores later changed the spelling of her first name to DeLois on the recommendation of her husband, Rev. Frank Campbell.

56. *Chicago Defender*, April 23, 1932, 6.

57. Ibid., April 30, 1932, 5; May 21, 1932, 6.

58. Charles Clency, interview with author, December 3, 2012.

59. Harris, *Rise of Gospel Blues*, 190.

60. *Chicago Defender*, August 19, 1933, A1.

61. For example, a 1969 recording of the First African Methodist Episcopal Church of Gary, Indiana's music department illustrates aurally that the gospel chorus employed many of the same formal singing conventions as the church's senior choir (Staff LP BP-3074).

62. *Chicago Defender*, July 30, 1932, 2.

63. Like Mahalia Jackson's, Roberta Martin's birth year is shrouded in mystery. In print, it is cited variously as February 12, 1907, February 14, 1907, and February 14, 1912. Her headstone at Burr Oak Cemetery in Chicago indicates a birth year of 1912, but a review of the 1910 and 1930 U.S. Census records suggests Martin was born in 1907. Roberta's brother told Irene V. Jackson that he was born in 1909, and Roberta was two years older than he was. Further, the 1910 U.S. Census that counted the Winstons while they were living in Arkansas identified Roberta as four-year-old "Birdie" [Bertie]. The fact that she was alive to be counted at all disproves the 1912 argument. The 1930 U.S. Census registered Roberta as a twenty-two-year-old living in Chicago. While February 12 is sometimes given as Roberta Martin's birthday, there is also some question about its accuracy. Her son Leonard recalled that the family always celebrated her birthday on Valentine's Day, February 14. See also *Chicago Defender*, December 4, 1948, 25.

64. I. V. Jackson, "Afro-American Gospel Music," 89.

65. Ibid., 90.

66. Ibid., 89.

67. Ibid., 90–91.

68. Anthony Heilbut, email communication with author, September 6, 2012.

69. On the 1940 census, Roberta Martin indicated her educational status as two years of college completed. See 1940 U.S. Federal Census, database available at http://www.ancestry.com.

70. Leonard Austin, interview with author, March 20, 2007. In conducting research for her dissertation on Roberta Martin, Irene V. Jackson could not find any record of Roberta Winston attending Northwestern University. The author was also unsuccessful in finding a record of Roberta Winston or Roberta Martin in the Northwestern University school registrar's files. Entering but not graduating Northwestern would have classified Martin as a near alumna, and many universities do not keep records of near alumni from more than eighty years ago.

71. Eugene Smith insists that Martin was recruited by Frye from Arnett Chapel AME

in Morgan Park in 1932. On the other hand, Martin told Horace Clarence Boyer in a 1964 interview that she was playing for Pilgrim at that time. The two circumstances are not necessarily contradictory. It is possible Martin was fulfilling both responsibilities and other music assignments at the same time. Further, the 1930 Census shows Roberta and Bill Martin living on 108th Street in Morgan Park, near Arnett Chapel.

72. Horace Boyer, "Roberta Martin: Innovator of Modern Gospel Music," in Reagon, *We'll Understand It Better*, 276.

73. Another popular explanation for how Roberta Martin became the accompanist and director of the Ebenezer Junior Chorus involves her auditioning unsuccessfully to be a vocalist for the Ebenezer Gospel Chorus. A deeper consideration of this theory renders it highly improbable. First, it is unlikely that anyone auditioned for the Ebenezer Gospel Chorus. Second, Martin had a lovely voice and, given her training, would have had no problem blending well with other altos. Third, she was known for her piano skills and, if anything, would have been persuaded to accompany rather than be one of many singers.

74. Eugene Smith, interview with author, January 10, 2008.

75. Song published by Thomas A. Dorsey but written by Ezekiel Gibson and Elmer Ruffner.

76. Information gathered from two interviews with Eugene Smith, both conducted by the author. One was broadcast on *Gospel Memories*, WLUW-FM Chicago, June 5, 2005; the other took place on January 10, 2008. Although conducted nearly three years apart, the interviews complement each other in terms of consistent information.

77. Eugene Smith, interview with author, January 10, 2008.

78. *Chicago Defender*, March 14, 1936, 7. Davis, incidentally, maintained a steady presence in the music departments of the city's South and West Side churches during the 1930s. In addition to directing Greater Mount Olive's gospel choir, established in 1934, Davis directed gospel choirs at Coppin Chapel AME and at Zion Hill Baptist Church Choir as early as 1936. His wife directed the Mount Sinai Baptist chorus on the West Side, and son John Walters Davis led the Wayman AME gospel chorus. John Walters Davis wrote the gospel song "I'm Tired, Lord, My Soul Needs Resting" (see I. L. Johnson, "Development of African American Gospel Piano Style," 155). Davis wrote, sang, and directed. When his wife died in late 1936, he moved to Philadelphia, where he married gospel singer Mary Johnson. Mary Johnson Davis (1899–1982) became a popular soloist and group leader whose influence on her gospel singing contemporaries was far more profound than the paucity of biographical information on her career suggests. Anthony Heilbut calls Mary Johnson Davis "the first significant gospel soprano" (see Heilbut, *Fan Who Knew Too Much*, 257).

79. *From a Rough Stone.*

80. Smith, *Life and Works*, 38.

81. In another account, Dorsey identified the singer traveling with him as Luschaa Allen.

82. Harris, *Rise of Gospel Blues*, 216.

83. Thomas A. Dorsey Collection, 1932–1982, Fisk University Library.

84. Harris, *Rise of Gospel Blues*, 217.

85. Ibid., 217–18.

86. *Chicago Defender*, September 3, 1932, 2. DeYampert citation from *Chicago Defender*, October 30, 1937, 10. By 1937, DeYampert was directing the choir at the Metropolitan Baptist Church at Warren Boulevard on the city's West Side.

87. Smith, *Life and Works*, 96–97; also quoted in Harris, *Rise of Gospel Blues*, 218.

88. "Precious Lord, Take My Hand." Web site, accessed September 5, 2008, www .preciouslordtakemyhand.com/pltmhhymnhistory.html. An announcement for the grand opening of the Chicago branch of Poro College was advertised in the *Chicago Defender*, March 17, 1928, B6.

89. Harris, *Rise of Gospel Blues*, 228–29.

90. Ibid., 237–38.

91. Ibid., 241.

92. Boyer, *How Sweet the Sound*, 76. Her name also appears on the 1938 sheet music of the song. Historian Horace Maxile has confirmed this fact.

93. Dixon, Godrich, and Rye, *Blues and Gospel Records*, 370.

94. Anthony Heilbut, email communication with author, September 6, 2012.

95. Thomas A. Dorsey Collection, 1932–1982, Fisk University Library.

96. Lena Johnson McLin, interview with author, June 15, 2007.

97. Ibid.

98. Ibid.

99. Ibid.

100. Smith, *Life and Works*, 38, 44.

101. *Chicago Defender*, April 11, 1936, 9; April 18, 1936.

102. Ibid., November 2, 1935, 22; November 23, 1935, 10; April 25, 1936; 8.

103. Ibid., June 22, 1935, 20; October 26, 1935, 22; November 23, 1935, 10.

104. Ibid., February 11, 1933, 3.

105. Ibid., April 1, 1933, 24.

106. Ibid., July 8, 1933, 7.

107. Ibid. (national ed.), August 19, 1933, A1.

108. Ibid., September 9, 1933, 15.

109. Lewis-Butts marriage information from *Cook County, Illinois Marriage Index 1930–1960*.

110. *Chicago Defender*, September 9, 1933, 15; August 10, 1946, 31. The site of the headquarters, 4048 South Lake Park Avenue, was finally secured around 1947.

111. Ibid., September 9, 1933, 15.

112. Ibid. (national ed.), September 30, 1933, 10.

113. Ibid.

114. Ibid., June 3, 1933, 1. Margaret Bonds (b. March 3, 1913, Chicago) would become a world-renowned composer, arranger, and classical pianist until her death in 1972 at the age of fifty-nine.

115. Eugene Smith, interview with author, January 10, 2008. The Wise Singers' technique of holding the note of the first syllable "I," in "I Can Tell the World," can be heard on the Silver Leaf Quartette's June 1928 recording of the song on OKeh 8594 and reissued on Document DOCD-5352. According to the reissue CD's liner notes by

Kip Lornell, the Silver Leaf Quartette toured extensively in the northeast, frequenting Philadelphia. Thus, the Wise Singers may have learned this particular arrangement from the Silver Leafs, or vice versa. See also Pearl Williams-Jones and Bernice Johnson Reagon, "Conversations: Roberta Martin Singers Roundtable," in Reagon, *We'll Understand It Better*, 303.

116. *From a Rough Stone.*

117. Background on Willie Webb from I. L. Johnson, "Development of African American Gospel Piano Style," 144.

118. *Chicago Defender*, October 24, 1936, 24.

119. Pearl Williams-Jones and Bernice Johnson Reagon, "Conversations: Roberta Martin Singers Roundtable," in Reagon, *We'll Understand It Better*, 297–98.

120. Eugene Smith, interview with author, January 10, 2008. Many gospel groups (e.g., Duncanaires, Pattersonaires, Brewsteraires) were named after the pastor of the church from whence they came or the group's spiritual or musical leader.

121. *Bowles Favorite Gospel and Spiritual Melodies*, no. 3; *Bowles Favorite Gospel Tidings*, no. 14; *Frye's Special Gospel Song Book*, no. 6.

122. Eugene Smith, interview with author broadcast on *Gospel Memories*.

123. As of June 1935, the Roberta Martin Singers were still known as the Martin-Frye Quartet; see "Dr. Hawkins Speaker at St. Luke's Church," *Chicago Defender*, June 8, 1935. Despite the group's name change, the press would refer to the Roberta Martin Singers as the Martin and Frye Quartette throughout the 1930s.

124. Eugene Smith, telephone interview with author, June 11, 2008. See also *From a Rough Stone.*

125. Daniel, "Ritual in Chicago's South Side Churches," 126.

Chapter 7. Across This Land and Country: New Songs for a New Era (1933–1939)

1. Eugene Smith, interview with author, January 10, 2008.

2. Daniel, "Ritual in Chicago's South Side Churches," 124–25.

3. Ibid., 15.

4. Ibid.

5. *Chicago Defender*, December 24, 1938, 17.

6. Ibid., August 11, 1934, 13. Nothing more is known of the Four Fryes.

7. Standifer, interview with Sallie Martin, September 19, 1981.

8. Ibid.

9. Smith, *Life and Works*, 80–82.

10. *Chicago Defender*, June 9, 1934, 18; October 6, 1934, 4.

11. Ibid., March 2, 1935, 13.

12. Smith, *Life and Works*, 40.

13. Ibid., 40–41.

14. *Chicago Defender*, July 6, 1935, 22.

15. Drake and Cayton, *Black Metropolis*, 670.

16. *Chicago Defender*, January 11, 1936, 16.

17. From a photocopy of the June 30, 1935, First Church of Deliverance bulletin, courtesy of Bishop Otto T. Houston III and First Church of Deliverance.

18. *Chicago Defender*, May 23, 1936, 17.

19. Ibid., May 8, 1937, 2.

20. Ibid., February 4, 1939, 6.

21. Ibid.

22. Horace Boyer, "Kenneth Morris," 309–10; Boyer, *How Sweet the Sound*, 72–73.

23. Dixon, Godrich, and Rye, *Blues and Gospel Records*, 880.

24. *Bowles Favorite*, no. 6, 10–11.

25. Kenneth Morris, interview with Bernice Johnson Reagon, 1987, in Reagon, *We'll Understand It Better*, 332.

26. Fishman, Brylawski, and Maguire, "Biography of Jack Kapp."

27. "Ivy League Black History."

28. Goreau, *Just Mahalia, Baby*, 72–73.

29. The discs were credited solely to "Brother" Son Bonds.

30. The Mound City Jubilee Quartette sides can be heard on *Vocal Quartets, Complete Recorded Works*, vol. 4: *K/L/M—1927–1943*, Document DOCD-5540, CD. The Silver Leaf Quartette's version of "Sleep On Mother" is on *The Silver Leaf Quartette of Norfolk: 1928–1931*, Document DOCD-5352, CD.

31. Dixon, Godrich, and Rye, *Blues and Gospel Records*, 670. The Four A Melody Men performed into the 1950s, remaining true to their a cappella jubilee singing style after quartets added hard-singing leads and backing musicians.

32. Ibid., 411; released and unreleased tracks by Professor Hull's Anthems of Joy can be heard on *Singin' the Gospel*, Document DOCD-5326, CD, liner notes by gospel quartet scholar and author Kip Lornell.

33. Godrich, Dixon, and Rye, *Blues and Gospel Records*, 305; additional personnel listed on *Golden Eagle Gospel Singers (1937–1940)*, Eden ELE 4-200, LP. The group photo that graces the cover of the Eden Records reissue depicts nine individuals, not seven. The six women and three men, dressed in Sunday finery, appear middle-aged.

34. Funk, liner notes to *Swinging Gospel Sounds*.

35. Ibid. The April 25, 1936, *Chicago Defender* reports that the "Golden Eagle Female Quartet" sang on a program at Grant Memorial on April 19, 1936. It is not certain whether these two aggregations are at all associated with each other. Anthony Heilbut posits that "He's My Rock" was written not by Kenneth Morris, as has often been attributed, but by the Soul Stirrers.

36. *Chicago Defender*, March 22, 1941, 8; January 17, 1942, 7; Funk, liner notes to *Swinging Gospel Sounds*.

37. Dixon, Godrich, and Rye, *Blues and Gospel Records*, 314.

38. Goreau, *Just Mahalia, Baby*, 73.

39. Ibid.

40. I. L. Johnson, "Development of African American Gospel Piano Style," 271.

41. Goreau, *Just Mahalia, Baby*, 74.

42. Ibid., 79.

43. Ibid., 87–88; I. L. Johnson. "Development of African American Gospel Piano Style," 156.

44. Goreau, *Just Mahalia, Baby*, 76.

45. Ibid., 115.

46. *Chicago Defender*, January 29, 1938, 22.

47. Ibid., April 2, 1938, 3; April 30, 1938, 6.

48. Ibid., April 2, 1938, 3.

49. Ibid., February 12, 1938, 19. This event is described as announced in the article.

50. First Church of Deliverance may have been inspired by Elder Lucy Smith to build its own church. Her new building was the first black church in Chicago in some time to be built from the ground up.

51. *Chicago Defender*, May 25, 1937, 10.

52. Ibid., May 27, 1939, 4.

53. Ibid. Bailey had little time to admire his work because he succumbed to tuberculosis two years later.

54. United States Patent Office, 1,956,350: "Electrical Musical Instrument," 1–3, available at http://www.google.com/patents/US1956350.

55. Hammond Organ, www.thehammondorganstory.com, accessed May 4, 2007.

56. *Chicago Defender*, January 11, 1936, 10.

57. Ibid., April 22, 1939, 10; January 29, 1938, 6. Lennie Ellis was the funeral home's house organist. It is unknown who was the organist for St. Edmond's.

58. Daniel, "Ritual in Chicago's South Side Churches," 77, 79. In the late 1930s, Daniel refers to the organ's role in the services of the "ecstatic cults" (i.e., Pentecostal, Holiness, and Spiritual churches) as aiding "in the swinging of the songs" as well as the "staccato and swinging effects produced by the singers and by the instruments accompanying them."

59. U.S. Patent Office, 1–3.

60. Kenneth Morris, interview with Bernice Johnson Reagon, 1987, in Reagon, *We'll Understand It Better*, 337.

61. Ibid., 338. Since the now-iconic Model B3 (and the C3, with its "modesty panel") was not introduced until January 1955, the organ that Reverend Cobbs purchased for First Church must have been the Model A.

62. Hammond Organ, www.thehammondorganstory.com.

63. Lester, "Lauren Hammond and Don Leslie"; Olsen, "Leslie Speakers and Hammond Organs."

64. Obituary, *Pasadena Star-News*, September 4, 2004.

65. Kenneth Woods Jr., interview with author, November 15, 2011.

66. Anthony Heilbut, email communication with author, September 6, 2012.

67. Baldwin, *Chicago's New Negroes*, 158.

68. *Chicago Defender*, February 25, 1939, 18.

69. Mr. and Mrs. Mack Marshall, interview with author, May 28, 2010.

70. Daniel, "Ritual in Chicago's South Side Churches," 143.

71. Ibid., 48–52. In a chart of the "Orders of the Semi-Demonstrative Service," Daniel

depicts one church as having two collections during the service, both accompanied by a gospel song (48).

72. Ibid., 63.

73. Ibid., 65.

74. Ibid., 66.

75. *Chicago Tribune*, January 7, 2006, 1.1

76. This event is described as it was scheduled to take place, according to an article in the *Chicago Defender* (December 30, 1939, 5).

77. Ibid. (national ed.), June 17, 1944, 18.

78. Thomas A. Dorsey Papers, box 1.

Chapter 8. From Birmingham to Chicago: The Great Migration of the Gospel Quartet

1. Quoted in Darden, *People Get Ready!*, 137.

2. Melvin Butler, "Gospel Quartets," in McNeil, *Encyclopedia of American Gospel Music*, 156.

3. Lornell, *Happy in the Service*, 18.

4. Ibid., 11–15.

5. Butler, "Gospel Quartets."

6. Dixon, Godrich, and Rye, *Blues and Gospel Records*, 215.

7. Seroff, liner notes to *There Breathes a Hope*, 5.

8. Abbott and Seroff, *To Do This*, 223. Abbott and Seroff's book provides greater detail on the history of the glee club and jubilee quartet communities active in Chicago during the prewar era.

9. Lornell, *Happy in the Service*, 21.

10. Brooks, *Lost Sounds*, 92.

11. Ibid., 92.

12. Ibid., 92–93. 95–96.

13. Romanowski, liner notes to *Earliest Negro Vocal Groups*, vol. 2.

14. Dixon, Godrich, and Rye, *Blues and Gospel Records*, 859.

15. Brooks, *Lost Sounds*, 97.

16. Ibid., 100.

17. Giovanionni, liner notes to *Lost Sounds*.

18. *Chicago Defender*, May 11, 1935, 20.

19. Lornell cited in Portia K. Maultsby, "The Impact of Gospel Music on the Secular Music Industry," in Reagon, *We'll Understand It Better*, 21.

20. Regarding the Pullman Porters Quartette, see Abbott and Seroff, *To Do This*, 223.

21. *Chicago Defender* (national ed.), December 1, 1923, 10; Abbott and Seroff, *To Do This*, 220–21.

22. Abbott and Seroff, *To Do This*, 221.

23. Reported in *Chicago Defender* (national ed.), December 13, 1924, 8.

24. Ibid., February 9, 1924, 6.

25. Reported in *Chicago Defender* (national ed.), December 6, 1924, 6.

26. Ibid. When Paramount advertised its spiritual line in the newspaper, it focused on singles by the Norfolk, Paramount, and Sunset Four jubilee quartets.

27. This fact was verified by Dick Rosemont for his Originals Project, http://www .OriginalsProject.us, accessed January 19, 2012, and confirmed by a review of recorded versions listed in Godrich, Dixon, and Rye, *Blues and Gospel Records*.

28. *Chicago Defender* (national ed.), August 14, 1926, 7; September 11, 1926, 7.

29. Ibid., November 5, 1927, 8.

30. Ibid., April 10, 1926, 7; September 29, 1928, 7.

31. Seroff, liner notes to *Birmingham Quartet Anthology*.

32. Seroff, liner notes to *Jesus Hits like the Atom Bomb*; Seroff, liner notes to *Birmingham Quartet Anthology*.

33. Seroff, liner notes to *Jesus Hits like the Atom Bomb*.

34. Ibid.

35. Ibid.; Seroff, liner notes to *Birmingham Quartet Anthology*.

36. Abbott and Seroff, *To Do This*, 234.

37. 1920 U.S. Census, database available at http://www.ancestry.com.

38. Seroff, liner notes to *Jesus Hits like the Atom Bomb*.

39. Abbott and Seroff, *To Do This*, 235.

40. Ibid., 235–38.

41. Ibid., 245.

42. *Chicago Defender*, August 6, 1932, 10.

43. Abbott and Seroff, *To Do This*, 238.

44. Ibid., 240, 245–46.

45. *Chicago Defender*, September 27, 1941, 1–2.

46. Ibid., August 6, 1932, 10.

47. Ibid., July 28, 1937, 12.

48. Ibid., September 27, 1941, 1–2.

49. Ibid.

50. Ibid., 11.

51. Ibid., July 10, 1948, 20.

52. Ibid., February 21, 1953, 38.; Hayes and Laughton, *Gospel Discography*, 135.

53. Abbott and Seroff, *To Do This*, 130.

54. Butler, "Gospel Quartets."

55. Seroff, liner notes to *Birmingham Quartet Anthology*.

56. Ibid.

57. Godrich, Dixon, and Rye, *Blues and Gospel Records*, 254.

58. Abbott and Seroff, *To Do This*, 149.

59. Carpenter, *Uncloudy Days*, 383.

60. Mark Burford, "Soul Stirrers," in McNeil, *Encyclopedia of American Gospel Music*, 356; Boyer, *How Sweet the Sound*, 95–96.

61. Wolff et al., *You Send Me*, 44.

62. Boyer, *How Sweet the Sound*, 95–96.

63. Godrich, Dixon, and Rye, *Blues and Gospel Records*, 263.

64. Quoted in Heilbut, *Gospel Sound*, 75–76.

65. Anthony Heilbut, email communication with author, September 6, 2012.

66. Wolff et. al., *You Send Me*, 45.

67. Heilbut, *Gospel Sound*, 79–80.

68. Ibid., 80.

69. Burford, "Soul Stirrers," in McNeil, *Encyclopedia of American Gospel Music*, 356.; Wolff et al., *You Send Me*, 46.

70. Heilbut, *Gospel Sound*, 77.

71. Others assert that the switch lead was invented by Silas Steele of the Famous Blue Jays.

72. *Chicago Defender*, October 22, 1938, 17.

73. Ibid., March 25, 1939, 8.

74. Godrich, Dixon, and Rye, *Blues and Gospel Records*. 264.

75. *Bowles Favorite Gospel and Spiritual Melodies*, no. 3.

76. Abbott and Seroff, *To Do This*, 155.

77. Seroff, liner notes to *Birmingham Quartet Anthology*.

78. Regarding the Soul Stirrers' broadcast, see Abbott and Seroff, *To Do This*, 263; regarding the Blue Jays, see *Chicago Defender*, October 24, 1942, 9.

79. *Chicago Defender*, February 7, 1942, 11; January 17, 1942, 7.

80. Ibid., September 2, 1944, 8.

81. Ibid., January 26, 1946, 8.

82. Seroff, liner notes to *Jesus Hits like the Atom Bomb*; Seroff, liner notes to *Birmingham Quartet Anthology*.

83. Anthony Heilbut, email communication with author, September 6, 2012.

84. Wolff et al., *You Send Me*, 42.

85. Abbott and Seroff, *To Do This*, 158.

86. *Chicago Defender*, January 5, 1946, 8.

87. Liner notes to *Don't Let the Devil Ride*.

88. Ibid.

89. *Chicago Defender*, March 14, 1942, 10.

90. Ibid., September 19, 1942, 10.

91. Abbott and Seroff, *To Do This*, 240–41.

92. *Chicago Defender*, February 14, 1942, 10; Abbott and Seroff, *To Do This*, 237.

93. Anthony Heilbut, email communication with author, September 6, 2012.

94. *Chicago Defender*, July 4, 1946, 27.

95. Heilbut, *Fan Who Knew Too Much*, 29.

96. *Chicago Defender*, November 13, 1948, 31.

97. *Chicago Daily Defender*, March 6, 1963, 16.

98. Cook County, IL, Marriage Index, 1930–1960, database available at http://www.ancestry.com.

99. *Chicago Defender*, October 13, 1951, 51.

100. William Roberts is not the same person as Bishop William Roberts of Fortieth COGIC.

101. *Chicago Defender*, March 23, 1948, 8; December 25, 1948, 30.

102. Hayes and Laughton, *Gospel Discography*, 327.

Chapter 9. Sing a Gospel Song: The 1940s, Part One

Epigraph taken from Daniel, "Ritual in Chicago's South Side Churches for Negroes," 134.

1. November 1957 *Newsweek* article quoted in *Chicago Defender*, January 4, 1958, 25.

2. Rev. Dr. Issac Whittmon, interview with author, July 6, 2008.

3. Southern, *Music of Black Americans*, 476.

4. I. L. Johnson, "Development of African American Gospel Piano Style," 145.

5. Samuelson and Peters, "Landmarks of Blues and Gospel," 12.

6. *Chicago Defender*, August 14, 1948, 31.

7. Ibid., May 20, 1944, 5.

8. Ibid. (national ed.), May 29, 1943, 16.

9. Uncredited liner notes, Myrtle Jackson, *Sings Songs of Hope and Inspiration*.

10. *Chicago Defender*, January 1, 1944, 8.

11. Aldrea Lenox, interview with author, January 8, 2011.

12. Heilbut, liner notes to *Soul of Chicago*.

13. *Chicago Defender*, March 22, 1947, 13. Mary Morris was widowed when Edna Mae was young and lost her own life in a 1946 house fire.

14. Ibid., December 20, 1941, 10.

15. Ibid., August 30, 1947, 18.

16. Anthony Heilbut, email communication with author, September 6, 2012.

17. *Chicago Defender*, November 20, 1948, 34.

18. Robert Sacré, "Robert Anderson," in McNeil, *Encyclopedia of American Gospel Music,* 10.

19. Carpenter, *Uncloudy Days*, 18.

20. Heilbut, *Gospel Sound,* 207.

21. Goreau, *Just Mahalia, Baby*, 96.

22. Eugene Smith, interview with author, March 30, 2009.

23. *Chicago Defender*, July 27, 1941, 7.

24. Ibid., October 19, 1940, 11.

25. Ibid., April 18, 1942, 10.

26. Anthony Heilbut, email communication with author, September 6, 2012.

27. *Chicago Defender*, June 14, 1941, 9.

28. Vernon Oliver Price, interview with author, April 11, 2007.

29. *Chicago Defender*, January 22, 1944, 8; Alexander, liner notes to *God Bless the Child*.

30. *Chicago Defender*, April 13, 1946, 10.

31. Ibid., October 23, 1943, 10.

32. Ibid., June 22, 1946, 20.

33. Rev. Dr. Clay Evans, interview with author, January 18, 2007.

34. Additional Rawls biographical information from *Chicago Defender*, November 5, 1953, 34.

35. Ibid., May 4, 1946, 27.

36. Ibid., August 10, 1946, 30.

37. *Chicago Defender*, July 4, 1946, 27.

38. Ibid., March 15, 1947, 6.

39. Ibid., April 3, 1948, 30.

40. Ibid. (national ed.), September 24, 1938, 6.

41. Ibid., October 11, 1941, 3.

42. Anthony Heilbut, email communication with author, September 6, 2012.

43. *Chicago Defender*, November 29, 1941, 4.

44. Ibid., September 2, 1944, 3.

45. Senator Ethel Alexander, interview with author, November 8, 2007.

46. Goreau, *Just Mahalia, Baby*, 94, 100–101. Mahalia Jackson traveled with Dorsey from 1939 to 1942 or 1943.

47. *Chicago Defender*, May 10, 1941, 5. From time to time, Johnson invited Louise Lemon, another Johnson Singer, to appear at Gammon.

48. Goreau, *Just Mahalia, Baby*, 91.

49. During the author's August 30, 2008, interview with Donald and Geraldine Gay, Donald said that COGIC Bishop A. A. Childs, for whom Mahalia worked tent revivals, was the first to refer to Mahalia as "Empress."

50. *Chicago Defender*, May 25, 1940, 11; May 8, 1943, 9; *Just Mahalia, Baby*, 95, 99.

51. *Chicago Defender*, April 15, 1944, 11.

52. Goreau, *Just Mahalia, Baby*, 102.

53. Ibid.

54. *Chicago Defender*, April 29, 1943, 8; June 3, 1944, 16.

55. Pearl Williams-Jones and Bernice Johnson Reagon, "Conversations: Roberta Martin Singers Roundtable," in Reagon, *We'll Understand It Better*, 298.

56. Ibid.

57. DeLois Barrett Campbell, interview with author, March 22, 2007; see also Williams-Jones and Reagon, "Conversations," 299.

58. DeLois Barrett Campbell interview with author, March 22, 2007.

59. Ibid.

60. I. V. Jackson, "Afro-American Gospel Music," 101, 137–38.

61. L. Stanley Davis, interview with author, March 1, 2007.

62. Heilbut, *Gospel Sound*, xxix.

63. I. L. Johnson, "Development of African American Gospel Piano Style," 334.

64. Ibid., 360.

65. Harold Bailey, interview with author, February 19, 2007.

66. I. L. Johnson, "Development of African American Gospel Piano Style," 141.

67. Bertha Burley Melson, interview with author, July 28, 2011.

68. Ibid.

69. *Chicago Defender*, September 13, 1941, 26.

70. Vernon Oliver Price, interview with author, April 11, 2007.

71. Jerome Burks, interview with author, November 13, 2013.

72. Heilbut, *Gospel Sound*, 206.

73. Carpenter, *Uncloudy Days*, 87–88.

74. Heilbut, *Gospel Sound*, 207.

75. Ibid., 207; Heilbut, *Fan Who Knew Too Much*, 34.

76. *Chicago Defender*, December 19, 1942, 5.

77. Carpenter, *Uncloudy Days*, 87–88.

78. Heilbut, *Gospel Sound*, 207.

79. Floriene Watson Willis, interview with author, July 5, 2013.

80. Rev. Dr. Clay Evans, interview with author, January 18, 2007.

81. Ibid.

82. Ibid.

83. Ibid.

84. *Chicago Defender*, June 8, 1946, 27; in a November 15, 2011, interview, Kenneth Woods Jr. told the author that when he saw Cleveland in the Lux Singers, Evans was not a member.

85. Anthony Heilbut, email communication with author, September 6, 2012.

86. Rev. Dr. Clay Evans, interview with author, January 18, 2007.

87. Bertha Burley Melson, interview with author, July 28, 2011.

88. Ibid.

89. Report, *Seventeenth Annual Session*, 31.

90. Jerome Burks, interview with author, November 13, 2013.

91. *Chicago Defender*, October 11, 1941, 4.

92. Ibid., April 4, 1942, 23.

93. Ibid., October 27, 1945, 23.

94. Jerome Burks, interview with author, November 13, 2013.

95. Ibid.

96. Heilbut, liner notes to *Soul of Chicago*.

97. Some of the biographical information on the Gay Family comes from an unpublished document written by Gregory Gay. Other data comes from Donald Gay and Geraldine Gay Hambric in discussion with Aaron Cohen and the author, August 30, 2008. After winning a one-hundred-dollar bond on the show in February 1952, Donald was invited to return to *Quiz Kids* several times thereafter. See *Chicago Defender*, February 23, 1952, 32.

98. Goreau, *Just Mahalia, Baby*, 163.

99. Donald Gay and Geraldine Gay Hambric, interview with author, August 30, 2008.

100. Ibid.

101. Ibid.

102. Ibid.

103. After Donald formally joined, the ensemble was renamed the Gay Singers.

104. Donald Gay and Geraldine Gay Hambric in discussion with author, August 30, 2008.

105. Ibid.

106. Robert Sacré, "Gay Sisters," in McNeil, *Encyclopedia of American Gospel Music*, 137.

107. Donald Gay and Geraldine Gay Hambric, interview with author, August 30, 2008.

108. *Chicago Defender* (national ed.), September 14, 1946, 17.

Chapter 10. "If It's in Music—We Have It": The Fertile Crescent of Gospel Music Publishing

The title of the section on Thomas A. Dorsey is taken from the title of one of his song folios.

1. Heilbut, *Gospel Sound*, xxx.

2. *Chicago Defender*, November 23, 1946, 27.

3. Ibid., July 1, 1946, 6.

4. Ibid., December 15, 1945, 6; August 3, 1946, 27.

5. Ibid., August 10, 1946, 31.

6. Report, *Seventeenth Annual Session*, 4.

7. Horace Clarence Boyer, "Take My Hand, Precious Lord, Lead Me On," in Reagon, *We'll Understand It Better*, 144–45.

8. Ibid., 143.

9. Smith, *Life and Works*, 47.

10. Boyer, "Take My Hand," 145–46, 149, 158, 160.

11. Ibid., 146, 163.

12. Biszick-Lockwood, *Restless Giant*, 176–77.

13. Eugene Smith told the author ca. 2007 about Martin starting her publishing business in the basement of her Bowen Avenue home. The Bowen Avenue address appears on Martin's "Didn't It Rain," copyrighted in 1939, her second year in the publishing business.

14. "I Know the Lord" was credited to Roberta Martin Singer Eugene Smith, but Anthony Heilbut told the author that Robert Anderson once confessed to him that "the song was composed by him and Roberta Martin, and assigned to Eugene Smith for vague contractual reasons." Heilbut, email communication with author, September 6, 2012.

15. "I'm Just Waiting on the Lord," Apollo 285; I. V. Jackson, "Afro-American Gospel Music," 113.

16. I. V. Jackson, "Afro-American Gospel Music," 106.

17. Ibid., 132.

18. Ibid., 121.

19. Leonard Austin, interview with author, March 20, 2007.

20. Anthony Heilbut, email communication with author, September 6, 2012.

21. *Chicago Defender* (national ed.), September 18, 1943, 20; (city ed.) May 6, 1950, 29.

22. *Chicago Defender*, November 20, 1943, 10.

23. Ibid. (national ed.), June 30, 1945, 9B.

24. Ibid. (city ed.), December 17, 1949, 27.

25. Ibid., September 23, 1950, 37.

26. Since he joined Bowles Music House in 1939, Carey Bradley may have been Kenneth Morris's replacement. When Bradley joined the Kings of Harmony in 1941, he introduced the quartet to some of the gospel songs being published by Bowles. By making some of the songs popular on the quartet circuit, the Kings of Harmony helped encourage other groups to adopt the new gospel songs into their repertories. See Abbott and Seroff, *To Do This*, 185.

27. Herndon, liner notes to *Living Legend.*

28. It is not known whether Cobbs's seed money was a loan, an outright gift, or an equity stake in Martin and Morris, or whether it was from his personal resources or the church's.

29. Martin and Morris Collection, Collection 492: Series 2—Business and Financial Records, Smithsonian Institution Museum of American History, Washington, DC.

30. Ibid.

31. Waterman, "Gospel Hymns," 87.

32. Dixon, Godrich, and Rye, *Blues and Gospel Records,* 598; Boyer, *How Sweet the Sound,* 92–93.

33. Dixon, Godrich, and Rye, *Blues and Gospel Records,* 598.

34. *Chicago Defender* (national ed.), January 16, 1943, 1; December 11, 1943, 16.

35. Martin and Morris Collection, Collection 492: Series 1—Correspondence 1942–43, 1944, Smithsonian Institution Museum of American History, Washington, DC.

36. Morris, "I'll Be a Servant for the Lord," 333.

37. Martin and Morris Collection, Collection 492, Series 1—Correspondence 1950–51, Smithsonian Institution Museum of American History, Washington, DC.

38. Morris, "I'll Be a Servant for the Lord," 333.

39. Ibid.

40. Letter from Rev. W. Herbert Brewster to Kenneth Morris, September 28, 1945, Martin and Morris Collection, Smithsonian Institution Museum of American History, Washington, DC.

41. Boyer, "Kenneth Morris," 313.

42. Ibid., 321–22.

43. Ibid., 323.

44. Martin and Morris, *Twelve Gospel Song Hits,* 2.

45. Ibid., 6.

46. Ibid., 10. Morris mentions that he had just married when he learned of his diagnosis, so it is possible that the affliction he refers to is different from his earlier bout with tuberculosis and occurred closer to the 1940s.

47. Morris, "I'll Be a Servant for the Lord," 339.

48. Ibid., 333.

49. Ibid., 336. Roberta Martin dedicated her 1938 "God's Amazing Grace" to "my dear friend, Mrs. Lula Butler Hurse, National Gospel Singer, Kansas City, Mo." Anthony Heilbut confirmed in a conversation with the author that Lula Mae Butler Hurse was the mother of William Hurse and that Mahalia Jackson and DeLois Barrett Campbell were fond of Mrs. Hurse's soprano singing.

50. Boyer, *How Sweet the Sound,* 75.

51. Eugene Smith shared this version at a board meeting of the Chicago Gospel Music Heritage Museum where the author was present, in 2008 or 2009.

52. Sheet music, "Just a Closer Walk with Thee."

53. Dixon, Godrich, and Rye, *Blues and Gospel Records,* 786, 912.

54. Born in Canada of Japanese ancestry, Hayakawa taught at Illinois Institute of Technology, in the heart of Bronzeville, from 1939 to 1948 and lectured at the Univer-

sity of Chicago from 1950 to 1955. He went on to serve as president of San Francisco State College and became a U.S. senator, representing California from 1977 to 1983.

Chapter 11. "Move On Up a Little Higher":
The 1940s, Part Two

1. The five-year contract was presumably a management agreement, as Sellers never recorded for the brothers' Coleman label.

2. Hayes and Laughton, *Gospel Discography*, 298.

3. Pruter and Campbell, "Miracle Records."

4. Edwards and Callahan, "Apollo Records Story."

5. Goreau, *Just Mahalia, Baby*, 107–10.

6. Ibid.

7. I. L. Johnson, "Development of African American Gospel Piano Style," 386; Heilbut, *Fan Who Knew Too Much*, 278.

8. I. L. Johnson, "Development of African American Gospel Piano Style," 329.

9. Goreau, *Just Mahalia, Baby*, 114–15; Hayes and Laughton, *Gospel Discography*. 185.

10. Goreau, *Just Mahalia, Baby*, 116–17.

11. Schwerin, *Got to Tell It*, 67.

12. Goreau, *Just Mahalia, Baby*, 116.

13. Ibid., 118.

14. *Chicago Defender*, August 28, 1948, 27. According to Goreau, "Dig a Little Deeper" neared the million sales mark (*Just Mahalia Baby*, 118).

15. *Billboard*, December 25, 1948, 38; Goreau, *Just Mahalia, Baby*, 116.

16. Schwerin, *Got to Tell It*, 63–64.

17. *Billboard*, August 20, 1949, 20.

18. I. V. Jackson, "Afro-American Gospel Music," 126. The author has both self-produced Martin discs mentioned in the text.

19. The Religious Recordings sides were later purchased and released on Fidelity, a Specialty Records subsidiary. It is possible that these releases were reissues of Martin's original independent discs. For example, "Jesus" and "Only a Look" as recorded on Martin's own label are aurally the same as those released on Dolphin's of Hollywood. Until the remaining independent releases are found, or more information is unearthed, this premise cannot be verified in its entirety.

20. I. V. Jackson, "Afro-American Gospel Music," 122–23.

21. Heilbut, *Fan Who Knew Too Much*, 123.

22. Portia K. Maultsby, "The Impact of Gospel Music on the Secular Music Industry," in Reagon, *We'll Understand It Better*, 31.

23. I. L. Johnson, "Development of African American Gospel Piano Style," 361, 367.

24. Hayes and Laughton, *Gospel Discography*, 229.

25. *Billboard*, November 19, 1949, 106.

26. *Chicago Defender*, August 9, 1952, 15.

27. Hayes and Laughton, *Gospel Discography*, 155.

28. Ibid., 13.

29. Ibid., 137.

30. Heilbut, *Fan Who Knew Too Much*, 258.

31. Ibid., 15.

32. Hayes and Laughton, *Gospel Discography*, 391.

33. Ibid., 36.

34. *Chicago Defender*, December 8, 1951, 33. Second Timothy Baptist Church was later renamed Stone Temple Baptist Church, in honor of its pastor, Rev. J. M. Stone. In 1952, Weber became choir director at Forty-Fourth Street Baptist.

35. *Chicago Defender*, March 1, 1952, 36.

36. Ibid., November 19, 1949, 9.

37. Ibid., 36.

38. Pruter and Campbell, "Premium Records."

39. *Chicago Defender*, February 24, 1951, 40.

40. Pruter, Campbell, and Kelly, "Hy-Tone Records."

41. Pruter, *Doowop*, 16–17.

42. *Chicago Defender*, January 24, 1942, 13.

43. Ibid., June 20, 1942, 10.

44. Ibid., September 18, 1943, 7; June 30, 1951, 39.

45. Ibid., March 20, 1947, 16.

46. James and Ritz, *Rage to Survive*, 17.

47. Eugene Smith, interview with author, January 10, 2008.

48. *Los Angeles Times*, May 15, 1994, accessed August 27, 2013, http://articles.latimes.com/1994-05-15/news/ci-58147_1_choir-sings-gospel.

49. Etta James, interview with the author, *Gospel Memories* radio broadcast, WLUW-FM, aired December 4, 2005.

50. James and Ritz, *Rage to Survive*, 16.

51. Ibid., 18–21.

52. Johnson, "Development of African American Gospel Piano Style," 157.

53. Mr. and Mrs. Mack Marshall, interview with author, May 28, 2010. Mack Marshall, Frye's nephew, recalled his uncle traveling to Los Angeles to train a church choir, though he could not recall the name of the church.

54. Hayes and Laughton, *Gospel Discography*, 293–94.

55. *Billboard*, July 29, 1950, 13.

56. Ibid., November 19, 1949, 106.

57. Heilbut, liner notes to *When Gospel Was Gospel*.

58. *Billboard*, February 4, 1950, 104.

59. Kenneth Woods Jr., interview with author, December 13, 2011.

60. *Billboard*, October 15, 1949, 19; Hayes and Laughton, *Gospel Discography*, 231.

61. *Billboard*, November 19, 1949, 106.

62. Ibid., July 29, 1950, 13.

63. Hayes and Laughton, *Gospel Discography*, 230–31.

64. Ibid., 231.

65. Hayes and Laughton, *Gospel Discography*, 293.

66. *Chicago Defender*, April 18, 1942, 10.

67. Ibid., June 20, 1942, 26; September 19, 1942, 10.

68. Ibid., April 18, 1942, 10. Fortieth COGIC, the mother church for the Church of God in Christ in Illinois, had the denomination's largest congregation at the time.

69. Ibid., June 20, 1942, 26; September 19, 1942, 10.

70. Ibid., September 23, 1950, 37.

71. Ibid., May 26, 1951, 40; August 28, 1954, 6; October 30, 1954, 28.

72. *Billboard*, October 15, 1949, 19.

73. *Chicago Defender*, May 26, 1951, 40.

74. Ibid., August 28, 1954, 6.

75. *Chicago Defender*, August 4, 1945, 7.

76. Ibid. (Gary ed.), March 1, 1952, 4. It is possible that the pianist was Bertha Lewis.

77. Biographical information from uncredited liner notes to Robinson, *This Is My Story*.

78. I. L. Johnson, "Development of African American Gospel Piano Style," 326.

79. Hayes and Laughton, *Gospel Discography*, 126.

80. *Chicago Defender*, June 12, 1954, 2; June 19, 1954, 12.

81. Ibid., May 2, 1959, 30.

82. Aldrea Lenox, interview with author, January 8, 2011.

83. *Chicago Defender*, August 4, 1945, 7.

84. Ibid. July 21, 1945, 23; August 2, 1952, 33.

85. Much of the biographical information comes from the Louise Overall Weaver Papers (1946–1984), Chicago History Museum Archives.

86. *Chicago Defender*, December 3, 1955, 24.

87. Ibid., August 20, 1949, 9; September 24, 1949, 33.

88. I. L. Johnson, "Development of African American Gospel Piano Style," 172.

89. Floriene Watson Willis, interview with author, July 5, 2013.

90. *Chicago Defender*, April 4, 1953, 36.

91. Ibid., January 5, 1946, 8; August 3, 1946, 7; November 26, 1949, 29.

92. Ibid., November 26, 1949, 29.

93. Ibid., November 11, 1950, 1.

94. Ibid., November 11, 1950, 1.

95. Bishop Jerry L. Goodloe, interview with author, September 26, 2013.

96. Delores "Honey" Sykes, interview with author, March 29, 2012.

97. Ibid.

98. Ibid.

99. Barlow, *Voice Over*, 56.

100. *Chicago Defender*, March 5, 1949, 4; May 28, 1949, 35.

101. Barlow, *Voice Over*, 149.

102. *Chicago Defender*, July 16, 1949, 27.

103. Ibid., February 18, 1950, 33.

104. Ibid., May 9, 1959, 29.

105. Ibid., April 10, 1954, 20; June 5, 1954, 15.

106. Ibid., August 5, 1950.

107. Goreau, *Just Mahalia, Baby*, 122.

108. Kenneth Woods Jr., interview with author, November 15, 2011.

109. *Chicago Defender* (national ed.), September 5, 1953, 12.

110. http://www.carnegiehall.org, accessed October 26, 2011.

111. Goreau, *Just Mahalia, Baby*, 130–31.

112. Much of the information on the First Annual Negro Gospel Music Festival comes from a report in the Carnegie Hall program database at the Carnegie Hall Archives. Special thanks to Rob Hudson, associate archivist at Carnegie Hall, for providing this information.

113. The Belleville A Cappella Choir was from the Church of God and Saints of Christ, a denomination that considers itself "the oldest African-American congregation in the United States that adheres to the tenets of Judaism." Members of 1950s vocal harmony group the Flamingos also came from that denomination. See the Church of God and Saints in Christ Web site, accessed August 28, 2013, http://www.cogasoc.org/main .html. Regarding the program, see *Chicago Defender*, October 21, 1950, 2. It is likely that the Gospel Clefs appearing on the Carnegie Hall program were the Gospel Clefs of Newark, who, under the leadership of Leon Lumpkins, became successful recording artists for Savoy Records later in the decade.

114. Anthony Heilbut, email communication with author, September 6, 2012.

115. Donald and Geraldine Gay, interview with author, August 30, 2008.

116. Ibid.

117. Goreau, *Just Mahalia, Baby*, 138–41.

118. From the First Annual Negro Gospel Music Festival program database, Carnegie Hall Archives.

119. *Chicago Defender*, October 21, 1950, 2.; Goreau, *Just Mahalia, Baby*, 141.

120. Reported in *Chicago Defender*, October 14, 1950, 9.

121. Goreau, *Just Mahalia, Baby*, 142.

122. *Chicago Defender*, October 14, 1950, 9.

123. Goreau, *Just Mahalia, Baby*, 148–50.

124. Ibid., 150.

125. *Billboard*, November 25, 1950, 30.

126. Ibid., 24 March 1951, 32; Robert Sacré, "Gay Sisters," from McNeil, *Encyclopedia of American Gospel Music*, 137.

127. *Chicago Defender*, January 19, 1952, 30.

128. Donald Gay and Geraldine Gay Hambric, interview with author, August 30, 2008.

129. *Billboard*, July 28, 1951, 36.

130. Martin and Morris, *Sallie Martin's Gospel Song Book No. 2*.

131. Lorenza Brown Porter, interview with author, *Gospel Memories*, WLUW-FM, aired January 1, 2006.

132. *Chicago Defender*, February 16, 1952, 33; May 14, 1955, 34.

133. Not to be confused with the Southern Sons quartet that recorded in the 1930s for Bluebird.

134. Information about the session from Ryan, liner notes to *In the Spirit*.

135. Hayes and Laughton, *Gospel Discography*, 18.

136. *Chicago Defender*, August 4, 1951, 41.

137. Ibid., July 12, 1952, 33; September 6, 1952, 7.

138. Ibid., August 11, 1951, 11. It is not known which Willie Webb record attendees received. It may have been his latest Gotham release, "Eyes Have Not Seen," with Alex Bradford as lead vocalist.

139. Robert Wooten Sr., interview with author, March 22, 2007.

140. *Chicago Defender*, April 14, 1951, 11.

141. Ibid., July 10, 1948, 20.

142. Leonard Austin, interview discussion with author, March 20, 2007. Eugene Smith also remembered the cabins.

143. *Chicago Defender*, December 17, 1949, 17.

144. *Chicago Tribune*, December 11, 1949, A11.

145. *Chicago Defender*, December 17, 1949, 17; Thomas A. Dorsey Papers, box 1.

146. Report, *Seventeenth Annual Session*, 75.

147. Ibid., 80, 86.

148. Ibid., 79.

Chapter 12. Postwar Gospel Quartets: "Rock Stars of Religious Music"

The section title "Music in the Air" is taken from a lyric in Sister Rosetta Tharpe's "Up above My Head, I Hear Music in the Air."

1. *Chicago Defender*, October 22, 1949, 1.

2. Lemann, *Promised Land*, 70.

3. *The Encyclopedia of Chicago*, www.encyclopedia.chicagohistory.org/pages/878 .html, accessed July 27, 2012.

4. Young, *Pilgrim Jubilees*, 16.

5. Abbott and Seroff, *To Do This*, 191.

6. Ibid., 196.

7. Personnel on the Aladdin singles from Hayes and Laughton, *Gospel Discography*, 323.

8. *Billboard*, June 22, 1946, 33.

9. Ibid., November 2, 1946, 21.

10. Hayes and Laughton, *Gospel Discography*, 323.

11. Anthony Heilbut, email communication with author, December 11, 2012. Several members of the Norfolk Singers, in fact, experienced greater success elsewhere, among them soul superstar Lou Rawls, who sang with the group between his tenure with the Chosen Gospel Singers and the Pilgrim Travelers. Robert Kelly, who came to the Norfolk Singers from a southern quartet called the Brookhaven Jubilees, went on to become a founding member of the Victory Travelers.

12. Wolff et al., *You Send Me*, 76.

13. *Billboard*, March 11, 1950, 36; February 25, 1950, 30.

14. Heilbut, *Gospel Sound*, 82.

15. Guralnick, *Dream Boogie*, 61.

16. Ibid., 61.

17. Wolff et al., *You Send Me*, 64.

18. *Chicago Defender*, February 3, 1951, 5.

19. Ibid., November 11, 1950, 34.

20. Guralnick, *Dream Boogie*, 35–36.

21. Ibid., 36.

22. Lornell, *Happy in the Service*, 85.

23. *Chicago Defender*, June 21, 1947, 10.

24. Wolff et al., *You Send Me*, 43.

25. Ibid., 41; Guralnick, *Dream Boogie*, 5.

26. Guralnick, *Dream Boogie*, 31.

27. Ibid., 8; Wolff et al., *You Send Me*, 19.

28. Wolff et al., *You Send Me*, 28.

29. Ibid., 28; Guralnick, *Dream Boogie*, 20.

30. Guralnick, *Dream Boogie*, 27.

31. Wolff et al., *You Send Me*, 59.

32. Ibid., 51–52.

33. Guralnick, *Dream Boogie*, 54–55.

34. Wolff et al., *You Send Me*, 60.

35. Anthony Heilbut, telephone communication with author, December 11, 2012.

36. In Wolff et al., *You Send Me*, Robinson came up with the idea (65). Guralnick reports in *Dream Boogie* that Crain claimed the idea was his (62).

37. Wolff et al., *You Send Me*, 65.

38. Ibid., 65–67.

39. Ibid., 68–69.

40. Ibid., 71–72.

41. Ibid., 78.

42. Ibid., 81.

43. Ibid., 33; Guralnick, *Dream Boogie*, 90.

44. *Chicago Defender*, September 27, 1952, 36.

45. Ibid., September 24, 1955, 32.

46. *Billboard*, December 20, 1952, 19.

47. *Chicago Defender*, January 16, 1954, 16.

48. Ibid., March 8, 1952, 36.

49. Ibid., April 28, 1951, 10.

50. Hayes and Laughton, *Gospel Discography*, 62.

51. Ibid.

52. *Chicago Defender*, November 13, 1948, 31.

53. Hayes and Laughton, *Gospel Discography*, 134.

54. Ibid., 134

55. Ibid., 62.

56. Wolff et al., *You Send Me*, 99. Some of the Highway QCs thought Sam had been doing his yodel when he was with their group. Singing Sammy Lewis recalled hearing it when Sam sang with the Singing Children.

57. Guralnick, *Dream Boogie*, 95–96.

58. *Billboard*, October 2, 1954, 45.

59. Bosn and Crume, *Perfect Song*, 11, 27.

60. Ibid., 101, 384.

61. Ibid., 140.

62. Ibid., 141–42.

63. Hayes and Laughton, *Gospel Discography*, 62; Leroy Crume was the guitarist.

64. Bosn and Crume, *Perfect Song*, 352; Guralnick, *Dream Boogie*, 120, 130.

65. Wolff et al., *You Send Me*, 115.

66. Guralnick, *Dream Boogie*, 114; Hayes and Laughton, *Gospel Discography,* 324.

67. Guralnick, *Dream Boogie*, 116.

68. Hayes and Laughton, *Gospel Discography*, 174.

69. *Chicago Defender*, March 24, 1956, 28.

70. Hayes and Laughton, *Gospel Discography*, 179.

71. Spencer Taylor, interview with author, June 25, 2009.

72. Ibid.

73. Hayes and Laughton, *Gospel Discography*, 174–175.

74. In baseball parlance, a "farm team" refers to a Minor League franchise, often located in a smaller town or city, which provides its best players to the professional team with which it is associated.

75. Betty Lester, interview with author, March 12, 2010.

76. *Chicago Defender*, April 19, 1958, 15.

77. Ibid.; Guralnick, *Dream Boogie*, 156.

78. Hayes and Laughton, *Gospel Discography*, 324.

79. Biographical information on James Phelps from an April 19, 2009, interview with Bob Abrahamian on *Sitting in the Park* on WHPK-FM, http://www.sittinginthepark .com, accessed August 25, 2012. The Spiritual Five is not the same group as the Spiritual Five of Chicago.

80. Heilbut said that Anderson helped train the young singer (telephone communication with author, December 11, 2012).

81. *New York Times* (New York ed.), October 30, 2010, A21.

82. Nations, liner notes to *Ring Them Golden Bells*.

83. James Phelps, interview with Bob Abrahamian.

84. Ibid.

85. *New York Times* (New York ed.), October 30, 2010, A21.

86. Much of the following history comes from Roscoe Robinson, interview with author, June 4, 2009.

87. Ibid.

88. *Chicago Defender* (Gary ed.), October 28, 1950, 19.

89. Ibid., November 5, 1953, 1. Dixon later sang with the Rockets, a vocal harmony group that recorded for Al Benson's Parrot label, though the single identified the quartet as the Rockettes.

90. Roscoe Robinson, interview with author, June 4, 2009.

91. Ibid.

92. Carpenter, *Uncloudy Days*, 354–55. Roscoe Robinson repeated this story to the author during their June 4, 2009, telephone interview.

93. Cohodas, *Spinning Blues into Gold*, 305–06.

94. Carpenter, *Uncloudy Days*, 355.

95. Roscoe Robinson, interview with author, June 4, 2009.

96. Young, *Pilgrim Jubilees*, 30–33.

97. Cleave Graham, interview with author on *Gospel Memories* radio show, WLUW-FM, aired February 3, 2008.

98. Young, *Pilgrim Jubilees*, 51; Rev. Cleve Minter, interview with author, March 10, 2010.

99. The Pilgrim Harmonizers never recorded "Life's Evening Sun" commercially, but collector David Frost found a copy of it on an MBS Recording Studios acetate in Pine Bluff, Arkansas. The acetate coupled "Life's Evening Sun" with "Jesus Is All the World to Me."

100. Young, *Pilgrim Jubilees*, 56.

101. Ibid.

102. Ibid., 239. Young states that the NBC record was released in 1954, but Robert Pruter, Armin Büttner, and Robert L. Campbell believe that it came out in late 1953. Pruter, Büttner, and Campbell, "Chance Records."

103. Young, *Pilgrim Jubilees*, 57.

104. Anthony Heilbut, telephone communication with author, December 11, 2012.

105. Young, *Pilgrim Jubilees*, 61–63.

106. Ibid., 62.

107. Hayes and Laughton, *Gospel Discography*, 336.

108. Ibid., 269; Young, *Pilgrim Jubilees*, 66–67, 70.

109. Young, *Pilgrim Jubilees*, 71.

110. Ibid., 73–74; Cleave Graham, interview with author on *Gospel Memories* radio show, WLUW-FM, aired February 3, 2008.

111. Cleave Graham, interview with author on *Gospel Memories*.

112. Young, *Pilgrim Jubilees*, 78–9.

113. Ibid., 94–96.

114. Goggin, "Kelly Brothers," 46.

115. Ibid., 65, 47.

116. Most of the information about Offe Reese comes from an unpublished 2011 interview that Robert Sacré conducted with Reese. I am indebted to Sacré for providing a copy of his interview for my reference, as well as a copy of the *Juke Blues* article by Martin Goggin, which also informs this section.

117. Sacré, unpublished interview with Reese. Titles of songs from Hayes and Laughton, *Gospel Discography*, 207.

118. Goggin, "Kelly Brothers," 47; Hayes and Laughton, *Gospel Discography*, 207.

119. Goggin, "Kelly Brothers," 47.

120. Ibid.

121. Fox, *King of the Queen City*, 67.

122. Goggin, "Kelly Brothers," 47.

123. Hayes and Laughton, *Gospel Discography*, 207.

124. Goggin, "Kelly Brothers," 48.

125. Ibid., 48–49.

126. *Chicago Defender*, May 10, 1952, 33.

127. Nations, "Norfleet Brothers of Chicago," 14.

128. Ibid.; *Chicago Defender*, March 30, 1963, 14.

129. Campbell et al., "JOB Label."

130. Nations, "Norfleet Brothers of Chicago," 15.

131. *Chicago Defender*, March 30, 1963, 14.

132. Ibid.

133. Ibid., February 6, 1960, 26.

134. Deacon Reuben Burton, interview with author, May 11, 2007.

135. Rev. Cleve Minter, interview with author, March 10, 2010.

136. Robert Dixon, interview with author, August 13, 2009.

137. Members of the Willing Four, interview with author, June 11, 2012.

138. Young, *Pilgrim Jubilees*, 173–74.

139. Ibid.

140. Zadella "Mama" Curtis, interview with author, June 18, 2009.

141. Rev. Cleve Minter, interview with author, March 10, 2010.

142. Zadella "Mama" Curtis, interview with author, June 18, 2009.

143. Willing Four, interview with author, June 11, 2012.

144. Robert Dixon, interview with author, August 13, 2009.

Chapter 13. The Gospel Caravan: Midcentury Melodies

The epigraph is taken from I. L. Johnson, "Development of African American Gospel Piano Style," 128.

1. See chapter 1 for an explanation of the semi-demonstrative and the deliberative churches.

2. Reagon, *If You Don't Go*, 13.

3. *Billboard*, February 4, 1956, 55, 61.

4. J. A. Jackson, *Singing in My Soul*, 78; Wald, *Shout, Sister, Shout!*, 37–39.

5. Morris, *Improving the Music*, 46.

6. Ibid., 43.

7. J. A. Jackson, *Singing in My Soul*, 78.

8. Ibid., 83.

9. Green, *Selling the Race*, 56.

10. Red Saunders Research Foundation, accessed September 15, 2012, http://hubcap .clemson.edu/~campber/rsrf.html. Other gospel artists who recorded for Allen included the Staple Singers, the Little Lucy Smith Singers, and the Genesa Smith Singers of St. Louis.

11. Nellie Grace Daniels Smith, interview with author, July 12, 2012.

12. Ibid.

13. Ibid.

14. Ibid.

15. Rev. Darryl Reed, interview with author, April 17, 2011.

16. Ibid.

17. Pastor Ray Allen Berryhill, interview with author, April 8, 2010.

18. Betty Lester, interview with author, March 12, 2010.

19. Irma Gwynn, interview with author on *Gospel Memories*, WLUW-FM, Chicago, February 2004.

20. Ibid.

21. Rev. Darryl Reed, interview with author, April 17, 2011.

22. Nellie Grace Daniels Smith, interview with author, July 12, 2012.

23. Story provided by an individual who asked to remain anonymous.

24. Cook County, Illinois, Birth Index, 1916–1935, database available at http://www.ancestry.com.

25. United States Federal Census Records for Illinois, 1930. The Walker family's migration is estimated based on Walker's brother Walter being born in Georgia around 1915 and brother George being born in Illinois around 1920.

26. Ibid.

27. *New York Times*, October 9, 2010, A22.

28. Goreau, *Just Mahalia, Baby*, 101–2.

29. Ibid.

30. *Albertina Walker.*

31. Ethel Harris, interview with author, December 1, 2011.

32. Hayes and Laughton, *Gospel Discography*, 13.

33. Nellie Grace Daniels Smith, interview with author, July 12, 2012.

34. Rev. James Herndon, interview with author, October 20, 2012.

35. Ibid.

36. Goreau, *Just Mahalia, Baby*, 175.

37. Aldrea Lenox, interview with author, January 8, 2011.

38. Sherry Sherrod DuPree, "The Caravans," in McNeil, *Encyclopedia of American Gospel Music*, 62.

39. Rev. James Herndon, interview with author, October 20, 2012.

40. Nellie Grace Daniels Smith, interview with author, July 12, 2012.

41. *Chicago Defender*, May 14, 1955, 34.

42. Harrington, "Shirley Caesar," 63.

43. Heilbut, *Gospel Sound*, 132.

44. Carpenter, *Uncloudy Days*, 165; Hayes and Laughton, *Gospel Discography*, 328, 159. Spencer Jackson, Griffin's husband, is not the same person as the Chicago choral director identified earlier in this book.

45. Carpenter, *Uncloudy Days*, 165; *Chicago Defender*, October 27, 1951, 17.

46. Heilbut, *Gospel Sound*, 136.

47. Rev. Dr. Stanley Keeble, interview with author, February 22, 2007.

48. Heilbut, *Gospel Sound*, 139.

49. Hayes and Laughton, *Gospel Discography*, 159.

50. Heilbut, *Gospel Sound*, 140.

51. Carpenter, *Uncloudy Days*, 165.

52. Anthony Heilbut, telephone communication with author, December 11, 2012; I. L. Johnson, "Development of African American Gospel Piano Style," 345.

53. Cohen, *Amazing Grace*, 19.

54. Bailey, *Criminal Just Us System*, 66.

55. Carpenter, *Uncloudy Days*, 88.

56. Almond Dawson, interview with author, December 5, 2012.

57. Nellie Grace Daniels Smith, interview with author, July 12, 2012; Hayes and Laughton, *Gospel Discography*, 51; Harrington, "Shirley Caesar," 61.

58. *Billboard*, February 5, 1955, 46.

59. Rev. James Herndon, interview with author, October 20, 2012.

60. Aldrea Lenox, interview with author, January 8, 2011.

61. Middleton, *Golden Era Gospel Blog*.

62. Rev. James Herndon, interview with author, October 20, 2012.

63. Ibid.

64. *Billboard,* January 29, 1955, 68.

65. *Chicago Defender*, April 9, 1955, 16.

66. Rev. James Herndon, interview with author, October 20, 2012.

67. Hildebrand and Nations, liner notes to *Great 1955 Shrine Concert*. In the 1970s, Specialty released selections from the program on an LP called *Gospel Stars in Concert*, but the songs had overdubbed instrumentation.

68. *Chicago Defender*, December 10, 1955, 24.

69. Carpenter, *Uncloudy Days*, 314–15.

70. Hayes and Laughton, *Gospel Discography*, 51. The single was left in the can by States and issued by Savoy after it acquired the Caravans' contract and masters for its Sharp and Gospel subsidiaries.

71. Carpenter, *Uncloudy Days*, 315.

72. Ibid., 18–19.

73. Margaret B. Fisher, "Inez Andrews," in McNeil, *Encyclopedia of American Gospel Music*, 12.

74. Emmett Price, "Shirley Caesar," in McNeil, *Encyclopedia of American Gospel Music*, 57; Harrington, "Shirley Caesar," 50.

75. Harrington, "Shirley Caesar," 53–54; Carpenter, *Uncloudy Days*, 65.

76. Harrington, "Shirley Caesar," 95.

77. Ibid., 56.

78. *Billboard*, October 13, 1958, 46.

79. Ibid., November 10, 1958, 3.

80. Hayes and Laughton, *Gospel Discography*, 51–52.

81. Uncredited liner notes to *The Sincere Gospel Sounds of Delores Washington* and *The Gospel Princess*.

82. Carpenter, *Uncloudy Days*, 71.

83. Harrington, "Shirley Caesar," 70.

84. Rev. James Herndon, interview with author, October 20, 2012.

85. Ibid.

86. Ibid.

87. Ibid.

88. Uncredited liner notes to *The Gospel Princess*.

89. Guralnick, *Dream Boogie*, 96.

90. Hayes and Laughton, *Gospel Discography*, 36.

91. Anthony Heilbut, telephone communication with author, December 11, 2012.

92. *Billboard*, March 27, 1954, 35. The other two were "Jesus Is a Rock in a Weary Land" by the Original Five Blind Boys and "He's My Friend until the End" by the Soul Stirrers.

93. Heilbut, *Fan Who Knew Too Much*, 27.

94. Willie James McPhatter, interview with author on *Gospel Memories* radio show, WLUW-FM, November 2, 2003.

95. Ibid.

96. Woods and Mason, *Graceful Journey*, 6–7.

97. Robert Wooten Sr., interview with author, March 22, 2007.

98. Woods and Mason, *Graceful Journey*, 15.

99. Robert Wooten Sr., interview with author, March 22, 2007.

100. Woods and Mason, *Graceful Journey*, 10.

101. Rev. John Wesley Moore, interview with author, April 5, 2007. Donald Smith was the only member not from Morgan Park; he lived in Bronzeville and attended First Church of Deliverance, where his mother, Anna Smith, was a pastor and member of the missionary board.

102. Woods and Mason, *Graceful Journey*, 20.

103. Nations, "Maceo Woods," 9.

104. Ibid.; Woods and Mason, *Graceful Journey*, 21.

105. *Chicago Defender* (Gary ed.), March 14, 1953, 3.

106. Barlow, *Voice Over*, 149.

107. *Chicago Defender* (Gary ed.), March 14, 1953, 3; October 30, 1954, 5.

108. Ibid., December 13, 1952, 5.

109. Ibid., October 30, 1954, 5.

110. *Chicago Defender*, December 26, 1953, 13.

111. Kyles was born September 26, 1934, in Shelby, Mississippi, and sang with Rev. Milton Brunson's Thompson Community Singers prior to joining Woods's group.

112. Nations, "Maceo Woods," 9.

113. *Billboard*, October 22, 1955, 46; Heilbut, *Fan Who Knew Too Much*, 116.

114. Nations, "Maceo Woods," 9.

115. *Billboard*, January 29, 1955, 69.

116. Woods and Mason, *Graceful Journey*, 29.

117. I. L. Johnson, "Development of African American Gospel Piano Style," 169.

118. Woods and Mason, *Graceful Journey*, 32.

119. *Chicago Defender*, January 20, 1961, 11.

120. Ibid., June 23, 1956, 18; April 25, 1959.

121. Ibid., May 10, 1958, 22; April 4, 1959, 14; Woods and Mason, *Graceful Journey*, 31.

122. *Chicago Defender*, April 18, 1959, 2.

123. Nations, "Maceo Woods," 10. The Vee Jay LP was titled *Sunday Morning*, after the radio broadcast.

124. Donald Smith, interview with author, March 5, 2010.

125. Woods and Mason, *Graceful Journey*, 36.

126. *Chicago Defender*, May 5, 1956, 2.

127. Ibid., April 27, 1957, 35.

128. Lynda Rutledge Stephenson, "Staple Singers," in McNeil, *Encyclopedia of American Gospel Music*, 373–74.

129. *Jet*, January 8, 2001, 52; *Ebony*, September 1965, 81.

130. Carpenter, *Uncloudy Days*, 388.

131. Stephenson, "Staple Singers"; Carpenter, *Uncloudy Days*, 388.

132. *Chicago Defender*, September 30, 1961, 15.

133. Carpenter, *Uncloudy Days*, 388–89.

134. *Chicago Defender*, September 30, 1961, 15.

135. Anthony Heilbut, telephone communication with author, December 11, 2012.

136. Hayes and Laughton, *Gospel Discography*, 339.

137. Ibid.; Carpenter, *Uncloudy Days*, 387.

138. *Billboard*, December 19, 1953, 38.

139. Nations, "Maceo Woods," 10.

140. Donald Smith, interview with author, March 5, 2010.

141. Carpenter, *Uncloudy Days*, 389; Hayes and Laughton, *Gospel Discography*, 339.

142. Hayes and Laughton, *Gospel Discography*, 339.

143. Mavis Staples in informal conversation with author at Black Ensemble Theater, Chicago, circa early 1990s.

144. *Ebony*, September 1965, 81.

145. *Chicago Defender*, February 3, 1962, 13.

146. Robert Darden, "Black Gospel Musicals," in McNeil, *Encyclopedia of American Gospel Music*, 36.

147. Quoted in Darden, *People Get Ready!*, 267.

148. *Chicago Defender*, December 1, 1962, 16.

149. Viale, *I Remember Gospel*, 69.

150. Ibid.

151. Ibid., 68–70.

152. Rev. Walter J. Butts, interview with author, October 1, 2008.

153. Heilbut, *Fan Who Knew Too Much*, 130.

154. Hayes and Laughton, *Gospel Discography*, 53.

155. *Chicago Defender*, November 19, 1955, 8.

156. Delores "Honey" Sykes, interview with author, March 29, 2012.

157. Ibid.

158. Ibid.

159. *Billboard*, October 19, 1963, 30.

160. Ibid., August 27, 1966, 8.

161. *Chicago Defender*, September 22, 1956, 5.

162. Ibid., August 3, 1946, 7; Romance Watson, interview with author, July 24, 2009.

163. I. L. Johnson, "Development of African American Gospel Piano Style," 160–61.

164. Charles Clency, interview with author, December 3, 2012; DeLois Barrett Campbell, interview with author, March 22, 2007.

165. Charles Clency, interview with author, December 3, 2012.

166. Autobiographical information on Floriene Watson (Willis) is from an interview with author, July 5, 2013.

167. Doris Sykes, interview with author, June 30, 2007.

168. *Chicago Defender*, February 22, 1947, 27.

169. *Billboard*, December 17, 1955, 62.

170. *Chicago Defender*, November 3, 1956, 7.

171. Anthony Heilbut, email communication with author, October 31, 2012.

172. *Chicago Defender*, August 17, 1963, 12; November 3, 1956, 7.

173. Ibid., October 19, 1963, 31.

174. Ibid., March 29, 1952, 23; November 8, 1952, 19.

175. Ibid., May 21, 1955, 34.

176. Ibid., December 25, 1954, 54; Hayes and Laughton, *Gospel Discography*, 217.

177. *Chicago Defender*, December 19, 1964, 36.

178. Ibid., October 5, 1963, 16.

179. Pastor Ray Allen Berryhill, interview with author, April 8, 2010.

180. *Chicago Defender*, October 5, 1963, 16.

181. Goreau, *Just Mahalia, Baby*, 151. Among the songs that the Gospelaires performed were the Roberta Martin Singers' "Only a Look" and "Old Ship of Zion."

182. Ibid., 162.

183. Ibid., 163.

184. Ibid., 167.

185. Ibid., 168–70.

186. Ibid., 177–78.

187. Ibid., 179.

188. *Billboard*, April 9, 1955, 136.

189. Ibid., August 21, 1954, 18; April 17, 1954, 24.

190. Ibid., September 18, 1954, 18.

191. *Chicago Defender*, January 15, 1955, 6.

192. Schwerin, *Got to Tell It*, 84–85.

193. Ibid., 199–201.

194. Ibid., 85.

195. Goreau, *Just Mahalia, Baby*, 186, 189, 195.

196. *Billboard*, January 22, 1955, 34.

197. Ibid., January 22, 1955, 36.

198. *Chicago Defender*, January 15, 1955, 6.

199. Information on Columbia single releases from Hayes and Laughton, *Gospel Discography*, 187.

200. *Billboard*, January 29, 1955, 68.

201. Goreau, *Just Mahalia, Baby*, 199.

202. Ibid., 202.

203. Quoted in *Chicago Defender*, February 11, 1956, 11.

204. *Billboard*, February 26, 1955, 27.

205. *Chicago Defender*, February 10, 1962, 10.

206. *Jet*, April 17, 1958, 45.

207. Schwerin, *Got to Tell It*, 114–15.

208. *Billboard*, February 2, 1957, 24.

209. Romance Watson, interview with author, July 24, 2009.

210. Ibid.

211. Heilbut, *Gospel Sound*, 273; Pearl Williams-Jones and Bernice Johnson Reagon, "Conversations: Roberta Martin Singers Roundtable," in Reagon, *We'll Understand It Better*, 304.

212. Williams-Jones and Reagon, "Conversations," 304.

213. *Billboard*, April 14, 1958, 12.

214. Anthony Heilbut, telephone communication with author, December 11, 2012.

215. Pruter, *Chicago Soul*, 31, xi.

216. Butler and Smith, *Only the Strong Survive*, 23.

Chapter 14. "He Could Just Put a Song on His Fingers": Second-Generation Gospel Choirs

1. *Chicago Defender*, July 4, 1959, 23.

2. Charles Clency, interview with author, December 3, 2012.

3. Heilbut, *Fan Who Knew Too Much*, 118.

4. *Billboard*, July 25, 1960, 38.

5. Charles Clency, interview with author, December 3, 2012.

6. Rev. Walter J. Butts, interview with author, October 1, 2008.

7. *Chicago Defender*, July 4, 1959, 23.

8. Charles Clency, interview with author, December 3, 2012.

9. B. C. Johnson, *Change Is Gonna Come*, 61–62.

10. Viale, *I Remember Gospel*, 92.

11. Charles Clency, interview with author, December 3, 2012.

12. *Chicago Defender*, March 29, 1952, 36; L. Stanley Davis, interview with author, March 1, 2007.

13. *Chicago Daily Defender*, August 27, 2009; L. Stanley Davis, interview with author, March 1, 2007.

14. Uncredited liner notes to Thompson Community Singers, *I'll Trade a Lifetime*.

15. Carpenter, *Uncloudy Days*, 58.

16. *Chicago Daily Defender*, August 27, 2009.

17. Ibid.

18. *Chicago Defender*, February 23, 1952, 33; October 29, 1953, 41.

19. Vernon Oliver Price, interview with author, April 11, 2007; *Chicago Defender*, January 21, 1950, 29; October 22, 1955, 31.

20. Dolores "Honey" Sykes, interview with author, March 29, 2012.

21. *Chicago Defender*, December 29, 1962, 20.

22. Vernon Oliver Price, interview with author, March 29, 2012.

23. Uncredited liner notes to *I'll Trade A Lifetime*.

24. Carpenter, *Uncloudy Days*, 58; Christ Tabernacle Missionary Baptist Church Web site, accessed November 25, 2012, http://www.christtabernaclembchurch.org.

25. *New York Times*, September 26, 2011, A25; Charles Clency, email communication with author, August 18, 2013.

26. *New York Times*, September 26, 2011, A25.

27. *Billboard*, February 20, 1965, 14.

28. Ibid., February 6, 1971, 12.

29. Viale, *I Remember Gospel*, 174; *Billboard*, June 9, 1973, 28.

30. *Billboard*, August 16, 1969, S16; L. Stanley Davis, interview with author, March 1, 2007.

31. *Chicago Defender*, February 20, 1954, 25; I. L. Johnson, "Development of African American Gospel Piano Style," 165.

32. *Jet*, March 6, 1975, 38.

33. Robert Wooten Sr., interview with author, March 22, 2007.

34. Ibid.

35. Ibid.

36. Ibid.

37. Almond Dawson Jr., interview with author, December 5, 2012.

38. Ibid.

39. Betty Lester, interview with author, March 12, 2010.

40. Ibid.

41. Doris Sykes, interview with author, June 30, 2007.

42. Ibid.

43. Rev. Cleophus Robinson, gospel singer and Peacock recording artist, assumed Reverend Sykes's St. Louis pastorate.

44. *Chicago Defender*, November 9, 1957, 18. The author has yet to come across a copy of the disc to confirm its existence.

45. Ibid.

46. Unless otherwise noted, biographical information on Helen Robinson comes from Marovich, "Here's to You, Mrs. Robinson."

47. *Chicago Defender*, October 13, 1962, 17.

48. Marovich, "Here's to You, Mrs. Robinson."

49. Ibid.; *Chicago Defender*, August 27, 1955, 4; November 30, 1957, 26.

50. Marovich, "Here's to You, Mrs. Robinson."

51. Ibid.

52. Margaret Aikens Jenkins, interview with author, May 21, 2007. The family lived in Morgan Park, but Margaret was born in Lexington, Mississippi. Marie found it easier to return to Lexington's black community to give birth than to endure the unblinking prejudice of Chicago hospitals.

53. Ibid.

54. Ibid.

55. Rev. Charles Walker, interview with author, *Gospel Memories*, WLUW, January 8, 2011.

56. Margaret Aikens Jenkins, interview with author, May 21, 2007.

57. Marovich, "Here's To You, Mrs. Robinson."

58. Rev. Willie A. Treadwell, Pastor Emeritus, Eighty-Second Birthday Celebration Resolution, City Council of Chicago, Illinois, presented by Alderman Emma Mitts on February 13, 2013, record R2013-243, Office of the [Chicago] City Clerk.

59. Rev. Willie A. Treadwell, Pastor Emeritus, Eighty-Second Birthday Celebration Resolution; *Chicago Defender*, July 18, 1959, 23.

60. Zadella "Mama" Curtis, interview with author, June 18, 2009.

61. Rev. Willie A. Treadwell, Pastor Emeritus, Eighty-Second Birthday Celebration Resolution.

62. *Chicago Defender*, April 20, 1957, 32.

63. *Chicago Sun-Times*, October 14, 1962.

64. Ibid., October 13, 1951, 3; November 24, 1951, 20; March 14, 1953, 27.

65. Bishop Jerry L. Goodloe, interview with author, September 26, 2013.

66. LouDella Evans Reid Papers, Vivian G. Harsh Research Collection, Chicago Public Library.

67. Rev. Stanley Keeble, interview with author, February 22, 2007.

68. I. L. Johnson, "Development of African American Gospel Piano Style," 128n.

69. Ibid., 385.

70. Floriene Watson Willis, interview with author, July 5, 2013.

71. I. L. Johnson, "Development of African American Gospel Piano Style," 353–54, 383.

72. *Chicago Defender*, March 21, 1964, 19.

73. I. L. Johnson, "Development of African American Gospel Piano Style," 344.

74. Rev. Stanley Keeble, interview with author, February 22, 2007.

75. *Chicago Defender*, April 9, 1960, 4. Idessa Malone Nelson is a fascinating figure, deserving of her own full-length study.

76. Ibid., June 10, 1950, 37.

77. Woods and Mason, *Graceful Journey*, 128; Charles Clency, interview with author, December 3, 2012.

78. *Chicago Defender*, August 25, 1956, 8.

79. Rev. Dr. Issac Whittmon, interview with author, July 6, 2008.

80. Doris Sykes, interview with author, June 30, 2007.

81. Rev. Stanley Keeble, interview with author, February 22, 2007.

82. *Jet*, April 17, 1958, 46.

83. *Chicago Defender*, April 5, 1958, 30; January 18, 1958, 36; January 31, 1959, 24.

84. Ibid., April 5, 1958, 30; *Jet*, April 17, 1958, 46.

85. Rev. Dr. Issac Whittmon, interview with author, July 6, 2008.

86. *Chicago Defender*, December 13, 1958, 30.

87. This song is also known as "Just like Fire Shut Up in My Bones."

88. Jessie M. Woods funeral program.

89. Viale, *I Remember Gospel*, 171.

90. *Chicago Defender* (Gary ed.), November 12, 1949, 17; *Chicago Defender*, March 28, 1959, 23.

91. Viale, *I Remember Gospel*, 171.

92. Except where otherwise noted, historical information on Charles G. Hayes and Cosmopolitan Church of Prayer comes from author's interview with Charles G. Hayes, February 11, 2007.

93. Ibid.

94. *Chicago Defender*, June 16, 1962, 13.

95. Charles G. Hayes, interview with author, February 11, 2007.

96. Charles Clency, interview with author, December 3, 2012.

97. Dennis Cole, interview with author, February 2, 2007.

98. Ibid.

99. Charles Clency, interview with author, December 3, 2012.

100. Charles Clency, email communication with author, August 18, 2013.

101. Charles Clency, interview with author, December 3, 2012.

102. Chedwick Allen Cathey, interview with author, December 3, 2009.

103. Ibid.

104. Woods and Mason, *Graceful Journey*, 42, places the gathering at White Castle, but Clency remembered that it was at Gladys's soul food restaurant on the city's South Side.

105. Ibid.

106. Ibid., 48.

107. Ibid., 48–50.

108. *Chicago Defender*, November 19, 1960, 15.

109. Hayes and Laughton, *Gospel Discography*, 402.

110. *Billboard*, June 15, 1963, 32.

111. Woods and Mason, *Graceful Journey*, 128–29.

112. Hayes and Laughton, *Gospel Discography*, 402.

113. Woods and Mason, *Graceful Journey*, 129.

114. Doris Sykes, interview with author, June 30, 2007.

115. Dennis Cole, interview with author, February 2, 2007.

116. Almond Dawson, interview with author, December 5, 2012.

117. L. Stanley Davis, interview with author, March 1, 2007.

118. I. L. Johnson, "Development of African American Gospel Piano Style," 128.

Chapter 15. "God's Got a Television": Gospel Music Comes to the Living Room

The chapter title is taken from the title of a 1955 Charles Taylor and Gospel All Stars single.

1. *Ebony* article quoted in Bodroghkozy, *Equal Time*, 17.

2. *Chicago Defender*, April 30, 1949, 1.

3. Ibid., July 9, 1949, 2. Whether the youth television show was ever produced is unknown.

4. Ibid., April 17, 1954, 13; May 15, 1954, 30.

5. Ibid., December 22, 1951, 3.

6. Ibid., January 19, 1952, 5.

7. Ibid., August 16, 1952, 36.

8. Goreau, *Just Mahalia, Baby*, 197.

9. *Chicago Defender*, March 12, 1955, 3; March 19, 1955, 7; Goreau, *Just Mahalia, Baby*, 198.

10. *Billboard*, April 16, 1955, 4.

11. Goreau, *Just Mahalia, Baby*, 203–204.

12. *Chicago Defender* (national ed.), May 31, 1958, 19.

13. Goreau, *Just Mahalia, Baby*, 227.

14. Ibid., 228.

15. Ibid.

16. *Chicago Defender*, November 13, 1958, 8; December 5, 1959, 15.

17. Goreau, *Just Mahalia, Baby*, 310–11.

18. Twelve *Mahalia Jackson Sings* episodes are available on the 2-DVD *Soul of the Church*, Hollywood Select Video, 2010.

19. Goreau, *Just Mahalia, Baby*, 319.

20. Ibid., 324.

21. *Chicago Defender*, October 31, 1959, 7.

22. Ibid., July 23, 1960, 16; August 13, 1960, 29. The William Friedkin who coproduced the program is quite possibly the same person who directed the award-winning motion pictures *The French Connection* and *The Exorcist*. The motion picture director is reported to have worked at WTTW in the 1960s.

23. Ibid., July 22, 1961, 28; the Halo Gospel Singers' pianist was Alma Androzzo, composer of the popular gospel song "If I Could Help Somebody."

24. Ibid., July 17, 1963, 16.

25. *New York Amsterdam News*, September 29, 1962, 17.

26. Ibid.

27. *Chicago Defender*, September 29, 1962, 29.

28. Ibid., February 2, 1963, 21.

29. Ibid., October 17, 1964, 28.

30. This episode can be viewed on the DVD *Spirit of the Church*, vol. 1.

31. *Chicago Daily Defender*, July 17, 1963, 16.

32. Myrna and Cheryl Ordower, interview with author, June 6, 2007.

33. *Chicago Defender*, August 10, 1963, 34.

34. Ibid., May 13, 1962, 2.

35. Donald and Geraldine Gay, interview with author, August 30, 2008. Ozie Vincent died in early February 1963 during an altercation with his wife, Betty. Accusing Vincent of seeing a married woman, Betty "stumbled over a stool, causing the .38 calibre pistol in her hand to go off." Evelyn served as the hostess of Vincent's funeral

services "until she became overcome with emotion." See *Chicago Defender*, February 9, 1963, 18.

36. Donald and Geraldine Gay, interview with author, August 30, 2008.

37. *Chicago Defender*, February 16, 1963, 20.

38. Steven Ordower, interview with author, March 29, 2007. Sid Ordower lost his first wife and child during the war.

39. *Jubilee Showcase* website, http://www.jubileeshowcase.com, accessed December 1, 2012.

40. Steven Ordower, interview with author, March 29, 2007.

41. Ibid.

42. *Chicago Daily Defender*, April 8, 1963, 3.

43. By 1964, the program was moved to 8:00 a.m. Sundays.

44. *Chicago Defender*, February 16, 1963, 20.

45. Ibid., February 16, 1963, 23.

46. Ibid., March 2, 1963, 28.

47. *Chicago Defender TV Fare*, March 9 and March 16, 1963.

48. Steven Ordower, interview with author, March 29, 2007.

49. *Chicago Defender*, August 10, 1963, 34.

50. Ibid.

51. Myrna and Cheryl Ordower, interview with author, June 6, 2007.

52. Ibid.

53. Steven Ordower, interview with author, March 29, 2007.

54. Myrna and Cheryl Ordower, interview with author, June 6, 2007.

55. *Chicago Defender*, August 10, 1963, 34.

56. *Chicago Defender TV Fare*, March 28, 1964.

57. Steven Ordower, interview with author, March 29, 2007.

58. *Chicago Defender* (national ed.), December 19, 1964, 10.

59. Ibid., December 21, 1963, 31; November 23, 1963, 28.

60. Quoted in *Chicago Defender*, February 22, 1964, 24.

61. Ibid., February 8, 1964, 33.

62. *Jubilee Showcase*, Episode 1-JS-65.

63. Darden, *People Get Ready*, 267.

64. L. Stanley Davis, interview with author, March 1, 2007.

65. *Chicago Defender*, September 25, 1965, 15.

66. *Chicago Daily Defender*, December 30, 1969, 13.

67. Steven Ordower, interview with author, March 29, 2007.

68. Inscribed on the Emmy Award, which author viewed during Steven Ordower interview, March 29, 2007.

69. Vernon Oliver Price, interview with author, April 11, 2007.

70. DeLois Barrett Campbell, interview with author, March 22, 2007.

71. Ibid.

72. Ibid.

73. *Chicago Defender*, September 19, 1964, 32.

74. Ibid., October 10, 1964, 12.

75. Ibid., October 3, 1964, 11.

76. Ibid., October 3, 1964, 15; October 24, 1964, 13.

77. Ibid., March 27, 1972, 16. WCIU was the television station that launched *Soul Train* with host Don Cornelius a year later.

78. Ibid., March 19, 1969, 18.

79. Viale, *I Remember Gospel*, 179–80.

80. *Chicago Daily Defender*, November 22, 1969, 39; March 1, 1969, 15; March 15, 1969, 18.

81. Quoted on Museum of Classic Chicago Television's YouTube Web site, accessed January 21, 2013, http://www.youtube.com/watch?v=_Z4fS24nlOY.

82. *Chicago Defender*, June 25, 1970, 16.

83. Ibid., December 13, 1969, 26.

84. Rev. Walter J. Butts, interview with author, October 1, 2008.

85. "Samuel Patterson," *The Black Gospel Blog*.

86. Lornell, *Happy in the Service*, 61.

87. *Chicago Daily Defender*, September 13, 1969, 35.

Chapter 16. "Tell It Like It Is": Songs of Social Significance

1. Schwerin, *Got to Tell It*, 14–17.

2. *Chicago Defender*, November 7, 1964, 13.

3. Schwerin, *Got to Tell It*, 109–10.

4. Viale, *I Remember Gospel*, 210.

5. Harrington, "Shirley Caesar," 8.

6. Goreau, *Just Mahalia, Baby*, 218–19.

7. Ibid., 231; Louise Overall Weaver Papers, box 1, Chicago Historical Society.

8. Oates, *Let the Trumpet Sound*, 116.

9. Ward, *Just My Soul Responding*, 181.

10. *Chicago Sun-Times*, October 14, 1962.

11. *Chicago Defender*, October 6, 1962, 32.

12. *Chicago Daily Defender*, May 27, 1963, A1.

13. Goreau, *Just Mahalia, Baby*, 347–52; *Chicago Daily Defender*, May 27, 1963, A1; May 28, 1963, 3.

14. *Chicago Defender*, October 19, 1963, 16.

15. Ibid., December 28, 1963, 1, 3.

16. Ibid., August 24, 1963, 8.

17. Branch, *Pillar of Fire*, 131.

18. Bennett, *Day They Marched*.

19. Schwerin, *Got to Tell It*, 140.

20. Keiler, *Marian Anderson*, 310.

21. Branch, *Parting the Waters*, 877.

22. Schwerin, *Got to Tell It*, 142.

23. Branch, *Parting the Waters*, 882.

24. Schwerin, *Got to Tell It*, 144.

25. Oates, *Let the Trumpet Sound*, 260.

26. Stefanie Minatee, email communication with author, January 31, 2013. Charter members of the Angelic Choir told the author in October 2013 that the session was not held at First Baptist Church, as has often been surmised, but at Trinity Temple SDA in Newark because a new First Baptist facility was still under construction on the spot of the original church.

27. Woods and Mason, *Graceful Journey*, 129.

28. Stefanie Minatee, email communication with author, January 29, 2013.

29. *Billboard*, March 5, 1966, 40, 42.

30. Ibid., February 29, 1964, 20.

31. Ibid., March 27, 1965, 6.

32. Oates, *Let the Trumpet Sound*, 358, 373.

33. *Chicago Defender*, February 12, 1966, 11.

34. Oates, *Let the Trumpet Sound*, 392–93.

35. *Chicago Defender*, July 7, 1966, 1.

36. Oates, *Let the Trumpet Sound*, 394.

37. Ibid., 398–99.

38. Fellowship Missionary Baptist Church was in need of funds because the holders of the loan to complete construction took umbrage at Reverend Evans's endorsement of King's 1965 visit to Chicago. They held up the loan's approval, causing work delays. Dorothy June Rose, *From Plough Handle to Pulpit: The Life Story of Rev. Clay Evans*, cited in Hallstoos, "Windy City, Holy Land," 304–5.

39. Ward, *Just My Soul Responding*, 203.

40. *Billboard*, October 24, 1964, 10.

41. Ibid., September 4, 1965, 32.

42. Hayes and Laughton, *Gospel Discography*, 341.

43. *Billboard*, August 10, 1968, 3.

44. *Chicago Daily Defender*, December 15, 1964, 6.

45. Rev. John Wesley Moore, interview with author, April 5, 2007.

46. *Chicago Defender*, December 19, 1964, 1.

47. Ibid., January 23, 1965; February 13, 1965, 3.

48. Delores "Honey" Sykes, interview with author, March 29, 2012.

49. Oates, *Let the Trumpet Sound*, 156.

50. *Chicago Defender*, March 2, 1963, 28.

51. Robert Dixon, interview with author, August 13, 2009.

52. Ibid.

53. Cohodas, *Spinning Blues into Gold*, 196–97.

54. *Billboard*, October 12, 1968, 19, 88.

55. Robert Dixon, interview with author, August 13, 2009.

56. Chicago, Checker 5048, 45 rpm.

57. *Billboard,* April 6, 1968, 27.

58. Robert Dixon, interview with author, August 13, 2009.

59. Oates, *Let the Trumpet Sound*, 471–72; *Jet*, May 23, 1968, 56.

60. Frady, *Jesse*, 227.

61. Ibid., 231, 232; Oates, *Let the Trumpet Sound*, 472–73.

62. *Chicago Defender*, April 6, 1968, 22.

63. *Chicago Daily Defender*, April 9, 1968, 3.

64. Oates, *Let the Trumpet Sound*, 475.

65. Ibid., 477.

66. *Chicago Tribune*, May 19, 1968, H57.

67. *Billboard*, May 18, 1968, 2.

68. Ibid., June 8, 1968, 42.

69. Rev. Jesse Jackson's Operation Breadbasket Choir became the Operation PUSH Choir (People United to Save Humanity) when the organization changed names. Gospel artists such as Jimmy Jones of the Harmonizing Four and Jacqui Verdell of the Davis Sisters soloed on the Operation PUSH Choir's regular radio broadcasts.

70. *Billboard*, May 18, 1968, 3.

71. Ibid., June 22, 1968, 25.

72. Shirley Wahls, interview with author on *Gospel Memories* radio show, WLUW-FM, May 1, 2010.

73. Blue Candle 1511, 1976.

74. Hayes and Laughton, *Gospel Discography*, 295.

75. Details of the *Jubilee Showcase* episode and transcription of Jackson remarks from Hallstoos, "Windy City, Holy Land," 283, 287, 329; *Chicago Daily Defender*, April 3, 1969, 20.

76. *Chicago Daily Defender*, April 8, 1971, 16.

77. *Billboard*, October 12, 1968, 19, 88.

78. Ibid., August 16, 1969, S16.

79. Hayes and Laughton, *Gospel Discography*, 288. A photo of the group, circa 1966, shows five members.

80. Ward, *Just My Soul Responding*, 182–83.

Chapter 17. One of These Mornings: Chicago Gospel at the Crossroads

1. Uncredited liner notes for *Praise God* by the Roberta Martin Singers.

2. I. V. Jackson, "Afro-American Gospel Music," 98.

3. Ibid. Newspapers printed Roberta Martin's birth year erroneously as 1912, and therefore her age as fifty-six.

4. Interestingly, James Austin and Little Lucy Smith Collier attended both the Elder Lucy Smith and Roberta Martin funerals as immediate family members of the deceased.

5. Leonard Austin, interview with author, March 20, 2007.

6. *Chicago Defender*, January 15, 1969, 1.

7. Leonard Austin, interview with author, March 20, 2007.

8. Eugene Smith, interview with author, January 10, 2008.

9. I. V. Jackson, "Afro-American Gospel Music," 97.

10. Goreau, *Just Mahalia, Baby*, 591, 594.

11. Ibid., 609.

12. *Memorial Tribute to Mahalia Jackson.*

13. Schwerin, *Got to Tell It*, 177.

14. Heilbut, *Gospel Sound*, 304–5.

15. Schwerin, *Got to Tell It*, 179; *Memorial Tribute to Mahalia Jackson.*

16. *Chicago Daily Defender*, February 2, 1972, 3.

17. *Memorial Tribute to Mahalia Jackson.*

18. Heilbut, *Fan Who Knew Too Much*, 22.

19. *Chicago Daily Defender*, February 2, 1972, 3.

20. Schwerin, *Got to Tell It*, 182.

21. Goreau, *Just Mahalia, Baby*, 609.

22. *Chicago Daily Defender*, February 5, 1972, 1.

23. Heilbut, *Gospel Sound*, 307.

24. Laurraine Goreau Collection.

25. Schwerin, *Got to Tell It*, 176.

26. Carpenter, *Uncloudy Days*, 180–81.

27. Ramsey quoted in I. L. Johnson, "Development of African American Gospel Piano Style," 340.

28. *Billboard*, January 15, 1972, 14.

29. Cohen, *Amazing Grace*, 7.

30. Ibid., 143.

31. *Billboard*, January 29, 1972, 4.

32. Ibid., October 2, 1971, 35.

33. Chedwick Allen Cathey, interview with author, December 3, 2009.

34. Cohen, *Amazing Grace*, 53–54.

35. Rev. Dr. Issac Whittmon, interview with author, July 6, 2008.

36. Bernice Johnson Reagon, "Pioneering African American Gospel Composers," in Reagon, *We'll Understand It Better*, 7.

37. Lena McLin, interview with author, June 15, 2007.

38. *Jet*, August 3, 1998, 34.

39. *Congressional Record—House*, October 19, 1988, 26802.

40. *Congressional Record—House*, June 3, 1998, 10844.

41. Uncredited liner notes to Donald Vails and the Salvation Corporation, *Until . . . The Rapture.*

42. Kenneth Woods Jr., interview with author, November 15, 2011.

43. *Sweet Sisters of Zion.*

44. DeLois Barrett Campbell, interview with author, March 22, 2007.

45. Betty Lester, interview with author, March 12, 2010.

46. Ethel Harris, interview with author, December 1, 2011.

BIBLIOGRAPHY

Primary Sources

Archival Collections

Collier, Lucy Smith. Papers. Vivian G. Harsh Research Collection. Chicago Public Library.

Dorsey, Thomas A., Collection, 1932–1982. Special Collections and Archives. Fisk University, Nashville, TN.

Ebenezer Missionary Baptist Church Archives. Vivian G. Harsh Research Collection. Chicago Public Library.

Goreau, Laurraine, Collection. Hogan Jazz Archive. Tulane University, New Orleans.

Martin and Morris Collection. Smithsonian Institution Museum of American History, Washington, DC.

Reid, LouDella Evans. Papers. Vivian G. Harsh Research Collection. Chicago Public Library.

Weaver, Louise Overall. Papers. Chicago History Museum.

Interviews

All interviews were conducted by the author unless otherwise noted.

Alexander, Senator Ethel. Chicago, November 8, 2007.

Austin, Leonard. Miami, (telephone) March 20, 2007.

Bailey, Rev. Harold. Chicago, February 19, 2007.

Barnes, Frances Pace. Chicago, October 15, 2010.

Bell, George. Chicago, June 20, 2008.

Berryhill, Pastor Ray Allen. Chicago, April 8, 2010.

Burks, Jerome. Chicago, November 13, 2013 (with Cherli Montgomery).

Burton, Deacon Reuben. Chicago, May 11, 2007.

Butts, Rev. Walter J. Chicago, October 1, 2008.

Campbell, DeLois Barrett†. Chicago, March 22, 2007.

Cathey, Chedwick Allen. Chicago, December 3, 2009.

Clency, Charles. Evanston, IL, April 5, 2009; (telephone) December 3, 2012.

Cole, Dennis. Chicago, February 2, 2007.

Curtis, Zadella "Mama." Chicago, June 18, 2009.

Davis, L. Stanley. Chicago, March 1, 2007.

Dawson, Almond. Chicago, December 5, 2012.

Dixon, Robert. Oak Park, IL, August 13, 2009.

Evans, Rev. Dr. Clay. Chicago, January 18, 2007.

Gay, Donald, Gregory Gay, and Geraldine Gay Hambric†. Chicago, August 30, 2008 (with Aaron Cohen).

Goodloe, Bishop Jerry L. Chicago, September 26, 2013 (with Cherli Montgomery).

Harris, Ethel. Chicago, December 1, 2011.

Hayes, Rev. Charles G.†. Chicago, February 11, 2007.

Heilbut, Anthony. New York, (telephone) January 2011; September 12, 2012.

Herndon, Rev. James. Durham, NC, (telephone) October 20, 2012.

Houston, Bishop Otto T., III. Chicago, January 2007.

Jenkins, Margaret Aikens†. Hawthorne, CA, May 21, 2007.

Jones, James. Gary, IN, April 10, 2009.

Keeble, Rev. Dr. Stanley. Chicago, February 22, 2007.

Lee, Antoinette. Minneapolis, (telephone) October 27, 2009.

Lenox, Aldrea. Chicago, January 8, 2011 (with Pastor Lamont Lenox).

Lenox, Pastor Lamont. Chicago, March 24, 2010.

Lester, Betty. Chicago, March 12, 2010.

Marshall, Mr. and Mrs. Mack. Chicago, May 28, 2010.

Mason, Elder Mack C. Chicago, March 5, 2007.

McLin, Lena Johnson. Chicago, June 15, 2007.

Melson, Bertha Burley. Chicago, July 28, 2011.

Minter, Rev. Cleve†. Chicago, March 10, 2010.

Mobley, Rev. Dr. Wealthy L., Sr.†. Chicago, April 10, 2010.

Montgomery, Pastor Louis. Chicago, November 16, 2010.

Moore, Rev. John Wesley. Chicago, April 5, 2007.

Morson, Bossie, Jr. Chicago, October 11, 2012.

Ordower, Myrna† and Cheryl. Chicago, June 6, 2007.

Ordower, Steven. Chicago, March 29, 2007.

Price, Vernon Oliver. Chicago, April 11, 2007.

Reed, Rev. Darryl T. Chicago, April 17, 2011.

Roberts, Mother Alva. Chicago, March 5, 2007.

Robinson, Roscoe. Birmingham, AL, (telephone) June 4, 2009.

Smith, Donald. Chicago, March 5, 2010.

Smith, Eugene. Chicago, January 10, 2008; (telephone) June 11, 2008; (telephone) March 30, 2009.†

Smith, Nellie Grace Daniels, and Bernadette Smith. Decatur, GA, July 12, 2012.

Sykes, Delores "Honey." Chicago, March 29, 2012.

Sykes, Doris. Chicago, June 30, 2007.

Taylor, Spencer. Washington, DC, (telephone) June 25, 2009.

Watson, Romance. Philadelphia, (telephone) July 24, 2009.

Whittmon, Rev. Dr. Issac. Chicago, July 6, 2008.

Willing Four (with Robert Sacré). Chicago, June 11, 2012.

Willis, Floriene Watson. Redwood City, CA, (telephone) July 5, 2013.

Woods, Kenneth, Jr. Chicago, February 19, 2007; November 15, 2011.
Wooten, Robert, Sr. †. Chicago, March 22, 2007.

† indicates deceased.

Newspapers and Serialized Sources

Billboard
Chicago Daily Defender
Chicago Defender, city edition, 1925–67
Chicago Defender, national edition, 1920–30
Chicago Sun-Times, 2005–6
Chicago Tribune, 1929, 2006, 2010
The Crisis
Ebony
Jet
New Music Review and Church Music Review, December 1920
Southtown Economist

Radio Programs

Gospel Memories, 2001–11.
Wade in the Water: African American Sacred Folk Traditions, 26 parts, produced by Bernice Johnson Reagon and originally broadcast over National Public Radio in 1994.

Secondary Sources

Abbott, Lynn. *I Got Two Wings*. Montgomery, AL: CaseQuarter, 2008.
Abbott, Lynn, and Doug Seroff. *To Do This, You Must Know How*. Jackson: University Press of Mississippi, 2013.
Abrahamian, Bob. *Sitting in the Park* radio show, WHPK-FM, accessed August 25, 2012, http://www.sittinginthepark.com.
Albertina Walker: The Queen of Gospel. Eric Peterson Productions, 2010. DVD.
Alexander, J. W. Liner notes to Princess Stewart, *God Bless the Child*. Gary, IN: VJ International VJS 18000, 1963. LP.
Ankeny, Jason. "Rev. F. W. McGee." *All Music Guide*. Accessed January 12, 2007. http://www.allmusic.com.
Baer, Hans A. "The Metropolitan Spiritual Churches of Christ: The Socio-Religious Evolution of the Largest of the Black Spiritual Associations." *Review of Religious Research* 30, no. 2 (December 1988): 140–50.
Bailey, Rev. Harold E. *The Criminal Just Us System*. Charleston, SC: BookSurge, 2006.
Baldwin, Davarian L. *Chicago's New Negroes: Modernity, the Great Migration, and Black Urban Life*. Chapel Hill: University of North Carolina Press, 2007.
Barlow, William. *Voice Over: The Making of Black Radio*. Philadelphia: Temple University Press, 1999.
Bennett, Lerone Jr. *The Day They Marched*. Chicago: Johnson, 1963.
Best, Wallace D. *Passionately Human, No Less Divine: Religion and Culture in Black Chicago, 1915–1952*. Princeton, NJ: Princeton University Press, 2005.

Biszick-Lockwood, Bar. *Restless Giant: The Life and Times of Jean Aberbach and Hill and Range Songs*. Urbana: University of Illinois Press, 2010.

Black, Timuel D., Jr. *Bridges of Memory: Chicago's First Wave of Black Migration*. Evanston, IL: Northwestern University Press, 2005.

———. *Bridges of Memory: Chicago's Second Generation of Black Migration*. Evanston, IL: Northwestern University Press, 2007.

Bliss, P. P., and Ira D. Sankey, eds. *Gospel Hymns and Sacred Songs*. Chicago: Biglow and Main/John Church, 1875.

———, eds. *Gospel Hymns No. 2*. Chicago: Biglow and Main/John Church, 1876.

Bodroghkozy, Aniko. *Equal Time: Television and the Civil Rights Movement*. Urbana: University of Illinois Press, 2012.

Bosn, Donna J., and Arthur Lee Crume Sr. *The Perfect Song*. Bloomington, IN: Xlibris, 2010.

Bowles Favorite Frye's Special Gospel Song Book, no. 6. Chicago: Bowles Music House, 1940.

Bowles Favorite Gospel and Spiritual Melodies, no. 3. Chicago: Bowles Music House, 1939.

Bowles Favorite Gospel Tidings, no. 14. Chicago: Bowles Music House, n.d.

Boyer, Horace Clarence. *How Sweet the Sound: The Golden Age of Gospel*. Washington, DC: Elliott and Clark, 1995.

———. "Kenneth Morris: Composer and Publisher." In Reagon, *We'll Understand It Better*, 309–28.

Branch, Taylor. *Parting the Waters: America in the King Years, 1954–63*. New York: Simon and Schuster, 1988.

———. *Pillar of Fire: America in the King Years, 1963–65*. New York: Simon and Schuster, 1998.

Brennan, Sandra. "Rev. D. C. Rice." *All Music Guide*. Accessed January 12, 2007. http://www.allmusic.com.

Brooks, Tim. *Lost Sounds: Blacks and the Birth of the Recording Industry, 1890–1919*. Urbana: University of Illinois Press, 2004.

Broughton, Viv. *Black Gospel: An Illustrated History of the Gospel Sound*. Poole, Dorset, England: Blandford Press, 1985.

Brown, Robert M. "The Mississippi River Flood of 1912." *Bulletin of the American Geographical Society* 44, no. 9 (1912): 645–57.

Burford, Mark. "Mahalia Jackson Meets the Wise Men: Defining Jazz at the Music Inn." *Musical Quarterly* 97, no. 3 (2014).

Butler, Jerry, with Earl Smith. *Only the Strong Survive: Memoirs of a Soul Survivor*. Bloomington: Indiana University Press, 2000.

Calt, Stephen. "The Anatomy of a 'Race' Label, Part II." *78 Quarterly* 1, 4 (1989): 9–30.

Calt, Stephen, and Gayle Dean Wardlow. "Paramount Part 4 [The Advent of Arthur Laibly]." *78 Quarterly* 1, no. 6:8–26.

Campbell, Robert L., George R. White, Robert Pruter, Dr. Robert Stallworth, Tom Kelly, Jim O'Neal, and Armin Büttner. "The JOB Label." Red Saunders Research Foundation. Accessed September 6, 2012. http://hubcap.clemson.edu/~campber/job.html.

Carpenter, Bil. *Uncloudy Days: The Gospel Music Encyclopedia*. San Francisco: Backbeat Books, 2005.

Cohen, Aaron. *Amazing Grace*. New York: Continuum Books, 2011.

Cohodas, Nadine. *Queen: The Life and Music of Dinah Washington*. New York: Pantheon Books, 2004.

———. *Spinning Blues into Gold*. New York: St. Martin's Press, 2000.

Corcoran, Michael. Liner notes to *He Is My Story: The Sanctified Soul of Arizona Dranes*. San Francisco: Tompkins Square TSQ 2677, 2012. CD.

Daniel, Vattel Elbert. "Negro Classes and Life in the Church." *Journal of Negro Education* 13, no. 1 (Winter 1944): 19–29.

———. "Ritual in Chicago's South Side Churches for Negroes." PhD diss., University of Chicago, 1940.

Darden, Robert. *People Get Ready! A New History of Gospel Music*. New York: Continuum, 2004.

Dixon, Robert M.W., John Godrich, and Howard W. Rye. *Blues and Gospel Records, 1890–1943*, 4th ed. Oxford: Clarendon Press, 1997.

DjeDje, Jacqueline Cogdell. "Los Angeles Composers of African American Gospel Music: The First Generations." *American Music* 11, no. 4 (Winter 1993): 412–57.

Drake, St. Clair, and Horace R. Cayton. *Black Metropolis: A Study of Negro Life in a Northern City*. New York: Harcourt, Brace, 1945.

Du Bois, W. E. B. *The Souls of Black Folk*. New York: Tribeca Books, 2013.

DuPree, Sherry Sherrod. *The African-American Holiness Pentecostal Movement: An Annotated Bibliography*. New York: Garland, 1996.

Dyja, Thomas. *The Third Coast: When Chicago Built the American Dream*. New York: Penguin Press, 2013.

Edwards, David, and Mike Callahan. "Apollo Records Story." Accessed June 28, 2012. http://www.bsnpubs.com/nyc/apollo/apollostory.html.

Evans, David. Liner notes to *Pace Jubilee Singers*, vol. 1: *1926–1927 & Four Harmony Kings: 1921–1924*. Vienna, Austria: Document Records DOCD-5617, 1998. CD.

———. Liner notes to *Pace Jubilee Singers*, vol. 2: *1928–1929 & the Remaining Titles of the C. & M. A. Colored Gospel Quintet*. Vienna, Austria: Document Records DOCD-5618, 1998. CD.

Fishman, Karen, with contributions from Samuel Brylawski and Marsha Maguire. "Biography of Jack Kapp." Jack Kapp Collection, Motion Picture, Broadcasting and Recorded Sound Division, Library of Congress Washington, D.C. 2008. Available at http://hdl.loc.gov/loc.mbrsrs/eadmbrs.rs008001, accessed April 27, 2012.

Fox, Jon Hartley. *King of the Queen City: The Story of King Records*. Urbana: University of Illinois Press, 2009.

Frady, Marshall. *Jesse: The Life and Pilgrimage of Jesse Jackson*. New York: Random House, 1996.

From a Rough Stone to a Polished Diamond, 1902–1977. Chicago: Ebenezer Baptist Church, 1977. In Ebenezer Missionary Baptist Church Archives, Vivian G. Harsh Research Collection, Chicago Public Library.

Funk, Ray. Liner notes to *Swinging Gospel Sounds*. Vienna, Austria: Document DOCD-5377, 1995. CD.

Giovanionni, David. Liner notes to *Lost Sounds: Blacks and the Birth of the Recording Industry, 1891–1922*. Champaign, IL: Archeophone 1005, 2005. CD.

Goggin, Martin. "The Kelly Brothers." *Juke Blues* 65 (Spring 2008): 46–49.

Goreau, Laurraine. *Just Mahalia, Baby*. Waco, TX: Word Books, 1975.

Gospel Pearls. Nashville: Sunday School Publishing Board, 1921.

Green, Adam. *Selling the Race: Culture, Community, and Black Chicago, 1940–1955*. Chicago: University of Chicago Press, 2007.

Grossman, James R. *Land of Hope: Chicago, Black Southerners, and the Great Migration*. Chicago: University of Chicago Press, 1989.

Guralnick, Peter. *Dream Boogie: The Triumph of Sam Cooke*. New York: Back Bay Books, 2005.

———. Liner notes to *Sam Cooke's SAR Records Story: 1959–1965*. New York: ABKCO 2231-2, 1994. CD.

Hallstoos, Brian James. "Windy City, Holy Land: Willa Saunders Jones and Black Sacred Music and Drama." PhD diss., University of Iowa, 2009.

Harrington, Brooksie Eugene. "Shirley Caesar: A Woman of Words." PhD diss., Ohio State University, 1992.

Harris, Michael. "Conflict and Resolution in the Life of Thomas A. Dorsey." In Reagon, *We'll Understand It Better*, 165–82.

———. *The Rise of Gospel Blues: The Music of Thomas Andrew Dorsey in the Urban Church*. Oxford: Oxford University Press, 1992.

Hayes, Cedric J., and Robert Laughton. *The Gospel Discography, 1943–1970*. West Vancouver, BC: Eyeball Productions, 2007.

Heilbut, Anthony. *The Fan Who Knew Too Much*. New York: Alfred A. Knopf, 2012.

———. *The Gospel Sound*. 4th ed. New York: Limelight Editions, 1992.

———. Liner notes to *The Great Gospel Men*. Minneapolis: Shanachie/Spirit Feel 6005, 1993. CD.

———. Liner notes to *The Soul of Chicago*. Minneapolis: Shanachie/Spirit Feel 6008, 1993. CD.

———. Liner notes to *When Gospel Was Gospel*. Minneapolis: Shanachie/Spirit Feel 6064, 2005. CD.

Herndon, James. Liner notes to Sallie Martin & Evangelical Choral Chapter, *The Living Legend*. Newark: Savoy SL 14242, 1969. LP.

Higginbotham, Evelyn Brooks. "Rethinking Vernacular Culture: Black Religion and Race Records in the 1920s and 1930s." In *American Studies: An Anthology*, edited by Janice A. Radway, Kevin K. Gaines, Barry Shank, and Penny von Eschen, 225–32. Malden, MA: Wiley-Blackwell, 2009.

Hildebrand, Lee, and Opal Louis Nations. Liner notes to *The Great 1955 Shrine Concert*. Los Angeles: Specialty SPCD-7045-2, 1993. CD.

Holly, Ellistine Perkins. "Black Concert Music in Chicago, 1890 to the 1930s." *Black Music Research Journal* 10, no. 1 (Spring 1990): 141–49.

Hurston, Zora Neale. *The Sanctified Church*. New York: Marlowe, 1981.

I See the Lord. First AME Church of Gary (IN). Gary, IN: Staff BP-3074, 1969. LP.

"Ivy League Black History," Biography of J. Mayo Williams. Accessed February 15, 2008. http://ivy50.com/blackHistory/story.aspx?sid=12/26/2006.

Jackson, Irene V. "Afro-American Gospel Music and Its Social Setting with Special Attention to Roberta Martin." PhD diss., Wesleyan University, 1974.

Jackson, Jerma A. *Singing in My Soul: Black Gospel Music in a Secular Age*. Chapel Hill: University of North Carolina Press, 2004.

Jackson, Mahalia, with Evan McLeod Wylie. *Movin' On Up*. New York: Hawthorn Books, 1966.

James, Etta, and David Ritz. *Rage to Survive*. New York: Villard Books, 1995.

James, Josephine. Funeral program. In author's collection.

Johari, Jabir. "On Conjuring Mahalia: Mahalia Jackson, New Orleans, and the Sanctified Swing." *American Quarterly* 61, no. 3 (September 2009): 649–69.

Johnson, Alonzo, and Paul Jersild, eds. *Ain't Gonna Lay My 'Ligion Down: African American Religion in the South*. Columbia: University of South Carolina Press, 1996.

Johnson, Barry C., Sr. *A Change Is Gonna Come: The Transformation of a Traditional to a Contemporary Worship Celebration*. Bloomington, IN: AuthorHouse, 2008.

Johnson, Idella Lulumae. "Development of African American Gospel Piano Style (1926–1960): A Socio-Musical Analysis of Arizona Dranes and Thomas A Dorsey." PhD diss., University of Pittsburgh, 2009.

Keiler, Allan. *Marian Anderson: A Singer's Journey*. New York: Scribner, 2000.

Kempton, Arthur. *Boogaloo: The Quintessence of American Popular Music*. New York: Pantheon Books, 2003.

Kennedy, Rick, and Randy McNutt. *Little Labels—Big Sound*. Bloomington: Indiana University Press, 1999.

Kindleberger, Charles P. *The World in Depression: 1929–1939*. Berkeley: University of California Press, 1973.

Klatzko, Bernie. Liner notes to *Memphis Sanctified Jug Bands*. Vienna, Austria: Document Records DOCD-5300, 1994. CD.

Lawrence, D. H. *Studies in Classic American Literature*. London: Penguin Books, 1971.

Lemann, Nicholas. *The Promised Land*. New York: Vintage Books, 1991.

Lenox, Mary F., *Living in Faith: A History of the Greater Holy Temple Church of God in Christ*. Chicago: TBL, 2008.

Lester, Charles Richard. "Lauren Hammond and Don Leslie." Accessed May 18, 2007. http://www.137731.com/hammond/leslie.html.

Levine, Lawrence W. *Black Culture and Black Consciousness: Afro-American Folk Thought from Slavery to Freedom*. New York: Oxford University Press, 1977.

Lewis, David N. "The Rainbow Records Discography: 1920–1926." *ARSC Journal* 39, no. 1 (Spring 2008): 41–79.

Lieb, Sandra. *Mother of the Blues: A Study of Ma Rainey*. Amherst: University of Massachusetts Press, 1981.

Lornell, Kip. *Happy in the Service of the Lord: African-American Sacred Vocal Harmony Quartets in Memphis*. 2nd ed. Knoxville: University of Tennessee Press, 1995.

Mapson, J. Wendell, Jr. *The Ministry of Music in the Black Church*. Valley Forge, PA: Judson Press, 1984.

Marks, Carole. *Farewell—We're Good and Gone: The Great Black Migration*. Bloomington, IN: Indiana University Press, 1989.

Marovich, Robert M. "Bon Temps and Good News: The Influence of New Orleans on the Performance Style of Gospel Singer Mahalia Jackson." *ARSC Journal* 42, no. 1 (Spring 2011): 50–62.

———. "Here's to You, Mrs. Robinson: The Helen Robinson Youth Choir Turns 53." 1999. In author's collection.

Marsh, Dave. *The Heart of Rock and Soul: The 1001 Greatest Singles Ever Made*. New York: Plume, 1989.

Martin, Sallie, and Kenneth Morris. *Twelve Gospel Song "Hits" and Their Stories*. Chicago: Martin and Morris Music Studio, ca. 1945.

———. *Sallie Martin's Gospel Song Book No. 2: The Argo Singers*. Chicago: Martin and Morris Music Studio, 1961.

Mason, Mack C. *Make Room for the Holy Ghost*. Hazel Crest, IL: Faithday Press, 2006.

———. *Saints in the Land of Lincoln*. Hazel Crest, IL: Faithday Press, 2004.

Maultsby, Portia K. "Music of Northern Independent Black Churches during the Antebellum Period." *Ethnomusicology* 19, no. 3 (September 1975): 401–20.

McGee, Rev. F. W. *Rev. F. W. McGee (1927–1930)*. Vienna, Austria: Eden ELE 1-200, n.d. LP.

McNeil, W. K., ed. *Encyclopedia of American Gospel Music*. New York: Routledge, 2005.

Memorial Tribute to Mahalia Jackson. In author's collection.

Michaux, Elder Lightfoot Solomon. *Happy Am I Spirituals*. Washington, DC: Elder Lightfoot Solomon Michaux, ca. 1935.

Middleton, Joseph. *The Golden Era Gospel Blog*. Accessed October 10, 2012. http://goldeneragospel.blogspot.com/2011/09/o-johneron-davis-i-finally-found-ya.html.

Misiewicz, Roger. Liner notes to *Rev. D. C. Rice: Complete Recorded Works in Chronological Order: 1928–1930*. Vienna, Austria: Document Records DOCD-5071, 1997. CD.

Morris, Kenneth. "I'll Be a Servant for the Lord." In Reagon, *We'll Understand It Better*, 330–32.

———. *Improving the Music in the Church*. Chicago: Martin and Morris Music Studios, 1949.

Nations, Opal Louis. Liner notes to *Ring Them Golden Bells: The Best of the Gospel Songbirds*. Nashville: AVI/Nashboro NASH4518-2, 1995. CD.

———. "Maceo Woods: The Vee Jay Years." *Blues Gazette* (Fall 1996): 9–10.

———. "The Norfleet Brothers of Chicago." *Blues & Rhythm: The Gospel Truth*, no. 207: 14–16.

Oates, Stephen B. *Let the Trumpet Sound: The Life of Martin Luther King, Jr.* New York: Mentor, 1982.

Oliver, Paul. *Songsters and Saints*. Cambridge: Cambridge University Press, 1984.

Oliver, Paul, Max Harrison, and William Bolcom. *The New Grove Gospel, Blues, and Jazz*. New York: W. W. Norton, 1986.

Olsen, Harvey. "Leslie Speakers and Hammond Organs: Rumors, Myths, Facts,

and Lore." Accessed May 18, 2007. http://www.mitatechs.com/leslierumors.html.
Online 78 RPM Discographical Project. Accessed November 11, 2010. http://
www.78discography.com.

Peterson, Bernard L., Jr. "Shirley Graham Du Bois: Composer and Playwright." *Crisis* (May 1977): 177–79.

Piper, David K., ed. *A Handbook of the Community Church Movement in the United States*. Excelsior Springs, MO: Community Churchman, 1922.

Pitts, Walter F. *Old Ship of Zion: The Afro-Baptist Ritual in the African Diaspora*. Oxford: Oxford University Press, 1993.

Pruter, Robert. *Chicago Soul*. Urbana: University of Illinois Press, 1992.

———. *Doowop: The Chicago Scene*. Urbana: University of Illinois Press, 1996.

Pruter, Robert, Armin Büttner, and Robert L. Campbell. "Chance Records." Red Saunders Research Foundation. Accessed August 11, 2012. http://hubcap.clemson.edu/~campber/chance.html.

Pruter, Robert, and Robert L. Campbell. "Miracle Records." Red Saunders Research Foundation. Accessed January 24, 2011. http://hubcap.clemson.edu/~campber/miracle.html.

———. "Premium Records." Red Saunders Research Foundation. Accessed October 21, 2011. http://hubcap.clemson.edu/~campber/premium.html.

Pruter, Robert, Robert L. Campbell, and Tom Kelly. "Hy-Tone Records." Red Saunders Research Foundation. Accessed October 21, 2011. http://hubcap.clemson.edu/~campber/hytone.html.

Reagon, Bernice Johnson. *If You Don't Go, Don't Hinder Me: The African American Sacred Song Tradition*. Lincoln: University of Nebraska Press, 2001.

———, ed. *We'll Understand It Better By and By*. Washington, DC: Smithsonian Institution Press, 1992.

Report. *Seventeenth Annual Session, National Convention of Gospel Choirs and Choruses, Inc.* 1950. Personal collection of Kenneth Woods Jr.

Roberts, Alva D. *My Life with Brother Isaiah*. Hazel Crest, IL: Faithday Press, 2009.

Romanowski, Ken. Liner notes to *Preachers and Congregations*, vol. 7: *1925–1928*. Vienna, Austria: Document Records DOCD-5567, 1997. CD.

———. Liner notes to *The Earliest Negro Vocal Groups*, vol. 2: *1893–1922*. Vienna, Austria: Document Records DOCD-5288, 1994. CD.

Rowe, Mike. *Chicago Blues: The City and the Music*. New York: Da Capo Press, 1975.

Ryan, Marc. Liner notes to *In the Spirit: The Gospel and Jubilee Recordings of Trumpet Records*. Chicago: Alligator Records/Acoustic Archives, ALCD 2801, 1994. CD.

"Samuel Patterson." *The Black Gospel Blog*. Accessed June 19, 2012. http://www.theblackgospelblog.com/2004/10/saint-samuel-patterson-1920-2004.html.

Samuelson, Tim, and Jim Peters. "Landmarks of Blues and Gospel." *Cultural Resource Management*, no. 8 (1995): 11.

Say Amen, Somebody. New York: Ryko Filmworks, 1982, 2007. DVD.

Schwerin, Jules. *Got to Tell It*. New York: Oxford University Press, 1992.

"The Secret History of Chicago Music: Blind Joel Taggart." *Chicago Reader*, February 23, 2012, B11.

Sernett, Milton C. *Bound for the Promised Land: African American Religion and the Great Migration.* Durham, NC: Duke University Press, 1997.

Seroff, Doug. Liner notes to *Birmingham Quartet Anthology.* Stockholm: Clanka Lanka CL 144,001/144.002, 1980. LP.

———. Liner notes to the Sterling Jubilee Singers, *Jesus Hits like the Atom Bomb.* New York: New World Records 80513, 1997. LP.

———. Liner notes to *There Breathes a Hope: The Legacy of John Work II and His Fisk Jubilee Quartet, 1909–1916.* Champaign, IL: Archeophone Records ARCH 5020, 2010. CD.

Shaw, Arnold. *Honkers and Shouters: The Golden Years of Rhythm and Blues.* New York: Collier Books, 1978.

Shaw, Malcolm. "Arizona Dranes and OKeh." *Storyville* 27 (February/March 1970): 85–89.

Simmons, Martha J., and Frank A. Thomas, eds. *Preaching with Sacred Fire: An Anthology of African American Sermons, 1750 to the Present.* New York: W. W. Norton, 2010.

Smith, Lucy. "The Biography of Lucy Smith." Manuscript, ca. 1928–29. Lucy Smith Collier Papers, Vivian G. Harsh Research Collection, Chicago Public Library.

Smith, Ruth A. *The Life and Works of Thomas Andrew Dorsey.* Chicago: Prairie State Press, 1935.

Soul of the Church. North Hollywood, CA: Hollywood Select Video, 2010. DVD.

Southern, Eileen. *The Music of Black Americans.* 3rd ed. New York: W. W. Norton, 1997.

Spaulding, Norman W. "History of Black-Oriented Radio in Chicago, 1929–1963." PhD diss., University of Illinois at Urbana-Champaign, 1981.

Spencer, Jon Michael. *Black Hymnody.* Knoxville: University of Tennessee Press, 1992.

Spirit of the Church. Vol. 1. Boca Raton, FL: Green Apple Entertainment, 2013. DVD.

Stamz, Richard E., with Patrick A. Roberts. *Give 'Em Soul, Richard! Race, Radio, and Rhythm and Blues in Chicago.* Urbana: University of Illinois Press, 2010.

Standifer, James. Interview with Sallie Martin, September 19, 1981. African American Music Collection, University of Michigan School of Music. Accessed April 28, 2007. www.umich.edu/~afroammu/standifer/martin.html.

Sutherland, Robert Lee. "An Analysis of Negro Churches in Chicago." PhD diss., University of Chicago, 1930.

The Sweet Sisters of Zion: DeLois Barrett Campbell and the Barrett Sisters. Sherman Oaks, CA: DIAP-Do It All Productions, 2013. DVD.

Titon, Jeff Todd. *Early Downhome Blues: A Musical and Cultural Analysis.* Urbana: University of Illinois Press, 1977.

Tyler, Mary Ann L. "The Music of Charles Henry Pace and Its Relationship to the Afro-American Church Experience." PhD diss., University of Pittsburgh, 1980.

Uncredited liner notes to Delores Washington, *The Gospel Princess.* Newark: Gospel MG-3094, 1970. LP.

Uncredited liner notes to Delores Washington, *The Sincere Gospel Sounds of Delores Washington.* Newark: Gospel MG-3089, 1969. LP.

Uncredited liner notes to Donald Vails and the Salvation Corporation, *Until . . . the Rapture.* Detroit: Sound of Gospel, 1986. LP.

Uncredited liner notes to Eddie Robinson, *This Is My Story, This Is My Song.* Highland Park, IL: The Sirens, SR-5019, 2011. CD.

Uncredited liner notes to Mattie B. Poole, *Mattie B. Poole Memorial Album.* Private press, 8–9401, n.d. LP.

Uncredited liner notes to *Myrtle Jackson, Sings Songs of Hope and Inspiration.* Newark: Savoy MG 14074, 1965. LP.

Uncredited liner notes to Roberta Martin Singers, *Praise God.* Newark: Savoy MG 14197, 1968. LP.

Uncredited liner notes to Thompson Community Singers, *I'll Trade a Lifetime.* Detroit: HOB HBX 2101, 1969. LP.

Uncredited liner notes to Windy City Four, *Don't Let the Devil Ride.* [Chicago]: Peace LP 1148, n.d. (ca. 1969). LP.

Van der Tuuk, Alex. "Wabash Rag: Paramount's Chicago Studios." *Blues and Rhythm,* no. 131 (1998): 6. Available at http://www.paramountshome.org.

Viale, Gene. *I Remember Gospel and I Keep On Singing.* Bloomington, IN: Author-House, 2010.

Wald, Gayle F. *Shout, Sister, Shout! The Untold Story of Rock-and-Roll Trailblazer Sister Rosetta Tharpe.* Boston: Beacon Press, 2007.

Walker, Rev. Charles. *Miss Lucie.* Nashville: Townsend Press, 1993.

Ward, Brian. *Just My Soul Responding: Rhythm and Blues, Black Consciousness, and Race Relations.* Berkeley: University of California Press, 1998.

Wardlow, Gayle Dean, and John Fahey. Liner notes to *American Primitive,* vol. 1: *Raw Pre-War Gospel (1926–36).* Austin, TX: Revenant 206, 1997. CD.

Washington, Joseph R., Jr. *Black Sects and Cults.* Lanham, MD: University Press of America, 1984.

Waterman, Richard Alan. "Gospel Hymns of a Negro Church in Chicago." *Journal of the International Folk Music Council* 3 (1951): 87–93.

Wilkerson, Isabel. *The Warmth of Other Suns: The Epic Story of America's Great Migration.* New York: Random House, 2010.

Williams-Jones, Pearl. "Afro-American Gospel Music: A Crystallization of the Black Aesthetic." *Ethnomusicology* 19, no. 3 (September 1975): 373–85.

Wolff, Daniel, with S. R. Crain, Clifton White, and G. David Tenenbaum. *You Send Me: The Life and Times of Sam Cooke.* New York: William Morrow, 1995.

Women of Faith. Part 1: *Lottie Woods Hall.* Rev. Harold Bailey, producer. New York, PCC Studios, 2013.

Woods, Jessie M. Funeral program. Previously available online.

Woods, Rev. Maceo L., with Mack C. Mason. *A Graceful Journey.* Hazel Crest, IL: Faithday Press, 2010.

Woodson, Carter Godwin. *The Rural Negro.* Washington, DC: Association for the Study of Negro Life and History, 1930.

Young, Alan. *The Pilgrim Jubilees.* Jackson: University Press of Mississippi, 2001.

———. *Woke Me Up This Morning: Black Gospel Singers and the Gospel Life.* Jackson: University Press of Mississippi, 1997.

GENERAL INDEX

INDEX OF SONGS

Robert M. Marovich hosts "Gospel Memories" on Chicago's WLUW 88.7 FM and is founder and editor-in-chief of *The Journal of Gospel Music*, www.journalofgospelmusic.com.

MUSIC IN AMERICAN LIFE

Only a Miner: Studies in Recorded Coal-Mining Songs
Archie Green

Great Day Coming: Folk Music and the American Left
R. Serge Denisoff

John Philip Sousa: A Descriptive Catalog of His Works
Paul E. Bierley

The Hell-Bound Train: A Cowboy Songbook
Glenn Ohrlin

Oh, Didn't He Ramble: The Life Story of Lee Collins, as Told to Mary Collins
Edited by Frank J. Gillis and John W. Miner

American Labor Songs of the Nineteenth Century
Philip S. Foner

Stars of Country Music: Uncle Dave Macon to Johnny Rodriguez
Edited by Bill C. Malone and Judith McCulloh

Git Along, Little Dogies: Songs and Songmakers of the American West
John I. White

A Texas-Mexican *Cancionero*: Folksongs of the Lower Border
Américo Paredes

San Antonio Rose: The Life and Music of Bob Wills
Charles R. Townsend

Early Downhome Blues: A Musical and Cultural Analysis
Jeff Todd Titon

An Ives Celebration: Papers and Panels of the Charles Ives
Centennial Festival-Conference
Edited by H. Wiley Hitchcock and Vivian Perlis

Sinful Tunes and Spirituals: Black Folk Music to the Civil War
Dena J. Epstein

Joe Scott, the Woodsman-Songmaker
Edward D. Ives

Jimmie Rodgers: The Life and Times of America's Blue Yodeler
Nolan Porterfield

Early American Music Engraving and Printing: A History of Music Publishing in America from 1787 to 1825, with Commentary on Earlier and Later Practices
Richard J. Wolfe

Sing a Sad Song: The Life of Hank Williams
Roger M. Williams

Long Steel Rail: The Railroad in American Folksong
Norm Cohen

Resources of American Music History: A Directory of Source Materials from Colonial Times to World War II
D. W. Krummel, Jean Geil, Doris J. Dyen, and Deane L. Root

Tenement Songs: The Popular Music of the Jewish Immigrants
Mark Slobin

Ozark Folksongs
Vance Randolph; edited and abridged by Norm Cohen

Oscar Sonneck and American Music
Edited by William Lichtenwanger

Bluegrass Breakdown: The Making of the Old Southern Sound
Robert Cantwell

Bluegrass: A History
Neil V. Rosenberg

Music at the White House: A History of the American Spirit
Elise K. Kirk

Red River Blues: The Blues Tradition in the Southeast
Bruce Bastin

Good Friends and Bad Enemies: Robert Winslow Gordon and the Study of American Folksong
Debora Kodish

Fiddlin' Georgia Crazy: Fiddlin' John Carson, His Real World, and the World of His Songs
Gene Wiggins

America's Music: From the Pilgrims to the Present (rev. 3d ed.)
Gilbert Chase

Secular Music in Colonial Annapolis: The Tuesday Club, 1745–56
John Barry Talley

Bibliographical Handbook of American Music
D. W. Krummel

Goin' to Kansas City
Nathan W. Pearson, Jr.

Blue Rhythms: Six Lives in Rhythm and Blues
Chip Deffaa

Shoshone Ghost Dance Religion: Poetry Songs and Great Basin Context
Judith Vander

Go Cat Go! Rockabilly Music and Its Makers
Craig Morrison

'Twas Only an Irishman's Dream: The Image of Ireland and the
Irish in American Popular Song Lyrics, 1800–1920
William H. A. Williams

Democracy at the Opera: Music, Theater, and Culture in New York City, 1815–60
Karen Ahlquist

Fred Waring and the Pennsylvanians
Virginia Waring

Woody, Cisco, and Me: Seamen Three in the Merchant Marine
Jim Longhi

Behind the Burnt Cork Mask: Early Blackface Minstrelsy and
Antebellum American Popular Culture
William J. Mahar

Going to Cincinnati: A History of the Blues in the Queen City
Steven C. Tracy

Pistol Packin' Mama: Aunt Molly Jackson and the Politics of Folksong
Shelly Romalis

Sixties Rock: Garage, Psychedelic, and Other Satisfactions
Michael Hicks

The Late Great Johnny Ace and the Transition from R&B to Rock 'n' Roll
James M. Salem

Tito Puente and the Making of Latin Music
Steven Loza

Juilliard: A History
Andrea Olmstead

Understanding Charles Seeger, Pioneer in American Musicology
Edited by Bell Yung and Helen Rees

Mountains of Music: West Virginia Traditional Music from *Goldenseal*
Edited by John Lilly

Alice Tully: An Intimate Portrait
Albert Fuller

A Blues Life
Henry Townsend, as told to Bill Greensmith

Long Steel Rail: The Railroad in American Folksong (2d ed.)
Norm Cohen

The Golden Age of Gospel
Text by Horace Clarence Boyer; photography by Lloyd Yearwood

Marian McPartland's Jazz World: All in Good Time
Marian McPartland

Robert Johnson: Lost and Found
Barry Lee Pearson and Bill McCulloch

Bound for America: Three British Composers
Nicholas Temperley

Lost Sounds: Blacks and the Birth of the Recording Industry, 1890–1919
Tim Brooks

Burn, Baby! BURN! The Autobiography of Magnificent Montague
Magnificent Montague with Bob Baker

Way Up North in Dixie: A Black Family's Claim to the Confederate Anthem
Howard L. Sacks and Judith Rose Sacks

The Bluegrass Reader
Edited by Thomas Goldsmith

Colin McPhee: Composer in Two Worlds
Carol J. Oja

Robert Johnson, Mythmaking, and Contemporary American Culture
Patricia R. Schroeder

Composing a World: Lou Harrison, Musical Wayfarer
Leta E. Miller and Fredric Lieberman

Fritz Reiner, Maestro and Martinet
Kenneth Morgan

That Toddlin' Town: Chicago's White Dance Bands and Orchestras, 1900–1950
Charles A. Sengstock Jr.

Dewey and Elvis: The Life and Times of a Rock 'n' Roll Deejay
Louis Cantor

Come Hither to Go Yonder: Playing Bluegrass with Bill Monroe
Bob Black

Chicago Blues: Portraits and Stories
David Whiteis

The Incredible Band of John Philip Sousa
Paul E. Bierley

"Maximum Clarity" and Other Writings on Music
Ben Johnston, edited by Bob Gilmore

Staging Tradition: John Lair and Sarah Gertrude Knott
Michael Ann Williams

Homegrown Music: Discovering Bluegrass
Stephanie P. Ledgin

Tales of a Theatrical Guru
Danny Newman

The Music of Bill Monroe
Neil V. Rosenberg and Charles K. Wolfe

Long Lost Blues: Popular Blues in America, 1850–1920
Peter C. Muir

Hard Luck Blues: Roots Music Photographs from the Great Depression
Rich Remsberg

Restless Giant: The Life and Times of Jean Aberbach and Hill and Range Songs
Bar Biszick-Lockwood

Champagne Charlie and Pretty Jemima: Variety Theater in the Nineteenth Century
Gillian M. Rodger

Sacred Steel: Inside an African American Steel Guitar Tradition
Robert L. Stone

Gone to the Country: The New Lost City Ramblers and the Folk Music Revival
Ray Allen

The Makers of the Sacred Harp
David Warren Steel with Richard H. Hulan

Woody Guthrie, American Radical
Will Kaufman

George Szell: A Life of Music
Michael Charry

Bean Blossom: The Brown County Jamboree and Bill Monroe's Bluegrass Festivals
Thomas A. Adler

Crowe on the Banjo: The Music Life of J. D. Crowe
Marty Godbey

Twentieth Century Drifter: The Life of Marty Robbins
Diane Diekman

Henry Mancini: Reinventing Film Music
John Caps

The Beautiful Music All Around Us: Field Recordings and the American Experience
Stephen Wade

Then Sings My Soul: The Culture of Southern Gospel Music
Douglas Harrison

The Accordion in the Americas: Klezmer, Polka, Tango, Zydeco, and More!
Edited by Helena Simonett

Bluegrass Bluesman: A Memoir
Josh Graves, edited by Fred Bartenstein

One Woman in a Hundred: Edna Phillips and the Philadelphia Orchestra
Mary Sue Welsh

The Great Orchestrator: Arthur Judson and American Arts Management
James M. Doering

Charles Ives in the Mirror: American Histories of an Iconic Composer
David C. Paul

The University of Illinois Press
is a founding member of the
Association of American University Presses.

Designed by Jennifer S. Holzner
Composed in 10.5/13 Minion Pro
with Univers Condensed display
by Jim Proefrock
at the University of Illinois Press
Manufactured by Sheridan Books, Inc.

University of Illinois Press
1325 South Oak Street
Champaign, IL 61820-6903
www.press.uillinois.edu